Defending Gary

Mark Prothero
with Carlton Smith

Defending Gary

Unraveling the Mind of
the Green River Killer

JOSSEY-BASS
A Wiley Imprint
www.josseybass.com

Published by Jossey-Bass
A Wiley Imprint
989 Market Street, San Francisco, CA 94103-1741   www.josseybass.com

Jossey-Bass books and products are available through most bookstores. To contact Jossey-Bass directly call our Customer Care Department within the U.S. at 800-956-7739, outside the U.S. at 317-572-3986, or fax 317-572-4002.

Jossey-Bass also publishes its books in a variety of electronic formats. Some content that appears in print may not be available in electronic books.

Library of Congress Cataloging-in-Publication Data

Prothero, Mark, date.
  Defending Gary : unraveling the mind of the Green River Killer / Mark Prothero, with Carlton Smith.— 1st ed.
      p. cm.
  Includes bibliographical references and index.
  ISBN-13: 978-0-7879-8106-8
  ISBN-10: 0-7879-8106-0
  1. Ridgway, Gary Leon, 1949- 2. Ridgway, Gary Leon, 1949——Trials, litigation, etc. 3. Serial murders—Washington (State)—Green River (King County)—Case studies. 4. Serial murderers—Washington (State)—Green River (King County)—Psychology. 5. Trials (Murder)—Washington (State)—Green River (King County) I. Smith, Carlton, date. II. Title.
  HV6533.W2P76 2006
  364.152'3092—dc22

                                                                          2006001253

Printed in the United States of America
FIRST EDITION
HB Printing   10 9 8 7 6 5 4 3 2 1

⟞⟝ Contents

For the victims—the living as well as the dead.

—CS and MP

To the memory of my dad, Bob, who passed away on November 7, 2005, and to my mom, Shirley.

And to Kelly, Sean, and Marley. I would never have had this chance without their enduring love, support, and guidance.

—MP

⁓⁓ Acknowledgments

There are many people I wish to acknowledge and thank for their support, encouragement, and help in writing this book.

First and foremost, I want to thank my co-counsel, Todd Gruenhagen. Not only is he a great lawyer, he is a great friend. I don't know if we could have achieved this resolution without him.

Thanks to another great lawyer and great friend, Greg Girard, for calling me on November 30, 2001, and for partnering up with me to venture into private practice. And for carrying the load for us while I worked on this book.

One of the best parts of this experience was having the opportunity to work with Tony Savage. He calmly steered Team Ridgway through some tough passages and handled every situation with an abundance of class. Thanks, Tony.

Thanks to my coauthor, Carlton Smith, for his patience and wisdom. This was truly a collaboration and Carlton's insights were invaluable. And for taking my words and making them into something readable.

Thanks to my agent, Jane Dystel, for making this all happen.

Also, thanks to Alan Rinzler from Jossey-Bass for all of his insights and constructive criticism. Thanks to all the people who worked on this project at Jossey-Bass and John Wiley & Sons.

Many stories and names had to be left out of this book because it was getting so long. During my twenty years at ACA, I was fortunate to work with the best, hardest-working attorneys, investigators, and staff of any public defender office you'll ever come across. I learned so much and had a great time in the process. Thanks to everyone at ACA, and especially to my good friends Dave Chapman, Don Madsen, Lou Frantz, Martha Walton, Jim Robinson, Fabian Acosta, Carl Luer, Dennis Hough, Byron Ward, and George Eppler. Also, former ACA director, Roy Howson. And ACA's founder and mentor to all of us, the late Irving Paul.

Thanks to everyone on the Ridgway Defense Team:

Lawyers: Todd, Tony, Suzanne Elliott, Eric Lindell, Michele Shaw, Dave Roberson, and Fred Leatherman (also, thanks to attorneys David Zuckerman, Roger Hunko, and Rita Griffith for their insights and materials).

Investigators: Bettye Witherspoon, Denise Scaffidi, Lis Frost, Jay Joslin, Susan Stafford, Mary Boben, Jerry Esterly, Lynn Erickson, and DNA investigator Susan Herrero.

Paralegals: Janna Witt-Richards, Donna McDougal, Amy Wadley, Rebecca Allen, Ariella Wagonfield, Joe Baker, Gordon McKendry, Stacy Wilson, Kelsey Case, Erin Curtis, Anna Frandsen, and Fauzia Suleman.

Accountant: Vanessa Baird.

Certus Consulting: Norman Yee and Kathi Wilkerson and all the "discovery readers."

Experts: Mary Goody, Judith Becker, Mark Cunningham, John Thornton, Craig Beaver, Sterling Clarren, William Logan, Alan Cohen, Dan Spitz, Neal Haskell, Stephanie Kavanaugh, Chet Dettlinger, James Hudson, Randy Libby, Elizabeth Johnson, and Larry Mueller.

Thanks to the King County prosecutor and his staff. This historical resolution would not have been achieved without the courageous decision by Norm Maleng. The difficult process was bearable due to the professionalism of all those working for the prosecution: Jeff Baird, Patricia Eakes, Brian McDonald, Sean O'Donnell, Ian Goodhew, Mark Larson, Dan Satterberg, and Kelly Rosa.

Likewise, the members of the Green River Task Force were first-class all the way through: Tom Jensen, Randy Mullinax, Sue Peters, Jon Mattsen, Kevin O'Keefe, the late Jim Doyon, Jim Graddon, Ray Green, D. B. Gates, Malcolm Chang, Ross Nooney, Mike Brown, Roger Kellams, Jeff Thomas, Scott Click, Laura Hoffenbacker, Rafe Crenshaw, and Tony McNabb.

Thanks to everyone at the King County Office of Public Defense, especially former directors Jim Crane and Anne Harper, as well as our Special Master, Kate Pflaumer.

Thanks to all the attorneys and staff at Hanis Greaney, especially Mike Hanis and Susan Paepke, for your support and for bearing with me while I tried to write a book and start a private law practice at the same time.

A huge part of my life involves swimming. There are far too many people to name (and I would probably forget to mention someone), so I'll just say thanks to all the swimmers and their parents at Kent

Swim and Tennis Club, Kentwood High School, and King Aquatic Club. Also, thanks to all my fellow coaches, parents, and volunteers involved in Pacific Northwest Swimming and USA Swimming.

A few of these people need to be singled out: Keith Ure, Sean Hutchison, Dan and Kalany Benoit, Eric and Adrienne Lindblad, Chuck and Jo Bizzell, Rob and Mary Munsch, Erin and Tracy Eronemo, Peter and Jaapje Kukors, and Ted and Suzanne Rychlik.

Some swimmers also deserve special mention: Courtney Eronemo for making me look like a great coach; Ariana Kukors for her constant "How's the book coming, coach?"; Brianne Lindblad, Phoebe Bizzell, Matt Benoit, Kevin Munsch. Their drive and dedication continually inspire me.

A variety of great assistant coaches—Tricia Olson, Charlie Mitchell, Jessie Rykels, Aaron Vaughan, Kit DiJulio, Meredith Plumb, and Kyle Munsch—covered for me time and time again during this ordeal. I couldn't have done this without their help.

Thanks also to my good friends Doug and Linda Lumbard, Brad and Tina Campfield, Jan and Debbie Bergman, Cameron Watt, and Les McDonald. Also to Shannon Henderson for all of her help and support.

Last, but not least, thanks to my family: Kelly, Sean, and Marley—you are my life—and Mom and Dad and Blake, for all of your unconditional love and support. We miss you, Dad.

About Our Sources

Much of the information in this book was obtained through inter-views, transcripts, and personal recollections, many of those based on my written notes of, for example, conversations with Gary, meetings with other team members, and various other meetings. Many of my observations were recorded in my journal, which I kept from the first night all the way through sentencing.

Gary Ridgway himself was a source for this book. His cooperation and agreement to allow me to use confidential conversations were critical to the project.

Defending Gary

PART ONE

The News

1

The practice of law can drive you crazy sometimes: what starts out as logical can end up surreal. Objections, objections to objections, sidebars, interminable wrangling over the meaning of words: a voyage into tedium by way of monotony, broken occasionally by moments of sheer panic. Judges drone, lawyers groan, defendants moan, and at the end of the day you pack it all up and get ready to start again the next day, as justice grinds forward, exceedingly slow.

When it starts to get nuts, that's when you have to take a break—get out of your daytime skin to do something completely different. That was why, in the darkening hours of the last day of November 2001, a Friday evening, I was on the pool deck at Kent-Meridian High School, about twenty miles south of the city of Seattle, in the State of Washington, shouting encouragement to a six-lane pool full of teenaged boys, as they swam their way through a hard workout. When I put down my briefcase and picked up my stopwatch, I had transformed into Coach Prothero, of the Kentwood High School Conquerors swimming team. Once I hit poolside, the thrust and parry of the courtroom receded, and the craziness of the legal system assumed much more manageable proportions.

On this last day of November, the gray concrete roof over the pool served as a giant hollow echo chamber for the splashing; with the odor of chlorine permeating the atmosphere, I was about as far away from the formalized setting of a courtroom as I could get every afternoon. In a way, I could put one reality aside, exchanged for another, at least for a while.

The varsity, including my son, Sean, was kicking and pulling through the last of their series of 25-yard freestyle sprints, when my Other Life broke in. As I walked along the side of the steaming pool, my shirtsleeves rolled up, dripping with sweat, yelling to be heard, I saw someone near the door, waving at me and peering at me with a peculiar expression. It was Jon Morrow, the father of one of our team members.

"Did you hear the news?" Morrow asked me when I approached.

"No. What news?"

"They've arrested the Green River Killer."

"No way!" I said, disbelieving. But I saw at once that Jon Morrow was serious.

The police had been trying for nearly twenty years to catch the most prolific serial killer in American history, suspected of murdering forty-nine women. At least until that day, they had repeatedly failed. Almost everyone had concluded long ago that the horrible case would never be solved.

"Yeah, it's all over the news, the radio, TV," Morrow told me. "He's a truck painter from Auburn."

My first reaction was that this had to be some sort of mistake, that it was some sort of weird rumor that had seeped out of the gossip mill, and from there onto the news waves. *Not now,* I thought: not after the two decades since the murders had first begun in 1982.

But my intuition told me it was true. It wasn't like the news, or the police, to be so specific—not unless something real had happened. As far as I could recall, this was the first time in history that someone had actually been arrested in connection with the nationally notorious crimes, as compared to only questioned as "a person of interest," as the phrase had it. And my next thought was this: if the police really had actually *arrested* someone for the murders, the chances were pretty good that he'd need a lawyer.

And then, almost at once, I found myself musing over two questions: *Where the hell has this supposed killer been all these years? And how is it that the cops have just now arrested him?*

"Yeah, they said it was a DNA match," Morrow told me. He gave me the look again. "You'll probably get him, since you're the DNA guy."

The DNA guy. Jon had that right. The lawyer who often got the DNA cases assigned to our publicly funded criminal defense agency. Me. The one who had to explain what all those numbers and computer printouts and all those *peaks* and *stutters* cast up by the overhead projector meant. Evidence that the accused was (or was not) one in a quadrillion or some other astronomical number that the human brain couldn't fathom. If the police really *had* arrested someone from Auburn, based on a *DNA match,* that meant I might be one of those called upon to try to save whoever it was from what would be an almost certain fate: execution by lethal injection—or possibly, even hanging.

To try to save whoever it was from the death penalty. Even if he *had* killed forty-nine women.

———

I'd grown up in south King County, in the State of Washington, near the Seattle suburb of Renton. As a criminal defense lawyer in the 1980s, I'd watched as authorities found skeleton after skeleton of young female murder victims in that decade, most of them strewn across the isolated, wooded hillsides of the rural southern portion of the county. The sheer number of victims was staggering: How could only one person—if it really *was* only one person—kill so many and not have been caught, sooner or later?

Or just as important was this: What *kind* of person could do this—kill again and again and again, with seeming impunity? For years, the speculation had been rampant. Various scenarios had it that the killer was an angry vice cop, hiding in plain sight; or a psychopathic security guard; or maybe a frustrated probation officer. In any event, someone with some sort of logical if emotional motive, however twisted, for killing troubled young women who had violated his sense of order. As a defense lawyer, I knew that people tended to look first for sensible reasons for the unexplainable. It's human nature to seek the obvious answer to complicated problems.

But I also knew that the killer most probably had no such official or even semiofficial occupation. Anyone in officialdom would almost certainly have been detected years earlier. Instead, it was far more plausible that the killer had been living an ordinary, unofficial life, unnoticed by his neighbors, his coworkers, and even his own family, if he had one. How else had he managed to elude detection for so long, other than by appearing to be utterly, unremarkably normal? It was my guess that he probably seemed just like anyone—except for a hidden, dark streak, some quirk that only emerged from the shadows when in the company of women who worked as prostitutes—his prey of choice.

But now, there had finally been an arrest, and if Jon Morrow was right about "the DNA guy," I might draw the biggest case of my career. Like anyone else in this situation, I wanted to know more.

As soon as swimming practice was over, I went to the nearby house of my friends Jan and Debbie, first to rehydrate myself with a beer, but mostly to see what the television people were saying about the arrest of this accused killer, this truck painter from Auburn, who'd been living and working right in our community for more than two decades.

———⟋⟍⟋⟍———

As I suspected, the television news people were frantic with excitement, rolling videotape of the authorities' announcement of the arrest, along with jumpy pictures of some suburban neighborhood where the alleged killer had been living for years. The television had tape of King County Sheriff's Department deputies walking to and fro over property that was obviously being searched. Then the usual interviews with shocked neighbors. All of this was backstopped by file footage from twenty-year-old crime scenes: generally, green-jacketed cops wandering around in the woods with rakes and buckets, which had been used to pick up the bones of the dead years before, along with a by-now oft-played loop of the removal of a body from the sluggish current of the turgid, indifferent Green River.

The story of the arrest dominated the afternoon and evening broadcasts, even national broadcasts, which came as no surprise. The Green River murders were the largest unsolved serial murder case in the history of the country, so the coverage had a certain breathless quality that accompanied unique events. Since the summer of 1982, the discovery of skeleton after skeleton, combined with law enforcement's failure to identify the elusive killer, had given the mysterious murderer near-mythic proportions. Gradually, the unknown fiend had become almost an evil Einstein in the public mind, for his propensity to kill, and kill, and kill again. Expert opinion—psychological profilers from the FBI and other mavens on serial murder—had opined that the deadly puzzle would never be solved; it was simply too old, too complex, to ever result in an arrest. Many of the same experts had also suggested that the perpetrator was either dead or in prison for another, lesser crime and so was now beyond identification and apprehension. In other words, the case was at a definite dead end. So much for the expert opinion, I thought.

As I watched the television news roll on, I also realized that no one—at least no official—was saying that the arrested person was *the* Green River Killer, only that he'd been arrested in connection with *some* of the crimes.

Was there, in fact, only *one* person who'd committed all of the crimes? All forty-nine of them? This had never been clear, and in fact, I knew this had long been one of the central puzzles of the case: Which murders were the work of only one person, and which were coincidentally similar crimes, murders that had been erroneously attributed to the Green River Killer, thereby making the total number of deaths seem far larger?

And second, was someone else involved—perhaps another killer or killers acting independently of the first person, or perhaps, at least occasionally, in concert? This was unclear, and an arrest on only some of the murders shed no useful light on the critical, larger issue: arresting someone in connection with only *some* of the murders left open the possibility that there was, in fact, another killer, possibly someone far more predacious, still out there.

That evening, the face of the accused appeared on all the evening newscasts: a roundish, somewhat florid, middle-aged face, mustachioed, facing the camera dead-on, stoic of gaze from under a neatly trimmed helmet of dark hair. The man's eyes were slits, and his lips were grimly pursed. On the basis of the photograph alone, he looked almost as lifeless as the long-dead faces of those he was supposed to have murdered.

Could this really be the face of the long-sought Green River Killer?

The worst serial murder case in the country had first come to public awareness in the summer of 1982, when the bodies of five young women, all strangled, were found in or on the banks of the Green River, as the river passed through the city of Kent, a small farming community that by the early 1980s was being transformed into a bedroom suburb of Seattle. The discovery of the victims, including three on the same day, had at the time jolted the entire Pacific Northwest.

The river began high in the Cascade Mountains to the east, then meandered down to a valley flood plain running north to Elliott Bay, Seattle's front yard. By the time it reached Kent, twenty miles south of the big city, it was a medium-size stream about one hundred feet across. Its twenty-foot banks were covered with thick brambles of blackberry bushes, high grass, and other dense growth. The water level in the river varied; some months heavy rain in the mountains caused the stream to swell almost to its brim, while at other times, a flood control dam far upstream lowered the river to the size of a lazy creek.

On July 15, 1982, the naked body of fifteen-year-old Wendy Coffield had been found in the river, hung up on a bridge piling just past Meeker Street, which was the main road into Kent from the west. She had been strangled, and her jeans had been tied tightly around her neck. A month later, on August 12, 1982, the body of twenty-two-year-old Debbie Bonner had also been found in the river, just about a half-mile south of where Wendy's body had been found the month before. Three days after that, on August 15, 1982, three *more* victims were found, and with those discoveries, the case had first become a public sensation. Two of the victims found on August 15, 1982, Marcia Chapman and Cynthia Hinds, were discovered under the water, weighted down and secured in place with heavy rocks; whereas the third, Opal Mills, had been found in the tall grass on the riverbank, not far away. As with Wendy Coffield, Opal's jeans had been tied around her neck.

Because of their close proximity and similar manner of murder, the authorities quickly announced that they were looking for a serial killer, and the appellation *Green River Killer*—a creation of the news media—followed almost immediately.

At the time, it was thought that the killer was using the river's waters to wash his victims of trace evidence, much as had happened in the Atlanta child murders of the previous year, 1981. The Green River channel had therefore become an early focal point in the investigation of the crimes. But over the next seven years, the remains of thirty-seven other young women, most of them just skeletons by the time they were found, had been discovered in isolated spots in the woods in a wide arc southeast of Seattle, miles away from the river's frequently sluggish course. These killings, too, had been attributed to the Green River Killer, although there were notable differences between the victims found in the woods and those found originally in the river. Another seven young women were eventually described as missing, presumed dead at the hands of the same killer.

Over the ensuing twenty years, a number of police task forces had been formed in sporadic efforts to identify the murderer. But like many such efforts that don't meet with immediate success, steadfast political support withered and eventually faded entirely. Despite the expenditure of millions of dollars and untold hours of investigation over the decades, despite having had hundreds if not thousands of potential suspects, as the new millennium began, the police seemed no closer to naming the deadly predator than they had in the summer of 1982.

This lack of progress was mostly due to the background of the victims. Many had been teenaged runaways living shadowy lives as casual prostitutes at the time they were last seen. The brutal fact was, many voting citizens were indifferent to the killings: being murdered was seen as an inevitable outcome of dangerous, even "immoral" conduct. The lesson was clear to the law-abiding: if you didn't want to run the risk of being murdered, all you had to do was not commit prostitution. Of course, it wasn't that simple. Most of those who had been killed were prostituting because they had other troubles: drug addictions, mental illness, bad family relationships, all sorts of self-destructive behavior that stemmed from deep-seated social dysfunctions. The real question wasn't whether the victims deserved to die—no one did—but whether the society as a whole would mobilize resources to stop it. And for a while, at least, the community's political leaders accepted the challenge.

But as the years elapsed without a resolution, the social concern about these kinds of crimes inevitably diminished. Eventually, police administrators, responding to political pressures, had insisted that as far as they could tell, the last murder had taken place in early 1984.

However, as we would all learn, this was far from the truth.

—❦—

It turned out that Jon Morrow's late-afternoon hunch about "the DNA guy" was on the money. When I stopped in at my office later that evening, there was a message for me from Greg Girard, my supervisor at Associated Counsel for the Accused (ACA), one of four non-profit law firms that handled criminal defense for the poor in King County, and my employer.

"Hey, Mark. I'm heading down to the RJC," Greg had recorded, using our short form for the Regional Justice Center, located just a few blocks from our public defender office in Kent. "They arrested somebody for the Green River murders and he's asked for a lawyer. If you're around, I'd appreciate it if you'd join me, because two heads are better than one. See you there." The message had been left just before 6 P.M.

I looked at my watch. It was just past seven. Greg's message meant that whoever had been arrested for the murders had probably been in police custody for several hours, possibly much of the afternoon, before Greg had been able to talk to him. That could be a problem: Who knew what the arrestee had told the police before Greg had been able to get there? There isn't a criminal defense lawyer in the country who wants to hear that his client, or even prospective client, has been talking to the police without him or her being present.

It isn't what you might expect—that the lawyer simply wants to get his client off, regardless of his guilt. The problem is, sometimes police make mistakes. They may arrest the wrong person. But once the police-prosecution bandwagon gets rolling, an innocent person who talks innocently may find his words used against him. The exonerations based on forensic DNA have clearly demonstrated that there have been many convictions, even death sentences, obtained on false confessions.

Yet the number of people wrongfully convicted because they cooperated with the police still seems to be growing. Some in law enforcement seem more interested in getting someone, anyone, than getting to the truth. Every few months seems to bring out more cases, some of them involving the death penalty—as this one surely would—that are reversed because of shoddy police work that targeted the wrong person. Once an individual was charged, there often seemed to be no way to go backward. So I was anxious to see this person that the police were claiming was responsible for so many murders—well, some of the murders, if the television news people had it right—to see what, if anything, he had said to them upon his arrest. I immediately headed over to the jail at the RJC.

The jail is a large concrete box attached to the Regional Justice Center, which also houses fifteen superior courts, along with a number of courtrooms used for district court and juvenile cases. As the south county's population exploded over the previous twenty years, it had become imperative to bring more justice facilities to the population. And that included jail facilities. That's why the Regional Justice Center had been opened in 1997.

I arrived just after seven that night and went first to the front counter of the jail. As with most modern lockups, visitors were separated from the jail staff by a large shatterproof glass window, with a metal speaker set in the middle. This civilian area was festooned with various announcements and rules, along with posters decrying domestic violence and drunken driving—by far the largest part of any modern jail's clientele. By that time of the evening, and on a Friday night, there was only one person behind the counter, and she was not in a mood to be helpful. As soon as I asked her about the whereabouts of the person arrested in the Green River case, I could see she thought I was just another pesky news reporter. I told her that I was a lawyer who'd been asked to see the new prisoner.

"He's not here," she told me. "They're taking him downtown."

I realized I was going to have to do a little detective work of my own. I called Greg's wife at home, with my cellular phone. She told me that she thought Greg was with the arrestee in the King County Sheriff's detectives' offices, which were nearby in the adjacent court building. I made my way there but found the door to the court building locked.

A long, lean, mustachioed man wearing jeans and a windbreaker was leaning against a wall, smoking a cigarette. He watched me trying to get in.

"Can I help you?"

"Uh, yeah," I said, not at all sure who this jeans-wearing cigarette smoker was or whether he really could help me. "I'm Mark Prothero. I'm with ACA. They arrested someone, and I understand he asked for a lawyer."

"You with Girard?"

"Yeah."

"Just a second." The man squashed his cigarette into cinders, then called on his own cellular phone. Pretty soon, someone came to the door and let us in.

"Follow me," the tall jeans-wearing man told me, and I now realized he had to be a detective with the King County Sheriff's Department. He wasn't anyone I knew, though, and after almost two decades handling criminal cases in King County, I thought I knew just about every detective by face, if not by name.

I followed this unknown detective down several hallways, ever deeper into the county detectives' secretive inner sanctum. Eventually, we came to a closed door. The blue-jeaned man knocked, opened the door, and ushered me in with an impassive nod. The interior of the room was stark—no window, nothing but concrete block walls painted slightly off-white, the usual fluorescent lighting on the ceiling. One edge of a small, square table was pushed up against the wall. Three plastic chairs were arranged around the three other sides. I heard the door close behind me and the click of its lock.

My colleague, Greg Girard, had his back to me on the near side of the tiny table, and catty-corner from him, sideways to the door, was a very ordinary-looking, compactly built man in his early fifties, dressed in blue jeans and wearing a plaid shirt. He had a nearly full head of brown hair, just beginning to thin a bit on top, but not a tinge of gray. A small, neat mustache covered his upper lip. He wore tortoise-shell glasses that seemed a little too big for his face, which made him look gentle, harmless, and even a little nerdy. He seemed very calm—actually, quite detached. I saw his resemblance to the man whose photograph I had seen on television, but in the flesh he somehow looked different, almost benign, and certainly inoffensive.

"Mark," said Greg, gesturing with his hand, "this is Gary Ridgway. Mr. Ridgway, this is Mark Prothero."

"Hello, Mr. Ridgway," I said, reaching out to shake his hand.

"Hi." He nodded his head, almost shyly, and smiled politely. We shook hands.

This was not at all what I had been expecting. Not only did his physical appearance surprise me, but he also seemed extraordinarily, unusually polite. I looked for something, anything—anger, sadness, embarrassment, fear—but I could sense nothing.

They must have got it wrong, I thought, as I released his hand. This can't be *the* Green River Killer! He's too ordinary! He's too small. He's too calm. He's too polite! He can't possibly have murdered forty-nine women. They can't be serious! They must have screwed up!

I didn't realize it then, but I was right. Gary Ridgway hadn't killed forty-nine women. He'd killed even more than that.

2

After his introductions, Greg Girard gave a quick run-down on the events that had led to Gary Ridgway's arrest that day. Gary had been at his job as a painter at Kenworth, a truck manufacturing plant in Renton, just south of Seattle, when two detectives came to ask him some questions. I learned that it wasn't the first time Gary had talked to the police about the Green River case. He'd been a suspect in the case as far back as the 1980s, and his house had been searched in 1987. But unlike others who'd attracted the attention of the police during the twenty-year nightmare, Gary Ridgway's name had never been published or broadcast. That was why I'd never heard of him before that day.

Greg told me he'd already advised Gary that he'd probably have to spend time in jail, at least until things could get sorted out. Gary had told him that his family might hire a private lawyer. As Girard summarized these points, Gary nodded agreeably. He seemed to be paying close attention.

At this point, I wanted to know exactly what had happened when Gary had been arrested, but in Gary's own words. I also wanted to hear this supposed killer talk: maybe then I might see some emotion or get an idea from his personality or his presentation, which might give me some idea of whether he was really capable of murdering anyone, let alone forty-nine women.

"Let's go over everything that happened today, OK?" I suggested. "Everything that everybody said or did, as best as you can recall."

"Oooh-K," he said with a grin, in a friendly, folksy way, stretching out the *O* sound a little longer than usual, and truncating the *K*. "Oooh-K." It was as if I'd suggested that he try the starter again on his car. This was a Gary Ridgway idiosyncrasy that I would become very familiar with over the next few years.

At about 11:30 that morning, Gary told us, the police had come to the Kenworth plant in Renton, just south of Seattle, and pulled him away from his work area in the truck painting section to ask him questions. A female detective did most of the asking, Gary said.

"What did she ask you?"

"She showed me a couple of pictures of this woman. She said it was Carol Christensen and wanted to know if I'd ever had sex with her."

From the reports I'd seen on television, it seemed that the police had acted because they had DNA evidence linking Gary to at least one of the murders, and if they were showing pictures of and asking about someone named Carol Christensen, I guessed that she might be someone they thought Gary had murdered—or least one of them.

"What did you tell her?"

"Well, I didn't recognize the woman, so I said no."

"Was that true?"

"I can't say for sure," Gary said. "The pictures were old. It was a long time ago. I mean, I *could* have had sex with her, but it was so long ago that I wouldn't have been able to recognize her from the pictures. Like I said, the pictures were old and weren't really that good. It didn't even look like the same woman in both pictures." He looked over at me to see if I understood his uncertainty. I nodded.

"But you didn't tell the detectives that?"

"No, I just said no." Now Gary displayed a somewhat sheepish grin, and I had the feeling that he was just realizing that he had made a mistake in giving the police a flat denial. Either that or he was testing me to see how I'd react to the idea that he might have been impishly less than candid with the police. I was just starting to get a glimpse of the multiple faces of Gary. One could never be quite sure when he was being deceptive—or just simpleminded.

"Then what happened?"

"Well, the cops left after about half an hour," Gary said. "I went back to work." But later that day, just after three as he was leaving the plant, two other detectives had arrested him as he was walking to his truck.

"There was no big scene," he said.

Once Gary was handcuffed, these detectives drove him to their offices in the Regional Justice Center, the same place where we were now sitting. No one said anything or asked him any questions while they were driving to the detectives' offices, Gary said. Once they arrived, they'd placed him in an interrogation room. At that point, one of the detectives told him that he was under arrest for the murder of Carol Christensen and for the first time read him his rights under Miranda: the right to remain silent and the right to speak first with an attorney.

"I said I wanted to talk to a lawyer," Gary said. One of the detectives then handed him a telephone book. Gary said he'd found the number of a lawyer who had represented him in the past and called it, but there was no answer. Then, Gary said, he'd tried the number of a downtown Seattle law firm that employed his sister-in-law, Dorene, as a paralegal. The office was closed for the weekend. By that time it was after five. One of the detectives then told Gary he'd call the Office of Public Defense for him, to see if they couldn't find a lawyer for Gary. Gary said that was fine with him.

"They seemed to relax after that," Gary said. One of them—Gary wasn't sure what his name was—told him that now that he'd asked for a lawyer, they wouldn't be able to use anything he said anyway, at least not in court. That wasn't actually true, but I guessed this wasn't exactly the time to point out the finer points of the latest interpretations of the Miranda decision to Gary. However, Greg Girard and I both knew it wasn't an unusual tactic on the part of the police to try to induce a confession from a suspect by pretending the conversation was "off the record."

"Was this interview taped?"

"Not that I saw."

"No tape recorder?" I could hardly believe this. In such an important case, it seemed incredible that no one had tried to get Gary's own words down permanently—and indisputably—on tape.

"No."

"No video camera?"

"No."

"OK, how long did they talk to you, before Greg Girard arrived?"

"A couple of hours. Maybe a little more."

"What did they ask you?"

"They said they wanted me to tell them where the other bodies are. 'Where should we look?' That's what one of them wanted to know."

"What'd you tell 'em?"

"I told 'em I didn't know, but maybe they should look where other bodies were found, 'cause, you know, maybe that's where he woulda left 'em." It sounded like Gary was suggesting that he'd been trying to help the police. I was thinking, "whoops." "*How should* I *know?*" That would have been the best response to that sort of question. Gary's response suggested that maybe he *did* know something about the crimes. Maybe. Here it was again: the subtle dichotomy between Gary the innocently naïve and Gary the guilty—you could take his answers both ways.

Gary described more of the questions, and Greg and I could both see the detectives were trying to psychologically stampede him into confessing. Sometimes the questions suggested that there was a witness who'd seen Gary drive away with one of the victims. At other times, they suggested that continuing to deny things would only make matters go harder for him. It was clear that, having told Gary that they wouldn't be able to use anything he said in court (untrue), they hoped Gary would relax enough to tell them what they desperately wanted to know: whether they were *right*. Sometimes, when confronted with what seemed to be overwhelming evidence, and with the assurance that nothing could be used against him, a suspect will give up the burden of secrecy almost as a relief.

"'Tell us where to look,'" Gary said they insisted. "'We're gonna dig up your yard, so we're gonna find anything if it's there.'" Gary said he told them to go ahead, that they wouldn't find anything. But the questions kept on coming, and Gary soon refused to say anything at all, he said.

"'Why'd you put three of the victims in the Green River and the rest in the woods at Star Lake and Maple Valley?'" Gary said he was asked. These were places, I recalled, where a number of the skeletal remains of victims had been found in the previous decades. I couldn't recall offhand just how many, but I knew there were a lot.

"'Why'd you put the trout on Carol Christensen? Why did you leave her with the bottle of wine?'"

"'Where do you go to church? You're *really* religious, aren't you? You were probably cleaning up the area, getting rid of these women, weren't you?'"

At one point, the three detectives showed him pictures of corpses, apparently taken near the Green River.

"Is that your work?" they demanded. Gary said it wasn't.

Gary remembered all of these questions and assertions from the detectives' interrogation, and he had no trouble realizing that they were trying to bait him into talking. Having Gary say anything, even denials, was better for the detectives, because any engagement at all gave them a chance to hit a possible raw nerve.

"'Look, Gary,'" he said one of the detectives told him, "'if you're willing to show remorse, take responsibility for what you've done, and tell us where the other bodies are, this is your one chance to avoid the death penalty. We know that not all the bodies are yours, that someone else was killing these women too. Why don't you just tell us, which ones were yours?'"

"What did you say to that?" I asked.

"Nothing," Gary said. "I told them I didn't do it. Then one of them called me a monster and told me all about lethal injection, how they put the needle in your arm. . . . He said he wanted to be there when they gave it to me, but they said if I could bring some relief to the families of the victims, some closure, that's what they said, then I had a chance to get life in prison instead of the death penalty."

So now I knew Gary had denied to the police that he was the killer. I decided not to press him on this. I rarely ask clients first thing up front if they are guilty. How can you expect to get an honest answer from someone who doesn't know you from Adam? And in this case, on something he has kept secret for eighteen years, assuming that he might actually be guilty. Expecting honesty at that point was premature.

Some attorneys prefer to ask for the client's "version" right at the beginning: "So, tell me what happened," an attempt to get the client to explain why he's attracted the suspicion of the police. I've learned that in most serious cases, it's best to see the allegations and evidence first, to get at least some of the official version of the facts, before getting the defendant's detailed account of what happened. I like to see (and I like my client to see) what the police have, so I can gauge the reasonableness or truthfulness of the allegations and the strength of the state's case. Of course, I also need to know about any statements my client may have already made to the police.

Also, I want my client to trust me, to have faith that I'll know the right thing to do. I need to have his trust so he'll tell me the truth. Besides all this, once my client has made a firm denial to me, then he's essentially locked in to that story, which makes it a lot harder for him to back off later, when it might really count. With all these factors in mind, I've just found it much safer and more productive to wait on the crucial question of possible culpability. I presume innocence and wait to see what the state can prove.

Anyway, it didn't matter. If Gary Ridgway was going to cooperate to save himself from the death penalty, he would have talked to the cops when they first invited him to tell all, instead of requesting a lawyer. Once he'd asked for a lawyer, the ball was in our court. It was up to us. If Gary said he wasn't the killer, that would be our position too—for as long as it was tenable.

Over the course of a couple hours, as Gary was telling us about the events that had brought him to the attention of the police, I noticed that he seemed to swerve between time periods, combining events and questions he'd been asked years earlier, in the mid-1980s, when he'd first been contacted by the police, or in 1987, when his house had been searched for the first time, although it wasn't always clear which event or question and answer belonged to which time period. The disparate events seemed to run together in his mind, and pretty soon both Greg and I were a bit confused about what had happened that day and what might have taken place years earlier. Gary seemed to think that Greg and I already knew a lot about him and the Green River case, probably because the search of his house fourteen years earlier had been big news, even if his name hadn't been published at the time. So his story assumed that we already knew things, even if we weren't really clear on what he was actually talking about.

"I've dated a lot of prostitutes," Gary said. "More when I was single." But he admitted that he'd continued "dating" right up to the present time. In fact, he told us, he'd been arrested just two weeks earlier, when he'd made the mistake of soliciting a police decoy. When he was being booked at the jail after his last arrest, he'd even given the old Green River Task Force as a reference!

On the whole, though, he seemed remarkably calm and collected. He maintained normal eye contact with both of us and smiled when it was appropriate. But then, every once in a while, his conversation would stray off the subject, sometimes even in mid-sentence, leaving us to wonder what he was talking about and just how it related to the charges against him. These seeming non sequiturs made me wonder if the disconnects were only the surface manifestations of deeper, possibly more ominous hidden brain damage.

As Gary finished describing the events of the day, I once again did not let myself think very much about the central issue, which was whether Gary was responsible for all of the murders, or even any of them. It wasn't something I needed to think about right then, because he had already denied killing anyone, at least to the police. My deeper, unvoiced instinct about his complete innocence, however, was skepticism. The report on television about the supposed DNA match (if it were true) suggested to me that the police had potentially solid evidence tying Gary to at least one of the victims, probably this Carol Christensen. But one murder, however reprehensible, was a far cry from being *the* Green River Killer, even assuming there were only one such person and not a series of improperly connected murders. Greg and I knew we'd have to wait to see what evidence the police actually had. Relying on Gary's version, or the reports on television, just wasn't going to be very helpful at this stage.

"It was Marcia," Gary told us. "She was the one who told the task force the things that weren't true."

"Who's Marcia?" I asked.

"My wife," Gary said. "I mean, my ex-wife. Judith is my wife now. Marcia is Matthew's mother. Claudia and I got divorced in 1971."

That was pretty much a sample of Gary's conversation that night. He skipped around from event to event in a way that often left us mystified.

Bit by bit, we began to form a picture of Gary's life. He told us that he'd grown up in the south King County area, not far from SeaTac International Airport, the very epicenter of all the murders. Both his mother and his father were dead. He had two brothers, one married to the paralegal who worked for a large Seattle law firm; that was one reason he thought his family might hire private counsel. He had been married three times, first to Claudia, then to Marcia, and last to Judith, to whom he was still married and with whom he lived in a paid-for house in Auburn. He was the father of one adult son, Matthew, who was serving in the Marines near San Diego.

Gary had worked continuously for Kenworth Truck Company from the time of his honorable discharge from the Navy in the early 1970s. All three Ridgway sons had been in the military at the same time. Gary had served in Southeast Asia during the Vietnam War, as had his younger brother, Ed, who'd been in the Army. His older brother, Greg, had been in Korea, also with the Army. Overall, except for his peculiar tendency to twine together disparate events as if they were all happening at the same time, Gary seemed utterly normal and certainly nothing like the evil Einstein everyone had expected the Green River Killer to be.

I explained to Gary that now that he'd been arrested, there was no way to speed things up. It would take many months, maybe even years, to get to the end of what had just begun to happen to him. That was simply the nature of the beast, in such a notorious case. Gary said he understood, that he was prepared to be patient.

"Eventually," I said, "after we get to know each other, we're gonna have to have some hard discussions. But those will be down the road."

"Oooh-K," Gary grinned. I wasn't sure that he actually appreciated what I was trying to suggest—that at some point in the future we would probably have to have some difficult, even traumatic, discussions about whatever evidence the police had against him, and whatever it was he might have done. Much, much later, I realized that Gary at some primal level actually was eager to have those candid talks. It was as if there was something inside of him that wanted to let out secrets—some of them anyway—that he'd kept bottled up for decades. But it would be more than a year before we came to that eventuality.

Greg and I explained that the law required that he be taken to court for a preliminary appearance, where a judge would determine if there was *probable cause*—some reasonable, factual grounds—to hold him in connection with the murders. We also explained that in a normal case, bail would usually be set, but in a case involving a potential death penalty—like this one—a suspect would be held without bail, which meant he'd have to stay in jail for the foreseeable future. He understood this and voiced no complaints.

This preliminary appearance would probably happen the next day, we told him, and the chance that his first appearance in court would turn into a news media free-for-all was a certainty. Gary had to expect that his picture would be taken over and over again and that his name would be made public. His family would probably be subjected to a barrage of calls from news reporters from all over the country, if they hadn't already been.

This seemed to be the only moment that Gary appeared sad. Clearly, the prospect of such unwanted notoriety for his family upset him. I asked Gary if there was anything I could do for him right away. Tears began to well up in his eyes, and he asked me to call his wife, Judith, and his brother Greg Ridgway, to let them know what was going on. I assured him that I'd make the calls.

At that point, there was a knock on the door. It opened, and a man with silver-gray hair entered the room. This was Dave Reichert, the King County Sheriff. Almost everyone in Seattle knew Reichert's story: he'd been the detective initially assigned to the Green River case nearly twenty years earlier, when the first five victims of the supposed killer had been found in or near the river. Over the previous two decades, he'd worked his way up the hierarchy of the Sheriff's Department, until he'd been first appointed, then elected, Sheriff. Now Reichert was a politician, not just a cop, and the arrest of the first official suspect in the nation's most notorious, unsolved murder case had to be even more of a triumph—one that might grow electoral legs, a fact that had already drawn comment from the television news people.

"Sorry to interrupt," Reichert told us, "but we were wondering how much longer you wanted to go on. Some of our guys have been up since early this morning, and we want to wrap things up for now, if we can." Reichert said plans had been made to move Gary to the large jail in downtown Seattle, where he'd be kept in protective custody until it was time for court. I looked at my watch; it was nearly nine.

Greg and I said we were done—for the moment. We gathered up our notes, and Gary was escorted by deputies to another room to prepare him for transportation to the main jail.

On the way out of the detectives' offices, Greg and I spoke briefly with Reichert and Detectives Jim Doyon and Randy Mullinax. They'd been among the investigators who'd asked Gary most of the questions that afternoon. I'd had cases with the compact, intense Mullinax before. In my view, he'd always been a straight shooter, not one prone to shade the facts for anyone's advantage. But because we still didn't know for sure exactly what Gary would be charged with, Reichert, Doyon, and Mullinax were less than forthcoming with hard facts—like, just *which* of the forty-nine Green River murders, or even how many, the police intended to say Gary had committed. Reichert told us that the case had been assigned to a highly regarded, veteran King County deputy prosecutor, Jeffrey Baird, and that Baird would handle all the official information. We'd have to get everything we wanted from Baird, he said. Sorry.

Greg Girard and I left, walking out the same door I had gone in through almost two hours earlier. Leaning against the wall, smoking another cigarette, drinking Diet Pepsi, was the same guy in blue jeans and a windbreaker who had let me into the offices when I'd first arrived.

"Excuse me, detective," I said, extending my hand. "I just want to introduce myself. . . . I'm Mark Prothero. . . . I've been a defense attorney for quite a while, but I don't think we've ever crossed paths before."

"Tom Jensen," the guy with the Pepsi said, shaking my hand.

"How come we've never met before? Where've you been hiding?"

"This case," Jensen said. "I've been on this case for seventeen years."

"Just this case?" I was astounded. "Seventeen *years*?"

"Just this case. Oh, there were a couple other homicides here and there, but mainly this was it."

I tried not to let my shock show. Somehow, some way, this one detective had worked on only *one* case for almost as long as I'd been a lawyer. . . . It hardly seemed possible, at a time when police detectives, even homicide detectives, routinely had more cases than they had fingers and toes to count them on. But not this guy, Jensen. I had to guess that this one detective knew more about the Green River murders than anyone else in the world—except, the killer himself.

"And all you're drinking is Diet Pepsi?" I asked him. "You're so calm. . . . They'd be scraping me off the ceiling, if I were you!"

"We did that already," Jensen said. "Now I'm just tired. I've been up for, like, two days straight. Right now, I just want to get some sleep."

———

Girard and I adjourned to the two-story, nondescript modern building of glass and stucco that served as ACA's south county office, a few blocks away from the jail. I made telephone calls to Gary's brother Greg Ridgway and to Judith Ridgway, his wife. Both calls were picked up by answering machines, and I left brief messages. We guessed that Gary's brother and his wife had already received so many telephone calls that they were no longer bothering to pick up the phone. After you hear from the news media that your brother or husband has just been arrested in connection with the worst unsolved serial murder case in the United States, "How do you feel?" would make anyone ignore the ringing.

I raided one of the refrigerators in the office kitchen for a couple of beers and gave one to Greg. At first we just looked at each other, both thinking to ourselves: *my God, we've been sitting with somebody who might actually be* the *Green River Killer!*

"Wow, that was weird," Greg said after he'd swallowed some of his beer. We were both stunned at Gary's placidity, even docility, under the extraordinary circumstances. He'd been so damn *polite*—hardly the demeanor one might expect from a man who might be accused of more than four dozen murders, the supposed evil genius who had flummoxed the police for almost twenty years. Under the circumstances, I wouldn't have been at all surprised to see someone ranting at anyone within shouting distance.

Neither Greg nor I needed to discuss whether we thought Gary was guilty—of one or even *all* of the killings. It was far too soon for that. We'd have plenty of time later to evaluate Gary Ridgway's potential culpability. Right then, all we needed to do was make sure that we'd done everything necessary to protect his rights. One thing was for sure, Gary wasn't going anywhere, any time soon.

I asked Greg how he'd heard about the arrest.

"I got a call from Todd." Todd was Todd Gruenhagen, another ACA lawyer who worked in our office in downtown Seattle. "Todd said he'd gotten a call from Jim Crane." Crane was the administrator of the Office of Public Defense, the government bureaucracy that handled the county's contracts with the nonprofit public defense agencies, like ACA.

"Crane heard about it on the radio or someplace and called Todd to see if ACA would represent whoever it was who had been arrested. Todd said we would and then tried to find out the guy's name and where he was being held, but the Sheriff's Department wouldn't tell him. Then he heard that Reichert was going to hold a press conference, so he tried to watch that, but some deputy wouldn't let him in." It sounded as though the Sheriff's Department had wanted to keep Gary to themselves for as long as possible that afternoon.

"After that," Greg continued, "Todd guessed that Gary was probably being kept at the sheriff's detectives' offices at the Regional Justice Center here in Kent." Todd then called Girard, reasoning that Greg could probably get to the prisoner sooner than he could. By then, it was just before six. Greg had left his message for me, then he called Colleen, his wife, to let her know where he was going. After that, he'd rushed over to the RJC to see the new arrestee.

It wasn't terribly unusual for the police to dawdle a bit before arranging for an arrestee to consult with a lawyer. Both Greg and I thought, from Gary's description of the events, that no real harm had been done. I did think it was odd that according to Gary no tape recording of the initial police interrogation had been made. One would think that would have been standard operating procedure in a case of this magnitude.

As Greg and I considered what we needed to do next for our new client, the potential enormity of the case began to sink in. We'd both tried difficult cases before, but nothing like this. The sheer possible size of it boggled the mind. Forty-nine separate murders, allegedly committed over an eighteen-month period—that is, assuming that the authorities were actually intending to say that Gary was in fact *the* one and only killer. If so, the volume of evidence would be staggering—hundreds of thousands, maybe even millions, of pages of reports to go through, compiled over almost two decades of seemingly fruitless investigation. A ton of physical evidence—possibly even literally. Enough photographs, probably, to pave all the sidewalks from Seattle to Chicago, or maybe even further than that. Thousands of potential alternate suspects, each of whom would have to be reinvestigated by the defense, just to make sure the police hadn't overlooked something that might tend to indicate that Gary hadn't committed all, or even one, of the crimes. Even more daunting, there would be a huge amount of news media attention, copiously ladled on top of a jury pool sick to death of the murders, and possibly, just aching to end the whole thing with a quick conviction.

There wasn't a place in the state and probably even the nation that hadn't heard of the murders. Where could we expect to find anyone who was unbiased? To do this case right, to get justice, promised to take years and cost millions of dollars.

And then there was Gary himself: so placid, so cooperative. We'd admonished him over and over again while we were with him to keep his mouth shut. We explained that there were people in jail—other inmates—who would be anxious to tell the authorities that Gary had "confessed" to them. He had to keep himself under control and say nothing to anyone about the charges against him. Could he do it? Or would he be swept up in his new celebrity-monster status and start playing the role of serial murderer for other inmates, even if he hadn't killed anyone? It wouldn't be the first time an innocent person had foolishly bragged his way onto the gallows.

Still, one thing was sure: whatever his tendency to conflate past and present events, Gary seemed to know what was at stake. His questions to us had been sensible, even reasonable, under the circumstances. On first impression, a mental disease or defect defense appeared to be out. In fact, it was Gary's very calmness that was most unnerving. Usually, it was my experience that an innocent person accused of a terrible crime was on the ceiling, with a volatile mixture of outrage and panic. Not Gary.

This made both Greg and me guess, at least to ourselves, and largely unspoken that night, that there might be something substantial behind the charges and that it was just a matter of time before the whole ugly story came out, despite Gary's initial denial to the police. But even then, we were unprepared for the awful details that were eventually to come from Gary's own lips.

3

I left the ACA office about nine-thirty that night. I called my wife, Kelly, at home. We'd planned to get together about seven, but obviously I hadn't made it. I began to explain about Gary Ridgway and his arrest, but Kelly interrupted.

"I knew it," she said. "I saw it on TV." Then she reminded me that we'd previously agreed to visit our friends Brad and Tina that night, so I told her I'd meet her there.

When I got to Brad and Tina's half an hour later, the television in their living room was on, still blaring about Gary's arrest. The broadcasters were running the same old file footage, as well as indulging in energetic speculation about what might happen next. I saw a clip of Dave Reichert saying no one was claiming that his detectives had actually arrested *the* killer, only that an arrest had been made in four of the forty-nine cases. That cautionary note was largely skipped over by the television people, who quickly moved on to the prospect of additional charges being filed in the near future. One thing seemed clear: the public, at least as articulated by the broadcasters, wanted the case to be finished, and sooner rather than later. That wasn't good—not if you wanted an unbiased jury.

"Mark," my friend Brad said when I arrived, "are you really gonna do this case?"

"It looks that way." I explained that I'd just seen the man of the hour in the King County Sheriff's detectives' offices at the RJC.

"What's he like?" Tina asked. "Was he creepy?"

"He seemed really nice," I said. "Normal, polite. He wasn't freaked out at all. He was a little stressed. He wanted me to call his wife and his brother."

"He's *married?*"

"Three times," I said.

Tina, who'd been one of Kelly's best friends since grade school, asked Kelly what she thought about my defending the supposed Green River Killer. Kelly had no moral objection to an accused serial murderer having his constitutional right of representation. She understood what my job was; her misgivings were much more practical. She'd already guessed that such a case might take over our lives.

"I know I'm going to be a single mother for the next five years," Kelly told Tina, in an exaggerated mixture of defiance and resignation. I laughed this off, but later, when we got home around midnight, I asked her what she'd *really* felt about my taking the case.

"You know what *I* think," Kelly told me. "I know you're going to be gone for long hours, and it's going to go on like that, for months, or maybe even years. But I also know you. It's something you want to do, and I know you won't be happy if you don't do it, and I don't want you to be unhappy. So you might as well do what you want. Besides, you'd just do it anyway." Kelly was kidding, but I could sense some real concern under her teasing.

—⁓—

Over nineteen years of marriage, Kelly and I have had our differences. What husband and wife haven't? I knew what Kelly worried about: the case would become so consuming that despite my best intentions, it would disrupt our lives, foul up all our established routines. But I also knew that whatever I decided, Kelly would back me all the way.

We'd first met at Renton High School in 1972, when I was a junior and Kelly was a freshman. Because we started out as best friends, we've always been able to be each other's harshest critics. She might hold a grudge longer than me, but never for very long. She can give someone the truth without stinting, and she wasn't about to let me get so full of myself that I'd lose my way. Being honest with each other was the bond that held our marriage together.

Kelly and I married in 1982, a few months after I'd passed the bar. Sean, our first child, was born in 1985, and Marley, his sister, five years later. Now our lives together were centered around our home, our children, their school, and swimming competitions, along with the many friends we'd made through these activities.

Swimming competitively has always been an important part of my own life. Probably because both my father and grandfather were expert boatbuilders—Prothero wooden boats are known all over the world—and everyone in my family had to learn how to swim at an early age. When I was seven, my older brother, Blake, and I joined the summer swim team at Lakeridge Swim Club. At age nine, I started to swim year-round, and by high school, I'd gotten pretty good. I qualified for my first senior nationals when I was seventeen, won a state high school title in the 200-yard individual medley in 1974, and then went to the University of Washington on a swimming scholarship. While at the "U-Dub," I finished third in the 400-meter individual medley at the summer nationals in 1976 and fifth in the same event in 1977. As a result, I was chosen to represent the United States in competitions in Argentina in 1977 and Paris and Amsterdam in 1978.

I knew that my experience as a competitive swimmer had taught me a lot about what it takes to be a good lawyer. Competitive swimming teaches people to work hard and to be patient for the reward. It teaches you how to struggle when you're working your ass off but not making any headway, while your opponent seems to have success without any obvious effort.

That in turn tells you that doing your best is really up to you, and in that way, it's just like the law. It teaches you to separate competition from friendship, showing you that someone who might be your opponent in the pool (or in the courtroom) can still be your friend, outside those places. Most of all, it teaches you to deal with frustration—to be persistent in spite of obstacles. There were plenty of times on the pool deck when I remembered that those lessons were fundamental training for any lawyer.

That night, though, I slept in fits and starts, juggling my initial impression of Gary Ridgway with random thoughts about Kelly, our kids, the needs of the Kentwood swimming team, and ideas on how a multiple murder case might be defended. At the same time, another part of me kept trying to turn my brain into a memo pad: reminders to check into this, or not to forget about that, or to consider still other things. As these thoughts streamed in and out of my consciousness with alarming rapidity, I found my brain spinning away.

If I went forward on the case—if I wasn't replaced by private counsel, as Gary Ridgway thought would probably happen—I knew that this would be the biggest case of my career.

And if ACA *did* defend Gary, the notoriety of the murders, with the number of years between the crimes and his arrest, along with the life-and-death stakes involved, would certainly bring intense public scrutiny to both me and my family.

Do I really want to do this? Is there something weird about wanting to do it? Is it fair to Kelly? Is it fair to Sean and to Marley? I know I'm going to be consumed by the thing. What if the trial takes a year and it's moved to, say, Spokane? Can I handle Ridgway, coaching the swim team, being a husband and father, all at the same time?

Even as these questions ran through my head, my rational mind quickly supplied answers, possibly rationalizations: *If I have to, I can give up coaching for a while. And I know I can be a good dad and husband. I'll work extra hard at that. I won't let this case hurt my family life in any way. It won't be like Ken Ford's case, where I had to learn all the capital case law from scratch. I've already learned it! Well, most of it anyway. I have a good idea of what I'll have to do.*

Or do I? Am I kidding myself? Am I in over my head? And then came some calming self-reassurance. *No. I'm not. This is exactly what my training and experience has led me to. There's a reason this came my way. I've had great luck at ACA and this is why—to get ready for this huge case! It's a beast, but I want it. It's my challenge, it's what I do. And Kelly knows this.*

She'll be with me on this, I told myself. *She'll support me because she knows everything I do will be scrutinized. Three times. So she knows I'll want to do my very best work. And she knows I'll throw myself into it. She'll see. I'll show her. I can do both. I can be a good husband, and a good dad, while handling this case. Besides, we probably won't get to keep the case anyway. Gary said his family would probably hire a private attorney. Once that happens, we'll be out. . . . So let's just see what happens . . .*

With all of these thoughts streaming through my mind, I got up the next morning, Saturday, December 1, 2001, just after six. The high school swim team had a regular workout scheduled for seven. As the sun was just coming up, I put my Coach Prothero hat back on, and Sean and I drove to the pool. Our boys' team had only a week or so to go before their first meet, so this was no time to let down, even if I hadn't had much sleep.

On the way to the pool, I asked Sean if he could find a ride home after the workout. I told him I had to cut short my coaching that morning and go to downtown Seattle.

"Yeah, Mike can take me home," Sean told me. "Or Ryan. Why are you going downtown?"

"I've been assigned the Green River guy," I told him.

"Wow," Sean said, impressed. "Really?"

"Yeah. What do you think?" I asked. "I mean, this could come back on you. People are gonna want to see this guy executed, and I'd be fighting it." I had an unformed worry that Sean, and maybe Marley, would catch some grief from their schoolmates over the fact that their father might be trying to save the supposed Green River Killer from being executed. In the present climate, it might not be all that popular.

"Hey, I think that's really cool," Sean said. "That's a big case. It was all over the news last night."

"Yeah, but would you be OK with it if I represented him?"

"Sure. All my friends know what you do, and I think they respect you for it. *I* do. No. It wouldn't be a problem for me."

At the pool, we had a quick team meeting. I let the guys know what was going on. The comments ranged from "He's gonna fry!" to "I didn't know Coach was a lawyer." I explained why I do what I do— how the Constitution gives every person the right to a fair trial and that a fair trial requires that a person accused of a crime be provided with a lawyer, even at public expense. And that otherwise, it wouldn't be a fair trial—it would be nothing but a railroad.

Not surprisingly, for high school boys, it appeared a strong majority of the team favored the death penalty. I explained that I did not expect the case to affect my coaching. I'd try as hard as I could to continue with the team. I hoped this would be the case, but I also knew some of those questions were out of my hands. Except for Sean and a couple of seniors, it appeared as if most team members didn't really care that I was going to try to defend a man arrested in connection with nearly four dozen murders. But then, most high schoolers have a rather more immediate focus.

After about an hour of practice, I turned the workout over to my assistant, Tricia Olson, who was an English teacher at Kentwood High

School, not far away. I'd coached Tricia herself, back in the early 1980s. Now she was grown up and was actually a teacher, for Pete's sake, which brought home to me how many years Kelly and I had been in Kent—from one generation to the next.

Just before eight, I left the pool and drove to Seattle to see Gary at the downtown jail.

To the rest of the country, Seattle is probably best known for rain, Starbucks, Microsoft, and Boeing. For those of us who live here, though, the Pacific Northwest remains one of the most livable regions of the country—a unique blend of nature and culture.

To the east of the city, the fir-shrouded Cascade Mountains run north and south through the middle of the state, like a huge, green-coated spinal column, separating the wetter west from the drier east. The mountains, a wall of forested, snow-capped peaks, are punctuated in the south by the steaming flattop of Mt. St. Helens, and in the north by the picturesque, semi-dormant volcano, 10,775-foot-high Mt. Baker. In the middle, the even yet more ominous, hulking dome of 14,411-foot Mt. Rainier dominates the Seattle skyline.

Seattle had once been a wide-open, frontier waterfront town, a place that had grown up on the shore of one of the largest natural harbors in the world, Puget Sound. The Sound is a labyrinthine tangle of inlets, straits, bays, and sloughs, which in turn means that no one in western Washington is ever very far away from water. Seattle had begun as a commercial nexus between sea lanes and rail lines—timber and fish going out, cheap labor coming in. It had long enjoyed (or suffered) a reputation for loose morals, particularly during the 1900 gold rush to the Klondike, when brothels were among Seattle's most profitable as well as prominent businesses. For decades, well into the twentieth century, the vice trades had operated more or less with the acquiescence of local law enforcement, who figured that organized dissolution was at least a bit more controllable than the alternative, and which at least had the advantage of keeping the politicians flush with cash, if not necessarily proud.

All this had started to change in the 1970s, however, with the advent of the birth control pill, the illicit drug culture, and the new Alaska rush—the one for oil. By the early 1970s, the flesh trade was rather completely disorganized, much of it occurring in "strolls" along a portion of Pacific Highway South, old U.S. 99, which ran along the top of a ridgeline southeast of the city proper, and just above and to the west of the Kent Valley, which lay directly under the shadow of Mt. Rainier. Most of this prostitution activity took place near the region's busiest airport, SeaTac International. The airport, a major stopover on the way to the Alaska pipeline project that took off in the early to mid-1970s, generated waves of lonely travelers willing to spend a few dollars for various kinds of entertainment on the way to and from the North Slope.

As the 1980s unfolded, Pacific Highway South also became local Seattle's motorized den of iniquity, the place where even the good went when they wanted to be bad. A number of these generally law-abiding, if hypocritical, patronizers of prostitutes, in fact, lived in Kent, down in the valley below the heavily trafficked ridge. As it turned out, the ridge and the valley became the very heart of the Green River Killer's killing ground.

Gary Ridgway had been living in the middle of this almost his whole life.

—⁓—

The downtown King County Jail in Seattle was a towering, eleven-story, fortress-like structure that had been built during the first Reagan administration, in part because the old jail built atop the 1920s-era King County Courthouse had become a threat to life and limb. A beige metal skybridge extending from the top floor, more than a hundred feet up and looking like a long series of steel shipping containers welded end-to-end, connected it across Fourth and Fifth Avenues to the old courthouse, which was a twelve-floor pile of gray bricks in imminent danger of collapse during an earthquake. Within four years after the new Reagan-era jail opened in 1984, it was already overcrowded, mostly because the laws had changed: in the eighties and nineties, we locked up far more drunk drivers and domestic assaulters than anyone had ever imagined when the place was first designed.

By 1990, things had gotten so bad with the crowding in the "new" jail downtown that the county politicians had to build another "new jail," which was why we had the Regional Justice Center in Kent. Still, both jails were often overcrowded, as the increase in jail population always seemed to race ahead of our ability to make new cells.

At the downtown jail, I went to the third floor, where the county corrections officers process the paperwork needed for *face-to-face* visits. *Face-to-faces*, as they are called, where you and your client sit at a table, physically together in the same room (unlike regular attorney visits and visits by relatives and other visitors, where you have to talk to the inmate through a glass window via a telephone hookup), usually require advance notice to the jail personnel.

In this case, though, probably because only a few hours after his arrival, Gary was already one of the most notorious prisoners ever lodged at the main jail, a sergeant was contacted, and I was allowed to have a face-to-face with Gary. This would be only the first of what would turn out to be many similar meetings in the jail over the next two years.

The corrections officers also told me that Gary's first court appearance had been scheduled for one o'clock that afternoon, in one of the high-security courtrooms on the first floor of the jail. They said they were expecting a huge news media gang in the courtroom and told me that television trucks were already beginning to arrive on the street outside the jail.

Now it begins, I thought.

4

Gary had been temporarily lodged in a single cell on the seventh floor of the lockup. I knew this was the floor generally used for those with health issues—physical and mental—which meant that Gary was under a suicide watch. The worst thing right then, for everyone, would be for Gary to do himself in, before any questions could be definitely answered.

A small room on the seventh floor was designated for the face-to-faces for prisoners housed on that floor. Inside the face-to-face room was the requisite plastic furniture, along with a fluorescent light that buzzed continuously. A long, narrow, vertical, wire-mesh window was set in the door to permit the guards to look in from time to time, whenever they wanted. A few minutes after I sat down in this face-to-face room, Gary was escorted in, shackled by hand and plastic-sandaled foot, wearing a red cotton prisoner's jumpsuit, with King County Jail stenciled on the back, just in case anyone forgot where he was.

Apart from being slightly disheveled—he hadn't been allowed to shave—Gary seemed as normal as he had the day before. He smiled at me pleasantly, and his gray-blue eyes seemed welcoming behind his large, semi-nerdy glasses.

"Good morning, Mr. Ridgway. How are you doing?" I asked. "How'd it go last night?" I knew the first night in jail could be traumatic for some people—*The Shawshank Redemption* had that part right.

"Oh, pretty good. I didn't sleep real well, but I was fine. I've always been a light sleeper." He smiled again.

I asked him if he'd had any thoughts about doing himself harm. I had no specific indications that Gary was thinking about committing suicide. That was just my standard operating procedure with someone who recently learned he could be facing the death penalty. But I could see he was, rather incredibly, in a good mood.

What's going on here? Some part of my brain registered the anomaly. *Either he's absolutely innocent and knows it, or . . . maybe he's happy that things are coming to a head? . . .* I wasn't sure how to interpret this behavior.

We talked about what to expect at his first court appearance that day. I explained the judge would undoubtedly find there was probable cause to hold him and would deny setting any bail in this case. That meant he'd have to stay in jail.

"Oooh-K," he said. The prospect of prolonged incarceration didn't appear to bother him much. His main concern seemed to be about his family.

"Did you reach my wife or my brother and let them know what was going on?"

"I was only able to leave them messages. I didn't actually talk to either one."

"I'm worried about Judith," he said. He guessed she was probably going through hell at that point. "They [the police] told me they would probably be putting her up somewhere while they searched the house," he said. "In a hotel somewhere, I guess." His eyes filled with tears as he thought about his wife and what she must be experiencing: being removed from their house, taken to a strange place by strange people, having to read and view and listen to increasingly lurid stories about her absent husband. Again I was struck by how ordinary this all seemed and how unlike a supposed remorseless serial killer Gary's all-so-normal behavior actually was. His feeling for Judith was completely genuine, not feigned in the least. In fact, when I thought about some of my other aggravated murder cases—Jim Cushing, Roy Webbe, for instance—I didn't recall *them* shedding any tears. But they each had chronic, well-documented mental problems. Did Gary's weeping indicate that he hadn't killed anyone?

One thing was sure: Gary was not acting like the unfeeling, con-scienceless, degenerate serial killer he was supposed to be, at least if one believed in the popular image of such predators. This was defi-nitely not Hannibal Lector.

We talked a little more. I reminded him of the importance of not talking to anyone about his predicament. . . . *Anyone*. He said he un-derstood. We also talked about the fact that death penalty cases—and this was definitely going to be a death penalty case—could take a long time, years even, to get to trial. Given the history of this case, it might take even longer than normal. Gary said he understood all this, too. In fact, he seemed perfectly at ease with what was happening to him. I realized that Gary had probably been imagining how these events might unfold for years before they had actually happened, or at least since the search of 1987, which was probably why he was so accepting of his situation.

I left in mid-morning, telling Gary I'd be back around noon to help him get ready for his first court appearance. I told him yet again that he had to understand he was the object of intense curiosity and that the news people were certain to want to take pictures of him.

"I know, I know," he said.

Once out of the jail, I collected editions of the Saturday morning newspapers, then went to Lemieux's Restaurant at First Avenue and Lander Street, not far from Safeco Field, where I ordered breakfast. While eating a plateful of scrambled eggs, bacon, hash browns, toast, and black coffee, I also devoured the front-page stories from the three major dailies.

The coverage was both emphatic and voluminous, although it would later turn out that at least some of it was in error. Still, I learned more about the Green River murders in that hour and a half at Lemieux's than I had ever known before then. Even though I also knew better than to believe everything I read in the papers, I felt like I was beginning to get a tentative grip on the essentials of the case. I also learned quite a bit of background about Gary Ridgway, or at least what the newspapers were saying was his background.

Each newspaper had multiple stories about the events of the pre-vious day. The two Seattle dailies, the *Times* and the *Post-Intelligencer,* each led off with a story attributing Gary's arrest to newly processed DNA evidence. According to the papers, an oral swab taken from Gary at the time of the 1987 search had been matched to DNA found with Marcia Chapman, Cynthia Hinds, and Opal Mills, three of the killer's victims, whose bodies had been found in or near the Green River in 1982. The match had finally been made because of advances in DNA technology that had taken place over the last few years. In other words, the police had possessed all the samples of DNA for many years but had just been unable to match them until now.

The *Times* reported that the police had actually made a DNA match with three of the victims—the victims found in or near the river, Chapman, Hinds, and Mills. Both papers quoted Sheriff Reichert as saying that the authorities did not have a DNA match with Carol Christensen, whose body had been found nearly nine months later, far away from the river. In fact, the papers had Reichert telling them that they had "other evidence" to link Gary to Carol Christensen.[1] Was that why they had shown Carol Christensen's photograph to Gary? Did they have evidence proving that Gary had in fact known Carol Christensen and were using Gary's denial to implicate him?

Another newspaper factoid caught my eye: according to the *Times*, at least, the police had made the DNA matches *two months* earlier. They'd had Gary under surveillance since then, according to Reichert. But they hadn't decided to pull him in until Gary had been coincidentally arrested in mid-November, when he'd solicited the undercover policewoman posing as a prostitute, and even then had waited for two more weeks—for what? Did that mean they had doubts that Gary was the killer?

On the other hand, the idea that the police had DNA evidence from *three* of the victims, and not just one, *was* worrying. Gary might reasonably claim to have once had sex with one of the victims, but three? What were the odds that one person's DNA would be coincidentally found with three people who would shortly afterward be murdered? One, maybe. But three?

The DNA information naturally caught my attention. It appeared that the Sheriff's Department had subjected the DNA samples it had from the victims—probably semen, I guessed—and compared it with the DNA taken from Gary nearly five years later, in 1987. The papers indicated that the samples had been subjected to STR testing—the latest technology in the burgeoning field of forensic DNA. Essentially, STR—an abbreviation for *short tandem repeats*—allowed experts to take a very small amount of DNA and test it for certain molecular characteristics at thirteen different areas, or *loci*, on the human genome. A DNA profile could be produced that could be traced to a single individual with an accuracy often in the quadrillions. Up until the previous few years or so, earlier types of DNA testing required much more DNA or were significantly less discriminating than that provided by STR, which made such evidence extremely exact. That was why a lot of old cases that hadn't resulted in matches to suspects were now beginning to be solved, all across the country. The question was whether the DNA that had been tested had been handled properly, according to agreed-upon laboratory protocols. If it hadn't, there was a possibility that we might attack the DNA tests as flawed. Of course, the fact that it had supposedly matched in three of the cases suggested that no mistake had been made.

One thing was sure: the day before had been a red-letter day in the life of Sheriff Reichert.

"This has got to be one of the most exciting days in my entire career," the sheriff had told the news media as he'd announced Gary's arrest. The DNA found with the victims had been "conclusively linked" to Gary, Reichert had added. But then Reichert had hedged on whether that meant Gary was *the* Green River Killer. "I cannot say with certainty that Gary Ridgway is responsible for all those deaths, . . . but boy, have we made one giant step forward."

The *Times* pretty much ran right past that caveat: "For nearly 20 years," the paper reported in its lead story, "detectives hunting for the Green River Killer knew in their hearts that Gary Leon Ridgway was probably their man."[2] The paper quoted a retired deputy prosecutor, Al Mathews, as saying that although most people involved in the investigation had believed that Gary was the killer, no one wanted to prosecute him in case the evidence was insufficient to sustain a conviction. Because of the constitutional ban on double jeopardy, Mathews had said, they would have had only one shot at convicting Gary, and no one wanted to mess it up by bringing a weak case.

Although Gary had never been named in any of the news media stories about the search of his house and cars that had taken place in 1987, it appeared that many of those who knew Gary also knew that he had previously been the focus of the Green River investigation. The *Post-Intelligencer* reported that Gary's coworkers at Kenworth even joked about this, nicknaming him "Green River Gary," or sometimes simply "G.R." But no one really thought he'd actually had anything to do with the murders. The nickname was all in fun. At least, until he'd been arrested yesterday.

The papers had gone to the usual sources whenever anyone was arrested in connection with an infamous crime—neighbors and coworkers. No one had anything bad to say about Gary. Almost everyone described him as pleasant and easygoing. One former manager at Kenworth called Gary "a steady Eddie," . . . a very normal employee, very trouble-free.

"I wouldn't say he was shy," the former manager had told the newspaper, "but he wouldn't go out of his way to engage people. Socially, he got along, but if you'd have told me yesterday he was a serial killer, I would have said, 'no way.' Nothing in his behavior would suggest that."

Unfortunately, that remark itself suggested that people were now prepared to believe that Gary *was* the killer. That was the power the police had—to influence the public mind by the very fact that they'd made an arrest. People gave lip service to the idea of being innocent until proven guilty, but the simple fact that police obviously believed they had the culprit—why else would they have arrested him?—tended to make people secretly believe the accused had to be guilty. All in all, the papers carried very little that might suggest that Gary was innocent. About the only leavening came from my friend and fellow Senior Trial Attorney at ACA, Todd Gruenhagen, who'd tried and failed to get into Sheriff Reichert's press conference, and who'd manage to alert Greg Girard to the fact of Gary's arrest. The reason the reporters hadn't tried to call me was that no one knew that it was Greg Girard and I who had first talked to Gary, not Todd.

"Ridgway's court-appointed lawyer, Todd Gruenhagen of Seattle, complained yesterday that police hadn't let him talk to Ridgway and wouldn't even tell him where he was being held," the *Times* reported.[3] "Gruenhagen declined to speak specifically about the case but cautioned the public not to assume Ridgway is guilty just because Reichert says he is." That was just about it, for our side.

I checked my watch; I still had a couple of hours before Gary's scheduled initial appearance. I decided to go into the ACA Seattle office, located near the downtown jail, to see if I could connect with Jeff Baird, the deputy prosecutor that Reichert had told us had been assigned to the case. I wanted to hear what Baird had to say about Gary's arrest and to let him know that I'd be representing him at the first court appearance.

—◁◁◁—

Just outside the ACA offices, across from the courthouse, I ran into Jim Robinson, ACA's assistant director. He'd decided to come into work that Saturday just to make sure that Gary's first appearance in court would be covered by a lawyer. It was apparent that things had happened so fast that our group still wasn't completely organized on how to respond to the new case.

Before he'd become one of our administrators, Jim had been a veteran public defender. He'd defended two notorious Seattle death penalty cases, one the so-called Wah Mee Massacre, in which two robbers had methodically gunned down thirteen people in a Seattle after-hours gambling club, and another case in which a bank robber had murdered a police officer during the crime. The bank robber was sentenced to life in prison, and the death penalty for the Wah Mee robber was eventually reversed on appeal. So Jim had plenty of experience with high-profile cases, and I trusted his judgment implicitly.

Jim asked about Gary, and I told him that I'd already been to see him that morning.

"How's he acting?"

"That's the funny thing . . . he seems so calm. He's very polite, not at all panicked. He's a bit upset about all the publicity, but that's what I would have expected."

We went into the office, Jim locking the door behind us. "I've been thinking about this," he said. "Why don't we waive the client's presence at the first appearance? The judge is going to find probable cause, and there's no way he's going to get bail. The only people who are going to get anything out of him actually being there is the news media. They'll show him answering the charges in his jail jumpsuit, and it doesn't do him any good because it just makes him look guilty. So let's see if he'll agree to waive his presence at the first appearance."

By waiving the appearance, Jim was suggesting that Gary simply stay in his cell during the court proceedings. That way, the media wouldn't be able to take pictures of him in the traditional garb of a prisoner. I saw the wisdom in Jim's proposal. "Sounds good, let's ask him," I said. "But first I want to call Jeff Baird."

I'd had experience with Baird on other cases. I knew him to be a very smart, very organized lawyer, who rarely let anything slip by. Like many others in the criminal defense bar, I also knew that Baird happened to be an opponent of the death penalty. Or, at least, he wasn't a proponent of the death penalty. Just why the prosecutor's office would assign someone opposed to the death penalty to a case in which the ultimate sanction was certain to be sought escaped me, however.

Baird wasn't in, so I left a message. Minutes later, he called back. We engaged in some casual banter. I told him I'd picked up a new case.

"Oh," he asked, "anything interesting?" An initial encounter with the opposition often started off this way, deadpan, both sides holding their cards close.

"Seriously, I thought we ought to chat before the hearing."

"Yeah, that's probably a good idea," he said. "I'll have a copy of the probable cause for you at the hearing."

The "probable cause" Jeff referred to was the sworn document produced by the police agency that contained the supposed facts leading the authorities to believe that the accused had committed the crimes, and as such, it would be our first chance to find out what the police knew—or thought they knew—about Gary. Once this document was filed and the defendant held in custody, Baird and the prosecutor's office would have up to three days to formally file criminal charges against him.

I decided to prod Baird a bit, to see if there was something he wasn't telling me.

"How come you're doing this case? It's going to be a death penalty case. I thought you didn't do death penalty cases."

"I'm just going to convict him," Baird said. "I won't do the penalty phase, . . . although, if there ever was a case for the death penalty . . ." He didn't have to finish his thought. If Gary had really committed forty-nine murders, there probably wasn't any way to keep the state from killing him. If he was guilty, and they let him live, how could they ever ask for the death penalty for anyone else, ever again?

I decided to show Baird that we had every confidence in the innocence of our client.

"You're not objecting to a PR, are you?" A PR was legal shorthand for a *personal recognizance* release from jail, in which a person merely promised to show up for future court appearances. No bail was required. Of course, a PR was absurd under the circumstances, but Baird went with my feeble attempt at humor.

"No, that's fine," he said. "He's lived here all his life, has had the same job for thirty years, just the one misdemeanor on his record . . . I have no problem with a PR."

So much for black humor. Baird was going to give as well as he got.

But then Baird said something unexpected.

"You know, down the road, after we get to know each other better, trust each other, we'll have to sit down and have a chat about where this case is headed," he said.

What did *that* mean? Where this case is headed? Where else might it be headed except to death row? Was Baird suggesting that the prosecutor might be willing to take a plea—without insisting on the death penalty? I knew what that would probably entail: information about unsolved cases in exchange for a life sentence. Would the prosecutor's office really go for this when the Green River case might involve as many as four dozen murders? It didn't seem possible.

I tried to cover my momentary confusion over this cryptic remark by maintaining my casual demeanor.

"Sounds like a plan," I said. "See you at the hearing."

I hung up and turned to Jim Robinson.

"Baird just said, 'Down the road we'd have to get together and talk about where this case is headed.'" I asked Jim, "What d'you think he means? Hanging or lethal injection?"

The State of Washington had two legal means of execution—lethal injection or hanging by the neck until dead.

Jim snorted. "Don't get your hopes up. Norm will never *not* seek the death penalty in this one. He could never ask for it again if he doesn't ask for it here."

"Norm" was Norman Maleng, the elected King County Prosecutor and Baird's boss. He'd held the job since 1978 and was practically an icon of legal probity in the Seattle area. He usually ran unopposed for reelection. If Maleng said the case required the death penalty, there was no way that even anti–death penalty Jeff Baird would be able to talk him out of it even if he wanted to.

Still, Baird's phrase kept running through my head: ". . . where this case is headed . . ." Did that mean that Baird himself had doubts as to Gary's guilt? Or that Baird believed that even though they might convict Gary of one of the murders, they'd never be able to convince a jury that he'd done forty-nine? Was Baird really suggesting a plea negotiation? I didn't know what to think.

I went back to the jail, this time accompanied by Jim Robinson. We sat down in a new face-to-face with Gary, who seemed as placid and trusting as ever. It was almost as if Gary were a patient about to go into surgery, and Jim and I were the doctors who were going to operate on him. He'd placed himself in our hands, the experts, and was agreeable to whatever we suggested.

"We've been thinking about waiving your appearance," Jim said. "If that's all right with you."

"It doesn't mean anything," I told Gary. "All your actual appearance will do is give the news media a chance to see you in your jail jumpsuit and take your picture. Which we want to minimize, if we can."

"Oooh-K," Gary said.

———∿∿∿———

Down on the first floor of the jail, in the high-security courtroom that had been constructed when the jail had been built, Jim and I found our way into the courtroom. The news media had jammed its way into the spectator section, sealed off from the rest of the courtroom by a thick glass partition. Baird, a lean, neatly dressed man with short, dark hair and a precise way of speaking, was already there. He passed us copies of the probable cause, the formal document that contained the facts that the authorities said justified the charges against Gary. It was six pages long, single-spaced, authored by Detective Tom Jensen. We skimmed through it; Gary was being accused by the sheriff's detectives of four counts of first-degree murder. It appeared that the detectives were saying that DNA they had taken from Gary in 1987—the saliva sample—had finally been matched, in October 2001, to DNA found in 1983 with Carol Christensen; that it was "consistent" with DNA found with one river victim, Marcia Chapman, on August 15, 1982; and that Gary could "not be eliminated" as the person who had left DNA with Opal Mills, found on the river bank that same day nineteen years earlier, August 15, 1982.

"DNA evidence links Ridgway to the murders of Mills, Christensen and Chapman," the affidavit contended. "In addition, strong circumstantial evidence links Ridgway to the murder of Cynthia Hinds—her body was discovered in the Green River on the same day and within feet of Chapman, and like Chapman, a rock was found in her vagina at the time of autopsy."

This was a prima facie case, all right. There wasn't any need at that point to say anything about the other forty-five victims of the killer. The authorities had enough to hold Gary for the foreseeable future, if they chose to file formal charges, which they certainly would, given those facts. It would be up to us, his defense lawyers, to find some weakness in this fundamental evidence, all the while hoping that more evidence didn't come in to tie Gary to still more of the murders. If that happened, Gary was sunk.

Now that we had the probable cause certificate, and Gary had waived his appearance, the main purpose of the hearing had been achieved. Within a few minutes, the whole thing was over, much to the disappointment of the news media, who had come to see Gary, who had never shown up. It also appeared that someone had forgotten to turn on the courtroom's sound system, so they didn't get any audio, either.

As Baird attempted to exit the courtroom, he was swallowed up in a mosh-pit of reporters, cameras, and microphones. Jim had a better idea.

"Follow me," he said, and he led me to a side door that gave us a clear shot at the jail's outer exit, beyond the scrutiny of the reporters. Still, one of them spied us as we got to the outer door.

"Mr. Gruenhagen? Mr. Gruenhagen?" he shouted, thinking one or the other of us was Todd, who had been identified in that morning's *Times* as Gary's "court-appointed" lawyer.

"No," Jim said, quickly walking away.

"Not me," I said. We made our escape from the puzzled reporter. *Who were those guys?* I imagined him asking himself.

Afterward, I drove to north Seattle to watch Marley swim. She had her best times in the 200-yard freestyle, the 200-yard backstroke, and the 100-yard individual medley. Clearly, having a father who was defending the supposed Green River Killer wasn't going to cramp Marley's style.

Later that night, I had a conversation with my parents, who had financed my way through law school. I told them I'd been appointed to the Green River case and asked them if they had any objections to the Prothero name being associated with the notorious case. Not a bit, they said, and they told me they were proud of me. They knew that defending any person accused of a crime was an important job, one vital to our freedom.

Like a lot of lawyers of my generation, I'd grown up watching *Perry Mason* on television, along with other lawyer shows—*The Defenders,* for example. In school, I'd found myself drawn to history and government—and just how the United States of America had grown into the greatest democracy the world has ever known. By the time I was in college in the early 1970s, I'd come to feel that many of our national problems—the war in Vietnam, Watergate, the excesses of the drug war, abuse of the environment, consumer rights, in fact many significant issues, could be addressed best through the legal system. I saw that law was the vehicle through which our society corrects those wrongs and improves, progresses, and moves forward.

By the time I was in my senior year in college, I'd decided that I wanted to be a lawyer. After graduating from the University of Washington with a degree in history in 1978, I attended the University of San Diego School of Law, graduating with a J.D. in 1981.

At first, I wanted to be an environmental lawyer, but I soon discovered that demand for earth-saving litigators was somewhat limited. In private practice, I discovered that I was spending 45 percent of my time trying to sell myself; another 45 percent trying to collect from friends, relatives, and others whom I tried to help with a variety of legal problems; and maybe 10 percent of the time actually being a lawyer. Slowly but surely, I'd found myself taking more and more criminal cases—mostly drinking and driving cases at first, and then other types. I slowly realized that I had a flair for defense work—in part because I thought I could empathize with a client's predicament.

I use the word *clients* instead of *suspects* because, as a lawyer for the accused, it's my job to make sure the accusers prove the case beyond a reasonable doubt. In fact, I don't much like the word *suspects,* because these days it's almost tantamount to saying someone did it. Suspicions are easy to come by, and actual legal charges are almost as easy to make. What should count in America, though, isn't mere suspicion, or even official accusation, but *proof.* Making sure that proof is real and substantial is what I was paid to do, and when the government was footing the bill, as it does with public defenders, I intended to give the taxpayers their money's worth. You'd expect no less if the authorities were saying *you* or one of your loved ones were the accused. That's why I prefer the word client, because until a jury and not the police—or the news media—says someone is guilty, that person is actually and legally innocent.

Although it's not particularly fashionable these days, I also don't believe that people are "born evil." Generally speaking, when they come to me, they have problems, sometimes big problems. A lot of the time, these problems are mental: drug and alcohol abuse, or some other form of psychological dysfunction, including loneliness, depression, or wild, unfocused anger. They don't usually want to do bad things, but they're often just caught up in a web of troubles, many of them of their own making, because of judgment that's been impaired, either by self-infliction or by circumstance. The way I see things, the client needs help. That's why he or she has come to me—for help. And it's really not much different than if your neighbor came to you and said his house was on fire. You wouldn't tell him to get lost. You'd help him put the fire out. That's what clients with criminal problems are: people whose houses are on fire and who need help putting the fire out. If things worked out, we could get the flames extinguished and get the person back to being a happy, healthy, and contributing member of society. And if that wasn't possible—if the crime was too severe—we could at least stop him from causing further destruction to himself or others by helping him arrive at a humane and just resolution.

Even from where I'm sitting, I can hear you saying, "Oh, yeah? What about guilty people who go free?" I admit that it happens, sometimes. But in my observation and experience, it's far more likely for an innocent person to be found guilty than for a guilty person to be found innocent. That's just the way the system works, even with all the rights we theoretically afford the accused. And I suppose I would also add this: it's really far more endurable to our society for one guilty person to go free than it is for our government to limit all of our rights to make certain of catching all of the guilty. That's the path to dictatorship.

And in the broadest sense, what we do as criminal defense lawyers is act as quality control for the criminal justice system: to make sure it operates under the rules we'd all agreed upon, more than two hundred years ago in our Constitution. In a significant way, our most important client is the Constitution itself.

By 1983, when I'd decided to get out of private practice and join ACA, I found great satisfaction in trying to help people cope with their problems, some of which, I will admit, were rather ghastly, including about a dozen murder cases, a few of which generated a fair share of publicity.

One was the rather lurid case of the so-called Queen Anne Axe Murderer, in which a mentally retarded and mentally ill man, James Cushing, had terrorized Seattle from March to September 1990. Jim Cushing wasn't "born evil." He was mentally ill and needed help. Cushing's mother had begged the state's mental health authorities to keep him hospitalized and medicated, but he was nevertheless released to the streets, in part because the state simply was unwilling to bear the expense of taking care of him. Within a few weeks, he'd stolen an axe from the back porch of a house on Seattle's Queen Anne hill and used it to kill a sixty-eight-year-old woman in her sleep.

Over the course of that summer, Cushing entered six other homes, often leaving an axe behind, along with messages scrawled on the walls in crayon, such as "The killer's back" or "Kill the bitch." Needless to say, this left the entire city very nervous. By September 1990, however, he was arrested based on fingerprints he had left behind at one of the houses he'd broken into. We advanced an insanity defense, but it was rejected by the jury, even though there was no doubt that he was severely disturbed. In fact, just after the verdict was returned, he turned to me and asked, completely oblivious to what had just happened,

"What's for lunch?" He wasn't evil. He was mentally ill! Jim is now serving a life sentence in a state prison, so the state wound up taking care of him after all; it's too bad it didn't do it when it would have done some good.

As it happened, while Cushing was terrorizing the community but before he was apprehended, I was selected from among five senior ACA lawyers for training in the newly emerging technology of DNA typing. At the time, the process of obtaining genetic material from crime scenes was in its infancy, and ACA wanted to have someone who knew what it was all about. My name was actually drawn out of a hat, and on March 15, 1990, the same day Marley was born, I left to attend a DNA seminar in Washington, D.C., presented by Barry Scheck and Peter Neufeld, who would later gain fame as O.J. Simpson's DNA experts. Scheck and Neufeld are also founders of the Innocence Project, organized to use DNA to exonerate people who had been wrongfully convicted.

Over the next decade, I had handled a number of other cases in which DNA evidence was critical to the prosecution's case. In 1992, I was successful in convincing a judge that DNA evidence offered by the prosecution should not be admitted in a rape case because the statistical methodology used by the State was not scientifically sound. The rape charge was dismissed but the State appealed and the judge's ruling was reversed two years later, as the statistical methods gained acceptance among statisticians and population geneticists. When the case came back on remand, my client pled guilty to a lesser charge.

In 1994, I was appointed to defend a man named Kenny Ford, who had been accused of a triple murder at a north Seattle tavern. Blood from one of the victims had been found on shoes belonging to Ford, a young man of well-under-average intelligence and enduring alcohol and drug problems. The case was peculiar mostly because of the legal wrangling. Realizing that the prosecutors had failed to charge Ford with aggravated murder, a prerequisite to asking that he be given the death penalty, his first ACA lawyer had him immediately plead guilty in an effort to preclude the prosecutor from rectifying his mistake. Acceptance of the plea on the spot would have had the effect of barring the State from seeking death. After a great deal of pushing and shoving in the courts over the next three years, the prosecutor's office eventually gave in and agreed not to ask for death for Ford.

And for most of the past year and a half before this last day of November 2001, I'd been working on the case of Roy Webbe, a thirty-one-year-old native of the Virgin Islands, who had been arrested for the horrifying rape-murder of a woman named Deborah Funk, who had been accosted in her Seattle-area apartment. Following a struggle, Webbe had gone to work on her with a steak knife, eventually sawing his way through her spinal cord.

For weeks after his arrest, Webbe had refused to meet with any lawyers or indeed have any conversations with anyone, and it soon became clear that he suffered from severe mental disturbance, so much so that we thought he was incompetent to assist in his own defense. Tragically, Webbe had served a prison term for a previous rape but had somehow been lost by the state's parole system. By that week, the same week that Gary Ridgway had been arrested, I was trying to finish a brief arguing that his mental condition was so bad that he could never receive a fair trial, in preparation for a critical competency hearing that had been scheduled for mid-December.

Which raised a new question in my mind: Could I give enough attention to Gary Ridgway? My first obligation was to Roy Webbe, and if it looked as though Webbe's case was going to take most of my time, I would feel obligated to step aside from Gary's case.

And there was the prospect that any defense of Gary Ridgway might well be fruitless. When the client is accused of being a monstrous serial murderer who had supposedly taken the lives of more than four dozen young women, the potential for a climate of nearly hysterical revenge is very high. An innocent person might well be found guilty under those circumstances, even if the evidence was merely suggestive and not beyond a reasonable doubt. Was there anything anyone could do to head this off?

And if the wrong person was convicted, that would mean the real killer was still out there.

5

The next day, Sunday, I went back to the Kent office to work on my Webbe brief, which was due the following week. Pretty soon, however, the telephone began to ring. The reporters hadn't given up. By now, someone had fingered Jim Robinson and me as lawyers for Gary after we'd shown up for the hearing.

The first call was from an Associated Press reporter, Janie McCauley. She was very pleasant, but I kept my remarks to a minimum. I suddenly realized that our home phone number was in the book. That probably meant that reporters would be calling our house all day and that Kelly, being the polite person she is, would be telling them that I was at the office. In turn, that also meant I'd probably be getting still more telephone calls as the day wore on.

I decided to call Greg Girard and Todd Gruenhagen. I knew we needed to come up with some sort of strategy to deal with the news media, even if Gary was going to retain private counsel. We'd all agreed to have a meeting on Monday to decide how to handle the case, as long as ACA continued to represent Gary. But this couldn't wait. If reporters were likely to be calling all day, we needed to figure out what to say.

Both Greg and Todd agreed that we should be polite, but non-committal: we needed to stay away from definitive statements like, "He didn't do it" or "Mr. Ridgway is outraged by these charges and denies any involvement and plans to sue for false arrest." Prosecutors kept track of that sort of thing, especially if the statements made them look bad. The right tone was to be polite, friendly, and say nothing of any news value. For one thing, formal charges still hadn't been filed. And who knew? Maybe something would happen over the next few days that might change the prosecutor's mind. At the very least, we needed to get more information ourselves. Todd, for one, was very suspicious of the news media. Besides getting facts wrong (already we had discovered that the media report that no DNA had been found with Carol Christensen was in error), the reporters were usually allies of the police and prosecutors, whether wittingly or not.

Having agreed to keep to the soft-stonewall strategy, I went back to the Webbe brief. Soon, however, the telephone began to ring once more, and I tried to dance my way through the media minefield by being friendly and pleasant without saying anything that might come back to bite our now-notorious client in his caboose.

"He has maintained his innocence for eighteen years," I told a reporter for the *Times*. "He still does. He wasn't particularly surprised to be arrested, because of what happened in the search in 1987." I didn't get into the DNA evidence, but the reporter asked me if the defense might attack its validity. I said it was too soon to settle on a possible defense strategy.

And so it went.

—⁓—

On Monday, December 3, Greg Girard and I drove down to the main jail to meet again with Gary. As a felony supervisor at ACA, Greg had already decided not to have further involvement in the case; he had enough to do, supervising staff trial attorneys like me. He told me that Todd Gruenhagen would probably be assigned to the case with me, that is, if we kept it.

I'd known Todd since I'd first joined ACA in 1983. We'd hit it off almost from the start because Todd had also been a competitive swimmer in school in California. Although he was forty-seven by the fall of 2001, he was still in terrific shape, at five-eleven, two hundred pounds. With his goatee and short hair, and his prominent nose, he looks a bit like a cross between Eric Clapton and Pete Townshend, if either of them wore thick glasses like Todd. He rides a Harley and is somewhere to the left of Michael Moore, politically speaking. He is an avid outdoors person, into fishing, hunting, scuba diving, and skiing. He owns a variety of firearms and loves the Second Amendment as much as any card-carrying member of the National Rifle Association. He raises bird dogs. He's also extremely well read and one of the smartest people I've ever met. What's more, he has a wicked sense of humor and takes great pleasure in elaborate practical jokes.

The main thing about Todd is that he's aggressive and tough. He's also a "true believer," as in the 1989 movie of the same name, starring James Woods as a criminal defense lawyer, loosely based on colorful San Francisco attorney Tony Serra, in that he sees it as his mission in life to hold the institutions of government, particularly the police, accountable for their actions. Todd can fix you in your steps when he stares into your eyes, and by drilling his finger emphatically on your chest, he can make you think twice about taking him on. As a lawyer, he's tough, persistent, and certainly the person I want in my corner if I ever get into trouble.

In any event, when we got into the face-to-face room to meet with Gary, Greg Girard explained to Gary why he'd be leaving the case and that he'd soon be replaced by another ACA lawyer, who hadn't been selected yet. Gary accepted this news placidly, as usual; at some level, he realized that he didn't have any real choice in the matter. I tried to assure him that ACA would do the very best we could for him, no matter what happened.

"Oooh-K."

By now, Gary was well aware that his name and video of his house had been plastered all over the news media, even if he hadn't actually seen any of the coverage. Prisoners on the seventh floor were denied television and newspapers. Naturally, he was curious about what the various news outlets were saying about him.

The papers that morning had given a lot of space to the searches that the Sheriff's Department had conducted over the weekend, one at Gary's house in Auburn, and others at houses he'd previously lived in, as well as the house his parents had lived in before they died. All of the houses, except his current residence, were located not far from where many of the Green River victims had last been seen in the 1980s, along Pacific Highway South near the SeaTac International Airport. The detectives had called in a backhoe to dig up the yard of one former house, "after body-sniffing dogs were alerted to something in the yard," according to the *Times*.[1]

Good grief. Now even the *dogs* were accusing Gary! It only helped a little that the Sheriff's Department admitted that they hadn't found anything. "We're pretty sure there's nothing there, and we're done digging," the sheriff's media spokesperson, John Urquhart, told the paper. But Urquhart also said the detectives planned to dig up the backyard at the Auburn house, too.

We gave Gary a brief description of the coverage so far, including the fact that the sheriff's deputies had been videotaped tearing his house apart and digging up his backyard. Gary grimaced and shook his head; he seemed humiliated to hear about these developments. If he was innocent, the highly public investigative exercise was well on its way to ruining his life. He asked again about Judith and his brother Greg, and I again had to tell him that I hadn't talked to them, that I had left messages, but they hadn't called back yet.

Whatever the stress of being jailed as an accused serial murderer, Gary seemed to have settled into a routine at the jail. He'd had no problems, he said, and even the jailers agreed that he seemed to be a model prisoner. We reminded him once more to keep his mouth shut—that just about anything he said could be twisted by someone if they wanted to help themselves by making him look bad.

"I won't," he said. "I mean, I will. Not say anything, I mean."

Oooh-K.

Afterward, Greg and I went across the street to the ACA offices for a meeting with Jim Robinson. Todd Gruenhagen was also there, along with two other ACA lawyers, Robert Williams and Gary Davis. The main topic was who on our staff would represent Gary, assuming we weren't relieved of the case by the private lawyer that Gary still thought his family might retain. We all agreed that we should still begin to form a defense team, even if we were eventually replaced.

Although ACA at that point had almost sixty trial attorneys on its staff, only Gary Davis and I were officially *capital qualified*. This was a relatively recent state innovation, in which attorneys who represented potential death penalty defendants had to demonstrate their expertise in the arcana of death penalty law and be on a State Supreme Court–approved list to practice it. The state's reasoning was sound: it didn't want to have to retry death penalty cases, because of appellate reversals grounded in claims of ineffective assistance of counsel. As it has developed over the years since it was reinstated in most states in (or after) 1977, death penalty law has become increasingly abstruse; in fact, it's almost a body of law unto itself. Todd, although he was probably more qualified than I was to represent a death penalty defendant—he had one such case before the "approved" list was required—had in his usual contrarian way simply refused to jump through the Supreme Court's hoops to get on the list. Now, because Gary Davis was up to his briefs with a triple murder case, it seemed clear that I would be Gary Ridgway's co-lead attorney, along with Todd—that is, if the Ridgway family didn't retain private counsel. So far, though, I hadn't heard anything from either Greg Ridgway or Gary's wife, Judith.

But I also knew that a case as large as Green River would be beyond the capacity of just two lawyers; in a situation involving up to forty-nine murder cases, we'd be swamped. In fact, we knew we'd need to evaluate *all* the cases on the chance that there might be someone else who was a better suspect than Gary Ridgway for the four murders we expected he'd be charged with. That's called giving an accused an adequate defense.

"How many lawyers do you think you'll need?" Jim Robinson asked, when we were all assembled in his office.

"At least six," I said.

Jim blanched at this prediction but said he'd circulate a memo to the other lawyers on the ACA staff to see who might be interested in joining Todd and me. But, he warned, we'd have to talk to Dave Chapman, the ACA director, before anyone could commit to that level of legal firepower. Dave just happened to be on vacation in Hawaii right then. Jim agreed to assign the primary defense of Roy Webbe to Robert Williams, my co-counsel on Roy's case, if we kept Gary Ridgway, which relieved me of that anxiety.

Now we turned to the matter of all the publicity that had gushed forth over the weekend, which had been massive, as well as almost uniformly negative, at least from the Ridgway point of view. It was immediately clear that we had a sharp difference of opinion on how to handle the tsunami of bad ink. I was beginning to think our soft-stonewall strategy was a mistake.

"We're getting crushed," I said. "If we continue to refuse to comment, they will print or broadcast more and more anti-Ridgway stuff. Not that we can stop it, but if we at least talk to them, maybe we could get 'Ridgway' and 'innocent' in the same sentence."

"Yeah, right, like that will have any effect on slowing down or stopping the negative stuff," Jim said, doubtfully. "Besides, everyone would expect his defense lawyer to *say* he's innocent. They don't care what we say."

"I'm thinking we ought to at least remind them that he's *presumed* innocent and that by rushing to the judgment that he's guilty, that he's the Green River Killer . . . well, there'll be no way he could get a fair trial," I said. "And everyone should agree he should at least get a fair trial." If the publicity got really bad, Gary might be able to base an appeal on actual media prejudice, as in the notorious Sam Sheppard case. That might cause a reversal and require a retrial. But our primary concern at the moment was trying to get him a fair trial, so it was within our scope of effective representation to try to dampen the negative press. And we should point this out to the media, too. Even if Gary were to be found guilty, they wouldn't want to be responsible for having his conviction thrown out because of media excesses, I suggested.

"It's refreshing, but you are so naïve," Todd put in. "He's *the Green River Killer!* You think people care whether he gets a fair trial or not? You think they'll care about the presumption of innocence? If you say he's 'presumed innocent,' most people will take that as just lawyer talk for 'he's guilty.'"

"Yeah," I said, "but we're not in a position yet to proclaim he's actually innocent. It's too early to go out on that limb, when we may be taking some other position down the line in order to save his life. We've got to maintain some credibility, so nothing can come back to bite us in the ass. I don't see the harm in telling people, and reminding the press, that he's presumed innocent and they are hurting the system with all this prejudicial stuff."

"The press only cares about headlines that sell papers or lead-ins to the five o'clock news," Jim said. "They really don't care about 'fair trials' and 'the presumption of innocence.' They just want to get people to buy papers and watch their broadcasts. I think we should stick with 'no comment.'"

Greg Girard weighed in with his opinion. "I agree it probably won't help, but I also agree that it wouldn't do any harm to remind people that he's innocent unless it's proven that he's guilty. Plus, you don't want to alienate the press to the point where they won't listen to you when you want them to. I say, give 'em a nibble, give 'em a little something to keep them happy. That will let them know that we're not afraid of talking to them, just that we don't really have anything to say yet. Say nothing but say it to them nicely." This was a sweetened variant on the soft-stonewall.

"Norm [Maleng] says he'll be having a press conference on Wednesday," Todd pointed out. "Let's think about our response to the press *after* he announces the charges. They'll want some kind of comment from us, and it would look worse if we continue to avoid them. So let's wait. I'm thinking maybe after that, we could prepare a statement and put media boy up there, so long as he stays within the script."

Todd looked over at me. It was clear he meant me with the "media boy" jab. He raised his right index finger and pointed it at my chest. "And I'll be standing right there, to make sure you don't stray," he said, with a mock glower.

"Hell, *you* can do it," I said. "It doesn't have to be me." But Todd despised the press. He had always considered reporters the enemy—allies of the authorities because their continued access to official sources depended on their making the officials look good.

"Nope, I can't do it," Todd said. "I hate the media. You love seeing yourself on TV."

I agreed we should continue with the soft-stonewall until at least after Norm Maleng's scheduled press conference. I knew Todd was right. The smart thing to do was to wait to see the charges actually filed by the prosecutor and what he would say about it, before considering any media offensive of our own.

The following day brought even more bad press for Gary. "**Ridgway once tied to 5 other victims**," the *Times* reported.[2] And worse in the next column: "**80 unsolved slayings to get new look by investigators**."[3] Eighty other cases! In addition to the forty-nine "official" victims. By my count, that made up to 129 murders that Reichert's Sheriff's Department had every incentive to lay on Gary Ridgway. And the sheriff himself wasn't at all coy about asserting that his department's evidence against Gary was "very strong": "**Case against Ridgway solid, sheriff says**," read *that* headline.[4] "**BC prostitutes say they saw Ridgway on streets**," the *Post-Intelligencer* reported, referring to streetwalkers in Vancouver, British Columbia, where another forty-five women were either dead or missing.[5] Forty-five! And Portland, Oregon: seventeen streetwalking prostitutes were dead, murdered. Was Gary Ridgway really responsible for up to *181* murders? It was absurd, beyond belief.

But I noticed an interesting observation by Reichert. Asked if he'd be willing "to trade the death penalty if Ridgway offered to cooperate in closing other cases," the sheriff answered, "When we come to that bridge . . . I will consult with Norm Maleng, and we will make a decision then."

When we come to that bridge? That sounded to me like Reichert had already looked down the road and had seen a yawning chasm ahead. As far as I could tell right then, the authorities had only one possible case of murder against Gary, along with three maybes. And Gary: too small, too polite, too ordinary. Every time I saw him in another face-to-face, he'd peer up at me through his owlish glasses, brows knitted together in earnest concentration, as if he were really, really trying, trying as hard as he could to be cooperative, and utterly puzzled as to how this had all fallen in on him. I looked again and again for the murderous mean in Gary, but I could never see it.

6

On Wednesday, December 5, the prosecutor's office filed four first-degree, aggravated murder charges against Gary Ridgway. Aggravated murder: "To wit," as the charging document filed in court had it, "there was more than one victim and the murders were part of a common scheme or plan." Four aggravated murders meant that the prosecutor could seek the death penalty.

The key to the charges was the aggravating circumstance: that the murders charged were part of a "common scheme or plan." The charges would require the state to present evidence that the murders were tied together, the so-called *common scheme* or *plan*. In turn, that meant that evidence from *all* of the official forty-nine murders might be used to demonstrate that there actually was a common scheme or plan, even if only four of the forty-nine were actually, legally charged as crimes. Whatever the common scheme or plan was, it wasn't directly specified, but it seemed clear that the state was alleging that Gary's "scheme" was to kill prostitutes—as many as possible.

So in addition to the physical evidence possibly tying Gary to three of the murders—DNA with Carol Christensen, Marcia Chapman, and Opal Mills and the circumstantial evidence linking him to the death of Cynthia Hinds—the state also wanted to present circumstantial evidence from some or all of the remaining murders to show that it was Gary who had committed the charged four. And even though the sheriff had said that no one was saying that Gary was responsible for all of the murders, the prosecutors' charging document had just essentially alleged that the authorities believed that Gary was in fact *the* Green River Killer.

The implications of this were immense: it meant that any defense of Gary would have to reinvestigate the entire twenty-year history of the case, if Gary were to receive a fair trial. That singular fact moved the Green River prosecution and defense into an entirely new universe, a place no legal proceeding had ever gone before in America. The sheer size of the case would be unprecedented. Which in turn meant—so would the costs.

Meanwhile the negative news coverage about Gary continued unabated. In fact, it seemed to be getting worse, at least from the defense perspective. "**DNA expert says science is pointing to Ridgway**," read a new headline, this one over a story reporting that "one of the nation's top independent DNA experts" had said the DNA found with Carol Christensen could only have come from one person in "tens of billions—far more than the world's population." The DNA found with Marcia Chapman had come from one person out of a possible 645 million. As for Opal Mills, that DNA had come from "at least two men," the paper reported—and Gary Ridgway could not be excluded as one of the contributors. On the other hand, once again, this was a tantalizing hint that there might be someone else involved in the killings. The "independent expert" consulted by the newspaper warned the defense to "stay away from attacking the science of DNA testing through the STR process, calling it "a waste of taxpayer money."

"A waste of taxpayer money . . ." I shuddered when I read that. It might be true that DNA testing through the STR process was scientifically valid, but that didn't mean it couldn't be attacked. It all depended on how the DNA samples had been preserved for the past decade and a half and whether they might have been contaminated or if the crime lab had properly processed it. Using the words "a waste of taxpayer money" made it sound like Gary was so guilty that even having a trial would be a "waste of taxpayer money."

That morning, I again went to see Gary in the jail, this time accompanied by Todd. It was the first time that Gary had met Todd. We both wanted Gary to begin to feel comfortable with the two lawyers he would have to depend on as this mammoth case unfolded. Todd would eventually become our "enforcer" with Gary. From that point forward, just about every time Todd came to visit Gary, Gary would know he was in some sort of trouble—often because he had been talking too much to the other prisoners, whose tales about Gary inevitably worked their way back to us. Todd would excoriate Gary for running his mouth, and Gary would meekly promise to say no more. Gary seemed impressed by Todd's forceful personality. I think if Todd had instructed Gary to start banging his head on the floor in four-four time, Gary would have done it. Later, I realized that this deference to authority—whether police detectives or jailers, or even his own lawyers—was a prominent facet of Gary's personality.

The spate of news media coverage continued to trouble us. After Todd and I finished with Gary, we went to see Dan Satterberg, who was Maleng's chief of staff. We wanted to get him to convince Reichert and the sheriff's detectives to stop giving press interviews. Satterberg had a brush mustache with a square jaw and a muscular physique. He had a piercing gaze and a rather sardonic style and was perceived by many as Maleng's "hit man"—the guy who did all the hard things that good-guy Norm didn't want to be blamed for, even if they were necessary. Todd and I had known Satterberg for years. He'd become a deputy prosecutor at about the same time we'd joined ACA, so we had sort of grown up together, although on opposite sides of the courtroom. I'd also played a lot of basketball against him, and on one great day in the not-too-distant past, my wife, Kelly, had robbed him of a sure over-the-fence home run in a softball game against ACA. So we'd always had a fairly friendly relationship, although one usually tinged with competitiveness.

"We'd like you to say something to the sheriff," Todd told Dan, when we were in his office in the courthouse. "The coverage is getting out of hand. We're concerned that it might be affecting our client's right to a fair trial."

"I don't see anything wrong with the coverage," Dan said. "I think the coverage has been great." His eyes glinted in devilish merriment at our predicament.

So much for that idea. Later, however, we were told that Maleng and Satterberg had tried to tone down Reichert's enthusiasm for Gary's guilt shortly after the arrest, but they hadn't had much success.[1] After all, Maleng's office had to try the case, and they didn't want to have a change of venue to some place outside King County, where a trial less influenced by all the publicity might be had, assuming such a place existed. Of course, Reichert's initial ebullience after the arrest was understandable, given the long years that had passed with no solution in the case. I just wished he'd been less celebratory and more respectful of Gary's right to an unbiased jury. On the other hand, if the sheriff kept on gabbing, the tipping point might soon be reached where we might be able to argue that Gary could *never* get a fair trial, anywhere, so badly had the well of potential jurors been poisoned by officials and the news media.

Unsatisfied by Satterberg, Todd and I left and went to the downtown ACA office across from the courthouse. At least we fired a shot across their bow, I thought. *Maybe from now on, they'll tone it down a bit. . . . At least they're on notice.*

That Wednesday, December 5, Todd and I and many of the ACA staff gathered around a television in the ACA offices across from the courthouse. Prosecutor Maleng was at the podium in front of the cameras.

At sixty-three, Maleng was probably the most publicly recognizable law enforcement figure in the state. His sandy hair and slightly ruddy face, with his wire-rimmed glasses, gave him a friendly, open appearance. Twice a candidate for governor, he was also well-known for his soft-spoken reasonableness. Certainly, he was no firebrand when it came to dispensing criminal justice. His cherubic countenance and pleasing smile had stopped any electoral challengers in their tracks in years past, and although he could evoke a stern, almost religious demeanor when the occasion called for it, he was never ideological in his approach to his job.

But now, on television it appeared that Maleng was assuming the vestments of vengeance.

"I will not bargain with the death penalty," Maleng said. "The mission of this office is to seek justice."

That certainly suggested that in Maleng's mind, justice could only be achieved by putting the Green River Killer to death. And in turn, that also suggested that the only way the defense could save Gary's life would be to convince a jury that he was simply not guilty of the murders.

That's just great, I thought, he's eliminating the possibility of a plea deal right up front. It's politics, that's what it is. My initial reaction to this was disappointment with Maleng.

"He had to make some sort of announcement about the death penalty," Todd said as we watched. I knew Todd was right. If Maleng hadn't said anything about the death penalty, the reporters certainly would have asked him, and the only reasonable response at that point was to deny any intention of negotiation.

We knew—or at least we guessed—what Maleng was thinking about. A little more than a year earlier, on the east side of the state, a confessed serial killer, Robert L. Yates, had received a life sentence despite evidence linking him to thirteen murders that had been committed in three counties over a period of years. Although authorities had evidence in about half of the killings, prosecutors in Spokane County as well as two others had agreed not to seek the death penalty in return for Yates's complete confession and cooperation in helping them resolve the unsolved cases. With the deal in hand, Yates had admitted all of his crimes and led authorities to the remains of one of his victims. When it was announced, the Spokane agreement with Yates set off a huge controversy: How could law enforcement authorities ask for the death penalty for someone accused of one or two murders but *not* ask for it when someone was accused of thirteen? To a lot of people, it didn't make any sense. The Yates case was one reason the reporters wanted to know Maleng's intention about any possible plea bargain.

While being held on the Spokane crimes, Yates also was charged with two murders in a fourth county, Pierce, just south of King County and Seattle. His lawyers argued that the Pierce County crimes were covered by Yates's agreement with the Spokane authorities, and the Spokane prosecutor agreed, eventually testifying that he understood the Pierce County officials had authorized him to make a deal on their behalf. But Pierce County authorities denied giving the Spokane County people any such authority and eventually brought Yates to trial in their county, a well-publicized proceeding that resulted in Yates receiving the death penalty for the Pierce County crimes. This "other jurisdiction" problem was to bedevil our Ridgway defense thinking almost from the outset: we wanted to make sure that what had happened to Yates didn't ever happen to Gary.

But there were several wrinkles to the Yates case that many people didn't think about when they rushed to condemn the Spokane County officials for their "deal." One was the expense of trying a death penalty case based on thirteen homicides. A trial on a single death penalty murder count often costs more than $1 million in tax money; thirteen counts was certain to be much, much more. Second, the state's law on *aggravated murder* was unclear on whether it actually applied to serial killers, at least in the Spokane prosecutor's view, and that meant even the prosecution thought a death penalty might be thrown out by a higher court, which would mean all the money to try the case would essentially be wasted.

Both of those factors—extreme cost and uncertain results under the aggravated murder statute—would be present if the state persisted in charging Gary with aggravated murder. If anything, with forty-nine possible victims instead of thirteen, the costs of trying the Green River case would be gargantuan, somewhere in the multiple millions of dollars. And just like the Yates case, there was some chance that the "aggravated" portion of the charges might eventually be thrown out. Where, after all, was the common scheme or plan that the statute required? The Spokane prosecutors in the Yates case had admitted that they had no evidence of a common scheme or plan in Yates's killings, all of which seemed to have been committed on impulse, without scheming or planning—just as it arguably appeared that the Green River murders, whether four or forty-nine, also were not part of any common scheme or plan. The fact that some saw this as a flaw in Washington State's aggravated murder statute didn't necessarily mean that the law, as actually written by the state legislature, did not apply to cases like Yates's or the Green River Killer. Pierce County authorities contended that the state's aggravated murder statute did apply to serial murders like those attributed to Robert Yates (and potentially, Gary Ridgway), whereas Spokane prosecutors weren't so certain. Needless to say, we agreed with the Spokane officials.

That afternoon, Todd and I held our own press conference at the Regional Justice Center in Kent. We wanted to slow down the rush-to-judgment juggernaut by putting *Ridgway* and *innocent* in the same sentence.

Todd and I stood behind a podium set up in the third-floor rotunda of the Regional Justice Center, with the domed ceiling above. As I took a deep breath and looked out at the gathering, there must have been twenty reporters and cameramen surrounding the podium in a semicircle, looking at us and anxiously awaiting our comments.

As planned, Todd went first and took a whack at the news media for overreacting to the news of Gary's arrest and making it seem like Gary had to be guilty because of the DNA reports. That was my cue.

"We're just saying, 'wait a second,'" I added. "Let's thoroughly review this. DNA evidence isn't unassailable. It's a technology that's susceptible to contamination, and there are human beings involved in the DNA testing process. People should not make the assumption that just because Gary Ridgway has been arrested, that it means he has to be guilty. Nothing's been proven yet, and it may never be. Just imagine if your husband, father, or brother was in this situation. Try to hold back on the judgment that law enforcement wants you to rush to."

"Doesn't the DNA evidence suggest your client was involved with the victims?" asked one reporter.

"It's just too early to say," I replied, trying to explain how the process works. "We need to have the evidence reviewed and scrutinized by our experts. We're not just going to accept what the state tells us. We have to review everything and may have to analyze it ourselves."

"Do you think Maleng will seek the death penalty?" shouted another reporter.

"Well, we certainly hope not, but based on his comments today, it sounds like he may have already made his decision."

"Will you be moving for a change of venue?" asked another.

"It's too early to say for sure," Todd said, "but with the amount of publicity the case is receiving, that's a real possibility."

"Do you think Mr. Ridgway can get a fair trial in King County?"

I paused, gave a sigh of exasperation, thinking *That's a stupid question,* but I held back and just shook my head. "No," I said, trying to decide how far I should go with that one. We didn't want to be accused of doing anything to exacerbate the prejudicial publicity problem. I decided to go for the truth. "There's no way he could get a fair trial in King County."

This was all a bit like trying to stop a fully loaded 747 on its takeoff roll, though. Our warnings to the news media barely registered. Todd and Jim had been right. The reporters treated our remarks as if they were obligatory, not to be given too much significance or weight. The amount of television time and newspaper space devoted to the defense press conference was minimal compared with Norm Maleng's. It was disappointing, because it was a *press conference* after all—our chance to say *Ridgway* and *innocent* in the same sound bite. But that stuff mostly ended up on yawning editors' cutting floors.

Even as I headed home to watch the news coverage, the media had already picked up a new court document that shoveled more blame onto Gary.

This was the affidavit of King County Detective Sue Peters, filed in court to justify the searches of Gary's property, and this document's thirty-three pages in effect trebled the evidence against Gary Ridgway—or at least gave the news people three times as much to write about, or broadcast.

Peters's affidavit contained numerous statements from Gary's two former wives, and from four former girlfriends, most of them focused on Gary's alleged sexual proclivities. According to Peters, Gary's first wife, Claudia, had told the police that she and Gary had sex outdoors and in his vehicle not far from Pacific Highway South, the epicenter of most of the Green River disappearances that were to occur later. Gary's marriage to Claudia lasted just two years, according to Peters, and ended when Claudia fell in love with another man. Later, Peters said, Gary had told another woman that his first wife had become a prostitute and that she had given him a venereal disease, although Claudia told Peters that neither claim was true.

According to Peters, Gary's second marriage, in 1973, to Marcia, lasted longer. Marcia was the mother of Gary's son, Matthew. Marcia told the police that she and Gary had sex in the tall grass on the banks of the Green River, and in several other places where victims' remains were later found. They had often gone camping or hiking where still other remains were later located. Gary, Marcia told police, spent many of his weekends at his parents' home near the SeaTac airport. She thought that Gary, his two brothers, and his father had all been dominated by Mary Rita Ridgway, Gary's mother.

"Marcia stated that Ridgway's mother ran the household, and that she was continually yelling at his father," Peters's affidavit claimed. "As an example, Marcia related an incident that occurred while she and Ridgway were both at his parents' house. In this incident, Mrs. Ridgway was upset with Mr. Ridgway [Gary's father, Tom], and became angry. She broke a dinner plate over Mr. Ridgway's head while he was seated at the table. Marcia stated that Mr. Ridgway did not retaliate in any manner, only got up and left. Marcia also stated that the first time she saw Mrs. Ridgway, she did not believe that she was Ridgway's mother because she was wearing a lot of makeup, tight clothes, and to her, looked like a prostitute."

As the 1970s came to a close, Gary's marriage to Marcia deteriorated but not before, at one point, Gary had come up behind her and attempted to choke her with his hands, according to Marcia. In fact,

Marcia had told the police, Gary liked to hide, then sneak up behind her and put her neck in a police-type chokehold with his elbow and forearm. Later, she said, Gary had accused her of going to motels on Pacific Highway South with other men. This was untrue, Marcia told the police.

Although none of this was evidence tying Gary directly to the Green River murders, taken together it comprised a portrait of a personality that was consistent with what all the behavioral experts had predicted, at least insofar as it encompassed the killer's predicted family history: a parental home dominated by an abusive mother, strong feelings about marital fidelity issues, sexually experimental, and often verbalized contempt for prostitutes.

But then, I knew that the police had over the years compiled a number of speculative "psychological profiles" of the unknown murderer; it looked to me that Peters had merely taken reputed aspects of Gary's life that fit with these psychological profiles and used them to suggest that Gary was in fact the killer. Left out of the affidavit, possibly, were all the ways that Gary did *not* fit the psychological profiles.[2]

The real meat of Peters's affidavit, however, was in the circumstantial evidence that purported to tie Gary to six other victims of the Green River Killer besides the four he had been formally charged with. Witnesses had placed either Gary or his truck near the places where Green River victims Alma Smith, Gail Mathews, Kimi-Kai Pitsor, and Kim Nelson had all last been seen in 1983. In addition, police had old records showing that Gary had once been questioned by the Port of Seattle Police while in the company of yet another listed victim, Keli McGinness. Even more damning, the boyfriend and father of victim Marie Malvar had actually traced her to Gary's old house and had made a complaint to police about Gary, accusing him of having done something to make Marie Malvar disappear. The complaint had not been taken seriously by the police at the time. In any event, this evidence, when combined with the DNA found with Marcia Chapman, Opal Mills, and Carol Christensen, and the proximity of Cynthia Hinds's body to that of Chapman, potentially tied Gary to ten of the forty-nine victims. Even more significant, the range of these potential victims included most of the varied geographical locations where the victims' remains had subsequently been discovered. If Gary had in fact killed these ten, it was powerful evidence that he'd killed all the others as well.

Altogether, these news reports were definitely a toxic blast, further damaging Gary Ridgway's right to a fair trial. If it kept up, the chance of finding anyone in King County who hadn't already decided Gary was the killer would become virtually nil.

Just after the news was over, I called my office to check for messages.

"Mark," said a recorded voice I immediately recognized, "this is Tony Savage. The family of Gary Ridgway has retained me, so I'll be taking over his case. Please give me a call. Thank you. Good-bye."

7

Tony Savage was a legend in Seattle legal circles. I had long admired him for his style, and most especially his unwavering commitment to his clients. A tall, lumbering, gray-bearded bear of a man, Tony was seventy-one years old, and in his long and distinguished career he had defended some of Seattle's most notorious, even infamous, people. Like almost all criminal defense lawyers, Tony was a vociferous opponent of the death penalty.

"Everyone of these [condemned] guys has something to offer," he once said, while defending a notorious triple murderer. "And I don't think we ought to be in the business of killing them."

Tony was the son of Anthony Savage, who had served as United States Attorney for the district of Washington back in the 1930s. Having grown up in Seattle, Tony was as much a part of the fabric of the community as the Lake Washington floating bridge. After becoming a lawyer in the late 1950s, he'd joined the King County Prosecutor's Office; but after obtaining a death penalty conviction of a man accused of beating a bowling alley operator to death, he'd seen the light: he'd asked that he be assigned no more death penalty cases. He was grateful to have lost that one death penalty victory on appeal, Tony said later.

Over the years, as a defense lawyer, he'd defended some of the most infamous accused killers in state history, including Charles Campbell, who'd broken out of a halfway house and had returned to the place where he'd committed his original crime—rape—and murdered the witnesses who had testified against him; David Rice, who had killed four members of a prominent Seattle family with a steam iron because he was under the delusion they were communists; a union official accused of hiring professional hit men to take out two union rivals; and even members of The Order, a neo-Nazi movement accused of numerous crimes.

"People say, 'how can you defend a guilty man?'" Tony once told the *Seattle Times.* "'How can you fight so hard for him?' But they know the answer to that. I'm not defending murder or rape. I'm merely seeing that the man accused of murder or rape gets a fair trial. My client's guilt is not *my* guilt."

From Tony's point of view, there was no such thing as "inherently evil."

"I don't believe we're born into this world to become murderers," he had said. "Charley [Campbell] had a miserable, miserable childhood. And to just snuff out these misfits ignores the basic problems. I can go on and on. How many of these guys are broke, half nuts, minorities . . . ?"

In addition to his long experience with the legal system and his unwavering commitment to his clients, no matter how publicly odious, Tony had two other attributes that would stand him in good stead as Gary's lawyer: he had a way with juries that was probably unmatched among King County attorneys, and—this was no small thing in Gary's prospective case—he had a terrific relationship with the news media, who almost universally loved him for his pithy, often humorous quotes. One wall of his downtown Seattle office featured the large, stuffed head of a gigantic moose, which kept unblinking watch over all who gathered there—a reminder of the Pacific Northwest's prized roots in frontier culture.

The next morning, December 6, I called Tony back and told him I had received his message that Greg and Dorene Ridgway had hired him to defend Gary.

"That's fine, Tony," I said. "Good luck with it. If you need anything from us at ACA, don't hesitate to call."

After hanging up, I was aware of a curious feeling about this development. On one hand, it would relieve my anxieties—whether I would have enough time and energy to deal with a case of such magnitude—and ameliorate my still-lingering concern about Kelly, Marley, and Sean. But at the same time, I felt a keen sense of disappointment. It was like being called into the big game to pitch, only to be removed by the manager even before finishing your warm-up tosses. The truth was, whether Gary was guilty or innocent, I *really wanted* to do the case.

———⌇———

I spent the rest of the weekend coping with the letdown. I'd already worked out an imaginary plan for the resources we'd need to defend Gary—all the lawyers, the investigators, the paralegals—and who would do what. Now it appeared that I'd never get a chance to put this paper plan into operation.

On Friday night, Todd and I attended the annual dinner of the Washington Association of Criminal Defense Lawyers (or WACDL) at a downtown Seattle hotel. Most of our colleagues in the defense bar commiserated with us for Gary's family's decision to switch lawyers, although some thought we would be relieved. Todd was, as usual, philosophical about the whole thing. The decision had been made, so there was no sense stewing about it. That was his take.

Still others commented on several statements that Tony had made to the news media about the case, once the news seeped out that he was taking over.

Asked how he intended to defend Gary, Tony had responded with a rhetorical analogy: "How do you eat an elephant?" he'd asked. "One bite at a time."

And about the DNA: "Prostitution is a contact sport. You don't do it fifty feet apart. That's the object of prostitution. The male customer wants to leave his DNA. If true, all the DNA proves is that he was a customer, not a killer."

Tony had also been asked how long it might take before the case came to trial.

"I think we'll be able to start trial in about a year, by next December," Tony had said.

What? It was my guess that just obtaining all the evidence from the prosecution would take at least a year, let alone trying to figure out what it all meant. I thought Tony was being wildly optimistic. *Either that,* I thought, *or he doesn't yet understand how big an elephant he really has on his plate.*

And as to the place where the trial should be held: "I feel lukewarm at best" toward a venue change request, Tony told the *Seattle Times*. "I don't want to leave Seattle. There's no better place in the state to try a murder case than Seattle. Omak and Coupeville are wonderful places, but not for a murder case." Tony's reference was to two small Washington State tourist destinations—both nice places to visit, but neither the right place for a major murder trial.

My fellow defense lawyers marveled at Tony's public comments. Some thought they showed that he hadn't yet fully appreciated all the aspects of what would certainly be the largest and most convoluted murder trial in the history of the United States. Predicting that the case could go to trial within a year was a bit rash, many thought, and so was the remark about the place where the case should be tried. Later, when it became apparent that much more time would be needed to produce a defense to the charges, as it surely would, or when a change of venue motion might become imperative, the prosecution could point to Tony's initial remarks as support for the notion that no additional time was needed, or that the case could remain in Seattle.

Most of all, though, I wondered what Tony's remarks might do to Gary's case in the event that he was convicted at trial and then appealed on these or other issues. If Gary was eventually convicted, he would undoubtedly be appealing any rulings (denials) by the judge of his motions for change of venue or motions for continuances of the trial date. Having Tony, his lead attorney, on the record claiming he wanted a trial in Seattle in one year would make it even harder for the appellate lawyers to argue that the King County jury was biased or that his lawyers hadn't had enough time to prepare for trial.

Tony's statements could come back to haunt Gary, I thought. That's why these death penalty cases need to be planned with the long view in mind—with an eye toward a future court of appeal reviewing the entire record, including off-the-cuff statements to the press by the defense attorney. Or was I just being paranoid and hypercritical after getting replaced by Tony?

Other lawyers told us they thought that perhaps this time, Tony had bitten off more pachyderm than he could chew by himself. From one colleague I learned that Tony had called Tim Ford, one of the most prominent legal experts on the death penalty in Seattle, indeed in the United States, to ask how he should get started. According to this colleague, Ford's advice to Tony had been to get Todd and me back into the case as soon as possible.

This took some of the sting out of being replaced—at least some people thought we public defenders had something to offer.

———✺———

The rumor about Tony consulting Tim Ford, and Ford suggesting that Tony get ACA back on the case, must have had some validity. Early on Monday morning, December 10, I took a call from Tony himself.

"Say," Tony said, after we had dispensed with the usual pleasantries, "I was wondering whether you and Todd would want to come back on the case with me, if I can convince OPD [the Office of Public Defense] to appoint you. I think . . . well, I know . . . this case is going to need more than one attorney. And I think I've made Mr. Ridgway sufficiently indigent. I know nothing about DNA, and I don't have any inclination to learn at this point."

I gathered from Tony's remark that his fee arrangement with Gary, Greg, and Dorene had probably wiped out most of Gary's assets—chiefly, his paid-off house in Auburn. As that amount alone would be insufficient to pay for an adequate defense, by demonstrating that Gary was now for all practical purposes indigent, the way would be cleared for the Office of Public Defense to authorize expenditures for Gary's additional defense needs—including a lawyer who knew something about DNA.

I didn't tell Tony how pleased his request made me. The cloud from the weekend instantly vanished.

"Tony, I'd be happy and honored to work on the case with you," I told him. "I can't speak for Todd, but I would guess that he's interested, too."

Tony responded agreeably. "I've got a meeting with Jim Crane (the OPD administrator) this afternoon. Why don't you talk to Todd, and I'll call you after I speak to Crane." Tony meant that he would try to convince Crane to have his office pick up the additional expense of defending Gary. If Crane refused, that meant Tony would have to defend the case on whatever money Gary and his family might raise. That would probably bankrupt Tony, if not kill him outright from overwork. I had a hunch that Crane would agree to appoint at least Todd and me and maybe others to work with Tony. The court rule was very clear: any death penalty case had to have at least *two* defense lawyers. And case law informed us that if adequate representation wasn't financed for a person who couldn't otherwise afford it, a huge issue would be opened up for appeal.

I called Todd almost immediately. He was typically very casual about the whole thing.

"Sure," he said, when I asked him if he wanted back into the Green River case.

That same afternoon, Tony met with Jim Crane at OPD. Crane agreed that if Gary were to receive an adequate defense against the charge that he was the worst serial killer in American history, he would need more than one lawyer. He agreed to recommend to the court that ACA be reappointed to the case.

All we had to do now was figure out how to actually defend Gary. And as little as I then knew about the Green River murders, I did know that it undoubtedly would be a daunting task.

PART TWO

The Team

8

On the same Monday that Tony went to see Jim Crane about getting public money for Gary's defense, King County Prosecutor Norm Maleng told the King County Council, the county's legislative body, that he intended to spend whatever it took to get a conviction in the Green River murder case. Initially, Maleng told the thirteen elected members of the council that he intended to assign as many as four prosecutors to the case, including Jeff Baird. Sheriff Reichert had already announced the formation of a new Green River Task Force (the fourth in twenty years)—to reinvestigate the old cases to see if more evidence could be obtained, against either Gary or anyone else. Reichert planned to assign up to a dozen officers to the new effort.

Obviously, if he had any chance of defending himself against that scale of resources by the police and prosecutors, Gary would need access to far more money than was in his net worth. Even if he sold his house and left his third wife, Judith, destitute, it would only be a thimbleful of the money an adequate defense would require. Failure to provide the resources to attempt to level the playing field meant that any conviction in Gary's case would be susceptible to being reversed by an appellate court. So, in this way, providing the money now was the most cost-effective use of the resources. Crane agreed to find the money needed—or at least some of it—for Gary's defense. But final approval would have to come from the court.

While these arrangements were being finalized, I decided to do some basic research into the Green River case. Even though the newspapers and television reporters had covered—*over*covered, as Todd would say—the current events surrounding Gary's arrest, most of the background of the case was given comparatively short shrift. To get a better grip on the events that had brought us to this situation, I burrowed into my garage and dug out my old copy of *The Search for the Green River Killer,* a paperback book, written by Carlton Smith (my coauthor here) and Tomas Guillen, published in 1991 by Penguin-Onyx. Although over a decade old, this book provided a comprehensive look at the events surrounding the murders and their immediate aftermath, including the intense political maneuvering that accompanied the original investigation.

At least one thing became clear from my rereading of the old book about the murders: the main reason so many legal and investigative resources would be needed (by both sides) on the present legal case against Gary was the old murder case's sheer size and complexity. Not the least of the problems was the very fuzzy nature of the crimes themselves. No one had ever been able to say, for instance, which crimes were actually committed by "the Green River Killer," whoever he was, and which murders had only been put on the list merely because they seemed similar and were also unsolved. For that matter, it wasn't possible to say which murders that *hadn't* been put on the list ought instead to be *on* it. As one of the police investigators had said years earlier, "It's not as if the guy is leaving his driver's license at the scene of the crime." The fact was, there was something of an analytical continuum for including or excluding the murders. The victims found in or near the Green River were by definition the crimes of the Green River Killer, whereas female human remains found forty and fifty miles away were simply a matter of guessing.

Although the murders were supposed to have ended in early 1984, the fact was, there were as many as fifty similar crimes that had taken place between 1984 and 2001 that had never been put on the official Green River list, in part for reasons of politics: some elected officials simply didn't want the pressure to divert scarce police resources that admitting more murders might bring. And there were about a half-dozen similar murders that had been committed *before* the Green River murders that weren't included on the list, either. So there was no way to know for sure which crimes were legitimately Green River crimes and which were not. The only person who knew for sure was the killer.

Making all this even more inscrutable was the fact that the police borrowed a good part of their early thinking about the murders from another notorious Northwest serial case, the "Ted" murders, as they were called, of the late 1970s. Those were murders of college-age young women by the infamous Ted Bundy, although it was years before anyone in Seattle realized that the "Ted" murders had been committed by Bundy, who was essentially unknown as a suspect until he traveled to Utah after the Washington State murders. Bundy had grown up in Tacoma, Washington. Between 1973 and 1974, the one-time law student murdered at least ten and as many as thirty young women in Washington, Oregon, Utah, and Florida. When the Green River murders first came to public attention in the summer of 1982, police saw the person they were seeking in terms of the sexual psychopathy of Bundy. That meant they believed they were looking for a very clever sexual predator, someone who, like Bundy, read the newspapers and watched television to enjoy the sensational reports of his awful exploits; someone who kept jewelry and clothing from his victims as "trophies" to facilitate his fantasies about his crimes; and someone who was capable of posing as a trustworthy authority figure, or even as a good Samaritan.

In the days immediately following the discovery of the first five victims—Wendy Coffield, Debra Bonner, Marcia Chapman, Cynthia Hinds, and Opal Mills—in or near the Green River, the initial psychological assessment of the unknown killer posited that the murderer was someone who felt compelled to remonstrate verbally with prostitutes over moral issues, even as he felt sexually attracted to them. The killer's motive was seen as tripartite: not only to chastise the victims and to take sexual power over them but also to taunt the police for their inability to stop him. Some police, in fact, thought he was sending a message to them: they were inadequate in stopping prostitution, and he, the killer, was doing their job better than they could. Placing the victims in the river was seen as a means of both washing them of trace evidence and, in a bizarre, somewhat contradictory way, posing them for later private revisitation (hence the large rocks used to hold them in place under the water), or, conceivably, to shock people who might subsequently discover them. Still others thought that in using the river, the killer might be engaging in a bizarre form of baptism.

What wasn't immediately appreciated by the public, although the police themselves were acutely aware of it, was that the authorities had come exceedingly close to apprehending the murderer in the very beginning of the case. This became apparent to investigators in the week following August 15, 1982, when they realized that if they had taken the trouble to search the river adequately on the afternoon of August 12, the day that Debra Bonner's body had been found, they would have discovered the submerged remains of Marcia Chapman and Cynthia Hinds then, rather than three days later. Even worse, had they placed the river under covert surveillance from August 12 through August 15, they would have caught the killer red-handed, when he returned to the river with the body of Opal Mills, who had last been seen around 1 P.M. on August 12, on Pacific Highway South, just about one hour before Debra Bonner's body had been discovered in the Green River. So it appeared that the killer had come back to the river with Opal's body after the police had left on August 12, having removed Debra Bonner's body, but having failed to discover the nearby bodies of Marcia Chapman and Opal Mills.[1]

Reichert himself had discovered Opal's body on August 15, as he was searching the grassy bank of the river near the place underwater where the bodies of Marcia Chapman and Cynthia Hinds had finally been discovered around noon the same day by a man floating downstream on an inflated raft. The initial police investigation was subsequently directed at a group of people who were known to associate with the victims, principally pimps, drug dealers, cabdrivers, and other assorted types that were well-known to one another in the rough-and-ready street milieu frequented by prostitutes.

Within a few weeks of the discovery of the river victims, in August 1982, however, Reichert—then a relatively inexperienced homicide detective—had focused his investigative interest on a taxicab driver named Melvyn Foster, who admitted some acquaintanceship with all five of the victims. A former convicted auto thief, who had once served a short stretch in state prison, Foster's lifestyle was everything the religious Reichert despised; it appears that to Foster, Reichert's holier-than-you attitude was likewise anathema. Reichert became convinced that Foster had to be the murderer. Soon a large contingent of police officers was trailing Foster around on his peripatetic travels, and several searches were undertaken of Foster's house and vehicle in order to find physical evidence linking him to the murders, to no avail. It likewise became clear to me that Reichert and Foster had become locked into a personality conflict, which may have clouded Reichert's objectivity.[2]

But while Reichert and the other police investigators had settled on Foster as the guilty party, increasing numbers of young prostitutes continued to turn up missing on Pacific Highway South as well as from several similar prostitution-afflicted neighborhoods around the city of Seattle. Although a number of these disappearances were reported to police by family members and pimps, few in the police paid much attention to them, at least at first. Certainly, no one considered that the disappearances were related to the Green River Killer, who, after all, in Reichert's view, *had* to be Melvyn Foster: Hadn't the dumping of victims in the Green River stopped as soon as Foster was placed under surveillance? Didn't that show that Foster had to be the killer? Or so the police reasoning went.

It was not until the fall of the following year, 1983, that people began to literally stumble over the grim truth. Someone had continued to murder scores of young prostitutes but rather than returning to the Green River had left their bodies in vacant lots or wooded areas all around the airport and then even further out, in the forested, rural areas of the county. One by one, the skeletons began to be discovered under trees and brush, usually by hikers, mushroom hunters, or simple passersby alerted while exercising their dogs. By the time months had passed after these often-unreported disappearances, the victims' bodies had been completely skeletonized by the elements, enormously complicating the solution of their murder: after all, one couldn't begin to figure out who the murderer was until one first knew who had been murdered.

By early 1984, the county sheriff—in those days the Sheriff's Department was known as the King County Police—formed another task force to investigate the murders. It had become apparent that Melvyn Foster was probably not the killer—not, at least, if the Green River murderer was the same person who had killed the other victims whose skeletons had been found around the airport, and increasingly, farther out in the county's more rural areas. After all, Foster had been under surveillance when a significant number of the new victims had been killed. That seemed to let the by-then-former cabdriver out.

As 1984 wore on and a larger number of detectives were now reassigned to the case, another fact became obvious: even though the newly discovered victims hadn't been found in water (despite the prediction of some, who had contended that future victims would be found in other rivers), there *was* something of a similar pattern. With some exceptions, the dry land victims mirrored the situation of the river victims. There, the killer had dumped five victims in a relatively compact area, all within a half-mile of one another along the Green River. And in the dry land cases, the killer had similarly clustered his victims—some found in brush north of the SeaTac airport; some south of the airport; some in a wooded area known as Star Lake, southeast of the airport on Kent's west hill; others even farther out, in a ravine near a cemetery in Auburn, southeast of Kent; and still others very far out on Highway 410, which led to Mt. Rainier, or out I-90, the main highway to Spokane.

And further analysis of these dry land *clusters,* as they came to be called, showed a common pattern of usage: that the murderer would usually first test the cluster area with a single victim.[3] Then, when the first victim went undiscovered for some time, the killer might return with a flurry of victims—sometimes up to five more within a short period of time. Once the cluster was discovered, the killer left no more victims at that site.

There were some differences between the river victims and the dry land victims, though, that simply confused the issue: Were investigators looking for more than one killer? One killer responsible for the river victims, another killer responsible for the dry land victims? Or were there multiple killers? Were the dry land sites only superficially similar merely because there was so little evidence found at each? Or were copycat murderers at work? It was as much of a conundrum as it was a continuum.

And to really confuse matters, there was the case of Carol Christensen. Unlike the river victims, or the dry land victims, Carol Christensen's body had been found fully clothed—and by itself, far from any other victim. What was more, two trout had been placed on her body, some uncooked sausage on the back of her hands, which were clasped across her waist. An empty wine bottle was placed between her legs, its neck surrounded by her clasped hands. A paper sack from a Pacific Highway South supermarket was placed over her head. In further contrast to the other dry land victims, Carol Christensen's body had been discovered within a few days of her death. And in very marked contrast with all the other victims, usually so difficult to identify, her driver's license was found at the scene. In none of the other cases was the killer so helpful to the police.

On the continuum perceived by the detectives, then, if the Green River victims were judged to be the most likely murders of the Green River Killer, Carol Christensen was seen as the *least* likely. And yet, here in 2001, Gary Ridgway had been charged with killing the most likely Green River victims, yet the best evidence against him—the DNA—was found with the least likely.[4] It was a strange puzzle.

Eventually, eight separate clusters were identified: the Green River, with its five initial victims; a brushy area near a Little League field just north of the airport, with three skeletonized victims; a second brushy area south of the airport, where remains of five victims were eventually found; Star Lake, with remains of six victims; a ravine adjacent to Mt. View Cemetery in Auburn, southeast of Kent, with three victims; a stretch of Highway 410 to Mt. Rainier, far southeast of Seattle, with partial remains of three victims; several locations far east of Seattle along I-90, with six victims; and a rural area southeast of Portland, Oregon, where partial remains of four victims were discovered. In addition, there were eight other victims found where there were no clusters, such as Carol Christensen. Generally, once one victim in a cluster was discovered by chance, investigators soon discovered the other nearby victims as they searched the area. That wasn't the case with the singles, as some called the *unclustered victims.*

Besides those forty-two discovered victims, there were also seven young women who had gone missing during the period of the murders, who were thought to have been murdered by the killer, but whose remains had not yet been discovered.

Identifying the skeletons of the dead and determining who was still missing was not a simple task, because almost all of the victims had backgrounds in prostitution, which frequently entailed the use of aliases and false identifications. It was only by attempting diligently to reassemble the victims' milieu—places they had lived, roommates, jail acquaintances, pimps, previous customers, court and probation records, along with information from their families—that investigators were able to assemble a comprehensive look at the killing terrain. It took the news media about a year to catch on to the fact that it was the order of disappearance of the victims, rather than the discovery (which was after all merely a matter of chance), that was most important to understanding what was going on. It took even longer to realize that the murders were not merely a sensational crime story, but rather a serious public health problem, the deadly result of some mentally aberrant individual at large among the free-floating, often clandestine population of prostitutes and pimps.

At its height from 1984 to 1987, the Green River Task Force assembled a gigantic amount of physical evidence, most of it from places where victims' remains had been found. No one could say with any certainty whether the physical evidence was even germane to the case, as very little of it actually made it to the Washington State Crime Lab. That agency, woefully underfunded and overburdened with tests it had to make for "higher-priority" cases that had actually been charged, was simply unable to keep up with the workload.

Meanwhile, the task force had collected tips on thousands of possible suspects, many of them customers of prostitutes, sorting them into piles of possibility: A suspects, a very good chance; B suspects, possible but not likely; C suspects, very unlikely. At the same time, other detectives assembled detailed histories of the dead—no mean feat, considering that many were mere bones when they were finally discovered, and so first they had to be identified.

The investigators' idea was to try to match a suspect's whereabouts with a victim's disappearance. To help make these matches, the authorities collected hundreds of thousands of pieces of paper from various Puget Sound police agencies, courts, and other public bodies, as well as from private employers such as private guard agencies. These data were then manually entered into a computer database; this was in the prescanner era.[5]

These documents ranged from parking tickets and traffic tickets to reports of arrests, reports of investigation, and even patrol officers' routine contacts with motorists, known as *field interrogation reports,* or FIR. There were, in fact, nearly ten thousand of those. Everything was fed into the rudimentary mechanical maw, in an effort to winnow the chaff to find the elusive golden needle. That was why the investigation had generated nearly a million pieces of paper over the years.

During this stepped-up investigation, the King County authorities again consulted with John Douglas, an FBI psychological profiler, who was said to be the model for one of the characters in Thomas Harris's novel *Silence of the Lambs.* Douglas theorized that the Green River Killer was marginally employed, was familiar with the outdoors, drove vehicles that were not well maintained, and had strong feelings about sexual fidelity. In fact, Douglas had opined, seeing the women market themselves on the street "makes his blood boil." At one point in the mid-1980s, police, relying on portions of this profile, detained a fur trapper in connection with the murders but soon were embarrassed to discover that the unfortunate man had nothing to do with the crimes. Subsequently, local authorities' relations with the FBI were soured considerably.

By 1987, after a few false starts, the investigation's pointer had swung around to Gary. By that point, the investigators had discovered in their computer quite a number of unusual circumstances that put Gary right at the top of the *A* list.

All of this was summarized in *The Search for the Green River Killer,* along with a fairly cryptic section relating to Gary, who had not been identified by name by the authors, but referred to merely as "the truck painter."

―⁓―

Combining the information from *The Search for the Green River Killer* and the facts recited in Detective Peters's affidavit, I was able to get a tentative grip on Gary's previous involvement with the Green River murder investigation.

Gary's first encounter with the law came in May 1982, when he was arrested by an undercover policewoman posing as a prostitute on Pacific Highway South. This took place more than two months before the first victims were found in the Green River. This was a routine arrest, the sort of thing that happened once or twice a month along the highway, as the police attempted to damp down the flourishing sex trade with occasional arrests of johns, as prostitutes call their customers. Gary paid a nominal fine and the incident was largely forgotten, although the record of the encounter remained in the system.

A little over three months later, on August 29, 1982, Gary had been contacted by the Port of Seattle Police just after 1 A.M. while near his pickup truck in the vicinity of South 192nd Street near the airport— the same cluster area where four skeletons were discovered the following year. This date also happened to be about the time that two other Green River victims were last seen, one later discovered near Star Lake, and the other still missing. Gary told the officer that he'd had to urinate, and the officer let him go with a warning; no one thought at that time to connect him with the victims that had recently been discovered in the Green River.

Six months after that, on February 23, 1983, the Port of Seattle Police again had contact with Gary. This time, Gary was with a woman, Keli McGinness, who would later also be listed as a Green River missing person. Because this was during the time that the King County police believed that cabdriver Foster was the killer, nothing further was done about this, and this encounter too was simply filed away.

Then, on May 4, 1983, Gary was contacted at his house in Des Moines, a suburb south of the airport, by a Des Moines Police detective, Bob Fox. Fox had been told that Gary had been the person who picked up a woman named Marie Malvar from Pacific Highway the night before. Malvar had then disappeared. Malvar's pimp and her father had traced her to Gary's house by recognizing Gary's truck as the one driven by the person who had picked Marie up the night before. But Fox, who had known Gary personally years earlier—they had worked together at a local market when Gary was a teenager—accepted Gary's explanation that he knew nothing about Marie Malvar's disappearance. This report, too, was filed away and temporarily forgotten, at least until Marie Malvar was put on the Green River missing list some months later as a possible victim of the killer.

As it happened, Carol Christensen's body was discovered about thirty miles away in Maple Valley some four days after Fox visited Gary at his house in May 1983. At the time, most investigators did not connect this murder to the Green River series because of the case's weirdness, with the fish, sausage, paper bag, and wine. The Christensen case would not go on the official Green River list until almost a year later, and even then many investigators did not believe it was actually connected.

Six months after Marie Malvar's disappearance in May 1983, just as the newly discovered skeletonized victims were beginning to show up around the airport in mid-November, a member of Reichert's initial investigation team, King County detective Larry Gross, interviewed Gary. Gross was routinely following up on Bob Fox's report of his investigation on Malvar, which by then had worked its way through the area police paper chain to the King County department. Gary admitted to Gross that he patronized prostitutes but once again denied having any contact with Marie Malvar. Gross concluded in his report that Gary was probably not a viable suspect in the murders: among other things, he didn't seem to fit the psychological profile advanced by the Federal Bureau of Investigation, and he certainly did not seem at all like Ted Bundy.

But by early 1984, it had become apparent to most detectives that cabdriver Foster probably was not responsible for the murders nor was someone much like Bundy, especially if one believed that the same killer who had put the victims in the Green River was also responsible for all the skeletal remains that were by then being found in and around the airport. A new push was made among prostitutes to induce them to provide tips on oddball "tricks," and on February 3, 1984, one woman proffered Gary's name to detectives. Gary had picked her up on Pacific Highway South in late December, and to her way of thinking (by that time, the discovery of all the new skeletons was much in the news), Gary seemed far too edgy, so she had aborted her "date" with him. Because of all the publicity then circulating about the murders, she had subsequently called the police to tell them about Gary; she knew his name to be Gary Ridgway, she said, because Gary had showed her his driver's license to prove that he wasn't a police officer.

With this latest information, a King County detective, Randy Mullinax, opened a new investigative file on Gary. Mullinax soon discovered Gary's arrest for soliciting the undercover policewoman from April 1982, Detective Fox's encounter with Gary in May 1983, and Detective Gross's interview of Gary in November. Mullinax thought it worthwhile to interview Gary once more, and on April 12, 1984, Gary voluntarily came into the Green River Task Force headquarters near the airport and readily admitted having "dated" Keli McGinness in the past and also having once seen another missing woman, Kim Nelson, soliciting on Pacific Highway South. Gary also admitted talking with a friend of Nelson's a day or so later. Nelson's friend, Gary told Mullinax, had told him that Nelson was missing and that she thought the Green River Killer had gotten her.

Gary also told Mullinax that he had dated women on the Pacific Highway strip between five and ten times and that he had contracted a venereal disease at least three times.

To Mullinax, there was little that made Gary stand out from the run-of-the-mill john that were by then attracting most of the Green River investigators' attention. He arranged for Gary to take a lie detector test, and on May 7, 1984, Gary did just that. The county's polygraph examiner determined that Gary wasn't lying, and Mullinax recommended that further investigation of Gary cease.

Six months later, in November 1984, another young woman, Rebecca Garde, contacted the police to tell them that in early November 1982, an unknown man had choked her during a sexual encounter south of the airport. Eventually, the man in this encounter was identified as Gary, and once again detectives asked Gary about his activities. In a new interview on February 23, 1985, Gary freely admitted that he had been with the complaining woman, even that he had choked her, but he said he'd only done this after she'd bitten him during oral sex. Once again, the investigating detectives accepted Gary's version of the events, and no further investigation was undertaken.

Subsequently, however, the FBI reexamined Gary's 1984 polygraph, the one he'd volunteered to take after Kim Nelson's disappearance, and concluded that it had been incorrectly administered. Two FBI agents began a new investigation of Gary in early 1986 and had a new interview with him. Once again, Gary freely admitted patronizing prostitutes in the past but said he'd stopped because of the murders. He admitted choking Rebecca Garde but said it was the only time he'd ever assaulted anyone. In this interview, Gary contended that he had a compulsion to pick up prostitutes, saying that they affected him "the way alcohol does an alcoholic." He said he liked to talk to the women. The FBI agents offered Gary another polygraph, which he agreed to take. But then Gary hired a lawyer, David Middaugh, who told the FBI agents that he'd advised Gary not to talk to the police anymore and not to take the new lie detector test.

At that point, the FBI dropped its investigation of Gary. Significantly, the decision to drop Gary as an investigative target was taken after other FBI agents had advised the King County Police to concentrate their efforts on another man, a laborer and occasional fur trapper who lived near the airport. After a highly publicized search of that man's home—a search that yielded no evidence—the Green River Task Force was harshly criticized by political figures, and the investigation's momentum was significantly dampened.

Nevertheless, by August 1986, Gary's name floated to the top of the *A* list once more. This took place because detectives had finally succeeded in locating the friend of Kim Nelson who had seen Gary briefly on the highway just before Nelson disappeared in late October 1983. This friend, Paige Miley, was located while working as a prostitute in Las Vegas. Miley was able to help a police sketch artist draw a composite of a man who looked very much like Gary. She subsequently picked Gary's photograph from a photo array. Interestingly, she also told the detectives—Randy Mullinax among them—that she had turned the man's license plate into Reichert's original investigation team in 1983 but had never heard back from any of the original investigating detectives.[6]

With this information in hand, detectives located Gary's second wife, Marcia. At that point, Marcia gave them information that reignited investigators' interest in Gary, as recounted earlier. On September 14, 1986, Marcia accompanied the detectives on an auto tour of the southeast King County area, during which she pointed out a number of places where she had gone with Gary. Many of these were places where Green River victims were subsequently discovered.

After this, a redoubled effort was made to link Gary to the murders. When detectives checked their case histories for the victims, they discovered that in three different disappearances, witnesses had seen the victims get into vehicles that arguably were similar to vehicles driven by Gary at the time.

On April 8, 1987, the investigators obtained a warrant and conducted a search of Gary's Des Moines–area house and a number of vehicles, mostly pickup trucks, that he'd had access to. Gary also was asked to provide a saliva sample, which he did. During these searches, investigators found traces of what appeared to be pink glass—the same sort of substance that had been found at a number of the places where murder victims had been found. The substance was taken to the FBI crime lab in Washington D.C., where it was soon identified as a naturally formed mineral commonly found throughout the Pacific Northwest. It was therefore useless as evidence.

With that, the initial investigation of Gary came to a halt. For the next fourteen years, little more was done to attempt to implicate him in the murders. Then, in August 2001, the STR testing of the DNA samples found with Carol Christensen, Marcia Chapman, and Opal Mills was undertaken, along with similar DNA samples taken from onetime cabdriver Foster, Gary, and one other man. Of the three, only Gary's came back as a match.

9

While waiting for Jim Crane of the Office of Public Defense to decide whether Gary was "sufficiently indigent" to warrant expenditure of public funds on his defense, Kelly told me that she'd been confronted by the mother of a girl who attended school with Marley.

"I'll bet you're glad Mark's off that awful case," she'd told Kelly.

"I didn't want to get into it with her," Kelly told me later. "It was hard for me to explain why you wanted to do it."

I wondered momentarily if Kelly was having second thoughts about my taking on such an infamous client.

"You *do* understand why I want to do this, don't you?" I asked her.

"'It's your work,' she'd say, you do it for pay,'" Kelly said, quoting Bob Dylan from "Hurricane."

"Well," I said, "we *hope* so. That's up to Crane, though."

"It's just tough explaining it to people who think he should be shot as soon as possible," Kelly said. I understood. Sometimes it *was* hard to explain.

"Just don't forget about us," she added. "We need you here, too."

―⁓―

By Tuesday December 11, 2001, Tony was successful in convincing Jim Crane to foot some of Gary's soon-to-be-astronomical legal bills. There was really no alternative—not if the court didn't want to see the case come back for a second trial after an appeal.

That afternoon, Todd, Tony, and I met at the ACA office in Kent to get ourselves organized.

"I want to let you know right up front, it's not like I'm on some sort of pedestal," Tony told us. "I look at this as the three of us being equals, not like I have to be the 'lead attorney.' I know you guys know what you're doing. So I think we work this like a democracy. If the three of us don't agree, two out of three wins. The majority rules. If you two agree on something and I disagree, I'll shut up and go with the majority."

That sounded fine to Todd and me. We discussed Tony's recent comments in the press, and Tony agreed that he had probably said things he shouldn't have. But one thing was clear: we needed someone to take the point as far as organizing our team—that is, interacting with Crane and the other bureaucrats—and generally acting as an administrator.

"I have no interest in being an administrator," Tony said.

"If you've ever seen the state of Todd's office, you wouldn't want him to be the administrator, either," I said, needling Todd for his messy office.

"That's something that would interest an anal retentive asshole like you," Todd shot back, grinning wickedly. Todd's anarchistic tendencies were unabated.

So I agreed to become the team administrator, in charge of scheduling meetings, setting agendas, sending out notices, and riding herd on what looked like would have to be a very large budget.

We discussed how to divide up the responsibilities of the case.

We all knew that we needed to have a strategy for dealing with the news media, given the explosion of news coverage that had accompanied Gary's arrest. Because of Tony's stature and because of his quotability, we also knew that he would be the reporters' first choice: they'd call him whenever they wanted a reaction to something that popped up in the news. But that didn't mean that Tony had to talk to them immediately. It was important to speak with one voice; that is, be consistent in what we were telling the media. We agreed to always consult and that from then on, whenever possible, there would be two of us when it came time for speaking to the media. Todd didn't want to do it, so that left Tony and me. Or "media boy," as Todd put it.

The way all three of us saw the case, we had to start immediately by dividing the work into several broad areas: first, the guilt phase, which meant examining and attacking the state's evidence that Gary had to be the killer, including the DNA and other mounds of forensic evidence, and which necessarily involved trying to see if there were other, more viable suspects; second, the legal issues, such as attacks on the search warrants, the issue of getting a fair trial in King County, obtaining complete discovery, issues regarding the uncharged crimes, attempts to attack the charges as insufficient, and motions regarding the constitutionality of the death penalty and the common-scheme-or-plan aggravating factor; and third, the penalty phase, convincing the jury not to impose death, and directly related to that, the *mitigation package.*

The mitigation package is virtually a requirement in all death penalty cases in Washington. It was, in effect, our last line of defense: things we'd argue if our client was found guilty. Preparing such a package required an assumption that the client would be found guilty in the guilt phase of the trial and that the only remaining question was whether the defendant deserved the death penalty. The package was essentially an investigation into the possible reasons for the defendant's criminal acts and into the reasons why his life should be spared. Because the case law essentially required the defense to assemble this package in any potential death penalty case, the smart thing to do was get started on it as soon as possible. In doing so, we weren't conceding for a moment (and certainly not publicly) that Gary would actually be found guilty. It was just that we needed to get going on it as soon as we could, in case the worst eventually happened.[1]

Todd and Tony both wanted to handle the guilt phase of the case. That meant examining the evidence against Gary, except for the DNA, which would be my area. The guilt phase would include making opening statement, closing argument, and cross-examining the state's witnesses, including all the lay witnesses who might claim to have seen Gary somewhere incriminating, as well as the expected experts on fibers, paint, teeth, bugs, crime scene analysis, all the stuff one might see on *CSI;* in short, it would be Tony and Todd's job to poke as many holes in the prosecution's case as they could and to make those holes seem even larger by calling witnesses favorable to Gary.

As "the DNA guy," I was predetermined to handle the evidence from the DNA recovered from Carol Christensen, Marcia Chapman, Opal Mills, and Gary himself, as well as from any other sources. My job would be to examine the evidence collection and testing process to see if it couldn't be neutralized somehow. And I also wanted to oversee the mitigation effort. That left a lot of work for at least one other lawyer, someone who would ride herd on all the legal issues that were sure to emerge and keep in the prosecution's face about their obligation to provide us with all the reports from the two decades of investigation— already reported in the newspapers to be around a million pages. Plus photographs. And videos. And audio interview tapes. The amount of material that was potentially disclosable was simply staggering.

Even though none of us knew for sure just how much money we could expect the court to approve for Gary's defense, we had every hope that the resources would be substantial. Case law had made it clear that a court's failure to provide "reasonable and necessary" resources for the defense of an individual in a capital case was grounds for reversal. With the amount of discovery to review, the need for more legal talent was obvious.

Tony had done the math: with four lawyers, one more than we now had, and assuming that the million pages were divided equally between the four of us and that all of us could read, make notes, and understand the material at a constant rate of four minutes a page (impossible!) and that we would all read steadily for eight hours a day, including weekends, it would still take four of us more than *five years* just to read all the paperwork, let alone prepare a defense, which obviously meant generating a substantial number of pages of our own. In sheer size, the Green River case was truly in a universe all its own. There was Oklahoma City and there was the Unabomber but nothing quite like this had ever happened before in the history of the American legal system.

"I think we should ask for two more lawyers, up front," Tony said. "Then, if the prosecution asks for the death penalty, which it will, I think we should ask for more." Todd and I agreed with this proposal for five attorneys, although by then I was beginning to think that even the six lawyers I had first suggested to ACA's Jim Robinson wouldn't be enough. A million pages of reports, forty-nine official victims, another fifty or so that might be connected, thousands of pieces of potential physical evidence: this wasn't just an elephant, it was an entire ram-paging horde of elephants! We definitely needed reinforcements.

We kicked around some names of other lawyers we might ask to join us, and after some discussion, we agreed that the next lawyer we included should be a woman. We knew that our male perspective might blind us to things that would otherwise be obvious to the op-posite sex.

"How about Michele Shaw?" Tony asked. "She called me and asked if she could help on the case. I've never worked with her, but she seems pleasant and smart."

Both Todd and I had known Michele when she'd worked a few years before as a deputy prosecutor. Since leaving that office, she'd gone into private practice and in fact had recently helped defend a complex fraud case in federal court, one with voluminous documents. Besides being smart, she was charming, attractive, and kept herself in great shape, just the sort of person who might make an impression on a jury. When Todd and I agreed to ask Michele to come aboard, Tony said he would call her.

We kicked around some other names in case we got the money we would need. I suggested Fred Leatherman, a Seattle lawyer I knew who was also proficient in DNA litigation. I had an idea that if Gary had any hope of acquittal, our first line of defense would be to knock out—or at least discredit somehow—the DNA evidence. Tony nom-inated Eric Lindell, another Seattle lawyer that Todd and I had known and respected for many years. Like Todd, Eric was a very aggressive defender, who distrusted mostly everything the government said or did. Like Todd, Eric was also a whiz on forensic issues such as fibers and paints. From what we'd all read so far, we were pretty sure that sort of *trace evidence* might play a major role in any case against Gary.

We discussed bringing on Dave Roberson, an ex–public defender known for aggressive representation of his clients. We weren't sure how many lawyers we'd get so we had to wait and see. We also wanted to make sure all of the possible avenues of appeal were covered, so we decided to try to reserve a spot for a well-qualified expert on appel-late issues in death penalty cases. Some names were considered, but we decided to hold off on bringing anyone else aboard until we could see how we stood with the court, which after all would have to approve the expenditures.

Three days later, on Friday December 14, 2001, Tony, Todd, Eric Lindell, Michele Shaw, and I met at the ACA office in Kent. Michele was particularly grateful to have been invited to join us. And at the time, I was pleased to see her, too. She had had a lot of experience with cases involving voluminous documents and quickly volunteered to take on that aspect of the case. Already there was talk by the prosecutor's office of somehow converting all the mountains of paper to an electronic format, one that would be far more easily handled than the warehouse that the county had needed to store it in for two decades. Michele's experience covered just this sort of transfer to electronic pages.

"I'll do anything you tell me to do. . . . I'll defer to you guys . . ." Michele said when we first sat down to talk.

———*∿*———

I had another face-to-face with Gary over the next week while we set about trying to organize his defense. I explained that it seemed pretty clear that the state would be trying to execute him, so it was vital that we start work immediately by trying to assemble all the reasons he should not be put to death, the mitigation package, as it's called. To do this right, we'd have to bring in an expert, who would start from the assumption that he was guilty, even if he wasn't.

"I know it seems like we're putting the cart before the horse," I told him. "But it's really the only way to do this. It doesn't mean that we don't believe you're innocent. It just means we want to get prepared for the worst, if it ever comes."

"Oooh-K," Gary said. "I get you."

By this point, he'd had visits from his wife, his brother Greg and sister-in-law Dorene, as well as from Marcia and his son, Matthew, who was serving in the Marines. Communications with Gary's family were crucial. We wanted to be there for them, for whatever reasons, any time of day. However, neither Todd nor I had interviewed any of Gary's family at this point; the family had retained Tony so these communications were initiated with Tony. Because they had hired Tony and Tony had brought in Michele Shaw, who was very personable and really good at talking with Gary's family, we decided to let Tony and Michele handle these day-to-day communications. In turn, Tony and Michele periodically filled us in, Tony in short telephone calls and meetings, and Michele by e-mail, on how Gary's family was reacting to this horrible situation.

According to Michele, Matthew had been contacted by detectives from the Sheriff's Department at Camp Pendleton, California, on

November 30, told that his father was being arrested in connection with the Green River case, and asked if he could recall any behavior on Gary's part that might suggest that he had committed the crimes. Matthew was naturally shocked at the arrest, although he knew that his father had once been a suspect in the murders. He'd told the detectives that there was nothing he could recall in his father's behavior that suggested he might be the killer. The detectives had then asked if he might be willing to talk to Gary. They had some idea that if he saw his son face-to-face, Gary might admit to the murders. Matthew said he was willing to talk to his father, and the Sheriff's Department arranged for him and his wife to fly to Seattle. There Matthew met with his mother, Marcia, and the two then went to the jail to see Gary. At the jail, mother and son encountered Judith, Gary's current wife, on her own visit. Both women wept at Gary's predicament, even though Marcia's information about her former husband had been critical to developing the case against Gary.

Michele told us that by the middle of December 2001, she had sensed something of a split beginning to show in the ranks of Gary's intimates—with Greg, Dorene, and Judith believing that Gary's arrest was some sort of horrible mistake, with Marcia leaning toward the idea that Gary had in fact committed the murders, and with Matthew torn between the family poles. Making matters much worse was the release of the police search warrant affidavit: Marcia's characterization of Greg, Gary, and Ed Ridgway's mother, Mary Rita Ridgway, as "dominating" the family, and "dressing as a prostitute" ignited Greg and turned him and Dorene against Marcia.

"That's not true," Greg told me, when I happened to run into him outside the jail on December 17, a day before Gary was scheduled to appear for his arraignment on the four murder charges. Although this was the first time I met Greg—I'd only talked to him briefly on the telephone—I recognized him at once because of his resemblance to his brother.

"My mother dressed very nicely, and that thing with the plate—that never happened. It's just Marcia. She's trying to justify all the things she did to Gary when they were married." As for Judith, Gary's arrest, coupled with the massive publicity, had devastated her. Judith had long suffered from a nervous condition, and until Gary was arrested, he had been the main pillar in her life. Now, suddenly, all the comfort and stability was wiped away. Their house would have to be sold to pay some of Gary's legal fees, and Judith faced possible destitution. The Sheriff's Department, to keep her shielded from the news media, had paid for her to stay several nights at a south King County hotel, but that couldn't last forever. By the end of the first week of Gary's incarceration, Judith had moved in with Greg and Dorene, at least temporarily.

Michele and her paralegal-assistant, Donna, spent hours on the phone, offering their support and comfort to Judith.

———

On December 17, we had an unannounced (at least, to the news media) hearing in a downtown Seattle courtroom. The prosecutors wanted to transfer the case from Kent to the downtown courthouse. We objected, but it was fruitless: the state wanted to have the case tried in Seattle, in part because of the downtown courthouse's proximity to the main jail. The jail administrators had a policy of housing all capital defendants and high-security inmates in the Seattle jail and would not transport them to the RJC in Kent. It was a foregone conclusion. The case was transferred to Seattle.

The more important bit of business, at least for the defense, was obtaining the court's approval for our anticipated expenditures to defend Gary. Presiding Judge Brian Gain approved the appointment of two senior ACA lawyers, Todd and me, and the retention of Michele Shaw. He indicated that he would also approve more lawyers if and when the prosecutors announced they'd be seeking the death penalty. He also authorized the Office of Public Defense to provide the defense money to hire one investigator and one paralegal, to join another investigator, another paralegal, and a case clerk that ACA was to provide for the case. With those additions, Team Ridgway now had four lawyers, two investigators, two paralegals, and one clerk, with the prospect of others joining us once the prosecutors announced their decision on the death penalty, which everyone agreed was inevitable. Judge Gain also authorized $290,000 to hire experts.

Altogether, OPD's Crane said after the hearing, about $950,000 of public resources had so far been committed to defend Gary against the murder charges, a figure that was certain to go up once the prosecutor said it would seek death. Counting the money that had already been set aside for the prosecution and the Sheriff's Department for their renewed investigation, there was a realistic possibility that the entire proceeding might wind up costing between $8 million and $12 million before it was all over. Putting people to death properly—

constitutionally—in the United States of America can and should be very expensive.

The next day, December 18, the jumpsuited, manacled Gary was once again escorted to the criminal presiding courtroom. This time, the news media was out in force, along with a smattering of others we were soon to understand were relatives and friends of the long, sad string of Green River victims.

Tony stood at the bar before Judge Jeffrey Ramsdell. With their backs to the audience, Tony towered over Jeff Baird to his right. Gary shuffled into the courtroom that was packed with the media as well as other prosecutors and defense attorneys waiting to get along to the day's arraignment calendar, separated from the audience by a glass wall and armed security officers at a locked door.

Asked by Judge Ramsdell how he pled to the four murder charges, Tony answered for Gary.

"Mr. Ridgway pleads not guilty," Tony said.

Gary was asked if he understood what the charges were and if that was indeed his plea.

"Yes, your honor," Gary told the judge. He was appropriately polite.

Afterward court officials led a number of the friends and relatives out of the courtroom first, to enable them to avoid the pack of news media. But at least one lingered behind.

As we exited the courtroom, a woman who identified herself as the aunt of one of the victims accosted Tony.

"How can you represent that killer?" she demanded. "You should be ashamed of yourself." She was really very angry, and it was clear that she'd made up her mind that Gary had to be the murderer.

In his usual low-key way, Tony gently extricated himself from the encounter. But later, in the elevator, Tony turned to me.

"Where were you?" he demanded. "I expected some help there. You just left me there to be attacked!" His eyes were laughing.

"Yeah," I said. "I figured I'd let you take one for the team."

10

On the last day of the year, December 31, 2001, I had another face-to-face with Gary. By this point, after my previous face-to-faces with him, and after absorbing others' impressions of our client, I realized that far from being someone with Bundy-like intelligence, Gary was in fact someone with rather less-than-average intelligence—that is, if one measured intelligence with standardized IQ test scores. Gary had told me that he had been held back a couple of grades but did manage to graduate from high school. In early January 2002, we didn't know what those IQ test scores might be, but I did know that if they came in at or near 70, there was a chance we might be able to defend Gary on grounds of mental retardation. The origin of this apparent mental slowness wasn't clear, but by this time, Todd had pointed out that Gary had been breathing toxic paint fumes at his job for almost three decades. Was it possible that prolonged exposure to paint, possibly including lead, had played a role in Gary's apparent lack of mental acuity, or even the murders, if one assumed that Gary was in fact guilty? That was one reason we wanted the money for the experts: we needed to test Gary's intelligence and his neural system to see if a lifetime exposed to paint fumes might explain things.

Gary *was* dyslexic; he had always had a hard time reading, which could affect some IQ scores. But there was more to Gary's smarts or lack of them than just scores on whatever tests we intended to give him; there also seemed to be a piece missing, something vital that prevented him from following subtleties in conversation or abstract ideas. Gary, however, had long before learned to camouflage this slowness by adopting the earnest, brow-knitting, concentrating expression I'd seen so often before, presenting the face of someone listening and following things intently. This *mask,* as I came to think of it, was Gary's way of trying to fit in with those around him, to make them believe he was just as smart as they were. I would eventually learn that it was very important, almost vital to Gary's sense of himself, that he see himself in *average* terms. That was one reason it would later be so difficult for Gary to admit to some of his worst predilections when that time finally came, more than a year later.

I realized that in addition to the fact that Gary was adopting the overt expression of someone intently following another person's discourse, he had a second camouflaging habit: he tended to repeat the last few words of anyone who had been speaking to him, almost as if he were saying, "message received and understood," even if it wasn't. In this way, Gary's conversation partner assumed, sometimes incorrectly, that Gary really did understand what was being said to him—even when he didn't.

Although he'd had several visits from others on our team, including Michele, in the previous week, Gary seemed very glad to see me. I realized that far from being the loner that some popular caricatures have made of accused serial killers, Gary was an exceedingly sociable individual—talking was his way of seeming to be like everyone else.

"Good mood," I jotted down in my notes, when Gary was escorted into the face-to-face room. And in parentheses, "goofy, maybe." There was in fact a slight tinge of mania in his demeanor as he came in.

I filled Gary in on what Team Ridgway had been up to over the prior two weeks and again explained why we were going to go on two tracks simultaneously: trying to get him found not guilty at trial while at the same time preparing for the worst with the mitigation.

"Mitigation, uh-huh," Gary nodded.

"So, in order to do that, we're going to need to collect some of your records," I said. "Like, your school records, any medical records, stuff about your family, your time in the Navy, just about anything we can get our hands on that will help us in case we have to put on the mitigation. Like, if you've had any head injuries in the past."

"Head injuries," Gary said. "Yeah, once I got knocked out. There was this lady I saw down by the Safeway, the one on 216th [Street]?"

"On the highway, you mean?" This was a supermarket not far from Gary's old house and quite near where a number of victims had last been seen so many years earlier.

"The highway, yeah. Anyway, I think it was maybe in September, could've been 1983. So this lady, she wanted to get away from her pimp. And I was helping her, but the pimp hit me from behind, and the next thing I knew, like I woke up in this ditch, and someone had poured battery acid on my arm. See?"

Gary showed me a large scar on his right arm.

I hardly knew what to make of this story. On the surface, it sounded implausible: Gary rescues a prostitute, is attacked by her pimp, gets knocked out, winds up in a ditch, battery acid poured over his arm? That sort of thing didn't happen to most people, that was for sure. And it seemed to flit from event to event, from the Safeway to the battery acid, almost but not quite a series of non sequiturs.

"Did you report this to the police?" I asked.

"No," he said, explaining, "I didn't want the pimps mad at me." In other words, if he went to the police, he'd have some mad pimps coming after him.

I also recognized another one of Gary's traits, one that I'd first noticed on the evening of his arrest on November 30, which was Gary's tendency in extended statements to wander far off the point, to jump around, and to mash together different events and times. I made a note to myself, again in parentheses: "Sometimes his ramblings get disjointed, weird . . . the jail?" By this, I meant that the jail environment hadn't seemed to have affected Gary as it usually did others. Most inmates were usually subdued, emotionally down. But rather than being depressed, taciturn, Gary seemed slightly hyper, and I wondered if being the center of all the attention in the jail was perhaps responsible for the disjointed nature of his ramblings.

I asked Gary about his fellow jail inmates on his tier, his "neighborhood," as we called it: who the neighbors were, what they were in for, what they'd said to him. Gary gave me a brief rundown on his near neighbors in the "ultra" section of the jail.

"Rafael is in Lower A, 1 house. I'm in Lower A, 2 house." Gary was referring to his "neighbor" on 11, Atif Rafay, in custody awaiting trial for the murder of his parents and sister. Gary never could get Rafay's name straight—he always called him Rafael.

"Rafael says the guy in Lower A, 3 is a snitch," Gary told me.

"You've got to keep your mouth shut, especially with your neighbors," I reminded him. "Some of them will lie about you if they thought there was something in it for 'em."

"Lie, yeah," Gary said. He nodded, but I had the impression he wasn't really hearing me.

"Well, Gary, it's important," I told him.

"Oooh-K," he said. He grinned at me, agreeably, and once again I was struck by how polite, friendly, and un-murderous he seemed. There was a seemingly irresolvable contradiction: the police had damning evidence against someone who just didn't seem capable of murdering anyone.

Later, back at my office, I had a message from a lawyer who represented another inmate housed on Gary's floor.

"What's up?" I asked, when I returned his call.

"Sorry," my attorney-informant told me. "The word on the eleventh floor is that Gary has been talking a blue streak. He's very glib, talks all the time. He's even been giving autographs to the other inmates."

Great! I thought. *That's just what we need.* Under those circumstances, it would only be a matter of time before one of Gary's neighbors called the prosecutor and offered Gary's signed "confession" in return for a lesser sentence. I immediately called Todd and filled him in. Todd cursed, and in his role as our chief enforcer, he agreed to go see Gary that same afternoon to put the fear of Todd back in him.

———

By the first week of January 2002, our team had agreed to hire a nationally known specialist in mitigation investigation, Mary Goody of Wyoming. Criminal investigation concentrates on the facts of a crime or crimes. Mitigation investigation is different. The mitigation investigator's job is to *assume* that the client is guilty and to look for possible reasons for the *assumed* criminal behavior. Anything that had to do with the client's birth, childhood, education, health, marriages, children— all of it was grist for the mitigation mill. Mary Goody was one of the best in the business; she would eventually earn every penny of the nearly $90,000 Team Ridgway would pay her and her associates for their work on Gary's case over the next year and a half.

Although conducting a capital defense—that is, a defense in which the accused faced the prospect of execution, should he be found guilty—*required* us to do this exercise in mitigation, it was still difficult to explain to Gary's family. Greg, Dorene, Judith, and Matthew all believed Gary was *not* guilty. He was their brother, husband, father. Who could believe such a thing? So why were we preparing—asking about past negative impacts on Gary—as if we expected him to be *found* guilty? To Greg and Dorene, at least, that smacked of having no confidence in Gary, of cynical disbelief in his innocence. To them, at a basic emotional level, it was defeatism.

So this was tricky: how to get Greg, Dorene, Judith, and Matthew to cooperate with Mary Goody, who had to operate from the assumption that Gary *was* guilty if any benefit of a mitigation package was to be realized. And it was over this ticklish situation that Team Ridgway encountered our first pothole.

In the initial process of getting ourselves organized, Michele Shaw had wound up with the non-expert, or lay, witnesses portion of the mitigation responsibility. I wanted to have charge of the experts who might testify, such as Mary Goody, or any other professionals, such as psychologists and psychiatrists. But we'd need more than that. We'd need witnesses capable of testifying as to Gary's character and family background. Greg, Dorene, and Judith had hired Tony to represent Gary, and Michele had come to us through Tony. So Michele took primary responsibility for our contacts with the Ridgway family, and over time, she built the trust and rapport with Gary's family that would be essential if we ever got to a penalty phase. As the next two years unfolded, Michele did an excellent job of keeping Gary's loved ones informed about the legal proceedings and our various maneuvers. In addition, she was a very good listener when they voiced their concerns, always vital in such a traumatic situation.

But not long after she arrived in Seattle to work on Gary's case, Mary Goody realized that any contacts she would have with Greg, Dorene, Judith, and Matthew would be arranged through Michele. Mary was not happy with this setup: by necessity, the mitigation specialist usually winds up knowing more about the client and his family than any other member of the defense team and—as a requirement—needs to have unfettered access to the family.

But there Michele stood as the gatekeeper and one who apparently kept agreeing with Gary's brothers and sisters-in-law when they voiced their belief that Gary had *not* committed the crimes and assuring them that his lawyers were working hard to get him acquitted. So there was natural resistance on the part of Gary's immediate family to providing the critical mitigating information, which is usually negative by nature. If you believe that your brother is innocent, that this whole nightmare is some sort of awful mistake, who would you prefer to talk to? The lawyer who assures you that innocence will prevail or the mitigation specialist who has to assume that your loved one did the dirty deed, and who needs to know your darkest family secrets to possibly help him avoid the death penalty?

It's one of the dilemmas of capital litigation: Is the focus of the defense a not guilty verdict or avoiding the death penalty? Putting all the chips into Not Guilty, as in "somebody else did it," and trying to maintain that position during the penalty phase has been a fatal strategy in many death penalty cases, especially where the defense is precluded from arguing for residual doubt. *Residual doubt,* or *lingering doubt,* is that gap between *beyond a reasonable doubt*——enough to convict— and *absolute certainty*—which defense attorneys argue and most jurors find is necessary to impose death.

Mary Goody came to town on January 9, 2002, and conducted her first interview with Gary late that same day. Michele sat in on part of this, although Mary would have much preferred to go one-on-one with Gary. She was concerned that Michele's presence as a lawyer who had told Gary that we were working to have him found innocent might make him reluctant to reveal any of his secrets, which was what Mary really needed to get. Michele didn't seem to understand this, and the seeds were there and then sown for what would turn out to be an ongoing, if subtle, conflict for most of the next year.

From the start, Mary and I knew we had to hire a neuropsychologist as an expert, someone who could see if our client suffered from brain damage. Michele never quite understood this recommendation, it seemed. It was clear that Michele had adopted the position that Gary was innocent of the crimes, so why should we look for evidence of brain damage?

"Could you tell me again," Michele asked, "if Gary didn't do this, why are we getting a neuropsych done now?"

"It's for the mitigation," I explained. "If we can find some organic brain damage, we could use it at the penalty phase, if necessary. Not as any mental defense. Just for mitigation."

"I see," Michele said, nodding her head, but I could see that she still seemed troubled by the notion of having to assume guilt to prepare for the worst. Most of us who had spent years as public defenders thought this was rather naïve on her part—at least, we thought, it showed an unfamiliarity with requirements for a death penalty defense.

For her part, Mary Goody explained to Gary that she wasn't there to hear him explain how he was innocent, that evidence that showed he couldn't have been the killer wasn't her part of the program. Gary, in his usual fashion, nodded with feigned wisdom, even if he really didn't understand the distinction. But Mary was adept at drawing people out—that was her business, after all—and Gary loved to talk, particularly to women.

Two days later, Mary provided me with her first written report, this one primarily focused on Gary's family history, or at least the version of history that Gary could recall.

According to Mary's report, Gary told her that he'd been born in Salt Lake City, Utah, on February 18, 1949. His mother had been Mary Rita Steinman Ridgway, born January 22, 1928, and his father, Thomas Newton Ridgway, born April 9, 1923. Gary was vague on where each had been born, although he was pretty sure that his father had grown up in New Mexico and his mother had grown up in Kitsap County, across Puget Sound from Seattle. Both his mother and father were dead, with Mary Ridgway having died only the month before Gary had been arrested, or so Gary thought.

"Really has to think of this," Mary noted parenthetically in her report, meaning that Gary wasn't sure when his mother had actually died. "Thinks it was October—really doesn't know."[1] His mother had died at the Ridgway family home just east of the airport, with the whole family around her, Gary told her.

"It was terrible for everybody, really," Gary told Mary. "I think she might have just gave up." Gary said that he and his brothers had gotten all of her financial affairs in order just before she died.

"She wanted to make sure that everything was taken care of and that we kept the family together," Gary added. "She was worried that we'd move out of state and not talk to each other. It wasn't that we didn't get along. We all have separate lives, do different things. We'd get together during the holidays. I saw her every day. I'd stop by home every day after work."

It was clear to Mary that Gary had been quite attached to his mother. She wanted to find out more about Mary Rita Steinman Ridgway, particularly in light of the statements that had been made about Gary's mother in the now-infamous search warrant affidavit. She noted that Gary had a well-thumbed copy of that document, the one that had been repudiated by Greg Ridgway as a product of Marcia's sour grapes a month earlier.

Gary said he wasn't sure how to spell his mother's maiden name, but believed that his mother might have been born in Bremerton, in Kitsap County, where there was a large U.S. Navy base. His mother had finished high school, Gary thought, but had not gone to college. Mary Rita's parents were Ed and Clara Steinman, Gary told Mary; he remembered them very clearly. His grandfather Ed had owned a hardware store in Bremerton; Gary thought he had once served in the Navy himself.

"They lived below and we lived above the store for about a year," Gary told Mary Goody. "I think it was in like, 1959 or 1960. We were just there for a year, until we got a place in Seattle. My parents—my dad had a job with Greyhound first—he took the ferry over [to Seattle] every day for work. I was in the third grade then. Then in 1960, we went to Seattle. I went to elementary school there."

Mary asked Gary if he had helped his grandfather out in running the store. Gary said his grandfather wouldn't let him. "He was pretty strict about that," Gary said.

"He was a hard man?" Mary asked.

"Pretty hard," Gary said. "That's what I got from my mom when she talked about him. He kind of favored my brother [Greg] over me. He cared more for his store, though."

Gary recalled his grandmother Clara, his mother's mother, fondly. She was very nice and liked to cook, he remembered. "Even years later," he said, "she always had a cake for us or something like that. She was kind of under the control of her husband; he was really strict."

Gary knew less about his father, Thomas Newton Ridgway. He wasn't sure when he died. Mary watched as Gary looked this information up in his copy of the search warrant affidavit. The affidavit recorded this as having occurred in 1998. She thought it remarkable that he had to rely on the Sheriff's Department's affidavit for his own family history, particularly something as significant as the death of his father. Gary explained that he wasn't very good with dates. He did recall that his father had lived for a time as a young man in Roswell, New Mexico, and that he had several brothers and a sister, some of them still in Roswell. Both his father and his brothers at one time had lived in Utah, but none of them were Mormon, Gary said.

Gary recalled attending Catholic elementary school, so Mary Goody tentatively noted that Gary's family might have originally been Roman Catholic, although Gary said he had most recently attended a Pentecostal church.

Mary asked Gary about his school experiences.

"I was held back a grade," he told her. "I think, because of my age or because I wasn't learning good enough." He couldn't remember when this happened, but he remembered that there had been family talk about putting him in a special education class when he was in the fourth grade.

Gary told her that he'd graduated from high school in June 1969. Mary realized that if that were true, Gary was twenty years old at graduation—two years older than his contemporaries.

"What did you find hardest about school?" Mary asked.

"Just getting up in front of the classroom, giving speeches, speaking in front of other people," Gary said. "Probably homework. I didn't like it. I'm not the best on reading."

Gary said he liked sports, but because he was older, he usually wound up having to play with students in grades ahead of his. "That was just too hard for me," he said. "I quit. Worked a lot of the time. So . . . I was in shop and I really liked it, and I did a good job there."

Mary asked about Gary's medical history. He'd had asthma as a child, Gary told her, and suffered from allergies most of his life. His eyes were often swollen, and they frequently watered, which had made other kids tease him about crying all the time. Sometimes he got injections for these allergies.

Mary asked Gary if he'd ever had any psychological counseling, and Gary said he hadn't. Then he told Mary that he'd wanted his second marriage, to Marcia, "to work out" and that he'd suggested marriage counseling, but Marcia wasn't interested.

That was pretty much it for Mary Goody's first cut through Gary's history, on her search for mitigation. She would return in the following weeks to conduct additional interviews of Gary, each time probing a little deeper. But it would take Mary until the spring of 2003, more than a year, to fully develop a working theory of what made Gary tick and—possibly—what had gone so terribly wrong. Digging this hidden history up would turn out to be very arduous work.

11

While Mary Goody was getting acquainted with Gary and his family background, my own family was absorbed in the competition of the high school boys' swimming season. In a historic triumph, on January 8, 2002, my swimmers broke the 90-meet winning streak of our arch rival school, Kentridge High, also winning the league championship for the first time in our own school's history. This was, for us, like beating a UCLA basketball team back in the era of John Wooden.

My son, Sean, won the 200-yard freestyle and the 100-yard breaststroke. When we got home that night, I gave him a big hug.

"Sean," I told him, "you did it! We *all* did it." All the work the whole team had put in during the fall and winter had paid off, and I was gratified to realize I'd been able to handle the pressure of organizing the defense of the monster murder case without it affecting my coaching, despite my initial fears. It only went to demonstrate that in the water as well as in the law, there's no substitute for hard work. Preparation was always the key to success, and that held particularly true, not only in sports competition but also when it came to defending a criminal case.

In mid-January, Todd and I thought we should sit down and talk with Greg and Dorene so they would have a better idea of who, besides Tony and Michele, was representing Gary. Preparation, preparation. Michele made arrangements for Greg and Dorene to come to ACA to talk with Todd and me before our team meeting on Friday January 18. We met them in the ACA lobby and exchanged greetings and introductions. I had met Greg once before, briefly outside the jail, and had talked to both him and Dorene on the phone, but this would be our first opportunity to sit down and talk. We took the elevator up to the ACA library.

We sat at the conference table amid the bookshelves, cluttered with a variety of notebooks, case law reports, law books, and reference manuals. Greg looked quite a bit like Gary, except his face was fuller and he wore his dark hair down over his forehead. He was in good shape for being in his mid-fifties. Like Gary, Greg had a mustache and wore glasses. Greg looked like what you might expect a computer engineer to look like, but without the pocket protector. He wasn't nerdy at all, but he did appear very serious and straightforward, someone who would tell you exactly what he thought without a lot of beating around the bush.

Greg's wife, Dorene, was a paralegal, but she looked and sounded more like an elementary school teacher. She had short brown hair and spoke with a sweet, but not timid, voice. She was quick to smile and agree, but had no trouble speaking her mind if she disagreed.

"It's just ridiculous they're trying to blame Gary for all this," Dorene said, after we all sat down. "He'd never hurt anyone. He's the nicest guy you could imagine. He's always doing things for other people." It was clear that Dorene loved her brother-in-law. "They've obviously got the wrong guy.

"This just isn't Gary," she continued. "He's not some murdering monster. I know he's not perfect, but I also know he couldn't kill anyone."

I wondered if the "not perfect" comment related to Gary's predilection for prostitutes, but I wasn't going to ask at this point. I simply nodded.

The conversation meandered around and about: some talk about family history, some talk about present-day events and happenings. We discussed the defense team and how we intended to handle the defense.

"In a death penalty case," I explained, "someone on the team has to prepare for the penalty phase. That is, someone has to be ready for the sentencing arguments, should the jury find him guilty. Do you understand?"

"Sure. That makes sense," Greg said. "You have to prepare for the worst."

"That's exactly right," Todd agreed. "Prepare for the worst and hope you never get there."

"Well, we sure hope we never get there," Dorene said.

"I understand. We all hope that. But, having said that," I continued to explain, "that means I will be working, preparing for the penalty phase, as if Gary is guilty as charged."

I sensed some confusion. The look on Dorene's face said, *You're our brother's lawyer and you think he's guilty?*

"Like you said," I continued, nodding at Greg, "prepare for the worst and hope for the best. Well, the 'worst' would be Gary being found guilty. Then, how do we save him from the death penalty? That's something we have to be prepared to deal with, even though we hope we never get there."

Dorene still looked a little confused at the concept, but Greg nodded. His look told me he understood why we had to do it that way. However, it also told me he didn't like anyone "assuming" his brother was guilty, even if it was the prudent thing to do under the circumstances.

As our defense team started to arrive, we moved into the third-floor conference room. Greg and Dorene joined us for a few minutes and were introduced to everyone. However, recognizing their presence would inhibit the team's ability to talk freely about the case, they graciously excused themselves, allowing us to get down to the business of defending Gary.

—⁓—

The following week, Mary Goody sat down with Greg and Dorene. It was at once clear to her that Greg and Dorene were Gary's staunchest defenders. Greg was still upset at the news media reports on the search warrant affidavit, the one that had Marcia disparaging his mother, Mary Rita.

"They've been cruel and vicious," Greg told Mary Goody, meaning the news media. "Marcia said my mother looked like a prostitute. But she didn't, ever. She never went anywhere without being presentable. It's ridiculous."

His mother, Greg added, was one of the first of the working mothers—and this at a time in the 1950s when the norm was for mothers to stay home with their children. She got a job with JCPenney and worked in the men's clothing department for thirty years, eventually retiring as one of her store's icons of service. The local newspaper had even marked her retirement with a feature story.

"She was just a very strong woman," Greg said, meaning that Mary Rita was someone who knew her own mind and was very confident.

Greg told Mary that his mother had actually been born in North Dakota, not in Kitsap County, as Gary had thought. Her father— Greg's grandfather, Ed Steinman—had been born in Chicago. But Ed Steinman was capable of obscuring his past when it suited his purpose. "He led every one of us to believe he was the tough, rock-hard German who escaped right before Hitler," Greg said. "It wasn't true, though. My dad (Thomas Newton Ridgway, Gary's father) and I were the only ones he took under his wing. My dad was like his son. We lived over there (in Bremerton) above the hardware store for a while. Grandpa was very gruff. I think no one made me cry as much as he did. But through it all, I learned that's how you run a hardware store."

Mary Goody asked Greg about his own father, Thomas Newton Ridgway. "He always had a big smile on his face and always had a big joke coming out of his mouth," Greg said. "He was very, very hard working. He proved himself to my grandpa. He earned his respect."

Greg said that his father had been born in Kentucky but that he'd had to go live with his grandparents in New Mexico, because his own parents were too poor to raise him. Tom Ridgway had grown up on a farm near Roswell. During World War Two, Greg said, his father had been an aircraft mechanic in the Army Air Corps. He'd been married to another woman before meeting Mary Rita and had a son by that marriage, whom Greg had met briefly only once.

Mary Rita had met Tom at a USO dance, Greg thought, and they were married in early 1947. He himself had been born that same year, in October. After they'd married, Greg added, his mother and father moved to Preston, Idaho, where Tom Ridgway had driven long-haul trucks and worked on construction jobs during the summer. Gary was born in February 1949, and a third son, Thomas Edward Ridgway, known as Ed, or sometimes Eddie, was born in 1951.

Although Mary Rita was raised as a Catholic, Tom Ridgway was not. Greg told Mary Goody that the religious issue had caused problems with Mary Rita's family, particularly Ed Steinman. Mary Rita wanted her children to be raised as Catholics and convinced her husband to convert to Catholicism. "The priest came to him just after he'd gone through all the classes," Greg told Mary Goody, "and said, 'that's fine that you did this, but you can't get into the church.'" His father's previous marriage prevented him from becoming a Catholic, Greg said.

"Dad felt ostracized," he said.

Dorene agreed. "I think it caused havoc in the family until the day she died," she told Mary Goody.

Still, Mary Rita insisted that Greg, Gary, and Eddie be raised as Catholics and that they faithfully go to church. "She'd drag us kicking and screaming," Greg recalled. "All the way up until 1964 or 1965, until grandpa (Steinman) died. She kind of finally gave up and then we were saying we wouldn't go anymore." But Greg wanted Mary Goody to know that his mother, Mary Rita Ridgway, was an excellent parent and someone very concerned that her sons do the right thing.

"Even when I was dating in high school," Greg said, "she sat up, concerned about the time we came home. She made us responsible for what we did. One expression she had, sort of a key to my life, 'Don't ever date anybody you wouldn't want to marry.'"

—◇◇◇—

One thing was very clear to Mary Goody from her interview with Greg, and that was that Greg was brighter, far brighter, than his younger brother. Whereas Greg had graduated from the University of Washington with a degree in physics, Gary barely made it through high school, and even at that, he was two years older than most other members of his graduating class. Greg worked as a computer software engineer; Gary sometimes had trouble painting trucks. At one point, in fact, Gary had painted a design on a truck backward, and the Kenworth Truck Company had to spend $14,000 to fix the mistake. After this, Gary had become known around the truck plant as "Wrong-way Ridgway." Gary told this story on himself with a laugh, but Mary Goody could see that it hurt.

As Greg sketched in the early Ridgway family history, Mary Goody came to understand that while all three Ridgway boys were growing up in the 1950s, the family had been beset by extreme poverty. The family had rarely lived in separate accommodations but usually rented rooms from other families.

"Dad's income was not fixed," Greg told Mary. "It was easier for them to go and live with other people. Mom used to talk about when they first got married, all they had was a can of soup to split. Lots of times when we were growing up, we had the rice and beans diet." The family had never been on welfare, Greg said. "Dad believed in earning a living. He didn't mooch on other people and he always paid back his debts."

At one point while living in Idaho, Tom and Mary Rita had run a restaurant and bar. "Dad got tired of guys hitting on my mom," Greg said. "People wouldn't leave the bar. They liked it, but there were too many temptations. Got to be too much of a regular crowd." According to Greg, neither of the Ridgway parents smoked or drank. After getting out of the bar and restaurant business, Tom Ridgway had gone back to trucking and construction. "Dad was always gone," Greg recalled. "Always trying to do something to make ends meet."

The family found ways to cope with the acute shortage of money, Greg recalled. They often grew their own food, and both parents learned how to stretch a dollar, sometimes by scavenging spare parts from junkyards and other disposal sites. One of the worst sins a Ridgway could commit was to throw something away before it was completely used up. Tom Ridgway was notoriously frugal, as was Gary himself. Both of them hated to waste money.

In the later 1950s, when the family had been living in Utah, Tom had been on the road as a trucker when little Eddie had contracted a high fever. The fever had resulted in some brain damage for Eddie, according to Greg, and as a result, he was somewhat mentally retarded.

By 1959, the family had relocated from Idaho to Bremerton, where they lived for a time above the Steinman hardware store. Tom got a job driving tour buses for Grayline and, after that, driving buses for the Seattle-area transit agency, Metro. Mary Rita also found a job with JCPenney. From that point forward, things had begun to improve economically for the Ridgways. The following year, the family bought their own house for the first time, a small rambler with a large lot just east of the airport. It was there that all three Ridgway boys had spent their teen years, and it was where Tom and Mary Rita lived until they died.

Mary realized that Greg wanted to portray a somewhat idealized, "normal" view of his family. That was understandable: Greg loved his younger brother and couldn't bring himself to believe that Gary had murdered anyone, let alone forty-nine people. So even though it was Mary's job to dig for reasons for Gary's potentially murderous behavior, Greg almost involuntarily denied that any such reasons could ever have existed.

It *was* true, Greg told Mary, that Gary had difficulty in school. He thought that Gary had been kept back a grade so that there would be a year between the two brothers in school. Gary had trouble reading almost from the start. He had a tendency to reverse letters and had been assessed as *slow* by his teachers. This wasn't talked about much in the family, Greg recalled. Whereas he received praise for being smart, no one ever really discussed Gary and Ed's learning difficulties. Greg thought that his parents had treated all the brothers equally, not giving special treatment to Greg. This, of course, wasn't Gary's perception. He had always felt that Greg was the fair-haired son because of his academic success, and he and Ed were downrated for not being as smart.

In behavior, Greg told Mary, all three brothers were completely normal. "We would do the normal kid things . . . for fun we did everything [that kids usually do]. . . . We played in the slag pile from a [nearby] copper mine [in Idaho]. We played there and got ourselves messed up. Anything that three young boys can do. Jumping into piles of leaves, made scooters, built forts, made our own fun." When they got older, all played pickup sports—football and baseball, particularly.

Tom Ridgway never beat them, Greg told Mary, although he would sometimes get out his belt and act like he might, if they were misbehaving. Usually, Greg said, all their father had to do was look at them to get them to straighten up.

In junior high school, Greg said, Gary wasn't exactly a loner, but he was quiet. "He didn't necessarily talk a lot. He had trouble reading when he was younger. I don't think he felt he could keep up with the other kids." But Gary's social skills improved in high school, he added. Gary was certainly more successful with girls in high school than he was, Greg said. Gary was much better at conversation with the opposite sex.

All three brothers entered military service about the same time, Greg said. Greg went into the Army and was sent to Korea, while Gary joined the Navy. Greg said Gary had told him that he'd served aboard an aircraft carrier and, for a time, on river patrol boats "being shot at by guys hiding behind trees . . . the only thing they didn't do was paint a target on their back." (Neither of these stories was true, as we soon discovered; Gary spent his service years aboard a supply ship that shuttled between the Philippines and Vietnam and was never shot at while serving aboard a river patrol boat.)

Eddie had joined the Army and worked in a motor pool in Vietnam, Greg said. He was only seventeen years old. There had been a noncommissioned officer who had ridden Eddie unmercifully, according to Greg. "He rode him and rode him and Ed broke," Greg said. "He [Eddie] rigged an incendiary grenade in a jeep with a trip wire to the driver-side door. The guy [the non-com] hit the dirt, the truck blew up . . ." It appeared that no one was seriously hurt, though, because Eddie, after a summary court martial, was sent to military prison at Fort Leavenworth for only two years, according to Greg.

Mary asked Greg for his take on Gary's marriages. The first marriage, to Claudia, took place in 1969, just about the time that Gary had joined the Navy, Greg told her. "He was high school sweethearts with Claudia. They were in love and had a good time." Then they'd moved to San Diego, where Gary was assigned to a ship. While Gary was at sea, Greg indicated, Claudia began a relationship with another man.

"There was unfaithfulness," Greg said, "and that was the end of that one. Gary was the recipient of a Dear John [letter]."

After the marriage to Claudia ended, Gary met Marcia, in the early 1970s, Greg said. It was evident to Mary that Greg was still sore at Marcia for the things that she had said in the search warrant affidavit. Unlike Claudia, who was thin and attractive, Marcia was overweight, Greg told Mary. Marcia loved to cook, and Gary enjoyed her artistry in the kitchen. After the supposed unfaithfulness of Claudia, Greg thought, Gary had naturally selected a heavier woman, reasoning that she would be less likely to stray.

Gary and Marcia's son, Matthew, had been born in the mid-1970s, Greg continued. Then, Marcia decided to "have her stomach stapled—not only did she lose the weight but she lost her personality," Greg said.

Until that happened, Greg said, he'd thought Marcia and Gary were getting along well. "They were going to church and seemed to be a really together family. Marcia changed—mostly because of the operation." Greg said that as she began to shed the weight, "Marcia was beginning to be noticed by other men." Marcia started hanging out at a nearby Elks Club and began performing as a country blues singer. While Marcia was being chased by other men at the Elks Club, Greg said, Gary stayed home to take care of Matthew.

The marriage began to deteriorate, Greg said, and in early 1981, the two divorced.

"Having Marcia divorce him was the last thing that Gary wanted," Greg told Mary. "He wanted to be a father. She used Matthew as a lever against Gary. She'd make him pay child support and then not let him see the kid. Gary paid a lot—$350 a month." Gary became very frustrated with Marcia, Greg said.

After the divorce, Gary began hanging around with people from Parents Without Partners, Greg told Mary. From 1981 to 1985—the time when most of the murders were taking place, as Mary Goody knew—Gary had a relationship with Roxanne Theno, another member of Parents Without Partners. That relationship ended in 1985, when Gary began seeing Judith, who was another Parents Without Partners member. Judith had been married to another man for eighteen years and had two daughters from that marriage, who were by now grown up.

"He courted her for a while," Greg said. "They didn't get married until 1987 or 1988." Since then, Greg added, Gary and Judith had been inseparable, involved in a stable, loving relationship.

So there it was: outside of Gary's dyslexia and his difficulty with school, there seemed to be little that was abnormal about the Ridgway family, certainly almost nothing in the way of mitigation. Gingerly, Mary inquired of Greg as to Gary's potential penchant for fabrication.

That wasn't even a possibility, Greg told Mary. He, Gary, and Ed did not lie, Greg said. That was the way they had been brought up.

The following day, Mary returned to the jail for another session with Gary. By that time, Dorene Ridgway had collected a series of family snapshots of Gary. Dorene had noted that one of the early descriptions of a possible Green River suspect had noted that the unknown man might have had a tattoo on his right arm. The photographs of Gary, Dorene advised Michele Shaw, showed that Gary had never had such a tattoo. She thought this would be useful evidence that Gary could not be the killer.

The snapshots were pretty much what one might expect to find in any family photo album. Taken together, showing as they did a smiling Gary with other similarly smiling family members at holiday get-togethers, only added to the sense of unreality about the whole situation. How could this normal-seeming, happy fellow surrounded by beaming children even be suspected of committing the worst serial murders in American history? It was just hard to believe.

For this session with Gary, Mary Goody wanted to get Gary's own take on his marriages. Hearing Greg's version was useful, but getting the events described in Gary's own words would be far more valuable.

Gary said he'd met Claudia during his sophomore year in high school, when he and Claudia had both worked at a supermarket in Burien, just west of the airport. Claudia's father was a career military man.

"Claudia and I dated all the way up until 1969," Gary told Mary. "I'd pick her up on the weekends and we'd go somewhere on Saturday and Sunday." Sometimes they'd go to a movie at one of the military bases in Seattle. It only cost a dollar, Gary said.

"Or we'd go park," Gary said. "We did that a couple of times and got caught." He and Claudia had had sex in Gary's car before they were married, mostly because they had no other place to go.

Listening to Gary describe his first love was interesting to Mary. She realized that he had idealized Claudia—that they'd shared an innocence together for the years before their marriage. She sensed that it was the loss of that sense of mutual discovery or coming of age—and the concomitant special commitment that came with it—that Gary grieved for the most.

Gary had joined the Navy in June 1969, just after he'd begun working at Kenworth, but didn't have to go into the service until August of that year. He signed up for a two-year enlistment, with an additional commitment to four years in the Naval Reserve. Gary thought it was a better deal than being drafted into the Army. Because Greg and Ed, who'd also just joined the Army, were about to be sent overseas, the Navy had released him early from his boot camp training so he could see his brothers before their separation. During his ten-day leave in Seattle, Gary had seen a lot of Claudia. When he returned to the Navy, in San Diego, he and Claudia had written back and forth. "She was the first love I ever had," Gary told Mary. "I really loved her very much from 1965 to 1971."

In the Navy, Gary said, he'd been assigned as a deckhand on the USS Vancouver, a ship designed to carry and land Marines by landing craft or helicopters. The ship had a long rear flight deck. In addition to carrying about five hundred sailors, it also ferried about a thousand U.S. Marines. According to Gary, the USS Vancouver was based at Subic Bay in the Philippines for a significant portion of his enlistment in the Navy. While in port, the crew and its Marines usually had eight hours of duty and were then released for shore liberty.

"We mostly had our evenings free," Gary said. "You'd get your work done and you'd leave at five, and then you had to be back before five in the morning." Many crew members and the associated Marines stayed out all night, congregating in bars near the base.

"There was a lot of drinking," Gary told Mary. There were also a lot of women hanging around the bars.

"Prostitutes," Mary said.

"Prostitutes," Gary agreed.

"Did you go with them?"

"Yeah."

"How often?"

"Probably about ten times," Gary said. "The women would be at the bars. They'd have all different kinds of music. You could just pick them up. . . . You had to pay them, but not much. They would fight over you—they were small women, and they had tempers."

"Did you try any drugs?"

"I stayed away from that stuff," Gary said. "I tried marijuana once but it didn't do anything for me." Gary said he stuck with alcohol for the most part—"it was so cheap."

After time at Subic Bay, the ship sailed to Vietnam. Gary said he couldn't remember what the ship did there, although he remembered they were there for about a week. Later the ship stopped in Okinawa and then returned to San Diego. Gary was granted leave and he'd returned to Seattle. That was when he and Claudia had gotten married, he told Mary. He recalled that Claudia's parents were against the marriage.

After the ceremony—Gary wore his uniform—he and Claudia had driven to San Diego. They'd found a small apartment not far from the base, and Gary was able to spend most nights at home with his bride.

"I liked married life," Gary told Mary. "Somebody to come home to and security—somebody to talk to. Security—someone my age—to talk to. Lots of times, you can't just talk to a guy. Regular sex."

"What kind of sex?" Mary probed.

"Regular. Just me on the top, her on the bottom. At first, just once a day. I tried to get as much time as I could at home. . . . It was great."

Eventually, however, Gary had to go back to sea, which left Claudia on her own while he was gone. "She was always there for me the first two times," he said. "But after the third time, she had to move to another apartment because she couldn't afford it. She moved in with another lady."

"Did that bother you?"

"No, not really. I was maybe a little bit surprised, because she had a job and the service was sending my money back to her. Being gone and being in Vietnam was kind of scary at times."

"How?" Mary was thinking that if Greg's version of his Vietnam experience was correct—Gary on the river patrol boat, being shot at "by guys hiding behind trees"—it might account for post-traumatic stress syndrome, which would be potential mitigation. She wanted to hear Gary describe his Vietnam experience in his own words.

"One time, we went there and went into a bay," Gary said.

"In one of the patrol boats?"

"In the big ship," Gary corrected. "We were all on watch, and they had the Marines all along the sides, with machine guns, and guns mounted on turrets."

"What kind of guns?"

"We had three-inch or five-inch guns. There were rumors about some hospital ship that went down in that bay in, like, seven minutes. The VC [Viet Cong] had put bombs under the ship. I replaced a guy who'd had his neck broken by a rope." (Mary was learning that Gary's conversation sometimes drifted.)

"We got word when we were coming out there that a missile or something was coming out to sea, so we went on red alert."

"Were you ever on a patrol boat that went up a river?"

"Our ship went up part of the Da Nang River," Gary said, "but there was nobody shooting at us."

He'd been in the Navy for "twenty-three months and twenty-eight days," Gary said.

"Were you ever hurt? What's the worst thing that happened to you while you were in the service?"

"I got bit by a rat," Gary said.

"Did you have to go through rabies shots?"

"I can't remember. They couldn't find the rat. I had a tetanus shot, I think. I was treated twice for VD. Gonorrhea."

"Not syphilis?"

"No, not syphilis. In Subic Bay, they'd have a sheet with all the names of the bars, and they'd have names of the people and the women at the bars where there were problems."

When this sea tour ended, Gary returned to San Diego. There he discovered that Claudia's roommate had taken up with "a black guy." And Gary now discovered that Claudia had taken a boyfriend—"a friend of ours." Claudia didn't want to have sex with him anymore, Gary told Mary.

According to Mary's report, at this point in the interview, Gary began to cry.

Gary said that Claudia and the new boyfriend liked to drink together. He realized that in the past, they had told him they would go to the liquor store, which was right across the street, but be gone for an hour. Gary had become jealous, but Claudia had assured him there was nothing going on—until the return from the last voyage, when Claudia no longer wanted to sleep with him.

Mary realized that this experience—or at least Gary's perception of it—had left him humiliated, and with a gigantic reservoir of self-doubt.

Gary soon got out of the Navy, his hitch up, and returned to Seattle without Claudia. He returned to his old job at Kenworth, but he missed Claudia terribly.

"I was so bummed," he told Mary. He told Tom and Mary Rita that he and Claudia were having a trial separation, that Claudia would be coming back to Seattle once they'd worked things out. Gary hoped that once Claudia was back in Seattle, she'd be among old friends, and things would get back to normal. After a few weeks, Claudia came back to Seattle and spent a week with Gary. Again they did not have sex. Then Gary returned from work one day to find that Claudia had taken his car to the airport and had bought a ticket back to San Diego.

"Panic set in," Gary told Mary. "I thought about calling the airline to report a bomb threat." It was Gary's idea that if he could somehow prevent the plane from taking off, he could get Claudia back. But he did nothing, and Claudia flew out of his life.

Gary was deeply depressed at Claudia's action, which he took as a personal repudiation. "I felt like my life was going down the tubes," he told Mary. "I had my weekends free, but I had nothing to do. A friend of ours called me a week later and told me he'd seen Claudia with a black guy. . . . I was hurt. I would much rather have had her tell me that she was going with another guy. I still loved her and loved her for years afterward. I never got over it. I was stupid and called her a whore. Deep down inside, I knew she didn't like black guys. For years, if people asked me about her, I'd say she was a whore."

And with this, Mary began to get a faint glimmering into Gary's mind and his possible motivation—if in fact he was the killer. Not only had Claudia, the love of his life, dumped him, but she'd gone with a black man. Gary had called her a whore. Then, years later, real whores—many of them associated with pimps who were black men—began getting murdered. It wasn't difficult to conjecture that Gary might have been getting even with Claudia in a symbolic, if fatal, fashion: by depriving black men of their kept women, he was also punishing the black man who had once made him so unhappy.

12

Gary and Claudia were divorced in 1971, after a little more than a year of marriage. A year or so after that, Gary met Marcia. Marcia had been driving the Loop, a place where young people cruised, in Renton, a suburb south of Seattle, with a friend when Gary first saw her.[1]

"I pulled her over like a police stop," Gary told Mary. But Mary wasn't entirely sure: Was this something that Gary actually remembered, or had it been adopted as a memory from Marcia's description of the same incident in the now dog-eared search affidavit in Gary's possession? In other words, was Gary slowly succumbing to the authorities' description of him, a version of the Stockholm Syndrome (where captives come to identify with their captors and adopt the mind-set of their captors)?

And if so, did this mean that Gary might someday soon confess? Mary put this thought aside for the time being and listened as Gary described his marriage to his second wife.

Marcia was about sixty to eighty pounds overweight when Gary met her. Then, after Matthew was born, Marcia had the operation to shut off part of her intestine. The excess weight began to fall off. "She got down to about ninety-five pounds, and they had to hook her up again because she was losing too much weight," Gary said.

Up until the operation, Gary said, he was happy being married to Marcia. They moved several times, eventually settling in a house in Federal Way, halfway between Seattle and Tacoma.

"We just wanted a nicer home," Gary said. "And things were going good and the marriage was good. When we got to Federal Way, it seemed to be going good. I don't know when she had the operation." But after that, Gary said, he was assigned to work nights at the Kenworth plant, and Marcia began attending school during the day to train as a dental assistant. With their split schedules, they began to drift apart.

Marcia began going to the Eagles' Lodge, Gary said (not the Elks, as recalled by Greg). "She went to the Eagles, for some reason. She was out until 3 A.M. It was an active crowd she was with. She never told them she was married."

Once again, Gary felt repudiated.

"Marcia made the decision not to be married anymore," he told Mary. "One day, something was wrong. She said, 'Why don't you go out and have breakfast by yourself?' I thought it was kind of funny. There was woods in back of the house. I went around the block and walked back up through the woods. She had a van come out. She was moving out."

Marcia was leaving him and had apparently hoped to finish the job before Gary came back.

Marcia and Gary then entered into a cold war of sorts, with Matthew as the stakes.

"It was terrible for me," he told Mary. "Missed the boy. . . . She moved into an apartment in Kent. Several times, I'd go over there, and I didn't want to harass her. . . . I'd just go over and sit in the car a ways away. Didn't have the nerve to go and talk to her. Probably for a month, I'd go over, three hours a night. I didn't want to pressure her. . . . I wanted to be close to her. Kind of hard to explain to my parents. . . . It was hard to tell anybody."

Later, Gary said, he and Marcia attempted to reconcile. "Lasted about a month," he said. "She left. I sold the house. I wanted her back. I got $5,500 out of the house. I wrote her a check for this and sent it to her. Said this was for marriage counseling. A week later, it was never cashed."

So here it was again—Gary's almost palpable desire to have a "normal," almost made-for-TV, home life. And under that, a yearning to be mothered by a female, someone who would be loyal, never stray, and attend to his needs. Someone very much like Mary Rita Ridgway.

Mary Goody eased back into Gary's relationship with his mother.

"How did you get along with your mother?" she asked.

"Good," Gary said. "I think a woman is much more closer to her sons. I was close to her." As Tom and Mary Rita had aged, Gary said, he spent more time with his parents. After Tom had died, he tried to spend at least a little time every day with Mary Rita.

Mary Rita had been the primary caregiver in the family when he and his brothers were growing up, Gary recalled. He remembered Mary Rita's home remedies for childhood illnesses. "If we'd get an ear infection," he recalled, "she'd get a cigar and blow smoke in your ear. Or put a pair of old socks with Vicks around your neck if you got a cold. That was one of her favorites. I still use it today."

Before he'd married Claudia, Gary recalled, Mary Rita had tried to talk him out of it.

"Why?"

"I think maybe she thought Claudia was a little wild," Gary said.

——— ⟶ ———

Mary kept probing, and as the session went on, she sensed that Gary was beginning to trust her. She realized that underneath his painfully erected façade of normality, Gary had enormous contempt for himself.

"He was the quintessential chubby little kid with glasses and the runny nose when he was growing up," Mary told me a few days later, when we were discussing her impressions of our client. She said, "The kid that everyone always picks on, the one who's always the last to figure out what's going on. Until Judith, the only woman who ever loved him was his mom. He thought women were always trying to put one over on him, and sometimes, they were."

Mary also told me that, as the interview came to a close, Gary came very close to revealing something vital, something shrouded in darkness. Something had happened in the past, he told Mary, in 1969 in the Philippines. Something that he'd fantasized about for years afterward.

"I never got it out of my system," he told Mary. "I probably should have had counseling. . . . I said to Marcia that it probably would have helped me more than anyone else. The $5,500 would have been worth it."

What was this thing that happened in 1969, in the Philippines, the thing that he'd never "got out of my system"? Gary wasn't exactly clear.

Mary came to believe that whatever it was, it was critical to understanding Gary's predilection for prostitutes—and possibly much more. This hint would come up again and again over the next two years, as various psychologists attempted to pry this obsession out of Gary, but to no avail. It remains one of the last mysteries of the Green River murder case.

After this session, Mary was certain about one thing, though, and that was that Gary was clinically depressed and probably had been for years. There in jail, Gary was trying to hold himself together, to put on a brave front. But underneath he was weeping—and had been for decades—she thought. Finding the origin of the depression and coming to understand how Gary had developed psychic methods of coping with it, promised to shed considerable light on just why Gary was in jail, having been accused of being the worst serial killer in American history, Mary suggested.

Although we agreed with Mary on many points, Tony, Todd, Michele, and I compared notes, and none of us had seen any signs of serious depression in Gary. We had all dealt with clients with clinical, diagnosed depression, and we were on alert for that with Gary. Despite Mary's concerns, none of us felt he was clinically depressed.

Mary recommended to our team that Gary have a full-scale neurological workup; she was convinced that his dyslexia, his mental slowness, and his inability to concentrate, even to keep to the same subject in conversation, were the direct results of neurological deficiencies, some of them likely inherited from his parents, and others perhaps the result of the impoverished early childhood environment—the sort of place where a mother was reduced to treating her child's ear infection with cigar smoke because of the lack of money for doctors, for example. And Mary agreed with the concern raised by Todd, and later, Fred Leatherman: What might the cumulative effects be of breathing paint fumes for more than thirty years? Surely, there was likely to be some toxicity that might cause brain damage. That might stand up as mitigation.

Over time, Mary became worried about Gary's mood. Even though he affected a stiff upper lip about his situation, and indeed about his whole life, Mary said she believed that he was nearing some sort of breaking point. He wouldn't show this to men, she thought, but when conversing with women, Gary might allow himself to let much more of his emotion show. Mary suggested that we get the jail to give Gary some medication to ease his depression.

A few days later, Mary wrote us a brief memo and included the notes from her last discussion with Gary:

"Several things I call to your attention," she wrote. "One is, he is very interested in talking about his use of prostitutes, which began very early for him in the Philippines. It doesn't sound much from his explanation of his military service that he did much in Vietnam except hang out on a ship and deliver goods. But in the Philippines . . . the men had a lot of time ashore. He did not appear to change in any way in demeanor or appearance while discussing this. His use was huge—as you probably know . . ."

Gary had told her the story about the attack of the pimp and the battery acid burn. "Which is very weird," Mary remarked. "One can't help but believe there was perhaps a pimp who didn't like him—for whatever reason. Greg and Dorene really commented about how cheap he was, and Gary himself describes himself as a penny-pincher. He really hated to pay more for the sex than $20 and cheaper if he could get it. More pieces to the puzzle . . ."

Mary wanted to see any and all records about Gary's past—among them his school records, his military history, and his work records from Kenworth. She also wanted to review the prior employment records of Tom Ridgway and Mary Rita Steinman Ridgway; she had an idea that these would shed even more illumination on Gary's behavior, and in this she would be right.

—⁓—

I made it a practice to visit Gary after Mary's encounters with him, in part to see how he was reacting to her attempts to delve into his personality. In his interactions with me in the face-to-face room, Gary seemed bright, even upbeat. With me, he seemed to want to talk about the evidence the police had cited in their affidavits—in other words, the case. He found things that weren't true about the authorities' assertions and wanted me to know about them—as if these errors would prove that he wasn't the killer.

"How could anyone have sex on the riverbank?" Gary asked, apparently attempting to cast doubt on Marcia's recollection of sexual encounters in the outdoors with Gary. "It's impossible. The banks are too steep. You'd roll into the river!"

Or "How long could a DNA sample last? I read in an article it was something like twenty years. Well, it's been twenty years." Perhaps the DNA evidence was no good, he suggested.

On another occasion, Gary wanted to know how the police could tell a Green River victim from any other victim.

"How did a victim get on the list?" Gary wanted to know. "What was the profile of a Green River victim?" Maybe some girls shouldn't be on the list, he said. And maybe, there were some not on the list who should be.

All the while, I sensed he wanted to find out as much as he could about the case: the more details, the better. That seemed natural to me at the time. If someone had accused you of being a notorious serial murderer, wouldn't you want to know what the evidence was? He was entitled to know. But I kept having to tell Gary that the evidence, except for the DNA, wasn't my part of the case, so I didn't know enough details about the facts of each charged case to discuss them at that point. That didn't blunt Gary's interest, however; he peppered others who visited him for details about the murders and the police investigation.

Gary also had interest in what the rest of the world was saying about him. Although inmates in the "ultra" section of the jail did not have access to TV—most were allowed out of their cells for shower and exercise purposes on an extremely limited basis—old newspapers and magazines did filter through. So did stories from visitors who'd seen things on TV or heard things on the radio. The day before Mary's first face-to-face with Gary, for instance, Gary said he'd been told that a Seattle television station had aired a program about the Carol Christensen murder, along with speculation that the man who'd left the fish, wine, and sausage with her body might be a "religious fanatic."

"I'm not a religious fanatic," Gary told me, and I could tell he wasn't. He'd never once tried to proselytize me, for instance, or anyone else he met with, as far as I know.

Besides these snippets of information from the outside world, Gary had also begun attracting letters, most of them from perfect strangers who had read or heard about him. One man from Florida had even deposited $20 to Gary's commissary account—twice. Ever polite, Gary wanted to write these people back. We wanted to head this off if we could: our paranoia about Gary communicating with outsiders led some of us to worry that one of Gary's correspondents might turn out to be a spy for, say, the FBI. I told Gary that we lawyers would write these people back and advise them that in the future, all their correspondence should be directed to Gary's attorneys.

By this time, I'd spent enough time with Gary to understand that although he wasn't anywhere near the evil genius that the Green River

Killer was supposed to be, he wasn't *obviously* stupid. Although his writing skills and spelling skills were rudimentary—something I would have expected from an undiagnosed dyslexic—his tendency to feign understanding things, particularly abstract concepts, concealed whatever reasoning weaknesses he had, at least from the nonexperts. It was only when you paid attention to what he was saying and realized that he hopped around from topic to topic like a flea on an electric hot plate that you realized he suffered from some mental deficits. Was this the result of the paint fumes? Or something that had taken place earlier in his life, or perhaps even before birth, like fetal alcohol syndrome? A head injury? It wasn't clear.

His socialization skills, however, were excellent. He was proficient at making eye contact, he could tell and appreciate jokes, and he knew more about the inner workings of a motor vehicle than I ever did. If you sat down next to him at a tavern or a ball game, you'd never think of him as dumb. He was just like a genial neighbor. "Hot enough for ya?" he might ask, grinning, and you'd immediately assume that this was one friendly person. If you asked him to explain why the South lost the Civil War, though, he'd probably change the subject before you realized that he'd done it. But Gary's social skills were so smooth that you might not even notice this.

There were some experts who suggested that Gary's hippity-hoppity thinking might have stemmed from an earlier head injury. A New York psychiatrist, Dr. Dorothy Otnow-Lewis, had proposed some years earlier that many convicted murderers had suffered traumatic brain injury in the years before their crimes. Dr. Lewis had consulted with the Robert Yates defense team and seemed eager to work on Gary's case, too. That was one reason we'd asked Gary about head injuries. But outside of the pimp-who-hit-me-from-behind story and Gary's recollection that as a kid he'd once fallen out of a tree, there didn't seem to be much help. There just didn't seem to be any really traumatic injury—certainly nothing that had put Gary into a coma or required his hospitalization. Still, Mary Goody was insistent that *something* was off in Gary's neural network. "Something's up with Gary," she told me in a brief telephone conversation.

By the end of January 2002, Mary was convinced that Gary had some significant mental deficits—neurological problems that, when combined with the environment of his upbringing, were at the root of whatever was going on. Again she urged us to hire a neuropsychologist, suggesting that lead in the paint as well as all the solvents and thinners that Gary had worked with for so many years at Kenworth might indeed have caused some organic brain damage, which could be useful mitigation.

In early February 2002, we retained Dr. Craig Beaver, a neuropsychologist from Boise, Idaho, who specialized in neuro issues, to conduct a series of tests. Mary began to assemble Gary's written records, from school, the Navy, and Kenworth. Gary readily agreed to authorize us to collect these.

With this in mind, as the first month of Team Ridgway came to an end, some of us—but not all of us—began to accept the possibility, even the likelihood, that Gary *was* in fact *the* Green River Killer, hard as that was to fathom.

However, other members of our team, notably Tony and Michele, along with investigators Lis Frost and Denise Scaffidi, continued to work from the premise—and cling to the possibility—that Gary, our nice, simple, working-man client, was indeed wrongfully accused of these crimes.

As Greg Ridgway kept insisting to us, his little brother simply didn't seem capable of committing so many murders, and, more, getting away with it for so long. He just didn't seem nearly clever enough for that.

But as we were later to learn, there were different kinds of cleverness, and not all of them could be scientifically measured, including some that could not even be guessed at.

13

Discovery. To a lawyer, it isn't a credit card. And it isn't a television channel. To a lawyer, discovery is the heart of the art of doing justice. It's where the defender finds out what the prosecutor has and vice versa. It's where cases are made—or lost. And in the Green River case, we had a veritable Mount Everest of discovery that we had to climb.

Almost as soon as we'd come back into the case, Todd had asked the prosecutor's office to provide us with as much written information about the case as they could, and as soon as possible. In an extremely complex criminal case—which this one certainly was—getting this critical information from the other side has a lot in common with industrial management theories: mainly, the last-in, first-out method of inventory control. In other words, the first reports we got from the prosecution tended to be the most recently created. Which wasn't particularly helpful, as the four charged crimes had all taken place almost twenty years earlier. However, we were able to receive the most recent DNA reports, which were informative. And damning. On paper, at least, it looked like the DNA results were accurate. But there would be much more scrutiny ahead.

Sometime in January 2002, after reiterating our pleas for some paper to go on, we received four large, black, three-ring binders. Much of this material had to do with events that had taken place since Gary's arrest. Fully three of them contained telephone tips that had come in after all the publicity. Suddenly there were hundreds of people all over the country who were convinced that they'd seen Gary in Alabama . . . Florida . . . Ohio . . . California . . . the list went on and on, and almost all of these tips were useless, because Gary had rarely ever left Washington State over the preceding twenty years. One that sparked my immediate attention was a call that had come in from a probation officer in Thurston County, about an hour south of Seattle.

"I saw the news about the arrest of Gary Ridgway," she said. "I am Gary Ridgway's probation officer. I had him on a rape conviction."

But Gary had never been arrested for rape. We knew that because we had a copy of his entire criminal history, petty as it was, with only two arrests for patronizing prostitutes. But when we looked into the matter, we discovered that the probation officer had been referring to Gary G. Ridgway, not our Gary L. Ridgway. The power of television had convinced the probation officer that her probationer had to be the same person who had been arrested. Combining this with all the other erroneous sightings of Gary from coast to coast, I was convinced that the deluge of tips was one of the greatest testaments *against* eyewitness evidence ever accumulated.

Besides all these interesting but useless tips, there were copies of some—but not all—of the detectives' reports following up on Gary's arrest, and also of interviews with Greg, Judith, Matthew, and several of Gary's coworkers at Kenworth, all of which had been generated on November 30, 2001, or immediately afterward. It was only much later that we found that some critical information was not contained in this initial pile.

We also received a binder with all the search warrants that had been served and their returns; that is, the list of things that had been taken as possible evidence by the searchers. It was immediately apparent from the affidavits in support of the warrants that the investigators hoped to recover items of jewelry and clothing that might have belonged to the forty-nine victims. A long list naming each of the forty-nine, with items of clothing or jewelry that each was thought to have when last seen, formed part of the warrants.

Scanning the list of dozens of items taken from Gary at either his house, his locker at Kenworth, his pickup truck, or the motor home that he co-owned with Judith, I could see no obvious connection between any of the things sought and those that had been taken by the police, such as Gary's tools. All of this stuff, however, would have to go to the state crime lab for inspection and possible examination. In effect, Gary had lost possession of his property for the foreseeable future.

In another face-to-face with Gary, on January 31, 2002, Gary asked me, "Could you see about getting some of the money they took and get it to Judith?"

"What money are you talking about?" I asked.

"Well," Gary explained, "when I was arrested, I had about $55 dollars in my wallet. And in the motor home, we had about $300 hidden in there for emergencies."

"All right," I said. "I can check into it for you."

"I mean, it's not evidence or anything," Gary said. "She's going to be needing the money now, without me working and bringing home a paycheck." He started to tear up when thinking about the predicament in which Judith had been left.

"That's true," I responded. "I'll see what I can do."

Of all the subjects we talked about in these face-to-faces, the one that was sure to make Gary start to weep was his wife. Judith had come to see him in the jail on numerous occasions, usually accompanied by Greg and Dorene. To Gary, Judith was as vulnerable as she was dependent; her medical condition made her nervous about driving, which limited her ability to take care of herself. Everything that Judith had thought was stable in her life—her marriage to Gary, their house in Auburn, Gary's impending retirement from Kenworth—had been smashed to ruins. The house, the center of Judith's existence, was being sold to pay Gary's legal bills. Worse, for Judith, a wrongful death suit had already been filed against Gary and Judith by the Opal Mills family. Theoretically, any remaining assets belonging to Gary and his wife could be seized by the relatives of the killer's victims, if a court held that Gary was in fact the killer.[1]

For this reason, Gary and Judith had been advised to divorce, in part to protect Judith's financial future. Neither was happy about this, and even as late as January 2002, Gary was still trying to figure out if a legal separation, as opposed to a full divorce, would protect Judith.

Gary continued to deny that he'd ever killed anyone, as well as some of the assertions that had been made about him in the search warrant affidavits.

"How do you have sex on the bank of a river?" he asked me again, referring to assertions made in one of the search warrant affidavits, which quoted his second wife, Marcia, as saying they'd once had sex on the banks of the Green River. "It's not possible."

In my observation, Gary did not seem particularly depressed—at least, not compared with many others I'd seen in the jail over the years. Nor did others on our team think that Gary was suffering unduly or that he needed antidepressant medication, as Mary Goody recommended. Gary had put in a *kite*—a written request to the jail staff— for antidepressant medications, and in response a jail psychologist came to see him.

"He said, 'You're pretty upbeat, considering what you're in here for,'" Gary told me.

This made *me* nervous. I wasn't at all sure whether anything that Gary said to a jail psychologist might somehow come back to hurt him later. I told Gary that if the psychologist ever came back, Gary was to tell him that he couldn't speak to him without a lawyer being present. Gary said he understood. After the evaluation, the jail psych staff determined there was no need for antidepressants, so they were never prescribed.

Sometime around the first of February, Gary called Mary Goody, asking her to come back to the jail—he'd remembered some more things from his childhood, Gary told her.

Mary now began to worry that Gary's depression—or what she thought was his depression—was beginning to get the better of him. She wanted someone on our team to check on his mental well-being.

"I just got slightly nervous concerning the tone of his voice when he called," Mary e-mailed me, telling of Gary's request that she come back to the jail. "I didn't think it was because he thought I was cute or anything. . . . we probably should talk about how you guys would want me to handle some type of confession of any sort. What do you think?"

Well, there it was: the first overt suggestion by anyone on our side that Gary might someday admit to the crimes.

"Regarding any 'confession' tomorrow, or in the future, for that matter," I e-mailed Mary, "just let me know that we have to talk without telling me anything substantive until I ask." Confession might be good for the soul, but as a defense attorney, I also knew it might be bad for the body, particularly if it came at the wrong time. And at that point, we weren't anywhere close to being ready. At the very least, we needed to know what the state had as evidence. I'd heard of cases in which an accused person "confessed" to all sorts of things he hadn't actually done, sometimes just to get the waiting over with. That's why we had to get the facts first.

A few days later, before Mary could come back to town, we heard that Gary had been talking to, of all people, Barbara Kubik-Patten.

Barbara had been one of the helpful amateurs who'd gotten involved in the Green River case back in the very beginning, almost twenty years earlier. A self-proclaimed psychic, she had once discovered one of the forty-nine Green River victims, an event that shocked her as much as it had the police at the time. On Sunday, February 3, she came to visit Gary in the jail. Just how she got past the jail visitor screening process wasn't clear, but she proceeded to tell Gary that at one point in the past she'd been "associated" with the Green River Task Force. But Barbara's visit was cut short by the coincidental appearance of Dorene and Judith. It's difficult to imagine what the reaction of the police would have been if Barbara had emerged from the jail saying Gary had just confessed to her: first she'd discovered a body, when the odds against that happening would seem to have been a billion to one, and then, twenty years later, the accused killer confesses—and to *her*? No one would have believed it.

The next day, Michele saw Gary in a face-to-face. "He is fine," Michele noted in an e-mail to Mary, who was still worried about his mental state. Michele had heard of Barbara Kubik-Patten's visit with Gary, and this event bothered her. Who knew what Gary might be telling other such judicial rubberneckers like Barbara Kubik-Patten?

Michele returned to the office and called Todd. Todd put on his best glare and went up to see Gary, while Michele e-mailed Mary to tell her about the visit of the self-proclaimed psychic and asking her to reinforce Todd's message: Gary was to keep quiet with the unauthorized, no matter how entertaining it might be for him to talk, even to self-professed seers.

On February 7, 2002, Mary returned to the jail for her third interview with Gary. By then, I'd already told Gary that we wanted to bring in Dr. Beaver for neuropsych testing. Somehow, Gary thought that meant we'd have him taken to a hospital. Mary explained that the tests would be given in the jail.

"Looks very tired," Mary noted in a later report to the team. "Admits no sleep again."

Mary asked Gary about his childhood memories and whether he was ever picked on as a kid. Once he'd been beaten up by another kid, Gary told her, but that was it. Had he ever been in any fights as an adult?

"I got in a fight in junior high over a girl," Gary said. "Once, in the Philippines, a guy came at me with a bottle, and I hit him in the face with a chair." Gary said that money had changed hands to keep the incident quiet. Otherwise, he said, the tavern "would have been closed down." Mary asked about Gary's drinking habits. When he was younger,

Gary told her, he drank quite a bit—"just showing off," he told her. But after 1971, he had drunk much less.

What about girlfriends other than his wives? Gary had had fairly steady relationships throughout the early 1980s until he'd met Judith in 1985. Talking about Judith made Gary upset again. Judith had told him that the sheriff's detectives had asked her invasive, embarrassing questions on the night he was arrested.

"Judith is emotional anyway," Gary said. "To have [Detective] Sue Peters come over and ask you about your sex life—'did he ever beat you or try to choke you?'—that was too much for her." And in the search, they had seized a good deal of Judith's property, including her old tax returns. The whole thing had been very traumatic for Judith, Gary said.

The conversation returned to his relationships with women. Gary said he thought he had emotional problems and that these problems had affected his choices about women.

"The women I tend to love are heavyset people," he told Mary. "Claudia was pretty slim but . . . maybe I had a guilt complex about . . . the only thing I could pick up was a heavyset woman. My dad would say 'There's a lot of love in those hills.'

"That's why I paid to have the [thinner] women love me. Even just being in the car with them. I couldn't pick one up naturally." Gary began to weep. "That was one of the reasons I went out with them. I've got something penned up inside."

Gary tried to articulate, but as sometimes happened when he became upset, the words jammed up somewhere between his brain and his tongue. He started and stopped, started again and stopped again, trying to explain why he felt he could only get heavyset women, why he had hired so many prostitutes. Mary realized that Gary was saying that he wanted to have thin women but didn't feel he deserved to have them, or wasn't proficient enough, or wasn't attractive enough himself to have a real relationship with any thin woman who wasn't a prostitute. So he hired prostitutes and then despised himself for it, telling himself that he was a loser.

"I just couldn't get thin women," Gary said. "My way of paying for it was to get the satisfaction of paying for a beautiful woman. Sometimes I'd get them in the car and talk to them, and it was enough until I could find the right one—sometimes it was the money, too. Too expensive."

What was this? The disjointed rambling seemed part explanation, part admission. "It was enough until I could find the right one," Gary had said. The right one? What did that mean?

It had to have something to do with the fantasy, the thing Gary couldn't "get out of my mind," whatever had happened in the Philippines in 1969. Something that had to do with thin women, a prostitute, Claudia, guilt . . . but whatever it was, it was still stuck somewhere inside Gary.

Or was this just some story Gary had cobbled together to get sympathy from Mary, while trying to justify (or at least explain) his predilection for prostitutes? Some way of attracting Mary's attention and her sympathy? As time went on, I noticed that Gary's adaptive system of behavior involved, first, ascertaining the facts known by the person he was conversing with; second, adapting those facts to himself and his own history; and third, creating an explanation for those facts that cast himself as someone who was relatively "normal." It was part of the chameleon-like social capacity he had developed in order to fit in—in school, in the Navy, at Kenworth, in jail.

But examination of this rationale—he hired prostitutes because it was the only way he could get "thin women"—didn't really stand up to scrutiny. Though it was true that some prostitutes were thin, just as many were heavyset. As in other walks of life, there were all kinds. And when one looked at the list of the Green River dead—assuming, *arguendo,* as we lawyers like to say, that Gary *was* the killer, one readily observed that for every thin victim, there was a heavyset one. So if Gary *were* the killer, the thin woman–heavyset woman dichotomy certainly wasn't operative, or at least it had nothing to do with the killings.

Mary asked Gary if Judith had known about his dealings with prostitutes.

"She only knew when I got arrested [for prostitution in November of 2001]," he said. "A lot of emotional problems that I have, I still have, because . . ."

But Gary censored himself once more. Now he admitted that he'd lied to Greg about his experiences in Vietnam. Where he'd told Greg that he'd been up the river on a patrol boat, being shot at by "guys behind trees," it wasn't true. The terrible, awful truth was, he told Mary, he was an extremely emotional person. "Kramer versus Kramer," he said, referring to the movie about the divorcing couple. "I've seen it four times, and I still cry. It's hard for me. I can't say I'm a wimp around my brother. So that's where I got him to believing I had a hard time in Vietnam." If Greg believed that he'd suffered from horrible combat, then he'd allow Gary to cry.

He cried a lot, Gary now said. "Marcia said I used to read the Bible and cry and cry, and I go to church and I cry. I watch Billy Graham and I cry and watch 9-11 and I cry. I would cry four to five nights a week at shows and movies, and talking to people, sometimes, I get a little teared up. Sometimes because of anxiety. Maybe it's the joy that other people have that I don't have. You don't see two big heavyset people getting together . . . the ones I could never get, it's always Tom Cruise and the slim woman."

By now, Gary was really crying.

"I don't know why," he said. "My mom and dad were great. They argued a lot. Toward the end, they'd argue about babying Ed. One time, I think my mom and dad split up. We were all sent up to Washington to live with cousins. We went to Bremerton and then dad joined us later on.

"My mom had a temper," he said. "One time, she threw a camera at my dad. In the papers, Marcia said my mom threw a plate. He just walked away."

At his parents' funerals, Gary said, the three sons were each allowed to give testimonials to Mary Rita and Tom. "Greg talked a long time," he said. "There was no time left for me."

Gary sniffled for a while, then he seemed to recover himself. Mary asked him about his mother, Mary Rita.

"She was real active," Gary said. "Slender. She was really heavy into washing dishes. She used bleach. Our house was dust free."

Mary asked Gary if he'd ever talked to his parents about his crying. No, Gary said. He didn't like to show it. Not even to Judith.

"Feels no hope," Mary noted in her report to our team. Then, in capitals: "NEEDS MEDS."

Gary told Mary that he'd had bed-wetting problems as a kid.[2]

"What did they do?" Mary asked, meaning his parents.

"They just changed the sheets and would make sure I didn't have anything to drink the night before. I guess I was a hard sleeper. They'd get me up in the middle of the night and go to the bathroom, I guess. This lasted until maybe the fourth grade."

Gary left home for the first time when he'd gone to boot camp in the Navy.

"I was always screwing up," he recalled. "The directions wouldn't sink in. I was always having trouble understanding. I was sick for twenty-four hours after I got there. Lonesome. I never was the brightest. I only had one A in high school. I didn't read very well, especially at first. Later on, I wore glasses. There was the combination of kids knocking you and teasing you for wearing glasses and not keeping up with the class on certain things." Gary said he'd been placed in a special remedial reading class, and then he'd been held back for one grade. "It was hard for me," he said. "I was always being compared to Greg."

"What about Ed?" Mary asked.

"Ed didn't care," Gary said. "Mom pitied him, more than anything else."

Mary probed more. What did Gary want in a woman?

"I like the company of a woman who makes me feel like a family," he said.

———✺———

That same evening, Mary Goody went to see Judith. Judith was almost five years older than Gary. Her father was in the Army when she was born. He reenlisted and was killed in Korea in 1950, when Judith was six. Several years later, Judith's mother had married another man and bore him four other children. Judith had suffered from epilepsy up until the age of twenty-three. Because of this, she had not learned to drive until she was in her mid-thirties. That was one reason she didn't like to drive downtown by herself to see Gary. Driving made her anxious.

She'd first met Gary on February 21, 1985, Judith told Mary, at the White Shutters Inn on Pacific Highway South.[3] The restaurant–cocktail lounge had been the setting for a meeting of Parents Without Partners.

"I always wanted to go where there was country music," Judith told Mary. "My friend and I went. Gary was sitting across from us. We talked and danced. I tried to ignore him because I thought he was too young for me. But he was so nice and polite."

She and Gary had begun dating, Judith said.

"Each week, we'd go to the meetings, and he started courting me. We'd meet at McDonald's. He would buy me dinner and we'd sit and hold hands and visit. He was always nice and he was comfortable. I felt happy and trusting. He was on swing shift at the time [at Kenworth]. I would be coming home from work [Judith taught child care skills at a local high school], and he'd be on his way to work. That's why we met at McDonald's."

Gary was always kind to her and her children, Judith said. In 1987, one of her daughters and her husband and their two babies had moved in with them for a time. "Gary was great to them," Judith said.

In 1987, Gary had been searched for the first time by the police, Judith said. "That's when he got stopped and his truck looked suspicious," she said. "I was working at a day-care center, and four big detectives came in and took me to a parking lot. The house was searched and torn up. His mother and father [Tom and Mary Rita] took care of me. They came and got me and I stayed with them. He passed the tests. . . . I never wore green for a long time because I thought about it. After living with him for three years, I told him that I loved him and that we were getting married."

Since then, Judith said, they'd led very quiet lives, rarely going out to bars or restaurants. They enjoyed camping, raised dogs, and tended their yard.

"He's made me feel like a newlywed every day when he comes home," Judith told Mary. "He'll tease me and give me a big hug and kiss every day—he was always playful and teasing. He's sweet and kind to me, the best. He let me be me."

Judith had really liked Mary Rita, Gary's mother. "His mother was the best," Judith told Mary. "She died on my birthday. The whole family made me feel so comfortable. It didn't bother them that I wasn't educated or didn't finish high school. They stayed home a lot and we would go to their house on the weekends. . . . I was much closer to them than my own family." Gary made a point to check up on his parents' well-being after work, Judith said, and when Tom died, Gary continued to see that his mother was OK on a daily basis. Later, when Mary Rita died, he continued to do the same for Ed, who was still living with his wife at the old family home near the airport.

The news that Gary had been patronizing prostitutes even after their marriage had come as a complete surprise to her, Judith said. "He should have told me," she said. "I never told him no." But other than this aberration, there was nothing at all out of the ordinary about Gary, she said. The whole series of events from November 30 forward had been a huge shock, a tremendous stress on her. She had constant anxiety.

"My heart has been ripped out," she said.

—⁓—

Mary Goody's sensitivity to Gary's mental state was far more acute than the rest of us who saw Gary. What we saw was a person who seemed to be doing fairly well in jail, at least compared to some. I always tried to find out from Gary what other people in the ultra section were doing. Some of the stories that Gary told me about other inmates—people so depressed they couldn't even get out of their cell, for example, or who had engaged in melees with guards, or had smeared feces on the walls—made Gary seem utterly normal. But Mary believed that Gary had been battling severe depression his whole life, and she still thought that medication was called for. It was imperative that we get a neuropsychological evaluation done as soon as possible, Mary told us.

It was entirely possible, Mary told me, that Gary was on the edge of blurting out a confession; in her experience, this usually happened in one of two ways: either bits and pieces began dribbling out, increasing over time, until suddenly there would be a flood of admissions; or the whole story might come pouring out all at once, without the slightest warning.

Tony—certainly no babe in the woods when it came to criminal defendants—kept his own thoughts on this subject largely in reserve. There was a time to explore the possibility for confession—to whatever it was that Gary might have done—and that time was not yet propitious, Tony believed. So Gary and Tony carefully went over the allegations in each of the search warrant affidavits, and in the certification for probable cause, with Gary explaining each piece of evidence and generally behaving as if confessing was the furthest thing from his mind.

Yet others thought we needed to consider our options in case some sort of confession *did* come gushing out. In a February meeting in a closed ACA conference room between our lawyers and Mary Goody (the paralegals and investigators were excluded so they wouldn't be "tainted" by our candid talk), we had our first discussion of what we would eventually come to call "Plan B"—offering Gary's confession in return for the prosecutor's agreement to withdraw his request for the death penalty, if that turned out to be the only way we could save Gary's life.

"You know," Fred Leatherman said, "we ought to just go up and ask Gary point blank, 'Are you interested in a deal, if we could get death off the table?' I'll be the heavy. I'll let him know what his options are. Hanging or lethal injection. Or cooperating."

I disagreed.

"I think it's too early for that. He's not ready. *We're* not ready. We have to evaluate the discovery before we can tell him how shitty his case is."

"And we have to *get* the discovery before we can evaluate it," Todd added, pointing up the fact that all we'd had so far was the paltry three-ring binders. "It's way too soon for us to bring that up. He'd think we're trying to shove a guilty plea down his throat."

"I'm not so sure Gary's that far away from spilling something," Mary Goody said. "Sometimes I sense he's just wanting to tell somebody."

"I'm not sure that would do him any good," I said. "I understand confession is good for the soul, but I'm not sure it would do his life any good at this point."

"I agree," Tony said. "I don't see what advantage Gary would have in confessing that he killed anyone right now. Then what, plead insanity? We know how successful *that* can be with juries. Once he admitted he was *the* killer, he'd get the death penalty so fast it would make your head spin. We might as well argue self-defense."

"But you set up the penalty phase with a failed insanity defense at the guilt phase," Fred pointed out. "At least, your arguments are consistent."

"There's one minor problem. Gary's not insane. He has no history of mental health problems. He's a little weird, but no weirder than Mark."

"Thank you, Tony."

"I don't think we should confront Gary yet," Michele said. "I don't think he's ready. He's just getting to know us and trust us. I say we wait." Although she still believed that Gary wasn't the Green River Killer, even Michele knew that at some point, we were going to have to confront Gary on the evidence against him, if for no other reason than to prepare for trial. She just didn't think the time was right, just like most of the rest of us.

"Besides," David Roberson added, "right now the only way to save his life would be for a jury to find him not guilty . . . like, the 'he-didn't-do-it' kind of not guilty. You know, he had sex with prostitutes, but he didn't kill any. Like Tony says, leaving his DNA with the prostitute was the object." Dave had unofficially joined our team, in anticipation of the inevitable death penalty notice.

But there it was: even discussing a possible confession by Gary to any crime, let alone forty-nine, was simply not useful at that point. And even if we had a confession, there was simply no way the prosecutor would ever agree to any sort of deal that would spare Gary his life.

14

Obviously, none of this discussion about possibly confronting Gary with a proposal that he confess in return for spending life in prison ever seeped out of our conference room. That was one reason why we'd kept the discussion down to the bare minimum of participants. We had enough trouble with stuff leaking out about Gary from other sources without having to see something like this inadvertently make it into the public prints or on the airwaves.

Another ripple within our team involved a story that had just run in *TIME Magazine.* In this article, Greg Ridgway was quoted, implying that all the Ridgway boys had grown up in a happy home and that whatever problems Gary might have had, they stemmed from his horrific service on the river gunboats of Vietnam. Michele had arranged this interview back in December as part of an attempt to establish Gary's innocence, at least in the public mind. When we heard about this, Todd and I told Michele to stop arranging these interviews with Gary's family members at once—all they did was undercut our mitigation efforts. I could see a prosecutor in the future arguing to a jury, "The defense wants you to feel sorry for the defendant, because of his horrible childhood, . . . yet his own brother says everything was hunky-dory."

After we explained this to Michele, she agreed to arrange no more such interviews.

Another story that surfaced was broadcast by a Seattle television station. In what appeared to be a "sweeps week" hurrah in the second week of February, a woman who identified herself as "Cricket" appeared on camera but shadowed to conceal her identity and claimed that she was a prostitute who had picked Gary up one night while he was driving a van. Cricket had looked into the back of the van, she claimed, and had seen a rolled-up rug with some legs sticking out of it. That was when she'd decided not to get into Gary's van, she told the television station, an obviously wise decision.

The producer of the "exclusive" called me before running the story.

"We're going to break this story," he told me, "and I just thought I'd let you know it was coming and ask if you had any comment."

I told the producer that by then I'd heard of so many outlandish sightings of Gary, tips that had come into the police from all over the country, that I'd learned not to put any credence in any of them.

"This sort of hype serves no purpose except to damage his right to a fair trial," I said. "We're going to try this case in court, with sworn witnesses who identify themselves by their real names and who are subject to cross-examination. Otherwise it's simply unreliable." I offered to go on camera to say exactly that to the producer. He declined. The story ran anyway, and when I told Gary about it, he told me that he'd never owned a van, nor had any member of his family.

But that gave Gary another idea.

"Why don't you look for a stolen van?" he asked.

I felt like saying, Oooh-K, Gary, I wonder how many vans might have been stolen twenty years ago?

———

The prosecutor's decision on the death penalty—the court had given them up until the middle of April to formally make up their minds—was directly related to two critical issues for our side. Once the inevitable was formally announced, we would be on much firmer ground to finally get the scale of resources we needed to defend the case. But until that took place—officially, that is—no court was about to grant us the carloads of money we'd need to hire more lawyers, investigators, paralegals, and experts. So we were to some extent stuck, waiting for the resources we would surely need to do the job the way the Constitution required.

Besides this was the matter of the discovery—the estimated million or so pages that had been spawned by law enforcement over the previous twenty years. Just getting access to the stuff wasn't enough. We also had to have the resources needed to make sense of it. The prosecutors and police had an almost two-decade head start on us in terms of familiarity with the Himalaya of paper, although in other ways, they had it even worse than we did. For one thing, they had to figure out what they were required to disclose to us, by law, and what they could legitimately withhold as privileged or irrelevant. That meant somebody on their side had to review every page to make an initial determination of whether we were entitled to see it. Then, once that decision was made, copies had to be turned over.

Of course, that meant that if there had been one million pages originally, now there would be nearly two million pages. Then, when we generated our own paper that had to be turned over to the prosecutor, the mound of pulp would grow even higher. The authorities had stored much of their stuff in a large room in the detectives' suite at the Regional Justice Center and the rest of it in an archival warehouse. Once we started getting duplicates of the stuff, we'd be inundated with paper too. Before we knew it, we'd have to get our own storeroom, maybe even our own warehouse. There had to be a better way. There was.

By late January, both sides had agreed to hire an outside contractor to scan all the documents into an electronic page-form using computer software. Michele took on the task of representing our side in this process, meeting frequently with the outside contractor, the prosecutor, and the police to make sure the electronic documents would be usable.

The copying process began with the investigation files on the four charged victims—Carol Christensen, Marcia Chapman, Cynthia Hinds, and Opal Mills—as well as records relating to the years of investigation of Gary. Each of these files was voluminous, in some cases reaching several thousand pages. By early March 2002, about twenty thousand pages had been scanned and copied onto CD-ROM disks. The disks were then turned over to us. Each of the files was arranged in a computer folder, which, when opened, generated sequential pages in the order that they had been filed in the original police notebook. By clicking a mouse on a table of contents, a specific page could be examined; alternatively, you could start at the beginning and keep reading until you got to the end. The files could also be searched for text strings.

We weren't happy with this setup. We wanted to be able to search and sort all these documents through the use of fields for type of document, date, author, agency, and the like. After some wrangling, the prosecution agreed to establish a sort of super-index, which permitted this sort of searching. Though they groused about the extra effort, this so-called *objective coding* of the pages helped them, too.

By mid-March 2002, the state had provided us with all of the documents for the charged victims and Gary's *suspect file,* as well as the objective coding for the Christensen victim file. The objective coding for the other three was in the pipeline. But we still weren't satisfied. We wanted the state to provide us with *all forty-nine* of the victim files, objectively coded, along with all the suspect files, also objectively coded. Despite much gnashing of teeth in the office of the prosecutor because of the extra cost, this was agreed to as well. The inescapable fact was that we needed to examine *all* the reports on *all* of the victims and *all* of the suspects, in case there was some unnoticed fact that showed that Gary couldn't have committed the crimes. We certainly couldn't take the state's word for it that there was none; we had to do it ourselves.

Which brought us back to the subject of money again. By the middle of February, it was slowly dawning on the rest of the world—or at least the Seattle-area politicians—just how much this gargantuan case was really going to cost. Jim Crane of the Office of Public Defense had already suggested that the total cost of prosecuting and defending Gary might be somewhere between $8 and $12 million, assuming that the state wanted to put him to death.

Even worse, this gushing of tax dollars would take place at the same time the county and state governments were going broke. Years of tax-revolt initiatives and tax-cutting mania by politicians, combined with the economic downturn after 9-11, had emptied the public vault. By late February 2002, King County officials estimated that they'd be at least $50 million in the hole on the annual county budget of just under $500 million. Already a hiring freeze had lopped about a thousand jobs from the county payroll, all of the county's forty-four parks had been closed for the winter, and there were serious discussions about cutting back human services like day-care centers, health care clinics, and letting people out of jail early. One of the proposed cuts hit me where it really hurt: the county swimming pool system was to be closed down.

The county executive, Ron Sims, put it bluntly: "The fundamental fund structure for traditional county government services, largely the justice system, is broken." About $3 out of every $4 spent by the county went for justice: courts, cops, jails, prosecutors, and public defenders like us.

And now came Team Ridgway with our request—demand, really— for millions of dollars of unavailable money to defend a man accused of heinous crimes. Of course, our part of the spending was only a fragment of the estimated, initial budget for trying Gary: $1.4 million, a figure that was certain to double, triple, or even quadruple once the prosecutor made it official that he would seek the death penalty, but which was significantly eclipsed by the $2.6 million immediately needed for the Sheriff's Department for the case, and the $1 million needed to scan the mountain of reports onto the CD-ROMs, and almost certainly still more money later. But they were "the good guys." We were the ones who were trying to prove that the government was wasting its money in charging Gary. Needless to say, neither we nor our client were very popular that winter.

Already there had been ominous sounds from some of the politicians that our defense of Gary would be one of the scapegoats for the county's dismal financial situation. When one of the members of the King County Council, Cynthia Sullivan, was asked if voters would be asked to vote for higher taxes to help pay for the Ridgway case, she said that judging from her e-mail from voters, that was highly unlikely.

"They think we ought to shoot him," she said, "and it goes downhill from there."

—⁓—

For some weeks, we'd been wondering who the assigned judge would be. As a matter of general practice in the King County courts, large, complicated cases are preassigned to a trial judge, someone who would take the case all the way through, from the preliminaries to the final verdict, and if necessary, the sentencing. As early as late December, Tony had begun dickering with Jeff Baird from the prosecutor's office as to who this might be. This was a sort of hat dance: neither side wanted to be the one compelled to file an *affidavit of prejudice* against the judge ultimately selected, because it wouldn't look good; worse, the offending party had to worry that the presiding judge might choose someone even worse, just to get even for the rejection of his first selection.

Tony and Jeff each compiled separate lists of judges they would consider acceptable. For our side, a great deal of time was invested in discussing the merits and demerits of various choices. The day finally came in mid-March when both sides presented their lists. Surprisingly, three judges appeared on both lists. The mutually acceptable names were delivered to the chief criminal judge, Jeffrey Ramsdell, for his consideration. Then, to the surprise of both sides, Judge Ramsdell passed the decision on to the new presiding judge, Richard Eadie, who ignored these names and picked Judge Richard Jones, who hadn't been on either side's list.

Judge Richard Jones—brother of Seattle music icon Quincy Jones—was a fine choice to preside over the Ridgway case. He was a former prosecutor (we weren't too happy about that), but he was well respected for running a tight, yet evenhanded courtroom. While on the bench, he may sometimes seem forbidding, but in chambers he can be warm and understanding, especially when a lawyer has a difficult case. Most of all, he was respectful of defendants. This is a major plus because granting an accused person dignity can make the difference in how an entire trial unfolds. And from an earlier case—Kenny Ford, in fact—I had the idea that Judge Jones was no great fan of the death penalty, which might even out any unconscious biases that might have stemmed from his earlier career as a prosecutor.

Judge Jones was named to take over the case in the last week of March 2002. By that time, however, our side had realized that getting the resources needed to defend Gary was going to require some deft political footwork—a tango to get Jim Crane, the judges, and the King County Council, the legislative body that held the purse strings, off the political hook. After a meeting in Ramsdell's chambers, Crane came up with a possible solution: he'd propose to Ron Sims, the county executive, that Sims ask the court to appoint a *special master* to decide on our funding requests. Any decision by a special master would have the force of a court order, but it would have the advantage of being made by someone who wouldn't have to take the political heat—someone who wouldn't have to run for reelection.

"I want someone with credentials and so much respect and credibility that the County Council would have to fall in line," Crane said. "They're tired of me asking for more money."

"But they have to fall in line or the court will trump them, either now or later," I pointed out. "And later will be way more expensive."

"I know that. You know that. Some of the council members know that," Crane said. "But some others are going to try to make this a political issue. After all, money's pretty tight these days."

"We'll just have to educate them," I said. "Have 'em read a couple of those Ninth Circuit decisions." The federal Ninth Circuit Court of Appeals had strictly held that a defendant had a constitutional right to *all* necessary legal assistance, as well as all necessary expert witnesses. "It's in black and white," I went on. "They *have* to give us the resources or this will be back again. Why can't they understand that? It's cheaper in the long run to give us our money up front." I was saying things Jim already knew. He smiled at my political naïveté.

"If it were only that simple," he said. "It just isn't. But I really believe a special master will provide that extra layer of protection that will appease the council and get this—or most of it—approved." Jim said he was sure we'd get our resources. How soon was another question.

———

While all this maneuvering was going on, Mary Goody had been busy. On March 18, 2002, she had another interview with Gary. He seemed less emotional in this session, certainly less teary. He explained that he hadn't been feeling very well at the previous interview. But Mary noticed that Gary seemed to be in a self-disparaging mood. He just wasn't very good at things, he told Mary. Reading, certainly. When he wrote letters, he had to write them twice to make sure that the sentences had the correct formation. He had a long list of words he had trouble with, all the way from A to zebra, and showed it to her. In the Navy, he had trouble with terms like *flank* and *about face,* and he was always screwing up. At one point, he'd been a spotter for a deck gun but had fouled that up, too. About the only thing he was good at, Gary said, was his job—or at least showing up on time for it or working overtime when asked. Mary saw that he was very proud at having been able to work so steadily over the years, without getting fired. Nevertheless, he said, people at work had teased him, sometimes cruelly. Once, as the plant's safety monitor, he sent in suggestions for the safety program.

"They sent me back a roll of toilet paper. 'This is what we think of your ideas.'" Afterward, as a joke among his coworkers, Gary was named "safety man of the year."

"You learn to take it and you learn to give it out, too," Gary said. "But it did bother me. I had the problem with prostitution, and I didn't have anyone to go to. There was no way out. I paid for the warmth and someone to talk to." But he felt ashamed that he used prostitutes and tried to keep it as hidden as his dyslexia. Even after marrying Judith in 1987, Gary said, he'd continued to patronize prostitutes, an aspect of his life he'd kept hidden from everyone.

"Always in the past, I've had other people talk [first]," he said. "Then I could ask questions. I couldn't understand a lot of card games. I don't stand up for myself. Even when I was younger. I don't want to tell people I'm dyslexic. I've always been shy around people. I don't have a good memory. I have to think and not sound stupid. Otherwise people would know 'Wrongway' was here." This was the secret of Gary's chameleon-like quality of blending in so well, whether at work or when out on the Strip looking for prostitutes: he listened and reflected back the expectations that others placed upon him, whatever they were, and let the others define him. He was eminently adaptable. "I don't stand up for myself," he said, and though he meant this as a weakness, it was also the well-spring of his infinite, barely guessed at, capacity to deceive.

That same evening, Mary met again with Greg and Dorene. Greg indicated that he had always been protective of Gary, especially in school when other kids teased him about having "a stupid brother." Gary had problems, Greg said, especially with reading. And Dorene added that a lot of Gary's problems began when his marriage to Marcia had fallen apart.

By the end of the evening, Mary was convinced there was still more of Gary's story to be had. She was certain that at least some of the origin of Gary's emotional problems, and possibly his neurological deficits, might be traced to the circumstances that had confronted his parents, Tom and Mary Rita, so many years before. With Greg and Dorene's help, Mary made plans to dig far deeper into Gary's past, and the pasts of Tom and Mary Rita.

The next day, at a team meeting, Mary told us that Gary's physicality—among other things, his droopy, often puffy eyelids—might indicate some sort of organic brain dysfunction. Gary had told her he'd suffered from allergies that had made his eyes water from early childhood, and other kids had often ragged him for being a crybaby. We decided to hire another expert, Dr. Sterling Clarren, to explore the possible effects of prenatal birth defects on the functionality of Gary's brain.

15

Over the next few months, while the rest of Team Ridgway was wrestling with the intertwined issues of money and discovery, Mary Goody tracked down and interviewed a number of Gary's relatives, many of them from Mary Rita's side of the family. As always, it was Mary's task to look for information that might explain why Gary might have committed murder, assuming he had. The portrait of the Ridgway family that slowly emerged shed some light on how Gary came to be the way he was but offered us little real hope of mitigation. She found no evidence of genetic insanity or mental illness, no instances of clear sexual molestation, nothing that would engage a jury enough to say, "Oh, so that's why this happened," which is almost always a prerequisite for convincing at least one juror to "just say no" to death.

According to Mary's reports, which she sent to me as the team member in charge of the mitigation issue, almost everyone Mary talked to recalled Mary Rita Ridgway as a beautiful, very smart young girl in the years immediately following World War Two—a high school cheerleader, very socially adept, and quite popular among her crowd while growing up near Bremerton, across the Sound from Seattle. Gary's mother was one of five children of Edmond Joseph Steinman and Clara, his wife. Mary Goody formed the impression that Ed Steinman, at least, was a very, very conservative Roman Catholic, with strong, some even said harsh, views on women and sexuality. At one point, according to one of Mary Rita's surviving relatives, Ed Steinman had taken a hammer to his daughter's painted fingernails, breaking them. "He thought she was too much into that," the relative recalled.

Early in 1947, Mary Rita had become pregnant and soon thereafter married Tom Ridgway.

"Tommy had a hard life," one relative remembered. "His family lived in New Mexico. He was taken away from his family by an uncle. The Ridgway family had such hard times," one of Mary Rita Ridgway's family members told Mary Goody, particularly back in the years of the Great Depression. Growing up with his bachelor uncle in Kansas, Tom Ridgway had little experience with women, and feminine tenderness. "It was a Spartan upbringing," one of Mary Rita Ridgway's cousins believed.

Tom Ridgway, Mary Goody also learned, was seen by Mary Rita's family as rough-hewn, earthy, and slyly lascivious, if not a bit crude. Today people would call his behavior politically incorrect or even sexist. He seemed an odd match for the beautiful and vivacious, yet prim and proper, Mary Rita. He had been married before and had fathered a son in that marriage. Some recalled that Tom made many statements disparaging prostitutes—talking about them frequently enough to make some wonder whether he protested too much.

"I always looked at her and looked at him and couldn't figure out what she saw in him," said one of Mary Rita's relatives.

Not long after marrying Mary Rita, Tom and his new bride moved away from Bremerton and Mary Rita's family, first to Idaho, then Utah. For most of the next twelve years, Tom and Mary Rita lived in various small towns in Idaho and Utah, while Tom earned a meager living as a long-haul truck driver, and Mary Rita was often left to cope by herself with a family that soon included three young boys—Greg, born in 1947, Gary, born in 1949, and Tom Eddie, born in 1952. Money was very tight for the Ridgways. At one point, the baby, Tom Eddie, developed a terrible fever while Tom was out of town on a trucking run, and Mary Rita had no money for a doctor. She resorted to putting the child in a snowbank to cool him off. Later, it would appear that the high fever had caused some degree of injury to Tom Eddie's brain.

In 1959, Mary Rita apparently decided to leave Tom Ridgway. She called one of her sisters and her sister's husband to come to Idaho to help move the family back to the Bremerton area. Whatever the issue was between Mary Rita and Tom, it was later resolved, as Tom soon followed Mary Rita and the boys back to Washington State.

Tom soon found work as a driver for a tour bus line in Seattle. That job eventually developed into full-time employment with the Seattle transit agency, Metro. So by early 1960, Tom Ridgway finally had permanent and stable employment. The next year, Mary Rita took a job in the men's department at JCPenney, and the family's fortunes finally began to improve. In 1963, the family acquired their own house just east of the airport, the same house where all three boys grew up.

"Tommy had some very stoic ideas of how to raise children," one of Mary Rita's relatives told Mary Goody. "When they visited us, Tommy was very strict, especially with Gary and Eddie. What upset me was, one time they came and visited us, Gary had a bed-wetting problem. His father's idea of how to deal with that was to make him sit in about three inches of cold water. I told him I thought it was terrible, and he wouldn't do that again in my house."

Mary Goody asked if this relative had ever seen Tom spank the boys— she remembered that Greg had said this never happened, although Gary said his father had beaten him with a belt on perhaps ten occasions.

"Yes," said this relative "and not just his hand. He took a stick to them." But this mainly happened with Gary and Eddie, not with Greg. Most thought Gary and Ed were thoroughly intimidated by their father and that Mary Rita was loath to interfere, in part because it only tended to make Tom madder.

"Tommy liked to go through old rubbish heaps to collect things," one said. "He often found things, took them home, cleaned them up, and resold them. He used to talk about different places where he'd found the 'treasures.' It was a family trait." Later, Gary would take his own son, Matthew, on these foraging expeditions through junkyards.

Others thought that the boys had been treated differently by Tom.

"Greg could do no wrong. He was smart. He was everything," one relative told Mary Goody. "He looked a lot like his mother, was good-looking and quick thinking." Not so with Gary and Ed, who tended to follow rather than lead.

"I think Greg noticed the difference in the way their dad treated them, and he tried to keep them [Gary and Ed] out of trouble and away from Tom. . . . The boys got themselves into situations because they had so much frustration, from not being able to live up to what their dad wanted them to be. Greg was the one he set the standard by. He really talked up Greg and his grades."

When Tom made Gary sit in the cold water after the bed-wetting incident, "Gary acted resigned, as if he knew this was going to happen." No one could remember Gary crying at the time, though. Tom was intent on making sure his two younger sons could take it.

"He was so small," one remembered. "I think Mary [Rita] went outside. Mary said one time that the boys had to learn. She didn't interfere in the way Tommy disciplined the boys. . . . She didn't say anything to help them."

Gary was, in almost every way, Tom's son, one relative seemed to say.

———

By early April 2002, we were ready to submit our mitigation package to the prosecutor's office. After considerable discussion, we'd decided to submit rather less than what we actually knew about Gary at the time. We didn't want to get into the Tom and Mary Rita relationship, or the perceptions from the Steinman side of the family, for example. We would continue to delve into those matters to learn more and to see if that would be something we could use after a conviction, if or when that actually happened. Until then, there wasn't much sense to tipping the prosecutors off to the full contents of our hand. It certainly wasn't the type of mitigation that would deter Norm Maleng from seeking death. All that would do was give the other side a year or more before the actual trial to dig up information intended to counteract ours. Besides, our information could cut two ways: although it shed some light on Gary's personality, the prosecutors might also use it to suggest that Gary had in fact committed the crimes. We certainly didn't want to go *there*—not in Gary's case, where the best chance of saving his life was to make sure that he was found not guilty.

We did need to give the prosecution something, however. We decided to concentrate on Gary's obvious neurological and intellectual impairments. Dr. Craig Beaver came from Idaho and examined Gary in the jail. He found that Gary's IQ, using a variety of unwritten tests, came out to be 85. Average intelligence is 100. Gary's performance on other tests was discernibly below average as well.[1] "In short," Beaver said in his preliminary report, "eighty-four percent of similar-aged adults function higher than Mr. Ridgway." He ranked almost at the bottom in the ability to do arithmetic in his head—that is, without a pencil and paper.

"Currently," Beaver concluded, "Gary Ridgway is functioning in the low average range of intellectual skills. Academically, he also evidences significant limitations. His pattern of results is consistent with his history. Mr. Ridgway demonstrates both learning disabilities and attentional problems. Given his pattern of cognitive difficulties, I have concerns about organic brain impairments. Further neuropsychological and neurological evaluation will be needed to comprehensively assess this issue."

In a meeting with our team, Beaver tried to explain some of these neuropsychological findings, which he believed showed that Gary had "diffuse organic brain damage." This wasn't a case where Gary had been conked on the head and had physical trauma damaging some specific area of the brain. This was a more scattered type of brain dysfunction, primarily in the frontal lobe region of the brain. As Beaver put it to us nonexperts, the wiring in the front part of his brain was not working correctly; but it wasn't like there was one specific problem he could place the blame on. This *diffuse* type of brain damage is often seen in cases involving prenatal exposure to alcohol, drugs, or other toxins, Beaver said. It can also be seen in those who suffer chronic exposure to chemicals and toxins such as pesticides or even lead paint.

This led us back to the issue that we thought needed to be thoroughly explored—Gary's prolonged exposure to lead paint and other toxic fumes from his many years as a painter at Kenworth. We decided to find an expert in brain damage due to chronic exposure to lead paint. To validate this hypothesis, we would also need all of the Kenworth records regarding what safeguards were in place and their compliance with OSHA standards.[2]

Our main purpose in presenting this limited mitigation package to the prosecutors was to make sure that we were on the record—with the prosecutor and the court—that we had tried to convince the authorities not to ask for the death penalty for Gary, should he be convicted. We had considered not submitting a mitigation package at all, recognizing that it was an act of futility in this case. But some legal authorities have held that a defense failure to present a request for mitigation before the prosecutor files his notice of intent to seek death could be ineffective assistance of counsel, and we certainly didn't want to start off as "ineffective," so we agreed to file something, even if it was just the minimum.

Because everyone on our side knew this was just a formality—that Norm Maleng, the prosecutor, would "never *not* ask for the death penalty" in the Green River case, as Jim Robinson had put it—there was not much sense in giving anything away: no matter what we said, the death penalty notice from the prosecutors was inevitable.

We did, however, make another run at the *aggravating* factor—the so-called common scheme or plan. We were convinced we had a good argument that the state's aggravated murder statute didn't necessarily include serial murders. After all, the statute required the state to prove that the crimes were somehow connected together, and we just weren't convinced they would be able to prove that. We pointed out that at least two prosecutors in Washington State, including Spokane County Prosecutor Steve Tucker in the Robert Yates case, had publicly said they had concerns that the *aggravated statute* applied to serial murders, at least as it was written.

"There is no legal precedent or authority directly on point in Washington," we pointed out in our mitigation memorandum, which we gave to the prosecutor's office on April 7. In fact, we said, in every other case of multiple murder that the issue had arisen in the appellate courts thus far, all of the victims had been killed at the same time and place.

Well, it looked good on paper, but we all knew that it would bounce off the prosecutor's office like a pebble off an elephant's hide. Ever since they had essentially said, in filing the charges, that Gary was *the* Green River Killer, they had been politically compelled to ask for the death penalty.

Nevertheless, we tried to talk them out of it.

On April 9, 2002, Tony, Todd, and I brought our slimmed-down mitigation report with us and met with Norm Maleng and Dan Satterberg, his chief of staff. The five of us met in Norm's office on the fifth floor of the venerable old courthouse. Of course, Norm had a huge office, tastefully decorated, complete with a large oblong conference table. We sat down. I envisioned other meetings at that table—prosecutors sitting around the table discussing the merits of various cases or the terrible deeds of one miscreant or another.

As polite and formal as ever, Maleng got right down to business.

"Gentlemen, thanks for coming," he said. "I always welcome the defense input on these important matters. And thank you for the mitigation materials. We are still reviewing it, but thank you for providing the information."

"Thank you, Norm," Tony said, "but I'm thinking you might have already made your decision on this one." Tony smiled, as if to underscore his sympathy for the political pressure Maleng was undoubtedly feeling.

"No, I really have not made a decision," Maleng said. "Of course, it's a big decision and I've been giving it a great deal of thought. And I've had several meetings with some of my senior staff. But I haven't made any final decision on it yet. I am interested in listening to what you have to say."

Of course, no one expected Maleng to tell us that he wouldn't even consider the mitigation we had brought him. The law required him to consider it, and this was Maleng just making sure the record was clear. He *was* considering it—at least for fifteen seconds.

I went over some of Gary's background, but Maleng pointed out that we had no evidence of mental illness on Gary's part. Well, Tony had called that one: there wasn't any, at least not as defined by the insanity statute and case law in Washington. I said we were still investigating Gary's neuropsychological issues. Maleng nodded.

Then Todd suggested that Gary might be the wrong guy.

"There are some factual and legal issues that would justify not seeking death in this case," he said. "Factually, there were so many other suspects, a few of which look better than Mr. Ridgway, at least with respect to some of the victims."

We could tell from the look on their faces that they weren't about to agree with this. "Besides," Todd continued, "if the state seeks death, you will have a polygraph admitted at the penalty phase that will show Mr. Ridgway was not being deceptive when he denied killing prostitutes." Todd was talking about the 1984 lie detector test, the one that Gary had passed.

"But that one wasn't really valid, was it?" Satterberg pointed out.

"To seek death, there ought to be absolute certainty," Todd argued. "There won't be, given all the evidence of other possible suspects in this case."

"Wouldn't that be for a jury to decide?" Satterberg asked.

Tony picked up the ball.

"Norm," he said, "you've known me for . . . well, let's say, for years. You know I am morally opposed to the death penalty. I think it is an abomination in a civilized society. I just think it's shameful we even have it on the books. The government should *not* be in the business of killing its citizens."

Tony paused, then went on. "You know how I feel about it, we've had these conversations before. But I know you're going to do what you're going to do, and my opinion about the death penalty won't change that."

"As always Tony, I admire your honesty," Maleng said. "And I admire your passion for what you do. It's a tough business we're in, and you are always frank and to the point. And you are always a gentle-man."

That was it. We knew that Norm Maleng and his staff were going to ask for death for Gary Ridgway. We all rose and shook hands. Now it would be a battle to the end, however long it took, and however much it cost.

On April 15, the prosecutors filed their formal notice of intent to seek Gary's death with Judge Jones. Afterward, our team went into the hall-way outside the courtroom to give a statement to the news media. Tony, Todd, and I stood with our backs to the wall as cameramen and re-porters formed a swarm around us. I read from our prepared statement:

> We are disappointed and we disagree with Mr. Maleng's decision to seek the death penalty for Gary Ridgway. However, we are not sur-prised. We felt Mr. Maleng made his position clear back on December fifth, so we were expecting this decision.
>
> Gary Ridgway is innocent of these crimes. We will work hard, as hard as we possibly can, to make certain that Gary receives a fair trial, is found not guilty, and never receives the death penalty.
>
> Gary's family and friends stand behind him and will continue to provide their love and support.
>
> For our part, we have only begun to review the voluminous dis-covery. This will be a difficult and lengthy process but we must be, and we will insist on being, completely prepared to defend Gary's life.
>
> When a community, through its government, seeks to kill a human being for the sake of punishment and vengeance, it becomes an ex-pensive proposition, as it must. As the United States Supreme Court has stated: "Death is different." That is, death is qualitatively different than any other criminal sentence, even life imprisonment, because mistakes cannot be corrected. As a result, the appellate courts give cap-ital cases what is called "heightened scrutiny." Many death sentences in our State have been overturned, some because the defense did not do all that it could or should have done.
>
> The State's effort to execute a human being should not be easy, cheap, and quick. Gary Ridgway is innocent. We will do everything in our power to make sure he is found not guilty.

Well, we'd said what we were going to try to do. Now we had to do it.

16

Although we had formally opposed County Executive Sims's request that a special master be appointed to oversee the costs of defending Gary—we reasoned that it would stand a better chance of getting Judge Jones's approval if we weren't out in front on the issue—we were pleased when Jones agreed to the idea. After some consideration, he picked former United States Attorney Kate Pflaumer. At our request, he also ordered us to keep Pflaumer's name secret. By this time, what with all the cutbacks from the county's budget shortfall causing screams of outrage from various interest groups, making her name public might even put her in danger.

Afterward we had a meeting back at ACA. Tony wanted the case to speed up, to get to trial sooner rather than later.

"We don't have three or four years," he said. "What if one of us dies?"

"Tony . . . ," Todd said, somberly. "Don't say that. Mark's in good health."

"Well, some of us may get disbarred between now and then," Tony shot back, grinning.

I met with the special master, Kate Pflaumer, a few times over the next couple of weeks, arguing that to defend Gary properly, *all* the murders had to be scrutinized by our side, not just the charged four. Our reasoning was fairly straightforward. If the four charged murders were identical enough in common scheme or plan to charge Gary with aggravated murder, and if the four charged murders had been considered identical enough by the investigating police to the forty-five other murders to warrant being put on the Green River official list, then it was up to us to investigate the possibility that someone other than Gary had murdered the other forty-five. Heck, even *one* out of the other forty-five could be reasonable doubt. That way, if someone other than Gary committed one or more of the uncharged forty-five, the odds were much better that the police were wrong when they said that Gary had committed the charged four. It only stood to reason. Or so the argument went.

Kate had a little trouble with our thinking at first. Why couldn't we simply defend Gary on the four? But I pointed out that the prosecutors had already agreed to disclose information to us on the other forty-five, as well as the general intention to use circumstances from some of the uncharged murders to prove Gary's guilt in the four charged cases. It was clear, therefore, that even the state acknowledged, albeit reluctantly, that we were entitled to look at all the murders. And that, of course, is why it would take so long and cost so much.

On May 7, 2002, Kate Pflaumer approved $1.9 million of our request: most but not all of what we were asking for.[1] Once this money was in hand, we'd be able to finally formally hire Dave Roberson, Eric Lindell, Fred Leatherman, and the appellate expert, Suzanne Elliott, who had been essentially working without pay for almost five months, as well as get started on some of our expert witnesses. Unfortunately, my political naïveté still hadn't dissipated. The County Council, which had to approve the money, was about to borrow a line from Andrew Jackson—the court had made its decision, "now let 'em enforce it."

Pflaumer's approval made its way back to Jim Crane, and from there to Sims, and from Sims back to the County Council, together with similar supplemental appropriations for the Sheriff's Department and the prosecutor's office. Their two Ridgway supplementals passed with little comment—after all, they were the good guys. But the defense team's request set off howls of outrage from the politicians. Politicians love to defend the Constitution, except when it comes to defending the Constitution.

As the figures became public, Dan Satterberg couldn't resist taking a swipe at us—and at the money that Pflaumer had approved. Speaking after the County Council failed to approve Kate Pflaumer's recommendation that we be given more money, Satterberg said we didn't need the resources. All we had to do was investigate the four charged crimes, not the entire Green River list.

"The Constitution requires that you provide a Chevy or a Ford to a defendant," Satterberg told local news reporters, meaning a generic, no-frills defense. "This is not a Porsche [defense], it's an entire Porsche *dealership*."[2]

Very funny! The television stations played and replayed Dan's witty remark over and over again. Now not only were we defending the most unpopular defendant in the history of the county, we were wasting the taxpayers' money while doing it. Luxury litigation! And this at a time when the county was closing parks and swimming pools to balance its books. We discovered that a member of the County Council had taken an opinion poll on his Web site—it turned out that over 93 percent of the public thought we were wasting money. Of course, if you'd put any one of them in the spot that Gary Ridgway was in, they would have changed their tune in a hurry. Todd guessed that Satterberg's remark was a calculated attempt by the prosecutor's office to poison the potential jury pool with even more toxic spin; but it looked instead to me that Dan was simply doing what came naturally—taking a whack at defense lawyers, again. And there had been speculation that he had ideas of running for King County Prosecuting Attorney if and when Norm Maleng ever decided to step down.

For our side, Todd and Michele rushed to court with a request for a gag order to prohibit any more inflammatory statements like this. Judge Jones refused to approve it but scolded the other side for making inappropriate remarks. The statements by Dan Satterberg, comparing defense lawyers to car salesmen, were "offensive," the judge said, and "dangerously close" to a violation of the rules of professional conduct.[3]

Just as this issue blew up, Michele had received a telephone call from a reporter from the *Seattle Times*. The *Times* reporter, Lynn Thompson, told Michele that she'd learned the identity of the special master and that the paper intended to publish the name the following day. Michele formed the impression that the *Times* reporter had obtained this secret information from the prosecutor's office, although the reporter refused to disclose her source. That was one reason why she'd wanted Judge Jones to issue the gag order. Michele called a lawyer for the *Times,* trying to convince the newspaper not to publish Kate's name. After some jawboning by Michele, the paper agreed not to make Kate's name public, in part because of Judge Jones's earlier order sealing the information, but Michele had to tell them that the special master had a real concern about being identified. Only a few years earlier, an assistant United States Attorney working in her office had been assassinated by an unknown gunman, in part, some thought, because of publicity surrounding his work on what some perceived to be an unpopular cause in Washington State—gun control. The defense worried that some unbalanced person, angry at the closure of parks and pools and the funding of Gary's defense, might want to take a shot at Kate.

—◊◊◊—

I continued to see Gary every week, as did Michele, our investigators, and occasionally Tony. Mary Goody came back to town on several occasions to conduct more interviews of Gary's aunts, uncles, and cousins. By June 1, 2002, Gary had been the jail's most notorious inmate for seven months; yet, aside from the spell of weeping that he'd exhibited to Mary Goody, he seemed remarkably well-adjusted for someone who'd never spent an entire night in stir until his arrest. By June, though, I had come to understand this somewhat. Gary had been trained by his father to stoically accept whatever fate befell him.

Still, Gary continued to evince a sharp interest in the merits of the case against him.

Over the preceding weeks, while I was wrestling with the money people, I'd kept Gary up-to-date on everything that was going on. "Oooh-K," he'd nod.

Gary particularly looked forward to visits from three of our investigators, Lis Frost, Bettye Witherspoon, and Denise Scafidi, as well as Michele Shaw.

"When are the ladies coming?" he would ask, and I realized that these visits from female team members were the high points of Gary's week.

In his meetings with members from our team, Gary paid close attention to details about the crime scenes. By this point, we were just beginning to obtain the investigators' original reports in the four charged murders, which provided subtle facts that previously had not been publicly available. Gary was very interested in those details, but that wasn't my role on the team, so he and I didn't spend much time on that stuff. One thing in particular caught my attention: Gary wanted to know if the police believed that the killer had had sex with the victims after they were dead.

"I was wondering," he asked, "do they think the guy had sex with 'em after they were dead?"

"Well," I replied, "there had been some suggestion in the FBI's initial psychological profile that there might be some of that going on. But necrophilia is not uncommon in serial murders, so they probably just threw that into the mix. Nothing I've seen or read so far indicates that, but we haven't reviewed all the photos and autopsies yet."

Gary simply nodded, "Oooh-K."

He had interest in the fish, sausage, and wine found with Carol Christensen. The detectives had told him about this unusual staging of the body on the night they had arrested him. He thought these might be clues to the real killer.

"Was the fish fresh or store-bought?" he asked, suggesting that if the investigators could find out who bought the trout, they might get a line on the perpetrator. Gary said he didn't think there was any religious significance at all to the fish, sausage, and wine. "The guy probably left them there just to attract animals," he suggested.

He pointed out that three of the four charged victims were African-American women and suggested that in that respect they were different than Carol Christensen. The rest of the victims were of all races. "What is a Green River victim, anyway?" he asked. "What's the profile? How do they decide who's on the list and who's not?"

He wanted to know how the charged victims had been killed; I explained they had been strangled.

"Do they think they were killed where they were found, or someplace else?" he asked.

He suggested that maybe the killer had used a stun gun to immobilize the victim. "Maybe they should be looking for bruises," he suggested. "How long does a bruise last, anyway?"

He also was continuing to pay close attention to what people were saying about him. "I heard some guy on the radio was saying that you had a better chance to win the lottery than I do of being found not guilty," he told me. "I heard that some casino in the Cayman Islands has a betting line on my case."

The incessant publicity, I told Gary, was one reason we were exploring the idea of asking for a change of venue. Our initial polling had shown that even though people who lived in other counties were *less* likely than Seattleites to believe that Gary had to be guilty, they were *more* likely to vote to give him death should he be found guilty.

Meanwhile, people were continuing to insist that they'd had close encounters with Gary in the past. One woman surfaced in a British Columbia newspaper, claiming that she had "dated" Gary, his father, and his brother at the same time. That was ridiculous, Gary said; he'd only been to British Columbia a few times in his life, and certainly never with his brother and his father.

I told him that another television reporter had asked for an exclusive interview with him.

"I urge you not to do it," I told him, as dryly as I could.

—∿—

By June 2002, even as Dan Satterberg was comparing us to German sports car dealers, the CD-ROM system of discovery was fully cranked up. Once a week, the prosecutor's office would hand over to us disks containing images of thousands of pages from the humongous pile of paper that had accumulated in the case over the years; in turn, we loaded the contents of these disks into our own database.

Although this eliminated the need for our own warehouse, it only highlighted another problem: we still didn't know what the documents actually said, unless we read every electronic page. And as Tony had figured out back in the very beginning, with so many pages, once we started down that road, we'd probably all go blind or die of old age before the case came to trial. But Michele had a solution for this.

Drawing on her previous experience assisting in a high-document-volume case, Michele arranged for a second contractor, Certus Consulting, to take the CD-ROMs that were being burned every week and to load them into a gigantic database. In turn, Certus would hire a squad of thirty young lawyers (at $35 an hour!) to read the documents as they came in (in their electronic form) and then sort them into electronic, *virtual bins*—that is, to hit a key that placed a document that talked about a car or a truck into the *vehicle bin* or a report that mentioned a specific location, say, South 188th Street and Pacific Highway South, or, alternatively, the Red Lion Hotel (which was at that intersection), into a *location bin*.

Altogether, after much discussion and a little trial and error, we came up with about thirty such virtual bins to sort the documents:

names of victims, witnesses, suspects, girlfriends, boyfriends, pimps, vehicles, locations, forensics, DNA, hairs, bones, blood, swabs, paint, fibers, soils, polygraphs, hypnotism (many witnesses had been hypnotized years earlier during the investigation), and a variety of other common, and some uncommon, factors.

This *sorting bin* process utilized a computer software program designed for use by lawyers in cases with large volumes of discovery, called *Summation.* It would enable team members to sit at their PCs in their own office and have access to our growing database of discovery. I might sit at my desk in Kent, for example, click on the Summation icon on my computer's desktop, enter my password, and log into the database. I would then be able to enter a query. For example, I might enter "Dr. Himmick/DNA reports," and up would pop a list with all of the documents, say twenty-three documents, that had these two commonalities. There might be a DNA report written by Dr. Himmick in the Opal Mills case, found at page 357 of the discovery. The same report may also be found at page 17,944. Dr. Himmick's report from the Carol Christensen case might be in there several times as well, but at least the program made it easy for us to quickly determine if some document was a duplicate. In this example, I might also be directed to a document written by Detective Jensen that makes reference to "Dr. Himmick's DNA report." Depending on what you were looking for, just like any computer search, the more identifying features, the more discriminating the search. Although initially cumbersome and difficult for some of us noncomputer types to get up to speed, this process would give us the ability to manage an unmanageable amount of information.

The problem was, again, the money: until the County Council approved our supplemental, we couldn't hire our own outside contractor, and the contractor couldn't hire the young lawyers who would do the sorting. The County Council didn't want to approve the money until the Office of Public Defense used up the money it already had— even though that money had been earmarked for all the rest of the county's poor defendants. OPD wouldn't agree to leave everyone else without a nickel, just for Gary, and hope that the County Council made good on its obligation to fund defense for the indigent at some later point. Unless we got the money that we had to have, we were stuck reading the electro-pages just as they were when they came in. The text-string search capability wasn't particularly useful because it tended to generate so many different hits and often misread letters. Every passing reference, of course, was returned without regard to its significance, which made focused inquiry almost impossibly time-consuming.

One thing that had jumped out from this initial discovery process, however, was the account of a woman who had proved critical to the original Green River Task Force's 1987 search of Gary. This was Paige Miley. In 1983, Paige Miley had been a twenty-year-old prostitute working on Pacific Highway South. On the last day of October 1983—Halloween, the same day I'd first become a public defense attorney with ACA—she had been working the Strip in concert with another young woman, Kim Nelson, who used the street name of "Star." Star was a very tall blonde woman; she'd told Paige Miley that if the Green River Killer ever came after her, she'd make sure he regretted it. So the subject of the unknown killer, who had then been much in the news from the discovery of a flurry of victims' remains near the airport, was on the minds of both women.

Miley and Star had been plying their trade in a bus shelter across from the White Shutters Inn. At one point in the afternoon, Miley had been picked up by a john, and she left Star alone in the bus shelter. When Miley returned some minutes later, Star was no longer there. Miley assumed that Star had picked up her own trick and that she'd be back shortly. But she never returned that day—or any other.

A day or so later, Miley was again in the bus shelter when a man came by in a pickup truck.

"Where's your tall blonde friend?" the man in the truck asked Miley.

At that point in her career as a prostitute, Miley was sharp enough to recognize the implications of this statement—after all, she'd only been on the highway that morning with Star for a few minutes, so that meant the man in the truck had to have seen them together. She guessed that the man in the truck might be the killer, if one assumed that Star had fallen into the killer's clutches, which seemed to Miley to be a distinct possibility at that point.

Giving some innocuous answer to the man in the pickup truck, Miley was able to detach herself long enough to put in a telephone call to the police. The call was routed to the small task force that had then been working with Detective Reichert. Another detective, Ben Colwell, interviewed Miley. She told the story of Star's disappearance, described the man in the truck and—according to Miley—had provided a license plate number for the truck.[4] The description of the man in the truck, and the truck itself, matched Gary. And Gary, when he was interviewed by the police in the 1980s, admitted having had this conversation with a woman who might have been Miley.

Several years later, Nelson's skeletal remains were discovered far east of Seattle in one of the I-90 clusters. The significance of Miley's encounter with the man in the truck was therefore to link Gary to those clusters—just as the DNA had supposedly linked Gary to the river victims, and to Carol Christensen. Miley's account therefore suggested fairly strongly that Gary was in fact *the* Green River Killer.

By the spring of 2002, however, Paige Miley was in fairly bad shape. Twenty years of prostitution and a soul-devouring drug habit had made her an iffy witness for the prosecution—iffy in the sense that her credibility might be attacked by the defense, but especially iffy in that, given her lifestyle, she might well not live long enough to testify in any trial. As a result, the prosecutors wanted to fly her to Seattle from Las Vegas, where she was then residing in the Clark County jail, to give a videotaped deposition. But on the eve of the deposition, our side received a large number of facts about Paige's past—her drug use, her complete record of arrests, among other things—that needed to be checked out before we could conduct our side of the deposition. After considerable pushing and shoving in court, the deposition was postponed indefinitely, and Paige returned to Las Vegas, where she began a term in a state prison. Subsequent developments eventually made the taking of this deposition unnecessary, as it turned out. But the ability to test faded memories wasn't the only thing lost to time.

As part of the trial preparation, Todd and investigator Bettye Witherspoon went on a number of occasions to the Property Management Unit (PMU) to review, document, and photograph items of evidence. In his cluttered office one afternoon in May 2002, Todd told me about one of their earliest ventures to PMU.

"First, we waited in a room for Marc Church (evidence specialist with the Green River Task Force) to go get a box of stuff. He comes back in and puts it on the table. Of course, he's got his rubber gloves on. 'Some rats got to this one' he tells me and shows me the corner of the box. It was all chewed up and falling apart."

"Rats?" I wanted to make sure I heard him right.

"Yes," Todd was chuckling. "Rats. Bettye was all grossed out. So anyhow," Todd continued, "Church reaches in and takes out an old manila envelope, with evidence tape. He cuts it open, very carefully." Todd was demonstrating as he spoke. "He slowly pulls out a clear plastic enve-lope, trace evidence found with Opal Mills. Removes a folded paper bindle. It has some writing on it. I don't know what's in there . . . we're watching, waiting as he slowly unfolds the bindle . . . EMPTY!" Todd was holding an imaginary bindle in his hands, looking at it in disbe-lief. *Where did the evidence go?* Todd began to laugh loudly. "It was hilarious!"

As it turned out, there were many boxes of evidence that had been tampered with—by the ubiquitous rodents, who had made away with the stuff for the purpose of making nests. Whether the appetites of rats would do Gary any good in the long run, though, was much harder to say. They couldn't have eaten the entire case up—there was just too much of it.

17

By July 2002, the mud wrestling over money was in its final round. The longer the County Council delayed funding our supplemental, the worse off we were. In our case, money was time—time to investigate; time to identify, track down, and interview critical witnesses; time to find and employ all the experts we needed to test the state's evidence; time to make sense of the gigantic pile of electro-documents that were by now streaming in, at a rate of about sixty thousand pages a month. We had four lawyers working for us who really hadn't been paid for their work so far, and we had a platoon of high-priced experts who couldn't even open a file until we got the money we needed and had been promised.

We decided to go to court.

On July 1, we filed a motion with Judge Jones asking him to order the council to put up the money. "The delay in providing additional resources has continued to delay the preparation of Mr. Ridgway's defense," our motion said. "The defense is not only short-handed with regard to all the work that must be done, but additional work is also created, such as this motion, thereby diverting the work of the four

lawyers who are currently working on the case. Mr. Ridgway's constitutional rights are being ignored by the County Council. Their inac-
tion and delay is building a record for potential reversal if there should
be an appeal in this case. Additional resources must be provided to
ensure Mr. Ridgway's constitutional rights are not violated further."

We appended a report written by the council's own staff that noted:
"If the county were to refuse to provide the resources, the judge could
dismiss the charges. . . ."

No one on the council seemed to have read this staff memo carefully, however. More than two weeks after it had been received, the
supplemental still had not been approved. We were informed that
maybe, just maybe, the council might get around to it in a few weeks,
once the Office of Public Defense gave a formal explanation of why it
couldn't use the money it already had.

On July 3, Judge Jones issued an order to the council to show cause
why it should not be compelled to immediately appropriate the
money, on pain of contempt, or worse—even, possibly, dismissal of
the case.

Yikes! This was a threat that got the council's attention. How would
it look if the case against the most notorious defendant in the county's
history were thrown out because politicians had dithered over who
was going to pick up the tab? The council had its own lawyer respond,
posthaste, explaining that the council hadn't understood that the OPD
hadn't already used the money it had on hand to fund our requirements. Sorry!

On July 22, 2002, the council finally passed the "Ridgway supplemental," and the full Team Ridgway was finally up and running.

—◆—

We hadn't been twiddling our thumbs while all this was going on,
though. By May 2002, we'd already identified quite a lot of information that the prosecutors had in their possession but hadn't yet provided to us. One was the so-called Jensen Database.

For all the years when he'd been the only detective assigned to the
Green River case—mostly, from 1988 up until 2001—Detective Jensen
had patiently assembled a computerized record of virtually every tip
that had come in to the police since the day the case had begun in
1982. The records also included references to other murder cases that
weren't on the Green River list but arguably might have been included.
In fact, we had been provided with copies of several memoranda that

had been written by Jensen over the years, generally recommending that a number of other cases be added to the official list. Jensen's recommendations dated as far back as early 1993, almost a decade before Gary's arrest. In one memo, Jensen had asked the higher-ups of the Sheriff's Department to add as many as fifteen other victims to the official Green River list, some murdered as late as 1988. This request was turned down by the Sheriff's Department's brain trust, however, which continued to insist that as far as it could see, the Green River murders had stopped in early 1984.

We wanted all of the records in this database, reasoning that the police might have overlooked some tip that identified a better suspect than Gary; and we wanted the records on the other fifteen cases that looked like Green River murders, even to Jensen, but which weren't, at least according to the pooh-bahs of the Sheriff's Department. That was the only way we could check to make sure that the real killer hadn't somehow slipped past a Sheriff's Department that was by that time convinced, except for Jensen, that the killer had long since left the area.

We'd also developed a list of about fifty similar homicides, including all of those cited by Jensen, for which we wanted to see all investigative records. But the prosecutor's office essentially drew the line on this, saying they weren't part of the Green River case and therefore did not have to be disclosed in discovery. *At least voluntarily.*

Undaunted, Todd drafted a subpoena to the King County Medical Examiner's Office for their records, such as investigative reports and autopsies, on each of these fifty-some-odd cases. We were pleasantly surprised when the Medical Examiner's Office agreed to turn these records over to us. These cases, many of them similar if not quite identical to the Green River cases, gave us an alternate universe in which to search for other suspects, especially when there were commonalities that linked to names and locations in the Jensen database. If we could, for example, show that Gary could not have committed these other, similar crimes—we called them "Red River," to distinguish them from Green River—that would help us establish reasonable doubt that Gary was responsible for the Green River murders. And who knew? With a lot of work and a little luck, we might even identify "the real killer."

As our team filled out, Eric Lindell was put in charge of our other-suspects investigation. Investigators Denise Scafidi, Bettye Witherspoon, and Lis Frost led the team's concerted effort to evaluate these similar cases that had not made the official Green River list. Denise and Bettye made a map of the I-5 corridor through western Washington. They added a clear plastic overlay with a green dot everywhere a Green River victim was found. They made a second plastic overlay with red dots for all other similar unsolved female homicide victims. It was a powerful visual exhibit. Many, many red dots were found in close proximity to green dots. And many red dots were in remote areas, similar to the types of areas the green clusters had been found. In all, there were over a hundred dots on the map. But they weren't just dots. They represented over a hundred young female murder victims. It was a sobering demonstration.

In the first few days of the case, Jeff Baird had provided me with the Washington State Patrol Crime Laboratory's DNA results from the testing done on the Carol Christensen, Opal Mills, and Marcia Chapman murders. Once the County Council had approved our funding, we were able to send these reports, along with all their backup materials, such as photos from the tests and the scientists' lab notes, to our own experts for their evaluation. Even though the methodology of the tests that had linked the victims' DNA to Gary's DNA seemed to be properly done, we wanted to be sure *everything* was done correctly—that's why we had to have our own experts.

As it happened, the Sheriff's Department had included a Red River victim in these initial tests—LeAnn Wilcox, whose murder in early 1982 some thought had been the actual start of the Green River crimes, and who had been acquainted with some of the Green River victims. Over the years, there had been vigorous debate within the Green River Task Force on whether LeAnn should be included on the official "Green River" list. The state's tests of DNA found with LeAnn showed that Gary was *excluded* as a possible source. This gave us solid evidence that someone other than Gary Ridgway had been involved in strangling young women and dumping their bodies in rural areas of south King County and would almost certainly open the door for us to eventually request DNA evidence from any of the other "Red River" cases. If we could find DNA matches among the fifty or so Red River victims, we would have made an excellent start at finding a viable alternative suspect to Gary. Presumably, the state had already done this, and we would ask for everything they did. But in any event, we would have to do this ourselves as well.

As we came to grips with the evidence that had been warehoused by the state for so many years, we again realized what a mammoth undertaking it was to prepare for Gary's trial. The Green River Task Force had accumulated over 170 videotapes, 500 audiotapes, 15,000 photographs, and over 10,000 items of evidence. Each of these had to be inspected. Worse, the videotapes were not just an hour or two. Many were surveillance videos, sitting and watching a house and the various comings and goings over the course of a couple weeks. Some were videotapes of mitochondrial DNA testing. Have you ever watched paint dry over the course of three or four days? Fascinating stuff. That responsibility went to one of our outside DNA experts, Dr. Randell Libby of the University of Washington, who knew what to watch for.

The audiotapes were also a pain in the neck. If you have ever tried to listen to a twenty-year-old taped interview, you know you don't just play it through and hear and understand everything. You have to rewind. "What'd she say?" Rewind it again. Sometimes again. The sound quality can be very poor, which makes it just that much more difficult and time-consuming. But we had to review it all. Most of those tapes were of witness interviews. Listening to those would be the responsibility of Tony and the investigators working on the guilt-phase preparation for the charged cases of Mills, Hinds, and Chapman.

Eric Lindell and his investigator, Jay Joslin, were assigned to handle the Christensen case. It was so different from the others that we'd decided to try to have a separate trial on that count—a *Motion to Sever Counts* in legal terminology. None of us thought Judge Jones would grant it, but we all agreed it would be a good appeal issue.

If it's true that a picture is worth a thousand words, that meant that each of the fifteen thousand photographs had their own story to tell. Many of these pictures were skeleton recovery scenes, showing just how each victim had been found and what the investigators had done while recovering the bones and associated evidence. We retained a crime scene expert, John Thornton, a former forensic sciences professor from the University of California, Berkeley, and a nationally recognized expert, to review the crime scene photos for us. We sent autopsy photographs to Dr. Daniel Spitz, a nationally recognized forensic pathologist from Florida, whom Todd and I had met at a death penalty conference in Austin, Texas.

The inspection of the physical evidence, much of it contained in small envelopes, continued to be a time-consuming task. As our inspections continued at the county's warehouse, we took digital photographs of each item and later put these into our database.

Finally, there was also a huge trove of raw records, traffic tickets, jail records, motel registration cards, police field interrogation reports, patrol officers' notebooks, employment records for businesses located on the Strip or near places where skeletons had been found—a huge mass of potentially relevant information that investigators had once accumulated in an effort to mechanically winnow out the identity of the elusive killer back in the 1980s. Any one of these might prove useful to Gary's defense, once we understood what to look for. Most of these had been stashed in cardboard boxes at the task force headquarters—about 230 boxes, in fact.

At first, we wanted the prosecution to copy all this material onto CD-Rom, so we could stick it in our growing database; we reasoned that something in these seemingly extraneous records might give credibility to some defense witnesses we might call. The records might be used to verify their time and location at some critical point. The prosecutors balked at this. They said it wasn't relevant. Eventually, we worked out a compromise: they wouldn't copy it, but we could go to the task force headquarters to look up things if we determined it was necessary.

Another cache of useful information we received during this period of time was the complete follow-up reports of all the main detectives. Perhaps of most interest to us was the follow-up report of Sheriff Reichert. It had been Reichert, after all, who had been the original lead detective on the case, far earlier than when Jensen and the others had come into the case. It had been Reichert who was at the Green River the day that Debra Bonner's body had been found on August 12; it had been Reichert who had discovered Opal Mills's body on August 15, three days later, when it was too late to put surveillance up around the river area; it had been Reichert who had focused, erroneously, on Melvyn Foster in the initial weeks of the investigation; and it had been Reichert who was nominally in charge when the tip from Paige Miley, possibly including a pickup truck license plate, had been swallowed up in the chaotic maelstrom in the fall of 1983, right in the midst of all the murders. So we were very interested to see what Reichert had made of this monstrous case that had remained unsolved for so many years. Because it had been Sheriff Reichert, front and center, on November 30, 2001, basking in the hero worship of the man who "captured" the Green River Killer.

We made a number of requests for Reichert's complete follow-up report, but it wasn't until late in the spring that it finally arrived. Contained in another thick, black, three-ring binder, the follow-up report covered the critical period from August 1982 to July 1987—almost five years of Dave Reichert's life, typewritten, often single-spaced, and encompassed in nearly six hundred pages.

The most astonishing thing about the sheriff's follow-up report—essentially a log of everything that he'd done on the case during the five years he worked on it—was his apparent obsession with Melvyn Foster. It was clear that the former cabdriver occupied Reichert's thoughts on very nearly a daily basis. Reichert developed informants—among them some of Foster's own family members, and, surprisingly, Barbara Kubik-Patten, the self-proclaimed psychic—who kept him informed of Foster's movements and his moods. The smallest rumor about Foster made its way into Reichert's follow-up log—down to what Mel Foster was having for breakfast. Reading the report made it clear that Reichert had always felt that Foster was the killer. And no wonder. Foster, according to Reichert's report, had been given multiple lie detector tests about the case, and according to the county's polygraph examiner, had failed every single one.[1]

And Gary had passed his one polygraph test, given by the very same examiner.

—⁓—

Ever since the Sheriff's Department had grilled Gary for about two hours after his arrest on November 30, 2001, we had speculated about what had actually happened in those two hours before Greg Girard had arrived. We had recovered a report by one sheriff's deputy, who said he'd been detailed to take notes but that once Gary had asked to see a lawyer, he'd simply stopped his note taking. And then he had destroyed his notes.

Gary, of course, insisted that he had denied killing anyone, during this two-hour interrogation without a lawyer. Eventually, we learned that the Sheriff's Department had videotaped the encounter but claimed there was no sound. We asked for a copy of the videotape. Sure enough, there was no sound. Neither was there any evidence of the detectives beating Gary with rubber hoses, which I guess was why they had continued the video without the sound. After watching the videotape, Todd hit on the idea of hiring a lipreader to see if we could figure out what Gary had actually said. The effort was a bust; however, Gary kept holding his hand in front of his mouth, and the detectives' backs were to the camera, so we still weren't sure what Gary had actually said as opposed to what he'd told us he'd said.

Then, sometime in the fall of 2002, we encountered the follow-up report of Detective Jim Doyon. Doyon had been on the Green River Task Force off and on for years. With Tom Jensen, his onetime partner, he was one of the few detectives who knew the case inside and out. Doyon's follow-up report, actually filed in early February 2002, said that Gary had been shown photographs of the Green River victims on the afternoon of his arrest and had been asked, "Is this your work?"

Gary, according to Doyon, had responded with an "uh-uh," which Doyon interpreted as a yes. This, of course, was why the interview should have been taped: such a damning admission should have more than a detective's mere interpretation to back it up.

There was more. Doyon reported the following statement by Gary in reference to the large number of victims:

"I think you will find that not all of them are mine," Gary was reputed to have told the detectives.

Egads! If these statements in Doyon's report were true, they seemed to constitute admissions by Gary, only hours after his arrest, that at least *some* of the murders had been committed by him.

As soon as we discovered this potentially devastating statement attributed by Doyon to Gary, I hustled over to the eleventh floor of the jail for another visit in the face-to-face cubicle with our client.

After our greetings, I asked Gary about the statement. "Jeez, Gary, Doyon says you told him they would find that quote 'they're not all mine,' end quote! Did you say that?"

"No," Gary shook his head. "I didn't say that. I don't remember exactly what I said. They would kinda put words in my mouth. But no, I didn't say they weren't all mine." He seemed clear. "And besides," he went on, "the detectives had told me that once I asked for a lawyer, they couldn't use anything I said." Apparently, Gary had been listening when he was read his rights.

"Well, when the detective said they couldn't use anything you said, after you asked for a lawyer, that wasn't actually true," I told Gary. Now we finally had a discussion about post-Miranda remarks—the legal subtlety I had decided not to tell Gary about on the night of his arrest, so many months before. "As long as they don't coerce you—beat it out of you—they can argue it's admissible for rebuttal."

"Oh, admissible for rebuttal . . ." He nodded, seeming to understand.

"Which means if you testify, they can offer those statements they say you said to contradict anything you say if you testify. For example, if you testify at trial 'I had sex with prostitutes, but I didn't *kill* any,' the state could offer this other statement against you. Detective Doyon could get up and say 'Mr. Ridgway said, 'You'll find they are not all mine.' In comes the statement."

"Yeah, but I didn't say that," Gary said.

"But that'll be your word against Doyon and [Detective Randy] Mullinax," I told him. "We'll argue it should have been taped, and it shouldn't be admitted at all. But I imagine Judge Jones will most likely let them use it in rebuttal, if you testify."

"So you're saying I shouldn't testify?"

"I'm saying it's a problem. We'll have a pre-trial motion to get it thrown out, and Judge Jones will decide whether or not they can use it. Of course, we'll have to try to get that hearing closed, so the press doesn't blab it all over the world. But if the judge rules the state *can* use what they say you said, in rebuttal to any of your later testimony, then I would say it'd be a real bad move for you to take the witness stand. We'd have to see how everything is going before we make a final decision. Actually you . . . *you'll* make that decision. We'll advise you, but that's ultimately your call."

"Oooh-K."

But by now I was thinking, *What a quagmire!* First we'd have to argue this incriminating statement shouldn't be allowed in as evidence. To do that, we'd have to get a pre-trial hearing to suppress the supposed statement; and we'd have to get that hearing closed to the press, who would certainly object, because the last thing we'd want is for this supposed statement to be published or broadcast before trial, and the first thing the press would want was to find out what it was that we didn't want out. Truly a quagmire.

If the statement *did* come out publicly, it would probably cook Gary's goose for sure with potential jurors. We might not have wanted Gary to testify at his trial anyway, but this effectively robbed our side of that option. This was one of the reasons why defense lawyers want to get to the client as soon as possible. And also one of the reasons why the police like to postpone that representation for as long as they can. And also a good argument for requiring video and audiotaping of all police interviews, both witnesses and suspects.

18

We all thought we were finished with the fight over money, but we were wrong. In August, the *Seattle Times* was back. They still wanted to publish the special master's name, reasoning that the identity of a person recommending a governmental action spending nearly $3 million of the taxpayers' money for a single defendant ought to be a fact known to the public. They wanted Judge Jones to formally unseal Kate Pflaumer's name. Presumably, they would then attempt to interview her to get her to justify her decisions.

"The trial of Mr. Ridgway is obviously a matter of public interest," said the *Times'* lawyer, Marshall Nelson, in his brief to Judge Jones, "and the conduct and funding of his defense is a matter of intense public debate. At the vortex of that controversy is the process through which defense funding is reviewed and approved. Public officials and members of the press and the public have voiced frustration at the public cost."

Indeed they had. As the controversy over funding Gary's defense spread, even after the council had finally approved the money, but the actual cost began to sink in, people began to take potshots at just about everyone associated with the case—over the airwaves in broadcast talk shows, and in letters to the editor. A man identifying himself as W. A. Byers of Renton, for example, wrote to the *South County Journal,* our local paper in the south county:

> The judge who is telling us that we have to spend millions to defend Ridgway is way off base. Maybe he has a bunch of lawyer friends that aren't doing too well and has decided to put them to work on Ridgway's defense.
>
> I have never seen so many lawyers on one case to defend one man with the taxpayers expected to pick up the tab. Remember who that judge is and see if we can't get someone with more sense on the bench.[1]

There was also an editorial cartoon depicting the Ridgway defense pulling the switch on an electric chair holding the King County taxpayers, who scream, "Green River Killer? Make that the GreenBACK killer . . ."

The city council of Normandy Park, a small suburb just south of SeaTac Airport, unanimously passed a resolution criticizing the County Council for threatening to close pools and parks while spending millions of dollars on Gary Ridgway. A county councilman, the late Kent Pullen—my own representative—borrowed an image from Satterberg and called us a "Cadillac defense," and said the court's order to the council to put up the money amounted to "judicial theft."

It went on and on, for days, then weeks. We were being bombarded with negative reactions and prejudicial publicity. But eventually, we did get some support. Two prominent Seattle defense attorneys, Jeff Robinson and Irwin Schwartz, wrote a long letter to the *Times,* explaining why the costs were so high and why these bills needed to be paid, to avoid the possibility of a later reversal. Of course, this only precipitated more letters to the editor, rebutting Robinson and Schwartz and blaming them and their ilk for the death penalty reversals to begin with. Eventually, however, editorial writers for the three main local papers—the *Times,* the *Seattle P-I,* and the *Journal*—accepted the premise that the taxpayers *had* to pay up front to prevent potential reversal on appeal, and they pointed out that it would be much more costly to the community to have to have to try the case twice.

An editorial in the July 21 edition of the *South County Journal* read:

COUNCIL SHOULD OK MONEY FOR RIDGWAY DEFENSE

The King County Council is taking a serious risk as it hems and haws over approving more money for the defense of accused serial killer Gary Ridgway. . . . We know that the $1.9 million figure is a jaw-dropper and that many people question why so much money should be spent defending Ridgway. The answer is that Ridgway needs both an adequate defense and one equal to what the county is going to spend investigating and prosecuting the case. Anything less only sets up a future legal issue over whether Ridgway, if convicted, actually got a fair trial.

Coming at a time when the county faces a $52 million deficit, paying out $1.9 million to a defense team is sure to rankle many people. However, a person's life is at stake and the prosecution will be going all out for a conviction. When this case is finally settled, it needs to be settled once and for all.

Setting up a reason—any reason—for an appeal will only add to the county's final expense.

Not everyone accepted this reasoning, unfortunately. In late July, even after the money had been approved, Todd received an angry voice mail directed at the Green River defense team. The female voice started calm and rational, objecting to the huge amounts of taxpayer money spent to defend someone who killed women. But as the words came out, they grew angrier, more irrational, and loaded with profanity.

"Would they give this kind of money to a woman if she killed a man?? OF COURSE NOT!! But it's OKAY to kill a WOMAN!! We'll pay MILLIONS to fucking help him WIN and fucking WALK FREE!! You Fuckers . . . Fuck! FUCKING . . . fuck . . . FUCK!!!" The message ended with an abrupt slamming down of the telephone.

Todd made a tape and brought it to our next defense team meeting for entertainment purposes. Although it was sadly humorous, it was a little creepy to realize that irrational people were out there blaming us for our efforts to provide an accused person his rights under the Constitution.

Then it hit even closer to home, for me. During this same meeting, I got a call from Kelly. She had just opened our mail. We'd gotten an anonymous letter, she said, and read it to me.

It began with a quote from me that recently had been on a television news Web site: "Death penalty litigation is expensive," I'd said.

"Our community is putting its resources together to try to kill a human being. If the defense can't be funded, then you can't prosecute the man."

This quote apparently maddened the anonymous letter writer. He or she wrote:

> You are nothing but a criminal also. There is plenty of evidence to convict Mr. Ridgway already without you making a total charade out of this. Find another way to entertain and expose yourself . . . perhaps AT YOUR OWN EXPENSE!?
>
> There are people all over the state struggling to make ends meet; struggling to feed their families, while overpaid compassionless idiots like you spent 90% of your energies trying to rip us all off! How dare you try to spend our money so frivolously while trying to masquerade as a fair, caring, ethical human being! Do you not picture yourself answering to God some day like most of us envision? Are you some kind of atheist?
>
> I hope you and your family are highly embarrassed about your senseless comments and change your tune soon. Take a look around you. Take a look at reality. Yeah, we'd all like to demand $1.9 million a year for our jobs we're working on, but our conscience stops us. Hopefully, you will come to your sense soon. Just because you might stand a chance of getting by with it DOES NOT make it right!!!!!!
>
> Wisen Up![2]

I told the rest of the team that Kelly and I had received a weird anonymous letter at our home address. Everyone joked about it even though we all knew it raised serious concerns—especially the fact that it had been mailed to our house and that it had mentioned Kelly and our family. As soon as the meeting was over, I drove home.

As I headed south on I-5, I thought about all this negative publicity and how it might be affecting Kelly, Sean, and Marley. Kelly had been very patient, occasionally giving me a hard time about the money issues. We were in the middle of another summer swim season at Kent Swim and Tennis Club, with swim meets every Tuesday and Thursday nights. Up at six and going full steam ahead until ten or eleven at night. With everything that was going on, the summer was whizzing by, and I hadn't been able to spend as much time with Kelly and the kids as I had planned. And now this letter.

When I got home, Kelly was fine, but a little unnerved. Obviously, the author of the letter had his or her facts wrong. I'm not "compassionless," and I'm certainly not "overpaid." As senior lawyers for ACA, Todd and I both earned a little over $84,000 a year—a comfortable salary but one we'd have been paid whether we were defending Gary or someone else; Todd and I were not making an extra dime out of the money appropriated by the County Council for Gary Ridgway's defense. We'd get the same paycheck every two weeks, whether we were representing car thieves and drug dealers—or Gary Ridgway. It didn't make any difference. (So, to whoever wrote this letter, all I can say is "Wisen up!")

"Why do you think this letter was sent to our house?" Kelly asked, with understandable concern. "I mean, this sounds like a threat . . . 'answering to God someday' . . . I don't like it."

"I don't blame you, but I don't think it's anything to seriously worry about," I tried to sound reassuring.

"Do they think *you're* getting the $1.9 million?"

"Sounds like it," I said. "Jeez, I wish. Then I could retire after this is over. The person's obviously a nut," trying to alleviate Kelly's concerns.

"Exactly!" she retorted. "That's why I'm worried. They know our home address."

My attempt to mollify Kelly had backfired. "Yeah, but they're just venting their anger in the letter. I think a woman wrote it," I said, trying to change the direction of the conversation.

"I think it's a man," Kelly countered. "Obviously a God-fearing Christian man. Maybe you should start going to church." She was getting her feistiness back. I put my arms around her and squeezed her tight. She resisted at first then hugged me back.

I gave her a kiss and whispered to her, "You know I love you and will never let anything happen to you or Sean or Marley."

"I'm not really that worried about us," she said and pulled away to look into my eyes. "It's you I'm worried about. We need you around. I don't know what we'd do without you. Just be careful. Please." She gave me a kiss.

For the first time in my twenty years as a public defender, Kelly and I considered removing our names from the phone book. I had never been bothered at home before, so I had never ever worried about it until then. I took a certain pride in not being afraid to have my name, home address, and home phone number listed for anyone to look up.

After this "wisen up" letter, though, others on our team thought it might not be a good idea to be so publicly accessible. Anyone who was so sure what God really wanted might be dangerous. But I didn't want to change my existence, or that of my family, because of pressure from some nutcase who didn't have the guts to sign his own name. Kelly agreed.

"But do me a favor, please," she asked. "Watch your back. We want you around for a while. After all," she said, "*somebody* has to mow the lawn and take out the garbage."

19

I continued meeting with Gary throughout the summer, while all of this political pushing and shoving over the money needed to defend him was going on. Like others on our team who had contact with him, I continued to marvel at his demeanor. He simply was not acting like someone accused of being a heinous, multiple murderer. He showed almost no evidence of mental stress and was unfailingly polite and friendly. The jailers unanimously agreed he was a model prisoner—cooperative almost to a fault. He continued to deny that he'd ever killed anyone, although admitting that he had patronized hundreds, many even a thousand, prostitutes over the years, a fact that he also said made him ashamed of himself.

"You know, what you ought to do," Gary suggested, "is try to track down some of the ladies I dated. They'll tell you I was a nice, normal customer. I treated them well."

"You mean, to show that you weren't ever violent or dangerous?" I asked.

"Yeah, not violent or dangerous," he said. "They could show that I wasn't into killing prostitutes, just dating 'em."

"Yeah," I said. "That's not a bad idea." I wanted to give him credit for coming up with an interesting avenue of investigation. "I guess I'll have to hit the streets with your picture and see if I can find some of these women you dated." In my mind, I was seeing images of myself on the dark corners and shadows of Seattle, showing Gary's picture to all the aging hookers. After all, the twenty- and thirty-year-olds weren't in the business in the eighties.

"Yeah, you could do that," he said, smiling, with a twinkle in his eye. "Or, I thought, maybe you could just get the booking photos of all the prostitutes arrested in '82 and '83." He had another idea. "I could look at the mug shots and see if I remember any. That way, you wouldn't have to go looking for prostitutes. I don't think your wife would want you out there doing that," he said with a smile. On that point, he was surely correct.

During the course of our many face-to-face meetings in the jail, we'd exchanged information about our lives. Obviously, Gary's three marriages were an important part of understanding him, and I had no reluctance to talk to him about my own family. It was all part of putting a client at ease—to allow him to see me as a person not all that much different than him, except he was on one side of the bars and I was on the other.

In many of my face-to-faces with Gary, he seemed to adopt the persona of a strategist; that is, his posture was one of judiciously considering the various legal angles and possible solutions to those problems. In retrospect, I realized that he was merely reflecting back to me the way I came across to him. In other words, he was aping me—or at least his perception of me. I eventually discovered that Gary came across differently to others on our team. With women, he tended to be emotional, sometimes weepy, whereas with Todd, he could seem like a tough guy. It was uncanny how he could pick up someone's expectation and reflect it back unerringly.

In my face-to-faces, I always took pains to lay out the current situation and what our possible alternatives might be. I was always analytical in these discussions, and true to form, Gary's behavior mirrored my own, whether he understood the nuances or not. Even in his minor complaints about the jail, he tended to try to seem as though he grasped the longer view, at least in these conversations with me. For example, in complaining about an ingrown toenail that he couldn't seem to get the jail health staff to treat, he asked about medication, "but no sodium Pentothal," he said.

No sodium Pentothal—the truth drug. Ha! Ha! A joke, but one that indicated that Gary was trying to think as he thought I might think. This was classic Gary: to gather in the way others thought and then to try to conform his behavior to that expectation.

In March 2002, we'd hired a nationally known forensic psychologist, Dr. Mark Cunningham of Texas, to evaluate Gary. Whereas Dr. Beaver was a neuropsychologist, who specialized in organic brain damage, one of Dr. Cunningham's areas of expertise was in the realm of *future dangerousness*, also known as *risk assessment*. He studied and evaluated murder defendants to see what threat they may pose in the future if they were to receive a life sentence instead of the death penalty. His initial assessment, done in the spring as part of our original mitigation package, was that Gary had adjusted very well to incarceration and posed no future danger to other inmates or corrections officials—an important point for a jury to consider if we were ever to ask them not to vote for the death penalty.

In addition to his *future dangerousness analysis,* Cunningham also contributed heavily behind the scenes as a consultant on all of the mental and psychological issues. He had been involved in dozens of death penalty cases all over the country, and his insights had proved invaluable.

Cunningham returned for an additional interview of Gary in early September 2002. Afterward, he expressed puzzlement about Gary.

"Interviewing Gary is like trying to grab a cloud," he told me, meaning, just when you thought you had a handle on him, your fingers closed around something that wasn't really there. There didn't seem to be any core, or if there was, it was so well hidden, possibly even from Gary himself, that one might never find it. In a very basic sense, Gary was all outside, no inside—a human hologram, a practiced exterior image surrounding something that didn't seem to actually exist.

With the exception of the disputed "not all of them are mine" statement, and the DNA, our team had yet to see any other really strong evidence that Gary was the killer. True, the discovery process was still going on, with thousands of electro-pages now streaming in; but the vast bulk of this material had to do with the old investigation, and only a small fragment had to do with Gary. After all, he had been repeatedly discounted as a suspect throughout much of the period of the most active investigation. So while we were learning reams of information about the forty-nine victims, hundreds of other suspects, and the fifty-some-odd Red River cases, we were still committed to "Plan A"—convincing a jury that Gary was not the killer. Many on the team believed we could establish that there was reasonable doubt about Gary's guilt, if we could get an unbiased jury. Of course, *that* was a big if.

We were aware, however, that the state was still subjecting many old pieces of physical evidence to renewed testing. It was their hope that they could find more hard links between the victims and Gary, such as additional DNA, hairs, fibers, fingerprints, and the like. In July 2002, Jeff Baird from the prosecutor's office told us that a tiny bone fragment had been found in a vacuum cleaner bag at Gary's old house. The bone fragment was examined by world-renowned forensic anthropologist Dr. Alan Walker of Penn State University. The newspapers and TV reports echoed the preeminent expert's preliminary conclusion that the fragment likely came from a human skull. The prosecution wanted to take this bone fragment to an east coast laboratory for mitochondrial DNA testing. Mitochondrial DNA, or mtDNA, is passed on only by the mother. If the mtDNA from the fragment matched mtDNA from the mother or a maternally linked relative of one of the victims, this would be devastating evidence against Gary, strong evidence that Gary had kept a portion of one of his victim's skeletal remains in his old house. The problem was, however, that the fragment would have to be destroyed as part of the testing process.

Destroying the evidence in order to use it was one thing. We knew that sometimes it couldn't be avoided when the sample was so small. But we balked when the laboratory refused to allow our own expert to watch the testing. The test was so sensitive, the lab explained, that even the mere presence of a non-laboratory person in the same room could potentially contaminate the procedure. Eventually, Judge Jones issued an order permitting the destruction of the bone fragment and excluding us from observing. He did, however, order the laboratory to provide all documents about the test, including a videotape of the entire test procedure. The news media covered this pretest hearing with rapt interest, along with the speculation from Dr. Walker that the bone fragment might have come from someone's skull. Macabre sells on TV, we all knew that. In the obligatory after-hearing interviews in the halls of the courthouse, Tony and I both downplayed Jones's approval of the one-sided test.

"It could be a dog. I don't have any idea. I'm assuming it's not related to this case," I suggested.

"It's probably a chicken bone. Maybe they'll get Gary for Colonel Sanders's disappearance," Tony quipped. As usual, he had a way with words: the news people loved *that* one. And I hadn't even known that Colonel Sanders was missing.

As the fall of 2002 unfolded, then, our side kept waiting for the results of this critical bone fragment test, and other such forensic examinations then under way. We all knew that if any of these tests linked Gary to more victims, we'd probably be compelled to explore Plan B—trying to trade Gary's confession for life in prison—if we were to have any hope of saving Gary's life.

I explained all this again to Gary one day in another face-to-face.

"You know, we're trying to save your life," I told him. "On the team, it's my role to prepare for the sentencing phase. If the jury finds you guilty of aggravated murder, we proceed to sentencing . . . what we call the 'penalty phase' of the trial."

"Right. I understand."

"And saving your life is going to be tough if we get to a penalty phase. That means the jury will already have found you guilty beyond a reasonable doubt. So they're not going to be on your side. They'll probably want to impose death."

"Yeah, I know." Gary understood this all too clearly.

"So as it stands right now, the best shot we have at saving your life is raising a reasonable doubt about whether you're guilty. Because once they find you guilty, well, you know. So we have to try to raise doubt with the jury about who actually killed these girls."

"Oooh-K."

"But that argument will be much weaker if they find some other forensic link between you and any of the other victims. I mean, we're arguing now that you just happened to have had sex with these three victims. It was a coincidence, but you dated so much, it's possible. But I think that's the outer limit for believability."

"Well, I did date a lot."

"Yes, you did, that's very true. I'm just not sure if the jury will believe it was just coincidence. It's like you were either the world's unluckiest patronizer of prostitutes or the world's luckiest serial killer."

Gary nodded.

"But one more forensic link—like DNA, hair, fiber, paint, whatever—and it's going to wipe out the 'coincidence' argument."

He nodded once more.

"So all this testing that's going on . . . if they find something, anything linking you to another victim, you're screwed. But if they don't, if they keep coming up empty-handed on all these other tests they're doing, that's good. The absence of any additional forensic links would help the 'coincidence argument.' Do you follow what I'm saying?"

"Yeah, I know what you're saying."

"So . . . what am I saying?"

"That if these tests come up with some other evidence tying me to one of the other victims, I'm screwed."

"Yup, basically, that's it. And if that does happen, we'll be having some serious discussions, and we may have to look at other ways to save your life. You know what I mean?"

"Yeah." I saw that whatever his mental deficits, he knew exactly what I was talking about—the prospect of telling all in the hope that the prosecutors would drop the death penalty: Plan B.

But what did Gary actually *know* about the crimes? And if he really did know something, would it be enough to convince the prosecutors to take the death penalty off the table?

Somehow I didn't think that Gary's confession that he'd killed "only" one or two or three or even all four of the charged victims and didn't have a clue as to who'd killed all of the rest was going to convince Norm Maleng not to try to execute him. To get that far, for Maleng to even consider a deal, Gary would have to be able to provide evidence to convince the prosecutors that he had killed all or almost all of the victims. It was counterintuitive—that the more guilty he was, the better his chance of not being executed. But that would be the only prize worth trading for, we presumed, as far as Maleng was concerned: to clear as many unsolved cases as possible.

And what if Gary *hadn't* killed them but only claimed that he had? Was he capable of lying about this in order to save his own neck? Would anyone believe him?

I wasn't sure that even I could believe him, at least on that point. That was the problem with Gary, as so many on our side had by then observed: What was real and what wasn't? My brain kept arguing with my stomach. My stomach insisted that Gary had to have killed at least some of the victims. The evidence so far cited by the state suggested that. But my brain retorted that it hadn't been proven beyond a reasonable doubt. And as every week brought no news, no suddenly devastating report from some laboratory somewhere that further implicated

Gary, I went back and forth but ultimately began to think to myself that Gary in fact might actually *be* innocent.

—␣␣␣—

The other forensic tests that were taking place that summer and fall weren't the only efforts being made by the state to shore up their case. Earlier that year, we'd asked the prosecutors to tell us which of the forty-five uncharged cases they intended to use as evidence to support the idea that there was some sort of common scheme or plan in the murders. Baird and his fellow prosecutors were reluctant to do this, saying their investigation was still continuing, and they didn't want any list they might provide to be considered definitive. They wanted to reserve the right to present evidence from any of the uncharged cases to prove the common scheme or plan element, which was necessary to support the death penalty.

Eventually, however, the state did agree to provide us with a tentative list of cases and other evidence they would probably present to support their theory of the common scheme or plan tying the four charged victims together. This at least would enable us to get started in focusing on those supporting cases. If we could show, for instance, that someone else had killed one or more of these other victims, that would not only damage the state's contention that there was a common scheme or plan, it would also be reasonable doubt that Gary had killed *anyone*.

For its part, to prove that Gary had committed the four charged murders, the state wanted to present evidence from the murder of Kim Nelson, "Star" (chiefly the account of Paige Miley); the disappearance of Marie Malvar (tracked by her father and pimp to Gary's house in May 1983); the disappearance of Keli McGinness (Gary had admitted having a previous date with her, because the Port of Seattle Police had a record of seeing him with her); the murders of Wendy Coffield and Deborah Bonner (the two uncharged victims found in the Green River before August 15, 1982); and statements made to detectives by one of Gary's coworkers at Kenworth, a man named Gary Yager, who had asserted to detectives that Gary Ridgway had in the past made remarks (as Baird wrote), "expressing great hostility to prostitutes and threatening to do them harm."

It wasn't true, Gary said, when we asked him about these supposed remarks. Gary Yager, he said, was just another one of his coworkers who was trying to get attention for himself, just as some of his other fellow employees had told their stories about working with Gary to tabloids, like the *National Enquirer.* There was nothing to Yager's assertions, Gary told us.

The importance of these additional cases, and the significance of Gary Yager's claims about Gary Ridgway's attitude about prostitutes, stemmed from a rule of evidence known in Washington as ER404(b):

> Evidence of other crimes, wrongs, or acts is not admissible to prove the character of a person in order to show that he/she acted in conformity therewith. It may, however, be admissible for other purposes, such as proof of motive, opportunity, intent, preparation, plan, knowledge, identity, or absence of mistake or accident.

There was that troubling word, *plan.*

That meant, if upheld by Judge Jones, evidence about these other murders and disappearances, as well as the supposed remarks about prostitutes, could be admitted in a trial in order to demonstrate Gary's supposed motive, or common scheme or plan in killing the four charged women. The state had earlier told everyone what they believed Gary's "plan" had been: "His larger criminal purpose . . . [was] . . . a scheme to pick up and murder vulnerable women again and again." The serial nature of the murders, said the state, constituted a continuing criminal enterprise.

The prosecutors contended that there were "remarkable similarities" between the charged murders. "But," they continued, "the 'common scheme or plan' which linked these crimes was, ultimately, the defendant's calculated enterprise to commit a series of murders. . . . he successfully endeavored, not just to kill, but to kill again and again."

All this presupposed not just that Gary had committed the murders but that he had done so with calculation; that is, he had set off each time with the *intention* of committing murder in his heart and mind, that is, *planning.*

But from our point of view, we weren't convinced that Gary had ever planned much of anything, let alone serial homicide. After all, thinking ahead wasn't exactly one of Gary's greatest strengths. So even if he had committed two or more of the murders, we thought the state's evidence for the aggravation was somewhat weak and subject to legal attack, which could effectively blunt the state's argument for the death penalty.

This point—which had previously divided the Spokane prosecutors from their counterparts in Pierce County over the Robert Yates case—had yet to be decided by any higher court.

The argument was articulated in an interview with the *Seattle P-I* by Ferris County Prosecuting Attorney Stephen Graham: "I don't know that all serial killers use a 'common scheme or plan.' Their behavior is too sporadic, spontaneous, and impulsive. I would want some real certainty in the law before I charged ahead at incredible expense."[1]

We intended to fight on this issue as long as it took. If the state were ever successful in asserting the principle that serial murder inherently involved a common scheme or plan, it was tantamount to an automatic death penalty, no matter what the circumstances.

Unless we could convince a jury that Gary was not "guilty beyond a reasonable doubt."

———

The difficulty of pulling together a defense team composed of so many people—some with extensive experience as public defenders and others with experience as privately paid lawyers unused to bureaucratic procedures—began to show up that fall, as we tried to sort through the mountain of material that was by then streaming in. Counting our outside contractor, Certus, we had over fifty people working to defend Gary. It was inevitable that personality conflicts would erupt. If it's true that where there are two lawyers, there'll be two arguments, that was probably sixteen times the situation with our eight lawyers, not to mention our paralegals, private investigators, experts, and outside consultants.

As the team's de facto administrator, I wound up being in the middle of more of these disputes than I had the patience for. There were arguments over money—who was getting paid how much, as well as when the money might finally come in. There were the usual tactical disputes—when, for example, it would be most propitious to do a certain thing or file a certain document with the court. There were ruffled feelings about various hierarchical issues, which only grew in imaginary importance the longer they went unaddressed. We had meetings—meetings and meetings and meetings—and almost as soon as one trouble spot had been damped down, up would pop another one. As for me, I soon developed an unreasoning distaste for the e-mail system, as these warnings, complaints, alarms, and personal hufferies coursed through the computer network. Michele became a prolific e-mailer—just about every day would find a swarm of them beeping into my in-box, most of them raising problems that we couldn't do anything about, at least right then. Worse, Michele had a hard time keeping her focus on her part of the program, which was chiefly to deal with the ongoing discovery issues and to be the communication liaison with Gary's family. If it ever got to a penalty phase, Michele's job would be to call witnesses who knew Gary—such as Greg, Dorene, and Judith—to testify on his behalf. But Michele had always been a true believer in Gary's innocence. Partly prompted by the questions and concerns of those who loved Gary, she soon began to pepper the other lawyers on our team with questions, comments, and suggestions. In other words, she was "creeping in" on their part of the program with suggestions as to how they should do their jobs, and not surprisingly, some began to resent it.

Some of us were concerned, in fact, that Michele might be getting too emotionally attached to Gary and his family and losing the objectivity she needed—in effect, succumbing to the charming side of Gary's persona. The fact was, Gary loved being around women.

"He's always on the make," Todd observed. Gary didn't seem to be able *not* to try to get the approval of every woman he encountered.

If Michele ever fell completely for Gary's charming innocence, we feared, that would only make it harder to convince him, *if* the day ever came, that the only way he could hope to avoid a death sentence was through Plan B. Mary Goody, Todd, and I worried that Michele would inadvertently stiffen Gary's resistance to providing a confession if that was the only way to save his life. We wanted her to pull back a bit. And in our meetings, Michele would agree, but within a day or so, this advice would seem to have been forgotten.

The tension within our team began to mount as we struggled to get a grip on the best way to defend Gary. Minor squabbles erupted between Fred and me over one of his briefs; between Eric Lindell and Michele over *other suspect* discovery; between two of the paralegals over a project to get all the previous news media coverage loaded into the computer; between Todd and Michele over the evidence stored at the warehouse; between Michele and me over her serial e-mails. I began, unfairly, to think of Michele as "Chicken Little," mostly for the incessant deluge of incoming e-mails, which usually dealt with some topic or problem or "emergency" that wasn't in her assigned area. I had no doubt she had the best intentions, but the way she injected herself into every issue was rubbing some people the wrong way.

Meanwhile the state wanted to set some firm dates for when Gary's case would come to trial. Of course, this depended on the results of the new forensic tests—if that bone fragment, for example, turned out to be from one of the victims, the state would probably ask the court to be allowed to add a new murder count to the existing four. And if other tests came back positive, the total could go even higher. For our side, we wanted a firm cutoff date for the adding of any new charges. The worst scenario for us would be for the state to add at the last minute, say, eight more victims we'd be unprepared to defend against. We'd be put in the position of asking for another delay, which would be accompanied by a rise in costs. The public outcry would follow.

We asked Judge Jones to set a trial date for the end of 2004; that would give us a little more than two years to get ready. The state wanted to put Gary in the dock much sooner. They wanted to start by the end of 2003. Judge Jones set the case for trial on March 16, 2004, but said that the date could be pushed back if the prosecution chose to add any new charges. At that point, the prosecution offered to agree to a deadline of March 27, 2003, to add any new charges. If it turned out that more evidence tying Gary to still more victims came in after that date, the judge would consider allowing the addition of new charges and pushing the trial date back even further. But, he warned the prosecution, they would have to have something very powerful for that to happen.

We were hoping that not only would the state not be able to add any new counts, but even the ones they had already filed would evaporate under our hoped-for, relentless legal assault.

20

As the fall evenings were growing chillier, I found myself pulled in too many directions. To meet the growing money demands of Team Ridgway, I started shifting dollars around from inside our budget—pay raises for our investigators, making sure our private lawyers' bills got through the bureaucratic maze, settling the bills from our experts—while trying to get the Office of Public Defense to actually pay these expenditures. I also started work on the next year's Team Ridgway budget, which had to be submitted to the county's financial pooh-bahs by February 2003. At the same time, some of the same bureaucrats complained that we weren't spending the money we already had fast enough to warrant asking for still more the next year. And I'd thought they'd be pleased at how economical we were being!

Around September 15, I received a telephone call from Jeff Baird.

"I finally heard back from Mitotyping (the DNA lab) on the bone chip," Baird said, referring to what had been suggested was a part of someone's skull. "They weren't able to get enough to even determine whether or not it was human."

I guess that lets Gary off the hook on Colonel Sanders. . . . Tony will be pleased.

"OK," I told Baird. "Thanks for the news." This was definitely good news. Even though Gary had assured me there was no way that this bone fragment, found in a vacuum cleaner bag, could be part of a skull, it was great to find out he was right. I felt a surge of optimism.

And then there was Roy Webbe. The issue of Webbe's competency had finally been put to a jury in July, and I'd had to divide my time between Gary's case and the mentally afflicted steak-knife rapist-killer. At that point, *alleged* steak-knife rapist-killer. After three weeks of testimony by psychologists and psychiatrists, a jury was unable to reach a verdict on Roy Webbe's competency, so a second competency trial was scheduled for late September. At the same time, the county's money shortage had led the council to slash funds for the swimming pools: they wanted the cities to take over their operation. Before I knew it, I was involved in a campaign to get the city of Kent or the Kent School District (or both) to put up money for our local pool, where I was continuing to coach the boys and girls high school swimming teams.

"Save the pool! Save the pool!" became a war cry. Soon volunteers from the community organized to lobby the city to do battle for the pool with the county. From September to the end of the year, not only was I rushing downtown on Gary's case and the Webbe case, in the evening I was back in Kent, attending meetings late into the night, as the Kent Citizens for Water Safety tried to convince the City of Kent and the county to reach agreement to keep the pool open. Of course, it wasn't long before someone pointed out that the pool wouldn't be in jeopardy if we weren't spending all that money to defend Gary Ridgway, which, although it wasn't actually true, at least provided some people with a satisfying riposte to our pleas.

With all that was going on, I was gone from home quite a bit. Saving the pool was a major issue in our house. I coached there, Sean and Marley worked out there, and Kelly was employed there. So everyone was pretty understanding. The convergence of the Ridgway defense budget running head-on into the closures of the parks and pools was omnipresent. Our house, it seemed, was ground zero.

Despite this juxtaposition, my family never wavered in their support of what I was doing for Gary.

"I'm proud of you, Daddy," Marley told me. It doesn't matter how old they are, daughters can still call their fathers "daddy."

"How about your friends or people at school? Do they give you any grief?" I asked.

"No. Nobody says anything," she said. Then she smiled and added, "Except they'll say 'Hey, I saw your dad on TV last night.'" There was nothing negative, nothing that bothered Marley in the least.

———〰———

The second Webbe competency trial resulted in Roy Webbe being found competent to stand trial for murder, so then the actual trial on Webbe's guilt or innocence began in early November. For most of the next month, I found myself continuing to bounce back and forth between Kent and Seattle, from Webbe to Ridgway, while making as much time as I could for coaching the high school swim team and saving the pool. I was running down but wasn't really aware of it.

By early December, the Webbe trial was at its end. Although everyone agreed that Webbe was mentally disturbed, the state had been able to prove to a jury, first, that he was legally competent, and second, that he had in fact killed Deborah Funk. After closing arguments on December 6, I hurried back to Kent, where the Kent Citizens for Water Safety had a sign-making party at the ACA office. The following day, Saturday December 7, we held a "Save the Pool" rally at Kent City Hall. Then, on Monday, December 9, I was back in Seattle waiting for the Webbe verdict.

The jurors retired to deliberate shortly after 9 A.M. While a jury is considering your client's fate, there's nothing to do; at that point, there's nothing more you *can* do. I dropped in at the office of deputy prosecutor Jeff Baird to finalize our proposed schedule for the Ridgway case, setting dates for all the pre-trial motions we'd have to have, including the common scheme or plan dispute. As we sorted these scheduling details out, I thought I might see if we were already so far down the track with Gary that there was no longer any way to stop this train.

"I hope we're not closing the door, with all this setting of a trial date and scheduling stuff," I told Baird. He caught what I was saying.

"I think we should always keep the door open," he replied.

"Yeah, but I think your boss sort of precluded any kind of a resolution about a year ago. . . . It seems like he kind of painted himself into a corner on that one." I was referring to the "we-will-not-bargain" statement Maleng had made to the news media just after Gary's arrest.

"Well, you never know what could happen," Jeff said. "I'm certainly *not* saying he'd change his position. I just never say never."

Of course, Baird was known for being opposed to the death penalty. What had he said early in the case? "I'm just going to convict him. . . ." Meaning he wouldn't handle the penalty part of the case. But I sensed that Baird might be sympathetic to any effort on our part to negotiate a settlement that might spare Gary Ridgway's life.

"Good. Never say never. I like that," I said, and we wrapped up our scheduling business. As I left his office, my mind replayed the conversation and whatever messages or spin I might get out of it. *Are they coming up empty-handed?* I wondered, thinking about the forensic tests that still hadn't come back. If the state was hitting a dry hole on the new tests, that was good for Gary. It meant Plan A, trying to raise a reasonable doubt about Gary's guilt, was still viable. *Better yet,* I thought, *maybe they've linked someone else to one or two of the victims!* I knew Baird had to be aware that even if a jury found Gary guilty and sentenced him to death, the chance of an execution ever actually taking place was about 50-50, what with all the appellate issues that might be raised. *He also knows the state of their evidence after all these years. Given what he knows, maybe he has concerns about something,* I thought. Maybe the rats in the warehouse had eaten too much of the state's case. Maybe the DNA could be vulnerable.

The more I thought about Jeff Baird's remarks, the more optimistic I became. *Baird knows juries,* I thought. *He knows that just one goofy juror who has his or her own "reasonable doubt" can hang the whole group, 11 to 1. And he doesn't want to have to try this case more than once. The taxpayers would go nuts.*

Just running this through my brain got me excited. I rushed over to Todd's office to share Baird's remark with him.

"Groon," I panted, calling Todd by his nickname. "You won't believe this little conversation I had with Baird." I told him what Baird had just said.

"Yeah," Todd said, "*his* door's open, but not Norm's." He gave me his crooked, cynical smile. "C'mon, Mark. Norm Maleng will never do a deal. He's made that clear. Besides, if he doesn't seek death for our boy, who can he seek death for in the future?"

"Yeah, but maybe they're coming up empty," I said. "Or maybe they've linked someone else."

Todd shook his head. I could see he didn't think this was likely.

"Unfortunately, Jeff doesn't speak for Norm. You didn't get down on your knees and start begging for a deal, did you?" Todd raised his eyebrows and glared at me.

"No, I was actually pretty cool about it. It was a pretty informal conversation," I reassured him.

"Good, because the more I think about it, he was probably circling his prey, looking for a weakness to go after." Todd, the hunter, turning my strange but positive interlude into a hunting metaphor, with me as the prospective dinner.

"Well, at least he didn't laugh out loud and call me crazy." I tried to pump the optimism back into my balloon after Todd's puncture.

Todd just snorted.

By three o'clock, I was back in court with Roy Webbe. The jury had just come in. Guilty on all counts.[1] I was disappointed but hadn't gotten my hopes up too high. Roy's defense had strained credulity. Roy had insisted on taking the stand on his own behalf. He testified that he, a mentally deranged, drug-addicted transient with a head full of dirty dreadlocks, had consensual sex with the victim, a single mom whom he'd never met before. Then, later, someone else had come into her apartment and nearly decapitated her with a steak knife. So even though we had put up a good, hard fight, I wasn't completely surprised by the jury's verdict. And it wasn't much of a leap to recognize that although the characters were different, Gary and Roy's defense was very similar: *he* had consensual sex with the victim(s) shortly before someone else murdered her (them). It hadn't worked for Roy and I had my private trepidation that it wouldn't work for Gary either.

—⁓—

Maybe it was all the running around I was doing, piling up miles on my small pickup truck, getting up early and staying up late at night, but as Christmas of 2002 neared, I was running out of gas.

As fatigue crept up on me, I found myself succumbing to frustration more easily and occasionally not thinking things through adequately.

"I'm never getting anything *done*," I noted in my journal. No matter how hard I worked, it seemed as though nothing was really moving forward. Instead we kept running into new obstacles. The DNA analysis we'd undertaken wasn't giving us anything to argue about, and certainly nothing was leaping off the pile of Red River murders to suggest any strong "some-other-dude-did-it" scenarios. And despite all of Mary Goody's work, we still hadn't found much in the way of mitigation. Gary wasn't crazy nor could he be considered near enough to being "retarded" to imagine the jury not imposing death. Our efforts to determine if he'd suffered some form of traumatic brain damage from paint fumes, or head injuries, or fetal alcohol syndrome, hadn't borne any fruit.

About the only thing we had in the way of possible mitigation was a tantalizing hint from Gary about his mother, Mary Rita. Gary had first told us that he'd wet the bed until he was four or five. Later that age had risen, to seven or eight, then ten or eleven. Next, in a conversation with Mary Goody, Gary had said that he'd had enuresis until the age of fourteen or fifteen—and that his mother had washed him, including his genitals, at night, in cold water, in the family bathtub, up to that age. Mary Goody thought this intimate familiarity between mother and son was important. It was certainly unusual, she pointed out.

And at the same time, Gary had complained to Mary that "women always push me around . . . I never stand up for myself, with women."

This pairing was significant: his mother had treated him as a baby up until his mid-teens, and had even berated him for being "a baby" because of the bed-wetting. And in the same conversation, Gary complained about being "pushed around" by women . . . "I never stand up for myself." And after this, Gary had launched into a long story about two prostitutes who he said had stolen his wallet twenty years earlier and how angry it had made him.

A few days later, I asked Gary about this situation with his mother, the bedwetting and the bathing.

"Yeah," he said. "It was no big deal. It was pretty normal, you know?"

"Something like that could be part of what happened," I said, thinking that, perhaps, Gary was hinting at a sexual relationship with his mother. If that had happened, it might constitute mitigation. "If something else happened, you should tell us."

But even as I asked the question, I thought I could sense his backing off. It was as if he realized that he'd gone further and disclosed more than he wanted to. Or he felt I was making too big a deal out of it.

"No, no. That was all," he said. "There was nothing else. Nothing sexual or anything like that." Maybe there was nothing. But it was clear that whatever he might have done as an adult, Gary didn't want any dirt thrown on Mary Rita for her actions when he was a teenager. We had no other evidence of any type of abuse by Mary Rita. Whatever mitigation there might be for Gary there, it was clear he wasn't going to cooperate in helping us dig it up.

Discouraged because we didn't seem to be getting anywhere, I went into the holidays in a dour mood, which soon manifested itself.

—⁂—

"I thought you said you'd be doing more work at home," Kelly said to me, as we went Christmas shopping later that night. "You don't seem to make time for us anymore." She was right. Between the Ridgway case, the swim team, saving the pool, and the Webbe case, I'd spent more time on the freeway, in jail, in court, or in meetings than I had at home over the past six months.

This had been coming on for some time. Kelly had been patient throughout the summer and fall, but it was pretty clear that she was reaching her limit. Despite her kidding-on-the-square, back in the beginning of the case, that she'd have to be a single mother for "the next five years," she wasn't about to let me forget what was most important— our family.

"I'm so tired," I told her as we tried to make our way through the shopping mall, where a crush of last-minute shoppers like us dodged and weaved to avoid one another and tried to blot out the jingling bells and scratchy Christmas music blasting from the public address system. I tried to explain:

"It seems like there's always something more to deal with," I said. "The thing with the pool . . . the swim team. . . . Every time I turn around, there's something new with Ridgway. . . . And I don't know where we're going with the DNA there or any of the forensic stuff. . . . People on the team are either snapping at each other or giving each other the silent treatment. . . . I lost my temper with Michele. . . . It seems like every day there's some new problem with the Office of Public Defense and our budget . . . and I don't know where we're going with the mitigation. . . . Christmastime used to be happy. But now it's just depressing."

Bah humbug! Kelly peered at me as if she didn't know me.

"Ho, Ho, Ho," she said, glumly. "This is a lotta fun."

I realized that I was simply worn out; I had to dial it back a bit. I had to forget about the incessant e-mails and leave it to others to take care of their responsibilities.

"Why don't you take the weekend off?" Kelly suggested. "Like real people do." I could always tell when Kelly was being facetious.

I did even better than that. From the Saturday before Christmas to New Year's Eve, I called only one meeting, a sit-down with Michele and me at ACA to try to smooth over our differences. I apologized to her for some of the rude things I'd said and done. She accepted my apology and we agreed to put our disagreements behind us and move forward.

By New Year's Eve, *Kelly* was sick. Sean wanted to have a party for his friends at our house, so Kelly went over to her mother's house to avoid the teenaged din. Marley was invited to spend the night at one of her friends. I went up into our bedroom and shut the door, turned on the new TV Kelly and the kids had bought me for Christmas (doubtless hoping that it would induce their husband and father to stay home a bit more) and spent the rest of New Year's Eve alone, feeling only a little sorry for myself. I had to realize that things could be a lot worse. I knew of more than one hundred sets of parents who had lost their children, years earlier, just as I knew Gary Leon Ridgway was spending his second New Year's in jail.

By Monday, January 6, 2003, I'd recovered enough energy to get back into the fight. I went to see Gary in our first face-to-face since the sensitive bed-wetting discussion we'd had before Christmas.

"Michele came yesterday," he told me.

"Oh, yeah? What did she say?"

"She wanted to ask me about that thing you and I talked about, you know, the post-stuff."

"The post-Miranda statement you made back in the beginning?"

"Yeah, what Doyon said I said, but I didn't."

"So what'd you tell Michele?"

"I just said those detectives were asking questions all over the place. . . . They wanted to know why I changed my rugs. I just told them that the rug was worn out, it was old, so I changed it. She asked me if I'd really told 'em, 'I'll tell you what's gonna happen, a lot of these you are gonna find are not mine.' I told her I didn't remember saying that."

"Is that true? That you don't remember saying that?"

"I may have said it," Gary admitted. "Because, you know, I never stick up for myself."

We had no idea how many items had been sent to various laboratories for whatever tests. The only way we'd known for sure about the bone fragment was because it had to be destroyed as part of the test, so the state had to tell us about it. But with more than a year now elapsed since Gary's arrest and nothing new—that is, nothing inculpatory— from any of the labs (which we assumed included the Federal Bureau of Investigation), that seemed to suggest that nothing devastating had been found. Of course, the state had until March 27 to finish all these tests—that was the cutoff date for adding any new charges. If we could make it past the 27th, the chances were pretty good that we could defend Gary on Plan A, the SODDI defense: Some Other Dude Did It.

On February 7, 2003, the sheriff, Dave Reichert, gave a speech at the University of Washington. Todd got wind of it in advance and slipped into the audience to listen.

Of particular delight for Todd, who wanted to keep track of the Sheriff's public pronouncements for purposes of our venue motion, came this exchange during a question-and-answer session with the audience:

A student asks, "Sheriff, how many do you think Ridgway killed?"

"Well, you know I've got to be careful," Reichert said. "Currently, he's only charged with four murders, but personally . . . I think he's good for a hundred."

A hundred! Nothing like poisoning the jury pool, I thought, when Todd told me what Reichert had said. And that was even with the Sheriff being "careful."

Two weeks after this, Reichert, former Green River investigation consultant Bob Keppel, and best-selling true crime writer Ann Rule, a Seattle-area resident, spoke at Green River Community College in Gary's hometown of Auburn. Rule had said for years that she intended to write a book about the Green River murders. Several of us bought tickets and were spread around in the crowd. The place was packed and no seats were open. Arriving late, I slid in the back and slithered along the back wall, unnoticed and anonymous, just as I wanted it.

"Hi, Mark." The guy next to me nudged me with his elbow.

"Oh . . . hi Randy." It was Green River Task Force Detective Randy Mullinax, with about three or four other Green River Task Force detectives. Six hundred or so people in the place, and I ended up standing next to one of the Green River detectives. So much for being unnoticed and anonymous.

Mullinax filled me in on what I had missed.

"I think I saw Todd here," he said, "but when Dave [Reichert] asked if there were any defense attorneys present, no one raised their hand."

"Do you blame him? He probably didn't want to be a target." The atmosphere was like a high school pep rally, with Reichert the star again, just like he'd been at Kent Meridian High School, back in the day. During his talk about the case, Reichert received about three or four standing ovations. To see and feel the community fervor that he was generating was frightening. The impossibility of getting a fair trial in King County struck me once again, with full force this time.

The next day, I had another face-to-face with Gary. He was brought to the austere face-to-face room in the usual shackles. I waited while the jailer removed the cuffs and chains. When he left, closing the door behind him, I put on my most serious face.

"I think it's time for you and me to talk about the case they have against you," I told Gary. "I'm looking at this from the prosecutor's point of view." He peered at me from behind his overlarge glasses, his brow knitted in his most impressive *I'm-paying-attention* countenance.

"First, they have the DNA with Carol Christensen. Your DNA. And you denied that you'd had sex with her. You can call it faulty memory if you want. They'll call that a lie. Juries don't like lies—when they hear them, they're much more apt to vote to convict.

"Then there's the DNA with Marcia Chapman, also yours, and the rock in her vagina. That ties her to Cynthia Hinds, who was right next to her and also had a rock in her vagina. After that, there's the DNA with Mills—you can't be excluded—and she was found next to Cynthia Hinds and Marcia Chapman. You see where this is going?"

Gary nodded.

"After that, there's the incident with the woman who claimed you choked her—I mean, that you choked."

"After she bit me."

"Yeah, but you choked her. And when you say she bit you, what's the jury going to think? They'll remember that you lied about having sex with Carol Christensen, and they'll say, if you lied about that, you probably lied about the other woman biting you."

"Well, I'm not lying. She did too bite me."

"And for the kicker," I went on, "there's Doyon, the detective. He's going to say that you told him, 'I think you're gonna find that not all of them are mine.'"

"But I didn't say that."

"But you lied about Carol Christensen," I pointed out.

Gary didn't say anything to this.

"If they keep coming up empty on these tests, hopefully, they'll have nothing new to add," I told him. "March 27 is going to be an important date. If they do come up with new charges based on some other type of evidence from these tests they're doing, we're going to have to take another look. I mean, that could really change things. Hopefully, they won't come up with anything else."

"I understand," Gary replied. He knew exactly what I meant without it actually being spoken out loud. We were right at the tipping point for Plan A. We could, just barely, make the argument that Gary had only had sex with prostitutes but that he hadn't killed anyone. But any new evidence would virtually flush that argument down the toilet.

———

At 1:30 P.M. on March 27, Todd and I walked over to the court together. It was clear to everyone that something big was about to happen. The typical throng of reporters and cameras were there. In addition, the courtroom was packed with law enforcement and victim family members. That didn't bode well for our side. Deputy Prosecutor Patty Eakes handed us a copy of an Amended Information and the Certification of Probable Cause, the legal documents necessary to add the new charges. A quick glance at the Amended Information told us they were adding three new counts: Wendy Coffield and Deborah Bonner, as most of us had expected, and a surprise—Deborah Estes. To that point, no one on our side had thought she would be added as a charged count. Her skeleton had been found in Federal Way, far away from any of the clusters of other victims.

I quickly scanned the probable cause document, trying to find out why they'd added Deborah Estes. The words hit me like a bolt from above—their tests *had* found new forensic evidence: tiny, actually microscopic, paint spheres in the clothing that had been found tightly tied around the necks of Wendy Coffield and Deborah Estes. According to their expert, the paint in the clothing was identical to paint used at Kenworth in 1982, 1983, and 1984, the years of the murders. Dupont Imron paint.

My first thought was, *Oh, shit!* I realized there was more: a statement Gary supposedly made to his onetime coworker at Kenworth, Gary Yager, about how construction sites would make nice places to hide dead bodies. Deborah Estes's dead body had been left at a construction site.

I went out to wait for Gary to arrive on the jail elevator. I warned him about the new counts and reminded him that everyone was watching his every move, every emotion. He said nothing, simply nodded, accepting the situation. When he got to court, he had to act like this new information wasn't going to bother him in the least. He nodded again. Minutes later, when the new charges were formally read, he gave no discernible reaction. As soon as the hearing was over, Gary was escorted back to jail, shielded from the reporters by his usual phalanx of guards.

Afterward, the news media surrounded us in the hall, seeking our comments about the new evidence. We downplayed the significance of the paint and emphasized how this was just going to cause additional delays, because now the court would have to give us more time to prepare.

Todd, Dave, Eric, and I reconvened at Merchants' Café, a local watering hole. Over a few beers, we gazed over the utterly altered legal landscape. Prior to the hearing, we had a pool over what the state would do. As the winner, Dave bought the first round. No matter how we tried to spin it, it wasn't pretty for Gary. Despite our talking down the evidentiary value of the paint spheres to the news media, the prosecutors couldn't have found anything much worse for our client, short of a Polaroid picture of him strangling a woman. Even if the same paint was widely used at other Seattle factories, like Boeing or Todd Shipyards, Kenworth paint or paint consistent with Kenworth paint, in the ligatures of not one but *two* victims, would be enough to guarantee Gary's conviction—and therefore, his death sentence.

So the case had taken a grievous turn away from all our hopes and efforts. And as the beer sunk in, so too did the ultimate realization that our nice, polite, respectful client was in fact *the* Green River Killer.

21

Over the ensuing weekend, my mind raced. What to do now? Plan B loomed ever larger in my mind, despite Todd and Tony's often-expressed doubts about Norm Maleng's willingness to negotiate. How could we put Plan B into effect? How would we approach Gary with the idea? We'd talked about it in the abstract—how plea bargains were usually conducted—but never with any seriousness. Now it just might be the only way to save his life. How would even discussing it affect our attorney-client relationship? Would he even be willing to consider it? Would he be willing to admit that he was in fact the killer everyone had been seeking for so many years?

I tried to keep busy over the weekend. It started by taking Marley to swim practice on Saturday morning, followed by her soccer game. The girls won three to two and Marley, the goalie, made a great save in the last five minutes to preserve the win. After the game, we had pizza with Kelly's mom, Jean. I dropped Kelly, Marley, and Jean off at Jean's house and went home. Sean and I watched the NCAA basketball tournament on the new TV. Then he and I went out for Mexican food.

The next day, I slept in until 10:30, then I left and picked up Kelly and Marley at Jean's house. When we got home, Kelly and I agreed to clean out our garage—sort of a spring-cleaning project we'd ignored for a couple years. It was a daunting task but we had to start sometime. And this way, she could just tell me to do something and I could do it. Not a lot of thinking required on my part. Anything and everything to keep myself from dwelling on the unpleasant reality of where we now were. But then, Kelly and I would have an occasional dispute over some item of questionable sentimental value—keep it or toss it— and I couldn't help but hear Gary's voice telling me to keep it, scavenger that he'd always been. Try as I might, I couldn't *not* think about Gary and the case.

On Monday, March 31, we had a "lawyers only" meeting at 10 A.M. in our war room at ACA. All of the lawyers were present, Tony, Dave, Michele, Eric, Fred, Suzanne, Todd, and me. First, we discussed readjusting the case schedule. The three new counts meant we'd have to ask for a delay of the trial date. We also had to consider reorganizing. Three new counts meant even more intensive work on those cases. Dave Roberson would continue to handle the Coffield and Bonner cases, which were now actual murder counts instead of 404(b) evidence: that's evidence that tended to show that Gary's scheme or plan might have been responsible for the initially charged four murders. Todd would take over the Deborah Estes case and try to get a handle on the paint question, with the assistance of our forensic expert, John Thornton. Fortunately, Thornton had literally "written the book" (actually, a chapter) on paint analysis in one of the top forensic science texts. The evidence on which the three new counts were based meant something else: the realization sunk in to all of us, Tony and Michele included. Our client was not innocent. He was the killer, all right. There could no longer be any reasonable doubt of that.

We moved on to our first in-depth discussion of Plan B. As he had from the outset, Tony thought it would never fly.

"Norm [Maleng] will not, cannot do it," Tony said. "He'd never be able to seek the death penalty again. I think he should do it, but he won't, not in a million years. And in all of my dealings with Gary . . . well, I just don't think he'll be interested either."

"I agree with you about Norm," I said. "But I'm not so sure about Gary. He just might want to spill the beans to get it off his chest."

"Well, we've got to try," Eric Lindell said. "We've got to at least find out if he'd be interested. If not, we just move on."

"I think Mark ought to have the 'come-to-Jesus talk' with him," Todd said. "And we've got to do this while we still have a window of opportunity." Todd meant the thirty days the state had before they formally filed their death penalty notice on the new counts. We knew that once that was filed, it would be even more difficult to get the state to back off.

"Well, I agree with Eric and Todd on that," Tony said. "We ought to explore the possibility with Gary and then move on. We can't afford to wait on it. And Mark should be the one to have 'the talk' with Gary."

I turned to Michele.

"Michele, would you set something up with Greg and Dorene?" I asked. We all knew they would be important. We hoped they'd be in favor of Plan B. If they weren't, there would probably be no way to convince Gary. "I think we ought to talk to them about this plan."

"Certainly," Michele said. "I agree we should let them know what we're doing. I'll set something up."

"Let's do it at your office, Tony," I said. Greg and Dorene had retained Tony's services because of his great skills and reputation, and they had a lot of respect for him. Meeting in his office, rather than at Michele's or ACA, might make the prospect of Plan B seem more serious. Tony agreed to have the meeting in his office.

The next day, Tuesday, April 1, I coincidentally had contact with a task force detective. During a casual conversation, the detective made an offhand remark, something to the effect of, "I sure wish your guy would give us some information."

"Yeah, well I wish *your* guy wasn't trying to kill my guy."

"Hey, that's Maleng's decision," the detective said. "I just know there are a lot of families with questions they'd like answers to." The detective appeared to be distancing himself from the prosecutor's public pledge of no plea bargain.

"Well, these new counts certainly alter the picture," I said. "I just wish Norm hadn't backed himself into a corner like that."

"I know, I know. Don't get me wrong. I believe in the death penalty. If anybody deserves it, it's Ridgway," the detective said. "And I'm not saying what anyone else wants out of this. I'm only speaking for myself, nobody else. I just want the information he has. That's all. We need answers. We need to know where those missing bodies are. Their *families* need to know. The way this is going now, we'll never know."

Afterward, I tried to read more into the conversation. He'd made it clear he was only speaking for himself, not Dave Reichert or the detectives in general. But this was certainly an indication that at least some of the cops wanted information more than they wanted to see

Gary Ridgway dead. Would the sheriff himself support our Plan B if we got that far? Based on some things that Reichert had said in the newspaper at the time of Gary's arrest, I thought the detectives at least were probably more interested in getting answers than simply killing Gary. They had lived for years with the pain of the victims' families, with so many unanswered questions about what had happened to those daughters, sisters, and mothers.

I felt it would be helpful to have a better grasp of the sheriff's position with regard to a possible plea bargain. If his detectives were firmly against a deal, there would be no way that Norm Maleng would ever agree to one, even assuming that the prosecutor could be moved off his "no way, never" position. Clearly, the detectives working on the case would have significant influence on Maleng's office.

Ever the optimist, I was once more buoyed by this tidbit from the detective, although I knew Todd would probably bring me back to reality in a second. I called Todd and recounted my conversation with the detective.

"I bet the sheriff would support making a deal for information, if it was *real* information, stuff that would actually close some of the cases," I told him.

To my surprise, despite all his previous doubts, Todd thought the detectives might in fact support a possible deal.

"I think they want to end this for the families' sake," Todd said. "They know the trial and appeals will take ten or twelve years . . . or more."

"You know, if we had good solid information, I'm sure they'd want Norm to make a deal," I said. "Now we've just got to find out if our boy has any information."

"Oh, you *know* he's got it." Todd was sure now, too. "You just have to convince him to give it up." Todd meant I'd have to be convincing in "the talk" I'd agreed to have soon with Gary.

The next day, Todd and I went to see Gary to prepare him for the arraignment on the new counts. I mentioned to Gary that one of the detectives seemed open to the possibility of a plea bargain. Gary gave little reaction to this news but simply nodded in acknowledgment. His passive response encouraged me to think that Gary might actually be amenable to a deal, but I didn't want to broach the topic with him quite yet. These things always require the most delicate timing: the dance of the scorpions, as Todd calls it.

The next day, April 3, before the new arraignment, Todd and I met with Tony at his office. Tony still didn't think that the prosecutor's office would ever agree to a plea bargain, even after I told him about my conversation with the detective. He was sure that the detectives were indeed open to a deal—and just as sure that it wouldn't make a bit of difference to Norm Maleng. But he again agreed that we should at least try to figure out what Gary thought of even trying to make a deal.

"I just don't think we should waste too much time on it," Tony said. "I agree we need to try and I agree now is the time. Then, once everyone says no, we can put it behind us."

"I'm thinking we should give it a few weeks," I said. "I don't expect Gary to blurt it all out right away. I expect it to be a process." I was thinking of Mary Goody's advice: that when a confession came, it either came all at once or in dribbles. Gary's backing and filling on various details over the past year suggested to me that if he was to make a confession, it would be the dribbling kind. I thought of something else.

"In the meantime," I told Tony, "I don't think you or anyone else on the team should be going up and visiting Gary and talking about his defense and preparation for trial and getting a not guilty verdict." If suddenly everyone stopped talking about our effort to find Gary innocent, I thought he might get the message.

"I agree," Todd said. "No one else should visit him. Everyone should just stay away and let Gary stew on the stuff that Mark and he will talk about."

I was struck by another thought. If I thought Michele might have been an obstacle to getting Gary to confess, what would happen if Gary saw that she, too, was urging him to give it all up?

"I think it would be good to involve Michele in this," I said. "Gary really likes her, and she's developed a good rapport with his family. If she completely stopped seeing him, he'd freak out." Besides which, we'd have Michele committed to the new strategy, or so I thought.

"OK," Tony said. "So for the next week or so, we'll just have Mark and Michele go visit him and try to see if he'll cooperate." He shook his head and laughed again. "It's never going to happen."

"As far as anyone else is concerned," Todd said, "I don't think we should tell anyone anything. We just need to maintain the status quo, keep preparing for trial and doing everything else we need to be doing."

"Agreed," Tony said. "Except I think Greg and Dorene should be told we're exploring this idea. By the way, Michele set up the meeting with them for tomorrow afternoon at my office."

"Yeah, I think we should generally let them know, because we can't have them going up and talking to Gary. He'd have to maintain his not guilty attitude and that could be counterproductive. I also want to bring Mary Goody and Mark Cunningham into the loop. Not necessarily to go and talk to him. They've done so many of these, I think their insights could really help." Tony and Todd agreed.

Later that morning, amid the media circus we'd become accustomed to, Gary was arraigned on the new counts. Deputy Prosecutor Patty Eakes caught me off guard. She began to give notice of the state's intent to seek death on the three new counts. I interrupted.

"Your Honor, I would respectfully ask that we have the thirty-day statutory period to consider offering a new mitigation package with respect to the new counts." I was stumbling through this, but I didn't want them to serve notice right away. I wanted to buy some time. Somewhere in the back of my mind, I heard Jeff Baird talking about keeping doors open. If Plan B, that thing we had never taken very seriously, was to have any chance at all, we'd need some time to get it together.

"That's fine, your Honor," Patty told Judge Jones, as she glanced over at me with a puzzled look. She turned back to Judge Jones. "The statute does give that opportunity to the defense. We can set this over for a month."

"OK, we'll set the date for notice in thirty days," Jones said. "Thank you, counsel." And with that, the hearing ended.

As Gary shuffled away in his chains, I told him, "I'll be up to see you tomorrow."

"Oooh-K. See you tomorrow," Gary replied.

All of the attorneys on our team met after the arraignment. We wanted to update everyone on the new developments and firm up the steps we'd have to take with Plan B. The critical issue was the timing. A majority felt if a deal was ever going to be discussed, it was now or never. Michele was more cautious. She argued that we shouldn't rush into something this huge without having all our bases covered. She was particularly worried about Gary getting "Yates'd"—a new verb conveying the idea that some other county's prosecutor might be lurking in the weeds to go after Gary.

"It's too important," she said. "We've got to do this right. We should slow down and get some advice." Michele had previously suggested bringing someone else in to offer advice on various other matters. Naturally, it rubbed many of us the wrong way. It was sort of like suggesting that we didn't know what we were doing. We had eight lawyers on our team. Plus experienced investigators and nationally recognized experts. Our collective experience was good enough for me. Besides, outsiders wouldn't have the level of knowledge that we had after working on the case for almost eighteen months. But I didn't want to get into a confrontation with Michele at that point.

"I agree with Michele," I said. "We do have to do this right. But I disagree regarding the timing. I think we have to move forward right now." I turned to Michele. "We won't go too fast. Besides, it could take awhile for Gary to come around, if he does at all." I didn't need to add that I was against bringing in some outside legal advice. Michele already knew how we all felt about that.

Todd pointed out that once the prosecutor's office filed their notice of intent to seek the death penalty on the three new counts, the window for dealing would be slammed shut. "We've got thirty days to see if our boy wants to play," he said.

"We have to keep going forward like nothing else is going on," I said. If we stopped our trial preparation, somebody was sure to figure out that something was up. "But for the next two or three weeks, it will just be Michele and me going up to see him and talking to him about cooperating and making a deal. OK?" Everyone agreed, including Michele.

The next morning, Friday, April 4, I stopped in at Todd's office before going up to see Gary at noon. Todd gave me some ideas for approaching our client about the prospect of a confession.

"Tell Gary what our polling shows," Todd said. "What was it? About 90 percent in King County already have him convicted . . . and that was before the three new counts!"

"He knows it ain't a pretty picture," I agreed. "I just don't think he's afraid of the death penalty."

"Yeah, he's more afraid of having to admit to Greg and Dorene and Judith and Matt that he *is* the Green River Killer than any executioner."

"I want to make the argument that he'd be doing 'good' by providing information. That he could help some of the families that he destroyed, if he killed their daughter, just by letting them know the truth. I think that will have an impact on him."

"Well, you would know better than me what would work with him," Todd said. "But if he's a psychopath, who committed all these murders, I can't see how he'd have much sympathy for the families. I don't know, maybe he's changed over the years? He's just tough to figure out. Just don't let him say *no*."

Around ten in the morning, I crossed over to the jail and made my way to the face-to-face room on the eleventh floor. Gary wasn't in his usual jovial mood. The three new counts had caused a subtle change in his demeanor, somewhat more subdued and less talkative.

"Gary, I just want you to listen today," I told him. "I'll do all the talking. You don't have to say anything. You just listen and then think about what I say."

"Oooh-K."

"I told you that very first night we met that we'd eventually have to have some serious discussions about your case. Well, we've come full circle now. In any death penalty case, the number one goal is to keep your client from getting the death penalty. And you know, that's been my role. From the beginning, I've had to work from the assumption that you *are* guilty of these murders. And now, with these new charges, your case just got a whole lot worse. You know that."

"Yeah, I know."

"We met as a team, and we think there's a very small window of opportunity—before Norm Maleng states publicly that he wants the death penalty on these new cases. There's a window where we could go in and try to make a deal to save your life."

"It's just . . ."

I cut him off. I didn't want him slamming the door before he had a chance to think things through.

"You don't need to say anything today. In fact, I don't want you to. Just listen and think, but don't try to make any final decisions today."

"Oooh-K."

"The chances of winning at trial were slim to start with, and now there's probably *no* chance. And if they find you guilty, there's no doubt you'd get the death penalty."

Gary nodded and looked down.

"What we want you to think about is offering Maleng a deal. Plead guilty and give them information on the unsolved cases in exchange for a life sentence."

"Do you think there's a chance of that?"

"I don't know. Probably not. But maybe. Anyhow, I think it's your only chance to avoid getting the death penalty."

I again ran down the evidence against him: the DNA, the other contacts with the uncharged victims, and now the paint. And there was the "not-all-mine" statement.

"'They're not all mine.' That will keep you from taking the stand to testify. I mean, if that statement came in, you'd be toast. When you start adding things up, it just doesn't look good. Like I said, if we go to trial, we'll lose. If we lose, you'll get the death penalty. I want you to consider letting me try to make a deal. Don't decide right now. Think about it. We'll keep talking about it, keep all the options open. And don't worry, in the meantime, everyone else is preparing for your trial, full steam ahead."

"I do have one question," Gary said.

"Sure." I said, thinking, *Only one? That's a good sign.* "What?"

"Well, say I tell them I want to plead for a . . . you know . . . for the deal . . . for life. What if Maleng says no? Then they'll tell the jury I'd tried . . . wanted to plead guilty. Then they'd find me guilty for sure."

"Good question." Not only was it an intelligent question, but it also told me he was considering the possibility of talking. "Don't worry about that. There's a court rule that prohibits that. Evidence Rule 410, ER 410. Of course, the rule can't stop leaks to the media, but it says no one, on either side, can introduce any evidence regarding settlement negotiations. That would bring an end to plea bargaining, which would bring the whole system to a crashing halt." If the prosecution ever said a word, either publicly or to the jury, about any plea negotiations, they'd face severe sanctions—including possible dismissal of the case.

"Oooh-K." Gary was nodding and smiling. Everything was now very agreeable and comfortable. I realized he was not at all upset with me for bringing this up.

"The other thing I want you to think about is this: if you *do* have information about those unsolved cases, you could bring some healing, some closure to the families of those victims. And that would be a good thing, not only for them but for you too. You would feel a lot better about yourself if you knew you had helped bring some closure for some of these families."

Gary's eyes welled up with tears. I thought, *He does have some feelings.* He looked at me and nodded again.

"And if you had information that could close a bunch of cases, we're pretty sure the sheriff's office and task force would get behind doing a deal." Everyone knew there were still seven victims whose remains had never been recovered. If Gary knew anything about *those* cases, I guessed that the police would be anxious to support a deal.

"You think so?"

"Yeah, based on some casual conversations here and there—you know, off-the-record chats—I've heard that they just want information for these families. As far as I can tell, they're not all that committed just to seeing you get the death penalty.

"You just need to think it over. Like I said, it doesn't look good right now. I know Maleng said he'd never deal, but it can't hurt to try. That is, if you have information to trade."

I changed the subject for a while to let out some of the tension. Gary filled me in on the latest doings of the inhabitants of the eleventh floor, and I told him that I needed to take care of my yard, which had grown out of control over the preceding weeks. Sometimes bringing ordinary reality into an extraordinary conversation can be calming.

"Sleep on it this weekend," I finally said. "Think about it, and we'll talk some more on Monday."

"Oooh-K . . . sounds good," Gary said, smiling. The tension from confronting Gary with his options had left me exhausted. As I left, Gary told me, "Have a good weekend. Maybe you can get some yard work done." He smiled. It was amazing. Here we were, literally talking about life and death—*his* life and death. Yet he remembered I was frustrated over the length of the grass in my lawn.

PART THREE

The Deal

22

That afternoon, Michele, Todd, Tony, and I met with Greg and Dorene at Tony's. The reality of Gary's guilt was looming like a large, dark cloud over all of us. Tony, never one to beat around the bush, started out, "Gary's defense team believes these new charges may substantially impact his ability to prevail at trial." He was very serious, though understated. His demeanor told Greg and Dorene something they had anticipated might be coming.

"We understand what you're saying," Greg said. "I try to look at the evidence objectively. I know the strength of scientific evidence." He meant the paint. "It's tough, as you can imagine, to deal with the thought that he could, in fact, be guilty. But he's my brother and I love him. We don't want him to get the death penalty."

"We'd like to have Mark go up and talk to Gary to see if there's any information he has to offer to the prosecutors." Tony was almost wincing as he spoke. "It's a long shot, but we need to try."

Tony wasn't seeking their permission nor deliberately hiding the fact that I had already had an initial talk with Gary. I hadn't yet actually asked Gary if he had any information to offer, and Tony chose his words in a way to show the respect and deference that Greg and Dorene deserved.

Tony gently laid out Plan B to Greg and Dorene: talk for life.

"We'd also like you to stop visiting for a while," Tony added. "We'll have to see how things go. For the time being, we'd like to have Gary focusing on the remaining options."

Greg said somberly, "Well, we want to see him live. Anything you need to do, go ahead. Anything we can do, we will. We have a visit scheduled with him for Tuesday. We'll see him and tell him we love him. Then we'll back away and stop visiting him. I understand what you're saying." It appeared Greg was onboard with Plan B. So was Dorene.

"Anything we can do, just let us know," she said.

I sensed a palpable change in attitude from both of them. Dorene had always been convinced of Gary's innocence. In the beginning, she'd been angry over his arrest, convinced that it was simply absurd. But now, she had a much more solemn demeanor, as if she were re-signed to the dreadful reality that the brother-in-law she loved and cared about deeply was also the nation's most prolific serial killer. If this was true, as it now appeared to be, they would carry that for the rest of their lives.

With Greg, I had always felt—maybe incorrectly, I don't know—that he either didn't like me or didn't trust me, or both. Here I was, one of his brother's lawyers, and all along I had been planning a strategy for the penalty phase as if Gary were guilty. What kind of a defense lawyer starts from the premise that his client is guilty when his client proclaims innocence? Now, however, Greg realized what I had been doing and why. When he left, he shook my hand and thanked me. He'd done that before, but there was something different this time. I felt like he really meant it, from him to me.

Over the weekend, I tried to relax, but my mind was drained from the talks I had with Gary, Greg, and Dorene. I found myself composing conversations in my head—what to say, how to say it, anticipating Gary's possible reaction, strategizing on what approach to try next. Kelly knew what was going on, at least in general. She knew I was starting "the talk" with Gary that we'd anticipated we might have to have, almost from the beginning. She sensed that my stress level had gone up and gave me space to think about things. Marley and Sean spent much of the weekend hanging out with their friends. I did get to watch the NCAA basketball tournament for a while with Sean. . . . It was Final Four weekend. And, oh yes, between games, I managed to mow our lawn.

—◊◊◊—

Early Monday morning, I was back in the face-to-face room with Gary. After the usual exchange of greetings, I asked, "Did you get a chance to think over what we've been talking about?"

"Yeah, I did," he said. "I've been giving it a lot of thought."

"Good. What I'd like to do is have you repeat back to me, in your own words, what I was telling you last week." That way, I could see if I was getting the point across to him.

"Oooh-K." He nodded. "You told me I was probably going to be found guilty."

"Well, a little stronger chance than 'probably' in my opinion. I'd say 100 percent. Do you agree with that?"

"Yes. I'd say 95 percent chance of being found guilty." He was still holding out some hope for an acquittal. I wouldn't quibble with him over that. I knew he had to do this in his own way.

"And if you are found guilty, then what?"

"Oh, I agree they'd give me the death penalty." No argument there.

"OK . . . well, do you want to live?"

"Yes, I want to live. I just don't want to be known as the Green River Killer. I don't want to bring that kind of shame to my family." He was telling me, yes, I am guilty, but I just don't want to admit it. He would rather go to his grave denying it than try to save his life by admitting it.

"Gary, I'm afraid it's too late for that. You are *already* known as the Green River Killer. You'll be known as the Green River Killer forever." I paused—then finished my thought—with a raised voice. "Hell, you'll be known as the Green River Killer even if you're acquitted!" That was harsh, but it was probably true. Unless someone else came forward to take the blame, which hardly seemed likely at that point.

"I know. I know." He acknowledged the truth of what I was saying, looking down, hanging his head and gently shaking it from side to side, sadly. At the same time, he realized his excuse for not cooperating was pretty lame. "But I don't want to plead guilty. I don't want to make any deal." He shook his head, no. No grin this time.

I wasn't letting him off the hook that easily, but I wasn't going to get pushy at this point, either.

"Gary, we've got to keep all our options open. We've got to find a way to save your life."

"Look, Mark," he said, very serious. "I'm not afraid of dying. I'd probably die before all the appeals were done anyway."

This was an argument I was afraid of, because it made some sense. He could deny being the Green River Killer, be the center of attention in the biggest trial in history, and see how the legal stuff played out. He might think he could keep his "ace-in-the-hole"—his knowledge of where missing remains were—until he *really* needed it, such as when he'd exhausted all his appeals and was walking to the death chamber, although that strategy hadn't worked for Ted Bundy.

"But Gary, if you do have information about the murders, you could do a lot of good by cooperating and telling what you know. Think of the families of the victims. They need to know. Imagine if it was your daughter . . . ," I said, trying to reach that sliver of humanity that I knew he had inside of him. He looked down, in deep thought. Then he lifted his head and looked into my eyes.

"No deals."

"OK, that's fine . . . for now. But we're not ending this discussion." I wasn't going to give up yet.

"I know. That's fine." He nodded and grinned again, leaving me to believe the door was still slightly open.

Tony, Todd, Michele, and I met at Tony's office that afternoon. I updated them on the conversation with Gary. Tony remained pessimistic.

"Gary won't go along with any deal because he'd bring shame to his family," Tony guessed. "He'd rather die than do that to Judith and Greg and Dorene. Besides, he told me he didn't do it." The smile on Tony's face revealed he no longer was convinced of Gary's innocence, if he ever had been. Either that or it was his way of saying, "I told you so" regarding Gary's willingness—or lack thereof—to cooperate.

"I'm meeting with his family before they see him tomorrow night. I'll see how they feel," Michele said. "I think he really listens to what Greg says."

"If we can get Greg onboard, I think our boy will get onboard too," Todd said.

"Oh, I think the family's onboard. Obviously, they don't want to see him get the death penalty," Michele replied.

The next day, Tuesday, April 8, I stayed away from the jail. Gary would be meeting with his family that evening, and I didn't want to give him another opportunity to tell me he wouldn't plead guilty. The thing to do, I thought, was to let him stew for a while and see if Greg and Dorene might change his mind.

Late that afternoon, Michele called. She indicated that Greg and Dorene and Eddie and Eddie's wife, Tina, had visited her before going up to see Gary. There was some frank discussion about Gary's case and lots of tears among all of them.

"Mark, it was so emotional," Michele said. "We all cried. When they left, Greg gave me a hug."

"Whoa," I said. "I never saw Greg as the huggy-type of guy."

"I know. It's just so hard to imagine what they must be going through. They just said they love Gary, no matter what he's done, and that they don't want him to get the death penalty. Greg said they would support us any way they can to have Gary avoid the death penalty."

"Do you think they will be with us on this? It's gotta be tough on them."

"Yes. Greg and Dorene said they'd go up tonight and tell him they loved him and wanted him to live, no matter what he'd done. And tell him to listen to his lawyers. They said they'd wait until they heard from us before seeing him again."

"That's perfect," I told Michele. "Now we'll have to see how it goes. We may have to arrange a visit with Greg later, but let's see how it goes for now." I was thinking that if Gary continued to insist on a trial, maybe Greg would be helpful later in convincing him of the wisdom of Plan B. Just as when they were growing up, Greg would do what he could to protect his younger brother.

If Greg and Dorene and Eddie could convince Gary of the importance of trying to make a deal, much of the credit for that would belong to Michele, I knew. Our trust and credibility with the Ridgway family was Michele's greatest contribution to our team.

"It's overlooked," I told her, "but the time you spent communicating with them has been very important. They trust us—and our decisions—because they trust you. Because you took the time and made the extra effort. And you recognized what a difficult time this must be for them. That tends to get overlooked too. Good work."

—⁓—

After another restless night, I went to see Gary on the morning of Wednesday, April 9. He was much more subdued. His eyes were red and puffy. I guessed that he'd been crying.

"What's up, Gary? Are you OK?" I asked.

"Oh, I'm fine," he replied, trying to act as if nothing had changed.

"How'd it go last night?" I asked.

"Greg and Dorene and Ed and Tina visited." His voice started to crack and his eyes filled with tears. "They . . . told me . . . that they loved me." He lifted his head, dabbed his eyes, and composed himself. I knew he didn't want to break down and cry in front of me. What he could do in front of Mary Goody wasn't allowed in front of another man, at least in the world of Gary Ridgway.

"They told me they loved me no matter what," he went on. "And they said they didn't want me to get the death penalty." The fact that those closest to him had told him they didn't want him to die had moved Gary profoundly.

"So let me try to make a deal for you," I pleaded. "Not only would your family want you to do that but think of all the good that could come out of it." Although the "good" was far, far outweighed by the "bad" he'd done, it was something. It was something he could do that could be positive, in a case of overwhelming negatives. He nodded, silently.

Once again, I did most of the talking. If Gary tried to veer the conversation off onto some tangent, I brought us right back on topic. We reestablished our areas of agreement: 95 to 100 percent chance of being found guilty and 100 percent chance of getting death if guilty. I went through the litany of evidence against him all over again, from the most critical, the DNA and paint, to the least important.

"What do *you* think about all of the evidence against you?"

Gary immediately jumped on one of the least critical bits of evidence the state had, fellow Kenworth employee Gary Yager's assertion that he'd heard Gary make disparaging remarks about prostitutes.

"He's making that up," Gary told me. "He's lying because he thinks I turned him in for stealing." Gary started to get a little angry. "Yager got caught stealing thinner from Kenworth and thought it was me who turned him in. That's probably why he's lying."

This was absurd. *He's evading the really solid evidence to talk about this bullshit? I guess that's all he has to defend himself with,* I thought.

"How much thinner?" I wondered how much we were talking about.

"Oh, about a gallon. He got fired and blamed me. I called him about five or six times and told him it wasn't me. We'd been friends, but we never talked after that."

"So your friend, your ex-friend, gets fired for stealing a gallon of thinner. He thinks you told on him, so he tells the police some lie about you 'terminating prostitutes'? To get back at you?"

"Yes," Gary said, defiantly.

"So you're telling me Yager is so mad at you, he'll lie to help convict an innocent person, his former friend, of being the worst serial killer in history?" I allowed my incredulity to show.

"Well . . . yeah." Gary was a little hesitant, starting to realize that this explanation was ridiculous.

"Come on, Gary, that's lame and you know it. Why are we even talking about Yager? He's the very least of your worries. I'm not worried about Yager. But after hearing you say that, it makes Yager sound *more* believable, not less. That's absurd. It's bullshit and you know it." I decided that now was the time to be confrontational.

Gary glanced down sheepishly. His demeanor reminded me of the first night we met and he had denied knowing Carol Christensen or having had sex with her . . . kind of a nonverbal expression of "Oops."

I bored in for the first time in all of our face-to-faces.

"I think you're guilty." Gary nodded and showed no reaction, as if he knew I thought he was guilty all along.

"But that doesn't matter to me," I went on. "As a criminal defense attorney, it doesn't matter to me if you're guilty or innocent. If I couldn't represent guilty people, I wouldn't be in this line of work. As weird as it sounds, guilt or innocence really doesn't matter to me. I'm trying to save your life. I assumed from the start you were guilty. I've told you that from the beginning." I didn't distinguish between what I'd believed and what I'd assumed for the sake of doing my job. After all, up until the new evidence had come in, I had still hung on to a shred of hope that he might actually be innocent.

"Uh-huh. I know that."

"Cases get plea bargained all the time," I went on. "Probably 90 percent of the time, in fact. The state thinks they're all guilty. Otherwise they wouldn't have charged them. Some are innocent, but that's not the issue here. Right now, it's about saving your life. I've got to call you on your bullshit. It's not going to help you if I just agree, 'OK, well, Yager's a liar.' My question was about the evidence against you, but I was really thinking about the DNA and the paint spheres. And the long line of incredible coincidences and circumstantial evidence. This Yager stuff is just bullshit."

Gary furrowed his brow, frowned, and looked down. His shoulders slumped. I realized he was getting the picture. He wasn't going to distract me this time by going off on one of his goofy tangents. But was he ready to take the next step?

He lifted his head and looked me in the eyes.

"What if I don't have information for them?"

I read that as, "I did it but I don't remember everything," or "I killed some of them but not all." The way he said it indicated he might be willing to consider a deal but wanted to know how much information would be needed to escape the death penalty. It was a very good question and led me to believe he was coming around. It also led me to wonder if he was doing some calculation in his mind, regarding the amount of information he had, and the amount of information he would have to disclose to get the deal.

"Well, if you killed, say, Carol Christensen for example, but not the others, I need to know that. I'm not saying that would get you off from the death penalty, but you've got to let me know. You should tell me. Look, you're in trouble, legal trouble, the most serious legal trouble you can have. I mean, life-and-death trouble. Now if you had a life-and-death medical problem, you'd tell your doctors the truth so they could save you, wouldn't you? You wouldn't lie to your doctor. Would you?"

"No."

"Well, you're in life-and-death legal trouble. You need to tell your lawyer, your team of experienced lawyers, the truth. That's the most critical thing. That's the only way a lawyer can help you. You've got to tell us the truth."

I waited but Gary gave no response.

"Gary, you know that everything you say to me is confidential. That means I won't tell anyone else without your approval. That's why a defendant is free to tell his lawyer the truth, even if he thinks it's bad. To really be able to help someone, the lawyer needs to know the truth, and to make sure people tell their lawyers the truth, that's why we have the attorney-client privilege. So if you're at all worried about that, don't be. Anything you tell me is confidential. I won't tell anybody."

I got up and put my file into my briefcase. I put my hand on Gary's shoulder and said, "Think it over some more. Give it some serious thought. I don't want to rush you on this. Take all the time you need. But I think the longer we wait, the tougher it will be to convince Norm Maleng to do a deal. So keep thinking about it."

Gary said he'd think about it some more.

I went back to my office in Kent, wondering whether anything I'd said had gotten through to Gary. That afternoon, I received a call from Michele.

"I just met with Gary," she said. "I'm on my cell phone, walking from the jail to Todd's office. Will you be in your office? I want to call you right back when I get to Todd's." She made it sound important.

"I'll be here."

A few minutes later, Michele called back. She was with Todd in his office. They put me on speakerphone so all three of us could talk. Michele's voice had an excited, breathless quality.

"Gary told me he wants to cooperate," Michele said. "I cut him off and didn't ask for any details. I told him we'd talk it over and that you'd come see him tomorrow. You have another face-to-face with him tomorrow morning, right?" She blurted it all out in one shot. My mind began to do somersaults. *Alright! He's gonna talk!*

"Yeah. Yes, I do. So tell me, how'd it come out?" I asked.

"He told me about his visit with his family last night and how Greg and he had cried. He cried, I cried," Michele said. "He talked about how Greg and Dorene told him that they loved him no matter what and that they wanted him to do whatever he could to live. He said he wanted to live because they wanted him to live. It was pretty emotional." I could tell that much from her tone of voice.

"He asked about a no contest plea, and I told him that wouldn't be possible. I told him the only way the state would consider a deal would be if he told everything he knew," Michele added. "I didn't ask how many or why or any of the other questions that were going through my mind. We didn't go into anything like that."

"You've taken the first big step in saving his life," I told Michele. "We've got a long way to go, but at least it's possible. Without Gary coming around, he would have received the death penalty. You've done a great job." After all of the confrontations that Michele and I had had, it was tough for me to admit, but it was true. The trust and rapport she'd developed with Gary—and with Gary's family—was critical, probably more critical than all of our research and motions.

Of course, getting Gary to agree to talk was only half of what we needed. We also had to convince Norm Maleng to listen. Even if Gary was willing to spill, that didn't mean that Maleng would agree to back off his "no deals" démarche.

As I thought about this, I realized that Mary Goody and Mark Cunningham had been right all along—that at some level, Gary really was anxious to get everything off his chest. But saying he would talk was one thing, getting him to actually talk was another thing entirely. We needed details. Just how much information did Gary really have? What would the quality of this information be? I had the lingering notion that despite Gary's expressed willingness to come clean, getting the awful story out of him would be difficult. And if we were to have any chance of convincing Maleng to back away from death, we had to have it all.

23

We had another team meeting the next morning, Thursday, April 10, at Tony's office.

"Let's just see what Gary has to say," Tony told us. "He may have changed his mind already. Mark, you can go up there and see what he really has in the way of information. Then we can reconvene and figure out where to go next."

"If he says, 'I killed Carol Christensen, but nobody else,' that's not going to get us anywhere," I said. I still wasn't sure that Gary was clear on the concept of talking for a deal.

"I still think we ought to take it slow," Michele said. "There's no need to do it right now. We've been focusing up until now on the first four counts. There's a lot more we need to know about the others. And the Red River cases." Michele seemed to be suggesting that we do more work on the rest of the cases before confronting Gary.

In these circumstances, however, I disagreed.

"We need to find out generally what Gary's talking about. . . . You know, how many? And we need to get a grip on the quality of his memory. I'm curious to hear just exactly what he says he remembers. He's been a little spotty in some areas, like about his childhood, for instance. Usually, when he's asked about the past, he says 'Ask Greg. Greg would know.' This stuff all happened a long time ago. We need to get a sense of what he *does* remember."

"Let me make a suggestion, Mark," Tony said. "Tell Gary we will only talk about things he did in King County. They're driving the boat on this. We don't need to talk with him about anything that occurred outside of King County." There it was again: the Yates bugaboo.

"Absolutely," I said. "All we can worry about now is King County. There's no sense in talking about any other jurisdictions until we see what he has to say about the King County cases."

"By all means stick to King County," Todd said. "Don't worry," he added, addressing himself to Michele. "We *won't* rush into anything. But we *do* have this narrow window of opportunity before Norm files for death again. We've only got about three weeks left before the notice deadline. We can't rush, but we also can't drag our feet. We don't want to spin our wheels."

"It seems to me it shouldn't take too long to just see what Gary has to say," Tony said. "Then we talk about it and decide whether to make a pitch to Norm. If we decide to make an offer to Norm, we make it. And then Norm will say 'No, thank you,' and at that point we move ahead the way we've been going—getting ready for trial." Tony was still sure that any plea offer would be rejected. After all, he'd known Norm Maleng for more than forty years.

"If Gary does have good information, I think the Sheriff's Department will try to convince Norm to drop death," I said. "Reichert wants to resolve this and run for governor.[1] Maybe we should get a better read on their position." I thought Sheriff Reichert might have enough clout to persuade Maleng to agree to a deal. The rest looked at me expectantly.

"I could set up a meeting with one of the detectives I trust," I added. "I could feel him out on the sheriff's position."

"I think the cops would want answers if Gary had them," Tony said. "But our best shot is probably through Jeff Baird. I think we start with talking to Jeff and let him run it up the chain. I know Norm well enough to go talk with him directly, but I wouldn't want to step on Jeff's toes."

Todd said he agreed with me about approaching someone in the Sheriff's Department on a confidential basis to see what the reaction might be, but Michele had doubts.

"I don't think you should make a deal with Reichert," she said. "That's too risky. It could all blow up in our face. We'd look like fools."

"No one's trying to make a deal with the cops," Todd said, with a tinge of exasperation. "They can't make a deal anyway. Only Norm can do that. And anyway, we shouldn't be concerned about how we 'look' to other people. That doesn't even enter the picture. We make a decision *as a team* and let everyone else *outside the team* say whatever they want." As Todd implied, once the team had decided something, there was no room for dissension. And Todd's truculent individualism was coming out. The idea that we should make a decision based on what others might think of us rubbed him wrong.

"Well, that's exactly what I mean," Michele shot back. "The cops can't make any deal, so we shouldn't be talking to any detectives about this." Michele seemed to think I was going to rush off to the detectives to tell them that Gary had just confessed to being the Green River Killer. Then, when Norm later rejected the deal, the detectives would testify to what I had told them. Michele reminded us that any conversation a lawyer might have with the police would not be covered by the plea negotiation rule. But what this really came down to was a matter of trust. I certainly had no intention of blabbing any of Gary's secrets to the detectives, but I did want to see if I could get a better feel for the Sheriff Department's position on the death penalty for Gary. That was the *realpolitik* of what we were talking about.

I tried to explain this to Michele. "Everything we say and do at this point still presumes that this case is still going to trial. Nobody's going to say anything to anybody that will come back to bite us in the ass later. I'm just talking about getting information *from* them, not about giving them any information."

"I don't see any harm in Mark talking with the detectives about their position," Tony said, "but there's not much benefit either. You're not going to be telling them Gary *has* information. You're just discussing a natural topic of conversation, at least in this case. I've had similar discussions, just idle conversations, where they've indicated their desire for information outweighs their desire for a death sentence." That seemed to settle the matter.

"You have your conversation with Gary this afternoon," Tony told me. "Give me a call when you're done. If he really does have information he wants to give up, I'll call Baird and set up a meeting for Monday. In the meantime, I don't see a big problem with you talking to a detective."

"OK," I said. "I'll call you after I talk with Gary. If Gary agrees, then you contact Baird to set up a meeting."

"If we do talk to one of the detectives, I'll be there, too. If you don't mind?" Todd asked. Todd was trying to reassure Michele that I wouldn't spill the beans—that he would be a witness. It wasn't a bad idea to have four ears, not just two. That way, we would run a lower risk of misinterpretation of anything a detective might happen to tell us.

"OK, so we've got a plan for the next few steps." Tony rose out of his chair and started to gather his things. He had to be in court on another case, so our meeting adjourned.

―⁓―

After I left Tony's office, I went directly to the jail. Once more, I took my plastic chair in the stark white face-to-face room on the eleventh floor. A few minutes later, the guards led the shackled Gary into the room and then retreated so as not to eavesdrop on our conversation.

"Hey, Gary," I said.

"Hello," he said. "How ya doin'?" He seemed to be in good spirits. Upbeat even. The puffy red eyes of the day before were gone.

"Fine, I'm fine. So Michele says you'd like to try for the deal. I think that's really great. I'm glad. At least that will give us a chance to save your life." I hoped to get that in before he told me he'd changed his mind.

"Well, you know, I'm not so worried about getting the death penalty or dying myself," Gary said. "But when Greg, the other night . . ." His voice trailed off and his mood turned somber again. He started to choke up, trying to keep himself composed, but failing.

I had a sudden insight: for years, Gary had thought of himself as worthless and had lived with a deep shame he could never share. But now his older brother had told him that he loved him, that he didn't care what Gary had done, that he didn't want him to be executed. It was a sort of unconditional love that Gary had never before experienced from his own family, except perhaps from Judith. The support from Greg had touched Gary deeply.

"When Greg told me . . . he wanted to see me live . . . and that they loved me . . . you know . . ." His voice faded, he wiped his eyes with a Kleenex, then looked at me and nodded. "And I really want to try to do what I can for the families." He was trying to keep his chin up, trying not to let the tears flow.

"Well, you're doing the right thing." I put my hand on his shoulder and looked in his eyes. "It's not going to be easy. It'll be OK to cry. That's perfectly acceptable. You *are* doing the right thing. For Judith, for your family, and for the victims. And for yourself. You will feel better about yourself, because you'll be helping people get answers. We'll help you through this, every step." I continued to try to build him up, to praise him for making this decision. "So now I need to know what kind of information you have."

"Oooh-K." Gary kind of snapped out of the doldrums and quickly transformed back to the guy who first came in. He seemed anxious, almost pleased, to be able to begin to tell me about his murderous past.

"Remember the house in Federal Way I told you about, where I did some auto painting on the side?"

"Yeah . . . kind of." I vaguely remembered the conversation. He had mentioned this when Todd and I had visited him on April 2. Gary told us then that he'd done some auto painting for cash at a house where there was a lot of partying going on all the time. He had claimed that prostitutes and bikers hung out there and that sometimes, some of the guys had sex with the prostitutes in one of the bedrooms. But Gary had denied doing any of that himself. Just painted cars and got paid, he'd said.

But now he offered a different story.

"Well, there were other things going on at that house . . . drugs, stolen property, bikers, and ladies . . . you know, prostitutes, coming over," he said. "I never did any of that stuff there. But they were drinking and drugging and partying all the time."

"Whose house was this again?" I asked. In addition to the information he was telling me, I was trying to pay close attention to his nonverbal cues—demeanor, facial expression, eye contact, body position, what he was doing with his hands—those kind of things. Those indications, as well as the substance of what he was saying, would help me determine if he was being honest or not.

"The house belonged to R. J. . . . R. J. Wilson."[2]

"Do you know his first name?"

"No. I only knew him as R. J."

"All right. Go on."

"There was another guy who was always there, a friend of R. J.'s. His name was Al, or Alex, Nickels. He's dead now. He died in late '83 or early '84. There was also a guy named Jack Shevcock or something like that. And Dennis. And Terry. He was a blond guy. They hung out there all the time."

Gary continued. "One of the ladies who came by was a blonde named Lynn. She drove a beige 1970 Cougar." Details like that were giving this story a ring of truth. "Another lady who was there all the time . . ." He looked up, trying to recall her name. "I can't remember her name. She was a black lady, about my size."

As Gary talked, I listened patiently, trying to be unexpressive, nodding occasionally and taking notes. At this point, I wasn't going to press him on inconsistencies like a cross-examination. I just wanted to let him talk and not do anything that might slow him down or distract him.

Gary went on. "I went to some old, abandoned barn with them, six or seven of us. I'm not sure where it was. There was nothing else nearby. I got really drunk, which was unusual for me, even back then. I passed out and don't really remember much of what happened. When I woke up, R. J. was the only one there. R. J. showed me pictures they had taken of me having sex with the black prostitute. They had taken pictures of me with my hands around her neck. She was naked and her eyes were closed. She looked dead. R. J. told me she *was* dead. . . . Maybe I killed her." I wondered if he was now backing away from actually confessing to murder. After all, he was "passed out," she "looked dead," "maybe I killed her." The language he was using was giving him some wiggle room. With the words he was using, I was afraid he was heading for a continued denial. But as I scrutinized every word and movement, it certainly appeared to me that he was being honest with me. The details seemed so specific.

Gary said he was told the boys in the barn had videotapes, not just of him but others as well. He said he never saw the videos and had no idea who had them now.

"R. J. told me they had pictures of me with two dead prostitutes. They were both black ladies. One had pants around their neck and one didn't." I wondered if that had been Opal Mills and Cynthia Hinds. I also wondered if he was savvy enough to throw in a detail here and there that would match up with some fact he'd learned by our going over the discovery with him in order to give his story more verisimilitude.

"I don't know who has the pictures now," he said. This immediately made me wonder, *Are there pictures out there somewhere? And if they were, why hadn't they popped up before now?* I decided to let this go for the moment.

"OK. So you wake up, R. J. tells you this stuff. What happened next?" I wanted to keep him on track with his story.

"After midnight, more like one in the morning, R. J. had me help him dump her body in the Green River . . . on the bank."

He was getting closer to admitting to rendering criminal assistance or—arguably—being an accomplice to one of the Green River murders. And two guys made sense, particularly in the Cynthia Hinds and Marcia Chapman cases. Not to mention the Mills case, with its double load of DNA. Many had always believed that some of the murders were the work of two men. The DNA found in Mills came from at least two male contributors and according to the experts, Gary could have been one of them. Hinds and Chapman, the other two young black women discovered in the Green River on August 15, 1982, were also in that two-person category, in part due to the large rocks that had been placed atop their bodies to hold them submerged and in place. And the rafter who had reported the bodies in the river that day, Robert Ainsworth, had told the police that he'd seen two men nearby as he drifted down the river that summer day.

"Who did you help put on the riverbank?"

"The black lady in the picture," Gary said. He looked down. "Actually, he [R. J.] filmed or took pictures of two or three black ladies, and one white lady. I'm quite certain I remember Coffield. There's a good chance I had sex with her."

"OK . . . now I'm getting confused. Are you saying that you and this R. J. killed Wendy Coffield and two or three black girls too?"

"Yes," he said. He looked up at me.

"Do you remember which one was first?" I tried to keep my tone more quizzical than confrontational.

"Yes. I'm quite certain Coffield was the first." He nodded and looked directly into my eyes. I could see his eyes were welling up with tears. I could sense he was having a tough time. On the other hand, I wasn't convinced this wasn't an act. I remained cynical on the inside and tried to remain supportive on the outside.

"OK. That's good. The stuff about the black lady and helping R. J. take her to the riverbank. . . . Was that true or not? I mean, did that really happen, was it after Coffield, or what? You've got to remember a couple things: I'm here to try to save you from the death penalty. You need to trust me and tell me everything you did. The truth and nothing but the truth. Know what I mean?"

"Yeah, I know. It's hard." Now *that* had to be the truth.

"You know, like I said, this is just between you and me. I'll talk to Tony and Todd and Michele about it in general but no one else on the team will ever know if they don't have to. I mean, if we don't make a deal, none of this ever comes out. You know that, right?"

"Oooh-K." He perked up a bit. I could see he was regrouping himself for the next round of disclosure.

"So go ahead. Keep going."

"Well, we did Coffield, the three black ladies in the river. . . . There were some others. I don't know their names." He paused, apparently trying to recollect a name or something that could identify a given victim.

"How about Christensen? That's your DNA. Did you kill her?"

"R. J. killed her. I loved her. He was mad at me for some reason and killed her."

I pressed him for details about this.

"So where did he kill Christensen?"

Gary put his hand to his chin, closed his eyes, trying to remember. "I'm quite sure it was in a hotel room somewhere."

"But you say you loved her. Why can't you remember? If you loved this woman, I think you'd remember where he killed her. Come on!"

He mumbled something, then looked me in the eyes.

"It was me," he said. "*I* killed her. We were in a hotel on Pacific Highway, somewhere near the intersection with Kent-Des Moines Road. We were having sex and we started arguing about something. She was going to leave and I went into a rage and choked her." He looked down again. "I really . . . loved . . . her."

Gary started to cry. I thought I should move on, so I didn't ask him anything else, although I wondered, why had Carol Christensen been so different than the other victims—dressed, with her driver's license left behind, with the fish and the wine? Because Gary "loved" her? We sat there for a while, and he composed himself. He said he had to go to the bathroom and was allowed to make this trip unescorted to the bathroom.

While Gary used the bathroom, I wrote down the names of the forty-nine victims, placing them in categories according to the cluster site where their remains had been found: Green River; Star Lake; Enumclaw; SeaTac South; SeaTac North; Mountain View; I-90/North Bend; Oregon; Other South King County; and still missing.

After about five minutes, Gary returned from the bathroom.

I asked, "You all right?"

"I'm fine." Gary was back to normal, smiling, nodding yes, making eye contact again.

"I want to go through each of these cluster sites to get an idea," I said, as I showed him my note page with all the cluster sites and victims' names.

"Oooh-K." He seemed interested in the list, looking it over very carefully. My impression was that he was trying very hard to remember details about a specific victim or a cluster site.

"Let's start with the river cases. Wendy Coffield's a yes. Was it just you or you and R. J.?"

"Me and R. J."

"And the three black women—Chapman, Hinds, and Mills?"

"Yes. Me and R. J."

"How about Deborah Bonner? White girl, she was found in between . . ."

"Yes." Gary interrupted me before I could finish. "Me and R. J."

"How many others did you kill with R. J.?"

"Two. Or three. Christensen. One in Federal Way we left at a construction site." He had to be referring to Deborah Estes. Of course, she had just been listed as a new charged victim, one with paint, no less, so Gary knew the authorities would probably be able to prove that one.

"And . . ." He glanced at the names on the paper. "Do you have anyone on Auburn-Black Diamond Road?" He was referring to Yvonne Antosh. On my list, I had referred to her as being found near Soos Creek. I had made no mention of Auburn-Black Diamond Road, which indeed was the road Gary would have traveled on to dispose of Yvonne Antosh's lifeless remains. This was the first thing that Gary had told me that could be taken as unprompted, verified information.

I said, "Yeah, I believe you would be referring to Ms. Antosh. Soos Creek."

In my mind, this added to the veracity of what Gary was telling me. I decided to see what he had to say about his involvement in the Star Lake cluster.

"How about Star Lake?"

"Yeah. That was me alone. No R. J. I left five, no six, I think, over there." Nodding, but with a twinge of embarrassment.

I didn't flinch or recoil. He was on a roll and I didn't want to slow him down. "How about out on Highway 410 in Enumclaw?" I asked.

"No. Never went out there." He said this with certainty. "Oh, I've been out that way camping with Judith, but no, I didn't put any bodies out there."

Was he backing away?

"You can tell me, you know. It doesn't make a difference to me. In fact, if you did leave some out on 410, I need to know."

"No. I didn't leave any bodies out on 410."

I asked "Was it R. J.?"

"No, I don't think so. I don't know."

I decided not to press Gary on the Highway 410 victims—three of them, Debbie Abernathy, twenty-six; Mary Sue Bello, twenty-five; and Martina Authorlee, eighteen. I had two thoughts: one, if I started calling bullshit on everything he said, he might clam up entirely and go backward. The other was that it was entirely possible there were two or more different unrelated serial killers and that Gary in fact had no involvement in the Highway 410 cluster.

"How about the north end of SeaTac Airport?"

"No. Dated out there but never left any bodies there."

"OK. How about the south end of SeaTac Airport?"

"Yes. Those are mine. I left four out by the Tyee Golf Course, in the woods out there. Quite certain it was four. Maybe five."

This group included Connie Naon, twenty-one; Andrea Childers, nineteen; Kelly Ware, twenty-two; and Mary Bridget Meehan, nineteen. Mary Meehan had also been eight months pregnant. Once more, I was struck by how young all the Green River victims had been.

"Were those by yourself or with R. J.?"

"By myself. One I strangled with my socks and left my socks around her neck."

I knew this had to be Gisele Lovvorn, who'd only been seventeen when she was murdered in the summer of 1982.

He sort of grinned, not with pride but rather with embarrassment, and shook his head, implying he knew that had been stupid of him to leave evidence behind. I thought no one on our team had ever told him about the fact that Gisele Lovvorn had been found with a pair of black men's dress socks knotted around her neck. But then I realized that this fact was included in Detective Peters's affidavit in support of the search, which Gary had a copy of, so he could have gotten this information from that document. But then, why would Gary accept blame for something he'd only read about?

"Do you recall one of the victims was pregnant?" I asked, referring to Mary Meehan.

"No." He looked perplexed, slowly shaking his head in the negative.

"All right. How about in the gully by Mountain View Cemetery?"

"No." Again, looking into my eyes, shaking his head, apparently giving each of these a lot of thought.

"How about out where Highway 18 crosses I-90, and North Bend?" This would take us closer to Kim Nelson, "Star," last seen alive on the morning of Halloween 1983. There were five other victims in that cluster, too.

"No," shaking his head, thinking. "No. No one out there."

"How about Oregon? Did you ever take any remains to Oregon, just outside of Portland?" There were four victims in two Oregon clusters. Investigators were sure that some of those remains had been taken there by the killer to throw them off the track.

"No." That answer came quick. There was no need to even think about it.

"How about the one on the list that was found in Pierce County, just over the county line near Jovita Boulevard in Sumner?" This was Colleen Brockman, sixteen, last seen on Christmas Eve 1983.

"Yeah, I picked her up in Chinatown and killed her in my truck. I think she had braces." Colleen Brockman did indeed wear braces.

"Were you in King County when you killed her?" As soon as I asked that question, I wished I hadn't. That took us into the "Yates" area, where we didn't want to go, at least not yet.

But before I could tell him he didn't have to answer that, he said, "In Seattle. We parked somewhere about a block west of Rainier Avenue, behind a bunch of businesses."

"How about the girl found out by Green River Community College? Did you ever leave someone out there?" This was Cindy Smith, seventeen, the last listed Green River victim, who had vanished from Pacific Highway South in March 1984.

"No," he replied without hesitation.

"How about Seward Park?" Mary West, sixteen, had been found there, a large park in south Seattle.

"No."

"How about Cottonwood Park, a little farther north up Green River on Frager Road?" A set of partial remains later identified as coming from Tracy Winston had been found there, years after the murders had seemed to have stopped.

"No, I'd been there with Marcia before, but I never killed anybody there," Gary said. "Or left any bodies there."

"How about this list of girls who were never found? Did you kill any of those? How about Keli McGinness?"

"No. I didn't kill her." But of course, he'd already admitted to having "dated" her.

"Marie Malvar?" I continued down the list.

"No."

"Rebecca Marrero?"

"I don't remember their names. Lots of times, I never knew their name. Or they go by a fake name, you know." He looked at me with that half-grin, half-embarrassed look. As sad as it was, it made sense and I was sure it was true. And it would make this process a lot murkier and more difficult.

"Patricia Osborn?"

He shook his head.

"Pammy Avent?"

Again, he shook his head.

"Kase Lee?"

Again, he shook his head and shrugged his shoulders. Names meant nothing to him.

"April Buttram?"

"No. I did *not* kill her." He said that with a degree of certainty. That sort of piqued my interest.

"Oh, really? How do you know you did *not* kill her?"

"Her name. I never killed anyone named April." I wanted to smack him or laugh in his face while calling bullshit! I tried to maintain.

"Gary, not less than two minutes ago, you told me names meant nothing to you! Now that's the reason you know for sure you didn't kill April Buttram? Come on!" I'm sure he sensed some of my exasperation.

"That's true. Well, I don't *recall* ever dating anyone named April. I would have remembered that name, you know." Gary emphasized and stretched out the word *recall* which we all know, thanks to Oliver North among others, is a clever way of avoiding a true answer. He looked at me, nodding and smiling as if the answer had satisfied me. After all, April is also the name of a month, so *anyone* would probably remember if he had ever dated someone named after a month. No, the answer didn't satisfy me, but I didn't want to interrupt the flow so I didn't continue to press him on it.

"Any others they don't know about?" This would be valuable information, if it existed.

"Yeah, there's a couple of others. One is in the woods up behind K-Mart in Kent . . . in the woods off Kent-Des Moines Road. One is up by a hospital in the north end. She died of an overdose. R. J. and I dumped her there. There's one in the woodsy area over by Lewis and Clark Theatre [on Pacific Highway South, south of the airport]. I think there's a building there now. Or a parking lot. And one up toward Duvall."

"All right," I said. "That's what we need to know. You're doing great." Despite my doubts, I wanted to encourage him. It seemed as if it was getting a little easier for him to discuss this stuff.

"And there was a black guy. He's the only guy . . . you know, the only *man* we killed. R. J. shot him. It was self-defense. The guy pulled a gun on him. R. J. didn't want to get the police involved, so we dumped him in the river near the Duwamish Drive-In [in south Seattle]."

"When was that?" I asked, wondering if we might be able to corroborate this homicide.

"1982, I believe," Gary answered. "Oh, yeah, there was another male victim. Alex. Alex Nickels. I was there when R. J. shot him because Alex had taken some of the pictures and videos from R. J.'s locker. He shot him. We rolled him up into an old rug and dumped him in the landfill at 188th." *Gee,* I thought. *That's the same dump I use.*

"When was that?"

"Late in '83 or early '84. I don't remember exactly."

We had started at noon. It was nearly four. We were just about done. I had a couple more questions. "How come one girl was on the bank and the others were in the river?"

"Well, I had come back to put her in the river, but some guy came floating by, so I never got to it." He grimaced, recalling an event that nearly got him caught back in August 1982. "The guy asked if I had caught anything. I guess he thought I was fishing. I told him no and asked if he'd seen anything. Then I got outta there."

"What were the rocks in the vagina about?" I asked, casually. I wanted to touch this topic gently to see where it went.

"I don't know. That was R. J.'s thing. Something about the pyramid-shaped rock and money, like the pyramid on the back of dollar bills. I'm not really sure." I sensed he was not being truthful about this but again decided not to press him. We could pry into the deeper and darker recesses of his mind later—right now we had what we needed to send out feelers about a deal.

I wrapped up the session by complimenting him on his disclosures. It had to be a very difficult step to take but he had done it. I sensed he felt good that he was getting it off his chest. "I'll be back in the morning and we'll talk some more."

"Oooh-K. See you tomorrow."

As I left the jail, my head was spinning, buzzing with Gary's revelations, and the challenges that lay ahead. As I parsed through what Gary had just told me, I kept wondering how such an apparently nice guy could commit such depraved and inhuman acts of violence. The whole thing seemed so off-the-wall as to be unreal.

I went straight to Todd's ACA office.

"Groon," I said, "you've got to hear this."

"Talk to me. What'd our boy have to say, O enlightened one?" he asked.

We went to the Merchants' Café and picked up some pints. I was anxious to tell Todd what I'd just learned, or it was going to get away from me. It seemed enormous. I summarized most of the four-hour conversation with Gary as I reviewed my notes with Todd.

"Well, what do you think?" Todd asked me, when I was done. "Do you think our boy's for real?"

"Yeah, I do. This stuff had so many details, so many bizarre twists and turns. . . . Who could make that shit up?" But at some level, I was still trying to convince myself that Gary had told the truth. "And why would he confess to just twenty-five, if he'd really killed fifty? What would be the point in that? It has a ring of truth, under the circumstances."

"Maybe he was fucking with you and just wanted to see how you would react?" Todd was reaching for possible other explanations.

"If that's the case, the man is one fine storyteller." And that could be the case. I had already seen firsthand Gary's topic-hopping ability to craft stories intricate in trivial detail—although none of them until now had involved such murderous mayhem. "But how would he have known about remains on Auburn-Black Diamond Road? Unless he had talked to someone on the team about it."

"That's doubtful. Lis, and maybe Denise and Bettye, are probably the only ones who even know the name," Todd pointed out. "No. You're right. It fits that there were two guys. It's *got* to be the truth. It's too bizarre to be a fabrication. Actually, it's probably a little of both."

I called Tony but he was gone for the day. I left a message.

"Hey, Tony, I just finished with Gary. Things went very well, so we're going ahead with Plan B." I now drove back to my office in Kent, thinking about what Gary had told me and trying to think of additional questions for tomorrow. When I got there, I called Michele and let her know that Gary had essentially admitted to his involvement in about twenty to twenty-five murders. I wanted to bring her up to speed, because we had another face-to-face meeting with Gary scheduled for 8:30 the next morning. This time Michele would come too, to hear it directly from Gary himself.

"Oh, my god!" Michele said. "Did he really? That's amazing. Do you think he was telling you the truth?"

"I think so. I mean, how could that stuff be a lie? And a couple things . . . well, he just *has* to be telling the truth. We'll see what he has to say tomorrow. See you then."

I got home around seven and took Marley and some of her friends to watch a high school soccer game. I sat in my truck and watched the game from the parking lot. But I didn't really see anything. I kept going over and over all the bizarre things I'd heard that day. I could feel my heart pounding and pounding as I sat there in silence, my mind racing all over the place. An occasional roar of the crowd would redirect my attention to the game, but only momentarily.

Was this really the truth? Would it be enough to get a deal? How much of what Gary told me might be his bullshit, and how much more hadn't he told me at all? How could this pleasant, polite, mild-mannered guy have done anything like what he's already confessed to?

How would we take the next step? This was a deliberate process, one step at a time. But we had to move forward. Once we got the ball rolling, it was important to keep the momentum, keep progressing toward the goal. I suppose the soccer game unconsciously seeped into my thinking. I knew there was a lot more to get out of Gary.

When the game was over, I came back to reality. I was still Marley's dad, even if I had spent the afternoon with a confessed serial murderer. I took the kids for ice cream on the way home, and when we finally got to our house, I wanted to let Kelly know what had happened. But I knew I couldn't. I'd promised Gary I wouldn't tell anyone outside of those on our team who needed to know. Besides, I already knew Kelly didn't want to know. Over the years, she had grown sick and tired of hearing about all the horrible deeds my clients had committed. She actually preferred not to know.

I was still keyed up and had a hard time getting to sleep. When I did drift off, my mind filled with images of two men, leaving a lifeless young woman in a river, two feet under the water, weighted down with a big rock.

Had this really happened? Was this the sudden gush of confession that Mary Goody had predicted? I couldn't make up my mind. I did know we had a lot of hard work ahead of us if we were going to sell the prosecution on the merits of sparing Gary Ridgway's life.

24

The next day, Friday, April 11, 2003, I joined the morning I-5 rush-hour traffic for the hour-long crawl into Seattle from Kent. I met Michele at the jail lobby on the third floor, the place where the face-to-face paperwork was always sorted out. Despite our disagreements in the past, our greeting was cordial. However, I knew that Michele still doubted the wisdom of proceeding with Plan B so soon.

As we were waiting for clearance for the face-to-face, Michele handed me a copy of an e-mail she'd sent to Todd and me that morning. I scanned it quickly. In this e-mail, Michele still wanted to slow down. She didn't want us to have any off-the-record discussions with anyone on the task force. She still wanted us to consult with other Seattle-area lawyers from outside the team, to "advise" us. She said we would be "viewed as fools" and "viewed as idiots" and "I know I am right about this. . . . We will be viewed as *stupid* by everyone in the defense bar, as well as many practitioners across the country, if we don't give this more consideration. The most important issue, however, is that GR will lose his life. I know it."

I tried my best to remain cool.

"Michele, this is what we talked about yesterday at Tony's," I told her. "No one is going to say *anything* to any detective that will come back to hurt us. We would only try to get information without giving anything up. And there is no need to bring in anyone else on this. I agree that these people you suggest we get advice from are all great lawyers. But we've been through this. We don't need to go outside the team for a second opinion. We've got eight good opinions, eight experienced lawyers, on our own team right now."

I'm sure she could tell I was less than thrilled with her e-mail. She glared at me, clearly irritated by my continued resistance to her suggestions. We dropped the subject for the time being, and went up the elevator to the eleventh-floor face-to-face room to wait for Gary.

I definitely didn't want Gary to think there was any dissension on the team. Michele and I were chatting about something unrelated to the case and happened to be smiling when he came into the room.

"You're not going to be smiling when this meeting's over," Gary said, as he walked in and closed the door behind him. He nodded with his sheepish half-grin. I worked to maintain my composure.

"Why, Gary? What's up?" *Oh, shit,* I thought, *he's going to recant everything. He's changed his mind. He doesn't want us to do the deal!*

"I'm a con," Gary said. "I manipulated you all. . . . I'm a liar. I don't want to die," Gary said, in a very serious tone.

"What do you mean?" I thought, *Now he's going to claim he lied about killing those girls.*

"I killed 'em all," Gary said, very matter-of-factly. "All of them. And six more they don't know about."

A flood of emotions and thoughts immediately rushed through me, all at once. Revulsion—*all of them.* Skepticism—*this is different than yesterday.* Relief—*but at least he's not recanting.* Satisfaction—*Gary was trusting us enough to disclose more of the terrible things he'd done, which is what he needed to do to give us a chance at saving his life.*

Simultaneously, my instincts as a lawyer took over, in an effort to continue to extract more information—information we needed to make the deal happen. Without missing a beat, without letting him know that he'd actually conned me the day before, I said, "That's good Gary. That's the kind of stuff you have to be able to tell us. That's the stuff that can save your life. The truth about everything you did."

Inside, my mind was in turmoil, but I tried to let Gary see only my professional exterior. I wanted him to know that it was good for him to trust us enough to tell us his darkest secrets. And it was good that he wasn't turning his back on cooperating, which, I believed, was the only way left to avoid the death penalty.

"The more details and information you can provide, the better chance of getting a deal," I told him. "And the more healing you will bring to their families." I wanted to continue reminding him that he'd be bringing some closure, some healing, to the families of those he had murdered. He was doing a good thing by being willing to provide this information, and I wanted to reinforce that with him.

Michele nodded and added, "Mark's right, Gary. You've got to tell us everything. It's your best chance to save your life. And think about the families."

"I did them all by myself," Gary said. "There was no R. J. All that was made up. No black guy killed and dumped at the landfill. No barn. No pictures. I made it all up. I wanted to tell you the truth, but I couldn't get it all out. I've been lying for so long . . ." Gary's voice faded off once more. But just the fact that Gary admitted lying did not convince me that he wasn't lying when he said he'd acted alone. How could I know that he wasn't lying now, covering up for someone else? How could I believe him? The only way to resolve that critical question was to force him to be as specific as he could about each of the forty-nine murders—plus six others that the police hadn't yet found, according to Gary. Now, however, was not the time for confrontation.

We spent two hours going over the various cluster sites and the number of victims he had left at these. That was how he remembered the killings—where he left the bodies.

"There are six, or maybe more, out on Highway 410, one by SIR—you know, the race track out off Highway 18, Seattle International Raceway. And . . . uh, there's one up near Duvall, two more up in North Bend. I'm quite certain there's one more they never found up at Star Lake. Malvar is in a gully, south of Kent, up the hill off of West Valley Highway." He obviously had much more information than he had previously let on.

"They shouldn't waste their time and money looking over some half-acre area," he said, referring to the police searchers. He wanted to take the task force on a field trip to show them where the still-undiscovered remains were.

"I can take them right to the spot," he said. He really wanted to go on a field trip—after eighteen months in jail, who wouldn't? I thought that this prospect was highly unlikely, even if the state did agree to make a deal. It seemed just too "Hollywoodish" to me: serial killer leads his captors on a trek through the bush to find the victims he'd left behind two decades earlier. But who knew?

"And I'm quite certain I stopped in '85. Maybe I killed one in '85. Picked her up in Tacoma, killed her in Federal Way, and dumped her out on 410. She was the last one." He made it sound like it was the truth. I would soon come to learn that whenever Gary used the phrase "quite certain," he was hedging against his imperfect recollection of people and events. To me, the way he said it made it clear that he was anything *but* certain. The "quite" was a tip-off that he wasn't really sure.

While we were sitting there in the four-by-six-foot face-to-face cubicle, Todd called on my cell phone.

"Hey," he said, "did you get this e-mail from Michele? Can you fucking believe her?"

"Yeah, I got it," I told him, keeping a poker face. "I'm sitting here with Gary and Michele right now, so I'll have to talk to you about that later." My response was ambiguous enough, but even though she couldn't hear him, I hoped Michele knew it was Todd and what he was screaming about.

"Oh, shit!" Todd said. "She's sitting right there, isn't she? I guess you can't really talk about it, all right. Come see me when you get done. We've got a meeting with Tony. Come and get me first and we'll walk down together."

I could tell Todd was livid about Michele's e-mail. I wondered what she would do when she experienced the wrath of Todd. "Will do," I said and hung up.

Gary, Michele, and I continued to talk, in general terms, about his killing spree. We stayed away from specific cases, though.

"Tell us how it would work? How did you manage to kill so many girls and not get caught?" I wanted to see if he took some sort of pride in his depredations.

"They were prostitutes," he said. "I would always pay them first, then we'd have sex, then I'd choke 'em. Then I'd take my money back, you know? Twenty bucks, thirty bucks, whatever it was." The first of many references to the possible role Gary's frugality played in the killings. I had a sudden flashback to Mary Goody's reports, in which Gary's relatives had all remarked on what penny-pinchers Tom Ridgway and Gary both were, and Matthew's recollection of going with Gary to look for coins in the seat cracks of wrecked cars at the junkyard. The unavoidable conclusion was that Gary might have killed his victims simply because he was too damn cheap to pay them. A new breed of killer—the "psychofrugalpath."

Michele sat quietly and listened to Gary's admissions.

"Where'd you go?" I asked. I wanted to know where these murders had occurred.

"Oh, my house, a lot. I killed most of 'em in my house. And in my truck. In the back . . . you know. I'd get them to go into the back of the truck because there wasn't enough room in the front seat. And I had a canopy, so nobody could see us." Gary was nodding, making appropriate eye contact with both Michele and me. He wasn't coming across as boastful or taking pride in what he'd done. Nor did he come across as having much shame or dread about his actions. It was simply matter-of-fact. "And some of them I killed outside, at the spot where they were found."

"How?"

"Oh, I always choked them with my arm," he said, demonstrating his forearm chokehold around the neck of an imaginary victim, gritting his teeth as he applied imaginary pressure.

"How about ligatures?" I asked.

"Oh, yes, I also used ligatures—my socks on that one." He gave us one of those sheepish half-grins. "Clothes, towels, stuff like that. I got smarter after awhile."

"It's amazing you stopped." Michele finally spoke. "None of the so-called experts believe a serial killer will ever stop. But *you* did. And that's great. But . . . *how* did you stop?" This was, indeed, a very interesting question. This, and other aspects of Gary Ridgway and his case, made some of us believe that serial killer profiling was really pseudoscience, not worth the paper it's written on. I had a glimmering of why it had taken the police so long to identify Gary. The investigators were looking for someone who only existed in the minds of people who made their living telling others what to look for, however remote from the reality that might be. But Gary had a quick answer for Michele's question.

"I met Judith."

Immediately, the tears welled up in Gary's eyes and his voice choked up, as he struggled to get words out.

"I met Judith," he said again. That was the answer. He broke down and sobbed for a few minutes. The mere thought and mention of Judith brought Gary to immediate tears. He really did love Judith deeply. Unlike the prostitutes, whom he'd had to pay, Judith had accepted him as he was, no-questions-asked, unconditional love. It was an incredible juxtaposition. One minute, he was describing his killing spree, rather methodically and matter-of-factly. The next minute, he was sobbing at the thought of the wife he loved so much.

As we were getting ready to leave, Gary said, "By the way, I never said anything to anyone about killing prostitutes or 'terminating' prostitutes or dumping bodies. Gary Yager, and the others who said I said things like that—they're all liars. I almost wanted to face the death penalty, just to face those fucking liars."

Wow—Gary was really pissed. I'd never seen that side of him before. He rarely—very rarely—used the F-word. On the way out of the jail, Michele and I did not talk. Outside, she said, "I'll see you at Tony's."

"Yeah, see you there," I said. I was still doing a burn about her e-mail. I headed over to ACA to meet Todd first. Then we'd go Tony's, where we could hash this out with Michele.

Fifteen minutes later, we all gathered at Tony's to discuss our next step. I let Tony and Todd take the lead with Michele. I could tell from Todd's reaction over the cell phone that morning that his response to Michele's e-mail was the same as mine.

"I have some real concerns with the suggestions in your e-mail, Michele," Tony began. "We discussed it already, and we decided we needed to move forward on this now."

"I just don't understand why you always insist on trying to bring someone in from outside the team," Todd added. "You've done this before, and we've already discussed it. And this concerns me, that you still have this need to go outside our team, to get advice from someone 'smarter' than the rest of us. I'm really tired of it."

"I know you all have more experience than me, but with all due respect, you guys just don't get it," Michelle said. "I know we need to move forward. I just don't see any need to rush this. If Norm would do the deal now, he'd do it six months from now. It's too important. I really don't see what good can come from meeting with a detective. It's risky. They'll know something's up. We know Reichert just wants the information. And it wouldn't hurt to get another look at this from someone outside the team . . . someone with experience doing this kind of thing."

It was like talking to the proverbial brick wall—nothing we said seemed to get through.

"There is absolutely no reason to bring in anyone else," Tony said. "And I do feel that we should proceed expeditiously. There's no sense in dragging our feet. Of course, we need to take it one step at a time. I can see Michele's point about contacting the detectives, even though I don't think it will do any harm. I imagine the sheriff's office would be in favor of a deal if Gary really *has* any information."

I could see that Tony was trying to steer a middle course between Michele and me. He reminded us that the proper way to advance the notion of a plea bargain was by contacting the prosecutor's office, but he wasn't averse to my making informal contact with the Sheriff's Department to try to sound them out about their feelings as to a possible bargain.

"I'll call Baird to set up a meeting with him for Monday," Tony said. "They'll bring the sheriff's office formally into the loop if *they* want. I think we ought to stick to the protocol and make our formal contact through the prosecutor."

"I still think we're going too fast," Michele said.

"Your concern is duly noted, Michele, but right now, we're all agreed: this is the way we'll go," Tony said.

"All right, Tony," Michele said. "Whatever you say." I took the last statement as a jab at me. She would move forward with Plan B only if it was *Tony's* request or idea. She went on:

"I told Gary I'd be up to see him this weekend. We won't talk about the cases, though. I'll just let him talk about whatever he wants."

As far as we knew, we left with everyone in agreement.

———

After this summit, I went back to my office in Kent. Tony was going to call Jeff Baird, but that only made me start thinking just how were we going to float this proposition to the prosecutor's office? Legally, under the court rules, we knew any plea offer we might make to the prosecutor would not be admissible as evidence, so we weren't worried that it could be used against Gary. But there were other concerns.

If we did reach an agreement, we would certainly include a provision under Evidence Rule 410 to prohibit the use of anything Gary might tell the state, in the event that the agreement later fell through, and we had to go to trial after all. Independently, and perhaps for slightly different reasons, Tony, Todd, and I had, prior to Gary's confession, each reached the tentative opinion that if we did have a trial, we'd advise Gary not to testify. Now, after his confession to Michele and me, there was really no question that Gary would not be testifying if there was a trial. We were sure he would go along with that.

One obvious risk was letting them know—for sure—that they had the Green River Killer in jail. Not that they needed to hear it from us, but it seemed it might only increase their zealousness and desire to get the death penalty if a proposed deal fell apart. And then *they* would know that *we* know, at least some of us, that our client was the Green River Killer. That would change the dynamic of our relationship with the prosecutors while we prepared for the trial. It was a very slippery slope we were approaching. Michele was right about that. And we didn't want to give the information away for free; that is, give them every-thing they wanted and then have them say thanks, but no thanks. I shuddered when I had those thoughts. I could envision the following nightmare conversation.

"Hi, Jeff. We'd like to talk about a deal."

"Yeah, well, what do you have to offer?"

"Oh, about fifty murders. You know, the Green River Killer."

"We already know that. No thanks."

So to pull this off, there would be risks. And there would have to be a lot of trust. Because there was a second obvious risk in going for-ward on Plan B—leaks. We could only imagine the irreparable harm to the already slim chances of getting a fair trial. It didn't have to be an intentional act, just someone slipping up at a weak moment.

Nevertheless, Todd and I still wanted to take the temperature of the Sheriff's Department on a possible deal. That afternoon, we contacted another task force member that we both knew.

"You guys gonna drop any more cases on us? Man, we're never gonna get to trial," I started.

"That's exactly what you guys *want*," the cop riposted. "Continue this thing forever so you never have to go to trial." But there was some area of agreement: "It's crazy. It sure would be nice if we didn't have to deal with all this legal bullshit. We just want answers to questions. And we got a whole lot of questions."

"Yeah, but *Norm* has made it clear," I pointed out. "He's more in-terested in killing our client than finding answers to your questions."

"You're right. But no one from the sheriff's office has taken that position. Information, that's all *we're* after."

"So what *was* the sheriff's response back then?" I asked, meaning when Maleng had first made his no-plea proclamation.

"Oh, I think it was along the lines that he would wait and see what happens. I know no one in this office ever said what Norm said. The sheriff definitely left the door open. If he could get information, a lot of good-quality information, I think he'd take it over trying to get the death penalty. As cops, I think we all feel he should die for what he did but that it would do more good for everyone if he lived and provided some answers."

Afterward, Todd and I looked at each other with poker faces.

"I think that went well," Todd said with typical understatement, as he opened the door to his car.

"Yeah. Me too. Have a good weekend."

Quantity didn't seem to be an issue in this case. Quality, however, was still to be determined.

Later that afternoon, while I was back at my office, Tony called and left a message. He'd set up the meeting with Jeff Baird for 2 P.M. on Monday, at Tony's office.

———*vvv*———

That night, Kelly and I went over to Brad and Tina's for pizza and beer. I was bursting inside with anticipation. Was it possible we could resolve this whole thing in the next few days? After we left, Kelly said, "I can tell something's up. I understand if you can't tell me."

"I can't tell you, but you should mark this day on your calendar," I said, raising both eyebrows as if to say, *you know* . . .

"I gotcha. Wow. I don't think I want to know."

"I think you're right."

"So what did he say?"

"I can't tell you."

"Oh, yeah." She knew that Gary was confessing to at least some of the murders simply by this "nonstatement" and the vibes she could feel. When you've been married for twenty years, you get to know each other pretty well.

25

Monday morning started off with another slow crawl down I-5 to get downtown for another face-to-face with Gary and Michele. There was a huge jam on the freeway, and by the time I got to the jail, Michele was waiting for me. I resolved to be as cordial and as collegial as I could. I knew that Michele had met alone with Gary over the weekend. She'd sent yet another e-mail suggesting we slow down, which I had ignored.

"So," I said, "how was your meeting with Gary?"

"Fine. We just chatted about stuff. We didn't really talk about anything to do with any of the cases. He seemed to be doing fine."

We went up to eleven and waited for Gary for a few minutes. We'd already decided that we would just talk about the process, the options and possibilities, not specific cases today. That is, unless Gary had specifics he wanted to talk about with us.

"Good morning," Gary said, as he came into the face-to-face room. "Hello, Michele. Hello, Mark. How's everybody doing today?"

"We're good," I said. "What's up?" I saw Gary had something in his hand to show us.

"Well, did you see this?" He showed us a copy of a recent newspaper article, headlined, **Ashcroft wants more death penalties**, or something like that. Yes, we told him, we'd seen it.

"Oooh-K." Gary put the article away and changed topics. "With the flea bargain, will I be able to save all the assets for Judith, like the motor home?"

I started to correct him, *PLEA bargain, not flea bargain,* but couldn't bring myself to do it. That was just the way Gary talked.

"I would think so, but that's not my legal area. Let us check into that." I made a note to pass the concern on to Tony, who was more involved with those issues.

"I just want to make sure she's taken care of." Tears welled up in his eyes again at the thought of Judith.

We talked a bit more about recent news from the eleventh floor. Gary and another inmate had been discussing the recent legal problems of a Washington Supreme Court justice that had been in the news, as well as the cases of Charles Champion and Ronald Matthews, two other eleventh-floor residents, both facing the death penalty for killing police officers in separate incidents. The other inmate had convinced Gary that neither Champion nor Matthews should get the death penalty, because neither had the intent to kill. I reminded him to be careful with what he said to other inmates. Now that he was embarked on his confession trek, I was concerned he might let something slip to another inmate. He told me not to worry.

Michele then spoke up.

"Gary and I had a really long talk yesterday," she said. "I spent quite a bit of time with him." She handed me a typewritten letter, dated April 13, 2003. It read:

To The Ridgway Defense Team:

At this time, I do not authorize any lawyer representing me, or any expert working on my case, to have discussions regarding plea negotiations or settlement of my case with anyone outside of the defense team.

I do not authorize any lawyer, investigator, expert or paralegal to speak to any member of the Green River Task Force about settling or negotiating my case.

Gary L. Ridgway and Michele Shaw, Attorney for Mr. Ridgway

I knew I had to remain absolutely calm. As I was trying to think of what to say and how to say it, a variety of thoughts were bouncing around: *You are shitting me! What on earth is Michele doing? She waited until Gary was here to show me this!* A string of expletives ran through my head. *Great job, Michele! She had this all prepared. She must've either typed it for him and talked him into signing it. Or she suggested it to him, and he asked her to type it up for him! But he always handwrites his own stuff. If that were the case, she had to have done it on Saturday! What is she doing? I know she doesn't* want *Gary to get the death penalty. But there's no excuse for this. We decided* as a team, *now she's going against that decision trying to divide us! I've got to dance through this without letting Gary see how divisive I think this is.*

I looked up after reading through it again.

"What's up?" I asked, trying my best to sound unperturbed. I looked at Gary. He was looking to Michele for guidance. I looked at Michele.

"Go ahead, Gary." She was going to let him try to explain this himself.

"Well, you know . . . uh . . . I don't want . . . uh . . . you know . . . I don't want the team to fight." He'd certainly picked up something having to do with division or tension in our ranks. He wasn't really too sure what he was saying, though. He muttered some more.

"We really need to get some outside help," he said. "You know, like a national expert." *Gee, I wonder where he came up with that idea?* I thought.

Gary was at a loss for words. He didn't even seem to really know what he was doing or saying—or why.

"Well, this second paragraph is fine," I said. "No one is going to be talking to the task force about doing a deal. They can't make deals. Only the prosecutor. And we decided as a team that the only one we'd talk to about a deal would be the prosecutor, not the cops," I explained. "The conversations we were talking about having with the detectives? We weren't going to be making any deals. I just wanted to get some information about their position on the death penalty. So don't worry. Nobody on our team will talk to the cops about any deals. So," I said, "moving back to this first paragraph, do you want to cooperate in exchange for a life sentence?" I asked the simple, but $64,000, question.

"Yes. I do." He nodded and looked me in the eyes.

"Well, to do that we have to discuss it with the prosecutors, right? I mean, they are the ones we *have* to negotiate with, right?"

"Right. Yes." Nodding, getting more serious.

"And you want to try to do that, right? Make a deal for no death penalty? For a life sentence?"

"Yes. Right."

"Then, we'll just have to . . ." As I spoke, I removed the cap top from my pen and put a big black X through the first paragraph, ". . . cross this out. Here." I handed the pen to Gary. "Go ahead and put your initials right there."

First, he glanced at Michele. What could she say? Was this the point where she would interrupt and tell him he shouldn't pursue this deal? That he shouldn't sign anything? Would Plan B suddenly go down the drain? Instead, it appeared she nodded. Then, he initialed the crossed-out paragraph. Now it only read:

> I do not authorize any lawyer, investigator, expert or paralegal to speak to any member of the Green River Task Force about settling or negotiating my case.

I started to breathe again. The deleted paragraph, removing the prosecutor's office from Gary's attempted embargo, meant we could go ahead and talk to the prosecutors after all.

"OK," I said. "That's good. No problem." We'd slipped over that shoal. But now I had a new thought: *What are we going to do about what Michele did?*

"How about a national expert?" Gary was still clinging to one of Michele's suggestions.

"Well, I just don't know that we need another one at this point. We discussed this over at Tony's the other day, and it doesn't make a whole lot of sense to bring in someone who would have to start from scratch. Especially when you have the collective wisdom and perspectives of some pretty good people already on the team. Mary Goody and Mark Cunningham are as respected national experts on death penalty cases as you can find." I was still having to work hard not to lose my temper. It seemed to me that Michele's answer to every question was to ask for advice from someone else. Someone *really* smart. You might look "stupid" if you make a decision on your own.

"Everything we do," I continued, "we think through about ten times. We know everything we do is critical to saving your life. We will proceed with caution. But we have to proceed and not delay."

"Yeah, I understand. What if Maleng says no?" That was a fair question.

"Well, first off, we won't give up anything until or unless we have to. Our operating assumption is that he *will* say no and that there *will* be a trial. And there's really no reason to dawdle. We make an offer to settle. It's not admissible at trial under the rules. If Norm says no, we're back on track for the trial." I thought for a second, then added, "If he says no, there would still be other options to explore besides trial. We'd have to see how it all unfolds."

We hadn't really aired out all these other prospects in our team discussions, but there were things we could do, other than dealing or death. And because it was a life-and-death situation, we had an ethical obligation to continue to try to resolve the case with a plea for a life sentence. We might, for example, find some outside support to attack the prosecutor's death penalty decision on political grounds. By the time the whole thing was over and they succeeded putting a needle in Gary's arm, the government might have to spend as much as $50 million. It wouldn't be long before that issue would rise up and smite the politicians. Did they really want to spend that amount of scarce public resources simply to execute one man, a man who might well die of old age before they could finally kill him? Was that smart social policy? The political pressure would rise as the costs continued to climb, and someone would be sure to put that question front and center before the electorate.

Then there was the full-court legal press we would continue to apply. The issues for appeal would be staggeringly complex and time-consuming, given the uniqueness of the case. We would have to move to continue the trial, to get more time to prepare. On some important issues, we could seek appellate review of Judge Jones's pre-trial rulings. We would generally make it as difficult as possible to prosecute and convict Gary. The harder we fought the case, the longer it would take, the more money it would cost, and the more the political pressure to stop the budgetary bleeding would rise. There would be more negative media coverage, leading to a higher chance of a change of venue, which in turn would drive the costs up even more.

If the case took long enough, maybe the community would get fed up and Norm Maleng would be put in a position where the voters wanted the case to end. If he didn't offer a deal, he would be defeated when he ran for reelection. Or so one theory went.

But we hoped, in other words, that we had ways of getting them to talk. Well, more like ideas we hoped would bring them to the table. Obviously, no one wanted to get to Plan C.

"Maybe we should hire a psychic to see what Maleng's going to do," Gary suggested with a smile.

I laughed.

"There you go . . . that's another good idea . . . a psychic. How about Barbara Kubik-Patten?"

"I'm serious." His smile was gone. I realized he *was* serious.

"No. No psychics. That's not real science, Gary. Besides, I don't think the taxpayers are going to want to pay for a psychic to tell us what Norm's going to do. Our special master only approves stuff if it's 'reasonable and necessary.'" I was trying to maintain a cool, professional demeanor. It was tough. On one hand, I wanted to crack up at the absurdity of retaining a psychic. At the same time, I was furious with Michele for pulling her divisive little stunt.

Gary said, "Yeah, I know they wouldn't pay for it. I was just thinking, maybe we could ask."

"No psychics. I don't think I'd want to base an important decision like this on some advice from a psychic." I was losing my patience.

Michele and I gathered up our materials. I kept the crossed-out letter from Gary in my file. I stood up and put my hand on Gary's shoulder and said, "You're doing the right thing here, Gary. Don't lose sight of that. You've got a lot of good, hardworking lawyers protecting your legal rights. Don't worry about that."

Gary looked up at me, smiled and said, "I know."

I walked out of the small room and stood outside the door. Michele shook Gary's hand and said, "I'll see you later this week, Gary."

Gary smiled and said "Oooh-K. See you later."

As Michele and I rode the elevator down from the eleventh floor, I asked her, "Why don't you come down to ACA so we can meet with Todd." I wanted to hear her explain her actions.

"Certainly," she replied without hesitation, although I sensed a degree of irritation. Other than that exchange, it was an uncomfortably quiet walk to ACA. Unfortunately, from my perspective, perhaps fortunately for Michele, Todd wasn't there, so we had a tense but brief discussion before she left.

"I thought we'd made a decision as a team to move forward," I said. "This was a bad move. It made us look like we don't know what we're doing. It made us look, to Gary, like we can't agree."

"We're moving too fast," Michele said. She wasn't giving up. "He's going to get screwed just like Yates did. We don't know enough about the stuff in other jurisdictions. That's why we have to slow down. There's no reason to rush things. It's his *life.*"

"Well, first, we're not going to do things without thinking them through very carefully. We are well aware of what happened to Yates. Second, although he's consistently denied it, let's say, just hypothetically speaking, Gary told one of us, 'yes, I did kill someone, or more than one, in . . . oh, some other jurisdiction . . . it doesn't matter . . . San Diego, Snohomish County, Pierce County, anywhere they have the death penalty. That wouldn't stop us from trying to make a deal to save his life in King County. That's where his ass is on the line." I continued on my rant, less concerned about controlling my emotions.

"*And*, if we *were* to get King County onboard with our deal," I went on, "then we can discuss other jurisdictions. But there's no evidence he killed anyone in any other county or state or country. And he has denied it every time it has come up between him and me."

"Are you through?" She really didn't like me or anything I had to say.

"No," I continued, "I'm not through. One more point I'd like to make. The worst thing is, even if *you* are right and Tony, Todd, and I are wrong, we made a decision *as a team*. When you're on a team, you have to live with and support the team's decisions. Even if *you* think *you* are right and the rest of the team is wrong. You have to be able to trust your teammates. And you have to be loyal to the team. That's what being on a team is about. If you can't support the decisions of the team, then you shouldn't be on the team."

There, I'd said it: my offer to her to leave the team. But I knew she'd never leave voluntarily. I also knew that it would really upset Gary if she left or was kicked off the team. But I still had to say it, if only to vent.

"OK. I'm done now," I said. Without saying a word, but with a look that could kill, she left.

About an hour later, Todd returned to ACA, and I showed him the letter and told him what had happened. Todd was beyond irate. He called Tony, who had also received the letter. Apparently, Michele had dropped a copy of the letter off at Tony's office that morning before she met me at the jail. Tony hadn't had the opportunity to call Todd or me yet. Todd and I met with Tony that afternoon, just before Tony and I were scheduled to meet with Jeff Baird. Tony, for the first time, was visibly angry with Michele.

"Boy, I'm pissed," he said, as angry as I had ever seen him. But he had a different spin on it. "It has no effect. It's meaningless. We are ethically *obligated* to negotiate for a life sentence, regardless of our client's instructions. It would be ineffective assistance of counsel *not* to try to negotiate for a life sentence. To *not* talk to the state about this would be unethical, and it would be ineffective on top of it.

"Those lawyers she thinks we should consult for advice are all first-rate," Tony continued. "I just don't think we need to hire anyone else. I'll talk to Michele. I feel responsible. I asked to have her on the team."

"Yeah, but we made the decision to hire her as a team," Todd said. "It's not on you, Anthony." He was right. It had been a group decision, not Tony's. And she had done many good things for the team, so it wasn't a bad idea to have her in the first place. We all believed her intentions were good and her heart was in the right place. We just couldn't figure out why she felt she had to bolt on us now, especially after we'd fully discussed everything.

———

We were still fuming at 2 P.M. when Jeff Baird came to Tony's office for our first soundings on whether the state would agree to a plea bargain.

Before Baird arrived, the three of us agreed that Todd should make himself scarce. He and Jeff are both zealous advocates and sometimes bring out the combativeness in each other. We didn't want any personality clashes hanging over this first attempt to approach the opposition, so when Jeff arrived, Todd cordially excused himself and went back to his office to work.

"So what's up?" Baird asked.

"Well, we were wondering if you think there would be any way we could get Norm to take death off the table, if our client could solve some of these 'problems' . . ." That was typical Tony—always take the direct approach.

Jeff lifted his eyebrows, cocked his head, and gave off a small grin. I could see the wheels clicking into place in his brain, then the results, five apples lined up on the slot machine: *We got him. . . . The Green River Killer wants to plead guilty!*

Baird said nothing for a moment while we waited.

"I appreciate the directness of your approach," he finally said. "I was thinking maybe . . . I was wondering why you called this meeting . . . but I wasn't really prepared." Jeff's immediate grasp of Tony's allusion to the state's "problems" was no surprise; he never missed anything. And in this case, the "problems" were significant: seven victims still missing, a dearth of evidence on most of the forty-nine listed Green River cases, and the prospect that Gary's defense might bankrupt the county before it was all over.

"Do you think there's any way Norm Maleng would consider a deal?" I asked.

"I can't say," Baird said. "I wouldn't say no, but I can't say. If it were some vague, you know . . . 'I'll plead guilty to seven counts if you drop the death penalty,' he'd say no. If you come in, and say, solve . . ." He looked to Tony and me to fill in the blank.

Tony gazed at the ceiling of his office as if he were calculating or maybe just pulling a number out of thin air.

"Oh," he said, "let's say, twenty-eight." He was picking a number out of the air.

Baird nodded, almost imperceptibly.

"OK. Say you come in and tell Norm you could solve twenty-eight of these 'problems,' as you referred to them, then I think Norm would want to hear what you have to say."

"Do you think the cops would support it?" I asked.

"I can't speak for the sheriff's office but I think so," Baird said. "Of course, same thing goes. It would have to provide them with information to clear a significant number of these unsolved cases, not just the seven we've already got him on."

"Will Norm listen to Reichert?"

"Well, he'll certainly consult with him. But Norm makes the decision. Norm will consult with a number of advisers, but it's his decision."

"How about you? Would you support it?"

"As you both know, I'm no big fan of the death penalty. If I get a conviction and he's locked up for good with no appeals, I'm happy. That's all I want."

We discussed the process of putting an offer together for Maleng's consideration.

"The evidence rules protect these discussions, but it raises an interesting issue," Baird observed. "If Norm decides no deal, and you put your client on the stand, what's the scope of our cross-examination? It just struck me, I don't know the answer." Essentially, Baird was saying that perhaps the post-Miranda statement standard that might allow the state to use the "not-all-mine" remark Gary had supposedly made to Doyon after his arrest could also be used to get any admissions made by Gary while plea bargaining into evidence as well.

"Well, we can work through those types of things," I said. "But this could get interesting." This was an area of post-Miranda law that had never been tested in court, at least as far as I could recall. Presumably, we could protect Gary with a provision in the plea agreement.

"I think the more tangible, specific, real-quality information he provides, the better chance there is that Norm would say yes," Baird said. "I mean, if he had a chance to solve twenty-eight murders that would otherwise go unsolved, he'd have to consider it. It would be the right thing to do. On the other hand, if it's vague, he could just say, 'No, let the jury decide. Get back to work.' And then there's that gray area in the middle."

"I can tell you that the quantity might be high but the quality could be less than perfect," I said. "It's been twenty years. Plus, he never really knew names and faces."

"Yeah, I can understand how that might be."

"Why don't we meet again Wednesday and see where we are?" Tony suggested. "You have to talk to your guys, and meanwhile, we'll try to get you a little more specific information in regards to what our client has to offer."

Baird agreed to meet again in two days.

⸻

The next day, April 15, 2003, I saw Gary in the face-to-face room, just me and Gary. As I was the one who had built the trust and rapport by meeting with him over and over again for eighteen months, I would be the one to extract the awful truth from him. I began my debriefing of Gary in earnest. I had to get as much detailed information as he had to offer. I had to get an idea on the quality and quantity he had to offer. I had to nail down the information Gary had that we could trade to save his life. Gary began by discussing one of his earliest murders.

"I'm quite certain the second or third one would have been in the south airport cluster." Gary had adopted the term *cluster;* by 2003, the term was used by everyone, even the police, so it wasn't surprising that Gary started using it too. I pulled out a map we had of the south airport area. Gary put marks where he had left the bodies of Mary Meehan, Constance Naon, Kelly Ware, Andrea Childers, and Gisele Lovvorn.

"Right there, I'm quite certain it would be this one right here." Gary pointed to the place where Gisele Lovvorn's body had been found.

Gary looked at me, shaking his head, and sighed.

"What a dad . . . ," he said. Then he stopped, collecting himself. "I picked her up when Matt was in the truck." He stopped, looked down, and shook his head some more. "Must have been a Saturday or Sunday, because I only had Matt on weekends."

"How old was Matt?" I asked, thinking to myself, Poor Matthew. Will he remember this? Did he know she was a prostitute?

"Seven. Or maybe eight?" Gary said. We checked the date. Gisele Lovvorn had possibly last been seen on July 17, 1982.

"Oooh-K. Matt was born September 5, 1975, . . ." Gary was doing the math in his head. "Yeah. He was seven."

"Keep going." I was sorry I had distracted his train of thought, but it quickly returned.

"I saw her hitchhiking and we pulled over to give her a ride. I drove to this spot there . . ." Gary pointed to a spot near the intersection of 19th Avenue South and 202nd Street, an anonymous area south of the airport, stuck between an old cemetery and a then-poorly-maintained Tyee Golf Course. "I told Matt to stay in the truck while we went for a walk."

Gary continued. "We went into the woods. She gave me oral sex . . . a . . . a . . . a blow . . ." He was stuttering, almost a little embarrassed. ". . . a blow job. You know." His reticence about discussing sexual acts and body parts was both disarming and alarming. Gary could look me in the eye and discuss murder but was shy about using the crude four-letter slang for sex or other sex-related slang terms. *What's going on with this?* I wondered, and I recalled Gary being disciplined by his father with a stick for playing "doctor." I thought, *He comes from a family where sex was hidden, dark, dirty, not talked about—shameful.*

Gary went on.

"I asked her to turn around so I could enter her from behind, you know, from the rear . . . dog . . . doggie-style."

"Gary, I'm not a prude," I told him. "You don't have to try to be so delicate and polite."

"Oooh-K." Gary smiled and nodded. He knew he didn't have to be "delicate and polite" with me. He'd heard me drop a few F-bombs from time to time. It was his own difficulty with using vulgarities that guided his word choice, not my sensitivities.

"So I finish and say, 'Is that my son coming?' or something like that. "You know, to get her to lift her head up."

As he said this, he demonstrated, lifting his chin up and turning to look back over his shoulder.

"Then, I put my right arm around her neck and choked her. I took my socks off, black dress socks, tied them in a knot and wrapped them around her neck and twisted. Wanted to make sure she was dead, you know." He demonstrated as he spoke, gritting his teeth as he twisted the imaginary socks around the neck of the imaginary Gisele Lovvorn. "I tried to undo the knot but it was too tight."

"Why?" I asked.

"Well, they were good socks. I didn't want to just leave them there." Gary said with a sheepish grin, realizing his extreme frugality had re-manifested itself.

Story after story, victim after victim, this meeting continued. My goal was for him to tell me things that only the killer would know. Not things he'd heard or read or been shown. Things from *his* memory that would prove he was telling the truth about his role in the murders.

Todd and I knew there was a fine line between prompting or jog-ging Gary's memory and feeding him facts he could then utilize to bolster the veracity of his confession. However, I decided to show him the pictures we had of all of the victims. Many of the pictures had been provided by the families and showed the young girls in happier scenes. Sadly, for some of the victims, the only pictures the police were able to find had been booking photos. Page-by-page, photo-by-photo, Gary looked for something that clicked in his memory.

"No," Gary said, as he thumbed through the pictures. "These ladies don't look familiar. I just never paid much attention to their faces. That's why I choked them from behind. . . . So I wouldn't have to look at them while I was killing them." Gary seemed ashamed of himself, not for the murders, really, but more for not learning their names and faces before he killed them.

"I do remember having to strangle one from the front," he said. "We were in the cab of my truck, over by the woods behind the park-ing lot at Lewis and Clark Theatre. She was the only one I killed in the cab of the truck. She wouldn't get in the back. That's why I had to choke her from the front. I thought for sure someone would see us."

Gary continued to look through the pictures, looking for a face he recognized.

"There she is," he said. "Her hair's different, but I'm quite certain that's the Lewis and Clark Lady." He was pointing to the picture of Kase Lee. To Gary, she was the "Lewis and Clark Lady," because that was where he had left her lifeless body. I soon realized that Gary's main memory of each of his murders began with where he had left the body.

I moved him along. "Anything else that stands out? From any of your killings?"

Gary thought about it and said, "I broke Coffield's arm. She was the first one I killed. I don't know why I broke it. I was just in a rage when I killed her. I broke her arm after . . . after I killed her. I was kneeling on the riverbank . . . holding her across my lap. . . . I was crying, mad, upset. . . . I thought for sure I was going to be caught." Not so much concerned about taking a human life but upset at the thought of being caught. I felt a chill and shook my head as I took notes, wondering how this nice guy could have committed these monstrous acts.

Gary continued.

"I took pictures of Hinds and Chapman. I went back with a Polaroid and took pictures."

"Are the pictures still around somewhere?" I asked, hoping this would provide some pretty solid evidence to present to the prosecutors, whom we still had to convince.

"Noooo," Gary shook his head, definitely. "I kept them for a while, then threw them in the river. I hid them in the concrete beams in the underground parking lot at the Red Lion [Hotel] there on 188th [Street] and Pacific Highway [South]."

"Gone now?" I asked, disappointed. I needed to confirm they would not be available for us to deliver to the state.

"Gone. Unless some fisherman picked 'em up as they were floating by. I threw them away after about a month. I'd go and look at them, but then I thought it was probably too risky." He looked at me, nodding.

The meeting continued, as the twisted and bizarre details emerged from Gary for the first time.

"You know the *real* pretty one?" he asked.

"Depends. I think a lot of them were *real* pretty. Some were cute. Some were beautiful. Some looked a little rough for my tastes, at least in their booking photos," I said. "Which one? Was it one of these girls?" I produced the picture showing all of the identified dead and missing.

Gary immediately pointed and said, "Her. Constance Naon." Reading the name under the picture. "I bit her on the breast for some reason, after I killed her. She had a real nice figure. And I took her car keys, too." I knew she had remained missing for so long, there could not have been any evidence of bite marks left when her remains were finally located. *But the keys?*

"What about the keys, where are they?"

"Oh, I threw them out somewhere along the highway."

I kept taking notes, prompting Gary from time to time, sometimes switching to a different victim or different cluster of victims. And I had some specific questions.

"How about the time Detective Fox came to your house? Was Marie Malvar there?" I asked one of the many, many questions I had.

There was a professional purpose for my questioning, but there was also my own curiosity.

"No, she was gone. I never kept them at my house for very long." He paused, thinking about Marie Malvar. "She fought back really hard. She fought the most of any of the ladies. So I took her body out to a gully, south of Kent-Des Moines Road. Left her by herself." Gary thought some more. "It was off West Valley Highway, south of 292nd [Street] and Star Lake [Road]. But before you get to Peasley Canyon [Road]. Before you get to the road that goes up to Mountain View Cemetery. I'm quite certain that's where I put her."

"Why not in one of your clusters? Why out there?"

"Well, she fought so hard. I guess I wanted to kind of punish her." He looked down. "You know. By leaving her alone out there." He said it like it was logical. Then he looked up at me. I must not have had much of a poker face at this point because my facial expression obviously revealed what I was thinking.

He looked at my face.

"I know," he said. "Pretty psycho."

"Look Gary, I've heard it all." At least, I wanted him to think so. "Maybe not in this quantity, but I've had some clients do some pretty bad stuff. It was just kind of odd. I mean, you'd just killed her. Then you were going to punish her? She's already dead."

"I know," Gary said, shaking his head. "It was stupid. I was mad and upset."

I decided to leave the psychoanalysis to others. Gary and I continued to discuss, for the first time in detail, several more specific cases. We talked about Amina Agishev, a thirty-six-year-old woman, who had no known ties to prostitution and who may have been shot at some point. Bullet fragments had been recovered with her remains. Chronologically, it appeared that she was murdered even before Wendy Coffield.

"I'm quite certain I didn't kill her," Gary said. "Coffield, in the river . . . I'm thinking, she was the first one I killed."

At this point, I didn't want to interrupt the flow of information from Gary. But I was thinking: *What? You're "quite certain" you didn't kill her? You "think" Coffield was the first one you killed? I can understand maybe confusing some along the way, especially at the rate you were going, but the first person you ever killed? Wouldn't you remember?* I planned to get back to that topic. For now, I just wanted to keep it going.

I asked about any "trophies" or "souvenirs" he might have taken.

"Where's the jewelry and all their stuff? What did you do with that?" I wondered if it went into his many garage sales over the years.

"A lot of it, I would just throw out on the highway," he said. "But I used about four different places to put stuff. One was next to the guardrail at 192nd [Street] and Military [Road South], right at the bend where the guardrail starts. . . . It could be blacktopped over by now. I never went back and looked.

"Another place was off Military [Road], just north of Kent-Des Moines Road. Across from the RV place and the bakery outlet. There's a row of trees at the edge of the property. I buried some jewelry around the base of the tree. Someone's got to have found it over the past twenty years."

"Probably. Where else?"

"You know where Grandview Park is?"

I did. "Yes. Up on Military?"

"Yeah. There's a big rock near the entrance. I put a watch—a Timex—buried it on the left-hand side of the big rock. And the place I put the most stuff was by a telephone pole next to the hardware store on Pacific Highway. It's a parking lot for an IHOP now." Gary frowned, knowing there would be no hope of finding any of these items.

"One other place was in the parking lot at the Safeway there on Pacific Highway and 216th. But they remodeled and relandscaped their parking lot years ago, so nothing's the same anymore."

At one point, Gary described how he felt while disposing his victims.

"At first, I was really upset and crying, thinking I'd be caught, . . . thinking of turning myself in. I felt bad," Gary explained, looking down. He raised his eyes to mine. "Then, you know, I started to feel less . . ." he paused to think of the right word ". . . remorse . . . as time went on. I started to actually go out, pretty much knowing I was going to find a prostitute and kill her. I started to enjoy it."

When I heard stuff like that, coming out of his mouth as-a-matter-of-fact, I would be stunned. *He's a monster! No way could he have been such a monster! How could this nice guy . . .* Then came another bomb:

"I wrote them a letter, you know. Told them about the rocks in the vaginas. Told them about the fish on Christensen. Told them he smokes." He smiled, referring to the killer (himself). "I told them some stuff that was true so they knew it was for real. Then I told them other stuff that wasn't true, to steer them away from me."

This was the first time anyone learned of the existence of a letter from the killer.

"I'll have to see if we can find it in the discovery," I said. I couldn't recall hearing about any letter to the investigators claiming knowledge about rocks in the vaginas—a sure tip-off that the letter was from the real killer. That would be solid evidence for the prosecutor that Gary knew what he was talking about.

—————

That weekend, Todd, Dave, Fred, and I went on our own field trip. Armed with maps and descriptions of various locations given by Gary, we cruised all over King County. Gary's maps and markings of the general areas where he had left undiscovered bodies were incredibly, eerily accurate.

In our tour we covered:

- Lake Fenwick Road, just west of Kent, where many new housing developments had gone up over the prior twenty years
- A steep, heavily wooded gully at 292nd Avenue SE, some short distance from Star Lake
- Auburn-Black Diamond Road, where at least one Red River victim had been found some years after the Green River murders had ostensibly stopped
- Seattle International Raceway, near Auburn
- The interchange where Highway 18 meets Interstate 90, miles east of Seattle
- The marshy area behind Leisure Time Resorts, near Echo Glen, just north of the I-90/Highway 18 interchange
- Middle Fork Road, a small, two-lane stretch of blacktop paralleling the Snoqualmie River's middle fork near a truck stop out on I-90
- Highway 410, east of Enumclaw, on the road to Mt. Rainier, where Gary claimed to have left as many as four additional bodies
- The area behind Lewis and Clark Theatre on Pacific Highway South—an area that was now a parking lot

It was clear to us that it was going to be very difficult to find any remains or anything else related to the murders, for that matter. Twenty years of nature and the environment, as well as two decades of human encroachment and development, had significantly altered most of these places from the era when Gary had been a predator.

Even though Gary's maps took us right to these spots, we doubted that anyone could find anything now.

Over the next week, I continued to question Gary. It was soon clear to me that he had plenty of information to offer. We went through each case, cluster site by cluster site, trying to draw out significant details from his memory. The week was rather grueling. Quickly, I improved my ability to ignore the horror and depravity, as I heard the basic routine repeated matter-of-factly over and over and over:

He would cruise the Pacific Highway Strip for prostitutes on the way home from Kenworth. He would spot a young girl, make eye contact, and pull into a shadowy area or parking lot nearby. The young woman would approach and ask him if he was "dating." All he had to do was to say yes or just nod, and she would open the door and hop in. The young woman would ask if he was a cop and he'd laugh, say no, open his wallet and show her his ID, next to a picture of Matthew, his son. Soon, she was comfortable, safe and relaxed, as they exchanged small talk.

Then they would get down to the business they both had in mind. Gary would typically negotiate a price for the woman to have sex— usually, penile-vaginal penetration, "a straight screw," in the vernacular of the street, for between $30 and $50. Sometimes, the woman would agree to oral sex first—*half and half* it was called. Sometimes the woman would agree to vaginal intercourse but only perform oral sex. That would really anger Gary, I discovered.

After reaching agreement on price, they would need a place. Gary often took them to his house in Des Moines, not far from Pacific Highway South; that was his preference. Sometimes he offered more money, maybe $60, even $80, if they would agree to go to his house. After all, if things went as planned, he'd get his money back. Many of his victims felt safe enough to do just that and ended up being strangled on Gary's bed.

On other occasions, he'd park in a secluded spot, and they would hop into the canopy-covered bed of his pickup truck. On some occasions, primarily with the victims found at the south and north ends of the airport, Gary and his victim would find a secluded spot outdoors in some woods or area of natural overgrowth. By 1982, such areas abounded around the airport, as the Port of Seattle had removed adjacent houses to mitigate noise problems from the nearby jetliners landing or taking off.

Gary had a very simple routine that varied or changed only slightly as he gained experience as a serial killer. The two would take off all their clothes, or most of them, anyway. The woman performed masturbation and oral sex to get him hard. They would switch to sexual intercourse in the missionary style. After a period of time, Gary would suggest that he would climax sooner if he could enter her from the rear—doggie-style—in the vernacular. The woman would agree. After all, it was going to make it quicker, and time is money to a prostitute.

After some minutes, Gary said, he would climax, then immediately wrap his right forearm across the front of his victim's neck. He would use his left arm to pull on his right, using all the leverage he could muster. Sometimes he would put a knee into the victim's back to add to his leverage.

It was disturbing to see him concentrate on these memories, closing his eyes, reliving the events in his mind, gritting his teeth as he demonstrated how he would strangle his victims. It was disturbing to know what these poor young women—girls, really, most of them—went through in their final moments of life. It sickened me beyond words. Why does that happen? Why do humans treat other humans that way? Why do some men treat women as mere objects, property to have sex with, then kill? As I sat there, I knew Gary wasn't the only killer that ever lived. But the level of depravity was overwhelming. This human being—this nice guy—had killed at least fifty women with his bare hands. First, he'd used them as a sperm receptacle. Then, to demonstrate the control he had over them, he killed them.

I was nearly overwhelmed by the mix of emotions—sadness, anger, repulsion about what Gary had done, mixed with hope and anxiety about the deal, providing good information, finding missing remains, and saving Gary's life. As a lawyer, you are trained to put your emotions aside, to create good boundaries, but it's not always easy; sometimes it's downright impossible. I mean, we are human beings too.

But I had been doing this a long time. I'd seen a lot of sad, ugly cases, though nothing on this scale. But that experience and training prepared me professionally. This case was so big and so important that I knew I had to keep my emotions suppressed. So as Gary went on, I kept taking notes and encouraged him to tell me more and more.

The outdoor victims were left at or near the spot he killed them. The victims killed in his house or truck had to be disposed of. He described how he would take a victim from his house, rolled up in a blanket, and put her body into the back of his pickup truck. He would drive to one of the cluster sites—the Green River, Star Lake, Highway 18, I-90 at Exit 38, or Highway 410. He would take their lifeless bodies from the back of his truck and drag, haul, or carry the body to some location, twenty-five yards or so off the road, maybe more, maybe less, into the woods. Some he would conceal next to a fallen log; others received a shallow grave, dug with his hands in the loose soil. But most, he simply covered with leaves and twigs and other debris he found in the near vicinity.

He would then drive home, upset and crying, guilt ridden, yet tantalized and thrilled at the same time. He was tormented by what he was doing yet was enjoying it more and more as he became the infamous "Green River Killer." I was fascinated and mortified, sickened—just as anyone would be. Yet by Friday, April 25, 2003, I was hopeful of a positive resolution—that his macabre, dreadful confession would be enough to save his life.

That same Friday, I received a call from Norm Maleng's secretary. Our meeting with the one man who could keep Gary alive to tell all of his tale, and in a way that it might finally do some good, was scheduled for the following Tuesday, April 29, at 10:30.

Now all we had to do was convince Norm Maleng to listen.

26

I spent most of Monday night before this meeting running different potential dialogues through my head—questions that Maleng might ask and how I would respond to them. Lawyers are supposed to be able to think on their feet, to be able to "wing it" with élan, or so they say. But I never met one that didn't run through the imaginary exercise of what he or she might say many times in advance.

I drove into Seattle, found a parking spot, and went to Tony's office first. Todd soon joined us. We'd already decided to leave Michele out of these discussions because of her opposition to moving forward so quickly with Plan B. The three of us walked up the hill to the prosecutor's offices on the thirty-fifth floor of the Columbia Center, Seattle's tallest skyscraper, with its spectacular views of Puget Sound and the majestic Olympic Mountains. The prosecutors were temporarily located in those palatial digs while their regular offices, on the fifth floor of the shabby old courthouse, were being retrofitted for earthquakes.

Sue, the prosecutors' receptionist we'd all known for years, greeted us as graciously as always. She called someone to let them know we'd arrived and then directed us to the stairs leading to the next floor up.

Waiting for us at the top was Dan Satterberg, the man who'd once said we were the Porsche dealership of defense attorneys. He smiled. Now that we were talking about a possible deal, maybe it no longer mattered what sort of car we were pushing.

We followed Satterberg to a very nicely furnished, executive conference room—even Porsche dealers would have been impressed at the way the state was living—and sat down.

"Mark's going to join us too," he said, referring to Mark Larson, the Chief Criminal Deputy Prosecuting Attorney. "I'll go get Norm."

"Where's the bug?" Todd asked Dan, referring to a hidden recording device. "Don't make us damage this pretty furniture trying to find it."

"Well, we've got one under the table and one under each of your chairs." He leaned over the table. "Testing one, two . . . testing one, two. . . . Just kidding. We'll turn them off. I promise." He left. Todd and he were both joking, of course (I think), but both played it completely straight, not even a smile.

"Good morning, gentlemen," Norm Maleng, as polite and as formal as ever, entered the room, followed by Dan and Mark Larson.

As noted, Norm is sort of a cross between Jon Voight and a Lutheran minister—medium height, sandy, gray hair, a round face with wire-framed glasses and a warm smile. We stood up and exchanged greetings and handshakes. Everything was very cordial and friendly.

"I'll get to the point," Tony said, sounding remarkably like he had almost a year earlier, when we'd first asked Maleng not to seek the death penalty.

"We're here to see if you will consider guilty pleas and resolution to fifty or so cases in exchange for taking the death penalty off the table. It would include the vast majority of the cases on the Green River list and maybe ten others."

"Thank you, Tony," Maleng said. "As you all know, I have a long-standing policy in this office. I will *not* plea bargain the death penalty . . ."

Maleng paused. He wasn't done with his sentence, but he paused so long, I didn't know if he would ever finish it. I stopped breathing. Did this mean, despite our best efforts, despite all the right reasons to do a deal, Gary would be sentenced to death, after a long and costly trial, followed by long and costly appeals? That the information I'd just learned from Gary will have to stay between Gary and me—forever?

And—could I live with that?

As these thoughts ran through my mind, I realized that Maleng was still talking.

". . . but, in a case of this nature and this magnitude . . ."

He paused again, looking across the table first to Todd, then at me, then Tony.

". . . we have to be prepared to be flexible and give everything careful consideration," he finally finished.

I began to breathe again. *He didn't say no!* I worked to keep my face absolutely straight.

"I'll want to meet and discuss this with Mark, Dan, our trial team, and the Sheriff's Department, of course."

I thought, *Perfect.* They'll advise him to make the deal, and we'll have our foot jammed so far inside the door, they'll never be able to close it. I remembered the brief conversation I'd had with one of the detectives, who'd said they were much more interested in getting the answers than seeing Gary executed. I was sure Maleng would get pressure from the cops to agree to the deal. The only question was: Would that be enough to convince the prosecutor to take the death penalty off the table to settle the case?

"Of course," Tony was saying when I came to. "I'm sure Sheriff Reichert would be hurt if he weren't consulted."

Maleng agreed and said he'd set up a meeting with Reichert as soon as he could.

"We all know this case is unique," I said. "Historically, there's never been anything close and there never will be." I was already anticipating that Maleng would get significant criticism if he agreed to a plea bargain and was trying to suggest a rationale he might use to justify a deal. "There is substantial mitigation in Mr. Ridgway providing information and assisting in clearing up fifty cases. It would bring a sense of closure to lots of families, and really to our entire community." I'd practiced so many of my arguments the night before that this came out before I realized it wasn't entirely necessary: Maleng had already said he'd consider taking the death penalty off in return for Gary's truthful confession—"flexible," and "every consideration." At least they hadn't said "no, utterly no." I decided to shut up before they changed their minds and decided not to be "flexible."

"Yes," Maleng said. "Well, we'll discuss it and get back to you. Thanks for coming by." Norm rose, so we all got up. The meeting was over. Short and very sweet.

Tony, Todd, and I rode the elevator down to the lobby.

"He didn't say No. He didn't say No." I had to repeat myself as I was in a state of disbelief. "I think we've got a chance," I said.

"Oh, I imagine he was just being polite. I still can't see him going along with it," Tony said, still doubting that Maleng would ever actually agree to a deal.

We decided to stop downstairs in the lobby of the Columbia Center to have some coffee and debrief.

"I bet their wheels are turning now," Todd said, as he sipped his coffee. "Or should I say 'spinning,' as in figuring out the right political 'spin' to put on the deal. And see . . . ," he added, extending his right index finger and poking me in the chest, ". . . we didn't have to bring any damn bones to the table." Earlier, in our discussion with Baird, he'd suggested that we bring in some human remains or a "souvenir" to demonstrate Gary's good faith, a suggestion that our side had rejected, at least among ourselves, as an enormous and unneeded potential legal complication.

"Well, let's hope we didn't need to bring in any bones," I said. "Closing fifty unsolved cases ought to do it. But you can go ahead and say it."

"I told you so," Todd said. "There, I feel much better." He gloated, but with a laugh. With all the nervous tension accumulated over the past few weeks, with Gary's wavering and Michele's attempt at an end run, it felt good to relax and laugh a bit. We were all feeling pretty good at the moment, but Tony wouldn't let us get our hopes up too high.

He popped our swelling balloons of hope.

"I still don't see how he's going to do it," Tony said. "If he doesn't go for the death penalty for Gary, how will he ever be able to seek it again? I just don't see him doing it. He's smart, though. He couldn't just reject it out of hand. He'll have to think it over before he says no."

"Yeah, and he'll discuss it with the sheriff and Baird and Mark and Dan. They'll be able to find the right political spin to help Norm sell it to the public," I said.

"Norm is a very astute politician, make no mistake about it," Tony said. "The man knows what he's doing."

"Well, I think we can assume Reichert will want him to do the deal," I said. "Then Dave can get on with his political future without Green River lingering on and on. And he might have more political clout right now than Norm. Maybe he can convince Norm to do it."

"Norm will listen but he's going to make his own decision," Tony said. "He won't do it just because Dave Reichert wants him to. Norm has his own morals and ethics he'll follow."

"It's not just about Norm's morals or ethics," Todd said. "It's about politics and coming up with sufficient political cover, something he can sell to the voters of King County."

"I think the voters of King County would favor a deal rather than seeing millions of tax dollars spent on seeking the death penalty," I said.

"But Norm's decision won't be about the money." Tony reminded us that Maleng had always said the money didn't matter when he had to decide whether to ask for death or not. It was the crime that mattered, not the budget.

"Of course, money will be a factor in his decision," Todd scoffed, showing his independent, cynical side. "He'll just never say that publicly. Death penalty equals politics, which equals money. It always comes back to money."

"I don't know about that," I said. "I don't want to seem naïve, but I wonder how much of the money stuff really enters his decision-making process. It's there, obviously, but I would bet he intentionally tries not to let it influence his decision."

Todd grinned, shook his head, and patted me on the shoulder.

"Yes, you *are* naïve. Of course, it will influence his decision. It's definitely a factor that weighs in our favor, whether spoken out loud or not. And they gotta give us what we need. So keep asking for more money, Mark. 'That's what you're good at.'" Todd was borrowing a line from one of my all-time favorite movies, *Butch Cassidy and the Sundance Kid,* where Sundance tells Butch, "You just keep thinkin', Butch. That's what you're good at."

But at least now Norm Maleng was doing some thinking, too.

27

Over the next month, while Norm Maleng considered our offer, our side continued to move forward, just as if we were going to trial. For all we knew, Tony was right—Norm would say no. We did not talk of Plan B to the other members of the team; it was too risky. The more people who knew, the greater the chance of a leak. The very worst thing that could happen now was for these discussions to be made public. It would destroy any remnant of the possibility of an unbiased jury. So we maintained our façade, essentially lying to our overworked and underpaid investigators and paralegals.

I continued seeing Gary, Monday through Friday, for anywhere from two to five hours, trying to keep his brain focused on the horrible events from twenty years past. I soon learned that, as with faces, he had no knowledge of the victims' names. He said the names meant nothing to him, because most of the women and girls he dated used fake names. That was one possible explanation. Another was that Gary was a psychopath, who didn't think of his victims as people but rather property, even trash, that he could dispose of at will. He only knew the names of a few, and those only from what he had seen, read, or heard about the case, before and since his arrest.

These grim discussions continued through our meeting with Maleng and for several weeks afterward, all the way into late May. About once a week or so, I was joined by Michele. Despite our earlier disagreement, Michele and I managed to be cordial and professional during these sessions with Gary. He had previously sensed our friction, so Gary was happy to see Michele. We went over everything we could think of, and then we went over it again. And again. After the flood of information rushed out, smaller bits continued to float to the surface.

After we had talked and talked about the factual things, we eventually discussed his understandings of the other major questions: Why? Why did he start? Why did he come to enjoy killing young women? And—how did he stop?

Gary's answers to the "why?" question were superficial at best, but it gave some insight into what he'd been thinking at the time.

One morning in early May, I asked him, point-blank, "Why did you kill these women?"

Gary replied, "I was just so mad at Marcia. She treated me bad during the divorce. I just wanted to kill her."

"But you didn't kill Marcia," I said, but it was more like a question.

"If I had killed Marcia, I would have been the number-one suspect. I guess I just hated all women."

"So why prostitutes?"

"Well, I hated them if all they worried about was their money and time. Like, 'hurry up. I gotta get back.' That kinda stuff." He looked at me, nodding. "You know . . . that would kind of set me off into a rage. Those were the ones I killed." He seemed to be seeking encouragement or approval, so I nodded back as if it made perfect sense.

"But if she was nice and treated me like we were on a real date and not so worried about time and money, then I wouldn't kill her." He went on. "Sometimes I'd kill them so I wouldn't have to pay." He shook his head with his sheepish half-grin and said, "I know. I'm cheap."

This simplistic, cold-blooded explanation for serial murder rolled out of his mouth as if we were talking about rain in Seattle. How could someone's brain get so completely miswired? Chronic exposure to lead paint, perhaps? So I asked.

"How about paint fumes at Kenworth?"

"We didn't really have much protection until the eighties," Gary said. "There were vents and masks, but you'd be breathing the stuff all

day. We'd actually even heat up our food and soup in the paint ovens."
He laughed and shook his head at how unhealthy that sounded. The
whole issue of lead paint and brain damage would have to be explored
in depth in the event the deal did not work out.

From time to time, we'd venture back into the realm of "why?" Gary
consistently downplayed any unhappiness or traumatic events from
his childhood. He consistently stuck up for his mom and dad. It
seemed to me that even if they existed, he was not going to open up
any private family matters that would reflect poorly on his family.

On more than one occasion, we discussed another major question.

"When did you commit your last murder?" I asked.

"In 1985," he said, firmly. "I stopped killing after I met Judith. We
met at Parents Without Partners in February or so. I think she moved
in around June." He began to tear up, as he always did when Judith
arose. "We were together all the time after that. I didn't have the desire to kill anymore. I didn't want to get caught, you know." He was
sniffling and trying not to cry.

"This is very important," I told him. "You've got to tell me the truth.
It won't help if you don't tell the truth. There are victims out there,
after 1985, that look a lot like Green River victims. You've got to admit
them now—that is, if you *did* kill after 1985."

Gary looked me in the eye.

"No," he said, "I'm quite certain. I didn't kill anyone after 1985, after
I got together with Judith."

I asked for details about the 1985 murder, which would have been
after the police said the Green River murders had stopped.

"The last one," Gary insisted, "was in 1985. I went to Tacoma to get
some new tires. I saw this lady I'd dated before. She lived in Des Moines.
She needed a ride back to her apartment. I think . . . I'm quite certain
. . . I killed her in my truck, somewhere in Federal Way. I took her body
out to Highway 410. I remember, because the canopy flew off my truck
on Highway 18 on the way home."

I was convinced. He had sprinkled in enough details, and the
strange twist of losing his canopy. It sounded as if he knew what he
was talking about. This left *me* "quite certain" that his last victim was
killed in 1985. Now even I was doing it. But then I began to wonder,
what did "quite certain" really mean? Why did he condition his statements, almost subliminally, with "quite certain," or "I would have done
this," or "I probably did that"? Was this a manifestation of his psy-

Prothero swims way to U. of W.

Mark Prothero, Renton High School's state-champion swim star, has signed a national letter of intent with the University of Washington, his parents announced Friday.

Prothero, whose swimming prowess is matched by his classroom ability (4.0 GPA), will get a swim scholarship for coming West Coast power.

The Renton ace won the Inspirational Award, Team Captain, Outstanding Swimmer and All-NPSL honors, in addition to his first-place finish in the 200 individual medley at the state meet at the University of Washington.

Prothero is the son of Mr. and Mrs. Robert Prothero, Jr., of Lakeridge.

Prothero is the second "big name" NPSL athlete from Renton to sign a national letter. Steve McDaniels, football-basketball star for the Indians, signed on with Notre Dame earlier in the week.

Other top NPSL athletes to sign thus far include Evergreen football standout Jack Thompson (Washington State); Tyee's hoop "Player of the Year," Rob Thayer (Seattle Pacific); Kentridge gridders Leon Minter and Randy Westendorf (both Colorado); Kent-Meridian football star Lawayne Richardson (Mount Hood CC); and Fred Helser, Auburn football-track standout (Oregon).

MARK PROTHERO

SPORTS

Record-Chronicle

Jack & Jill adults meet

The second meeting of the Renton Parks and Recreation Department adult Jack and Jill Softball League will be held tonight at 7 o'clock at the Liberty Park Community Bldg.

The league, co-recreational in make-up, is slated to begin June 16 and all players and teams interested should plan on attending. League rules and playing dates will be discussed. Interested persons should call John Webley at 235-2560.

This was an article that ran in the May 22, 1974, *Renton Record-Chronicle* a few weeks before I graduated from Renton High School. It was about my getting a swimming scholarship to the University of Washington.

Swim team photo from my freshman year at the University of Washington, October 1974.

A family picture taken at my parents' house on my mom's seventy-seventh birthday, November 14, 2004: Bob, Kelly, Marley, me, Shirley, and Sean. Missing from the photo is my brother Blake, who apparently was taking this picture.

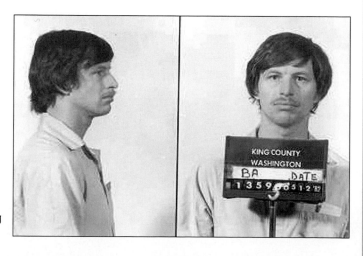

KING COUNTY
WASHINGTON

Booking photo of Gary Leon Ridgway, arrested on May 12, 1982, for patronizing a prostitute.

Wendy Coffield, the first victim of the Green River Killer, is taken from the river, July 15, 1982. (Photo by Duane Hamamura, *King County Journal*.)

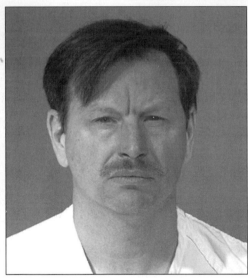

Gary Ridgway's booking photo from his arrest on November 30, 2001.

Todd Gruenhagen and me at our December 5, 2001, press conference at the Regional Justice Center in Kent. I think a reporter had just asked about getting a fair trial in Seattle. (Photo by Gary Kissel, *King County Journal*.)

Co-counsel Todd Gruenhagen on the second field trip, Saturday, June 14, 2003. (Photo by Malcolm Chang.)

Co-counsel Tony Savage on the second field trip, Saturday, June 14, 2003. (Photo by Malcolm Chang.)

Detectives Randy Mullinax, Jon Mattsen, and Tom Jensen question Gary at "the bunker," December 14, 2003. I took this photo from the seat I occupied from June 14 through December 17, 2003.

This was an editorial cartoon by Jeff Johnson in the *Skagit County Herald* on December 11, 2001.

These are not all of Gary Ridgway's victims, but only forty-eight out of at least seventy-five women whom he murdered.

 Wendy Coffield

 Gisele Lovvorn

 Debra Bonner

 Marcia Chapman

 Cynthia Hinds

 Opal Mills

 Terry Milligan

 Mary Meehan

 Debra Estes

 Denise Bush

 Shawnda Summers

 Shirley Sherrill

 Colleen Brockman

 Alma Smith

 Delores Williams

 Gail Mathews

 Andrea Childers

 Sandra Gabbert

 Kimi-Kai Pitsor

 Carol Christensen

 Martina Authorlee

 Cheryl Wims

 Yvonne Antosh

 Carrie Rois Summer

 Constance Naon

Kelly Ware

Tina Thompson

Debbie Abernathy

Tracy Winston

Maureen Feeney

Mary Bello

Delise Plager

Kim Nelson

Lisa Yates

Cindy Smith

Patricia Michelle Barczak

Roberta Joseph Hayes

Marta Reeves

Patricia Yellowrobe

Linda Jane Rule

Pammy Avent

April Buttram

Marie Malvar

Mary West

Becky Marrero

Patricia Ann Osborn

Kelly Kay McGinnis

Kassee Ann Lee

April 13, 2003

To The Ridgway Defense Team:

~~At this time, I do not authorize any lawyer representing me, or any expert working on my behalf, to have discussions regarding plea negotiations or settlement of my case with anyone outside of the defense team.~~ *GLR.*

I do not authorize any lawyer, investigator, expert or paralegal to speak to any member of the Green River Task Force about settling or negotiating my case.

Gary L Ridgway   4-13-03
Gary Leon Ridgway   Date

Michele Shaw   4-13-03
Michele Shaw, Attorney for Mr.   Date

This was the letter I was presented by Gary on April 14, 2003. I had him delete one paragraph and initial his deletion so the discussions could continue to move forward.

This was a letter from Gary to Michele and me, written April 24, 2003.

4-24-03

Michelle + Mark

I couldn't sleep last night. This part of the case is eating me apart. I have hid this for 19 years. I am sorry I can't figure out those first woman. I had so much hate and coverup Its in mind somewhere. I just don't know how to get it out.

I sorry I didn't tell you all that you wanted. Maybe I wanted to control the finding of the women. I just want to get it out and find all of them. It is going to be easer for me to show, then by a map. I don't want any of them lost forever.

Please help me find all of them. I get down on my nees and pray every night that we well.

4-16-03

I signed a paper to all my legal staff. Not to talk to the GRTF and the prosecuters.
Mark talked me out of the part about the prosecuters.

Gary L Ridgway

Gary sent all of his defense lawyers this letter to further clarify what had happened with regard to the April 14 letter.

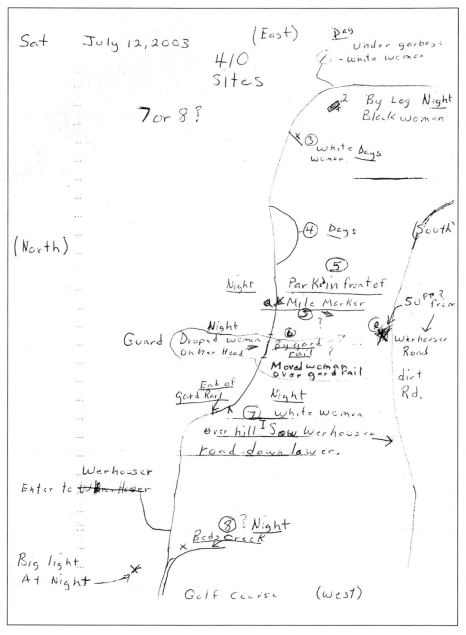

This is one of the maps of Highway 410 drawn by Gary for the investigators.
He drew this one on July 12, 2003.

Bettye Witherspoon, investigator at Associated Counsel for the Accused. (Photo by Elisabeth Frost, 2002.)

The Honorable Richard Jones, King County Superior Court, at the plea hearing on November 5, 2003.

Gary Ridgway's arrest set off a huge media frenzy, satirized in this editorial cartoon by Jake Dill, the *Daily,* December 5, 2001.

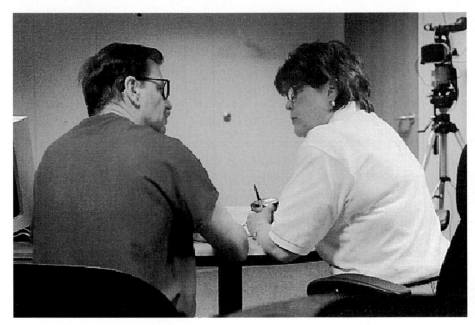

Dr. Mary Ellen O'Toole, of the FBI's Behavioral Analysis Unit, interviews Gary at the bunker on July 19, 2003. (Photo by Todd Gruenhagen.)

Investigators Denise Scaffidi and Lis Frost. (Photo by Bettye Witherspoon, 2002.)

On our field trips during the summer and fall of 2003, Gary would be escorted from the van to look for specific areas where he remembered leaving one of his victims some twenty years earlier. You can see that he has a chain around his waist, with handcuffs, as well as a chain between his ankles. (Photo by Ross Nooney.)

During breaks in the interrogation, Gary would turn his chair around to our table and confer with his lawyers. (Photo by Todd Gruenhagen.)

Senior deputy prosecutor Jeff Baird conducts the plea colloquy with Gary Ridgway, November 5, 2003.

In response to the criticism of the Ridgway defense budget by the prosecutor's chief of staff, Dan Satterberg, Todd came up with this idea. We sent Dan the picture as a little memento of the case. (Photo by Bettye Witherspoon; additional computer graphics by Fabian Acosta.)

Gary Ridgway listens to members of his victims' families at the sentencing hearing, December 18, 2003.

Tim Meehan, brother of victim Mary Meehan, addresses Gary at sentencing on December 18, 2003.

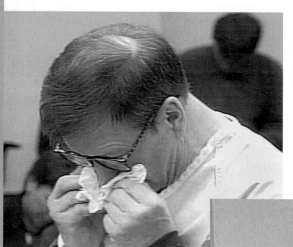

Gary Ridgway breaks into tears during his allocution at sentencing, December 18, 2003.

Gary and I stand at the bench before Judge Jones for the formal imposition of sentence.

Dr. Robert Wheeler interviews Gary at the bunker on July 2, 2003.
(Photo by Todd Gruenhagen.)

This editorial cartoon by Jeff Johnson appeared in the local *Kent Reporter* on
September 4, 2002. That's me on the left and our potential jurors in the chair.

Dr. Judith Becker, from the University of Arizona, interviews Gary at the bunker on December 8, 2003. (Photo by Mark Prothero.)

The Ridgway defense team lawyers at the post-plea press conference. From left to right: Eric Lindell, Todd Gruenhagen, Michele Shaw, Tony Savage, me, Fred Leatherman, David Roberson. Missing from the picture is our appellate expert, Suzanne Elliott, who was arguing a case in the court of appeals that day.

That's me coaching at the Seattle Summer Swim League championships on August 4, 2003. My team, Kent Swim and Tennis Club, won the league championship that summer. (Photo by Brian Martinet.)

The King County prosecution team, from left to right: Norm Maleng, Brian McDonald, Sean O'Donnell, Ian Goodhew, Jeff Baird, and Patty Eakes. (Used by permission of King County Bar Association.)

This editorial cartoon by Eric Devericks was in the *Seattle Times* on November 7, 2003.

chopathy? Was it a by-product of a lifetime of living a lie? Or was it a sign that he didn't really know and was making everything up, taking the blame for the murders that he knew he hadn't really committed?

On May 28, I was at a Ridgway budget meeting with the County Council budget staff person, Carrie Cihak, Anne Harper, as the new head of OPD, and Special Master Kate Pflaumer. Dan Satterberg also showed up. He came over and sat next to me during the meeting.

"Hey, Dan," I said. "Todd and I have a deal on Porsches this week."

"No thanks," he said. I guessed he already had one.

"Can we have a little chat . . . in private?" We found a corner in the hallway.

"Norm is still giving your offer very serious consideration," Dan said, after looking around to make sure we weren't being overheard. "He's likely to call you in sometime next week."

"How's it look?"

"I'd say the mood has shifted."

"Really," I replied. He was being intentionally vague, but from my perspective, the "mood" had previously been to reject our offer. I refrained from jumping up and down and screaming.

"It's just so big, so significant, so important," Dan explained, "that it's taking awhile."

"It's expensive, too," I added, although I knew that reason for doing the deal was an unspoken one.

"Yeah, well, we asked the state legislature for some of that Extraordinary Justice Act money. I think we asked for $6 million. They gave us about $700,000."

"Well that ought to cover *your* salary, but what about the Ridgway case?"

"*Almost* cover my salary," he shot back. "You should be hearing from us by Friday, maybe next Tuesday at the latest."

I relayed the conversation to Todd.

"Well, it's looking better," Todd observed, "but don't get your hopes up. It's all tied to money and the political spin they can put on it."

"There's so many good reasons to do it, though. Norm will be a political hero for having the guts to do it. He can blame the faulty death penalty statute. He can blame the legislature for underfunding capital cases. He can blame ultra-liberal, anti–death penalty federal judges. He should pull a Governor Ryan and be a Republican who speaks out for a moratorium on the death penalty." I was referring to the courageous act of then–Illinois Governor George Ryan, who put a moratorium on the death penalty in Illinois and created a blue-ribbon panel to explore why so many innocent men were mistakenly on Illinois's death row.

"I don't care why he does it or why he says he's doing it," Todd said. "He's getting political pressure from Republicans to deal with this budget destroyer. It's about politics, and politics is about money. Not faulty laws or high reversal rates. Politics and money. But Norm can say whatever he wants. That's up to him and his spin-meisters." Whether he actually believed himself or not, Todd loved to display his distrust of the government.

28

After Satterberg's comment, Todd and I were increasingly confident that Norm Maleng would accept our offer. Tony was hopeful but still thought Maleng wouldn't go through with it. Still, Todd, Suzanne Elliott, and I put together a draft *proffer*—a formal, legal document that essentially summarized what Gary would confess to if the prosecutors agreed to take the death penalty off the table in return.

On Monday, June 2, 2003, I received an e-mail from Satterberg late in the afternoon.

"Call me in the A.M.," it read.

The next morning, I waited until about a few minutes after eight and then called Dan.

"Dan, this is Mark. What's up?"

"Norm would like to meet with you, Tony, and Todd at two tomorrow."

"Great. We'll be there. Can you give me any hints?"

"No, I can't do that."

"Didn't think you could."

"I want to keep you in suspense."

"Thanks. I don't really like sleeping all that much. See you tomorrow."

"See you then."

I immediately called Tony and left a message. Then Todd. Todd had to come to Kent anyway for another matter, and when he arrived, we went into my small, cluttered office and closed the door. I told him that Maleng had reached his decision.

We were both hyped-up, but we had to keep it low key. We tried Tony again, but he was still unavailable. Todd went to his other appointment, while I tried to get some work done. It wasn't easy. *Why do more work preparing for trial? If Norm Maleng says yes, there will be no trial.* I was too nervous and excited to focus on anything else, anyway. I didn't even want to think about the alternative: Maleng saying no and then having to go to trial.

The next day, Tuesday, June 4, 2003, I had another face-to-face with Gary, this one with Dr. Judith Becker, a psychologist we'd hired to evaluate Gary. Judith Becker specializes in the study of serial rapists and serial murderers. I had scheduled the face-to-face on Friday, before I knew when the meeting with Norm would be.

I observed and took notes for a while and then excused myself for the meeting with Maleng. I told Gary I'd return to let him know Maleng's decision.

I walked the block from the jail to the prosecutor's office and rode up the elevator to the thirty-fifth floor. I had tried my best to avoid thinking about it, but the thought began to weigh very heavily: *if Norm says no, I will have detailed information from Gary that no one else in the world knows—details about unsolved murders and locations of remains of missing teenage girls that I will have to keep to myself because of the ethics of the legal profession.* Attorney-client confidentiality is sacrosanct and could not be violated if I wanted to continue to practice law. I had tried hard to keep these thoughts out of my consciousness, but now that the moment was at hand, it was impossible not to worry about this; I kept repeating to myself the many reasons why the prosecutor should accept our offer.

I got off the elevator and Tony got off another one at the same time. Was our timing a good omen?

Todd was already in the prosecutor's lobby waiting for us. As we walked up the stairs to the conference room, Tony asked, "Yes or no?"

I put my arm around his shoulder and said, "Yes."

Tony chuckled.

"Well, I still think he'll say, 'Thanks but no thanks.' Shall we put a bottle of something on it?" Tony liked to make small bets, usually involving expensive brands of scotch or other tasty potables.

Before I could take his bet, Mark Larson was there at the top of the stairs.

"Hello, gentlemen," he said. "We're meeting in the same room. Have a seat and I'll go grab Norm."

We sat around the big, beautiful mahogany conference table, in silence, just the three of us sitting there, lost in our own thoughts. Then Maleng, Larson, and Satterberg came into the room and closed the door. We exchanged handshakes and greetings.

"This is the hardest decision I have ever had to make," Maleng began. "Period. I have two choices: one is to say, 'No deal. No negotiations.' The other is to say, 'Yes. Let's accept the defense offer and try to negotiate a settlement.'"

I waited, frozen in the moment.

"I'm choosing the second option and saying yes to your offer."

The emotion of the moment was incredible and intense. I had no words to describe the sense of relief I had from hearing Maleng's choice. I realized he was still talking.

"My immediate reaction to your offer was no," he continued. "But your proposal had such huge implications for the people involved, and for the entire community, that I knew I had to give it very thoughtful consideration. I thought hard, and I realized that one of the foundations of our criminal justice system is to seek and know the truth and to do justice. I knew there were so many people who need to know the truth."

He went on:

"I recalled the passage from First Corinthians, chapter 13: 'For now we see in a mirror, dimly, but then, face to face.' I saw that this resolution could provide justice for the mothers, fathers, sisters, brothers, and the children of the victims. I decided yes, let's resolve this."

At this point, I felt deep gratitude and respect for Norm Maleng. He was first and foremost an elected official, a politician, but here he was, doing a 180-degree turn on a high-profile case, with his decision having widespread implications for the future of the death penalty in our state. And this after he had once adamantly—and publicly—rejected such a possibility. However costly it might prove to him politically, this was one of the most courageous decisions I had ever seen a political figure make. And my own relief was suddenly palpable. Someday in the near future, others would hear the gruesome details and learn of the locations of the still-missing remains. I wouldn't have the burden of carrying that information around inside me, prohibited from telling anyone else.

This wasn't just for Gary, although he was our client. It was for everyone—the beginning of the end of a nightmare that had held our community in an unfathomable curse for nearly a generation.

—⁓—

Todd, Tony, and I rode down all thirty-five floors in complete silence. There was another person in the elevator, so we couldn't talk about what had just happened. Being a lawyer means having to know how to control your emotions, so we were able to pull it off. We agreed to talk later and went our separate ways. I returned to the jail to give Gary the good news.

"Yes!" I said. "Norm Maleng said yes!"

"Oooh-K," Gary said. "That's good." He was so blasé about what had just happened, that I had a hard time believing it. *That's good.* Just another day. Ho hum. *Jeeeeezus Keey-riiiiist!! How can he take it so calmly!*

"Oh, well," I said. "At least one of us is happy."

Judith Becker, our psychologist, was still meeting with Gary when I came in. The three of us discussed some of the ways it might all play out. Maybe the news began to finally sink in, because Gary suddenly seemed to feel grateful, even magnanimous, now that his life would be spared.

"I want to start a Green River Victims' Fund," he said. "You know. If someone writes a book or makes a movie, I want some of the money to go to a fund for the victims . . . their families." Considering that Gary was a cold-blooded psychopathic serial killer, that sure seemed like a nice idea. Once again, the duality of Gary Ridgway: nice guy versus serial killer. I still could not make any sense of it. I couldn't because it didn't *make* any sense.

After my meeting with Gary and Judith Becker, I called Eric, Dave, Suzanne, Fred, Michele, Mark Cunningham, and Mary Goody from our team. They were told, in general terms, that Norm had accepted our offer and we were moving ahead with Plan B. Obviously, I stressed the need for confidentiality: a leak from our side could torpedo the deal, which might mean Gary could still get the death penalty. We also agreed to continue our investigation and trial preparation until the plea was formally entered, although in a reduced mode. We couldn't just shut everything else down, because whatever we did was being scrutinized. If we were seen to have stopped our trial preparation, the news media would know something was up. We needed to stay under the radar as long as necessary.

Over the next week, Tony, Todd, and I met with Jeff Baird and Mark Larson, working out the language of our formal written proffer and plea agreement. In writing the proffer, we realized that we had to give Gary some wiggle room; that is, some recognition in the document that Gary's memories were less than 100 percent accurate. What if Gary could, say, remember forty-six of the murders but drew a blank on the other three? Would that therefore entitle Maleng to renege on the agreement and insist on a trial and death sentence anyway? Even though that wasn't very likely, lawyers like to make things as complete as possible. In addition, we weren't really sure if the seven missing women on the "official" Green River victim list were included in the ten to fourteen additional victims that Gary had claimed. His memory for faces was very bad, and of course, he had no independent memory for any of the names. So the exact number of victims that Gary would be able to provide some information on had to be somewhat amorphous, although it appeared the totals might be as high as sixty—maybe even more.

By the end of the week, both sides agreed on the language of the proffer and plea agreement. One major dispute took a little longer than the others. The state wanted Norm Maleng to have the power to decide whether or not Gary had "substantially complied" with his end of the deal; that is, that he had given enough specific information to support the conclusion that the unsolved cases had been cleared. We insisted that Judge Jones should be the final arbiter on that issue, not the prosecutor's office. The state eventually conceded on this point, and with that we finally had a deal.

We had a conference with Judge Jones in his chambers and asked that the next hearing be postponed. Both sides realized that the judge sensed a plea bargain was in the offing. Why else would the usual monthly battle over discovery suddenly go on the back burner, especially after both sides had previously argued so vigorously over the most minute of points? We also saw that he was just fine with being kept out of the loop. Sometimes judges don't want to know all the gory details of settling litigation. Nevertheless, as nothing was formalized yet, Judge Jones continued working with the county's staff on the expensive technological improvements that would be needed for a Green River trial that now might never happen.

On June 10, we delivered our formal proffer to Norm Maleng.

> Enclosed please find our proffer. The proffer is being put forward in a spirit of good faith and with cautious optimism that we can achieve our mutual goal.
>
> As we discussed, all references exclude the seven presently charged counts and the case involving Ms. Garde.[1] We also want to explain that some of the responses are in terms of a range of numbers and/or an approximation. We do not want to overstate nor understate the quality or quantity of the information that can be provided. However, there are some variables that we cannot accurately address, including human activity and development, animal activity, and the inherent difficulties with recalling these memories after twenty years' passage of time. We believe Mr. Ridgway is being as truthful as he can possibly be. We also believe that he may be able to recollect more specifics if his memory is jogged as this process continues.

In the proffer, we said that Gary believed that he had killed between forty-seven and fifty-three women in King County between July 1982 and May or June 1985; that he was unable to identify any from photographs; that up to twenty-eight were killed in his house, between eleven and fifteen in his truck, and another dozen or so outside near the places where their remains had been found. We said that Gary could remember the places where he'd left virtually all of the bodies and that he could lead the police to between ten and fourteen of these victims that had not yet been found. We also said that Gary could lead the detectives to the personal property, such as clothing or jewelry, of between six and ten of the victims.

"In exchange for a promise not to seek the death penalty against him, the defendant is willing to plead guilty to 47 counts of aggravated first degree murder (excluding the presently charged counts)," the proffer said.

The seven charged counts were excluded, because at this point, we were operating under the presumption that there would still be a trial. The state did not want to deal with all of our motions to exclude evidence, and potential appeals, regarding the admissibility of evidence from those seven counts if they had been part of the settlement discussions and thereby protected under the evidence rules, specifically ER 410. This went back to Baird's puzzlement as to whether the state could use any admissions made by Gary while plea bargaining as so-called post-Miranda evidence, similar to the "not all mine" statement that Gary had supposedly made to Detective Doyon but that hadn't yet been ruled on by the courts, at least in the context of plea bargaining. Just avoiding the seven charged counts was one way the state hoped to dodge the issue. For our part, we didn't care: in fact, if the state blundered into the charged counts, we were going to be happy, because it gave us more to appeal about, if the deal somehow fell through.

Once the proffer was accepted, Gary would be free to meet face-to-face with the detectives to answer their questions. But first, we had to get Gary to sign a document that formally empowered Tony, Todd, and me to make the deal. We decided as a team that the three of us would run with the ball from here out, once the detectives began their interrogations of Gary. We wanted to keep our group as small as possible— on a need-to-know basis only. Besides, we had to maintain consistency and continuity. We couldn't have all eight of our lawyers taking turns sitting with Gary during the interviews, even if our side wasn't going to say much. No one would know what had been said in the previous interviews they hadn't sat in on, which would probably turn the detectives' interrogation sessions into a legal version of the Jerry Springer show—surprise and shock on a daily basis.

On June 12, 2003, our side met with the prosecutors to discuss timing and logistics. Baird told me, "We'd like to have the plea agreement signed tomorrow. The sheriff's office wants to move him out of jail tomorrow at the 2:30 P.M. shift change. Apparently, that's when it would attract the least amount of attention."

On June 13, Friday the thirteenth, we finalized the language of the plea agreement. The plea agreement formalized the conditions of the interrogation process and contained the key language:

> Upon complete, truthful, and candid disclosure by the Defendant of all crimes that he has committed in King County, Washington, the Prosecuting Attorney shall withdraw the notice to seek the death penalty on the currently charged counts and decline to seek the death penalty on any additional charges of Aggravated Murder in the First Degree arising from such crimes.

Todd, Michele, and I went up for a face-to-face with Gary. I went over the plea agreement. Slowly. Word for word. We answered his questions as we went along.

"Will you guys be there when I'm interviewed?" Gary asked.

"Yes," I answered. "One of us will be there every time they ask you a question. That's part of the deal. We get to be there with you."

"Where are they gonna take me?" Gary asked.

"That's a good question. Somewhere private and secluded, we hope," Todd told him. The risk of leaks was one of general concern for all involved, especially Gary.

"Will I be able to have visitors? Greg and Dorene?"

"Not for a while," Michele answered. "I think they want you to focus on trying to remember everything."

"When do we start?" Gary asked, obviously anxious to get the process moving.

"We don't know, but it could be as early as today. If some detectives come and get you this afternoon, don't be surprised," I answered.

"Oooh-K."

Gary seemed relaxed and ready to talk about everything he could remember. At about 1:30 in the afternoon, on Friday the thirteenth, Gary signed the agreement.

At about 1:45 P.M., Todd and I took the agreement over to Baird, who would then deliver it to Maleng.

"Thank you, gentlemen," Jeff said as we handed him the agreement that would spare all of us the biggest murder trial of the new century, or maybe even the last.

"OK," I said. "So where are we supposed to meet you guys?" We had been kept in the dark on where they wanted to put Gary, now that they were about to have him. Todd and I had thought it might be the Federal Detention Center in SeaTac, near the airport. Or maybe one of the local jails—say, Renton, or Kent. . . . Of course, that probably meant that Gary's agreement to cooperate would be blown within a week; other prisoners, if not the jailers themselves, would be almost certain to blab. Jeff smiled.

"Task force headquarters at Boeing Field," he told us. "They made a room up for him right there. Right in with the task force." Gary would be eating and sleeping—indeed, spending twenty-four hours a day with the same people who'd been trying to catch him for the last twenty years.

Todd and I both laughed and shook our heads. But why not? It was perfect, really. No one would ever think to look for him there. And if they did, I imagined the security would be pretty tight.

Just after 2:30 P.M., as the guard shift changed at the jail, two plain-clothes members of the task force quietly and inconspicuously went up to the eleventh floor, collected Gary, and drove him to the place where he would live for what would turn out to be the next six months.

PART FOUR

The Talk

29

Even though Gary was on his way to the task force, my own emotional roller coaster continued. My son, Sean, and his friends, the kids we'd come to know as they all grew up together, were graduating from high school the very next day. There was a lot going on with that. Yet here I was, tied up in the middle of the most sensitive part of this monumental case. I knew the whole deal could rise or fall on how cooperative Gary would be with his interrogators, once they had him in front of them, so the tension was high.

I did have a chance to sit down and have a heart-to-heart with Sean earlier that week, just before we got Gary's deal signed.

"I've been really busy lately with the case . . . ," I started to explain.

"I know," Sean said. "It's OK."

"You got all your English credits taken care of, right?" I asked because he had to do some extra work to make sure he had enough of the required English credits.

"Yeah. Done. Ms. Henderson confirmed everything," Sean nodded, smiling. "I'll be walking Saturday." Meaning he'd be in the graduation ceremony.

"Good. I knew it would work out." I hugged him. *Thank you, Ms. Henderson.*

I held him tight and he hugged me back. I whispered in his ear, "I love you, buddy. I'm so proud of the way you turned out. Keep it up and you'll have lots of success."

"Thanks, Dad. I love you too," he said. "Thanks for everything you and Mom have done for me."

I held my firstborn tight as the tears welled up in my eyes. These were tears of joy, love, pride, with some sadness that Sean was not a little boy anymore. And inside, I felt another source for my tears. I still couldn't help but think of the parents who hadn't had the chance for this moment with their daughters. I hugged Sean that much tighter. This parenting thing isn't easy, but it's really hard when you see your babies grow up so fast. With all those young girls—Gary's victims— weighing on my mind and heart, I realized how fortunate Kelly and I had been. I could not and still cannot begin to imagine the pain those parents must still live with. Many of Gary's victims were killed before they'd ever had a chance to finish high school.

—⁓—

I arrived at the Green River Task Force headquarters at Boeing Field, the airport immediately south of the city, at about three on the afternoon of June 13. I soon heard Baird and others working there referring to the place as "the bunker." It did have the feeling of being underground, because it actually was the ground floor of the old Federal Aviation Administration building, a classic utilitarian government building just north of Boeing's Museum of Flight: from the street-level parking lot, you had to go down a flight of stairs, which right away gave you the subterranean feeling. While Gary was in there, all the windows had been covered, to keep the outside world from catching a glimpse. No sunlight, locked entry with tight security: all that was missing were the series of automatic doors from *Get Smart.*

After descending from the parking lot, I knocked on the door. The door opened, and I was let in by none other than Tom Jensen. By now, after all the discovery our side had reviewed, I had come to appreci- ate the incredible effort that Jensen had put into the case almost from the start, and particularly over the previous decade when he'd worked virtually by himself.

"I remember the last time you let me into a locked door to see Mr. Ridgway," I told him. "November 30, 2001, I believe." Jensen smiled.

Now that he was about to get some answers, I realized that he could actually see the end of a case that had consumed much of his working life.

Todd and Tony soon arrived, and everyone exchanged handshakes and greetings. One of the things that immediately struck me was the number of people—task force detectives, prosecutors, and staff—who were there, and who obviously knew what was going on. We had all been so secretive that I thought the number of people who knew what was being discussed was a very small circle. Wrong. Our side was introduced to some of the task force members we would be working closely with during the interrogation process: Captain Jim Graddon; Detective Katie Larson (the media spokesperson for the task force); Detective Graydon Matheson, one of the evidence specialists; Sergeant D. B. Gates; Sergeant Ray Green; and Intelligence Unit Detectives Malcolm Chang and Ross Nooney, who would be video- and audiotaping almost everything that happened during the interrogation process.

They took us on a brief tour of the facility. The main space, perhaps one hundred feet by one hundred feet, had one row of small cubicles separated by partition walls along the west wall, where the five assigned prosecutors—Jeff Baird, Patty Eakes, Brian McDonald, Ian Goodhew, and Sean O'Donnell—worked. The center part of the space was filled with boxes of supplies, case files, and discovery materials, as well as copy machines, a barrier of paper, shelves, and boxes that extended over eye level. Another row of cubicles, for detectives, was on the east wall.

Along the south wall was a small room, almost a large closet, which had been set up for their special guest. This is where Gary would sleep. The door to the room had been taken off its hinges, and a desk blocked the opening. The room contained a cot, a chair; nothing else except for four bare, off-white, concrete walls. A video camera attached near the ceiling watched and recorded all of Gary's movements whenever he was in there, morning, noon, or night. Outside this improvised cell, two to four security officers, each of them with fully charged Tasers, kept watch over Gary at all times. All of them were members of either the King County Sheriff's Department's Intelligence Unit or SWAT team. In addition to their Tasers, they were heavily armed with weapons that could fire real bullets. Gary's odds of escaping this confinement were at absolute zero.

Next to Gary's closet was a bathroom with a toilet and sink. They had rigged up a "camping shower"—essentially a big plastic container filled with water, hung above. When the valve was opened, gravity could provide Gary with a cold shower on a daily basis. Along the wall next to the bathroom was the "kitchen": a sink, mini-refrigerator, coffeemaker, and microwave. Standard stuff found in most offices.

As we viewed these accommodations, we were told that we would not be allowed to walk around in those areas of the building in the future. That was fine and perfectly understandable. After all, it was the other side's work area. They had photos, maps, memos, lists, and assorted "work product" all over their desks and walls. We had no right to have access to their area any more than they had a right to ours, back at the ACA office. If the deal somehow came apart, they wouldn't want us making use of any of their internal stuff. That's what discovery was for.

However, this did lead to the ironic situation of our having to ask the prosecutors and detectives to fetch us coffee whenever we needed a cup or a refill. As time went by, asking the captain of the Green River Task Force to get me a java refill felt strange. But Jim Graddon did it with a smile and class, the way he handled everything, from sifting through dirt in ninety-degree weather, or taking out the trash at the bunker. Jim did it all, including the jobs others didn't want to do. He was the epitome of a leader who led by his own example.

Tony, Todd, and I were led back to the north wall of the bunker, where another door led to a conference room and then, the interrogation room. Part of this area would become the defense "office"— our own "home away from home" for the next six months, although at the time we had no idea how long we'd be there. They had also stocked a mini-fridge in the conference room with water, Coke, and 7-Up. They treated us very well, and everything was very friendly. A Todd-like thought ran through my mind—*Are they trying to be nice to lull us into dropping our guard?*

We then moved into the interrogation room. Video cameras and microphones had already been set up. Everything they recorded was piped out to Malcolm Chang and Ross Nooney on the other side of the wall, in the conference room.[1] There were two off-white tables and several chairs in the interrogation room. We were told that two detectives, two defense lawyers, and Gary would be in the room during the questioning; other detectives and the prosecutors would sit in another large office and watch on a TV monitor. If three defense lawyers were there, one of us would be in the conference room outside the interrogation room with Chang and Nooney, watching everything on a video monitor. After we looked this setup over, we went back into the conference room.

"Shall we get started?" Graddon suggested.

"Sure," I said. Two of the security guards left to bring Gary from his closet. A few minutes later, Gary came shuffling around the east corner of the prosecutors' cubicles, leg irons, handcuffs, and waist irons gently rattling. Knowing Gary, I thought it was more than was necessary: shackled and accompanied by somewhere between four and six armed officers, every time he moved. It seemed like something out of *Silence of the Lambs,* only minus the face mask-headgear. But I wasn't going to comment. Gary didn't object, and they were going to do it their way, no matter what we thought.

Gary saw us waiting for him as he shuffled into the conference room. He was smiling and looked pleased to be at this stage—and *on* this stage—under the circumstances.

We all greeted the man of the hour.

"Hey, Gary . . . how ya doin'?" I said.

"Good, thank you," Gary replied. "Everyone's been real nice."

Gary and his escorts stopped at the door to the interrogation room. His leg irons and handcuffs were unlocked, and he was led into the interrogation room.

Before Tony and I were allowed into the room, our briefcases were searched, and we were frisked and searched with a metal detector wand. This procedure was followed every time we entered the interrogation room over the next six months, typically two to four times a day. As a result, we got to know the security team pretty well, and they, us. Still, they always checked our baggage.

—⁄⁄⁄—

The discussion that everyone had been waiting for, for so many years, finally began just after 4 P.M. on June 13, 2003. We almost immediately ran into a snag.

The first thing covered was the formality of putting the plea agreement on the record. Brian McDonald handled that procedure for the prosecution team. He read from the proffer we had negotiated.

"At the very end, paragraph eighteen, it says, 'In exchange for a promise not to seek the death penalty against him, the defendant is willing to plead guilty to forty-seven counts of aggravated first degree murder, excluding the presently charged counts.' Is that an accurate statement?" McDonald asked Gary.

"Um, yes it is . . . or I mean it . . . it depends how many they . . . you find. I don't . . . I don't . . ."

"But is it pretty accurate?"

"It's pretty accurate," Gary said.

"Is it accurate or not?"

"Yeah, it's pretty accurate, yeah."

"Do you want to consult with your attorneys about that?"

The problem here was that the agreement called for Gary to be accurate in whatever he would tell the detectives. If he was inaccurate, the deal would go out the window, so Gary was trying to avoid being tied down to some specific number of victims, in case the prosecutor might later come back and say, sorry, you left one out, the deal's off. We had a quick discussion with Gary and assured him that if he missed one or two in the total number of victims the agreement would still apply, provided he was making his best effort to remember.

"I agree to, um, to, plead guilty to the counts that I committed, not the others," Gary finally said. He meant the three murders he'd denied committing, that of Amina Agisheff and Tammy Liles, and the unidentified remains found near Liles in Oregon. Gary had resolutely insisted that despite his earlier assertion that "I killed 'em all," he *hadn't* killed Amina Agisheff, or Liles, or the other unidentified victim found near Tammy Liles. With Agisheff and Liles and the unknown bones out, that meant the total was somewhere between forty-six, the minimum, and fifty-three, which included the seven charged victims that Gary wasn't formally bargaining on. The total number would depend on how proficient the detectives would be in matching Gary's spotty memory to the evidence. Also, by agreeing to the spread, Gary was admitting that there might be more murders that he couldn't immediately recall, just not Agisheff, Liles, and the unknown Oregon victim.

"Now, it says . . . you recall killing forty-seven to fifty-three individuals in King County. Is that accurate?" McDonald asked. Our proffer had lowballed the number to be on the safe side. Based on Gary's statements to us, we were still thinking the real number was around sixty—or even more.

"Yes, yes," Gary said.

"And then at paragraph eighteen, it says, 'In exchange for not . . . for a promise not to seek the death penalty against him, the defendant is willing to plead guilty to forty-seven counts of aggravated murder.'"

"Yes."

"Is that correct?"

"Yeah, around forty-seven, yes . . . or pretty clo . . . I . . . I . . . I don't, um . . . not 100 percent sure. I mean 99.9 percent."

"As to what?" McDonald asked.

"Is forty-seven."

"That is the number 'forty-seven'?"

"Yeah."

"Elsewhere the number is between . . . listed between forty-seven and fifty-three. Is that the ambiguity you have about how many murders you've committed?" McDonald asked.

"Yes, it is, I think."

"So it's somewhere between forty-seven to fifty-three?"

"Yes, it is."

So there it was, after more than twenty years, the first official admission by Gary that he was in fact the Green River Killer, even if the numbers were very loose.

Once this was completed, Randy Mullinax came in, reintroduced himself to Gary and then introduced the other detectives who would be conducting the interviews: Tom Jensen, Sue Peters, and Jon Mattsen.

Mullinax was short and stocky, dark-haired (what there was left of it), with a goatee; his eyes never seemed to blink. He usually wore blue jeans and either a T-shirt or golf shirt under a fleece vest. As the weeks of interrogations unfolded, it was often Mullinax who played the "bad cop" role; his intensity could be intimidating.

Sue Peters was short in height, with short brown hair; she'd been with the King County Sheriff's Office for almost twenty years and was in such great physical shape that she looked as if she were in her late twenties, but she was actually closer to my age. In her time, she had been a skilled high school and college athlete. She'd been in her first few weeks as a patrol officer at the Green River when the bodies were found in the summer of 1982.

Tom Jensen was tall, with light-brown hair, and a mustache. He was lean and laconic, although on occasion his indignation could make Gary cringe, as we were to discover. He usually wore blue jeans and a windbreaker.

Mattsen was the youngest of Gary's principal interrogators. At thirty-five, he had a boyish face that made him seem even younger, with short, light-brown hair, a quick smile, and a twinkle in his eye. He and Sue Peters often filled the "good cop" role as the interrogations progressed.

"Hello, Tom. Hello, Sue. Hello . . . J . . . Jon?" Gary obviously wanted to get their names right. He turned to me. "Maybe you could write their names down for me?" he asked.

"Sure." I said and wrote down the first and last names of each of the four detectives. Mullinax told Gary that the plan was for two of the detectives to interview him for an hour or two; then everyone would take a fifteen- to twenty-minute break. After this, more interviews, this time with the other two detectives, would start. In effect, they would come at him in relays. Gary said he was ready.

Peters and Mattsen now stepped out and closed the door. Jensen and Mullinax began the interrogations. It was about 4:30 P.M. As Jensen explained later, they had two primary objectives in this first post-confession interview: first, finding the remains of the seven women who were still missing, and second, verifying that Gary was in fact *the* Green River Killer, the one and only.

"What we'd like to start with is the bodies that are still out there," Jensen told Gary. "Every day that goes by, there's a chance that a house can be built on one, or a parking lot can be . . ." On our side, we'd already seen how true that was. Many of the places where Gary had claimed to have left the bodies of his victims had been developed or otherwise paved over.

"Yes," Gary interrupted. He knew exactly what Jensen wanted to know.

"So," Jensen said, "I think a good starting point would be for you to tell us about the first one you can recall and where it is."

"The . . . the first one I killed?"

"Yes," Mullinax said.

"Uh . . . I don't actually remember where I killed 'em," Gary said, "'cause I wasn't planning on killin' any of 'em. And what happens is, uh, I, I, I had uh, uh, sex with a lot of women, and I don't really know where every one I killed . . . I don't know where I killed the first one. It was Coffield . . ."

What we had here was a failure to communicate. What Jensen wanted to know was where the first undiscovered body was. What Gary thought Mullinax wanted to know was where he had killed his first victim. Both Jensen and Mullinax *did* want to know that eventually, but not right then. They wanted to find some new bones, not only to recover one of the missing but also to verify Gary's claim that he really was the killer. Right at the start, though, the interrogation had veered into the charged counts—which weren't, after all, formally part of the proffer, in case something went wrong. And Gary had just admitted to the police that he had in fact killed one of the charged women, Wendy Coffield.

Argghh!

Mullinax tried to start over. "Well, let's not talk . . ."

"Yeah," Jensen said.

"Oooh-K," Gary said, agreeable as ever.

"Let's go with the ones that we have not found, the ones that you know are still out there, the ones that have not been discovered. That's what we'd like to start with and pick which ever one you want to start with, whichever one is freshest in your mind," Jensen said.

"Oooh-K," Gary said. "The farthest one out is, I think it's over by uh, the Fall City exit, off of I-90." Gary had just given the detectives a location where no skeleton had previously been found, somewhere off a small road that led north away from I-90 toward the small town of Fall City, far to the east of Seattle. This was the farthest away from the big city that he'd ever left a victim, Gary said.

Over the next six hours, Gary described ten other locations where he believed no skeletons had ever been found.

These included a spot not far from the Leisure Time Resort, a privately owned campground that he and Judith had frequented out I-90, where he had left the remains of either April Buttram or Keli McGinness, he wasn't sure which. It was only a coincidence that years after he'd left a body nearby, he and Judith had joined the campground, Gary said. In early 1984, before meeting Judith, he'd returned to the site and recovered the skull. His idea had been to take it to Portland to throw the police off, he added. This victim would eventually become known as the "Leisure Time Lady," in reference to the nearby campground.

He'd left another body near Seattle International Raceway, Gary said. And one near the Lewis and Clark Theatre off Pacific Highway South. He thought it was probably Kase Lee, last seen in late August 1982. Another near a truck stop off I-90, some miles farther east from the campground. Perhaps three more bodies up Highway 410, the road to Mount Rainier. He'd left a body near Lake Fenwick, which was just to the north of Star Lake; he'd left one over the side of the hill some distance south of Star Lake, around 292nd Street, just to the southwest of Kent. He left a victim at Northwest Hospital in north Seattle. That one, he'd tried to set her hair on fire after she was dead but put it out because it was making too much smoke. (This turned out to be Linda Rule, a seventeen-year-old who'd been on our Red River list, but never on the Green River list.) He'd put a body out on Auburn-Black Diamond Road, to the southeast of Kent, and not far from where another discovered Green River victim, Yvonne Antosh, had been found; and he'd put yet one more over the side of the main road from the airport into Kent, Kent-Des Moines Road.

And Gary told the detectives of several locations where he'd left jewelry he'd taken from the victims. The clothes, Gary added, he'd simply thrown out of his truck as he drove down various highways.

But Gary had no idea of who was where. The names meant nothing to him, and neither did the pictures.

Mullinax wanted to know how he had killed his victims. It always happened in the middle of his "date," Gary said.

"Well, explain to me what you mean," Mullinax said.

"Well, I had so much uh, hate in my, in myself that, that I'd uh . . . 'cause I had a lot of things I didn't stand up for," Gary said. "So I . . . I dated a woman. If she would have sex—if it was a motel or whatever— if she . . . lied to me about . . . anything, or hurrying me and not enjoy- ing the sex, um . . . a culmination of all those, or, or some of 'em, uh, during the middle. And . . . and a lot of 'em were over by the airport— the, the uh, noise set me off. I know one of 'em . . . like a truck came by and, and it set me off. And plus, the, the woman lyin' to me."

Here was a smorgasbord of rationalizations from Gary. Women lying to him, hurrying him up, noise from airplanes, noise from a truck. About the only truthful thing in this was Gary's assertion: "I had so much hate . . ." It was clear that even though Gary might be willing to say what and where, he wasn't anywhere close to saying why.

I decided to encourage Gary to be a bit more forthcoming.

"I think that you should explain to them the physical position that you and the women were in," I told him. Gary nodded.

"When I pick up a woman, I usually date 'em. We agree on sex, and if she . . . she uh, en-en-enjoys it, it's . . . you know, she's prob'ly faking it. And I would be on t . . . on top of her usually, uh, face-to-face, and if I couldn't uh, have a climax, I would have her turn around and I would get her uh, from the back end, um, penis in the vagina, not, uh, rectum or anything, and uh, that is . . . sometimes I'd kill 'em, and sometimes I wouldn't. And just . . . the, I had a lot a rage at that time and that's uh, why I killed these women. I didn't plan on killin' 'em."

Gary said that as soon as he had killed someone, he'd begun cry- ing and almost immediately thereafter had become afraid of being caught. He always tried to get rid of the victim's body right away, he said. But we would eventually find out that that was hardly the truth.

"OK," Mullinax said. "All right. Did you take anything from this particular victim?" Mullinax wanted to go back to the first undiscovered victim to see if he might be able to identify her from a missing person report, which might describe her clothing or jewelry when last seen. "Take her clothing or anything?"

"Every one of 'em, almost, I took the clothing," Gary said, "'cause I, I . . . not to wear it or anything like that. It was just to . . . 'cause the, maybe the hatred of the women that I, uh—I like to have sex with no clothes on. So motel dates, I didn't kill anybody, mo . . . motel dates."

Jensen asked Gary what else he could remember about his murder of Kase Lee, whom Gary thought he had left in the brush near the movie theater on Pacific Highway South. Since Kase's disappearance on August 28, 1982, the failure to find her remains had been one of the detectives' largest frustrations.

Gary looked at Kase's photograph and said he was fairly certain that she had been among his first ten victims.

"First ten you did?" Jensen asked.

"I'm just guessin', ten," Gary said.

"Relatively early on in the series?"

"Yes, 'cause the first seven I did were in the river," Gary said.

"Just as a note of clarification," Mullinax said, "I'll go back just a moment. Did you say . . . that there were . . . *seven* women in the river, or five?"

"I'm just guessin' . . . five, uh, the, the clusters," Gary said.

This was no help—not as far as Mullinax was concerned. But he had only himself to blame for giving Gary the correct number.

As he had with me, Gary insisted that he'd stopped killing after taking up with Judith. "I stopped in, uh, in '85," he said.

"You know for sure, for certain?" Jensen asked.

"Yes."

"And so there's no possibility that any of this going into '86 or . . . ?"

"No."

But Jensen already knew that Gary either wasn't telling the truth about this, or his memory had failed. The body that Gary thought no one had found out by Seattle International Raceway was that of Patricia Barczak, who had been killed in 1986 and found later. Jensen kept this to himself for the time being, however, and the interview went on. As for me, I had no clue at that point that Gary wasn't telling the truth, the whole truth, and nothing but. I was only to learn later how hard that was for him.

———m———

By around 10:30 that night, we'd covered most of the what and the where: repeated murder by strangulation and where Gary thought he'd left the bodies, as well as the jewelry and clothing, although it appeared that the chance of finding anything that belonged to the victims other than their skeletal remains was very remote. Because Gary had no idea of the names of his victims, many became known to all of us—the detectives, the lawyers, and Gary himself—by some particular geographical or physical reference: the "Carnation Lady," the "Power Line Lady," the "Log Lady," the "Water Tower Lady," or some such description, always ending with "Lady." The Gary I had come to know never called his victims *whores.* They were usually simply *ladies.*

After Gary had been hooked up to his chains again, and taken to his closet, all of us—both the defense and prosecution, as well as the tag-team detectives—sat around the table in the conference room. By the end of this long day, Gary had formally admitted forty-six of the original forty-nine victims on the Green River list. He had also told the detectives about fourteen other sites where he claimed to have left bodies that had not yet been discovered. That meant sixty possible victims, maybe more. Now the question was this: Could any of what Gary had just said be verified?

"Tomorrow morning, we'd like you here at 6:30," Mullinax said. "We're going to go out on a little field trip to see some of these places he's told us about."

"Oh, boy, sounds like fun," I said, although I preferred sleeping in later than 5:30 A.M. on a Saturday morning whenever possible. "We'll be here." Then I remembered something very important. "How long do you think we'll go tomorrow? My son graduates from Kentwood High School tomorrow evening at the Tacoma Dome."

"We'll make sure you don't miss it," Captain Graddon said. "We want to work with your schedules too. But I think we all agree we want to get as much done this weekend as possible. Just let us know when you need to leave and we'll wrap it up by then." Everyone nodded and chimed in their agreement.

"Todd and I can be here, too," Tony said. "We can talk about it tomorrow."

"Thanks." I was relieved this wouldn't conflict with Sean's graduation and that they didn't plan on going until eleven *every* night.

I got home around 11:30 and went upstairs to see Kelly. She was still awake. I sat on the edge of the bed and explained why I was so late getting home.

"I can't tell you any details, but things just kicked into high gear. They have moved Gary from the jail so I'll be really busy . . . *really* busy . . . over the next few days."

Kelly protested. "Not tomorrow! It's Saturday and graduation is tomorrow."

"Yes, tomorrow. But I'll be home in time for graduation. It's not until seven. I promise you. I won't miss it! I wouldn't miss it for the world."

"You better not . . . or there'll be another victim." She turned away and turned off her light. The conversation was over.

However, I was still wide awake, buzzing with the events of the day—a Friday the Thirteenth that would forever be etched in my memory. I walked out to our deck with a cold Red Hook ale. It was after midnight, now officially June 14, but it was still pretty warm outside, the beginning of an abnormally warm summer in Seattle. I lay down on our chaise lounge, drank my beer, and gazed at the stars. Pretty soon, the thoughts of tomorrow's field trip racing through my mind began to slow down and I found my eyelids closing. Throughout the night, I had quick, wispy little visions of Gary leading a group of us into some wooded area, arm extended, index finger pointing . . .

30

We all gathered at the bunker the following morning, June 14, 2003, for the first of what would eventually turn out to be twenty field trips that Gary would be taken on over the course of the next five months. The plan was to put Gary in an extra-large, ten-seat van, surrounded by his lawyers, two prosecutors, several of the detectives, along with a videographer and a sound guy. Everything heard, seen, and said would go on tape. At the same time, we all wanted to do this as unobtrusively as possible, to prevent some citizen from recognizing Gary and then putting two and two together. If that happened, our secret negotiations would be blown at the very start.

Tony and I went along on this first trip, and all three of us went the next day, too, a Sunday. After that, due to space limitations in the van, only one defense attorney and one prosecutor would ride along. Because most of these trips originated in south King County, I was usually the defense attorney who got the field trip duty. Tony and Todd both lived about an hour from the bunker, even without traffic. I live about fifteen minutes away. Besides, we wanted consistency and continuity. It helped to have someone along who'd been there the day before. In the end, I went on probably about fifteen of the twenty trips.

The procedure on these treks typically involved a rendezvous at the bunker in the early morning hours, sometimes as early as 3:30 A.M., and never later than 6:30. Everyone dressed as if we were going to go hiking in the woods—which we usually were—and there was plenty of denim and fleece and a variety of hiking shoes and boots. Gary usually wore a light brown windbreaker over his jail coveralls, with a black baseball cap on his head, helping to hide most of his face from prying eyes. The main van was always driven by Task Force Detective Mike Brown, with one of the security team in the front passenger seat. When everyone was ready, I'd be escorted through the forbidden zone to a back door on the south side of the building. Mike would pull the van up as close as possible to the door and Gary would then be rushed out to the van. The rest of us would pile in, and we'd be on the road. The prosecutor and I often sat in the seat behind the driver. Behind us in the third seat were Gary, one of the detectives, and Ross Nooney, the video man. Another detective and Malcolm Chang, the sound man, filled the van. A caravan of two or three unmarked cars and a couple of SUVs full of task force members, maybe another prosecutor, and sometimes even Sheriff Reichert followed behind.

Typically, one of the detectives would start the recording of the trip by giving the date and time and introducing the people in the van and directing Mike Brown toward our destination of the day.

That first day, Randy Mullinax gave us our itinerary.

"The plan this morning, gentlemen, is to try to go to the Leisure Time [campground], and the Carnation-Fall City site, and maybe Ken's [the truck stop] as the third. Is that logical?" he asked Gary.

"Yes," Gary said. Gary the night before had said he was "quite certain" that there were undiscovered skeletons in these places that could be found. The area near the Leisure Time campground was the place where Gary thought he'd left either Keli McGinness or April Buttram.

But once we got out to the road behind the Leisure Time resort, Gary at first had a hard time finding the spot where he'd claimed he entered the woods.

Gary said quietly, almost to himself, "Looks a lot different . . . a lot different."

I was thinking, *Oh, no. First one and he can't recognize a thing.*

Gary asked, "I'm sorry, Mike. Could you turn around and go back. Slowly?" It was a question I would hear many times over the course of the summer, and every time I would cringe, I can only imagine how it must have gotten on Mike Brown's nerves. Still, he'd always respond with something like, "Sure Gary," or "No problem," and he'd turn us around without complaint.

Finally, Gary had us stop.

"Right here," he said. "This is where I went in. I'm quite certain."

We piled out of the van and tromped into the woods. Way into the woods. Deeper into the woods, over and around fallen trees, no real trail, other than the one Gary was now blazing, although he was still in his chains. He got to a spot—a swampy, marshy area next to a huge fallen log.

"Right there. I left her there. I'm quite certain it was April Buttram. Maybe McGinness, but I'm quite certain it was April Buttram." Gary pointed to the center of the marshy area, a shallow pond of water and muck, an area maybe eight-by-eight feet.

"Yeah, right," I said to one of the cops with a sarcastic snarl. It just seemed impossible that he could be directing us to *the* spot he'd left April Buttram, twenty years before, in 1983. I was somewhat skeptical of getting results from this site, but we were early in the process. There were many other sites to visit. Some of the detectives looked around, but there were no bones that were obviously visible.

Eventually, we headed back to the van. The detectives decided that the growth around the site and the changing of seasons over the previous twenty years might have obscured the bones, if in fact they were actually there. The chances were very high, too, that the parts of the skeleton had disarticulated—that is, come apart—over the decades and were probably scattered over a wide area. Some of the Green River victims that had been discovered in years past had their bones strewn over several acres, mostly from the action of rain and small animals. To find the bones, the detectives agreed, it would be necessary to eventually call in a special squad of task force detectives: the "Diggers and Whackers," as they were called—people to chop down the brush and to sift the exposed soil for human remains. The Diggers and Whackers, armed with machetes, rakes, shovels, and mesh screens, would strip the ground bare, looking for bits of bones or teeth or any other evidence of Gary's victims.

Our next stop that morning was on the eastern side of the town of North Bend, not far from the truck stop referred to the night before by Gary. This location was actually a few miles east of the truck stop, on Middle Fork Road, a beautiful, forested area running along the middle fork of the picturesque Snoqualmie River.

When we got there, Gary recognized the exact spot. Unfortunately, there was a parking lot where twenty years before he'd left his truck by the side of the road. And one of the large trees had been cut down. He thought he'd taken a small trail into the woods and had left the body covered with brush.

"I . . . I thought it was already picked up," Gary said, meaning that he thought the body had been found years before.

"You're saying this parking area was not here at that time, the shoulder wasn't even here," I encouraged.

"This parking here was never here. No. And there was a walkway in there for . . . it must've been for fishing. I don't know how far . . . and I didn't hear no water. It was at night, so I didn't pay no attention to water. And, uh, it was . . . the only place that had a walkway at it. I thought maybe it was an animal walkway, but I'm not quite sure it was . . . between this part and here."

"And back there?" Mullinax asked, as we surveyed the chopped-down trees and parking lot.

"And back there," Gary agreed, "and it's leveled in there."

"But for some reason you think that we found a body here?"

"You had to have, because Mark said that they . . . uh, there was a parking lot here. You had to have found one here. Or not you guys but . . ."

"Someone would," Mullinax supplied.

"Someone," Gary agreed.

But if there had ever been a body there, it was plain that it was long gone now. Or buried in the berm created when the parking area was created.

———

After striking out on Middle Fork Road, we got back into the van and headed back to the bunker. We returned at about noon, hot, sweaty, and generally disappointed with the day's results.

One of the more interesting aspects of these field trips was Gary's acute sensitivity to the presence of strangers. He was still in shackles, and he obviously did not want to be seen. But he seemed to have some sort of inborn radar that told him when passersby, ignorant of what was going on, happened to be in the area. On more than one occasion, curious passersby would ask what was happening, and the detectives would explain they were simply looking at real estate. But pains were taken to conceal Gary from onlookers—and also Tony, whose tall, bearded visage was thought to be instantly recognizable from his many years as a defense lawyer in King County.

When we returned to the bunker after this first field trip, both sides decided we needed to work out some sort of media strategy to explain Gary's sudden disappearance from the jail. We all expected the news to get out sooner or later. When Gary was put back into his closet, I met with Captain Graddon, task force spokesperson Katie Larson, and Deputy Prosecutor Patty Eakes to figure out what we'd say, once we started getting the inevitable questions from the news media about Gary's present whereabouts. We knew that Gary's disappearance from the jail was bound to be noticed by other inmates, and there was no way to stop them from talking about it. It would only be a matter of time before rumors made it to the media. All it would take then is for someone to recognize Gary on one of the field trips to put the story together and to jump to the obvious conclusion. That was one reason both sides wanted to start the field trips early in the morning. There was less chance we'd be noticed.

"We hope it stays under the radar," Graddon told me, "but in the event word gets out that he's not in the jail, we thought we'd better coordinate our response. Let's see if we can come up with some response or responses we can agree on, so we're not contradicting each other."

"I imagine the press will figure it out pretty soon," I agreed. "Someone in the jail will say something to somebody. I was going up to the eleventh floor once a week for eighteen months. Then I'm there just about every day for a couple months. Then, all of a sudden, Gary's gone. One of his neighbors or one of the corrections officers is gonna start thinking, *Hmmm? I wonder what's up?*"

"No one is going to be asking *us* anything," Patty Eakes said, meaning the team of prosecutors in the bunker. "You should probably talk to Dan [Donahoe, Norm Maleng's media spokesperson] just to coordinate with him."

"I'll do that," Katie Larson said. "My concern is, once the Diggers and Whackers get to work, the media's going to go nuts. They'll figure out Gary's been moved and start adding things up."

"As long as we stick with no comment, nothing can be confirmed," I said. "They can speculate all they want."

"Which they will," Graddon agreed.

"It sells," I shrugged.

"I'm going to let them know that these searches are based on a further review of all of the evidence," Katie Larson said. "Which is true."

"How about the inevitable 'Where's Gary now?'" Eakes asked. "That'll be the next question."

"If they ask where Gary is," Katie said, "I'll let them know he's in a secure facility. 'A secure, undisclosed location' [this was a well-known phrase at the time, in the post 9-11 climate]. I thought about saying he was in a secure area at Western State Hospital [the mental lockup], but we don't want to say he's at Western if he's not."

"We wouldn't want that either," I agreed. "It implies to the potential jurors out there that we're exploring a mental defense, like, he did it, but he's crazy. I don't think we want potential jurors exposed to *that*, in addition to the fact it's not true."

"No, they'd be able to find out he wasn't at Western and know we were lying."

Graddon agreed. "That would make things much worse, believe me."

"Let's get an order from Judge Jones, under seal, transferring Gary to a secure, undisclosed facility," I suggested. "That might keep the media at bay, for a while. If they ask us where Ridgway is, we're under a sealed court order not to say anything. Then they'll try to get the order unsealed, and if or when they do, it still doesn't really tell them anything." This was sort of like putting a riddle inside an enigma: if and when the news media convinced Judge Jones to unseal the order, there would still be nothing to find out.

"Sure," Patty Eakes said. "I think we could do that. Why don't you draft something up. We'll sign off on it, and one of us can take it to Jones and get it filed if he signs it."

I decided we should try some role-playing. I held my pen toward Katie Larson as if I were a reporter.

"So Detective Larson, the task force is out digging and whacking, and Gary Ridgway is not in jail. Is Ridgway leading the task force to these sites?"

Katie put on her best media poker face.

"We are searching these sites based on our ongoing investigation and review of *all* the evidence, thank you." She turned the "mike" on me by holding her fist, with an imaginary microphone to my face. "Tell the viewers, counsel. Is your client leading the task force to places he left his victims?"

"I don't know. Ask Katie Larson. She's got him locked up in some se-cure, undisclosed location. Or . . . maybe I just stick to 'no comment.'"

"I think that's a better idea," she said. "Or, there's, 'I cannot confirm nor deny the rumors . . .' or, 'We're prohibited from commenting under court order,' or something like that."

As soon as this was fixed, I rushed home, showered, and made it to Sean's graduation—emotionally whipsawed, between looking for re-mains of someone's dead child, and watching my own son take the first step into adulthood.

——⁓——

The next morning, though, a Sunday, we were back at the bunker at just before seven for another field trip. This one went to several new sites, the Lewis and Clark Theatre, where Gary had said he'd left the body of Kase Lee; five places where Gary had said he'd left some of the victims' jewelry decades earlier; Lake Fenwick, north of Star Lake; and two other locations just over the lip of the long ridge that separated the airport strip area from the Kent Valley. Two of these locations were incredibly steep; it seemed almost impossible that one person could have maneuvered a dead body over the side. Gary said he'd managed it simply by dragging the body downhill. As the detectives peered over the edge, trying to see anything, I saw Jensen trip and fall, disappear-ing from view over the steep embankment.

"Tom's down," I said.

"Oh, great," Sue Peters said. "Gary just made the lead detective fall, so . . ."

"Uh-oh," Gary said.

One of the detectives tried to contact Jensen over his handheld radio.

"TJ . . . TJ," he called.

A few moments later, Jensen emerged over the top of the embank-ment. The location was so steep and so overgrown as to be nearly im-penetrable. Here was another site for the Diggers and Whackers, it appeared.

Afterward we returned to the bunker for another debriefing. Hav-ing found nothing obvious, the detectives were becoming a bit irri-tated with Gary.

"OK," Jensen said. "Well, hey, first of all, let me tell you, Gary, I'm getting a little frustrated here. OK?"

Gary started to say something, but Jensen cut him off.

"Like, we're 0 for 2, 0 for 2 yesterday . . ."

"I know," Gary said, "I am too." Frustrated, he meant.

"And Todd [Gruenhagen] chastised me for saying that," Jensen added, "but I have to say, we're close to 0 for 12 now," meaning that we'd been to almost a dozen locations, including the five for jewelry and had found nothing.

"Uh-huh," Gary nodded.

"And it's getting a little frustrating, you know?"

"Uh-huh."

"I just, just want to let you know that."

"I know."

"If you're blowin' smoke up my ass, eventually it's gonna come out my ears," Jensen finished.

"No, it's not," Gary said.

"OK, all right, all right," Jensen said, but anyone could see that Jensen was beginning to entertain some serious doubts about Gary's true willingness to cooperate.

This frustration boiled up again late that afternoon, when Mattsen and Mullinax tried to pin Gary down. They wanted some verifiable information that he really was the killer.[1]

"Gary," Mattsen said, "you have to realize that we *know* you killed the seven women that you're charged with."

"Yes, I am," Gary said, meaning he was guilty.

"We have no doubt on that."

"Right."

"What we are trying to get information on is the *other* women that you have had contact with, over whatever time span."

"Uh-huh."

"As the agreement spells out, you're required to tell us about all the crimes committed in King County."

"Yes."

"Now we're going to ask you a very simple question: Can you tell me any information, a bit of information, that you could not have gained or gleaned from either the Green River book, the affidavit, the certification, or any of the discovery paperwork that you were provided by your defense attorneys? Can you provide me with something, essentially, that none of those would know about?"

"That only the Green River Killer . . ." Mullinax broke in.

"Only the Green River Killer would know," Gary finished. "Yeah, I can give you a couple of things. Uh, the airport site, uh Na . . . Naon . . . Naon . . ."

"Naon," Mattsen nodded

"Uh, on her right breast I had . . . I bit her breast. The . . . I could . . . you already know I told you the one about the, the river . . . the river . . . it comes back to the river victims. Oh, OK, I broke one of the arm of . . . had a rage . . . it was the first one I ever killed, the very first one of . . . I have trouble with names . . . uh, Coffield . . . Coffield. Uh, one of the woman I killed that is not [on the Green River list] . . . she has the left leg or right leg, either had polio, or it was deformed or broken. Had . . . a big limp, and she had a hard time getting into the car. Um, the lady with the accent, the European accent, uh, the lady I . . . I think from the ball field [north airport cluster], and I think she was under a log or by a log. She's not white, she's not black, uh, she's other . . . other race, I don't . . . if I might be able to figure out, I don't know. Uh, you already know about the sock, the sock has got my DNA on it." Mattsen's challenge seemed to rattle Gary.

"This sock?" Mattsen asked, trying to interrupt Gary's verbal wandering with a question.

"The sock that I killed the stronger woman with," Gary said.

"That you killed who?"

"I don't remember what her name was. Like I said, I don't know their names. The one that you guys got, I put a sock around her neck."

"OK."

"And I tied it with my own hands."

"What kind of sock is it?"

"And I . . . and I put a tourniquet in the back end of it. Black sock, um, I put a . . . a piece of wood that's by the site, a twig that I twisted so the wood . . . in there. Uh, what else?"

Gary said that at one of the sites south of the airport, he'd put a stick in the ground where he'd buried a body in a shallow grave.

"Which body is that?" Mullinax asked.

"Oh . . . one you guys already have. I don't . . . I can't remember what the address is . . . it's south of the airport. Uh, another one—is the one at the airport, there was a stick sittin' out of the one, the farthest one I buried, there was, uh, this stick sitting out. Uh, I don't remember. . . . You say there's rocks around Naomi . . . Naon . . ."

"Tell us about the stick," Mattsen insisted.

"The stick is . . ."

"What's the significance of the stick?"

"Just a stick I put in there."

"Put in?"

"Put in the ground, and it was on top of her, not into her skin, but just level there, and the branches were leaning up against it. It's all . . . did you find one there?"

"As a marker?"

"Not as a marker, just like a . . . a stick growin' out, maybe to throw you . . . maybe to throw you guys off, or something, I don't know."

"Well, you tell *us* why you put it there," Mullinax demanded.

"Probably to throw you off. Or not to mark it . . . it was a fresh dug and I think there was a mound there, I don't know. I didn't take a shovel. Uh . . ."

"You did or did not?"

"Uh, did not."

But as we were to discover, that wasn't true, either.

As this interview wore on, Gary tried to convince the detectives that he was in fact *the* Green River Killer by citing small bits of information that he thought only the killer and the detectives would know. He recalled picking up Mary Meehan at a nearby motel, then walking to the south airport cluster area with her. He admitted killing her but denied knowing that she was pregnant—although at eight months, this seemed hard for the detectives to believe. At the Mary Meehan site, the team recovering her remains had discovered a small item in the grave area that some had thought could have been either put or dropped there by the killer. Now Mullinax and Mattsen wanted Gary to tell them what this was. He couldn't do it.

By late that night, little progress had been made by the detectives in verifying that Gary was in fact *the* one and only killer. Both sides were getting discouraged.

Before we left for the night, Todd and I spoke with Gary alone. He was obviously distressed.

"I can't believe they're not finding anything," Gary said. "I'm sure those were the right spots. Do you think I'm going back to jail tomorrow?" he asked. He seemed resigned to failure.

"No," I told him. "I don't think they'll give up that fast. It's been twenty years. I think they know it's going to be hard, this stuff."

"Gary, I believe you're trying your best," Todd said, offering more encouragement. "That's all you can do. Just keep trying to remember things."

We believed he was trying and wanted to give him some support as he felt he was letting everybody down.

"I think you're doing good. Something's going to be found. You just have to remember the 'good' you're trying to accomplish and stay positive. Don't get down on yourself. They'll find something," I told him.

"And remember . . . ," Todd warned, ". . . don't tell any lies. Do *not* make shit up just to give them an answer. That's the worst thing you could do. If you don't know or can't remember, just say that. Don't feel like you have to provide an answer." This was critical because, for so much of his life, when Gary started to feel cornered, he would typically lie his way out of it.

Todd continued, "In this case, that would only compound your problems."

We didn't realize it then, but Gary had already told a number of lies. And before this was over, he'd have to take back an awful lot of them.

31

The field trips went on for the next few days, but unfortunately, nothing was found. Gary appeared to be sincere in his efforts on the field trips, frustrating though they were. Everyone was wondering why nothing—*nothing*—was turning up. All wanted to see something tangible, Gary more than anyone. First, his desire was to help the families of the missing girls find their remains. Second, the possibility always loomed that the state would repudiate the deal if he couldn't live up to his part of the agreement.

For the first few days, after the fruitless field trips, the detectives had concentrated on the where and when of the crimes, largely passing over Gary's motivation. But on June 17, 2003, four days into The Talk, the conversation veered into *why* Gary had killed so many young women.

Reasoning that Gary's anxiety about possibly generating their contempt might in some way be blocking him, the detectives decided to try a new approach. They told Gary that they realized that he had changed a lot in twenty years, that he was no longer the person who had done all those terrible things. They knew there was "a new Gary," they said, someone who was essentially a good person. But they needed to know what the "old Gary" had done. Todd and I sat quietly to the side, watching this stratagem unfold. We had already been asked not to help Gary out with suggestions, whenever he got stuck.

"*That Gary* is much different than the Gary that we are talking to and have talked to the last five days. It's apparent to us and we've had extensive conversations, as I'm sure you see us huddled around," Mattsen said.

"Uh-huh."

"That . . . that you are a bright individual and that when you speak to us, although you may have your own little way of thinking about things, you're able to recall a lot of details in these scenes and a lot of details about your activities twenty years ago. We want to get to where you were twenty years ago. We want to get to that person that is different than the person we have before us now. The person that's talking to us. . . ."

"Uh-huh."

"The person that's providing the information. The person that is really, sincerely trying to be helpful. But we want to go back to that individual of twenty years ago. We want to get that person and to figure out what he was doing during that time frame. Detective Peters laid before you a picture of you during that time frame."

This was a photograph of the "old Gary," one that had been taken in the early 1980s.

"And I think it's important for you to remember that that individual is different than this individual that we're talking to now, OK?" Mattsen continued.

"Yes," Gary said.

"On another kind of side note," Mattsen went on, "we've talked and I've got to tell you, I'm not totally comfortable that you're providing *all* the information that you have about some of these individual scenes. So I just want to make sure, and it's clear with you, that you can tell us anything about these individual scenes. That it's OK for you to tell us and that we're not going to be shocked about anything that you tell us, OK?"

"Oooh-K."

Mattsen said that he and Jensen wanted Gary to go over the Connie Naon site again.

Gary agreed. He said he'd made some notes to himself the night before, so he could remember to tell the detectives things he remembered about the killing of Connie Naon.

"I remember picking her up at . . . really close to the Red Lion or right at the Red Lion, across the street," Gary said, referring to the hotel that was at the corner of South 188th Street and Pacific Highway South, very close to the airport.

"OK," Jensen said.

"And we talked about sex . . . an issue she brought up . . . she had a Camaro, or later on she had a key or key chain that said Camaro, I'm not very sure which one. And we took it to that site and walked into the area where we had sex. I got behind her and . . . I couldn't climax on top of her. . . . I got behind her and climaxed and then after I climaxed I killed her. I dug the hole. Close to where she was. Maybe three or four feet, maybe five feet. Put dirt mostly on one side. I don't know how big the hole was. Big enough for her, and I put her in there face up and no . . . I covered her up with the rocks and stuff from the hole, and the dirt. Then I covered her with vegetation to make it look [like] the scene . . . area around it . . . around the grave. I was getting into . . . that's why the first few bodies, I was getting . . . I had to bury her because I had a tendency . . . not a tendency . . . of wanting to go back and screw them while they are dead. But I didn't do that. I had to bury her because I wouldn't go back. That's when I started burying them. I . . . when I took them . . . started taking them out to where I wouldn't go back. Not trying to get . . . keep away from the urge of doing that."

"You had an urge to go back and have sex with the bodies," Jensen said, putting it in a nutshell.

"I did have an urge, but I didn't do it and that was why I started burying them."

"That's not unusual, Gary. That's OK," Jensen said.

"'Cause I . . . I didn't want to do . . ."

"Didn't want to do that," Jensen finished.

Well, here it finally was, something that had been looming over the case almost from the start, like a small dark cloud. Gary had asked me very early on if the police believed that the killer had been having sex with the dead bodies of the victims—*necrophilia*. I'd thought he had heard something about the Yates case, where that had been alleged and apparently confessed to. But even after he'd confessed to me in April that he'd "killed 'em all," Gary had denied having postmortem sex with any of the victims. And when our side had received crime scene photographs in discovery showing some skeletons with the leg bones raised and bent, or even broken, I still hadn't believed that Gary had been engaging in sex with the dead. He just seemed too ordinary.

But now Gary was admitting that he'd had "the urge" to have sex with the dead, which was why he'd buried some or had taken some further away from Seattle, so he wouldn't succumb to the urge. He hadn't actually admitted having sex with the dead, but I knew him well enough to know that was about to come next.

I realized he was still talking.

"On the very first one, I didn't have a shovel," he said. "Whichever one I started burying first. I had to go back and get a shovel for the first one. And then I just kept the shovel in the back . . . because of that one reason, I had to bury them."

"The first few you didn't . . . ?"

"Bury them?" Gary asked.

"You *didn't* bury them?" Jensen asked again. The unspoken part of the question was, "well, if you didn't bury the first few, did you have sex with them?"

Here it comes, I thought.

"It got worser as I got going," Gary said. "I had the urge."

"You had more urges to go back?"

"Yeah and . . . that's why I wanted to get that in my mind. I was getting to a point where it was getting worse and worse."

Jensen probably realized that Gary had just crossed an important confessional threshold—giving up even the admission that he'd had the "urge" to have sex with the dead. He tried to encourage Gary to go on, trying to let him know it would be OK to tell everything.

"It's OK if you did," Jensen said, meaning, if Gary had had sex with the dead.

"Uh-huh."

"All right," Jensen said. "Nothing to be ashamed of. Thousands of people have done it before you. You're not the first one. And you're not the only one, and you're not going to be the last one."

"Uh-huh."

"So, that's one of the things that we need to know. If you . . . it's going to come out."

"This is . . . the Gary I was before . . . ," Gary said.

"I know it, but this is the guy we want to talk about," Jensen said. "If he went back, if he had an urge to have sex with their bodies after they were dead. That's him. That's not you. We need to know what *this* guy did."

"Uh-huh."

"OK and if . . . I know it was more than an urge. OK? I know that you went back to some of them. It's OK if you tried to stop and it didn't work. OK. It's all right. We've got to know that. That's one of the things we have to know. We have to understand you. We have to understand what you did. That's why it's OK to let it out."

"Uh-huh."

"We're very clear that on a lot of the scenes that we know about, and that we've recovered things from, and that we've been to, that there has been some stuff done to the victims after they died. That's common, Gary. And . . ."

"Yes, I did lie about that," Gary said. "I went back one time before and . . . on some of them . . . that I . . . like I said, got to give it out, I can't keep holding it in."

"No. It's building up inside you like a bad cheeseburger and you've got to . . . you need to take a shit," Jensen said.

"And that's why I had to bury them because I couldn't . . . they were in locations where I . . . that's why I went and took them further out, where I wouldn't be able to go. I buried them, and from there on out I stopped doing that. As far as I know, I don't know if I did or not. Not all of them."

"When did you stop doing it?"

"Having sex afterwards? As far as I know, I might of but not on all of them, because it was too far out to go back and have sex with them."

"Which ones did you have sex with, that you remember?"

"Which ones? Probably . . . um . . . in the river . . . um . . . one with the sock around her neck."

"Did you go back to the one with the sock around her neck?"

"One or two times I did, I think. Um . . . maybe later on I could figure out the rest."

"That's fine," Jensen said. Having gotten Gary over this very heavy admission, Jensen was willing to back off and give him some time to recoup. Not Mattsen, apparently.

"Good," Mattsen said. "Very good, Gary. You're doing very good."

"But we need to get to the bottom of this aspect," Mattsen continued. "We need to get . . . kinda figure out what's going on here, OK?"

"Uh-huh."

"You said that you had these urges?"

"Uh-huh."

"Explain those urges to me," Mattsen said. "Explain what's going on in your head."

"Uh . . ."

"This Gary, this is the Gary twenty years ago," Mattsen encouraged.

"Um . . . going back to have sex with them was a sexual release. Um . . . that I didn't have to pay for. Um . . . um . . . I don't remember what else, offhand. Um . . . power over them, maybe."

"When did you start having these urges?"

"I think it was after the first ones in the river. Coffield. Bonner, no. Uh . . . maybe . . . uh, at least one of the two in the cluster of three of them."

"Which cluster?"

"At the river."

"At the river?"

"There was three of them."

"Do you remember which one?"

"Probably, the first one was in the river and maybe the second one."

"So they didn't go into the river right away, then, did they?" Jensen said.

"They went in the river," Gary said. "I went back the next day and put them in the river. Just like I did the last one, Mills. They were on top, or something. It wasn't in the river. That one I didn't have time to, because of the fisherman down there. I drove away fast."

"So you had sex with them before you put them in the river?"

"I had sex with just the two in that cluster. I didn't have Bonner. I didn't have . . ."

"So you kept them aside for a day or so . . . ?"

"Yes."

"Then you had sex with them?"

"Then I had sex with them."

"Then you put them in the river."[1]

"Yes. Those two only at the time. The next day when I went back to put them in the river."

"And after that . . . ?"

"Put rocks on it," Gary said.

"Then, after that you decided you didn't want to do that anymore?" Jensen asked.

Gary sighed.

"I did it to any one of them that was close by," he admitted. "Probably that's when I probably started and I did to every one of them."

"Did you keep any of these girls at your house for a while?"

"Never," Gary said. "They were always taken out."

"So you . . . when you had sex with them a couple days later, you were always out[side]?"

"They were out within fifteen minutes," Gary said, still answering Jensen's previous question.

Jensen asked Gary how he'd managed to get the victims he'd killed at his house out of the house without anyone noticing. Gary said he'd usually rolled them up in a piece of carpet, then dragged the carpet to the rear of his pickup truck, then put them in the bed of the truck before taking them to the places where he'd left them.

"After you'd pick up these women, these prostitutes, and after you killed them, where would you keep them?" Mattsen asked.

"I . . . in the house. I'd take them and put them in the truck and go find a place to put the bodies. There was no . . . other than one . . . that it was real close to me that I didn't . . . I won't tell you that because it's something you guys don't need to know. Um . . ."

"Don't need to know what?" Jensen asked.

"Well, it's a charged count, so should I tell you about that?" Gary asked.

"Sure," Mattsen said.

"OK," Gary said. "Christensen. I dated her several times, three times, two times before and when I killed her she was . . . I knew she had a daughter and knew where she lived because I dated her three times. And the last one . . . one day I dated her in the back of the truck in a Schuck's [auto part store] parking lot, in the back, and the other time it was near . . . during the day . . . in the Midway swap meet. It was during the day, nobody in there, just Highline [Community College] parking. And everything went good there. We got naked and all those . . . when I brought her home she was into, the last time she was in a hurry, and she didn't . . . I thought being in the house would be more comfortable than dating her there than on the street, but she was in a hurry, and she wasn't . . . wasn't satisfying me, and it made me mad because she was very much in a hurry and I got behind her when we were having sex and ejaculated in her and killed her."

"How did you kill her?" Jensen asked.

"I choked her with my arm and some . . . either my arm or once or twice, I choked with a towel. There was on the . . . I didn't . . ."

"Let's back up. Let's back up a little bit, OK? Where's this date taking place?"

"It's taking . . . this date is taking in the house."

"In your house?"

"In the house, in the bedroom."

"How did you arrange the date?"

"I picked her up at night, right close by the Red Barn Tavern."[2]

"At night?"

"Yeah, I thought it was at night. It . . ."

"OK."

"I thought it was . . . I'll have to think more about it 'cause I dropped off her body. It was in the day, and I know I consumed that wine. I drank the whole bottle of wine."[3]

"Where'd you get it?"

"Out of the refrigerator. I don't know where I bought it. And the fish was . . . I don't cook . . . and the fish were in the refrigerator. Somebody gave it to me. I don't know who, my parents or somebody. I don't . . . at that time, I didn't cut the heads off the fish and . . . every time I had fish somebody always cooked it for me. And that's why I brought those to put on her body and the sausage I didn't cook so I . . . it was ground sausage. I took her out to that site and laid her face up and . . . I clothed her. I know I put her bra on backwards but I was . . . I didn't care, because the snaps in back and I didn't bother to go back and put the bra on backward because she already had . . . didn't have her shirt on yet or blouse. Um . . . then I thought I laid down with her a little bit and cried because of killing her. I know I did and . . . I don't know 100 percent sure if I picked her up at night or in the morning, but I knew I took her there during the day where I dumped her off. I took her to the site. I drove in and that, might have backed around where I was. Took her body out, laid her in plain sight under that . . . put the fish . . . I don't know if the fish were heads up or heads down and the sausage in hands and the bag over her head. As I was leaving there, I got to the . . . out the driveway, right next to me, an officer in a white State Patrol [car] was going out of the next dirt road, so I drove up to the . . . took a right, stopped at the stop sign and I . . . trying to figure out which way I went. I think I went to . . . that might come to me . . . and I looked in the rearview mirror to see if the cop was going into the spot where I just came out and that was . . . I just realized I clothed her, so I wouldn't want to go back and have sex with her, and I really cared for her because I dated her before, but this . . . it didn't turn out right."

"How long did you keep her?"

"I know I drank that wine, so it must have been maybe a half hour."

"Overnight?" Jensen asked. He didn't seem to be buying Gary's story that he'd consumed a whole bottle of wine in just a half hour.

"I don't know. You know when she came up missing. I don't know what time she came up missing."

"Did you keep her overnight, Gary? It's OK."

"It's um . . . I slept with . . ."

"Did you want to spend the night with her?"

"I think I slept with her and I picked her up at night."

"At your house?" Mattsen asked.

"At the house," Gary agreed.

"Then you had sex again?" Jensen asked.

"I don't think I had sex . . . might of. I don't remember."

"You did sleep with her? You cuddled with her?"

"Yeah, cuddled with her, and I cried because of killing her. Didn't want her . . . she'd always been nice to me before."

"She hurried you too much this time?"

"Hurried me too much and . . ."

"She had to go back to work?"

"Um . . . I don't know whether she said that or not."

"You need to release this, Gary, you need to bring this out," Mattsen said. "You need to talk to us and tell us exactly what happened. And you're doing great."

"Uh-huh."

"What made her special?" Mattsen asked.

"What [made] her special? She liked me touching her. She liked me . . . she um . . . she would make me come on top of her and this last time when I killed her, I couldn't come because of the hurryingness and . . ."

"Did you care for her, Gary?" Jensen asked.

"I cared for her, yes. I cared for her."

"Why?"

"Because she love . . . liked . . . she fulfilled my sexual desire to touch her, to feel her, to . . . she was . . . she liked sex, I think is what it was. The two times before and it made me feel good about being with her."

"She's beautiful," Jensen said.

"She doesn't look like her . . . the two pictures that you have of her . . . doesn't look like her."

"Yeah, they are lousy," Jensen agreed.

"And after seeing pictures of her . . . makes me sad for killing her. I blocked out the women's faces for so long that . . . until I see them here."

"You always remembered Carol's face, haven't you?"

"Always . . . because I liked her."

"She was good to you?"

"She was good to me except for that one time."

"Did she seem like she was in a hurry?" Mattsen asked.

"I didn't bother to ask her, and I knew about her daughter, but I didn't . . . I was horny and I wanted sex, so I just . . . just a one-frame mind. I had great times with her before, why not this time? She wouldn't take a shower with me and wouldn't . . . wouldn't . . . too much in a hurry. She didn't . . . being in the house is secure for me and scared outside, doing it, you know, a little bit."

"She wasn't responding?"

"She wasn't responding. Wasn't enjoying it. She had something else on her mind. Some place to go. Some place to hurry off, and I more and more. Every time she said hurry, I got madder and madder. I got behind her after I got on top."

"You had sex first?"

"I had sex when I was behind her. I climaxed and as soon as I climaxed I . . . that's when I choked her, while I was on the back of her."

"I mean, see, that's my question," Jensen interrupted. "You already know she's in a hurry, don't you? She's already told you."

"Yes."

"And you've done this, how many times before? Ten, fifteen, twenty times?"

"Yeah."

"You know what's going to happen if she pisses you off?"

"Uh-huh."

"And you *like* her. You're telling us all these things."

"Yes."

"Yet, you got into this, anyway."

"What's that?" Gary asked.

"Yet, you start having sex with her anyway."

"Yeah."

"Knowing full well it can end up in her death."

"Yes. Yes."

"Why?"

"What's that?" Gary didn't understand Jensen's profound question. We sat, shocked, as we realized that Jensen was weeping.

"You've touched me," Jensen said. "Why don't we take a break?"

Both detectives left the room. Gary, Todd, and I were left alone. Both Todd and I were stunned. This detective who had worked on the case without interruption for almost twenty years had let his emotions overcome him.

"That was strange," Gary said.

"Well, you know Gary, Tom's devoted his career to this case," Todd said, "and I imagine things can hit pretty hard, when you're that close to it. He's got emotions, too. Shit, it shows he's human."

"Gary, I have another problem," I said. I was a little perturbed. Gary had claimed he had been entirely honest with me during our debriefing sessions from April 11 to June 12. It was his information upon which we relied to make our formal proffer. If it contained a bunch of lies, we were in trouble. Now Gary had just admitted necrophilia, when he'd steadfastly denied it to me.

"How many other surprises are we gonna get?"

Gary looked confused and asked, "What do you mean?"

"How about screwing 'em after they were dead?" I asked.

"Oh, yeah." He grimaced. "I'm sorry about that. I was so ashamed. I just hoped it didn't have to come out. I only did it a few times."

"Gary, look . . ." I was incredulous. "If you can admit *killing* fifty women, you ought to be able to admit having sex with them afterwards." I took a deep breath. "But the important thing is that you didn't tell me the truth, and you said you would."

"Gary, you have wounded my friend Mark," Todd told him. "You lied to him, and I don't like that. He's trying, we're trying, to save your ass. Why would you lie to him? I don't like that. We have put you at risk, based upon you telling us that what you said was the truth. Now we don't know what we can believe. We keep telling you to tell the truth. You agree to tell the truth. And then a bomb like this. You've *got* to tell the truth."

"I know," Gary said. I think he felt bad for lying to me about the postmortem sex. "I was just embarrassed. I promise I won't hold anything back from here on."

"Well, I hope so," I said. "I mean, we're here now. Any more surprises? Did you kill anyone after 1985?" I was concerned now that the conventional wisdom—serial killers never stop until they're arrested or dead—might be true after all.

"No," Gary replied without hesitation. "I'm quite certain I didn't kill anyone after '85."

After the first few days of my post-April 11 interviews with Gary, I had noted the various ways Gary would qualify his answers: "I might have . . ." "Maybe . . ." "Probably . . ." "I must have . . ." "I had to have been . . ." "Something like . . ." "A lot of times I would . . ." "I'm quite sure I . . ." "I think I . . ." "I always . . ." "It's very possible I . . ." and my favorite, "I'm quite certain . . ." which I now knew to mean that he was anything *but* quite certain.

And as for me, I was now quite certain that we were going to have a few more shocks like this last one before the whole thing was over.

32

When we arrived the next morning, June 18, a Wednesday, Jim Graddon, the task force commander, called Tony and me over for a private chat.

"Gary has been acting strangely, pacing forward and backward around his room, . . . kind of muttering to himself. He looked kind of upset. We're not sure what's up. Just wanted to give you guys a heads up."

"Thanks," Tony said. He looked at me with a *What's this* look. I gave him my own *Hell if I know* look in return. Tony turned to Graddon and asked, "Could you have your folks bring Gary over, so we can see what's going on?"

"Sure," Graddon said. "We'll bring him right over."

They brought Gary to the interrogation room. We all sat down. I asked him how he was doing.

Gary seemed agitated.

"I didn't sleep very well. They tried to get me to remember what I was like back in 1982. I kind of worked it up, like I was the 'old Gary' and I'm ready to talk to them." Then he added, "Ask them to keep my handcuffs on . . . just in case I get real mad." He got up and started pacing back and forth.

Mattsen began the new round of questioning just after 8:30 that morning. After politely asking Gary if he'd enjoyed his catered breakfast of pancakes, sausage, and eggs (he had), Mattsen invited Gary to get whatever he had on his chest off it.

"I understand that you wanted to say something to us," Mattsen said.

"Well, last night I went to sleep . . . and the other Gary came into my mind the . . . the rage, the power, the control," Gary began. "Um, he's—he's . . . he's really, *really* pissed off about the, uh, not listening to me, not, uh, you, um, you guys are, um, uh, not listening to me about the, uh, the photographs that I . . . I . . . I tore up couple days later.[1] I never put a . . . I never put a body . . . left a body in the house. You guys are tryin' to control me, and I'm not gonna let you do it. I never slept with a woman overnight with a . . . a dead woman."

Tony was in the conference room, watching on the video monitor, and Todd and I were together in the interrogation room. We both realized that part of Gary's anger seemed to be coming from the detectives' previous suggestions that he was lying about not keeping photographs of his victims and that he was lying about not keeping Carol Christensen's body in his house overnight.

"Sure, I screwed 'em a few times," Gary went on. "Um, uh, fighting with the other . . . the new Gary, and the old Gary is both a . . . a . . . a . . . a . . . uh [I'll] give you as much as I can on the old Gary. But, um, not . . . I'm not mad enough to, uh, get it out. Um, um, that's where to start, uh, Christensen . . . don't, uh . . . new Gary wants me to candy-coat this stuff and I'm not gonna candy-coat it. I . . . I killed her because I *wanted* to. I killed her because I was mad. I killed forty . . . forty-nine to fifty people between '82 and '85. And I killed a . . . I killed a lot of 'em and, uh, just the rage, the anger of my ex-wife, everything that just came through on me. And I killed because I wanted to, I don't . . . it only didn't . . . I didn't kill any mo . . . people in motels. I'm tryin' to help you find these bodies, not workin' with me. I want . . . I wanna go out and look at these sites, but you . . . you talkin' to me, you . . . and I . . . I gotta get this out. I'm . . . I'm . . . I'm about 10 percent of what I was last night. I was really angry and this is just . . . just the beginning of it, and I'm not even halfway through and my mind isn't clear."

Todd and I saw that whether he was old or new Gary, he was giving them the full Gary, complete with the non sequiturs and the hot plate–jumping narrative that we'd become so familiar with in the past, what we'd come to think of as *Ridgway-speak*.

"On all the women I killed 'em because I wanted to, not be . . . and I was . . . hate . . . hated . . . hated 'em," Gary continued. "And, uh, still stuck between the two Garys. Um, um, it started with Coffield . . . Coffield, or whatever her name is. I . . . I killed her someplace, I don't know . . . I don't give a shit about where I killed 'em. And I'm not . . . uh, and I just . . . I can't . . . can't figure out where I've dated so many women that they, uh, and I didn't give a shit about them, I didn't give a shit about their jewelry. Just didn't want them to have it.

"Carol Christensen meant nothin' to me. The . . . the fish and the . . . were to attract the animals. The, um, I didn't care about their bodies. I'd drag them from their feet. I . . . um, I'd drag them. I knew . . . knew where I dragged them by markers. Uh, and, um . . ."

We could see that Gary was starting to wind down after this outburst. Mattsen apparently decided to stoke up the flames to get him going again.

"What did Carol do to piss you off?" he asked.

"I don't think she did anything to piss me off," Gary said. "I think all of 'em didn't do anything to piss me off. I was just mad that . . . just mad and wanted to kill 'em. A couple of 'em I wasn't mad enough to kill. I let 'em go and I didn't . . . I didn't even try to kill 'em."

Mattsen said something we didn't catch, but it seemed to set Gary off again.

"You're lyin' . . . you're lyin' to me about the damn, uh, only a few I had sex with 'em afterwards. When I took the ones outta my house, almost every one of 'em I never had 'em overnight, I never went back to their place to have sex with 'em. Um, that's why I took 'em far out, and I didn't give a shit about them. They were . . . they weren't human I guess."

"Let the old Gary out . . . let the old Gary out," Mattsen prodded.

"Uh, I am. . . . I'm trying. Um, I bit . . . I bit her because I was still mad when I bit that lady on the breast, uh, Naomi . . . Naon. I didn't . . . like I said, I didn't know that, uh, the one that was pregnant was pregnant, because I don't think I even screwed her after I killed her. Uh, maybe you can ask some questions and it might help me . . ."

Gary's venting had suddenly run out of steam. Jensen tried to get him going again.

"Does the new Gary feel the same way the old Gary does?" he asked.

"No, the new Gary is a candy ass . . . he's . . . he's a wimp."

"Who's . . . who's been talkin' to us all along?"

"It's been mostly him and candy-coating it too . . . to not knowin' . . ."

"The new Gary . . . the new Gary is not a wimp," Jensen said, "because the new Gary . . . a new man was born yesterday, and I think *that* was the new Gary. When he started lettin' this stuff go, that was a new man," Jensen said.

"Mean . . . meaning . . . ?"

"A *real* man."

This seemed to confuse Gary. Who was he, the old Gary or the new Gary? What did the cops want from him? I suddenly recalled what Gary had told Mary Goody back in the very beginning: "Always in the past I've had other people talk [first]," he'd said. "Then I could ask questions." In other words, it was Gary's way to let others define him first; then he would do his best to conform to this image. But Jensen's rejection of "old Gary" and his lauding of "new Gary" had thrown the real Gary off.

"The old . . . the old guy that . . . ," he stammered. Gary turned his body in his chair so he was no longer looking at the detectives. He kept his eyes closed, face pointed toward the floor.

"Whoever was talkin' to us yesterday was a *real* man," Jensen said.

"Yesterday, that was . . . that was the . . . that was the other Gary," Gary said, not raising his eyes. "This . . . this is me back in '82 . . . '82, not what he is. He . . . he didn't have any guts to stand up for himself. He . . . he let women . . . he used 'em, he let woman take control and I want control, I don't have to have him control. He's not anymore . . . he's just . . . he's just there for . . . I don't give a . . . he's the . . . the good side and I'm the bad side. He's . . . I'm the one that did it, he didn't do it, he's different then. And I, uh, I killed every one of them and . . ."

Gary seemed to find some mental footing again. He went back into his confrontational mode but still kept his face turned away from the detectives.

"You know, you're putting things in my mouth and I'm not gonna take it," he said. "I'm in control here and . . . and I'm . . . and I'm . . . I'm in charge, that's the way I wanna be . . . I never been that way, and then when I was . . . I was in charge when all these womens I killed."

"This is the old Gary?" Jensen asked, with seeming indifference.

"This is the . . . this is the old Gary, '82 Gary, not the new one. I . . . I hated 'em so much. I did take a picture, three . . . three or four pictures of the women, put 'em in that location under the SeaTac Red Lion. I did tear 'em up. Don't tell me I . . . it's hard to tear things . . . those up, because I did . . . or cut 'em, or . . . I did tear 'em up. I did write a letter, now that I remember I think I either . . . either wrote it to the, uh, police station or, um, *Seattle Times Magazine*.[2] I didn't hide any jewelry under the house, in the house. So you're gonna be wastin' your damn time by goin' over there.[3]

"You're gonna be wastin' your time goin' to the other houses, 'cause there's no jewelry there. I got rid of it. When I met Judith, I did kill two ladies after . . . uh, one lady I got outta Tacoma and I killed her. And I killed another lady, uh, I killed her in, uh, I dated her before one time and didn't kill her. And took her into Federal Way 'cause she wanted to go into Federal Way, and I killed her there. And that's . . . and I killed one lady . . . uh, that was the one in the pickup . . . in the . . . in the pickup with a . . . the . . . a Ford pickup with the damn, uh, uh, white camper on it, and I killed her on the floor of it. I used . . . I used my hand, my arm, I killed her and I pulled her back as I chokin' her. I used wire . . . I used extension cord on her . . . on some of the women's necks, and I pulled 'em tight. And all the rage and the . . . some of 'em I took . . . took the towel and wrapped around their neck and pulled 'em and killed 'em. Some I used, uh, uh, a tie and a towel, and I pulled 'em back and I put my legs in the back of her back on some of the women and just pulled as hard as I could to kill 'em. I, uh, I did it because I hated them. And I had . . . and after I killed 'em I mighta screwed a few of 'em, but I didn't give a shit. They were just pieces of trash to me. They were . . . they were garbage."

"Why'd you hate 'em so much?"

"Why did I hate 'em? Because I . . . they had . . . women had control over me and I don't like being controlled. And I always, we . . . uh, I always, uh, had all kinds of problems with the house, and I was not strong enough to get on my back legs and tell people to . . . to not take advantage of me and not to . . . not to, uh, use me. Back then I was just a . . . I was just a wimp, and then when I was . . . I had control when I was . . . when I killed the women. I got my rage out for the time. I did cry, yes, I did. And I . . . that was . . . that was the good part of me, I cried, but I still killed 'em, and I didn't care anything about 'em.

"I . . . the burn on my arm is not a burn. This is scratch marks. There's scratch marks here from ladies I . . . These are from Malvar. I killed her, she scratched me. When I was killin' her, she fought, she scratched me here. Uh, the acid is just a lie that other . . . other Gary is tellin' ya . . . tellin' that he's not me, I'm the one that did it, I the one that killed those women. I am the one that got the scratch marks."

This was the first time that either Todd or I had heard that the-pimp-who-knocked-me-out-and-burned-my-arm-with-battery-acid story was a lie. Gary said that he'd concealed the deep scratches on his arm that Marie Malvar had inflicted by pouring battery acid on his arm; it had hurt like hell, he said, but it was the only way he could explain the wounds. When Detective Fox, his old friend from the supermarket, questioned him, he'd hidden the injuries from him so he wouldn't see them.

"You wanna know other things about the women. One, I [was] still pissed off, I . . . I took her body out and pulled it over the top of the . . . the tailgate and I dropped her on her head. I pulled her over on the guardrail someplace and, uh, pulled her body where I was dumpin' her. I don't remember which one that was. I did roll that woman off the end all the way down there so don't . . . don't tell me what you think I did. I didn't pose nobody, I did not kill no damn dog.[4]

"Over to your right, goin' towards the ocean or, uh, west of there, under some logs and stuff, I put a body there. I don't know who she was. There . . . there . . . you say . . . somebody says there's a body up next to her, I don't know if that was mine or not, I don't give a shit. Uh, sorry, but that's just the way I feel about those women. I had control and that's what it . . . what it all comes down to, is control of those bitches. I told 'em to . . . to 'shut up and don't yell and I'll let you go,' but I kept on choking and didn't . . . I didn't give a shit about givin' 'em . . . givin' 'em . . . getting 'em up to . . . I didn't wanna get caught. I didn't have no love and I didn't . . . nobody loved me, so fuck 'em all."

—⁓—

As much as it appeared that Gary was trying to come up with a way to disclose more information, the "old Gary" seemed a bit like a bad actor trying to portray someone with multiple personality syndrome. Turning his face away from the detectives, closing his eyes, looking down at the floor—it was almost as if Gary was feigning some sort of trance: *The Three Faces of Gary*. If that's what his intent was, it was not very convincing; it was too forced, too contrived. But whipping himself into the "bad Gary" mode may have been the only way he could force himself to get the uglier details out, as he claimed, however phony it sounded to the rest of us. He was definitely trying.

The story of depravity continued. Gary told of returning to have sex with a dead victim while Matthew slept in the car. Another time, when he had a dead woman in the back of his truck while he went to work, he went out at lunch, drove his truck to a restaurant a few minutes away, and had sex with the corpse during his lunch break.

Sometimes, when he returned for "free" sex with a corpse, there were only a few maggots, so, as Gary described, he would just flick them off and have sex with the cold, decomposing corpse. Other times, there would be so many maggots that even he was too fastidious to have sex again. While listening to this, my mind was just dumbfounded. I don't get grossed out easily, but Gary had pushed me to the edge.

Todd leaned over and whispered, "You've heard of a three-dog night, right?"

"Yeah?" I knew Todd was referring to an Eskimo measure of how cold it was in the arctic.

"Now you've heard of a two-maggot fuck," he said with a straight face. I didn't know whether I wanted to cry, laugh, or throw up. However, it was this sense of dark, sick humor that we had to share to maintain our sanity, a defense mechanism we unfortunately share with homicide detectives, emergency room physicians, medical examiners, and morticians.

By the afternoon of June 18, Gary had already been caught in some significant lies. In addition to at first trying to deny the necrophilia, he'd had to go backward on the pimp-put-acid-on-my-arm story. He'd denied that he'd kept any dead bodies overnight in the house, which Jensen, for one, seriously doubted.[5] The lies only made the investigators doubt it even more when Gary insisted that there were no pictures, that there was no jewelry, that there was no clothing. The FBI's profilers had always maintained that serial killers kept "trophies," and the more insistent Gary was that he had not, the more the detectives believed he was lying. All they had to do was point to the lies that Gary had already recanted as evidence for this proposition.

During a break, Baird approached Todd and me and asked, "Can I talk to you guys for a second?"

"Sure," Todd said. We sat down at the conference table.

"I'd like to talk to your guy," Baird said. "Just me, with you guys present, of course, directly talking to him, telling him this is serious and that he cannot lie. That he's in breach of the agreement and the whole deal could go away. Just a warning, before he digs himself in any deeper. No questions. I don't even want him to say anything. Just listen."

"I don't see any problems if we stick to that," Todd said.

When Gary was brought back after the break, we told him Baird just wanted to tell him some things and that he wasn't going to ask Gary any questions.

"Oooh-K," Gary said. "That would be fine."

"We're the reason you're here and not in the King County jail," Baird told Gary when he was brought back into the interrogation room . . . "and the reason you are here is because you signed a contract and swore to tell us the truth and the whole truth."

"Yes."

"And the complete truth. Do you understand that?"

"Yes, I do."

"Now, I realize it has been a number of years since you committed these murders, . . . and I realize that you claim to have some problems with your memory . . . but you do know the difference between a truth and a lie, don't you?"

"Yes, I do."

"OK. I'm here to tell you that you're violating the terms of this agreement unless you turn this thing around. Because you have been lying."

"Uh-huh."

"Yesterday, you lied to us."

"Yes, I did."

"You came in here, and you said that these women hadn't injured you. You said that Malvar hadn't injured you. You told this story about how some pimp dropped battery acid on your arm."

"Yes."

"That's a lie."

"Yes, that's a lie."

"You've told that to your lawyers and you've told it to us . . . and you told it to the detectives. And when they asked you about it today, you said, 'Well I've been lying about that for years.'"

"I've been lying about that for years, yes."

"That's got to stop. Do you understand that? That's not a memory problem. Do you understand what I'm saying?"

"I know it's . . ."

"You haven't forgotten how you got that injury, have you?"

"No."

"You lied about it."

"Yes."

"Stop it. You understand me?"

"Yes, I do. I understand."

"Now we're going to let you talk to your lawyers for a little while, and we're not going to start talking to you again until you have a little change of attitude. You've got to start telling the truth. If there are things you don't remember, that's fine. But if there are things that you *do* remember and you're lying about, you've got to stop that right now. Do you understand me?"

"I agree."

After Jeff left the room, Todd asked Gary, "Do you think he's serious? Do you think he means business, Gary?"

"Yes," Gary said. "He means business."

"And that means, any more lies and the deal's off. Back to jail you go!" I wanted to make the point as well.

"Yes. I know," Gary nodded. "I understand. It's just . . . I've been lying so long. It's hard."

"Don't lie. Period. That's not hard." Todd wasn't letting him off the hook that easy. "Do *not* lie. Do *not* make shit up."

"Oooh-K."

After this, Gary seemed to be a bit more forthcoming with details of his crimes. He told of killing Linda Rule near Northwest Hospital in north Seattle in the fall of 1983 and setting her hair on fire.

"Did that excite you, to see her hair on fire?" Sue Peters asked.

"That would excite me to see her . . . um . . . she had beautiful hair and to hurt her more," Gary said.

"OK."

"To give her, not any more pain, because she's already dead, but it did excite me a little bit but I would have been more excited if I could have caught her hair all the way on fire."

"Had you ever done that before?"

"Never have."

"What about after that time?"

"No."

"Are you sure?"

"I am definitely sure."

Trying to burn off Linda Rule's hair, it appeared, was another way Gary was trying to take something his victims valued *away* from them—the same as he had done with their clothes, their money, their jewelry. As Gary would later put it, he didn't think the women deserved to have these things.

Whenever a victim would scratch him, Gary said, he always made sure to cut her fingernails short before he got rid of the body. He'd read books about serial killers, he said, and had watched television cop shows, so he knew that evidence could be found under the nails, which was why he always cut them after the victim was dead. He flushed the nails down his toilet, he said. When he'd moved three of the skulls to Oregon, he said, he'd worn cotton work gloves that had been issued to the painters at Kenworth. At one Oregon site, he said, he'd left a glove behind.[6]

Eventually, Gary said, he'd learned to use ligatures—ropes, belts, towels, anything used for leverage—to strangle his victims. That way, he said, it was less likely that he would be scratched.

Just before noon, Mullinax ended the morning's interrogation session.

"It's 1155 hours," Mullinax noted for the tape. "Gary, what would you like for lunch today?"

"Chicken," Gary said. "Or how about fish and chips?"

"Fish and chips again."

"Yes."

"All right," Mullinax said.

I looked at Todd and just shook my head. It was simply mind numbing how fast Gary could go from describing the most awful depravity to the utterly mundane.

—⌇⌇—

The June 18 session ended around five in the afternoon. Todd and I took refuge in a microbrewery a mile or so south of the bunker. As the summer came on, this became a ritual for the two of us. Over a pitcher of good beer, Todd and I would reprise each day's events and plan ahead for the next day. By then, the detectives were telling us ahead of time what they planned to discuss next, in part to get our insights on how best to approach Gary. While splitting our pitcher, we'd call Tony, if Tony hadn't been there that day, to let him know what had happened and what was planned. Todd and I were working only on Gary's case, but by this point, Tony had decided that our train was well down the track on the plea, heading toward resolution, so he resumed taking on new cases. This left most of the observation of these interrogations to Todd and me. But we kept Tony fully briefed on the events in the bunker.

As emotionally wearing as these interrogation sessions were, the conversations with Todd, and the beer, were the best way to wind down. After a day in the bunker, the normality of the alehouse helped make us human again. In fact, by the time I got home or to the pool and hooked up with Kelly and the kids, they'd never have known I'd spent the whole day with the worst serial killer in American history.

33

Over the next few days, the detectives tried to reinvigorate Gary's Swiss cheese memory by taking him back to his earliest murders—or what Gary had consistently said were his first murders, the victims found in or near the Green River in the summer of 1982. As we ventured into a discussion of the charged counts, not subject to the proffer, Todd and I made a strategy call. *If* the deal fell through, which was still possible, discussion of the charged counts would botch things up for the state a lot worse than it would for Gary.

These cases were considered critical to understanding how Gary had evolved as a killer. If indeed they represented the first time he'd crossed the line into homicide, understanding why and how he had done so could be invaluable. And as the discussion grew more intense, the language grew rougher.

"I want to go to the beginning and try to help you unlock memories by rewinding the tape," Jensen told Gary. He asked Gary to talk about the first time he had killed.

"That was Coffield," Gary said. "I picked her up at the . . . on Pacific Highway. It had to have been Pacific Highway. I had family living in the house, so I couldn't take her home.[1] So it was a night date.

Um . . . I don't really remember where. It was in the truck, back of the truck. In the . . . must have been the Riverton area. I don't remember where I killed her. It's not registering where I killed, like, the first six . . . first six."

To Jensen, this seemed hard to believe. How could Gary *not* remember the very first time he had ever killed anyone? It simply did not stand to reason.

"How can that possibly be?" Jensen demanded. "The first person you ever killed and you can't remember any details about it?"

"Um . . . I just can't picture a place where I killed her. She's just . . . I know the first one should stand out more than any, but that is the farthest one back and that is the hardest one to pick up, where I killed her."

"Gary, did you just fuckin' wake up that day and decide you were going to kill somebody?" Jensen asked.

"No, I think when I picked her up, I was going to kill her."

"You were?"

"Yeah, when I picked her up."

"What clicked?"

"Probably worked up to that," Gary said. "It wasn't probably just all at one time."

"Worked up from when?"

"Worked up from the stuff that happened to me at the house. Stuff that happened to me at work. Happened from me getting my wallet stolen. It could have been the day before that, that woman stole my money, eighty bucks."

"Eighty bucks?" Jensen's incredulity was obvious.

"Eighty bucks," Gary said. "It was in the backseat of my truck, behind the seat. I had money in there they stole, and somebody might have pissed me off at work that day. I screwed up."

In classic Gary-speak, he had somehow managed to edge away from the thrust of Jensen's questioning. *Could have, might have.* There was no there there. There was absolutely nothing from Gary's mouth to show that he'd actually killed Wendy Coffield—other than his claim—and even that was accompanied by either assertions that could not be verified or facts that were already known to him through his reading of the discovery. And when it came to the central point— why—trying to pin Gary down was, as our psychologist Mark Cunningham had observed, "like trying to grab a cloud."

After killing Wendy Coffield in the second week of July 1982, Gary said, he'd encountered Gisele Lovvorn (Gary consistently mispronounced her name as *Laverne*) in mid-July and had killed her, using his black socks, while his son, seven-year-old Matthew, waited for him, oblivious, in the nearby pickup truck. After that, Gary had returned to the Green River with the body of Debbie Bonner. Like Wendy Coffield, Gary said, he'd put Debbie Bonner's body into the river and watched it float away. He'd made no attempt to weight them down with rocks, as he did the next two victims, Marcia Chapman and Cynthia Hinds. The day after he'd killed Cynthia Hinds, Gary had picked up Opal Mills. After killing her, he'd taken her down to the riverbank and left her there, intending to return later to have postmortem sex with her. But when he'd returned, he'd been frightened off by someone floating by in the river.

"One thing for sure, I . . . I got stopped there at the end, when the guy comin' down the river saw me and I said uh, 'Have you seen anything yet?' And that meant . . . [from that] point on I stopped killing anymore [at the river]. He saw me. The bodies were found. I went on land to kill. I went back to Laverne's [Lovvorn] spot and killed a black lady there. And then I went [and] killed people in other areas. Took 'em different places. Never went back to the river until . . . Cottonwood Park" [Tracy Winston, last seen in September 1983].

Gary insisted that after the victims had been found in the river on August 15, 1982, he'd stayed away from the river, with the exception of Tracy Winston, at a different part of the river a year later. He'd put all of his other victims on dry land. He'd certainly never killed anyone in a motel, he insisted. There would have been too many witnesses, too much possible evidence.

"I wasn't lying about any of them. Not deceiving. That's what I . . . how my mind was thinkin'. I forgot all about the second one in the field [Lovvorn]. I didn't go back to . . . I don't think I even went back to have sex after. When I left her in there, that was it. Forgot all about her."

"You seem a little agitated," Jensen told him.

"No, I'm just . . . you're . . . you know you . . . I want to explain that the . . . I didn't kill anybody in the motel. I'd have to burn it down. There's witnesses all over [the] places."

"That would be dumb," Jensen said. "That would be really a stupid thing to do."

"That would be . . . that'd be the stupid thing to do."

I could see that Jensen now realized he'd found a new way to get useful details from Gary—by getting him to go over all his mistakes. Gary seemed happy to talk about these, and Todd and I suddenly saw a much more animated, conversational Gary.

"You never did anything stupid," Jensen began.

"Well, I did a lot of things stupid, but . . ."

"Name one," Jensen challenged. "Name one."

"Name one? Leavin' clothes on 'em."

"Why was that stupid?"

"Because eventually, you'll find some kind of DNA on it or some-thin'. Uh, not putting 'em all on the river when I killed 'em, instead of comin' back the next day. That was stupid."

"Why?"

"I went back to take the . . . any clothes off of 'em and have sex with 'em. Put the rock in the vagina. I did it with two of 'em. I was gonna put the third one in the vagina. No clothes in 'em down the river."

"Why was that stupid?"

"Because you got DNA off of uh, the . . . the last one on the bank. You got . . . you could've got somethin' off the clothes. Uh . . ."

"Tell me somethin' else that was stupid."

"A place where we . . . go have sex is might've been stupid. We got pick . . . picked up for prostitution, that's all." Gary meant the time he'd been contacted by the Port of Seattle while dating Keli McGinness.

"What else is stupid?"

"Uh . . ." Gary was running out of mistakes.

"You can't count stupid as anything that wasn't possible at the time. So DNA was like . . ."

"Unmentionable then," Gary agreed, meaning that when he'd first killed, the science of forensic DNA testing wasn't known.

"It did not exist," Jensen agreed. "So *that*'s not stupid, OK? So you can't go stupid on this."

"Well, the stupid part was talkin' to the guy down there and askin' if he found somethin' yet. Did you . . . instead of saying, 'Did you catch anything?' I said, 'Did you find something yet,' or somethin'." This was in reference to the rafter, apparently Robert Ainsworth, who found the bodies on Sunday, August 15, 1982—three days after Debbie Bonner's body had been recovered by the police.[2] "That was stupid," Gary added, "knowing that he's gonna find those bodies, 'cause they're right there."

The rafter could have identified him, Gary said. That's why he jumped into his pickup truck and raced away and never went back to the river until more than a year later.

Jensen eased into another area:

"Did you ever kill any kids?" he asked. In some cases, I knew, ser-ial killers actually began their murderous careers as teenagers, killing the first time at a very young age, then returning to the practice many years later. Gary had never told anyone on our side about any teenaged violence on his part.

"Nope. Never killed kid . . . no kids . . . killed the kids at all," Gary said.

"Why not?" Jensen asked.

"Just the . . . just the prostitutes. The kids don't . . ."

"Why only prostitutes?"

"They were accessible," Gary said.

"Why did you focus on prostitutes?"

"Because they . . . they weren't . . ." he mumbled something we couldn't catch. "Expendable," he said. "Maybe that was what the word is. Expendable. They were . . . have sex with 'em and . . . I couldn't kill an ordinary woman. I'd kill a prostitute."

"Couldn't kill an ordinary woman?"

"I couldn't, woman . . . uh, not ordinary, but I couldn't kill a, a woman with kids. The, you know, the . . . uh . . . uh . . ."

"Half of these prostitutes had kids," Jensen told him.

"Half the womans had kids," Gary agreed. "But they were prostitutes. They were prostitutes. And they were vulnerable and they were the . . . that's . . . there . . ."

"Some of the prostitutes were kids," Jensen pointed out.

"Yeah, a lot of 'em were kids, yes," Gary agreed. "Twelve to . . . or thirteen to sixteen, eighteen years old, yes. But they were prostitutes and they were . . ."

"So why not just any kid?"

"'Cause they're not prostitutes. Not . . . I'm gonna . . ."

"But I mean, killing's killing, isn't it?" Jensen asked.

"Killing is killing but it's not a . . . prostitutes were one of the causes of my problems. And that's . . . sex was a problem."

"Is anybody that you have sex with a prostitute, then?"

"Every woman that I had . . . that I killed was a prostitute. We agreed on sex. We agreed on how to do it. I paid her the money or paid it afterwards. And I killed her. Not one of 'em was a hitchhiker. *They* didn't want money. They were all into prostitution. They were all into . . . some of 'em were into drugs. I don't know if they were into drugs . . . which ones were into drugs . . ."

Gary seemed to be trying to throw the blame onto his victims, citing prostitution and then drugs. But Jensen wanted Gary to explain why the mere fact that a woman agreed to have sex for money justified Gary in killing her.

"You didn't answer my question," Jensen said. "Is every . . . is every woman you ever had sex with a prostitute?"

"No."

It was only women who agreed to take money for sex who were prostitutes, Gary insisted.

Jensen now pointed out that Gary had had sex with his wives, and all three had taken his money in the past, yet Gary hadn't killed them. Gary admitted that was true; but he also admitted that he'd felt like killing Claudia and Marcia in the past and that the only reason he hadn't killed Marcia was because he would certainly have been caught.

"One last thing here," Jensen said. "Why would you never have killed any men? Why not . . . why not pick on men?"

"Why not men?" Gary asked. "It's because I couldn't . . . it's easier to kill a woman, for one thing . . ."

—⁓—

After a short break, Detective Jensen returned, this time with Detective Jim Doyon, and resumed questioning about the Green River scenes. Jensen wanted to know why Gary had put the rocks in the vaginas of Marcia Chapman and Cynthia Hinds.[3] This had been a subject of considerable speculation among the detectives almost from the start of the case in August 1982.

"Why did you do that? Why did you put the rock in her vagina?" Jensen asked.

"Uh . . . um . . . might be symbolic," Gary said. "The woman would not have sex with anybody else. But I don't know. Keep anybody else from having sex. And you know not . . . not that they would because her . . . she's dead. But just to . . . just to . . . somethin' that I wanted to do. So I started on her. I was gonna do it . . ."

"Was it something that you'd thought of before, or . . . ?"

"Yeah, I thought of it just when I got there. Had sex. There's a . . . there's a rock. I'll put it in her vagina."

"Was there some sort of symbolism in your own mind, Gary, about getting your rocks off or getting their rocks off?"

"I didn't think about it. I think it was just . . . just a um, somethin' I was gonna do with her and the next victim. Yeah . . ."

"I mean," Jensen asked, "if there'd been a banana nearby, would you have done that?"

"Uh, if there was a banana [near]by, and if I thought about it, I would have. Or a . . . or even a beer bottle or something like that. A bunch of beer bottles were there, I probably would have . . ."

"Why a rock, though? I mean, why a rock? Any symbolism with . . . with regard to a rock?"

"No, I was goin' with Roxanne," Gary observed, "but I don't think that's any symbolism. It was just that it was a, a trademark or somethin', I dunno. I just didn't have no . . ."

"You were looking . . . you were looking to establish a trademark?"

"Uh, not really a trademark, just to block her . . . block her vagina with a rock," Gary said.

"Did you have any help?" Detective Doyon asked.

"No, I did not have any help. Not . . . no."

"One of the things that we thought of early on was this is either a really powerful person or it's a couple of people," Doyon told Gary. "Your brother never came down and offered to give you any help?"

"No, I didn't tell . . . he . . . I didn't get along with my younger brother that much."

"You didn't what?"

"I didn't get along with my younger brother in that period of time."

"Did you ever tell your brother about these things?"

"No, I never told anybody about this. Nothin'. Didn't . . . kept it away from everybody. It was my . . . my secret . . . my . . . and uh, that's why it bothers me . . ."

"Initially putting all these first five—well, I guess not the first five, but putting these five in . . . it didn't have any religious symbolism to you at all? Like uh, what do you call it? Baptism, or . . . ?"

"No, that didn't have anything like baptism, no."

"You didn't think of that at all?"

"No."

"You know, oh, you're washin' away their sins . . . down the river?"

"[I was] washin' away any evidence, was one thing," Gary said.

Jensen and Doyon turned to the issue of the heavy rocks placed atop the bodies of Marcia Chapman and Cynthia Hinds. Why, they asked, after he'd let the bodies of Wendy Coffield and Debbie Bonner float away had he decided to hold the next victims in place under water? Gary fumbled for the answer to that one.

"You have a lot of trouble with 'why' questions," Jensen told him. "Whenever I ask you a 'why' question, you go into . . . you go into a narrative of what you did. You don't answer me. OK?"

"'Cause I, uh . . ."

"Is it because you don't know why you do things?"

"That is a lot of reasons, yeah. I don't know why I put the rock in it [the vagina]. I don't know why I put the . . . took pictures and didn't put 'em in a scrapbook or you know, like what I . . . any other . . ."

"Is that a mistake you made?"

"A mistake to put a rock in? I don't think so. It was just . . ."

"Why don't you think so?"

"It was just uh, somethin' to uh . . . it might've been a mistake and that's probably why I tried to take it out. But it wouldn't come out. Um, I don't know if it was a mistake, but it's just a . . . just somethin' to do. She was a, a . . . a dead woman. And I've always had an idea of putting something in a woman besides grapes and a banana and beer bottle or somethin' like . . ."

"You always wanted to try somethin' like that?"

"Yeah."

"Ever try that before?"

"Never tried that before. Not with a, not with a rock, no."

"Well, what have you used before?"

"Oh, uh . . . I've never . . ."

"Use a beer bottle?"

"Uh, one time, a beer bottle at one time."

"On who?"

Gary told Jensen that he'd inserted a beer bottle into the vagina of one of his wives when she had passed out from too much alcohol years before.

"Stuck a beer bottle in her?"

"I tried to, yeah. And then I . . . and over in the Philippines I was always having women with . . . walkin' over with a beer bottle in their vaginas, bringing it over to sailors all the time. They'd do it."

"That's the way they deliver a beer?"

"That's the way they deliver beer a lotta times over there. But not to me. They did it to somebody else. And he liked it that way and . . ."

That was all, Gary said. That, and the rocks.

And even though the psychologists would later return to these beer bottles again and again, whatever their significance was to Gary and whatever their relationship was to the rocks would never be made clear.

But then, as our side already knew, Gary had a lot of trouble with the "why" questions.

34

Despite Baird's warning, frustration over Gary's cooperation mounted as the record hot and dry summer progressed. Nothing was being found, despite our repeated field trips, as many as four visits to the same area, and repeated confirmation from Gary as to the specific area to search. At one point, Gary told them about a human skeleton he and two Kenworth coworkers had supposedly found out near a campground east of Seattle in the summer of 1987, near a place called Greenwater. But Gary denied that he'd been responsible for this body and added that his coworkers had advised him not to report the skeleton, as it would only bring more unwanted attention to him after the search that had been made earlier that same year. Detectives decided to contact the coworkers to see if they would verify Gary's story. This took some time, however.

As June neared its end, we were all having second thoughts about Gary's credibility. Todd and I worried that the deal would come apart, and we'd have to have a trial anyway. Baird, I'm sure, was worrying that his side had bought a pig in a poke. Still, we kept on trying.

The emotionality of the bunker sessions was difficult to take at times, but Todd and I were able to help each other get through it—

often with the sort of deadpan humor we used to desensitize ourselves to the horrors we were hearing. At times, Gary's answers to the detectives' questions were ridiculous—it was obvious he was lying. When this happened, Todd and I would occasionally glance at each other, raise our eyebrows, or shake our heads. Sometimes, despite the grim topic, we had to suppress our laughter because of the absurdity of some of Gary's responses.

During these sessions, we defense attorneys sat just off camera, monitoring the questions and answers. Usually, it was Todd and me, sometimes Tony and me, and sometimes Todd and Tony. We frequently exchanged notes, some serious, some not-so-serious, as the interviews progressed. With the not-so-serious notes, the goal was to get the other guy to crack up, audibly if possible. If you laughed, you had to mask it into a cough or by clearing your throat; we couldn't be obvious, least of all to Gary. Again, these were our own psychological defense mechanisms at work, helping us cope with the dreadful stories coming from our client.

Meanwhile the dynamics of the interrogation sessions had profoundly shifted; under these circumstances, because we wanted the deal to go through, Todd and I essentially abandoned our traditional adversarial role and became allies of the interrogators. Our motives were different, but our end goals were the same. Both sides wanted to get the facts out.

Just before the beginning of one session, just after the detectives had failed to find anything at Grandview Park (where Gary had claimed to have left some victims' jewelry twenty years earlier), Mattsen spoke to Todd and me.

"I want to give you guys a heads up," he said. "Randy [Mullinax] and I are going to turn up the heat, shall we say. We're going to be more . . . confrontational. . . . We're gonna call him on his bullshit and tell him he's going back to jail unless we get some results. We're not there yet . . . yet . . . but we want to give him that impression. And we'd appreciate if you don't share this conversation with your client."

"No problem," Todd said. "Thanks for the warning."

Mattsen smiled. "Well, we didn't want you guys sitting there thinking the deal was off. We didn't want to do that to you."

During the next interview, the detectives did turn it up. They appeared very angry and upset . . . at or beyond their boiling point.

Mattsen and Mullinax wanted to know why Gary had lied to them about "loving" Carol Christensen. He spent much of June 17 trying to say that Carol had been special, that he'd cried after killing her, and that he wanted her to be found. Then the following day, "bad Gary" admitted that he'd hated her, that he'd hated all his victims, that to him, they were just "garbage."

"Why did you make the decision to lie to us?" Mattsen demanded.

"To make you feel like I'm not that bad of a person," Gary said. "Not that bad a person, just to pick up Christensen and by putting in the other things it made you . . . made me feel like I was much more your person, but I was lying to you and cuddling her and all that stuff. It made me feel more like a monster. That's what they call me."

"Who calls you that?"

"The newspaper and the press and everything. Killing all these people. It's got to be a monster doing that."

"Who had you told that story to, before?" Mattsen asked, referring to the good Gary's first tale about loving Carol Christensen.

"Mark, I think, I'm quite sure," Gary said, meaning me.

"Who else?" Mullinax asked.

"You guys."

"Who else?" Mullinax seemed not to believe that Gary would only lie to his lawyers.

"I think that's just about it."

"Did you spin that same story for Mark?"

"Yes, I did," Gary admitted.

"For what reason? The same reasons?"

"The same reasons that it wasn't that much of a . . . of a . . . of an evil person, to lie to 'em, just like I lied to you guys."

"But you're smart enough to know that you promised through this agreement to come in here and tell the truth, aren't you?"

"Yes, I am."

"OK. . . . So we're just trying to get into your head and understand why it was necessary for you to do that. It is hard for me to believe that you really give a shit about what I think about you. You know, it's not about what we think about you. It matters not what Jon and I think about you. This process is about getting to the truth. Finding out what the truth is. Not about our feelings or about what you've read in the newspaper and so, very honestly, with you, there are a lot of people who are very disturbed about what has occurred over here, over the last thirteen days.

"How is it that we are trying to make some decision about being able to tell when Gary is telling us the truth and when he's lying to us?

It is a process, quite honestly, that I never anticipated having to face, when you walked in here. I can't imagine why you would have walked in here and told one lie. You have a card in front of you that says you have a pass. So it makes no sense to us about why . . . why we have listened to so much B.S. from you for the last thirteen days. And there is no clear line in the sand for us to know when you stopped lying and when you started telling the truth. That's what we are trying to understand here, Gary."

"One of the reasons is because this is going into . . . I thought all this was going to be aired in a . . . in Ann Rule's book," Gary said. Like almost everyone in Seattle, Gary knew that Ann Rule intended to write a book about the Green River case someday.

"She has access to everything she ever does about a case. It always goes through the detectives, and it gets all this stuff here. And it's all documented, and I thought for sure this was going to be right there. She's going to go note for note in her book. And that would be hard for people to understand, the person not having any feelings for a person and that's . . . I figured this is gonna be . . . everything's going to be in a book. Everybody in the nation is going to buy this book."

Gary seemed to be suggesting that he wanted to satisfy the detectives' desire for details, so he made some up—details that made him look less like "a monster." But then, that had always been Gary's way: to find out what people wanted and then to try to give it to them. He'd admitted that as far back as his first conversations with Mary Goody. But Mattsen and Mullinax didn't want Gary to make them happy. They wanted the truth.

"Tell me the things that they [we defense lawyers] hit us on, when you first came in here," Mullinax said. "I remember hearing from somebody, 'Gary wants to talk about a foundation, . . . about doing good.' 'Gary wants to talk about doing the truth.' We want to hear what the truth is, not about what Gary wants to tell us. So you wasted, I don't know, all of these days."

"No."

"All of this shit on us?"

"Just, uh . . . what was it, six days," Gary said.

"Gary, why did you lie to us?"

"Because I was lying to my lawyers the same time, and it just kept on going."

"That's not the question. Why were you lying to us, when you had a free pass? When you had the opportunity to come in here and say what was on your mind about these killings? These killings that have . . .

so many people have invested twenty years of their lives in. You included. You had an opportunity. Why did you make the decision to lie?"

"To, uh . . . to make it less to look like a monster doing it."

"Gary, you killed sixty people," Mattsen said.

"I killed up to sixty people," Gary agreed.

"That's a biggie, Gary. That's pretty important."

"Yes."

"Why did you make the decision to lie to us in those crucial days, when we first started out?"

"It's hard for me to tell the truth. It's hard for me to tell the truth."

"Now maybe we are getting somewhere," Mullinax said.

"It is hard for me to tell the truth. I'm trying to get the truth out."

"Why is it hard for you to tell the truth? Why? That's the sixty-four dollar question. Why?"

"It's just hard for me to tell the truth. I'm trying to get . . ."

I thought Mattsen was actually starting to get mad. But then he caught my eye and gave me a wink, one that Gary couldn't see.

"Gary," he now said, "are you worried that Coffield may not be your first kill? Gary, are you worried that that may be . . . that that's the barrier? Is there something else out there that you're worried to bring up? Now I can accept it if you could sit here and tell me that you can't . . . that you don't want to talk about it. OK? I can accept that. But just tell me if there's something before Coffield. Is there something before Coffield that you're unwilling to discuss with me? But just be a man and just tell me that there's something before, so we can alleviate all of our other questions that we have, and we can move on to something else. Is there somebody before Coffield, Gary? Because you know what, everybody else in all these other rooms that are watching you sit here and spew this, whatever you're spewing [is wondering about that]. Is it that there's something else there? Coffield was not your first kill, was she, Gary?"

Gary started to deny this, but Mattsen cut him off.

"Maybe you were eighteen years old, living up by your mom and dad's house, and found some woman walking around, and you killed her or something and left her down on the hill somewhere. Maybe that was your first time, Gary. Maybe it was, you know, out with . . . doing something one night, and you see a girl walking along the street and you killed her. I don't know what it is. What I do know is, it wasn't Wendy Coffield. What I *do* know is, you remember the details, in great detail. That, you know, up here [pointing to his head], who it was you killed, the first person that you killed, and you need to tell us about it."

"Coffield's the first one, and that's all I can tell you," Gary said. "I don't remember killing anybody else before her. She was [number] one, like I said."

"Is there some monster that you're afraid that maybe . . . people seeing you for . . . what is going on? I mean, I don't understand this. Make us understand."

"Coffield was the very first one. That's all . . . that's all I know. She's the very first one."

That was Gary's story and he was sticking to it.

"That's what's in my mind, is just Coffield is the first," Gary insisted. "It's . . . the river was the first. The first one was the river, then the [river] bank, then back to the river."

"'Coffield's the first one,'" Mullinax parroted. "But yet, when Jon or anyone else hits you on specifics, you told us more details about killing your cat than you did about murdering the first person in King County. We got more details about the frickin' cat going in the cooler and coming back and looking at it the second day.[1] Give me a fuckin' break. A cat! I whipped out a picture of Wendy Coffield in here to put down in front of you. It wasn't a cat. We are talking about *people*."

"I took a life and . . ."

"Bullshit! Bullshit! Every *body*. This person. We want to know what you thought. What you felt. Why you did it. I don't give a shit about the neighbors or anybody else. You. What you felt. Why you did it. Where she was at. What you remember. What you did afterwards. The whys. The whys."

"She just . . . it's just that I killed her, and after a while I calmed down and knew that I killed a person but it's didn't . . . it's not a . . . it didn't relieve my urge to kill somebody else. So a couple of days later, I killed another person."

"Why did you have the urge in the first place?"

"The hate," Gary said. "I wanted to get even with 'em."

"Why?"

"Because she's a prostitute and not worth anything. Nobody would look for her."

"Nobody would look for her?"

"Nobody would . . . you wouldn't . . . an officer would not . . . that would be second [in police priorities] after looking after an ordinary woman. They wouldn't . . . they would look more harder . . . than a prostitute."

"We are back to generalities," Mattsen said, with exasperation. "You still can't say anything specific about your first kill in King County."

"It . . . it just did not . . . it just did not have any different feelings than the first one. The first one was the first one," Gary insisted.

"Ah, I'm not taking about Laverne [Lovvorn], OK?" Mullinax said. "I'm talking about, is there something that you are afraid of that, I mean, I don't understand. I mean, you're the Green River Killer, you know, it's like you have it on your hand. 'OK, I killed two in 1982 and 1985. 1982 and 1985.' Goddamn, Gary. Goddamn. You've got the opportunity, literally, of a lifetime here. And it boggles us to think that we are having to drag this out of you. You can give us all these truths, all of these things that you've done, when you live here. And we're gonna walk out of this room and feel good about it, but for some reason you're . . . like these boundaries or barriers that you cannot get around."

Gary said he thought he could do better with details if the detectives gave him a timeline of who was last seen and when.

"OK," Mullinax said. "The root thing here is, telling the truth [or] telling lies. I hope that, you know, you should maybe give us a little more credit. I mean we just didn't walk in here like, you know, the dipshit off the street, and start, you know, 'Gary, tell us about these people you killed.' We've been working real hard at this. We know a lot of stuff, probably, that you don't. And so when you sit here and blow smoke at us, it doesn't make us real happy, and it gives us absolutely no faith in you. No faith in you. We're trying. We're trying, but we're not there. We can't . . . we can't . . . it's hard for us to believe what you're telling us. So many times, because you admit one day that you lied about what you said yesterday, and the day before and . . ."

Mattsen cut his partner off.

"Gary, why are you here?" he asked. "Why are you doing this?"

"One of the reasons is because we made a contract to take the death penalty off," Gary said, honestly enough. "Other way of getting my story out the way, it is not the way somebody wants to put it, and I lied to you a lot of times. I admit. I have a lie in my head and it just kept on coming out . . . kept on coming out, and I thought it was the truth, and I kept on being . . . it got deeper and deeper into lying."

"Why should we believe you now?"

"Because I'm trying to tell you the truth," Gary said, and Todd, Tony, and I believed that he really was. It was just that he didn't want to remember.

—∿∿—

As this interview progressed, Gary continually referred to Gisele Lovvorn as Laverne, as had been his practice for months. Mattsen kept patiently correcting Gary, repeating her name, *Lovvorn,* slowly and distinctly. It didn't seem to stick in Gary's brain, and each time he again said *Laverne,* I could see Mattsen wince. But Gary never got it.

Later in the same session, Mullinax questioned Gary about his last victim. Gary said this victim, which he repeatedly referred to as "the last one," had been killed in 1985, just before Judith had moved in with him. During this "last one," the camper canopy on Gary's truck had suddenly detached and flown off the truck while he was on his way back from dumping the body way out off Highway 410. That's why he remembered it so clearly, he said.

Mullinax asked, "How did you quit? I mean, how'd you stop?"

Again, Gary attributed his reforming to Judith. Once she'd moved in, Gary said, he spent most of his time with her. So he didn't have as much time to kill—literally. Judith, it turned out, had a poodle named Peaches.

"Well, because one thing I had things to care for, animals," Gary said, in explaining why he no longer had enough time for murder. "We've always had animals, cats and stuff, so that brought me out of it. Had her [Judith], she was dependent on me."

"So," Mullinax said, "havin' a fuckin' dog, or Peaches the Poodle, or some fuckin' thing like that, is supposed to suddenly cause you to be cured of killin' prostitutes? We're suppose to sit here and believe that you're able to just bam, stop that urge! 'Cause you got Peaches ridin' around in your lap, and you got the motor home, you got Judith, you got a life? [But] still seein' whores?"

"Still seein' whores," Gary agreed.

"That's like stickin' a cigarette in your mouth, but no, you're not gonna light it up," Mullinax said. "I'm not gonna believe that shit."

"And the by-product of that," Gary added, "was I was . . . I was beatin' the system. I knew that nobody . . . very many people never stopped killing, and it was me to get back at you guys and have you guys waste your time tryin' to pin me on other murders. Yeah, that would be . . . that's one of the motives, too, but not the underlyin' motive of stoppin', 'cause I know you guys would keep on lookin' and keep on lookin' . . ." It pleased him, Gary said, that the police would think that he had to continue killing, like all the profiles said serial killers did, when he knew they could never find any new evidence against him, because he'd stopped, unlike all the other serial killers. His cessation itself was a form of taunting the police.

"Why the fuck should we believe that suddenly Gary Ridgway has got the will and the wherewithal to say, 'I'm done, that's it, not gonna kill any more prostitutes . . . sixty-three's my limit, that's it, can't kill anymore?'" Mullinax asked.

"You're not gonna . . . you're gonna be wasting a lot of taxpayer money, and you're gonna come up with zilch," Gary told the two detectives, about any efforts to tie him to murders after 1985. People in jail, he said, or prostitutes on the street would try to frame him for other murders that he had not committed. But the talk would never stand up, he said.

"You're gonna come up with maybe a DNA on somebody, or somebody's gonna lie to you and tell you that I beat 'em up, took a knife to 'em, shot 'em or . . . or, uh, hung 'em, or whatever you wanna . . . whatever they come up with, they're bullshit. And you're gonna find a lot of that, because they just, hey, 'here's my escape goat, I can use him.' Yeah, I drove . . . drove 'em down the road, and there's . . . 'he was the one that came over, and I didn't like him, because he helped me fix my tire, or he slowed by and drove by.' It's a bunch of bullshit, they're gonna bring . . . you're gonna bring up all kinds the low lives out there, they're gonna come up with any kind of thing to . . . to put on me."

"To pin it on you," Mullinax said.

"To pin it on me," Gary agreed, "and I'm . . . I'm right, and I'm just laughin' my head [off] because you guys are believin' 'em." Gary meant that he thought the detectives were giving credence to all the tips that had come in since his arrest.

He might have dated prostitutes after 1985, he continued, but he hadn't killed any.

"That's . . . that's when I stopped," Gary insisted once more. They could try as hard as they wanted, he said, but they'd never be able to show that he'd murdered after 1985, because of Judith and Peaches the Poodle.

"Fuck Peaches the Poodle," Mullinax glared at Gary. "With all your lies so far, you've made this job so much more difficult. Your credibility, you know, I really can't say you have any right now."

"Uh-huh," Gary said, polite as ever. "I agree with you." Mullinax ignored this.

"So you need to think about," Mullinax went on, "tonight, about how you could start building up some of that credibility, because our patience has worn very thin. We're here because we want to hear the true story. We want the truth about these things, not what we might suggest or not what your . . . anyone else has told you. We want to hear from Gary Ridgway what he did to all of these women. Do you understand that?"

"I understand that."

"One little piece of evidence, one bone, body find, one . . . one thing that only the Green River Killer would know or could provide—credibility."

"Well, if it goes in my mind as the memory, or if it goes into my mind as a . . . a lie, it comes out as a lie," Gary was saying. "If what I feel like . . . for instance that sign down there in Oregon, it says to me . . . my mind says it's Allstate. We go by it and it says, 'Allstate' every time. [The sign actually said State Farm, it turned out.] And then all of a sudden, it's not a lie. It's just been burned in my mind, and Laverne . . ."

Mattsen stood up, leaned across the table, and got in Gary's face. Like Mullinax, he too was tired and angry.

"Hey, you know what?" he said. "It's not *Laverne*. . . . It's *Lovvorn!*"

"Lovvorn," Gary said, repeating it. "Lovvorn."

"OK?" Mattsen said. "The lady's name is Lovvorn."

"Lovvorn," Gary repeated once more, drawing out the *o*'s.

"Gisele Lovvorn," Mattsen said. "If you need to write that down, then write that down, because, do not refer to her as *Laverne* again. This young lady was named *Lovvorn*."

"Seventeen years old," Mullinax said. "Lovvorn."

"Lovvorn," Gary said.

Over the next two days, we went on more field trips, and still nothing turned up.

Then at the end of June, Todd, Tony, and I were told that the state wanted to bring in a forensic psychologist, Dr. Robert Wheeler.

35

D r. Wheeler was about Todd's and my age, a full head of gray and black hair, wire-framed glasses, a very pleasant personality, and a quick smile. He was dressed in a shirt and tie, a little more formal than the rest of us, by this point. As a forensic psychologist, he examined people regarding their mental state as it related to various court proceedings and legal standards: incompetency, insanity, diminished capacity. In layman's terms, his specialty was, essentially, trying to determine if someone was crazy at the time he committed his crime.

Wheeler was to prove to be amazingly adept at penetrating into Gary's thought processes, and particularly his defenses. Again and again, he forced Gary to examine his own statements for lies and inconsistencies, parsing his illogic relentlessly, refusing to let his evasions slip by. As the next few days went on, Wheeler pruned away each of Gary's layered mental defenses, giving all of us a stunning, deeply disturbing look at the deep recesses of a serial killer's mind.

Wheeler made it clear that he wasn't there to help Gary with his emotional problems but to help him get to the truth.

"I'm not here . . . I guess I want to emphasize that I'm not here to do therapy with [you], right?"

"Uh-huh," Gary said.

"I'm not here to act . . . to stand in for the detectives. I'm here to assist the attorneys in understanding who you are. What made you tick. What your behavior patterns were, and I can do this, because you've got your attorneys, and those attorneys have an agreement."

"Uh-huh," Gary said.

Wheeler had an uninterrupted run at Gary for the better part of three days and would return later for more sessions. By uninterrupted, I mean that for the most part, all the detectives stayed in the conference room, watching on the video monitor. So the atmosphere in the interrogation room was somewhat different. Whereas the detectives had been trying to pull facts out of Gary's brain, Wheeler was trying to see how Gary's brain actually worked. By this point, Gary had remembered a few more locations for possible bodies, bringing the total to as many as sixty-three.

Wheeler asked Gary to describe the circumstances of his arrest on November 30, 2001. Gary said that Detectives Peters and Mullinax had come to Kenworth to talk to him first and that this had made him a little bit mad, "because I was tryin' to forget the Green River murders."

"Tell me how you feel when you're mad," Wheeler said.

"Uh, when I really get mad I uh, shake, and I haven't had that much problem. Um, sometimes I forget to breathe and uh, uh, things get blurry."

"What do you think about when you're mad, was my question."

"What do I think about it?"

"Yeah. What do you think about when you are mad?"

"Hm, um, just I get, I get frustrated and I can't uh, think proper."

"What kinds of thoughts do you have?"

"Uh, back, right now I don't have any thoughts of hurting anybody. But back then, in '82, I uh, wanted to kill somebody, kill a prostitute."

"When you got angry, you wanted to kill?"

"Yes."

"Besides prostitutes, who did you get mad at and want to kill?"

"Well, I got mad and wanted to hit somebodys . . . you know, people at work, but I, I couldn't because I'd lose my job and I just uh, held that, all that pressure . . ."

"Who did you want to hit?"

"Oh, uh, just uh, anybody that uh, you know, kidded me during the . . . for some reason, you know, kidded me or, or uh, I had problems with 'em, putting the right formulas in and so my da . . . back there I had to have a lot of uh, things just didn't si—sink in my mind . . . memory, and I'd put the wrong chemicals in and put the wrong combinations of it, and I ruined about three or four trucks during the day. So that made me mad, and I didn't have no way of uh, controlling that 'til later on, when uh, was around a prostitute. That's when I started killin' prostitutes, about that time."

"In what way do you mean, you had no way of controlling it? Controlling what?"

"Well, I . . . my, my anger. My anger uh, only came out when I was with uh, prostitutes and I, and I just kept it in during that period of time."

"And when you get angry, you want to hurt people, is that what you said?"

"At that time," Gary corrected. "This, I, I don't, I'm not into that anymore. Uh, that's just between uh, '82 and '85. But I . . ."

"Are you telling me that that suddenly in 1985 you no longer had problems with anger?"

"I still had anger, but I had ways of, of, you know, doing yard work and stuff like that just to help out."

"Doing yard work?"

"Doing yard work, and, and, and, and . . ."

"And?"

"Reading," Gary said.

"Mr. Ridgway, are you, excuse me, are you telling me that before 1985 you got angry and you wanted to hurt and kill people?"

"Um-hm."

"And then in 1985, you wanted to, you got angry and you did *yard work*?"

"I, I did other things to keep . . . myself busy and I, I, uh, had a new wife that cared for me. And . . ."

"Mr. Ridgway, excuse me," Wheeler said. "Are you telling me that before 1985, when you got angry, you wanted to kill people, and if I understand correctly, you actually did kill quite a number. Is that . . . ?"

"Yes, I did."

"And then all of a sudden in 1985, when you got angry, you, you raked the lawn?"

"No. I, I had, uh, uh, I had different uh, personality towards people," Gary said. "I had somebody to care for, and I love my wife. I didn't wanna do any more killing. I sl . . . I did slow down, I think the last one I killed was some time in '85. But I didn't have that uh, urge to go out and kill uh, uh . . ."

Wheeler's skepticism was obvious to everyone, even Gary. Wheeler tried another approach.

"Was it your general opinion that you would essentially never be caught? Did you feel like you had succeeded?"

"My general opinion, uh, yes, I didn't think I'd ever get caught."

"Had you always felt that way?"

"No. I felt, uh, when I first killed the first woman, I thought I'd be caught."

"Why was it that when you killed the first woman, you thought you'd be caught?"

"Uh, 'cause [they] usually catch somebody within twenty-four [hours], you know, a couple, couple weeks of the first killin'. And I always thought it was uh, Coffield, but it wasn't. It was somebody before her."

"So there was somebody that you killed before Coffield, and you assumed you would be caught?"

"Yeah. I did."

All of us watching the monitor—detectives and lawyers alike—didn't know what to make of this new admission. Three days after Mullinax and Mattsen, and Jensen and Doyon, had excoriated Gary for insisting that Wendy Coffield had been his first victim, Gary was now throwing that story completely overboard in this conversation with Wheeler. And what was more, he was claiming this was another victim he'd killed in his house, almost five months before any of the Green River victims had been found, and this one, like Carol Christensen more than a year later, had been re-dressed. Was Gary playing around with Wheeler? Didn't he realize that Wheeler would have been briefed about what Gary had already said—in fact, that he'd even seen Gary on videotape insisting that Wendy Coffield was first? Was this more lies, or was it the truth?[1]

Gary now told Wheeler that he'd told a girlfriend in February 1982 that he'd done something—he didn't tell the girlfriend exactly what—and that she might expect to see something about it in the newspaper soon. This was more than four months before Wendy Coffield was murdered.

"What did you tell her you had done?"

"I didn't tell her any, anything, you know, other than that."

"What had you done?"

"Well, that was the day I killed my first woman."

"And where did that killing take place?"

"The only thing I can remember is, uh, killing her at . . . my house, and putting some, putting some uh, putting her clothes on, I'm quite sure, with a, a uh, jeans and a shirt with a, a blouse with white buttons . . . about the size of a dime."

"Do you have a clear memory of that?" Wheeler asked.

"I have a clear memory of that, but uh . . ."

"And you've always had that memory?"

"Yeah," Gary said. "Uh, yeah, I almost always have it, yeah . . . you bring it out."

"Yeah," Wheeler said, dryly. "And you have always remembered that you dressed the woman that you killed in this blouse, and the blouse had white buttons the size of dimes?"

"I didn't always remember that. I, I thought that, that she was down, down the uh, like the fifth or the sixth one. And I've always thought the first one was Coffield. She was by the, by the river, but that didn't happen until Ju . . . July, so it had to been the one that I put the clothes back on."

"Whose clothes did you put on her?"

"Her clothes."

"Her clothes," Wheeler echoed. "And uh, so this was the first woman that you killed, as far as you can recall, as we sit here? . . ."

"Yeah."

"I don't know whether there's something that I'm doing that's causing you to sort of jerk me around a little bit," Wheeler told Gary. "Are you telling me that you killed this woman, this was the first woman you killed, and you're gonna tell me now you can't remember where she is?"

"I'm . . . it might be up by uh, uh, Highway 18."

"So exactly where is this spot?"

"Uh, it must be the one out on, I get this also from the uh, uh, the uh, task force has the discovery, and they said one a the womans was up on Kensington Road, or some'n like that, up on . . . and that might be where she is.[2] I don't . . . I just don't remember where I put the first one. I remember, I don't even remember where I put half, you know, I put . . . last couple days there was three victims I don't even know, remember killin'—where they put 'em."

"Mr. Ridgway, would you agree with me that it's pretty unlikely that someone would forget about the first person they ever killed in their life? I mean, for most people, that should be a fairly significant event, wouldn't it?"

"Yeah, but most . . . yes, it was."

"I mean that's not like the first time you had a McDonald's cheeseburger, right?"

"Right."

"What would you conclude if a person said they didn't [remember their first kill]? What would you conclude about that person?"

"I'd conclude they're, uh, not telling the truth, or they just don't, don't remember."

"And is that what you want me to conclude about you, that you're not telling the truth?"

"Not that. It's just . . . uh, I been [tainted] with the discovery and I don't uh, I don't wanna taint and say it's that place."

Wheeler asked Gary why he thought he'd been brought in to see him. Gary said he'd been told that Wheeler might help him remember things.

"OK. So you wanted me to help you. You thought maybe I could help you bring out some information?"

"Yes."

"What information would you like me to help you with?"

"Well, uh, why I can't remember a lot of this, where I can't remember putting bodies."

"What if I said to you, 'I think that you *can* remember.'"

"I guess maybe you have a way to help get it out. I don't know."

Wheeler approached this by trying to get Gary to focus on why he'd agreed to cooperate. Gary said he wanted to help the detectives recover the bodies of his victims so their families could have closure.

"How can you take responsibility? What specifically can you do to demonstrate your trustworthiness and to take responsibility for what you've done?" Wheeler asked him.

"Confess to all my killings and to lead 'em to any bodies they haven't found."

"And have you led them to bodies they haven't found?"

"I've led 'em to bodies they haven't found, but there's no, so far they haven't found anything."

"No bodies."

"No bodies."

"Are you a little concerned about that?"

"I'm really concerned about it, and . . ."

"Well, what is your concern?"

"I'm concerned that there's uh, somethin' wrong with my mind and . . . goin' to one site and there's two bodies there instead a one, and I forgot there's a body there."

"Are you concerned about possible consequences to yourself?"

"Yes."

"What are your concerns?"

"That they're gonna put me back in jail. And uh . . ."

"Did you, are you expecting that you're gonna not be in jail?"

"I've been, every, every morning I uh . . ."

"All right. You mean, move you from here, back [to jail] . . ."

"Move me back to jail, yeah."

"What would be the meaning of that?"

"Meaning, they haven't found anything and meaning, too, that . . . that uh, they think I'm blowin' smoke up their rear end."

"And what would happen then? What would happen to you?"

"I'd go, go through trial and get convicted."

"And then what would happen?"

"Get the . . . death sentence."

"Does that concern you? Are you concerned about potentially facing the death penalty? Does it concern you that you might face death?"

"It, it, it has, but . . ."

"Have you thought about it?"

"Oh, I've thought, thought a lot about it, but . . ."

"Tell me some of what you thought."

"Well, I've read up a little bit about it, injection. And, and then uh, could take seven or eight years before getting it. Plus, the books say it's just, it's a process that you just go to sleep and your heart stops, so there's very little pain."

"So one thing that you were concerned about is whether it would be painful."

"Um-hm."

"What are you thinking about dying versus living? Tell me the truth."

"That uh, that, that I confessed to where the bodies are and, and uh, prayed that I'd go to Heaven."

"Do you have a preference as to whether you live or die?"

"Yes, I'd . . . I'd rather live."

"How confident are you in that?"

"Real confident."

"Pretty confident?"

"But it, it doesn't, uh, it really doesn't bother me if uh, if I go to trial. It's gonna be a lot of pressure."

"What's the pressure of going to trial?"

"The pressure of every day goin' in there and havin', uh, people come up there, and witnesses, the pictures . . . the, the process of . . ."

"How does that affect you? Why is that of concern?"

"Because of, it, it's just more and more pressure comin' down on me from the uh, jury lookin' me and tryin' to keep a, a poker face, and not to express my feelings and . . ."

"Are you afraid you'll blow up, lose your temper?"

"Um-hm."

But I thought that Wheeler had missed what bothered Gary most about going to trial. He wasn't afraid that he'd lose his temper but rather that he'd somehow look foolish—stupid, even: his long-abiding fear of speaking in public, of revealing his mental slowness, of being identified as Wrongway Ridgway.

—⁓—

Wheeler asked Gary why he'd made the agreement to confess.

"Why'd you enter that agreement?"

"Why? Because uh, my uh, let's see. My uh, my brother cried . . . uh, they had a meeting with the lawyers, and he uh, cried to them. He didn't want me to be executed, for one thing, so he got me to thinkin' what uh, how, how I can help to uh, give the information out, to make a deal for uh, gettin' the death penalty off, by telling the, uh, detectives and the attorneys that I did kill all these women."

"You mean, are you saying that you entered into it because your brother . . ."

"Well, my brother and . . . and then I got to thinkin' the families would like to know where their, where their daughters are . . . buried and, and, and how they died. Where, uh, where they, where they died, and to help them out . . ."

This led Wheeler to ask whether, when he was first arrested on November 30, 2001, he was afraid that he'd finally been caught.

"I'm asking you at the time you were arrested, did you feel like, 'They still haven't got anything on me? I'm going to get off on this'?"

"Yeah."

"So you were pretty self-confident?"

"Yes."

"You didn't want to be caught?"

He hadn't wanted to be caught, Gary said, and by the time he was arrested, he'd tried hard for years to forget all the murders.

"I wanted to, basically, wash most of it away from life. I didn't think too much of it. I didn't fantasize on it."

"How about earlier on? How did it affect your view of yourself?"

"I had really low self-esteem. I didn't like myself when I was killing them. I didn't like myself. I didn't have anybody that I thought didn't love me. And going through the divorces that I had before. Being rejected by other women I went with."

"Help me understand," Wheeler said. "So you're saying you felt unloved and had been rejected and dumped by other women?"

"Yeah."

"Is that right? My question is, how did the fact that you were so successful at the killings affect your view of yourself and your self-esteem?"

"Well, I was in a way a little bit proud of not being caught doing . . . like removing the clothes. Not leaving anything . . . any fingerprints on it, using gloves. Changing tires on my vehicle one time after I . . . I think after I dropped Christensen off. I think I removed the truck tires. Not bragging about it. Not talking about it." It fed his self-esteem to be so clever, Gary indicated, and it became a source of secret pride.

"So you weren't talking or bragging about it, but you felt, as you said, proud of yourself. Proud in what sense?"

"Proud that I didn't get caught, but later on, proud that I didn't get caught and I could live a better life . . . but I still had that sex draw to prostitution."

Wheeler now tried to uncover some of the ways that the murders stimulated Gary. He asked about Gary's sexual habits, including masturbation, and suggested that Gary had taken photographs of his victims for purposes of recalling the pleasure that the murders had given him. But Gary had a hard time admitting masturbation. To him it was shameful.

"I took the pictures just . . . not for . . . I didn't masturbate on the pictures or anything like that," he said. "I took some pictures of some by the river, and then I hid them and went back a few times, but I didn't masturbate. If I wanted to, I could just go out and kill another woman instead of masturbating. It's always been in my mind that masturbating in one way is wrong, but I did it anyway. It's better to go to a prostitute than to masturbate."

"How do you understand in your own mind . . . when you say to me that rather than going and masturbating because that was something you felt was a little bit wrong, even though you did, you could just . . . instead of doing that, just go kill another woman? Tell me, what does that say in your mind, about you?" Wheeler asked.

"Maybe I misquoted by saying [that]," Gary said. "It's not necessary to kill a woman but going to a prostitute instead of masturbating, and in the '70s I went to prostitutes because I didn't have a girlfriend at the time or . . . and I didn't masturbate."

"But nonetheless you were aware that you were killing human beings?"

"Yes, yeah."

"And that that's against the law?"

"Yes, it is."

"And that you could go to jail for it?"

"Yes, I know that."

"Did you think that?"

"I thought about all that but . . . thing was to kill and I didn't have remorse. I had remorse sometimes, but not all the time."

"You had morals sometimes but not all the time?"

"No, remorse."

"Remorse."

"But I didn't try to think about it."

"So when you thought about yourself and you thought about killing these women who wanted to live, and then it being morally wrong and legally wrong, how did you square that away with your desires and intentions to go ahead and kill them?"

"My desire was to have sex with them and to kill them and that was my gratification. Morals, there was no morals involved in it. I think . . ."

"No morals involved?"

"No."

"So you didn't really experience any moral deterrent? Do you know what I mean when I use the word *deterrent*?"

"Uh-huh."

"So you didn't feel any deterrent by taking another human life or breaking the law?"

"No, there's was no deterrent. That sometimes I let [a] woman, before I even thought about killing them, I thought about it and told them they were too nice to kill or something like that, and let them go, but it would cost me to do that, because I was planning on killing them. Got them in the car and told them, 'get out of here, you're too cute.' Probably, after I talked to them a little bit . . . talked about something, maybe it got to me and I let them go."

Like what, Wheeler asked? What would they say that would cause Gary to let them go?

"I don't know if there's anything that I can give you to believe about that, 'cause I . . . that's the way I . . . maybe it was . . . could have been the way they dressed, if they were in a dress. Maybe it made a difference, I don't [know] . . ."

———

Wheeler now asked Gary about any physical or neurological disorders. Gary recalled getting lost on several occasions as a small child and generally experiencing a sense of befuddlement.

"Besides getting lost, were there any other developmental, medical, or social problems that you had that you were . . . told about?"

"I had allergies and I wet the bed a lot at the time and had all kinds of allergies and bronchitis and . . ."

"Until what age did you wet the bed?"

"Until eleven," Gary said.

Todd and I were both aware that Gary was shading this information. After all, he'd told Mary Goody—and then me—that he'd wet the bed up until his mid-teens. This was apparently something he did not want to share with Wheeler.

"So up until age eleven, you never completely stopped wetting the bed for any period of time?"

"I don't remember if I did or not."

"You don't remember?"

"No."

"You don't remember whether, for example, you were able to go for some period of time without wetting the bed and then started up wetting the bed again, versus whether you never completely quite made it past the stage of wetting?"

"It was frequent as far as I know. Sometimes I wouldn't wet the bed, and sometimes I would."

"But there was never a period, as far as you recall, months or years, that you didn't wet the bed, until you were age eleven?"

"No, I don't remember."

Wheeler asked Gary what he could remember about his early childhood, and on this subject, Gary was far more animated and emotional.

"And do you have any memories of life before the age of five, or let's say, six? Do you have any memories at all?"

"Only . . . no, not very many memories, no."

"Tell me what you can remember."

"I can remember of my brother getting . . . we had three little ducks, and I had one, Greg had one, and my brother had one, and my brother, younger brother, liked to carry them around by the neck and, of course . . ."

"Probably pretty hard on the ducks?"

"Pretty hard on the ducks and they . . . I think he killed all of them that way. Got to walking around . . ."

This was probably Gary's first experience with death, and it seemed to have made an impression on him.

"What are your memories of what the weather is like in Pocatello? What's the climate?"

"The climate was hot. I can remember going up in the mountains with my parents and taking the dog with us, and he was kind of . . . vaguely . . . go after rattlesnakes, and he wouldn't get bit. He'd swing them back and forth and kill them. And . . ."

"And what do you remember about your relationships with your mom and dad during those years? Just during those years?"

"That's when I was learning to ride a bike. Dad was teaching me."

"Do you remember your dad teaching you to ride a bike?"

"Uh-huh."

"Tell me what you remember."

"I can remember he . . . putting me on the bike and me falling off a couple times and remember coming home . . ."

Gary started crying.

"This is bringing up some memories, isn't it?"

Gary nodded. He continued remembering events from his childhood.

"Our dog was in a dogfight with German Shepherd and the German Shepherd biting Duke all up. And uh . . ."

"That must have been pretty sad and traumatic for a young kid?"

"And all they could do was put Duke to sleep," Gary finished.

"Yeah. That was a really big event in your life back then?"

"Yeah," Gary said, weeping.

"Did you see them put Duke to sleep?"

"No. They took him someplace, and Greg got bit in the leg by the other dog or both of them. I don't know which one. My dad had to something . . . sew it up by himself or something, and Greg getting his foot caught in the bike one time when my dad was driving. My dad forcing him to walk on it. It was painful but it had to be done. They didn't take him to the doctor's."

Gary said that he'd always had difficulties in school and that Greg, his older brother, often had to stand up for him, because Gary wouldn't stand up for himself. Just thinking about Greg made Gary weep again.

"What was the worst behavior you can ever recall doing?" Wheeler asked. "What can you recall that you did that you were ashamed of during those years? First, second, or third grades?"

"The worst thing," Gary said, recovering himself slightly. "OK, one, I was playing with matches in the back of a garage, and I burned the garage down."

"Burning the garage, that's a big event. Was this in Pocatello?"

"That was in Pocatello, somewhere close to our house. I ran and hid in the basement."

"Did the garage actually burn down?"

"I don't know. I heard the fire engines and stuff, but I was in the basement . . . I think somebody saw me come out. I don't know if I got a spanking for it or not."

"Do you recall setting the fire?"

"Yes."

"Did you set other fires?"

"Later on, I started one fire in . . . another fire over in Long Lake, my grandfather had some property. A grass fire."

"How old were you then?"

"Fourteen, I think, maybe. Thirteen or fourteen."

"And why did you set that fire?"

"Just playing with matches."

"By this time, your difficulties in learning were bothering you?"

"Uh-huh."

"In what way did they affect you?"

"Well they . . . they were . . . I went to a psychologist or somebody, and they tried to hypnotize me and that didn't work."

"Why did they try and hypnotize you?"

"To find out why I couldn't read and why I couldn't write and I guess that . . ."

"Just an approach to diagnosis for reading problems?"

"Uh-huh."

"I never heard that one before," Wheeler said.

"And why I kept on coming up with 'I don't know, I don't know.'"

"That would be your answer to everything, 'I don't know'?"

"Not that . . . they came right . . . they wanted to put me . . . they did want to put me in a special program called Woods . . . Woodside?"

Gary was crying again.

"Woodside, that's in Seattle, isn't it?"

"Uh-huh."

"Isn't that a special ed program?"

"Uh-huh. It was for . . ."

"You're crying as you remember that," Wheeler said. "Why are you crying?"

"Because I didn't want to go."

"Why was that?"

"That was a school everybody made fun of."

"So this was . . . you were already a kid that was getting sort of singled out as a slow learner, and this was just gonna, like, put a badge on your head that says 'slow learner'?"

"Uh-huh, and when the buses come by, a kid I knew in the fourth grade, he was put in that bus, and every time it came by, everybody else I was with made fun of it and the people in there."

"'The retards'?"

"The retarded people," Gary agreed.

"Were you being made fun of in that way?"

"Um . . . not really . . . I just . . . I wasn't being made fun of. Sometimes I was but it wasn't that much, and I just barely sneaked through to graduate."

"So you aren't being taunted or teased or singled out, but you just felt like . . . you felt slow compared to the other kids?"

"Uh-huh."

"Did that bother you at all?"

"It bothered me a lot. I wouldn't answer questions because sometimes I'd say the wrong thing, and they'd laugh, or you weren't reading your book right so I never answered any questions [in class]. I kept to myself all the time, in that way."

It was especially hard, Gary said, because Greg was so much better of a student than he was. Gary thought his mother and father favored Greg.

"How would they favor Greg?"

"They didn't show it too much, but he would . . . it used to be we always got clothes that was handed down, which it didn't bother me, they were clothes, but I'd go to school and, 'you're not like your brother.'"

"Who would say, 'you're not like your brother'?"

"Teachers."

"Oh, so they would compare your . . . was your brother a better student?"

"Uh-huh."

"And so they would kind of point out to you that you were slower than your brother?"

"Uh-huh."

"And how would you feel when that happened? Did that bother you?"

"Yeah, it bothered me I couldn't make it up to his standards . . ." Gary started crying again. "But I just, you know, brushed it off. I didn't try to keep a grudge or anything. Get by, get out of school."

"It doesn't cause you to feel resentful or angry?"

"Yeah, it . . . a little bit angry, but it didn't last."

"What was the anger? Describe that."

"Just the anger of not being able to be like my older brother."

"When you were killing women, did you ever wonder what your parents would think about you, when they discovered or learned that you were killing all these women?"

"They would probably deny it. They would probably . . . probably deny it all the way."

"So you thought they would never believe it was true, even if you were caught? Did you ever think about the possibility that you might get caught and that you would have to have . . . and that your parents would learn that you were a serial killer?"

"Well, I think . . . thank God they're dead, right? Because it . . . it'd bother me. Would bother me a lot."

Wheeler said he believed that Gary did have some significant memory problems, although he did not believe that Gary couldn't recall the details of the first time he killed.

"OK. In addition to or aside from any memory problems, have you ever been concerned about other mental problems or psychological problems that you might have or have had?"

"Uh, might be the, um, well . . . uh, somewhere along the line, maybe a, uh, um, forget what they call it, uh, [but] tell the difference between a lie and a truth, maybe . . . that mighta been somethin' . . . But I know that's a . . . that's a problem, or is it just . . . but I don't know what . . ."

"Do you think you can't tell . . . between truth to a lie? Or do you think you sometimes just choose to lie?"

"Just choose to lie."

"OK. You believe that?"

"Yeah. I don't think it was a problem. I think it's just tryin' to make up for my memory and . . ."

"Yeah, you . . . you . . . you fake it, at times," Wheeler said, meaning that sometimes Gary lied simply to make up for the fact that he couldn't remember, or when he didn't know the correct answer.

As Wheeler delved more into Gary's past, some new details came out about Gary's adolescence. When he was sixteen or so, he had regularly exposed himself to a neighborhood teenage girl, who essentially ignored it, Gary said. This went on for about three months, while he and she watched cartoons on television together. One night, he'd rapped on her window, thinking he might convince her to come out and have sex with him, but the girl had instead called out to her father. Later, when he was confronted about this by the girl's father, Gary denied he was the one who had tapped on the window.

Around the same time, Gary said, he'd gotten angry over being rejected by another girl and had gone over to the elementary school he'd attended and broke "fifteen or twenty" windows in the school. He was arrested on the spot, and his mother and father had to pay for the damages, he recalled. He also had episodes of excessive drinking in high school and once got a negligent driving ticket after he'd piled a car into a ditch after a drinking binge. He'd broken into at least two houses and once thought about stealing a motorcycle.

Later in high school, he'd met Claudia, and his first regular sexual relationship began. By the time they were married, Gary said, they were having sex "three times a week" while Gary was on shore leave from the Navy. Wheeler called him on that one; he told Gary that the detectives who had interviewed Claudia said she'd told them that she and Gary had sex "two or three times a day."

Gary admitted that this was possible and said he thought he might have been "wearing her out" with his sexual demands.

Gary readily told Wheeler about his experiences with the prostitutes in the Philippines. Usually, Gary said, he was drunk. Sometimes he used a condom and sometimes not.

"So the brain was a little impaired?" Wheeler asked.

"The brain was a little impaired and . . . and horny and watching them dance and stuff like that. Come over and sit on your lap, rubbing me up. Turn you on, so . . ."

"Did you harm any of those women in any way?"

"No. I really liked one of them real well but I didn't bring her back."

"I appreciate that. Did you harm any of them?"

"No. No . . ."

"Were you starting to have fantasies about harming?"

"No, I didn't have any fantasies about harming them."

"How confident are you of that judgment?"

Gary said he was confident that he hadn't choked anyone in the Philippines. He then told Wheeler the beer-bottle-in-the-vagina story and said that he'd always had a fantasy about inserting objects in women. Wheeler asked if he'd done this after leaving the Navy, and Gary told him about the two rocks with the Green River victims.

Wheeler next asked Gary about all the relationships he'd had with women, not prostitutes, between his marriage to Marcia and his meeting Judith. In none of these was there any violence, Gary said.

"All right," Wheeler said. "And people's sexual desires also develop in certain ways, and there's certain things we know about them, and you know what, you don't get struck by a bolt of lightning and go out and kill a prostitute. So let's just talk about it. Just tell me . . . the truth about when you started fantasizing, the first time, about killing them. I don't know whether it was when you were in high school, or in the Philippines, or in Singapore."

"I thought it was right after all . . . the divorce with Claudia first."

"OK. So you started having fantasies about killing people after divorcing Claudia?"

"I don't think I had . . . just a touch of it."

"Just tell me what they were. What were the fantasies?"

"I might have had some kind of fantasy. I don't know where it started from."

"Just tell me what it was."

"Maybe just hurting a prostitute or something."

"Why did you have that fantasy? What caused it?"

"I don't know what caused it. 'Cause they're vulnerable and something I can do to them that I can't do to an ordinary woman."

"What did you have in mind that you could do to them that you couldn't do to an ordinary woman?"

"Hurt them in some way."

"OK. What caused you to want to hurt the prostitutes in the first place?"

"Because women hurt me and I was just . . ."

"What woman hurt you?"

"Claudia did. Marcia did."

"Do you remember having temptations, thoughts, fantasies, urges, desires, cravings to hurt prostitutes after breaking up with Marcia? Shortly after?"

"The choking of Marcia was one of the major things," Gary said.

"That turned you on, right?"

"That turned me on."

"Yeah. Did you get a hard-on doing that?"

"No, I didn't get hard-on."

"But afterwards, you incorporated that into some of your sex play with Marcia, didn't you?"

"Yeah."

"Yeah. So you would . . . you would sort of strangle her and then have sex, and that was part of your sex play, right?"

"That was a little bit of it, yeah. And to sneak up on her."

"And you enjoyed that, didn't you? You enjoyed that because it gave you a sense of, kind of control, and it really emphasized your power and her vulnerability, didn't it?"

"Uh-huh."

"So you were in charge?"

"Uh-huh."

"OK. So was it during that period of time after you strangled Marcia that you then began . . . did the fantasies generalize? Did they expand then to hurting prostitutes at that point?"

"Yeah, it expanded."

"Tell me how they expanded."

"Well, after that I wanted to have sex with a prostitute and kill her doing that."

"Say that again."

"Sex with a prostitute and kill her."

"After what? After Marcia? After you'd strangled Marcia that time?"

"After, yeah."

"OK, that's fair enough. What was the pleasure in killing?"

"Pleasure in killing is to uh, get . . . you know, be [in] control. To ha . . . have sex with 'em if I wanted afterwards, and to uh, take away uh, uh, another woman that, so she won't hurt anybody else."

"So she won't hurt anybody else?"

"Yeah, like, like uh, my ex-wives did, and everything."

"These women have nothing to do with your ex-wife. Why . . ."

"Well, they were my s . . . they were my escape goat. Uh, I couldn't kill an ordinary . . . uh, my ex-wife I couldn't kill."

"'Cause you, you'd get caught."

"'Cause then I'd get caught. I could kill a, a prostitute and have a lot less chance of . . ."

"Getting caught."

"Getting caught, 'cause uh, you know, you don't know 'em. They don't know you. They're, the police won't look as hard as they would, if it was a senator's daughter or some'n, you know? And they were uh, their life history—they, you know, they, they wander a lot and so they don't know where they're killed."

"So the pleasure in it is because you can take out the anger you felt towards Marcia."

"To, for Marcia and Claudia, and anybody else that . . ."

Killing, Gary said, was his way to get even with everyone who dumped on him.

———◊◊◊———

Wheeler wanted to know if the killing itself had made Gary feel proud.

"I know . . . I killed those women and, with my bare hands, and with a li—lig . . . [Gary tried to say the word ligature, but couldn't find it] . . . uh, ropes and everything else, that it uh, gave me the satisfaction of takin' a life, or . . ."

"Tell me about that satisfaction of taking a life. I want us to know all about that."

"Well, that made me feel uh, uh, made me feel uh, like, I guess, better after doing it, and . . ."

"What felt good?"

"Uh, the uh, the uh, um, the little fear of uh, people, you know, watchin' the prostitutes and uh, seein' if I can get one without somebody bein' seen . . . me and her. Uh, the uh, the adrenaline, maybe uh, flowin' more when I got a woman in the car, and anxious to, to kill her, and, and uh, not killing her when I first get her in the car. It had to be after I have sex. Um, hm, just that uh, just to get a, uh, another woman dead."

"Another woman dead. You mean just like a-notch-in-your-belt type of thing? To be the best serial killer of all time?"

"No, that, that wasn't in my mind. It was just that the, it might've been in my mind a little bit, but just the idea, 'cause when I start killin', just kept on killing. Wanted sex and, and it was easy and, and uh, I didn't have no morals and everything, so that didn't, conscience didn't stop me."

"Why do you think you didn't have any conscience or morals? Do you think you were born without it?"

"I . . . I had conscience and stuff back when I was younger, but after a while it, it just hardened up and it didn't happen anymore."

"Where did they go?"

"Back in my brain someplace, or, you know, some place . . ."

"What caused that?"

"Prob'ly all the uh, times people uh, kidded me uh, things I did wrong, and not knowing uh, the memory and everything just . . . I mean I was in con . . . control of my life when I was out killing, and there was nobody, nobody uh, could tell me what to do. Uh, my morals, I didn't have any remorse. Could just go out and kill one person and act pretty normal the next day, and . . . and uh, some uh, maybe I didn't even need a reason to kill a person. I finally got to a reason where hey, in . . . in the morning, I'm gonna kill somebody and, and look and look and look. And sometimes I . . . I would and, there's nobody out there, I'd, I'd wait 'til the next day, 'til I found somebody."

Wheeler suggested that they make up a list of reasons for why Gary had murdered.

"So you, you've talked about, gosh, let's see if we can make a list together, OK?"

"Oooh-K," Gary agreed.

"You help me out. My brain's getting foggy. You listed, uh, didn't wanna pay for sex, right?"

"Didn't wanna pay for sex," Gary agreed.

"You listed, mad at women."

"Mad at women," Gary nodded.

"Were you mad at your mom?"

"Not . . . not, no," Gary stammered. "It's . . . she was, just uh, during that time she was just. There was nothing . . . mad a . . . mad about her."

"So this mad, being angry at women, how does that, how is that becoming, in your mind, how does that affect your killing when . . . aren't, aren't your mom and Judith the two most important women in your life?"

"Um-hm."

"So maybe I ought to be thinking that what you were doing was getting back at them?"

"But if that was it," Gary said, "then why did I stop it?"

"Well, I guess I have an open mind on that question, if you want to be perfectly . . ." Wheeler meant he wasn't ready to believe that Gary really *had* stopped killing in 1985.

"Um-hm."

"If you want me to be perfectly honest," Wheeler finished.

"Yeah," Gary said. "Well, for one thing, Judith cared."

Wheeler went back to his list making.

"So you've said, not wanting to pay for sex . . ."

"Not wanting to pay for sex," Gary agreed again.

"Anger at women."

"Anger at women."

"What are the others?"

"Uh," Gary said, "once I got into it, I couldn't, couldn't uh, couldn't stop."

"OK. You became compulsive, in the sense that it felt really, really good?"

"It felt really good to . . . um . . . uh, they couldn't hurt anybody else. I don't know if that would be uh, that wouldn't be in there. Uh . . ."

"Gary, they couldn't hurt anybody else. These women had never hurt *you*. You keep sayin' they couldn't hurt anybody else. Jesus, it was you who killed them. To listen to you, you'd think it was *them* who killed *you*. What do you mean when you say they couldn't hurt any . . ."

"Well . . ."

"Is that, is that just something that you've picked . . . have you been reading some true crime magazine, or something, to pick that up?"

"No, I just . . ."

"Well, what? . . ."

"I just, uh, just said it because it's, it . . ."

"Came into your head?"

"And . . ." Gary started, but Wheeler cut him off.

"I mean, Christ, we've been here for like, God knows forever. Can you tell me one or two things that are truthful?"

"I thought those things there, were, were truthful that I told you about, other than couldn't hurt anybody else. But . . ."

"So that wasn't truthful."

"That wasn't . . . that wasn't truthful. That's just some'n I, that came into my mouth—it came out."

"OK. Yeah, I appreciate that. It's . . . is it true that that was not truthful?"

"That's n—not truthful, yes," Gary said.

"All right. So, so that one's off the table. So where does the 'angry at women' one stand? Is that on the table or off the table?"

"Um, that'd be, that'd still be . . . I'm still angry, still angry at women. Maybe it should be narrowed down to my ex-wife and . . ."

"She must be a powerful lady. Which ex-wife? You have . . ."

"Two of 'em."

"Two of 'em. Which one? Which one's the . . ."

"Marcia."

"So she was one powerful lady."

"She has a lot of control over me, you know? Wanting more child support . . . wanted . . ."

"Now you're saying she turned you into the world's most prolific serial killer."

Gary started backing off from this.

"Isn't it sort of ironic that she took all the control?" Wheeler asked.

"Well, maybe I'm just usin' her as an escape goat for it. I don't know . . ."

"OK. So you didn't wanna pay for sex. You were angry at women. You got, you got, once you got started it was just too much fun to stop. What other reasons?"

"Think that's, that's it, I think."

"What does, what does the fact that you're saying that one of the reasons you killed sixty-three women was because you were too cheap to pay for sex? What does that say about you as a human being?"

"It says that, uh, money was more valuable than, uh, a woman."

"Yeah, that says, apparently, that tells us something about your economics. But what I'm asking you is, what does it say about you as a human being?"

"What it says is, it's, uh, I'm a, I'm a killer. Um, I'd rather kill a woman, not, not to have sex with, or not to, uh, pay for sex. Um . . ."

"Do you remember when I asked you earlier today if you thought you had ever had any psychological problems or mental problems?"

"Yeah, I said I did have, I think I do have some."

"So what I'm asking you now is, do you think the fact that you're too cheap to pay for sex and therefore found it easier to kill women reflects a mental or psychological problem?"

"Yes, it does."

"What is the problem?"

"Just com . . . comes down to the, uh, I just loved killin' women, maybe. Money didn't . . ."

"You just said, it comes down to 'I love killing women.' Right? Would I be correct to believe that you have cravings to kill women, desires, thoughts about killing women, urges to kill women, that have continued through the 1990s?"

"I'd tell ya you're wrong. I'd, I'd tell ya that uh, I stopped . . ."

"I'm not asking whether you stopped . . . you just told me, 'I love killing women.'"

"I love killing women . . . then."

"You didn't say 'I love killing women *then*.'"

"Yeah," Gary said, and it was evident to everyone that whatever it was that drove Gary to kill women was still in there.

Afterward, Tony approached Wheeler. Tony asked if Wheeler had seen the "bad Gary session," in which Gary seemed to be trying to channel "old Gary."

"Now, I'm not tryin' to tell you it was a split personality, like the Four Faces of Eve and all that," Tony told Wheeler. "But, uh, he just . . . put on a wingding for about forty-five minutes, the likes of which I've never seen."

"That's what I think is bull," Wheeler told Tony.

36

When we finally finished on the first day of Wheeler, Baird and Mullinax approached us.

"We want to shake things up with your client," Baird said, "and we'd like you guys to go along with it."

"What do you have planned?" Todd wanted to know.

"We think Gary is getting way too much enjoyment out of the field trips," Mullinax said. "And we're not getting anything, which is starting to get on everyone's nerves. I mean, those guys [the Diggers and Whackers] are going out there and working their asses off, and they're not finding anything. So we're going to take his field trips away from him. Not permanently, just temporarily. But we'd ask you not to tell him the plan."

I looked at Todd. We had previously agreed to turn up the heat on Gary ourselves and cooperate with any strategies or tactics, within reason, that the state wanted to try. After all, we wanted them to verify Gary's story as much as they did.

"Sure," I said. "We can go along with that." Todd nodded his agreement.

"OK," Baird said. "Tomorrow morning, we'd like you here at 5:30, just like we're going on a field trip. Business as usual. Just when we're about to leave, Detective Crenshaw will come up and get in Gary's face and call off the field trip."

"*Five-thirty?*" I groaned.

"Yeah." Mullinax smiled, understanding my reluctance to get up at 4:45 in the morning just for pretense. He explained, "We want to have him think he's going, which we know he likes, then yank it away from him. We want to see how he reacts. Or if he'll come up with more information in the next few days in order to get the reward of another field trip."

"OK. I'll be here," I said.

—◦◦◦—

I got to the bunker at 5:30 A.M. After a few minutes, we organized ourselves for a typical field trip. As Gary was being escorted from his room and wired for sound, one of the task force detectives who'd been with us on most of the field trips, held him up.

"Wait a second, Gary," he said.

"Uh-huh," Gary said.

"We're not leavin'," the detective told him.

"OK," Gary said.

"Not till we get the word."

"OK, we're ready," Sue Peters said.

"Oooh-K."

At that point, Rafe Crenshaw, another task force detective, one of the Diggers and Whackers, approached Gary.

"Mr. Ridgway," Crenshaw said, "I've been looking for you." Crenshaw told Gary that detectives had finally been able to check with Gary's two coworkers to verify the story that they had once found some bones near Greenwater and that they'd supposedly told him not to report them to avoid getting in trouble.

"Why did you give us those names?" Crenshaw demanded, meaning the Kenworth coworkers.

Gary again said they could verify that they'd been with him when they happened to "discover" some bones. "I forget what it was," he added.

"Well, I just got off the phone with those two guys," Crenshaw said, "and I'm not happy, because I've been wastin' my time, OK. Why are you wastin' my time? They're callin' bullshit on your story."

"What . . . what story?" Gary asked.

"They're callin' bullshit about you findin' some remains or some clothing or bones over in Greenwater."

"I did, uh . . ."

"It's a bunch of crap," Crenshaw said. "It's a bunch of crap and you know it, and you got me out here spendin' my time for nothin', right? I got a wife and kid at home I could be spendin' my time with."

"Uh, I . . ."

"The bullshit about the jewelry over on 188th Street and Military, that's bullshit, too," Crenshaw went on, referring to Gary's claims that he'd left some of the victims' jewelry in that area near a guardrail. "You wanna know why it's bullshit? Because I spent a whole fuckin' day out there diggin' fifty-one posts on that guardrail for nothin'. Is that what you want me to do, want me to waste some of *your* time?"

"That . . . that's where I put jewelry," Gary said.

"No, that's bullshit, and you know it's bullshit. Grandview Park, the big rock, I spent a day out there diggin'. Metal detector. Not one fuckin' piece of jewelry. Why? 'Cause it's bullshit, and you know it's bullshit."

"No, I don't."

"Yeah, that's bullshit. Gai's Bakery, I spent a whole day in that guy's yard with a metal detector lookin' for jewelry. Bullshit . . . more bullshit you're tellin' us."

"It's not bullshit."

"It's bullshit, and you wanna know how I know it's bullshit? Because you can't even look at my eyes and tell me that bullshit. That's why it's bullshit, you're fuckin' lyin' to me. You got me out here spendin' day after day, followin' up your little bullshit stories."

"It's not bullshit."

"It is, it's bullshit and you fuckin' know it, and you just keep spinning a web and tellin' us another lie, and another lie. It is, it's bullshit, Grandview Park, the big rock, nothin'. Gai's Bakery, at the bottom of a tree, bullshit, nothin'. The guardrail, 188th Street, nothin'. I spent the last weekend on Kent-Des Moines Road in ninety-degree weather, choppin' down trees and clearin' brush and brush . . . why? 'Cause another one of your bullshit stories. There's no fuckin' body out there. You know what we found?"

"What?"

"We found a skeleton of a possum, little bitty possum's skeleton, that's it. No body, no skull. Why, because you're bullshittin' us, you're tellin' everybody a fuckin' lie, and you feel like once you started to lie, [you] gotta continue with it. You're not goin' anywhere. Take his ass back to his fuckin' cell, and when you wanna start tellin' the truth, you let us know. That's it, you're not goin' nowhere today."

Gary mumbled something inaudible.

"That's it, I don't wanna hear it, I don't wanna hear it, go back."

"Gary," said the other detective, "let's go . . . let's go back."

"'K," Gary said, thoroughly subdued.

They stripped Gary of the sound equipment and put him back in his closet. Nothing more happened that day, and Gary was left alone to ruminate.

―᠆ᨆ᠆―

The next day, Wednesday, July 2, Wheeler was back. Wheeler wanted to find out why Gary was having so much trouble telling where he'd left his victims. He suggested that Gary wanted to keep these secrets because they were "his," as if they were prized possessions.

"Why was it important for you to know that, that that was a body, that there was a body there that you knew about that you had killed? In what way was that important to you, to be able to, to know that, to have that?"

"Um, just memories of uh, when I was out killin' women."

"So it brought back those pleasant memories of killing?"

"Well, it was pleasant, and sometimes it turned into nightmares over . . . I remember always havin' dreams about putting some person someplace and looking for it and I never could find it . . ."

"So you were worried about the possibility that you might put a body and then not remember where to find it?"

"Yeah, that's . . . and several times I looked and I couldn't find bodies."

"And why was that so troubling to you?"

"I lost her. I lost, I lost . . ."

"You lost . . . you lost possession?"

"Possession," Gary agreed. "Lost . . . um, thing that bothers me now, [is] going out to lookin' for 'em . . . and they're not there . . ."

"So you kinda miss them. Is that right?"

"Yeah. I miss 'em, and . . . I get visions in my eye where I put 'em, and, and they're not there."

"Tell me, when you say you miss them, tell me what you mean."

"I miss the, the power, the uh, knowing I killed a woman there, pu . . . uh, put her there . . . I worry they get, they get found and they get taken away and they wouldn't be where I put 'em."

"And how would that affect you if that happened?"

"Well, I lost one a my . . . victims . . ."

"And so that . . . tell me more about why that . . . was painful to you to think about, losing one of 'em."

"I'm just painful more now than then, but it is painful because I lost a . . . maybe a part a me that's . . . for years . . . I always thought she was there and, and she's not there."

"So this was somebody that became a part of who you were."

"Yeah. Somebody that, I don't know, a, a woman just was uh, meant some'n to me, uh, as . . ."

"Go ahead, tell me."

"As somebody I killed . . ."

"What did she mean to you?"

"She meant . . . a beautiful person that was my property, my . . . my uh, possession. Some'n only I knew and, and I missed when they were found or wh—where I lost 'em."

"How did you feel back . . . in the '80s when the bodies were found and taken away, those times when they were discovered? How did that feel?"

"It felt like they were takin' some'n, some'n a mine that I put there."

"It's almost like they were stealing from you?"

"Yeah, they, they found 'em and I, I couldn't . . . couldn't . . . have that feeling and, of them . . . being where I put 'em and my, my, my possession . . . my . . . my property."

"When did you first begin to want to have women become your property, the dead women? How did you come to feel that way?"

"I, I don't remember. I mean in, in, in a way, yes, Marcia was my property. Claudia was. Prob'ly before I met Claudia, maybe . . . right after I met her or some'n like that. Didn't want her to leave, so she was . . . prob'ly smothered her, or . . . and . . ."

"So you smothered the body?"

"Yeah, I smothered, in a way of not wanting anybody else to have her. The same way with Marcia. She was my, my property."

"I'm just curious again," Wheeler said. "I think I asked you about this, but I don't remember what the outcome was. It occurred to me that given how easy it was becoming for you to kill women and have sex with them and that you knew that you were going to be doing it again—what was it about having sex with a dead body that you preferred, over just going out and getting another woman to kill?"

"Well, one thing, you'd have to pay for it, and she was already dead," Gary said. In other words, it was more trouble—and riskier—to find another victim than to simply return to the last person killed.

"But you would have got the money back from the next woman, because you weren't paying," Wheeler pointed out. "Were you experiencing really, *really* strong, horny urges to go back and have sex with them? Or were you just really, like thinking, getting all hot and bothered thinking about the women and the bodies?"

"No, it was kind of getting to me, and I tried to get the urge out by putting the bodies out further and further. I mean . . ."

"How do you mean, it was getting to you?"

"'Cause I felt it wasn't right, and then the cold body didn't turn me on as much as a . . . a woman warm . . . a warm body to have sex with," Gary said.

In other words, Gary got no perverted satisfaction from having sex with the dead. It was just less bother, not his preference.

Later, Wheeler tried to get Gary to explain why he'd let the body of Wendy Coffield float down the stream, rather than weighting her down with rocks.

"Let's just stay on Coffield," Wheeler told him. "I'm not trying to walk you into some sort of trap. I'm trying to get you just to tell me what your thoughts and feelings are. If you push Coffield down the stream . . . it would seem like this wasn't one you were putting somewhere where you could keep and go back and visit. That's what I'm wondering."

"I realized I had a problem killing, and in one way I wanted her to be found, but in another way I was mixed up. I wanted her to be found so . . . to help me stop but it didn't help me at all."

"Tell me how you would remember that. That you wanted her to be found, to help you stop."

"Well, I pushed her towards . . . within a couple hundred yards from the bridge and knowing that she'd be . . . get hung up there or something like that."

"Why did you want her to be found?"

"Because a little bit, I wanted to quit and another I wanted to be caught, because I had a little bit of a conscience, and I knew it was wrong but I still killed. I didn't really care for myself. I just had the feeling that something's going to stop me, because I'm doing wrong. I'm fighting inside my head, of killing them. On the other hand, wanted to be caught. Wanted them to be found. Wanted to be caught, but then I *didn't* want to be caught."

Gary said he thought his urges to kill came from pressures, particularly at work. He thought he'd been taken advantage of—that, as he had repeatedly said over the past two years, he didn't stand up for himself.

"How were you getting taken advantage of at work?"

"Well, I'd be put on a different shift and be on there for . . . what they told me on Halloween of '83, you can either go on night shift or you can quit . . . and it was an alternative. You go on night shift or you quit. So I went on there with another lady who was supposed to go on there for a couple months, and as soon as she got on there, she was on there for one month, and I got stuck on there for two years or three years or something like that."

"So you were angry?"

"Angry at her . . . angry at her for having . . . women getting told to get on night shift and then they are only on there for one month, and then a guy gets put on days and they get a little better . . . get a little bit better job preference."

"Why were you angry at them rather than the person who put them on there?"

"Well, she was a woman and I didn't have no control over men. I had control over prostitutes and women. Not over women at work, but prostitutes, so I could . . ."

"But why were you angry at the woman at work. She was just doing what she was told the same way you were, wasn't she?"

"Yeah, but here I go and get stuck on there for . . . and then she comes off [nights] within a month, which made me mad, because we were both told to go on nights."

"Well, I can see why that made you mad," Wheeler said. "What I don't understand is why didn't it make you mad at the person who did the shift scheduling? She wasn't the person who scheduled the shifts, was she? She was just someone like you who was getting told when she had to work."

"Yeah, but she was a woman and that's what . . . yeah. Women that take advantage of people and me."

Gary seemed to be saying that he resented it when he perceived that women used their sexual allure to get advantages.

"And wreck the system," he added. "Work the system."

"Are you saying that by this point in your life, your mind was so shaped in a certain direction that you just hated women and felt that all women took advantage of you?"

"Yeah. Yeah, that's . . . they took . . . they had women down there . . . some women always took advantage of the situations and schedule things to make it easy on them and make it harder on the guys. It was my way of getting back at women."

"Was to kill the prostitutes?"

"Kill prostitutes," Gary agreed. To get even with women generally.

—∿∿—

In the next session, Gary continued to insist that he'd stopped killing women after meeting Judith in early 1985. Wheeler made it clear that he still didn't believe him. He tried to get Gary to explain what was in his mind when he supposedly stopped killing. Gary soon admitted that he'd had urges to kill women after he'd supposedly stopped, especially the prostitutes that he continued to frequent. Wheeler zeroed in on Gary's admission that he'd still had the urge to kill after 1985.

"Tell me about . . . what the urge was. What was the circumstances?"

"Here's . . . here's a woman in my car," Gary said, trying to re-create the mood that led to the urges. "Here I have the ability to take her out and kill her."

"So you're thinking that? 'I've got that power?'"

"I've got the power to do it. I have the power not to do it too . . . the power not to do it was stronger than the power to do it and to ruin my . . . get caught, a witness or something like that and to ruin what I worked into a nice house. It's paid for, everything's paid for, I don't want this over my shoulder. I want to get this out. I want . . . I don't want to get caught. I want to be . . . retired and never get caught. And if I do this, I'm going to get caught. Eventually, I'm going to get caught. Somebody's going to escape again or something."

Gary said he resisted the urge to murder because he didn't want to lose everything he'd built up with Judith.

"So you're really doing . . . people in my business have a fancy name for that," Wheeler told him. "We call it *cognitive restructuring*, self-talk. So you're trying to talk to yourself, and you're saying, 'Gary, if you act on this urge, lots of bad things are going to happen. You've worked really hard to get a good life. Got a house paid off. Looking forward to retirement. Got a wife I love, and by God, if you slip back into the old ways, sooner or later they're going to catch up with you.'"

"Uh-huh. 'Cause I always thought that I wouldn't get caught, until new technology comes in and . . ."

"You were paying attention to what technological developments were?"

"Everybody is," Gary said. "Reading books and stuff like that. And then . . ."

"So you were worried about that? OK."

"Uh-huh. But the deal is I had . . . I had everything to win by not killing than by killing. Sure, I get satisfaction out of it, in killing, but I'm gonna get caught. I'm scot-free. Why take the chance and kill somebody, when you've gone for a streak like this and then go back into killing? And then, those pimps out there, they don't give a shit. They'll kill ya, they'll beat you up and do anything they want with ya, and they'll get away with it. Cops, they always got boundaries. They can't beat ya up."

Wheeler said he still thought Gary had been unable to resist the urge to kill after taking up with Judith.

"I don't remember killing any," Gary said. This, of course, was somewhat short of a firm denial. "I never . . . I don't remember going back and killing anybody after '87. I had much more to lose. I had a house, a family and everything, and I didn't have no reason to go back. Sure, I've had problems, but I had Judith as an anchor to watch me, still. I still had problems with prostitution, but that's . . . going back and killing, it wouldn't help me. I've got a space there where I beat the Green River Task Force. And they're putting all their efforts into trying to find more killings I did since '87, let's say '87, and they're spinning their wheels, and here I am sitting back sort of seeing prostitutes and everything, but not . . . not killing. I didn't have an urge to kill. A little bit of an urge but still it . . . I didn't."

Wheeler tried to convince Gary that the urge to kill was so deeply implanted in Gary's mind that he couldn't possibly have resisted it. He asked Gary if he'd ever given a pet dog a treat. He asked Gary how the dog had acted when Gary held out his hand with the treat concealed.

"Waggin' his tail," Gary said.

"Do you see the connection between the illustration with the dog and the sex and the killing?"

"Uh-huh."

"And you make that leap for me? Tell me what the connection is I'm drawing for you."

"Well, the connection of the dog wanting food and something as a woman, with sex . . . women go hand in hand with sex."

"Well I made that a little too . . . a little more complicated than I should of, and it wasn't the best example. So let me try and see if I can break it down. Your dog learned to expect food when you acted in a certain way, and he acted as though he was gonna get food, right?"

"Uh-huh."

"And the exact same thing happens when you went out with prostitutes, OK. That's just like the situation with your dog when he's expecting food. You went and put yourself back into the exact same situation where you had killed some fifty, sixty, sixty-three women before, right?"

"Right."

"It is not possible that you had no urges or temptations? Do you know what the temptation . . ."

"Yeah."

Wheeler slammed his fist down on the table, hard.

"You blinked," Wheeler said.

"Uh-huh."

"You could not *not* blink."

"Right."

"OK, because it's a reflex."

"Uh-huh."

"It happens . . . your brain is not involved."

"Right."

Wheeler said that Gary's instinct was to kill the women he picked up and that this instinct was so ingrained that he would always have it, Judith or no Judith. Gary again denied that he'd killed anyone after 1985.

"I'm not talking about killing them," Wheeler said. "I'm talking about *the urge* to kill them, Gary."

"I had the urge to kill, yeah."

"So . . . you're saying, 'I had the urge to kill but I didn't do it?'"

"Yeah."

"You didn't kill."

"I didn't kill."

"So you had to do something to resist that urge, right?"

"Yes."

"What did you do to resist the urge?"

"I . . . I don't know what I did to resist. You know, it was some special thing. I just didn't want to kill anymore. I wanted to have sex, pay for sex. It was just because I didn't want to ruin the sex I had with my wife, and it was . . . and if I did kill, I would tell. There's no . . . I've killed sixty-four, what's wrong with telling if I killed another thirty? There's . . . it's not going to hurt me to tell if I killed them, but if I didn't, why am I going . . . why am I trying to hide any that I killed in the nineties?"

By now, it was obvious that Gary never did have a good grip on exactly how many people he'd really killed. The number kept shifting—forty-eight, fifty, sixty, sixty-three, sixty-four. Who knew?

"All right," Wheeler said. "Why would you, maybe, *not* give up the information?"

"I don't know that there would be any reason why I wouldn't. There's nothing gained by it. If I give out that information, I get the deal. I don't give it out, then I don't get the deal."

"You're right about that, which should be of great concern," Wheeler told him.

"It is a great concern to me," Gary admitted.

"So why would somebody facing that very high risk that you're facing, why would that person not give out that information? What would be more important to that person than giving up the information?"

"Well . . . more . . . the guy is probably stupid and wants to keep his possessions. That would be one. That would be stupid."

"Bingo," Wheeler said.

"If I had them, I would give them up. That's why I'm here for."

"Unless you were wanting to be stupid and hold on to your possessions."

"That would be the stupidest thing for somebody to do," Gary said.

"Well, you know, sometimes people do the stupidest things."

"I know a lot of people do the stupidest things," Gary said. "But if I had that information, I would give it up. You know, they always think I've done all these others, but . . . it's stupid for me not to give them up, if I did them. Now, if that's a stereotypical . . . [that] every serial killer never stops killing, then I'm one of the . . . I'm lying to you about . . . anybody I killed in the nineties. I don't remember killing anybody in the nineties, is my position. I'm letting you have what I've got, and if I don't get this deal, I don't care. It's going to be off my conscience that I gave up everyone that I killed. If they say . . . if they say I'm a serial killer, never stopped, well, if I didn't kill in 2000, and 1990s, then there's going to be bodies. . . . It's not going to be mine. I've given everybody a note there, of where I put them at the time. I didn't kill any in the nineties. I don't recollect killing them in the nineties."

"You don't recollect killing them or you didn't kill any?"

"As far as I know, I didn't kill anybody."

"You can't control the fact that you've got urges to kill," Wheeler said, "and you can't control the fact that you would have some relapses. And all I'm asking you to do is to get moving quickly and get some of that stuff out, so you can get to where you say you want to go. . . . Do you want to think about whether you want to do that or not?"

"I've been thinking about it," Gary said.

"Do you know what you want to do?"

"I think I'm trapped in a corner. I'm thinking that . . . maybe . . . I thought that I stopped in the eighties. I know they think . . . maybe I should go . . . and everyone of these, they say, 'well, this could be yours.' 'OK, that's mine.' Should I go ahead and start volunteering and say I killed all these women, just to get the deal? I get pressured . . . my back against the wall, and if I'm telling you all along that I didn't kill, but you think I did kill, then maybe I should just go the opposite and just lie and say I killed all of them out there. When they come up and say, 'Hey, have you killed this one? That looks good enough.' They'll believe me, because they don't believe me of *not* killing them."

"Well, I think you're feeling a little bit sorry for yourself right now," Wheeler said.

"No, I'm feeling a little bit pressured into the corner. They do not believe me. I stopped and if I did relapse, then I'd tell them, if I did relapse."

But Wheeler was obviously skeptical and eventually got Gary to admit that he'd even had the urge to kill *Judith*. Wheeler said that only proved his point: the urge never really went away.

Wheeler suggested that Gary was keeping the later murders back so that Judith wouldn't know that he'd been killing after their marriage—that he was trying to protect her feelings.

"The hard question I refer to is, let's assume for the sake of discussion that there were some murders that occurred after 1987."

"Uh-huh."

"She's gonna find out about those too, correct?"

"She'll find out, but it . . ."

"I'm just hypothetically, I mean she'll . . . she's gonna find out, right?"

"All I know is, I was seeing prostitutes, that's all I know. I mean, I don't remember killing any more."

37

The following morning, July 3, we gave Wheeler our list of sixty-three possible places where Gary thought evidence might be found, including a number of locations where Gary had said he'd left victims or property of victims before 1985. The list wasn't exact, because Gary sometimes confused victims; some of them, we told Wheeler, might have been counted twice. We hoped that the list would help Wheeler jog Gary's memory.

After lunch, Jensen approached Todd and me before the new interrogation session.

"Remember when we went out to Highway 410 a couple weeks ago, and Gary pointed out the one we called 'Loop Road Lady' and the one up the logging road by the stump, 'Logging Road Lady,' or whatever?" Jensen asked.

"Yeah," I replied, curious about where he was going with this. "What's up?"

"Well," Jensen continued, ". . . he nailed both of those, perfect. I mean, he pointed right at the spots where remains were found." I understood that Jensen was referring to victims that had been found years earlier, not the missing that everyone was so anxious for Gary to pinpoint.

"That's good," I said, thinking that meant Gary was being honest and his memory was damn accurate, at least as to known Green River murders. But Tom had a weird look on his face, so I asked, "Right?"

"Yes, that's good, except . . ." Jensen obviously had something more to tell us. "Except the 'Logging Road Lady' was Roberta Hayes, and the 'Loop Road Lady' was Marta Reeves." I immediately knew what this meant: *Gary was still killing after 1985!*

"Roberta Hayes was last seen alive in 1987," Jensen went on, although I already knew what he was telling us. "Marta Reeves was last seen in 1990. Your boy may need to rethink his position on not killing after 1985. We were hoping he was going to do that yesterday with Dr. Wheeler, but he couldn't bring himself to it. I think he's thinking about Judith."

Ugh! The thoughts rushed through my weary mind. *This is bad news. That opens up the killing time frame another five years, at least, and there were quite a few Red River cases in that time frame!* I looked over to Todd. I could see his mind sorting through the possibilities, too.

"Shit," I said to Todd.

"Shit," Todd said, clearly at a loss for a more eloquent response.

"Yeah," Jensen agreed. "Shit."

"OK," I said. "What next?"

"We'd like you to keep this to yourself," Jensen said. "Let us bring it up with Gary. We're going to do that during this next session. We'd like to use it somehow, maybe see if we can get him to come clean on his murders after he was with Judith. I don't know. Hopefully, this will get him over the hump. We know he really doesn't want to hurt Judith, and that's why he probably said he stopped in '85."

"That's fine," Todd agreed. "We won't say anything to him."

"Well, the good news is that it shows he's being honest with you," I pointed out. Then I thought about it again. "That is, if you overlook the part about never killing after '85."

"We'll have to see what he says about that now. Kinda opens up a whole new can of worms, doesn't it?" Jensen said.

I had a sudden realization.

"I suppose that makes 'S.I.R. Lady' Patricia Barczak?" I asked Jensen, now remembering that Red River victim Patricia Barczak was thought to have been murdered and dumped in the woods near Seattle International Raceway sometime in 1986. Gary had admitted putting a victim near the raceway in his first interrogations, and although I knew that Patricia Barczak had been found in that vicinity,

I'd never considered that she'd been the victim Gary was talking about. After all, I knew that Patricia Barczak had disappeared in 1986, which was after 1985. I found myself wishing that I'd pressed Gary harder on the "SIR Lady" before we'd made our proffer. "Yes," Jensen said. So that meant at least three victims after 1985, including one in 1990. And it also meant there were probably more than that.

When the afternoon session started, Wheeler tried to convince Gary that he'd had a "relapse" in 1990. Jensen had tipped Wheeler off that Gary had pinpointed the locations of two post-1985 victims, so Wheeler increased his pressure.

"But I . . . told you that, generally, when people are trying to break a habit . . . they have slipups, they fall back for periods of time," Wheeler said.

"Um-hm."

"So I'm just giving you an opportunity now, if you want, to take advantage of it. Before the detectives come in, to talk about what might've been going on with you in 1990, and if you want to talk about any relapse."

"Uh, I don't remember any relapse in '90, so . . . it's a, big surprise to me. I mean, I . . ."

"Do you have any recollection? . . ."

"I don't have any recollection . . ."

Jensen now entered the interrogation room with a map that Gary had drawn for the task force a few days before, accompanied by Sue Peters.

"OK," Jensen said, showing Gary the map. "Remember drawing that map?"

"Yes, I remember this map, yeah."

"Remember when you drew it?"

"Just a couple days ago. I don't know what, uh, no date on it . . . just a couple days ago."

"All right. OK," Jensen said. "And on that map you've located, possibly what, how many victims at uh, Highway 410?"

"Uh, one, two, three, four, five, six, seven, eight or, eight or nine."

"OK. We're here to tell you that we have recovered bodies at two of those sites that are not on the Green River list."

Gary said nothing to this.

"This one here we have found," Jensen said, pointing to one of Gary's markings on the map.

"Oh, yeah?"

"We found her quite some time ago. This one *here* we found," Jensen said, pointing to another marking.

"Um-hm."

"OK? This lady right here is named Marta Reeves."

"Yes."

"She disappeared in 1990."

"OK," Gary said, "then I killed her then, yeah. I, I agree, I killed a woman there, yes. But I thought it was in '87, '87 or '88 . . . I, I admit getting a, killing a woman there."

Sue Peters broke in.

"So are you saying today to Tom [Jensen] and me that you actually continued to kill, but you slowed down?"

"I, I slowed down, but I don't remember the, the dates. But these are the ones that are, the map is accurate of the, of the women here. But, and you know they're accurate of the, the, but the years . . ."

"Well, 1990, Gary, isn't that long ago," Peters said.

"I know it's, it's . . . yes."

"And I want you to be able to look me straight in the eye . . . and tell me that you did continue to kill after 1985. Not that you might've, or you could've. For once in your life, be honest and own up to what you did."

"I did kill after '85, yes," Gary said.

"OK. Thank you . . . now, you probably even killed some later. We have some other ones after 1990 that we can talk about later."

"Yeah, we can talk about 'em," Gary agreed.

"OK. But the first step is admitting that you continued to kill and not just, you know, 'I quit in 1985 when I was with Judith,' because we already . . . we're past that, right?"

"We're past that, yes."

———

When this session was over, Todd and I had a two-on-one with Gary.

"Gary, it's been a long day," Todd began. "Hell, it's been a long, hard, couple of weeks. We're all tired. Now this? What were you thinking?"

"Well, like I said, I had my time frames mixed up," Gary said. "I thought I stopped in '85. I wasn't lying to you guys . . . I just didn't remember."

"Gary, I can understand when you say you didn't remember victim number twenty-five as opposed to number thirty-seven," I told him. "You were killing at a pretty rapid rate then. But if you slowed down to one a year, how do you forget you committed *those* murders? I don't understand."

Gary thought for a second, looking at Todd and me, slowly shaking his head from side to side. No sheepish grin this time. He was very solemn.

"I don't know," he said. "Maybe I blocked it out somehow, or lied to myself so much, I believed it. I didn't want to . . . hurt . . . Judith . . ." His voice trailed off and he started to cry.

"Look, Gary, in one way, this is a good thing," Todd said. "It shows them you are *trying* to be honest. If you were intentionally and knowingly trying to withhold information about killing after 1985, you wouldn't have acknowledged those two out on Highway 410." Todd was verbally patting Gary on the back for trying. Then Todd changed his tone.

"But you can't hold anything else back . . . *anything!* Because if they catch you in more lies, the deal will be off, and we'll be in trial."

Gary promised us once more that he would tell the truth. Then he was shuffled off to his closet for the long weekend.

Todd and I reconvened at the Pacific Coast Brewery for more commiserating and strategizing. Because it was a three-day weekend, for Independence Day, we made a choice *not* to call Tony and ruin his own weekend with the news. We hoisted a few more than usual.

"This isn't going so well," Todd said. "I think we've been a little *too* supportive."

"I think he's doing the best he can," I said. "He certainly knows what he has to do—tell the truth. Whether or not he can do that, I don't know. But I don't know what else we can do for him beyond what we've done. He's heard it over and over again from you and Tony and me."

"I don't mean we abandon him," Todd said, shaking his head. "But let's think this through. He lies when his back is against the wall. He's proven that. He lied to you for no reason, other than he was embarrassed. He's lied in the face of the possibility of this deal falling through, and having to face the death penalty. He can't help himself. We've got to do what we can to help him get the truth out, even if it means roughing him up a bit." Todd meant verbally, of course. Not physically, although that crossed our minds, too. An absurd image flashed through my brain of Todd and I whacking Gary repeatedly with our briefcases.

With revelation of these post-1985 murders, Todd and I decided to enlist our investigator, Bettye Witherspoon, to compile a notebook with all the information we had on the forty or so Red River cases that had taken place after 1985. We had the idea that we could use this to force Gary to tell us everything he was still keeping back. We all knew that this was worse than concealing something like necrophilia out of shame and embarrassment. The I-didn't-kill-after-1985 lie was a substantive omission that opened the door to an unknown number of additional cases—and victims. If Gary couldn't tell the truth about those, the whole deal might go down the drain. All our work so far would be wasted, and the worst of it was, we'd have a very hard time resurrecting our Plan A defense—that Gary hadn't done it. Damn near impossible, in fact.

Todd and I finished our beer and headed to our homes, both of us filled with doubts and foreboding.

38

The investigators were pleased that Gary had finally admitted killing after 1985, so they decided to reward him with more field trips. We went out again on July 9 and 10, but again nothing was found. On one day in mid-July, we returned to the Kent-Des Moines Road area, the main highway tying the airport to Kent. It was our second effort at that site, where Gary was "quite certain" he'd left the body of a victim down a slope off to the side of the road.

"Why are they looking over there?" Gary asked me, nodding at the place where the Diggers and Whackers were preparing to do battle with the underbrush.

"Gary, that's where you *told* them to look," I said.

"Oh, yeah," he recalled. "But that's not right. It's really over there." He pointed to another area perhaps seventy-five yards away. "I'm quite certain."

With this new information, the searchers started in anew, but struck out once more.

After this, the interrogators took a short hiatus. Then, on July 16, Jensen, Mattsen, Mullinax, and Peters returned to question Gary.

"You miss me?" Jensen asked Gary.

"Yeah, I missed ya," Gary said, and I thought he *had,* too. Sometimes it's better the devil you know than the devil you don't know, as the old adage has it.

"Oh, OK, I feel better," Jensen told him. "I thought I'd just bring you up to speed on what's been goin' on here. We had some debates on whether we were even going to bother to do this anymore."

"Oooh-K."

"We didn't feel like we were getting very far, and some people really wanted to just cut this off. We managed to convince people that we're making a little progress, even if it was slow, and it might be worthwhile to continue doing it for just a little while, anyway."

"Oooh-K."

"So we're back and we're gonna talk to you some more."

"Oooh-K."

At the end of this session, Jensen told Todd and me that an FBI agent from their Behavioral Analysis Unit would begin interviews with Gary the following day.

This was Dr. Mary Ellen O'Toole, and by the time she was finished with Gary, twelve days had gone by—almost two weeks of my life that I would never have back and that was long enough to drive almost anyone crazy. Except Gary. Ever-polite, Gary was cooperative to a fault, allowing her to put words in his mouth as if she were feeding sugar cubes to a horse. But Gary, as Todd had long ago pointed out, really responded to women. Wanting to please them was his fondest desire and was in fact at the core of his rage against women: his need to please them was lethal—to them. In fact, he just ate it up and probably would have liked to eat O'Toole herself up, if he hadn't been manacled hand and foot.

―⁓―

In contrast to Wheeler, O'Toole seemed to spend an inordinate amount of her initial interview with Gary trying to impress him with her FBI credentials. There must have been some strategy behind her methods, but it escaped me. Where Wheeler mostly asked questions in a sort of Socratic fashion, inexorably drawing Gary forward to admissions, O'Toole told almost as much as she asked. She said that the FBI's Behavioral Analysis Unit was engaged in very important work and that not just any serial murder case was worth their attention. She did things by the FBI's "book" on serial killers, we were told. The "book" had it that certain things were *always* true about serial killers.

"One of the things that our unit does, to dispel any kind of confusion is, we, we *do* study serial crimes, serial murders, and the people that commit these crimes," O'Toole told Gary, when she began.

"However, for me to undertake a case study for our unit . . . we are not particularly interested in the number of people that someone killed. We're not interested in the most prolific serial killer. What we're interested in is behavior, the most significant behavior, the most aberrant behavior that an offender uh, engages in at a crime scene.[1] So in order for our unit to be interested in a case, um, that's, that's the type of, of information that we look for. Does that make sense to you?"

"Yes, it does," Gary said, although he'd probably followed only about half of what O'Toole had just said. Apparently, O'Toole realized this.

"Do you understand that?" she asked again.

"Um-hm." Gary nodded, seemingly placid, as usual.

"Right."

O'Toole apparently wanted to put Gary on notice that he'd really have to impress her, if he wanted the attention of the FBI—the more aberrant his behavior, the better.

"All right. In order to . . . have your offenses and you as a person . . . be, uh, interesting enough to perhaps, at some point become a case study, in the area of interest particularly for our unit, what I would need to do is to put you through . . . what I would like to refer to as a 'verification process.'"

"Um-hm."

"By that, I mean, to be able to verify certain kinds of behaviors and verify um, information about you as an offender and about the kinds of behaviors that you engaged in at a crime scene."

"Um-hm."

"All right. The way that I like to work this is, to be able to verify information relative to your crimes to make it worth our while.[2] What I would like to do, um, is to, the way I do it with other offenders, uh, is to have you, as the person who was there, walk through the crimes with me as the, as the FBI profiler in very much of a clinical sense. Does that make sense to you?" Gary nodded.

"All right," O'Toole continued, "there are four stages to a crime scene. I'm going to give you a little bit of, of a lesson in, in um, serial killing."

I looked at Todd and raised my eyebrows. She was going to give *Gary* a lesson in serial killing? Like, he needed one?

"Oooh-K."

"All right? There are four stages to a crime scene that we study, that we have been studying. Uh, the first is the uh, pre-offense behavior—what does the offender do before the crime, and part of that is the victim selection process. How does the offender select particular victims? The second part of the offense uh, is actually the crime itself. How does the offender, that would be you, how does the offender interact with the victim, how is the victim interact[ing] with the offender. Because one thing that we've known over the years is that oftentimes the offender has to change his behavior, based on the personality of the victim—what the victim does at that crime scene—at the moment that they are being assaulted. Do you understand that?"

"Um-hm."

"OK. The other stage that we look at is post-offense behavior, um, and I understand that in your case there may be a significant amount of, of uh, uh, post-offense behavior that can be discussed. Does that make sense to you?"

"It's, that's after the crime?"

"Post-offense, yes."

"OK."

"Do you understand that?"

We were only five minutes into the session, and I thought if O'Toole asked Gary if she was making any sense to him one more time, I was going to need a bucket. Watching her manipulate "our boy" was excruciating.

"Um-hm."

"Have you read any of our research on serial killers?"

"No, I haven't."

"All right, Mr. Ridgway, you're going to find that in dealing with me, I cut right to the chase. And again, I want you to uh, look at what we're talking about from your perspective. It is through your eyes that I'll be able to complete this, this [verification] process to see um, how interesting this case is."

O'Toole now suggested that Gary had to have known that "something was, not quite right with you" from an early age. Gary said yes, he knew that.

"We have what we call in our unit, Mr. Ridgway, um, uh, the 'snap theory.' Would you like for me to explain that to you?"

"Yes."

The snap theory, O'Toole told Gary, was the idea that someone completely normal could one day wake up and go off on a serial killing spree. But it had never happened, she said.

"People do not wake up at twenty years of age and at twenty-five years of age and snap and go out and commit a series of homicides or series of sexual assaults. The snap theory, Mr. Ridgway, simply does not exist."

People who became serial murderers, "in every case," O'Toole continued, had "red flags" in their childhood that were indicators of future murderous behavior.[3] These were learned behaviors, O'Toole added. She tried to connect the "red flags" to Gary's acknowledgment that he'd known something was wrong with him from an early age.

"Let me ask you this, Mr. Ridgway. At what age did you realize that there was something wrong with you?"

"Uh, what age? Prob'ly, uh, ten or so, I guess."

"And what was the red flag that you saw?"

"Well, my learning and uh, forgetting things and . . . breathing and uh, allergy problems all the time, and depression."

"OK. That's not what I'm talking about, Mr. Ridgway."

"Oh."

"Are you familiar with the term um, *paraphilic behaviors?*[4] Have you heard that term?"

I thought O'Toole might just have well asked Gary if he'd ever heard of "philatelic behaviors." For all he knew, O'Toole could have been talking about stamp collecting.

"No, I'm not," Gary admitted.

People who exhibited "paraphilic behavior," O'Toole told Gary, were people with personality disorders.

"[It] generally starts," she continued, "based on the way a person is reared. And it is my experience that . . . the mothers are very influential in how these . . . offenders, making, that would be you . . ."

"Um-hm."

"How these offenders develop and begin to develop and evolve into the kind of serial murderer that they become, and, Mr. Ridgway, I want to get right to your mother."

"Um-hm."

O'Toole now showed Gary a photograph of his mother, Mary Rita.

"That's my, that's my mother, yeah," Gary said.

"Mr. Ridgway, was your mother a prostitute?"

"No. No, she wasn't," Gary said. "She uh, worked at Penney's and she was always dressed in nice clothes, most a the time, and, and she, I don't think she ever was a prostitute."

"Let me ask you that, Mr. Ridgway, in a different way. Is it, was your mother ever involved, was your mother—in your experience with your mother from a clinical point of view—involved in activities that someone else could look at and say, came close to uh, uh, sexual promiscuity?"

"I don't, I don't know of any, no. Uh, uh, uh, no. She . . . any, any, any problem with that."

"Does this style of dress and this presentation strike you in a particular way, Mr. Ridgway?" O'Toole asked, referring to the photograph, which depicted Mary Rita in shorts.

"Well, it's pretty uh, um, it's pretty um, risqué in a way, yeah, 'cause a the short uh, pants . . . or outfit." But his mother had never gone out of her way to be sexually exhibitionistic in public, Gary indicated. And from everything that we had learned from Mary Goody's interviews with Mary Rita's family, I was sure Gary was telling the truth about that, at least. If anything, sexuality was so repressed in Gary's family as to be one of the real causes of Gary's behavior. Using the photograph of Mary Rita, taken in the privacy of the Ridgway backyard and one not much different than one that might be found in a typical family photo album, was to conclude Fact Z from Exhibit A; it was simply too large a leap. But I realized that O'Toole's perception of Gary had been colored by the assertions of Marcia in the awful search warrant affidavits. O'Toole believed that Mary Rita had to have been a prostitute (or at least a "loose woman") to account for Gary's murderous behavior. She wanted Gary to validate this as part of the "verification process."

Gary observed that his mother had been thin, as well as attractive.

"You know," he said, "in that, in the way that she was, she was a woman that just m-most men would, would want for a wife. Um, sexually-wise, you know, the uh, ideal for a woman that uh, wasn't, wasn't fat, and she was very active. And uh, and she was around men all the time in the men's department at Penney's, so she was around men all the time. And she wore . . . she got the clothes at Penney's and she wore the, the best they had, you know, uh, flaunting her uh, her figure—flaunting her figure."

O'Toole seized on this.

"And how would she do that?"

Todd and I could see Gary getting a bit flustered. As usual, his language began to deteriorate when under pressure.

"She just come, come natural, to her to uh, to uh, to, to help people and to uh, make sales, and she, she was a real good sales, salesperson."

"Um-hm," O'Toole said.

"And uh, in that process she had to uh, measure people, measure men for uh, clothes and um, and, you know, some people might ask she what, what looks good on 'em, on 'em, you know, on her, on the guy or some'n like that, so she knew uh, what looks good. She'd pick out all of our clothes for us."

Gary was trying to establish that his mother was very sharp in her fashion sense—something he thought was one of her best points.

"Um-hm," O'Toole said. "Are you telling me that she would measure men for their clothing?"

"Yeah, she had to measure the instep, uh . . ."

"The instep?"

"The waist," Gary said.

"The instep is for a shoe."

"Uh, uh, in . . . up to the pants, to the crotch."

"Um-hm."

"And I guess up to the waist, I guess. And then uh, arm length, she'd measure that."

"All right. Mr. Ridgway . . . you and I are looking at this from a perspective of attempting to understand how, in part, what may have contributed to some of your develop[ment], you appreciate that, right, Mr. Ridgway?"

"Um-hm. Yes, I do."

"As you talk about your mom and the measurements, I think you may be on to some interesting behavior. Uh, how sexually, did you, inappropriate may your mom's behavior have been with you three boys?"

"I don't think there was any at all. Uh, she was the one that um, she was the one that uh, usually set the rules and uh, my dad gave out the discipline and . . . when younger, I mean. When we were smaller, if we got a spankin', she'd give it to us, but la-later on, if we did some'n wrong, my dad would be the one that, had to wait 'til he'd come home and get a spankin', if we needed it."

"Did you see your mother naked?"

"Did I see her naked? Uh, maybe once, maybe twice. I don't remember, don't remember that part of . . . uh, it's very possible I have."

"How, how old, what was your, your, your a . . . the, the oldest that you were when your mom saw *you* naked?"

"Thirteen or fourteen, prob'ly."

"What were those circumstances?"

"Those were uh, well, about thirteen when uh, when I had to go . . . uh, when I wet the bed and had to, uh, wash off in the bathtub."

"Tell me about that."

"Well, I was still wettin' the bed about that time and uh, I'd uh, get into the bathtub and wash off, 'cause we didn't have a shower . . . and I was um uh, embarrassed about it, about wetting the bed. But uh, I just couldn't, uh . . . they went to wakin' me up at midnight to go to the bathroom, and still sometimes I'd wet the bed. I don't know, know why."

"You're in the bathtub and, to wash off, to wash the urine off?"

"Yes, in the ba . . ."

"Who was in the bathroom with you?"

"M—my mom was, and maybe my brothers would walk through, and, they needed to go to the bathroom."

"Mr. Ridgway, I think that may be significant in understanding some of what ha . . . uh, has taken place in your development. What was your mom saying to you?"

"Hm, she'd be uh, upset that I wet the bed. And uh . . ."

"Describe that, please."

"Prob'ly uh, disgraced me or, you know, um, um, yell at me for wettin' the bed."

"Keep going."

"Um, and I'd have to go back and uh, put my clothes on and um, be uh, depressed all day because a that, you know, that part."

"What would your mother say to you, her words to you?"

"She, she would uh, uh, she would say things like, uh, 'Haven't you, ha . . . haven't you grown up to not wet the bed anymore?'"

"Um-hm."

"'Why are you um, only, only bed . . . babies wet the bed,' I think, what she said sometimes."

"What else?"

"Um, I don't remember too much more about that."

"Mr. Ridgway, I would, in my experience, I would expect to hear from you that your mother said more to you, more degrading comments about this experience."

This was a prodding that had ambiguous potential outcomes: it was clear that O'Toole believed that Gary was now censoring his recollections and that through this expression of disbelief, she might get deeper into the situation. But at the same time, it had the effect of encouraging Gary to provide what the interviewer wanted, even if it wasn't necessarily true. This had been Gary's wont all through the interrogations: giving his interviewers what he perceived they wanted and expected to hear.

Typically, Gary split the difference between the two alternatives.

"I think she said, then she'd say, 'Why aren't you like the re . . . Greg, or my younger brother, they don't wet the bed.' And um, 'Why are you doin' this to uh, to, to me,' or uh, um . . . 'Haven't you learned not to we—wet the bed,' and it's a, a, 'On—only babies wet the bed.' Um, 'Aren't you gonna grow up?' Um, uh, don't remember too much, I'm thinkin' even, even uh, um, the . . . the water wasn't that hot. It was cold, you know, because it takes time for the water to warm up in the bathtub, so it was, was not comfortable to be in there."

"I wouldn't think so," O'Toole said. "Were you standing or were you sitting in the bathroom?"

"I was sitting in the bath, bathroom, uh, wash—washin' off, and it was, it was cold and uh, was shakin'. . . . And she would be, be uh, s—speakin' to me that you um, I don't know if she used 'worthless' or, but she . . . you know, she uh, degraded me, uh, uh, not that way, that, it didn't uh, didn't feel, didn't feel love. Didn't feel that much love at that time."

O'Toole tried to suggest that Gary had had an incestuous relationship with his mother, but Gary resolutely rejected that idea.

"Mr. Ridgway, when your mother was in the bathroom and you were washing off, was she ever sitting on the toilet herself going to the bathroom?"

"She, she prob'ly, she could have. Um, maybe pee'n or some'n, but I . . ."

"And you would see that?"

"Oh, she'd be covered up. Uh . . . if, if she had to go, she prob'ly did, and I'm not worried too much about that. I was worried about getting washed off and uh, I, I don't remember."

"When you were in the bathtub and you were washing off, were you sexually aroused?"

"No. I was more d—depressed, uh, than sexually aroused."

"Do you remember times when you would look at your mom and feel sexually aroused or sexually stimulated?"

"Um, some . . . yeah. A little bit, yeah."

"Tell me."

"Well, here's uh, a woman that's um, like the ones outta the um, dirty magazines, the . . . and she's got um, smooth legs, smooth uh, figure and breasts, tight skin, um, uh, just uh, soft, soft uh, soft . . . type a woman. Uh, some'n sexual, some'n that's, could turn somebody on, turn me on a little bit."

"Keep going."

"Some'n um, that is uh, I li—like to, like to touch and feel and . . . um, to uh, experience with. Um, some . . . uh, maybe even have sex with her. Um, just some, just a uh, the opposite sex . . . just turn me on."

"Keep going," she said.

"Some'n to uh, have my first uh, experience with a, with a woman."

"Was with your mom?"

"That's what I thought, yeah."

"Tell me about that."

"Ju—ju . . . that she was a, a female, the opposite sex, and, and a, a woman that I'd like to of, um, been my f—first uh, sex partner. Um, somebody that uh, that was a, a, an ideal body and, and uh, right, the right padding and the right um, uh . . . physical characters of a . . . of a woman that'd be ideal to have sex with. Um, and I think it's almost about all, I think."

"What were the experiences . . . and I'm going from my . . . my background and my training and . . . and from listening to you. What were those experiences when you . . . you and your mom were in a situation that had a lot of sexual overtones to it? What were those situations like?"

"Uh, the sexual overtones, uh, I . . . I don't know if there was very many of 'em. I don't remember," Gary said.

39

The main trouble with O'Toole's approach to Gary, as far as I could see, was that she didn't know everything we knew about Gary's family and his upbringing. It appeared she didn't know about the early pregnancy, the difficult poverty, the strong Catholic morality, the absence of early medical care, or any of a host of other vital background facts that were necessary to understand the context of what she was learning from Gary. She apparently knew nothing about Gary's neurological deficits, which may have had something to do with his protracted bed-wetting. She knew nothing of his dyslexia or his speech problems, or any other organic brain damage, his below-normal intelligence, or his troubles with words. As to her "cutting to the chase," as she put it, Todd and I felt that O'Toole missed a large part of the plot.

Lost in the operation was any understanding of the broader context of Gary's development. And O'Toole had an enormous advantage— Gary *had* to answer her questions if he wanted to keep the deal alive. In some ways, it was shooting fish in a barrel for O'Toole: any admission by Gary was taken as truth, any denial as lying. I couldn't help but wonder how most people would stand up to similar probing under those conditions. Even Gary's admission that he was sexually attracted to his mother (not the sort of thing that most people would acknowledge because of the obvious social taboos) was seen as more evidence of paraphilia, when in fact Gary was simply trying to honestly answer O'Toole's pregnant question.

When O'Toole became available to do her interviews with Gary, everyone on the task force took great pains to suggest to him—and to us, his lawyers—that she was very, very important. They would tell us she wasn't in Seattle solely for the purpose of interviewing Gary or because of Gary's infamous deeds. No, we were just lucky that she was able to spare some time and drop by to help the locals.

It was hard for Todd and me to take. We both believed it was all an act, scripted in the hopes of getting Gary to reveal more details—that if he wanted her approval as someone worth her time, he'd "remember" more.

O'Toole's *m.o.* seemed to be to sit next to Gary, inching closer and closer as each of the interminable interviews progressed. She would stare into his eyes, and he would stare back. "Gaze" might be a better description of the way they looked into each other's eyes. From time to time, O'Toole would place her hand on Gary's arm as she locked eyeballs with him. From our vantage point to the side, Todd and I could see when their legs would actually be touching under the table. She was obviously entering Gary's personal space intentionally as part of her interview tactics.

As noted, O'Toole spent an abundance of her time telling Gary that the FBI profiling group, known as the Behavioral Analysis Unit, was the best in the world in studying and researching serial murders. But they were only interested in the "most impressive" serial killers. She would attempt to get Gary to reveal torture, dismemberment, cannibalism—something that would make him impressive enough, worthy of study by the FBI, who were, by the way, the smartest and best when it came to studying serial killers. But try as he might, Gary couldn't get himself to admit to any of the "very impressive" things the FBI wanted to hear.

At one point, O'Toole asked Gary, "Mr. Ridgway, on a scale of 1 to 5, with 1 being the least impressive and 5 being the most impressive, where do you put yourself?"

Gary reflected for a moment.

"Oh, a 3, I guess."

Todd and I looked at each other with a look of disbelief. *C'mon Gary . . . More victims than anyone! Not caught for twenty years! A 3?*

I passed Todd a note that read simply, "5."

Todd wrote back, "*very* impressive."

Presumably, there was a method to her madness. She must have used the same tried-and-true interview techniques on other serial murderers. But in this case, it was as difficult to watch as it seemed—to Todd and me—to be ineffective. All she demonstrated was that perhaps better than anyone else, she could get Gary to confess to a lot of things, even if he hadn't done them. And that was at the heart of the problem the task force was trying to sort out. Which of these ongoing confessions was real? Was he confessing to murders he hadn't actually committed? I wondered if, in some ways, her approach may have even hindered the process, putting ideas in Gary's mind, words in his mouth.

In her relentless search for paraphilia, O'Toole kept unearthing new incidents of aberrant behavior. It was as if by piling up the incidents, the point was proved; but, of course, it said little about the origin of the behavior. In my mind, all that was really established was that Gary was a nasty, tricky little boy who'd grown up to be a nasty, tricky, messed-up man.

The hot, dry summer continued, setting records for temperatures and lack of rainfall. It was odd. On some days, at 3:45 in the morning, I'd be out in the woods with my client, as he was describing another murder and pointing the detectives to another location, where he'd left a body twenty years earlier. By seven, I was on the deck of our summer swim club, Kent Swim and Tennis Club (KSTC), coaching boys and girls from ages five to eighteen through their morning workouts.

The six-lane, outdoor pool is nestled between two parks and an elementary school, with woods to the east and west. One of my favorite things to do was to stand on the west side of the pool deck, watching the sunrise over the treetops. Rays of sun would peek over the trees and come gleaming across the pool surface while the swimmers were doing their laps, and wisps of steam rose from the pool. Within a couple minutes, the sun would be above the trees and the entire pool would be flooded with sunlight. Another day was officially under way.

After the workouts were over, around ten, I usually stopped in at my office and then headed to the bunker for more interrogations. More afternoons of Gary describing what he enjoyed the most:

"Killing," Gary said matter-of-factly, one afternoon in another interview with the detectives. "Killing is the ultimate. The sex was there too, but it was the killing that was the best part. . . . I did like the fighters. They wanted to live. . . . It heightened the excitement. . . . I was the boss. . . . The fight. The kill. That was the best part."

After the interviews were over for the day, I would head back to the pool to work on our meet lineups or to coach if we had a meet that night. Our meets were on Tuesday and Thursday evenings. They started at six and went until about nine-thirty. By the time I'd get home, it would be about eleven. With the early morning field trips, this made for extremely long days.

The swim club was enjoying another undefeated season, while I was leading this double life and burning the candle at both ends. The parents on the club, and my three beautiful college-aged assistant coaches (Jessie, Kit, and Meredith) watched the TV and read the papers, so they knew something was going on. For the most part though, people knew I couldn't say anything, so no one asked any questions or pestered me for information. They knew that my time coaching at KSTC was my mental vacation from the Green River case.

Then, on Thursday, July 24, KOMO TV reporter Liz Rocca broke the story on the nightly news. Citing three unnamed sources, she reported that Gary Ridgway had entered plea negotiations with the state and that he was leading investigators to as-yet-undiscovered remains. I could only wish that it was so. Despite all the predawn field trips, the Diggers and Whackers had yet to find a single bone. Still, the cat was out of the bag.

Over the following week, the rest of the news media pack went wild. Another television station, KIRO, reported that their "investigations" had "discovered that Ridgway is not only talking with Green River Task Force detectives but has traveled with them in person to known body dump sites," which was only regurgitating what their competitor had already reported. They dressed their report up with a talking head, though.[1]

"This is pretty strong evidence, if he's at a scene," John Junker, a University of Washington law professor told them. "I wouldn't let him go to a crime scene unless there was something very valuable in exchange. That would be some understanding on the death penalty."

Two days later, headlines in the *Seattle Times* proclaimed, "**Ridgway reportedly in plea-deal talks**."[2] Tony was quoted: "The plea is 'not guilty.' That is still on the table. And I am still looking toward trial. End of statement."

Michele was contacted by the *Times* reporter, too. "We're under court order not to talk about anything that's under seal," she said. "We could be disbarred if we did."

A reasonable response but we knew it would only whet the reporters' appetites. If it was sealed, it had to be a secret, and if it was secret, they wanted it.

Over the next week, the media barrage continued. "**Ridgway secretly transferred**," screamed the August 1 front-page headline of the *King County Journal.* "**No one will say where accused serial killer is now**," read the sub-headline.[3] The article, written by Kathleen Merrill, quoted Craig Nelson, the King County Jail Commander, "I am hoping as a taxpayer that they don't have him in the Hilton."

I was interviewed for the article as well:

> Mark Prothero, one of Ridgway's eight defense attorneys, denied that Ridgway is cooperating with authorities.
>
> "When those rumors were first brought to our attention, we denied them and that has not changed," Prothero said. "We don't want to add any fuel to the fire. The reporting on the speculation and rumor is detrimental to my client getting a fair trial, so we're just not going to comment on them."

OK, I didn't actually lie. I said that we'd denied the rumors, which was true: we *did* deny them, and "that has not changed." But with the Diggers and Whackers striking out so far, we had to consider the possibility that the deal would fall through and that we'd be forced back to Plan A, as unappealing as that was at this late date.

The *Times* followed with a new front-page headline in their Sunday, August 3 edition—one that circulated among almost half a million subscribers: "**Ridgway discussing guilty plea in killings**," it read, with a sub-headline: "**Sources: Suspect would swap information on Green River slayings to escape execution**."[4] To the potential juror, reading these headlines, it looked as if Gary had to be guilty. If "sources" were saying that the notorious Ridgway was "swapping information," that implied that he knew something, which wasn't at all what a lawyer wants the public to know if his client is going to trial. However, within the smaller print of the article, it was revealed that there was no hard information behind the headline:

"The deal *could be* announced in *several weeks,* but *no final agreement* has been reached, *a source close to the case* said yesterday." [Emphasis added]

At the bunker on the following Monday, Todd and I met with Jeff Baird and Patty Eakes to figure out how to deal with the leak. And to speculate on where it might have come from.

"We've got to move this thing forward," Todd told them. "Let's get the plea done before the bottom falls out."

"Believe me, we'd like to be done with this as well," Baird said. "But this is about getting as much information from Ridgway as possible *before* we do the deal. I mean, I think we all know this is too far down the track to reverse direction." *Thank God for that,* I thought. "But Ridgway doesn't necessarily know that," Baird added. They wanted to keep the pressure on Gary to keep cooperating.

"It would be nice if Norm would just tell us it's a done deal," I said. "We wouldn't have to stop the interrogations. Just some reassurance. It's getting a little hairy not knowing. Especially with all this recent attention."

"It would help if we could find something," Eakes said, putting the ball back on our side of the net. "Here we are, six weeks into this, and we still don't have anything tangible to show for it. It's a little hairy for us too."

Patty's point was sharp and poked in the sorest spot for our side. So far, nothing physical had been found to verify Gary's story and certainly no remains of the missing, which after all was one of Norm Maleng's main motivations for agreeing to the proposed deal in the first place.

"So who the hell is the leak?" Todd wanted to get Jeff and Patty's theories on whom these unnamed "sources close to the case" might be. Todd's counterpoint to Eakes's jab was that the leak primarily benefited the prosecution, not the defense, because it had the effect of implying that Gary was guilty.

"I wish I knew," Baird replied. He and Patty were clearly as angry as Todd and I about the untimely disclosure. "There are a relatively limited amount of people who know, at least on our side."

"It didn't come from the defense," I countered. There was obviously no way we would have said anything about the deal.

"No," Baird said. "I wasn't implying that it had."

"Based on the information that's being reported," Todd pointed out, "it is definitely someone who's here at the bunker on a regular basis."

Patty Eakes agreed. "I think it's someone close to what's going on, and I don't think it's any of the lawyers."

Which left the cops.

"That was my hunch," Todd said. "We don't want leaks, and Norm [Maleng] doesn't want this stuff out there either. I bet Reichert is sending his cronies out [to leak], so he can wrap this one up and get ready for his next election campaign."

Neither Baird nor Eakes said anything to that. But from our perspective, we believed the source of the leak had to have been someone in the Sheriff's Department.

———∿∿———

While this media storm was breaking around us, O'Toole continued her interrogations of Gary, which we began to see as increasingly ineffective, mostly because she kept *telling* Gary what he was, rather than trying to find out. She spent almost as much time telling Gary that the FBI knew more about Gary than Gary as she did asking questions. Gary usually tried to assure her that she was right, naturally.

"We know what we know and it is what it is," she said, over and over. This became such a mantra that Todd couldn't resist penning an ode on the subject.

> "It is what it is."
> Unless what you say it is,
> is not what the FBI says it is.
> It depends on what your definition of "is," is.
> What is it?
> Putting the complexity of all human behavior
> Into the same pigeon hole.
> Putting a square peg in a round hole.
> A quantum of support for one's thesis
> Whether right or wrong.
> A brick in the wall of ignorance
> That law enforcement sequesters itself behind.
> An impediment to knowledge
> An offense to enlightenment
> An affront to reason
> An insult to science
> And, most significantly,
> A guarantee of failure in the future.

Todd meant that as long as the FBI continued to try to force serial killers to match their paradigm, through their "verification process," they would continue to fail to apprehend them.

O'Toole went on trying to trace the origins of Gary's "paraphilic" behavior to his mother, Mary Rita, frequently suggesting that Mary

Rita had engaged in incestuous behavior with Gary. Gary consistently rejected this but was really no match for O'Toole. Every admission by Gary that his mother had ever cleaned him up after one of his bed-wetting episodes became an exercise in maternal masturbation, despite Gary's denials.

O'Toole prompted Gary repeatedly to say that the origin of his rage against women stemmed from his relationship with his mother, presumably because of the supposed seductive behavior. Goaded in this fashion, Gary finally admitted that he felt like harming his mother, but not because she had "seduced" him. He was mad because she berated him for wetting the bed and failing in school, Gary said.

Gary said he'd taken his anger out on other things "instead a hurting her."

"Living things?"

"Living things. Killing, killing animals."

"OK," O'Toole said, doubtless mentally checking off the Animal Torture Box on her "verification" form.

"Killing animals. Um, I stabbed a kid one time."

Now both Todd and I sat up and paid attention. This was the first we'd heard of this.

"Stabbed a kid with a knife," Gary continued.

"Tell me about that," O'Toole prompted.

"Uh, it was down by . . . where I used to go to school, and a boy was playin'. I stabbed him in the side and . . . uh, didn't kill him. And uh, I, I was about um, sixth grade, or I think it was, go . . . it was seventh grade, and I, I uh, that was at the same time I was, you know, breaking out windows, throwin', was throwin' rocks at windows at school, but . . ."

"Not interested in that," O'Toole said, meaning the window breaking, not the stabbing.

"But that's what I took my ag—gression [out] on. I couldn't take it out on my mom. I had to take it out on my animals and . . . and the kids . . ."

Unaccountably, O'Toole did not follow this up right away.

"How many animals did you kill?" she asked, apparently going back to her "verification" list.

"I wanted . . . I killed a lotta birds, but uh, one cat—suffocated it in a, an ice chest."

"You couldn't take your aggressions out on your mom . . ."

"No, I couldn't."

"But you could think about it . . . What'd you think?"

"I thought a—about hurting her, uh, so she'd shut up and uh, leave me alone and . . ."

"How did you think about hurting your mom?"

"Killing her," Gary said, finally arriving at the place where O'Toole had herded him.

"And how would you do that?"

"I thought, uh, with my hands or, uh, I didn't have no guns or anything or, so that didn't . . . it had to been, uh, hands or uh, uh . . ."

"And then after she was dead, what were you gonna do—in your head?"

"In my head? I . . . I don't know what I would do. I just, just uh, just wanted her to stop. She . . . one time there they were gonna put me in a, a, a special school. I didn't want that. My dad and my mom were arguing about it all the time—and it was uh, for retarded people, and I didn't, wasn't retarded, I don't think, so I was mad at them for wanting to put me away from other kids. And wanting to hurt her or . . . and uh, my uh, hurt her bad."

"What does that mean, 'hurt her bad'? Help me to understand that."

"Just beat her up so she would leave me alone, and . . ."

O'Toole now attempted to link Gary's anger at his mother to his admitted sexual appreciation of her.

"And how did you think in your mind about hurting her in a sexual way?"

"Uh, in a sexual way? Um, I, I . . . at that time I don't think I knew anything about any way to hurt her in a sexual way uh, 'cause, wasn't really into uh, knowin' too much about sex, so it . . ."

"Let's go back. You're watching your mom and you said that that was sexual."

"Um-hm."

"But at the same time, you're angry at your mom. At some point, we know that sex becomes, uh, violence, and violent sex becomes erotic for a serial killer."

"Um-hm."

"That's a given. That's Profiling 101 for us."

"Um-hm."

"And we know that that does occur. And what I'm asking for you to describe for me is, in your circumstance, you're talking about you're, at age fourteen, you hate your mother. She's dressing provocatively, so you've got, you've got these two forces goin' on.[5] And I understand about only bein' able to understand having one thought in your head at the same time."

"Um-hm."

"But at some point, violence was erotic for you. We know that that happened. Would you agree with that?"

"Um-hm."

And here was another aspect of Gary's personality—rather than argue with someone, Gary would often simply say "Um-hm," not as a sign of agreement, but instead as a sort of signal: "I hear you, information received." In other words, "Um-hm," wasn't at all the same thing as an admission.

Still, for weeks Todd, Tony, and I had heard Gary repeatedly deny he'd ever stabbed anyone. "I don't like blood," he'd said over and over again. But under O'Toole's loaded prodding, Gary had finally, if offhandedly, admitted having committed violence toward a younger child when he was a teenager—pretty much exactly as Dr. O'Toole and the FBI's statistical profile had predicted.

———⁓———

Throughout the rest of July, from our point of view, O'Toole continued trying to make Gary measure up to the bureau's standards for serial killers. One of the most interesting exchanges occurred over the victims' jewelry. This was at least partly our fault. In wording our proffer, we'd said that Gary could lead investigators to places where he'd left the property of his victims. We hadn't made it clear that Gary wasn't claiming that he still *had* this stuff, just that he could take them to places where he'd left them. Because the FBI "book" on serial killers said that they *always* kept "trophies" of their crimes, when Gary denied that he had anything left, no one on the law enforcement side believed him. Repeatedly, the detectives, and then the psychologists, tried to induce Gary to give these "trophies" up.

O'Toole, for instance, told Gary that even if the missing skeletal remains were lost forever, he could redeem himself simply by telling the detectives where he kept his "stash." This again, was part of paraphilic behavior, according to O'Toole: serial killers *always* kept this stuff to facilitate reliving their perverted crimes.

Gary agreed that bringing the detectives to his "stash" would be one way to prove his desire to cooperate.

"But that, that is a problem," Gary added. "Is, what I did is, I didn't, I didn't save the items I got. Like I told ya, I saved a, a little bit in a couple places, but a small quantity and, and over, over twenty years, it, uh, they disappeared—like a watch disappeared. Um, uh, small amounts of jewelry, and what I gave at, you know, gave [at] Kenworth, and left at the airport, and stuff like that, it's just not . . . there is, there is no more. There is no, um, there's no jewelry, no, no clothes or anything. There's nothin'."

"See, I hear the words there," O'Toole said, "but based on my experience and my area of . . . expertise, I know that that's simply not the case. And all I'm suggesting to you is, um, that that is not, that's not factual, and that, um, you would have kept *some* things. And I think we talked yesterday about, you still have an emotional bond to some of your victims."

O'Toole returned to this topic numerous times, and Gary in each instance denied that he'd kept any items back. And I believed him: if he wanted the deal, and he was willing to admit to up to sixty-three murders, why would he still want to keep an old ring or necklace? If all he had to do was turn this stuff over to cross the finish line, why wouldn't he do it? This was another area where the paradigm about serial killers was off, in my judgment: not every serial killer kept "trophies," I thought.

So, too, was it off on another fragment of paraphilia: cannibalism.

"Because you know, again, as we go through this evaluation process," O'Toole told him, "it's up to you to want to work with me, and . . . the extent that you have the insight into your behavior is what's important. So to um, you know, it is what it is. That's our, that's what we say in our unit, so we can't go back and, and try and reclassify a behavior. If, if we put it out on the table, you look at it, you, you describe it, we must move on from there."

"Right," Gary said, as if he understood what O'Toole was talking about.

"All right," O'Toole said. "Cannibalism."

"I never did, uh, you know, you know, eat any a the bodies or, or uh, you know, cut 'em up, or anything like that," Gary said. "No, nothin' at all. Never saved body parts to, you know, uh, to uh, other than the heads—take the skulls to Oregon."

O'Toole didn't seem to believe him.

"As far as cannibalism, on that experimentation scale, it can be, experimenting can be something very mild. And it can be something that's um, really extreme." Didn't Gary just want to take a little nibble? Just to see what it was like, O'Toole's question implied.

"Um-hm."

"And it could be, even on one occasion, I need to be able to evaluate that paraphilic, the existence of that paraphilic behavior as far as . . . even if it existed only one time, or, if it just existed in your head on one occasion . . . if there were ever any *thoughts* of cannibalism."

"There was no, no thoughts at all about cannibalism . . . nothin' at all," Gary said. "Nothin' at all about no eating, or you know, taking any a the flesh or anything like that. Nothin'."

We know what we know and it is what it is—no matter what you tell us!

O'Toole also attempted to entice Gary to disclose additional grotesque behaviors by offering him an opportunity to "educate" others.

"We kind of like to characterize this as, you know, having a panel of serial killers, and . . . holding one seat, possibly for you, on this kind of panel of serial killers, where you can sit and educate people as to how things happened and evolved, and what you really were about, and who you are, Mr. Ridgway, as opposed to how somebody characterizes it. Is that something I think you told me you would want to do?"

"Yes. I would," Gary said.

Professor Gary Ridgway, holder of the distinguished Ted Bundy Memorial Seat on the faculty of serial murder. It staggered the mind. I couldn't help myself as I listened to this. The next thing I knew, watching this conversation unfold, I'd sketched a portrait of O'Toole's Blue Ribbon Panel of Serial Killers. It came out looking like a caricature of da Vinci's Last Supper, so I suppose O'Toole had in some way poisoned my own mind with her talk of cannibalism.

As far as Todd and I were concerned, the profiler from the FBI was less effective than the King County detectives at getting real, honest information from Gary, with the significant exception of digging out the child-stabbing story. From our vantage point, she sought the extreme, the sensational, the bizarre, the "very impressive," the devil incarnate, all to validate the bureau's statistical preconceptions. Instead she got lost in the vast sea of his nothingness and had to settle for plain and simple Gary Ridgway—killer of between sixty and seventy women, perhaps more, the one who'd gotten away with it for so long for the fundamental reason that he'd never been what anyone, especially his victims, ever expected.

40

As the last days of July rolled into August, we continued to discuss the apparent stalemate with the investigators, comparing notes on how to interpret Gary: when he was hiding things or when he simply couldn't remember; his usual circumlocutions and what they most often meant. And the cops gave us *their* take on Gary—fascination alternated with revulsion.

The detectives were still concerned that Gary was trying to claim murders he'd never really committed, in order to induce the prosecutors to go ahead with the deal. To guard against that possibility, on our field trips, the van would occasionally pull over at some area, not among any of the known Green River cluster sites, and also not among any of the Red River sites. On one of these excursions, Mullinax put Gary through his paces.

"OK, Gary. Take a look around and get your bearings. . . . Now tell us what you did here."

Gary turned and looked all around the area.

"Nothing," he said. "I don't remember doing anything here."

"Are you *sure,* Gary?" Mattsen asked. "Did you kill somebody and leave her body here? Take your time. Are you *sure* you didn't leave a body here?"

Gary pondered for a while, then shook his head.

"No," he said. "Nothing here. I'm quite certain."

At our next stop on the field trip, we all got out and took a short walk to the site they wanted to look at. As we were walking, I asked Detective Mullinax, "Who was the victim at that last site? I didn't have that location on any of my lists."

"We just threw that in to see if he'd confess to it," Mullinax said. "Nothing happened at that one. Sometimes we found victims at these spots. Sometimes not."

"Placebos?"

"Exactly." Then Mullinax looked at me. "Please don't tell him we're doing that," he said.

So sometimes Gary could be right, even when there was nothing there.

Still, everyone was growing more and more impatient—frustrated—with the fact that nothing was being found. On top of that, with the news media breathing hot and heavy down our backs, it felt like the whole thing might blow up any day. It was only a matter of time before one of the news organizations discovered us on one of our field trips. We were all caught in our dilemma: *they* wanted evidence; *we* wanted them to seal the deal.

One morning, Baird and Eakes asked Todd and me to have another chat about where we were and where we were headed. They waved us back to their corner of the bunker space, where there were some chairs and a coffee table.

"We really need to wrap this up," Todd told them, seizing the initiative. "If something is going to be found, it's going to be at a site he's already taken you to. I'm just concerned about the press and the publicity, and the possibility still lurking out there that this man may still need to get a fair trial sometime down the road."

"You know, this deal—I mean, *any* potential deal—will be scrutinized and criticized for years," Patty Eakes said. "And it's Norm Maleng's name and reputation that will be up front on this. He just wants to make sure it gets done right. We don't want to have to come back when Gary remembers something else if we don't have to."

"I can let you guys know, seriously, that I don't think this deal will unravel," Baird said. "Norm has been holding out, making sure we cover everything and do it right. But I share your concern, and that's why we wanted to talk. Let's look at the calendar and get a tentative date for a possible plea set with Judge Jones. I think it's time we let him know what direction this is going."

I kept my face impassive, while thinking, *Bring Judge Jones into the loop? That would solidify things even more. It's a done deal! Great idea!*

"That's probably a good idea at this point," I said, trying to low-key it. "He reads the newspapers. We can see what he wants or needs to know."

"How about September 16?" Patty asked, looking at her calendar. This was more than a month away.

"I was hoping for something a little sooner than that," Todd said. If you give Todd half a loaf, he'll want half of your half—that's what makes him a good lawyer.

"There's still quite a bit of ground the detectives want to go back over," Baird countered, "and some additional stuff they haven't brought up yet."

I had that sinking feeling again—*more surprises—what else do they know that Gary hasn't told us?* I sincerely hoped it wasn't cannibalism. I wasn't sure I could stomach any of that.

"Let's face it," Baird went on, "Mr. Ridgway is not the easiest person to get information from. He's part of the reason this process is taking so long."

"Point well taken," Todd said. He'd decided half a loaf was better than nothing. "September 16 works for us. Do you suppose you could give us some confirmation that Norm will do the deal?"

Baird and Eakes hesitated.

"Just let me and Todd know," I suggested. "And Tony. We won't tell Gary or anybody else. Except KOMO, KING, and KIRO," meaning the local network television stations. "And CNN." They knew I was kidding.

"As soon as I get confirmation from Norm, I'll let you guys know," Baird said. "I'll call Judge Jones to let him know what we've been doing." Jeff dialed the phone on the table as we sat there. Judge Jones came on the line.

"Judge, this is Jeff Baird. Uh, I've got you on speakerphone, because I'm sitting here with Ms. Eakes, Mr. Gruenhagen, and Mr. Prothero."

"Good morning, counsel." We could all hear Judge Jones's voice through the speaker.

"Judge, we'd like to discuss some scheduling issues with you. The parties are in agreement that we should strike the August status conference. We really have no active issues or disputes that need the court's attention."

We all knew that Jones had to understand what this meant, even if Baird didn't spell it out. Since when did a murder case involving seven charged victims and up to forty-two others, maybe even more, *not* have "active issues or disputes"?

"Good morning, Judge. Todd Gruenhagen here. We're in agreement with Mr. Baird's proposal."

"That's fine," Judge Jones said. "Fine. We can strike the August status conference."

"And we'd like to tentatively set a date of September 16 for a hearing that could potentially resolve the matter," Baird added.

There was a pause on Jones's part. "Potentially resolve the matter" meant only one thing.

"I see," Jones said, after a few seconds. "I've been following the news but . . . well, that's . . . very interesting. How much time on the sixteenth?"

"Hi, Judge. Patty Eakes here. I think we better reserve the whole day."

"OK. That works. I'll keep the sixteenth open."

"Judge, this is Mark Prothero. Do you need any more information at this time? We're obviously keeping everything under the radar as much as possible."

"Well, the press seem to have their sources. But no, I don't need to know any more at this point in time. I think I know where this is headed, so, for now, I'll just have you penciled in for the sixteenth and wait to hear from you."

The conversation ended; everyone knew we'd just taken an important step on the road to a formal plea, a resolution that would dispose of the whole case, with all the politics that this implied.

Todd and I joked around with Baird and Eakes for a few minutes, then we all returned to work, they to their cubicles, us to the conference room.

"I'm thinking this is a done deal," I whispered to Todd as we walked away.

"You would hope so," he said. "But what's this 'additional stuff' Jeff is talking about?"

"I don't know," I said. "I'm guessing we'll find out soon enough, though."

I kept trying to tell myself whatever it was, it couldn't be that bad. If it were, why would Baird have called the judge? But on the other hand, it still depended on Gary. Any more lies wouldn't help us—or him—at all. All Baird had to do was call the judge to scrub the date. In plea negotiations, it always takes two sides.

Tony joined Todd and me for the interrogation session later that afternoon. We filled him in on our earlier discussion with Baird, Eakes, and Judge Jones, along with the selection of September 16 for a possible plea date. Naturally, Tony was pleased with this news and the thought that this case could soon be winding up.

The security gang brought Gary over for the next session. As was the usual routine, we had some time to talk with Gary before the session started.

Gary turned to face Tony, Todd, and me. He had that sheepish grin we had become ruefully familiar with.

"I have to tell you guys something," he said.

Uh-oh.

"What is it, Gary?" Todd asked.

He looked over at me.

"You know that spot we stopped at, on the field trip last week? By South Park?" South Park was a neighborhood just south of the city of Seattle.

"Yeah," I said. "I remember. That place over by the McDonald's, right? What about it?"

"I *did* kill a lady there," Gary said, with a wince. "I've been thinkin' about it and thinkin' about it. I'm quite certain I killed a lady and left her there."

"When?" Tony asked.

There was a short pause while Gary searched his mental "wherehouse," as he so often called it.

"Um, I'm quite certain it was '90 or '91. I know I was married to Judith. I was just gonna date the lady. We got in the back of the truck, but she said I was taking too long. She got dressed and got out before I finished. I got really mad and choked her when she was opening the door to get in the truck." He shook his head. Was he sorry? Ashamed?

Nope. He was rueful for another reason.

"It was so stupid," he went on. "I just left her laying there. I was sure I'd get caught."

"Let's go tell Tom," I suggested, meaning Jensen.

—◠◠◠—

We asked Jensen to come and talk to us in the conference room. Gary waited in the interrogation room.

"What's up?" he asked.

"Well, it looks like Gary has another case solved," Tony told him.

"Oh, really?" Jensen said.

Apparently he wasn't expecting much.

"Which one?"

"You know the site we stopped by in South Park last week?" I asked him. "That one. He's been thinking about it, and he's 'quite certain' he killed a woman and left her there."

"You are shitting me!" Jensen was stunned.

"I know. A week later, and he remembers. Pretty strange," I said. I thought Jensen's reaction came from the delay in Gary's remembering.

"Yeah, pretty strange, all right," Jensen said, shaking his head. "We just took him by there as one of our *placebos*. The victim there was Patricia Yellowrobe, and she died of a drug overdose. Or so we *thought*. And guess what?"

"What?" Tony said, for the three of us.

"She was killed in *1998!*" Jensen said. I could see he was completely exasperated.

I was stunned and sickened. It felt like all the wind had been knocked out of me. *1998?? 1998?? That can't be! Now that opens things up for another decade! Another ten years of possible cases! We could be here for months!*

"So much for the September 16 plea date," Todd sighed.

A few minutes later, when Gary was questioned about this most recent case, he described what she was wearing, what happened during their encounter, where he left her, and the position her body was in. According to the detectives, Gary was 100 percent accurate in his descriptions. He had indeed killed as late as 1998.

41

While the news media continued to go crazy with their speculation and anonymous sources, we all agreed to take a short break from the field trips. There was no sense in giving the news people a chance to videotape Gary clambering over some hillside in his manacles, especially as the media were now in such a frenzy. Meanwhile, though, the Diggers and Whackers continued to hack away at various locations, looking for twenty-year-old bones, in what Jensen soon sardonically referred to as the "King County Deforestation Plan."

On August 4, Mattsen and Peters walked Gary through a videotape of their 1987 search of Gary's house—the search that hadn't found anything some many years before. After Gary's admission that he'd killed up to thirty of his victims in his own bed, this dwelling became known as the "PKH"—Primary Killing House, according to the detectives' jargon. The video tour was relatively uneventful, until we got to the kitchen. On top of the refrigerator was a box of cereal, the same place we keep our own cereal in the Prothero kitchen. Gary's favorite breakfast cereal was Total.

"For the fiber," Gary explained, as the camera zeroed in on the box. Perfect, I thought. I suddenly envisioned a new advertising campaign for General Mills, shoved along with an endorsement from Gary. I saw the commercial in my head, Breakfast-of-Champions style, and could even hear the voice-over:

Total . . . the cereal for serials.

Good Grief! I suddenly remembered another image—a cartoon I'd once seen, with a cereal box lying in the road, with a knife stuck through it. The caption read that the notorious "cereal killer" had struck again. Well, we were all getting a little crazy, which was about to be proven all over again.

At the end of another long, hard week of watching O'Toole and the detectives trying to squeeze information out of Gary, the strain on everyone was evident. Todd and I reconvened at our microbrewery refuge. We vented over a couple of beers, complaining about our client, complaining about the prosecutors, complaining about the cops, complaining about the length of the process—and the body-slamming fatigue of it all. On the roller-coaster ride that was this summer of 2003, we had both reached one of the lowest and slowest stretches of track. We finished our beers and headed to the parking lot.

"They're looking in the wrong place!" Todd insisted.

"Oh, yeah? Which 'wrong place' are you talking about?" I asked.

"That last one, as you're heading east, out 410," Todd said. "'Federated Forest Lady,' I think we were calling that one. When we went out there the second time, they had yellow crime scene tape up. Remember? I presume that was the area they were searching. I swear that was seventy-five yards off from the place Gary was talking about."

I realized we were all anxious for them to find some bones, but I thought Todd's obvious irritation was a little overdone.

Then Todd said, "I'm going out there and find some bones. Wanna come with me?"

"Yeah, *right*," I said, sarcastically. I could just imagine our digging up our own bones—the investigators were sure to say we'd "found" them to make sure the deal went through. They'd accuse us of sabotaging their investigation, and then where would we be? More important, where would the deal be?

"I'm serious," Todd insisted. "I'm going out there this weekend and look where they should have looked. Where do you want the bones? On your porch, or should I just bring 'em to the bunker?"

"Godammit, Todd," I said. "Don't be stupid. You can't go out there. If you have a problem with where they're looking, tell them. Don't go out there on your own. Are you nuts? Have a good weekend. See you on Monday."

We both got in our cars to drive home. I knew he was preoccupied, but then, so was I.

Early the next Monday morning, after dropping Marley off for her workout at the King County Aquatic Center, I called my office phone from my cell phone to pick up my messages. There was a message from Todd:

"Mark, call me when you get this message." Whatever it was, it sounded serious.

I dialed him on my cell.

"Hey Todd, what's up?"

"Hey. We've got to talk." It *was* serious.

"OK. Why? What's going on?" I felt my anxiety level going up. I tried not to think about all the things that could still go wrong with the deal. Had Gary tried to *escape?* Had they found evidence of a second killer that Gary had until now refused to admit existed? Had something awful leaked to the news media?

"Are you on your cell?"

"Yeah."

"This is pretty important . . . too sensitive to talk about on a cell," Todd told me.

Although my curiosity was now fully piqued, I was well aware of Todd's concern, bordering on Orwellian paranoia, about someone intercepting confidential cell phone conversations. So I didn't push him.

"Let's meet at the bunker at eight," Todd continued. "That'll give us a half hour to talk before the interviews begin."

"Sounds good," I said, and hung up. By now, I was really worried. *What the hell is up?*

—⁓—

Todd was waiting for me when I got to the bunker just before eight. He didn't say anything. Whatever it was, it had to be serious, based on Todd's demeanor. I followed him into the interrogation room, where we could be alone. He closed the door behind us, and we sat at our usual side table. Todd took a seat, frowning. I looked at him as I put my briefcase on the floor and sat down next to him.

"What is it?" I asked. By now, I was really worried.

Todd turned and looked directly at me. His face was grim—lips pursed, eyes slightly squinted, glaring in the manner he has when something has upset him. With his right hand, he placed an envelope in front of me without saying a word. I saw it was the sort of envelope you get photographs back in, once your film has been developed.

Todd was silent as I opened the envelope and started sorting through the prints. There were pictures of some forest; pictures of Todd kneeling down by a log; pictures of Todd pointing to something under the log. It wasn't until that moment that I remembered what he'd said on the previous Friday afternoon. *He went out on his own bone search! Oh, shit! He really went out there!*

"You didn't . . . ?" I asked. I didn't have to say any more.

"I *told* you," Todd said, "they were looking in the wrong place." He grabbed the photo of him pointing to the thing under the log.

"That's a part of a skull. And I'm betting it's human."

I could see an off-white, semi-rectangular piece of something, about three inches by four inches, obscured with dirt and leaves.

"Todd, are you shitting me? You really didn't go out there, did you?" I was starting to get upset. In fact, more than a little upset. I could imagine all sorts of problems with this unauthorized venture of Todd's. Starting with the detectives' accusation that we'd planted the partial skull out there just to seal the deal.

"Mark, they were looking in the wrong place!" Todd told me.

He really *had* gone out to look, just like he'd said he would.

"Godammit, Todd!" I was angry now. "*Godammit!* They're gonna be so pissed!" I started trying to figure out how we'd explain this to Baird and Eakes, not to mention Satterberg and Maleng. I couldn't see any way to make it all right.

"Pissed? Pissed?" Todd said, in disbelief. "They should be *happy!* I'm doing *their* job for them! They should *thank* me."

I continued to flip through the pictures.

"Oh, yeah, how about this one?" It was a picture of Todd, kneeling in front of the log and the partial skull. In his right hand, he was holding a sign that read "GRTF" (Green River Task Force) while his left hand displayed another "sign"—his middle finger. This was classic Todd versus the Police and Government.

"Well," Todd said, smiling a little, "we don't have to show them *that* one."

"Let's not," I agreed. "I don't think they're gonna be real happy with us as it is. I cannot *believe* you'd be so stupid!"

"What d'you mean, 'stupid'? *Who's* stupid? I found the fuckin' bones, didn't I!" I barely heard him.

"They're gonna be pissed at you for going out to a crime scene and messing with the evidence. That reminds me, you *did* leave everything alone, didn't you?"

"Yes, yes, of course, I didn't touch a thing," Todd said, with some asperity. Like, did I really think he would be stupid enough to actually *collect* the bones?

I was still looking at the pictures when something occurred to me.

"Who took these pictures?" I asked. *Did Todd bring someone else out there with him? Was there a* witness *to this insanity? Who else knew about this?*

"I used my tripod and timer," he reassured me. "No one else was with me. No one saw me out there."

"I really, *really* wish you hadn't done this," I said, stuffing the pictures back into the envelope.

"They'll probably kick us off the case, now. In fact, you'll probably get disbarred—interfering with an investigation, tampering with evidence, violating the plea agreement. They're gonna go ape-shit when they find out you did this!" The more I thought about it, the more upset I got.

"Oh, fuck you," Todd snapped "They oughta be happy. I'm doin' their job for their inept asses."

"We gotta show these to Tom and Randy. Right now," I said, and picked up the pictures, heading for the door. Just as I reached it, Todd called out to me.

"Hey, Mark . . ."

"What?"

"*GOT-cha!*" he chortled, and for a few seconds I didn't get it. Then it suddenly dawned on me that he'd pulled another one of his devilish practical jokes. And I was stupid enough to fall for it!

The next thing I knew, I was running across the interrogation room, whacking him repeatedly in his shoulder and back with my fist. I was furious and laughing and at the same time the back of my brain was thinking, *Thank god he was just joking!* He tried to turn away, but he too was laughing so hard he couldn't defend himself.

Ha Ha!

Well, we were all a bit crazy by then, even Todd.

Just as we anticipated, the news media soon encountered the Diggers and Whackers hard at work on the "deforestation" plan. On August 12, the *King County Journal* had pictures of Patty Eakes and deputy prosecutor Brian McDonald digging at the site off Kent-Des Moines Road, just west of Kent, the arterial up to the airport. This article was written by Dean Radford. To their credit, the *Journal* did not jump on the "unnamed sources" bandwagon, like the other papers and TV stations. Reporters Kathleen Merrill and Dean Radford, and their editor, Tom Wolfe, refused to go with the story of a plea deal without confirmation by a named source on the record. But the picture of the two deputy prosecutors out there with the Diggers and Whackers said more than a thousand words.

The frustration continued to grow as August wore on. We endured more questioning by the FBI's O'Toole. Every five minutes or so, we were reminded that her unit was the smartest in the world and only studied "interesting" serial killers and that she had happened to have a couple of spare minutes in her busy, important schedule to drop by to talk with Gary. Gary wasn't particularly awestruck by O'Toole's bona fides. In his view, it was just some other thing he had to do if he really wanted to get the deal.

Then, on August 13, Mullinax told Gary that he'd soon have a Very Important Visitor.

"Gary, do you know who Norm Maleng is?"

"Yeah, he's the prosecuting attorney. . . . He's a top man."

"He's *the* top guy," Mullinax agreed. "Pretty important in your life right now."

"Um-hm."

"In the next couple of days, uh, Mr. Maleng is gonna come down and observe this process . . . be down here to watch firsthand, um, how you respond to these questions. I think it would be fair for me to, probably characterize how he's feeling right now, is not too good. So far, we have not recovered a body; we haven't found one piece of jewelry."

Mullinax told Gary that they'd gone down to Portland to look for the skull he'd said he left by the insurance company office but had again found nothing.

"We found nothing," he repeated. "And it's another one of these things that Norm Maleng is having to chew on, when he is trying to process all this stuff. And what he's coming up with are *not* happy thoughts. . . . I can't stress to you how important it's going to be that no bullshit come out of your mouth. . . . And what you *don't* wanna do is make this mistake when Norm Maleng is gonna be watchin' on the other end of that camera."

"Um-hm," Gary said.

Oooh-K, Gary, I thought, *it's show time.*

That afternoon, we had another Team Ridgway meeting in ACA's large conference room—everyone, including the investigators, paralegals, and clerks, all sixteen of us, who were employed on Gary's defense. It was time, finally, to wind things down. Rather than moving forward, the rest of the team could shift to neutral. Todd explained we were now "quite certain" there would be no trial. We both hoped that Baird was right and that Maleng wouldn't decide to pull the deal off the table at the last minute. Everyone on our team knew what was going on. They could watch TV and read the newspapers like everyone else. But it was still somewhat of a stunner to have it confirmed.

We discussed the anticipated events, including the proposed September 16 hearing for the plea, as well as the continued need for confidentiality, despite the obvious leaks that had already occurred—we thought, from the Sheriff's Department. Other than Todd and me, everyone else could put the Ridgway case on hold, and take on new clients. There wasn't going to be a lot more to do; we could essentially shut down Team Ridgway and start saving the King County taxpayers' money.

Two days later, Maleng arrived at the bunker. It was certainly a coincidence, but that day's edition of the *King County Journal* included a letter to the editor, which attempted to make the point that women were not safe in King County, because Maleng only sought the death penalty when the victims of murder were *men.* I had to wonder if the writer was the same person who'd left the sputtering and obscene message on Todd's answering machine months before. But the letter made it clear that if Maleng gave final approval to the plea deal, it would be a decision with very political consequences.

Maleng got to the bunker around eight that morning. He was accompanied by Dan Satterberg. They watched on one of the monitors in a separate office while the detectives put Gary through his paces. Even before we started, Gary had told us that he'd remembered something new and wanted to let the detectives know right away.

"You've got something to start off with, Gary?" Mullinax asked him.

"The field trip on, uh, was it Sunday? And we went out and stopped in front of that guardrail, where I told there was a, a body, uh, out on 410?"

"OK," Mullinax said, doubtless aware, as was Gary, that Maleng and Satterberg were watching this performance on the monitor nearby. "All right."

"I believe that's that lady, with, um, the limp or, a black lady with the limp," Gary said. "And she's, I put it in, I, I pulled her in there, I killed her on days and I, I put her in there at night. And I drug her to the n-, uh, southeast, uh, uh, of that spot where I took you to. It's, it's more, a little bit more southeast, like I said, about fifty yards, or fifty feet."

"OK. Well, let's be sure we're talking about the right place, then," Mullinax said. "This was . . . by that gravel pit?"

"Gravel," Gary nodded, "right across from, the street from the gravel pit."

Mullinax didn't discernibly react to this new information, which didn't sound all that much different than other sudden "memories" that had cropped up with Gary before. Instead, he and the other three interrogators, Jensen, Peters, and Mattsen, led Gary through a discussion of the non-prostitute girlfriends that Gary had had before and during his killing spree.

After about an hour had gone by, Jeff Baird entered the interrogation room.

"Sorry to interrupt," Baird said. "Mr. Maleng is going to be leaving. He wants to know about the last prostitute Mr. Ridgway killed. And he doesn't want to hear the . . . he wants to hear about the last one Mr. Ridgway killed."

"Go for it," Peters told Gary.

"Um . . ."

"Did you hear what Deputy Prosecutor Baird just said?"

"Yes. I heard what he said. And I don't . . ."

"OK, the very last one," Peters insisted.

"Come on, Gary," Mullinax said, when Gary paused. "You are not a stupid person. . . . The question, very simply, was the last one, the most recent one. The one that you did last. Should be pretty clear in your mind."

"Uh, the, the last one would be, be in the, as far as I know, was in '88, uh," Gary said, getting rattled.

"Eighty-eight?" Peters asked, her disbelief obvious.

"Uh, '98, *ninety-eight,* the one over by South Park. I don't remember one prior than that."

"Doesn't tell us shit, Gary," Mullinax said.

"No, it doesn't," Gary agreed.

"You're talking about a body that we're, you're asking us to just, I guess, figure this out. *You're* the one that killed the person. What we're asking you is, who was she, where'd you pick her up, how'd you kill her, those kinds of things? We're asking you to give us the answers. Not for us to guess at what you did."

"That would have be, that would have been the one in '89 that, in South Park, where I picked her up in South Park, as far as I remember."

"OK," Mullinax said, obviously disgusted. "I'm sure Mr. Maleng is hustling out the door after that response. Thank you."

―――⁓―――

Afterward, Maleng and Satterberg approached Todd, Tony, and me.

"Welcome to the summer camp for wayward attorneys," I told them, striving for jocularity in the wake of Gary's lackluster performance on Maleng's only question. But I could see Maleng wasn't in a joking mood.

"Police, prosecutors, defense attorneys—we all have our rules," he said. "But it's also a criminal justice *system,* and that's what's at work here."

"It's been a very interesting experience," I added. "In a weird way."

"That's not the word that Jeff [Baird] used to describe it," Satterberg said.

The following day was Saturday, August 16. The early morning rambles through the bushes, followed by O'Toole's interrogations, then Norm Maleng's command performance appearance at the bunker, had sapped my energy. So had Gary's unceasing inability to remember the vital details of his murders, especially when it counted the most. I decided to sleep in. Maybe the whole thing would go away.

But at ten, I got up, and set off for Snohomish, about an hour to the north, to watch Marley play soccer. Her team lost, 5 to 0. *Oh, well,* I thought, *no one can win them all.*

I got home about five. Then I decided to stop in at the office for a few minutes. Just after I got there, my cellular phone rang. It was the reporter for the *King County Journal,* Dean Radford.

"I apologize for bothering you on a Saturday, but I was wondering if you had just a minute or two to talk," Radford said.

"Sure," I said. As far as I was concerned, Dean and his colleague at the *Journal,* Kathleen Merrill, had been the best, most fair reporters covering the case. "What's up?"

"Do you have any comment on the task force recovering remains in Enumclaw today, out on Highway 410?" Radford asked.

"No," I said, trying to remain calm. "I hadn't heard." My mind was racing through the possibilities, though. *What was he talking about? Remains found out on 410! Where? They gotta be ours! Please, please, let them be ours. . . .*

"Let me read you the report from the AP off the Web," Radford said.

> Human skeletal remains were found Saturday during a search officials said was part of the investigation into the deaths of at least 49 women in the 1980s.
>
> Detective Kathleen Larson said it was too early to tell whether the bones were linked to the Green River serial killings.

As he read the report, I put my computer to work searching the Internet for any other reports.

"Any comment?" Radford persisted.

"Well, no," I said, even as I frantically clicked from site to site. "That's news to me. I can't comment. I'd like to get some more information, talk to the prosecutors and detectives, before I say anything."

But my brain was shouting, *Yessss!*

"How about Gary's location?" Radford persisted. "Where are they keeping him?"

"I can't comment on that."

"I understand. How about all these recent searches and the reports of Gary's cooperation? Can you confirm any of *these* reports?"

"Sorry, Dean. I can't comment at all, except to say we know the task force is continuing to investigate all the uncharged cases." In my mind, I saw Katie Larson extending her fist at my face, microphone style, as we'd rehearsed two months before.

"Yeah, yeah," Dean said. "Sounds like Katie Larson's standard response. I understand you can't say anything."

"Yeah. But maybe soon."

I was elated. Now the deal would go forward for sure. Gary's life would be spared. And some victim's family was going to get the painful news but also—I hoped—some sense of resolution that comes with the knowledge. I even felt good for Jensen and Mullinax. Their patience and perseverance finally hit pay dirt, literally. Maybe Gary had come through after all. I called Todd and left a message. I called Tony.

"Tony," I asked, "did you hear? They found some bones."

"Yes, I heard," Tony replied. "Michele heard it on the news and called me."

"This is what we've been waiting for," I said. "The end is in sight."

"It shouldn't be much longer now," Tony agreed.

Over the rest of the weekend, I watched and read more news reports. Based on what I could see on television and determine from the descriptions of the area searched, I realized this had to be the victim that Gary had referred to as "Gravel Pit Lady"—dumped across the highway from a big rock quarry–gravel pit that served as his landmark, the one he'd told Mullinax about while Maleng was watching. On Monday, August 18, these remains were identified as one of the long-sought missing Green River victims, sixteen-year-old Pammy Avent. I learned this from KING television reporter Linda Byron. She called for a comment while I was driving to eastern Washington. I'd taken the day off from the bunker to drive to Ellensburg in central Washington with Sean for his freshman orientation at Central Washington University. Again I was struck by the tragic juxtaposition: here I was, taking my oldest child to college, while on the same day, some other family was finally finding out what happened to their own child so many years before.

The discovery of Pammy Avent—and her identification as "Gravel Pit Lady"—meant that at last the investigators finally had solid evidence that Gary was in fact *the* Green River Killer. With the discovery of Pammy's remains, the six still missing included Kase Ann Lee, Rebecca Marrero, Marie Malvar, Keli McGinness, April Buttram, and Patty Osborn. Gary had tried to lead or direct detectives to all of these sites, but until the discovery of Pammy Avent's skeleton, the detectives had failed to find anything. Now, even though six remained missing, Maleng had what he needed to justify the deal.

We wanted to share this good news with Gary, to let him know his efforts had finally accomplished something. He was as frustrated, or more frustrated, than anyone else, by the previous failures of the Diggers and Whackers. I also thought the positive news would help him, give him some confidence in what he was doing. But the interrogators didn't want us to tell Gary that he'd finally found one of the right spots. They asked us not to tell him, in an effort to keep the pressure on. As long as Gary thought he was failing, they believed, he would continue to try. With some reluctance, we agreed with the detectives' request.

42

Throughout the long hot summer in the bunker, Gary had occasionally asked about Sheriff Reichert. We'd seen the silver-haired Reichert from time to time at the bunker, and occasionally on field trips. Although he had a separate, small office at the bunker, he spent most of his time downtown at the King County courthouse, where the main office of the Sheriff's Department was located. Although he may have been overseeing the investigation, from our perspective he was less involved in its day-to-day activities. Most of former *Detective* Reichert's involvement with the case had taken place from 1982 to 1987; in fact, he'd been at every site where remains had been found. However, he left the investigation just about the time that Gary had first been searched in the spring of 1987, more than fifteen years earlier.

Since that time, Reichert had devoted most of his efforts to working his way up the sheriff's rank ladder—sergeant, lieutenant, captain, until his appointment (by County Executive Ron Sims, a Democrat, no less) as King County Sheriff. Most of the work on the case between 1990 or so and the eventual arrest of Gary had been done by Tom Jensen and Jensen's occasional partner, Jim Doyon.

Yet that hadn't prevented Reichert from riding the wave of popularity that accompanied the arrest of the most notorious serial killer in American history. And it was clear, to us at least, that Dave Reichert intended to let the case push his personal prospects as far as it could, which probably meant higher political office.

On our side, we couldn't help but feel there was something just a little too contrived about Reichert—but that may have been because he was a conservative, born-again Christian politician, who generally opposed the things we favored and stood in favor of all the things we were against. Like the death penalty, for instance. Yet, to his credit, Reichert had agreed to support our proposed plea deal.

Nevertheless, early on, in fact right from the beginning, we irreverently—but with all due respect—referred to Reichert by Todd's cynical nickname for him: "Hairspray." To go with his handsome, telegenic face, Reichert was readily identified by his head of silvery-white hair, always perfectly coiffed, and, we thought, always ready for the next photo opportunity. The hair, which contrasted starkly with his dark eyebrows, made him a natural target for wags bent on spoofing him. Political cartoons sometimes pinpointed the sheriff's apparent vanity, especially his hairdo. In one cartoon, published within two weeks of Gary's arrest, a mirrored vanity table occupied a prominent place in the sheriff's office, as a figure representing the bearded Tony Savage came through the front door, asking a grinning Reichert if he couldn't please borrow Gary's new, wall-mounted head, an obvious trophy for Reichert.

"He'll need it for his fair trial," the cartoon Tony said, meaning Gary's mounted head. "Don't you mean his fair *tribunal?*" the cartoon Reichert responded, grinning beneath his dark eyebrows and silver hair.

The day after taking Sean to Central Washington University for his freshman orientation, I was back in the bunker with Todd.

"So," I asked, "how'd it go yesterday?"

Todd shook his head from side to side, with a look of sheer resignation.

"You will not believe this one."

"What? Tell me."

"Before they started yesterday, they asked if Sheriff Hairspray could interview Gary, with Gary thinking it's just him and Dave, one-on-one. I could watch on a monitor, but they wanted to do it without me in there. They told Gary it was off-the-record, no tapes, no cameras. They acted like they wouldn't do it if we objected, but I agreed, so long as I could call it off if I wanted. Plus, I wanted to see if I had trained our boy properly."

"So what happened?"

"They pulled him [Gary] out and took him into Reichert's office [his bunker office]. Then they start gabbing away. Did he ask to speak to his lawyer? Noooo! Did it even . . . cross his mind? I doubt it! I could not believe it. Every day, every possible way I know how to communicate with him, and he doesn't get the most basic warning: *don't* talk without Mark or me there! I am so frustrated." Despite their assurances to Gary, they still taped the session, by use of a concealed camera and microphone, although Gary was in the dark on this.

"So what did he say?" I was wondering if anything new came out—maybe something really bad?

"Nothing," Todd reassured me. "Same old shit." But that wasn't the point, to Todd. Gary had talked to the cops on their terms, without first asking for his lawyer, a violation of Rule Number *One.* "They want to do the same thing again today for a couple more hours."

—⁓—

I tried to figure out just why Reichert wanted to go mano-a-mano with Gary. In the back of my mind, I wondered if this was for the purpose of getting some video for a future political campaign: *Sheriff Reichert Questions the Green River Killer.* It couldn't hurt him with most voters, that was for sure.

Todd and I sat with Malcolm Chang and Ross Nooney, watching on the monitor as Gary was led into Reichert's bunker office on Tuesday, August 19. After they greeted each other, Gary said, "Maybe I should talk to my lawyers?"

"Yessss!" exclaimed Todd. "Finally!"

They stopped the proceedings to "notify" us to come to the bunker, even though we were already there. Apparently, they still wanted Gary to believe no one was watching this private conversation. When I "arrived," I spoke to Gary.

"They want me to talk to Reichert, one-on-one," Gary told me. "We did it yesterday, too."

"Really?" I feigned ignorance. "Did you talk to Todd first?"

"No," Gary shook his head and grinned, an acknowledgment that he'd broken Rule Number One.

"Gary, Gary, Gary . . . how many times have we told you?" I was letting him know how disappointed we were.

"I know," he said. "I won't talk with him today without you or Todd."

"It's not that," I said. I hadn't intended to put a kibosh on the mano-a-mano gambit. "It's just that you should know to *always* consult— or ask to consult—with your lawyers first. Besides, is there anything you're telling him that you haven't already told to Tom, Randy, Sue, or Jon?"

"No," Gary replied. "He wants to know where the jewelry is, but I already told them every place I put it. I don't have anything new or different."

"Well, do you want to talk with him?" I asked.

"Sure. That's fine," Gary said, nodding and smiling. "Whatever they want me to do."

"OK," I said. "I'll be around here working on some other stuff." They still didn't want me to let him know that the session was being taped, apparently because they thought Gary would be more likely to part with the truth if he thought that only Reichert would be present.

"If you need me or want to talk to me about anything, just have them stop and we can talk."

"Oooh-K," he said. With that, I left Reichert's office and joined Todd back in the conference room. Gary was right. It was clear that Reichert wanted Gary to tell him something that he'd never revealed before, mainly about the jewelry.

Eventually, three days of bunker time were taken up with Reichert's attempts to cajole Gary into disclosing the whereabouts of the missing jewelry, which I had long ago concluded was a figment of the experts' imagination and their "book." I was convinced Gary had ditched it long before, as he kept insisting he had.

Later, Todd and I went over the tapes of the sheriff's sessions with Gary, and even though nothing really new was produced, the encounters did have some interesting and even amusing moments.

On August 18, for instance, Reichert compared himself to Gary.

"We've got a lot of things in common, kinda, don't we?" Reichert told Gary.

"Uh-huh."

"What do you think? What are some of things that we have in common?"

"Same age," Gary offered.

"Yeah," Reichert said. "I'll be fifty-three in a couple weeks. How old are you?"

"I'm fifty-three . . . fifty-four."

"So you're a year older than me."

"Yeah . . . we're about the same age."

"Um-hm. Did you know I was . . . I'm dyslexic?" Reichert asked.

"No, I didn't know that."

"Yeah. And that's . . . and you are too, aren't you?"

"Uh-huh."

"Now that's weird, don't you think?"

"That is weird, yeah," Gary said.

Besides being about the same age and both being dyslexic, Gary and he had other things in common, Reichert pointed out. Both had grown up in south King County, both agreed that their mothers had very strong personalities, and both had spent over thirty years at their jobs—Reichert with the Sheriff's Department, Gary at Kenworth.

Most of all, Reichert said, they had the murders in common. They had both stood on the bank of the Green River, almost twenty-one years earlier to the day, the one who'd put the bodies into the water and the other who'd helped take them out.

"They're always going to tie us together," Reichert said. "Our lives are tied together."

"Um-hm," Gary said.

Over the next three days, Reichert seemed to alternate between accusing Gary of lying and praising him for his cleverness in eluding capture for so many years. It was, in its way, somewhat schizophrenic, but I guessed that Reichert's primary intent was simply to prick something inside of Gary to make him expostulate. At one point, Reichert told Gary someone was certain to make a movie about the Green River case.

"But you watch, Gary. When the movies come out—and there will be—right?"

"Yeah, there will be movies," Gary agreed.

"Who's going to play you, do you think?"

"I don't know but, um . . . some new actor?"

"Who do you think? We can talk about this. Who do you think might play you?"

"They . . . maybe Tom Cruise."

Reichert asked Gary who he thought would play *him*. Gary fumbled for a minute, trying to think of what to call Reichert—"Dave," or "you," or . . . ? But he was momentarily flummoxed, trying to be polite, yet still engage with Reichert's pose of intimate familiarity.

"You can call me sheriff, if you want," Reichert suggested.

"I can call you sheriff, yeah. And they probably have you . . . they'd probably have you an . . . older . . . maybe George Clooney, they'd probably have somebody [like that] for you."

"How about Leslie Nielsen?"

"Leslie Nielsen," Gary agreed.

Reichert laughed.

"Yeah," Gary said.

Reichert told Gary that he'd interviewed Ted Bundy, years earlier, when Bundy had offered to help the police understand how the Green River Killer thought. But there was a big difference between Bundy and Gary, Reichert acknowledged. By the end of Bundy's series, he was taking big chances and had gotten very sloppy in committing his crimes, almost as if he wanted to be caught. But that wasn't true with Gary, Reichert said.

"You didn't do that. We had to catch you. No, you didn't do that."

Gary tried to say that at the end, when he'd killed in South Park in 1998, he'd made mistakes because he was "out of practice," as he had put it.

"No. No. No. I'm not buying it," Reichert said. "You . . . you are [an] organized, accomplished serial killer. I know that. I've been in this business for thirty-two years."

"Um-hm. There's still a lot of things that I screwed up on."

"Yeah, but you know what?"

"I got away with it," Gary said.

"Exactly. How did we get you? It took us twenty-one years . . . twenty years."

"Twenty years, and you would have gotten me earlier, if all these people would have turned me in, when I choked 'em." By this point in the interrogations, Gary had claimed that he had choked at least five or six victims who had survived and escaped but had never reported him to the police; there was only one verified case of that, however, that of Rebecca Garde.

"But yeah, but no," Reichert said, disagreeing with Gary that the police could have caught him much earlier. "Because you know why? Because you were smart enough to figure out a way to schmooze it up, you know . . . I mean, you were [intending to] kill her, you know, you did all those things that people let their guard down. Why do you think you were so successful? I've got several reasons."

"Why?" Gary asked, not sure what Reichert wanted to know.

"Why you got away with it for so long," Reichert clarified.

"With the women, they wouldn't expect somebody my size to be a serial killer," Gary explained. "They wouldn't expect it, where they get a guy that looks like Arnold [Schwarzenegger], maybe they figure, 'I'm not going anywhere with *that* guy.' Here's a guy not muscle-bound, not a weight lifter and you know . . .'"

"You don't give yourself enough credit," Reichert said. "You were good. I . . . you know, I don't know if I said this or not. I think I did. You were hunting, right?"

"Yeah."

"You were out there hunting."

And to this Gary agreed. He'd been an urban hunter, stalking his victims, just as a wolf in the woods might look for a deer. He'd checked the terrain for danger, sniffed the air, found ways to approach his prey, lulled them into relaxing, and then sprang upon them with a fatal surprise, a trick from a trick. Not everyone understood that about his method, Gary told Reichert. And one reason he'd gotten away with the murders for so long was that the police had never really approached their investigation with the understanding that they were looking for someone who loved to hunt.

"If they're not in that mode, they can't picture themselves in my body," Gary said. "Ask the right questions. Know what it feels like to track down some animal. Track down a . . ."

"So you're like an animal that we were hunting?"

"No, *I* was a hunter."

"Yeah, you were a hunter, but I was hunting *you.*"

"Um-hm," Gary said, not mentioning that Reichert had never caught him.

Reichert tried to find out why Gary lied so often. Gary said that with his dyslexia, he found himself habitually lying to cover up his inability to learn and retain things.

"Like I told them before, uh, uh, basically to get by, I had to be, 'cause a dyslexic, you know, I had to be a, a, a liar." Lying was his way of coping with the world, Gary said.

"But I, but I'm dyslec . . . dyslexic," Reichert pointed out.

"Hm."

"Now ya got me doin' it!"

"Um-hm."

"But I couldn't be a cop for thirty-two years if all I did was make up stories," Reichert said. "Somebody woulda found me out by this time, don't you think?"

"Hm, it's possible."

"I certainly wouldn't be the sheriff."

"No."

"Nobody'd elect me. Who would vote for me?"

"Well, I didn't," Gary said, grinning faintly, meaning he hadn't voted for Reichert.

"Yeah, OK . . ." Reichert got it. Gary was teasing him. "Very good," he said. "You got a good sense a humor, huh?"

"Um-hm."

"That's good," Reichert said. "You're gonna need it."

Over these three days, Reichert pressed Gary again and again to give up the jewelry. Gary resolutely insisted that he hadn't kept anything. Eventually, Reichert told him that he would go to hell because he hadn't fully confessed.

"And you're not being honest right now," Reichert told him, "so you, what you've done is, you just sentenced yourself to eternal life in hell. Your ass is just gonna burn the rest a your life. You, have you read Revelation? The Book a Revelation?"

"Uh . . . yeah."

"You oughta read the Book a Revelation. Not only will you be on fire, but you're gonna have sores and stuff happenin' all over your body."

"Um-hm."

"And you . . . and . . . and you can never stop it. It'll never heal. You'll be in constant pain and torture, that's what it says."

"Um-hm."

"I mean you, you even said that you were lying."

"I'm a natural liar," Gary admitted. "But I'll tell ya, I'm not lying about the, the jewelry. I'm not lying about it. . . . I can't . . ."

"But you are."

Gary said there was no way he could convince anyone that he was telling the truth about the jewelry—not if everyone insisted that the FBI's "book" said he had to be lying about it.

"And that's, that's what . . . I'll tell ya, it's like this wall," Gary said, of his interrogators refusal to believe that he did not still have the victims' jewelry. "I'll tell ya it's white and you keep on tellin' me it's black. And I know it's true, but I can just [say] it *is* a white wall."

"Um-hm."

"And you're tellin' me it's black. I'm not gonna change my . . . I'm not gonna change my story."

"I just want ya to tell the truth."

"And I'm *tellin'* the truth about the jewelry. There's no jewelry, no clothes, and that is the truth, and I'll go to the grave with it."

"I'm just gonna just sit here," Reichert said, staring at Gary.

"Um-hm."

Sheriff and serial murderer stared at each other without speaking for almost two minutes.

At the time, on Day Two of the Reichert Grilling, we could all see this live, as Reichert's stare got more intense. It was a stare-down contest. Reichert slowly, gradually leaned forward. Gary slowly, gradually leaned back. It seemed to go on and on. It was starting to get really weird when Todd broke our silence as we watched this in the conference room.

"Who's gonna break first?" Todd asked. "Who'll win the stare-down? I got five bucks on Hairspray!"

"I'll take that action. I got your boy," Nooney, the soundman, said. "Dave doesn't stand a chance. Gary, hell, that's all he does for several hours a day . . . stare at blank walls. I've seen him just sit there for hours. He's amazing."

Nooney knew what he was talking about. After what seemed like a very long period of utter silence, Reichert withdrew from the stare-down. Todd got a five dollar bill out and handed it to Nooney.

"That really wasn't fair," Nooney admitted. "I've *watched* Gary. I knew Dave was in over his head."

"So in that case, give me my five bucks back," Todd said, holding out his hand.

"Yeah . . . right," Ross said, as he pocketed Todd's fin.

When we looked back at the monitor, Reichert was talking.

"Ah, maybe I'll write a book," he said.

"Hm, you could," Gary agreed.

"What do you think I should title it?"

"Oh . . . you could title it uh, uh, 'Technology Caught the Green River Killer.'" Gary suggested.

"That wouldn't be very catchy, would it?"

"No, but it'd be honest . . . honest. Took all that time—I wouldn't been caught if it wasn't for technology."

Reichert persisted.

"What do you think I oughta title that book? Got any ideas?"

"'Catching of the Green River Killer,'" Gary offered.

"No. Some'n catchy . . . be a good title for the book."

"Let's see," Gary said, really trying to help. "Maybe uh, 'Solving of the uh, Worst uh, Murder Cases, uh, Serial Killer in, in uh, State's History, or Washington's History,' or some'n like that."

But Reichert didn't like that one either.[1]

"You mentioned somethin' earlier that you thought you heard somebody mention that I might be runnin' for governor," Reichert told Gary.

"Yes, I heard you're running for governor or some or some'n . . ."

"How did that make you feel?"

"Well, that would uh, that . . . at the time it made me feel like, uh, because I was gonna get the death penalty, that you [might] have the . . . sometimes a governor pardons people. Sometimes, yeah, but it wouldn't, you wouldn't pardon the Green River Killer, not with that many killings. One killing would be different than, you know, forty-seven, originally."

"Yeah. Did you figure that out on yourself, that if I was the governor I might have to . . . ?"

"Yeah, I figured that out . . ."

"Sign your death warrant?"

"Yeah. Um-hm."

"Boy, that would be odd, wouldn't it?"

"It would be odd, but it . . ."

"Lead detective and then the governor . . . and I sign your death warrant?"

"Um-hm."

"Boy, that coulda been, the [book] title could be . . . 'From Search Warrant to Death Warrant.'"

"Um-hm."

"Maybe that would be a good title."

"And have the last say in all the . . . because a this whole thing of the Green River Killer case," Gary said.

"Cuz a you," Reichert said.

"Of me, yeah. You could prob'ly . . ."

"I guess I should thank you."

"Be a shoe in. Be a shoe in."

"So you have that much confidence in me, huh? You think I could do a good job there?"

"I think you could, yeah. I think if you're runnin' as a Republican, maybe . . ."

Watching this on the monitor, I had to laugh, envisioning the headline: **Serial Murderer Endorses Reichert for Governor**.

"Yeah," Reichert said. "Are you a Republican?"

"I'm a, you know, you know, little Republican, yeah."

So Gary was in the GOP.

"You won't be able to vote, though, will ya?" Reichert said. "I guess I should thank you."

"Yeah, you prob'ly should, yeah if, if you're running."

Reichert was pulling Gary's leg, all right, but Gary seemed to pull right back. Gary now told Reichert he thought he'd do all right as a governor. They had a short discussion about politics and Reichert's prospects, as if Gary were some sort of precinct committeeman whose backing Reichert wanted.

"You might stumble a little bit, but I think . . . ," Gary offered.

"Ya think so?"

"Yeah."

"Why would I stumble?"

"Well, bein' not into the politician part . . ."

"Yeah," Reichert said. "Maybe I wouldn't be so good at it. Took twenty years to solve this case. Yeah."

"Yeah."

"Maybe if they had somebody smarter workin' on it, it mighta been solved a lot quicker. What do you thinka that?"

"No."

"No?"

"Well, uh, no, not smarter," Gary said. "If, if . . . I think the major part was the victims who got away were not, didn't come forward until after . . . and the six, six choking victims never reported—only one did, I woulda been gone a long time ago."

"Hm," Reichert said.

"And that's . . . that's the problem between the police and the uh, the, the prostitutes. The willingness of women to come in and, and give up that information without getting arrested, without . . . and then on top of it, some, some a these women, they'd go into [they might today] have a good job and everything, they don't wanna give up that, you know, didn't wanna go in the [police] office . . . 'write your name down,' 'Oh, yeah, I got choked by Mr. Ridgway,' you know, 'back in '82, when, uh . . .' 'I don't want this to [get back to] my husband . . . I don't want this on record,' and so a woman might not a come in for something like that. She may . . ." The fact that the police tended to arrest prostitutes, Gary suggested, discouraged them from becoming potential witnesses, which was one reason why he'd chosen them to kill.

"Hm, so had nothin' to do with the detectives, huh?" Reichert seemed to miss Gary's point completely.

"It has *a lot* to do with detectives," Gary said, meaning the police indifference if not outright hostility toward assault complaints from prostitutes. "But a lot of it has to do with the, the first victims."

"Hm."

"If they woulda [felt safe to come in and report the choking assaults], I woulda been in jail and not kill as many as I did." The fact that detectives tended to disparage and ignore complaints from prostitutes created the climate that allowed him to murder so many, Gary insisted again.

"If they woulda [come in and reported], I'd be watchin' my back slightly more, and I wouldn't uh [got so many] . . ."

Reichert asked Gary about the closest he'd come to getting caught, and Gary told the story once more about his encounter with the "fisherman," possibly the rafter Ainsworth, on August 15, 1982. After that, he hadn't dared to go back to the river, he said.

Reichert asked him if the fact that the television station had reported the subsequent surveillance of the river had scared him away. No, Gary said. It had been the fisherman. Which of course meant that if Reichert had put out surveillance after the discovery of Deborah Bonner's body on August 12, 1982, they would have had at least two days' worth of chances to catch Gary before the discovery of the bodies on August 15. So maybe it *did* have to do with the detectives . . . or one of them, anyway.

Reichert asked Gary what he thought of the FBI's O'Toole.

"She's kind of nice to talk to?"

"Kind of nice to talk to, yes, yeah," Gary agreed.

"She's not threatening?"

"She's not threatening. But she can . . . the same things that, uh, you know, the, that are, uh . . ."

"Well, you know, she's good at getting you to tell the truth."

"She's good at that, but it's also good at sw-, swaying me into, into other areas that I, I didn't do."

"Huh?"

"And I don't remember . . . the first night, I thought it was, I choked a woman from Sixth Avenue [in downtown Seattle]. But she says . . . that I had to go back in the '70s."

"Right. I'm with her," Reichert said. He agreed with O'Toole that according to "the book," Gary had to have killed the first time in the 1970s, years before Wendy Coffield. "I don't believe you."

"Well, I don't think anybody *does* believe me."

"They don't," Reichert nodded.

"Everybody's got to go by that standard of looking. You've got to have . . . you gotta go into, you know, 'you're a child killer' . . . 'you gotta kill animals' . . . 'you gotta set fires' . . . 'you gotta do this' . . . 'when you kill somebody, you [stash] all their stuff.' When somebody becomes a little bit unique, doesn't have the stuff, then they are 'a liar.'"

"I know that you can remember things. I know you're a lot smarter than sometimes people think you are. You're a smart guy," Reichert told Gary at one point.

Gary shrugged.

"I'm smart in some ways," he admitted.

"You know, one of the things I promised when I started this case is that I was never gonna give up."

"Um-hm."

"You know, you probably learned that about me over the years that I was going to keep on working."

"Yeah, I heard that you were maybe one time go for governor and decided . . . I heard somewhere, you wanted to stay with the task force."

"Right. That's it. That's my reason for staying right now."

"Um-hm."

"Yeah. Twenty years. Twenty-one years. What's the date today?"

"It's August 15."

"Eighteenth."

"Eighteenth already? No, I didn't know."

"So three days ago on August 15, twenty-one years ago, three days, twenty-one years ago on August 15, you and I were standing on that riverbank."

"Um-hm. The women were found."

"You and I, like I said, you know, when you go off to prison, you're gonna need a friend."

"Um-hm."

"And wherever I go . . . they're always going to tie us together. Our lives are tied together."

"Um-hm."

With this last, Malcolm Chang and Ross Nooney, watching in the conference room, broke into the well-known Carole King song:

When you're down and troubled, and you need a helping hand . . .
You've got a friend. Ain't it good to know. You've got a friend . . .
We all cracked up.

In his last interview with Gary on August 20, Reichert returned to the topic of writing a book. He suggested that Gary cooperate with him.

They could split the profits, he said, 75 percent for him, 25 percent for Gary. Once Gary got to prison, he added, he wouldn't be able to make any money anymore.

"You'll need some in prison," Reichert said. "Big money could help protect you."

"Yeah, 25 percent wouldn't be bad," Gary said.

"I get 75 because I did most of the work. My hair's gray now." This led Gary to a question he'd apparently been aching to ask Reichert:

"How come your eyebrows are dark and your hair is gray?"

"I dye my eyebrows," Reichert said, completely deadpan.

It took a few minutes before Todd and I could stop laughing.

From our perspective, Reichert should have left the interrogations to the homicide detectives: Jensen, Mullinax, Peters, Mattsen, and Doyon. In his run up the political ladder after his days as a detective, some of Sheriff Reichert's investigative skills had apparently gotten stale. His showdown with "the devil" amounted to nothing more than, as far as I could see, a protracted photo op for an ambitious politician.

Todd and I convened for beer after the last Reichert session, sharing some laughs over some of the weirdness of Hairspray's encounter with Gary. We also privately rejoiced in the discovery of Pammy Avent's longlost remains four days before, which we believed had finally made our proposed deal with the state inevitable. We were sure that nothing could go wrong now.

"Congratulations," Todd said. "Good work." He raised his glass of golden ale.

"Same to you," I replied, touching his glass. "Can you believe it?"

"Yes, I can," Todd said. "It's the right thing to do. But you gotta give Norm [Maleng] the credit."

We clinked our glasses and drank to Norm. And then to Baird, to Eakes, to McDonald, and to the other prosecutors. Then we raised our glass and toasted Tony.

"To Obi Wan Kenobi," I said.

"To Obi Wan," Todd replied.

Then we toasted the task force. Then Gary. Then we ordered another pitcher.

"Is this gonna be the end of the death penalty in Washington? What do you think?"

Until now, we'd tried to avoid that question. One river at a time, so to speak. Although it was not our primary motivation, it was certainly a nice possible collateral effect of what was about to happen.

"Well, Mark," Todd said, "*I* think so, but then I don't make those decisions. We'll have to pass that battle on to our fine appellate colleagues and the black robes in Olympia." Todd burst into a huge smile, his eyes now sparkling. He raised his glass for another toast.

"Here's to the end of the death penalty. In Washington, at least."

I smiled and clinked his glass. "I'll drink to that."

Dave Reichert might get elected governor, or so we expected, but the Green River case might be responsible for ending the death penalty in Washington State. It was ironic as hell that it might take the crimes of a multiple murderer to end capital punishment, which after all, was nothing more or less than arbitrary, state-sanctioned murder. But from our point of view, killing was killing: it was *all* wrong.

43

After the discovery of Pammy Avent's remains on August 16, there was a palpable change in the atmosphere at the bunker. It was as if a huge cloud had dissipated. Although everyone was now convinced that Gary was *the* killer, finding evidence beyond the river that only he could have known about relieved a lot of anxieties. From then on, there were more smiles and occasionally more laughter, relieving the grim subject. The interrogation sessions got shorter, simpler, and seemed more congenial, at least for a while.

On Thursday, August 21, Patty Eakes and Brian McDonald gave us more good news. The Diggers and Whackers had succeeded again.

"They found more bones at Kent-Des Moines Road," McDonald told us. "They're human. Just thought we'd let you know. Please don't tell your client."

"We won't," I said, then added, "Right where Gary said they would be."

"The *second* time," Eakes pointed out, recalling Gary's "Why are they looking there?" remark on our second field trip to the Kent-Des Moines Road site. Despite the two discoveries, the investigators and prosecutors were still convinced that Gary was holding back information. Assuming that the Kent-Des Moines Road remains were in fact one of the missing, that would leave five other possible skeletons still out there. That was one reason why the authorities didn't want us to tell Gary that he'd finally directed them to some remains—they wanted to use the still-theoretical possibility of the death penalty to keep him cooperating.

During a break in the interrogations on August 25, Gary asked Todd, "Have they found anything yet?"

Todd reflected briefly on our agreement with the state to keep this information back and reluctantly lied to Gary.

"No. Nothing yet." Todd wasn't happy about abetting the state in its continued coercion.

Before the detectives came in to resume questioning, Todd and I decided to go outside the room to have a chat with them. Deputy Prosecutor McDonald joined us.

"We've been asked point-blank by our client if anything had been found yet," Todd said. "Per our earlier agreement, I told him no. But it makes me very uncomfortable."

"We'd like you to please reconsider and tell Gary what's been found," I added. "It's really difficult, when we're put in a position to have to lie to our client. It sort of breaks down the trust we've worked so hard to build."

"We need you to tell him *now*," Todd persisted. "The credibility and trust we have with Gary is critical to this whole process. If he knows his lawyers aren't telling him everything or—even worse—affirmatively lying to him . . ." Todd paused. The danger of a resentful, bitter Gary simply deciding to permanently clam up was obvious.

"That's a good point," McDonald said. "We don't want you to be in a position of having to lie to your client."

"Yeah," Jensen added. "We certainly don't want to put you in a bad position, and we do appreciate your going along with us. We just wanted to use it to our best advantage . . . to pry out some more information."

"Who knows?" Todd pointed out. "Telling him might boost his confidence, validate his efforts. In any event, we don't want to have to lie to Gary anymore."

"OK, we understand," Mullinax said. "We'll talk it over and figure out how we're gonna let him know."

When the next session began, Tom Jensen began.

"Morning, Gary."

"Morning, Tom."

"I've been elected to bring you some good news."

"OK."

"You know what the Mendoza line is in baseball?"

"Wh—who? Mendoza?" I could see Gary was thinking this Mendoza had to be the name of another victim.

"The Mendoza line?" Jensen asked again.

"No."

"That's a barely acceptable batting average," Jensen explained. "Right around .200."

"Uh-huh." Arithmetic had never been Gary's best subject.

"You're up to about .100 now," Jensen said, meaning that Gary was 1 for 10.

"Oh, OK."

"We found some stuff. Kent-Des Moines site."

"Uh-huh."

"Found some bones," Jensen said, finally deciding to spell it out for Gary.

"Good," Gary said.

Todd and I said nothing, but we were relieved we didn't have to lie to our client anymore. And, I thought, Gary had actually caught up with poor Mendoza.[1] Of the ten sites that Gary had listed in the beginning, he'd actually now hit on two—although the detectives apparently decided to keep the news about the "Gravel Pit Lady," Pammy Avent, back from Gary. Two for ten was .200. And the Diggers and Whackers hadn't given up yet at the other sites.

Gary's spirits were obviously buoyed by Jensen's decision to tell him that progress had finally been made to verify at least part of his story. His demeanor brightened noticeably for the rest of the day.

—⁓—

We adjourned early. After Jensen left, Todd shook Gary's hand and said, "Good job, Gary."

"Thanks," Gary said. "Thank goodness they found someone." He was obviously sincere. What a puzzle—to spend years searching out and killing people with hardly a second thought, then years later to have what appeared to be an honest desire to give comfort to someone's still-grieving relative. Or maybe Gary was simply glad that someone could finally say he believed him after all the weeks of being called a liar.

"I hope you're feeling better about this now," I said to Gary. "What a huge relief."

"Yeah, it *is* a huge relief," Gary said. "Finally. I was starting to have some doubts they'd ever find anything. I knew I'd left her there." He looked at me, nodding. I could see tears welling up in his eyes. The stress he'd been keeping inside must have been nearly unbearable, especially after everyone had repeatedly condemned him for lying. My sense was that these tears were a mixture of remorse, happiness that the discovery would bring some closure or healing to the still-unknown victim's family, and overwhelming relief that they now knew he'd been trying to tell them the truth all along.

Todd and I got up to leave. I told Gary, "Have a good, restful night's sleep. You've done something good. You should feel good about it." I patted him on the back. We wanted to give as much positive reinforcement as we could to help Gary locate more memories in the "wherehouse" of his mind.

—⁓—

The interviews and field trips continued. On Saturday, August 30, at about 6 A.M., we visited the Star Lake site again. About twelve hours later, while barbecuing steaks with our friends Chuck and Jo, at home, I heard more good news. The television reported that bones had just been discovered at "92nd Avenue East, just east of Snoqualmie Parkway," which I knew as the Leisure Time site. It turned out that the bones had been found in the exact spot that Gary had pointed to on the very first field trip, June 14—the same swampy and mucky location where the Diggers and Whackers were complaining that they couldn't find anything and that had initially done so much to undermine Gary's credibility.

Although we didn't know who it was, Gary had always said this victim would be either Keli McGinness or April Buttram; he'd always confused them because they had similar body types. "Big boobs," was how Gary had put it. But the Leisure Time find put Gary's accuracy number up to three, counting Pammy Avent, which the detectives were still withholding from Gary. Tests were under way to see if these two skeletons matched anyone on the Green River missing list.

On Tuesday, September 2, Baird approached Todd and me as we waited for the morning's session to begin.

"We want to continue with the questioning for a while," he said. "It doesn't look like we'll be able to do the plea on the sixteenth. I'd prefer to get it done sooner rather than later, but when we set the date of September 16, your client had neglected to mention he'd murdered someone as recently as 1998. As I recall, he mentioned it later that same day."

Dammit! I thought. But we recognized that Baird had a point.

"How much longer?" Todd asked.

"I'm not sure right now," Baird said. "They want to keep talking as long as information keeps coming out, painful as that might be. Once we're done, it'll take us a couple weeks to get all the paperwork prepared."

"It would be fine if Norm would just make it official," I said, trying for something, anything, to cement the deal in place. "Set the plea for some date in the future." I suggested that making the deal public would have some significant budgetary consequences.

"I mean, we have a team of people preparing for trial," I pointed out, although in fact, our pre-trial work had slowed down considerably. "All of a sudden, they'll be out of a job. And we're putting out a 2004 budget that contemplates a trial. OPD and Judge Jones should know for budget purposes. Ask Norm to have a press conference before this goes much further. That way *he* can control the way the information comes out, instead of the media." I figured if Maleng made it public, it would be a done deal, and he couldn't change his mind. Anything to speed up the process.

"Who do you think is spinning the news through these planned leaks?" Todd said, meaning Maleng. "He's sending out his test balloons, checking the responses . . ."

Baird laughed at Todd's cynical notion—that it was Maleng himself who was the source of the plea deal leaks. Todd's pet theory was that the prosecutor was attempting to prepare the political ground for the eventual deal.

"I'd like him to make it official too," Baird told us. "I'll talk to him about it and get back to you at the end of the week. Although, I don't expect him to trek down here and tell you himself."

"No, but that would be nice," I said. "I guess we can take your word for it." I was teasing Baird.

Later, we called Judge Jones, struck the September 16 hearing date and tentatively rescheduled it for November 5.

The next morning, September 3, before the interrogation session began, Tom Jensen and Randy Mullinax met with Todd and me.

"Did either of you tell Gary about the other finds?" Mullinax asked.

"No," Todd and I answered at the same time.

"Good," Jensen said. "We want to give him the Leisure Time find today."

Tom and Sue walked into the interrogation room and sat down.

"Good news," Jensen told Gary. "Got a bone at Leisure Time."

"Good," Gary said. Gary said again, as he had from the beginning, that "Leisure Time Lady" had to be either Keli McGinness or April Buttram. He just couldn't remember which one. Months later, he said, he'd gone back to the place to pick up a skull. He'd read or heard that Keli McGinness—who'd by then been reported missing—had at one time been in Portland. That's why he'd taken the skull he recovered to Portland: to make investigators think that Keli had been murdered there, not near Seattle.

Keli McGinness had last been seen in mid-June of 1983, at a motel located not far from Gary's house, The Three Bears, which was the focal point of a number of Green River disappearances. But April Buttram had last been seen in Seattle in August 1983. As Gary had explained, those victims he picked up in Seattle rather than on Pacific Highway South were more likely to wind up out I-90, such as the Leisure Time site. The reason for this was that it was a more direct route to the disposal site from Seattle; if the victim had been taken from the Pacific Highway South, like The Three Bears Motel, they were more likely to wind up at Star Lake, Mountain View Cemetery, or up Highway 410, sites in the south county. That was especially true of victims he had lured to his house, Gary said. It was just more convenient.

To help clarify this question—which in turn might help experts identify the bone fragment—Jensen asked if Gary had kept the victim overnight. In other words, April Buttram might have been disposed almost immediately, whereas Keli McGinness was more likely to have been kept longer.

"Did you keep her overnight in your house?" Then he added, "We won't think anything less of you."

Todd jotted me a note that read "factual impossibility," meaning that Jensen and Mullinax had already reached the nadir in their thinking about Gary.

"I know that," Gary said. "No. I did not keep her overnight in my house."

If this was true, it suggested that the Leisure Time victim was in fact April Buttram. Gary admitted it was possible, as he tended to confuse eighteen-year-old Keli with sixteen-year-old April. Still, Gary said, he'd thought all along it was Keli McGinness, because that's why he returned for the skull—because of the news reports placing Keli in Portland.

This skull, of course, had never been found, despite all the searching that had taken place near the insurance office in Portland.

Gary now said he was "quite certain" that either Keli or April had been left at the Leisure Time site and that if it wasn't Keli but April who'd been left there, that meant Keli had to be the victim he'd left near Lake Fenwick. The Lake Fenwick site had never produced anything, but Gary continued to insist that he'd left *someone* there, and by now I believed him. It was just that the Diggers and Whackers had not been able to find anything.

Jensen and Peters now questioned Gary about a post-1985 victim that he'd admitted to Wheeler that he'd left off the side of Highway 410. This was "Federated Forest lady," in our macabre lexicon.

Jensen asked Gary how he could be so sure that he'd left "Federated Forest Lady"—who had not been found as yet—near a specific milepost on the highway, which was one of Gary's usual marking mechanisms.

Gary remembered picking up "Federated Forest Lady" quite clearly, he said, because he'd had to buy a new tire that same day. The old tire had gone flat, he remembered, and his spare was bald.

"I thought I was gonna get a ticket for bein' . . . havin' a bald tire on the back," Gary said. Gary was very conscientious, it seemed, worrying about getting a traffic infraction.

I smiled at Todd. Todd had to turn away. He passed me one of our notes: "Driving on bald tires could cause an accident and someone could get injured." I had to cough to suppress my laughter.

A few hours after getting the new tire, Gary said, he'd gone into Tacoma and picked up "Federated Forest Lady." She'd wanted a ride to her apartment in Des Moines. Gary was driving her there when he stopped somewhere in Federal Way and killed her. Then he took her body to Highway 410. That same day, the canopy had blown off the back of his pickup truck. That's how he remembered "Federated Forest Lady."

Could it get any more weird than this?

Well, yes.

"What do you want for dinner tonight, Gary?" Jensen asked. "Your choice. Since we found some bones out there at Leisure Time, you earned a dinner of your choice—something more than your typical cheeseburger and fries. What'll it be?"

"Oh, I don't know," Gary was caught off guard. "Salmon?"

"Salmon it is!" Jensen said as he closed his file, hopped up, and started to leave the room.

I raised my hand and shouted at Tom, "I'll take steak and lobster, thank you!"

"As soon as *you* come up with a bone!" Jensen said over his shoulder as he left.

"Well, Gary, nice job," Todd said. "And salmon. Good choice."

———

On September 12, after the interviews were over, I was approached by Randy Mullinax as we headed out to the parking lot.

"I just wanted to let you know you were followed here today by a TV reporter. I think he was from KIRO. Just to let you know." Apparently, the reporter deduced that if he followed me, I'd lead him to Gary, because everyone now knew that Gary was no longer in the jail.

"Really? I sure didn't notice anyone," I said.

"It's OK," he said. "No one's really worried too much about that, at this point."

As I got into my truck and drove away, I looked over my shoulder and kept an eye on my rearview mirror. I didn't see anyone following me. Then I wondered, *How did the cops know someone was following me? Are they following me, too? No, that couldn't be. Are they monitoring the cars coming into the parking lot?* I guessed they had people outside, watching.

On September 16, instead of entering the plea as we had hoped, Tony, Todd, and I met with Mark Larson and Dan Satterberg under the watchful eye of the moose in Tony's office. After exchanging greetings, we sat down.

"We're here for Norm," Larson said. "He feels Mr. Ridgway is finally fulfilling his end of the agreement. But the detectives still have additional questioning for him."

Tony let out a small groan.

"How much longer is this going to take?" he asked. "For heaven's sake, how many more questions could they possibly have?"

"They finally feel like they are getting good information from him now," Satterberg said. "Not the Mother Lode, but it's a good vein, and they want to work it as much as they can. They want him to continue to fear the death penalty, so they don't want you to tell him it's a done deal."

Which meant we'd get no public announcement of the deal, despite my earlier suggestion.

Tony sighed. "Understood," he said.

"Except it's not fear of the death penalty that's motivating Gary," I pointed out. Gary really and truly wanted to cooperate for the sake of the victims' families, I thought.

"I agree," Todd put in.

"We just want him to continue to talk and continue to have every incentive he can possibly have to continue to provide information," Satterberg said. We all recognized Satterberg's use of the word *incentive* as the operative noun.

"What's your boss's proposed time line for all this?" Todd asked—like O'Toole, cutting to the chase.

"Maybe the end of October, plus or minus a couple weeks, depending on your client," Larson said.

"How long after the plea until sentencing?"

"Probably three to four weeks," Satterberg guessed. "To get the victims' families lined up." Satterberg knew that this would be part of the political calculus. Having the families in favor of the deal would be a huge plus, and that would take some preparation.

"Is Norm going to say anything ahead of time?" Tony asked.

"Nothing public," Satterberg said. "There will be no press release prior to the plea. We have a strict policy in our office. We won't comment on a plea until the ink's dry."

"What about Judge Jones?" Tony asked. "What about the victims' families? What about Gary's family?" Tony meant that even if Maleng said nothing publicly, somebody was sure to let the secret out.

"Obviously, Judge Jones will have to be told," Satterberg said. "And we can talk to the detectives, to make arrangements for you to let Mr. Ridgway's family know."

"Norm will be contacting the victims' families," he added. "We'll just have to explain to them the importance of keeping it confidential. We wouldn't expect any of them to leak it to the press, anyway."

"That's a lot of people keeping a big secret," Todd pointed out.

"Well, it's not much of a secret anymore, anyhow," Tony observed.

"After the plea, the defense can address the press, then Norm and the sheriff will have a formal, joint press conference," Satterberg said.

"How about a three-way," I suggested, ". . . press conference, I mean." Ha, ha. I really did mean a three-way news conference—sheriff, prosecutor, defense. They weren't interested. I figured they didn't want Tony upstaging Maleng and Reichert.

"Will you be using any automobile metaphors at your press conference?" Todd asked Dan.

"No. No automobile metaphors. Metaphors can be very useful, but they can get you in trouble." He grinned, ruefully, I thought.

"What's Norm going to say when he's asked, 'If not Ridgway, who can you seek the death penalty for?'" Tony asked. "You know that will be one of the first questions."

"Sure. That's going to be a primary issue for Norm to address," Larson agreed. "We feel we've carved a path to maintain a fair and consistent position that the public will understand. And hopefully agree with."

In other words, no death penalty moratorium, I thought. *They think they can still seek the death of young black men who kill police officers. That will certainly piss off some members of the community. How can they ask for death for some killers, but not for the man who admitted murdering up to sixty-three women, or whatever the number finally turns out to be?* But I knew that was the elected officials' problem, not ours, and I certainly wasn't going to give anyone any arguments against giving Gary his life.

Larson and Satterberg left. The fifth day of November looked like a solid date for the end of the nightmare.

Still, the interrogations continued, although little new was coming out by this time. The detectives took Gary over and over his murderous spree, looking for contradictions, trying to get him to explain how and why. To some extent, it was mind numbing: endless repetition of depravity set against the anxiety that at any moment, some fragment might come skittering out of Gary's brain that would change the calculus of what we were doing significantly. Meanwhile, my private, weird dissonance continued: hearing all about gruesome murder by day, trying to have a normal home life by night. Yet for Kelly and me, there were also some significant changes.

On September 19, I drove Sean off to college for his freshman year. We got there just in time for us to quickly say good-bye, before he went to an orientation in his dorm. We got in a brief, teary-eyed hug, then he had to go. The emotion of the immediate moment, coupled with the emotion I'd been trying to hold in over the summer, hit me hard. After Sean departed, I sat in my truck in the parking lot and cried. As my son walked away and moved onto the next chapter of his life, I thought of the tears shed by the parents of the girls who had never lived long enough to make it to college, because my client had killed them. I sat there by myself and cried some more, needing to let it out.

—⁓—

On Saturday, September 27, we learned that the remains found at the Leisure Time site were in fact those of April Buttram; and on the day after that, still more bones were found, these at the 292nd Street site, just off West Valley Highway. By Gary's reckoning, these remains would be those of Marie Malvar, she who had fought so hard that Gary had later had to conceal the scratches she left with battery acid.

By now, after all the rumors and speculation that had been in the news media, reporters both broadcast and print were contacting Tony and me on a daily basis; we'd run out of creative ways to say no comment. On Monday, September 29, MSNBC contacted Tony to ask him to appear on *The Abrams Report*. He couldn't do it and told them to call me. I explained that I wouldn't be able to say anything substantive, but the producer said they would only ask questions I could answer. Nothing about confidential stuff, they said.

I was misled. I was on the show with Ann Rule, who now confirmed that she did intend to write a book about the Green River case, and the entire subject of discussion was the rumored deal—the very thing I'd told the producer I could not talk about. I was asked six different questions, and I had to say "no comment" six different times. My brain was strained trying to think of new ways to say nothing.

The next day, September 30, I followed my usual routine—ordinary, at least for non–field trip days: a stop at the ACA office in Kent before going to the bunker to see what the latest was with Gary.

Once I got to the bunker, I parked, got out of my truck, and walked toward the door. Out from behind a van popped a television reporter, Chris Halsne of KIRO, Channel 7 in Seattle. He approached me quickly, with a cameraman in tow.

"Wondering how you feel about the accommodations that have been set up for your client inside the task force headquarters here. Are they sufficient?" he asked, sticking a microphone in my face. I suddenly knew why some people lost their temper at people who used microphones like weapons. I tried to keep my cool.

"That question assumes my client is in there," I said, "and there's no comment on that, on the location of Mr. Ridgway."

"We have information that Ridgway, they're accommodating him here, so they can have easy access to talk to him. Would you deny that's true?" the reporter persisted.

"I can't comment on that one way or another."

"Is he secure?"

"Is he secure? Oh, yes, he's secure. No doubt about that, and we're able to have contact with him," I said.

"So, he's local? You don't have to go a long way?"

"That's fair to say." *OK, that's enough.* I thought. *Shut up.*

I was remembering what Mullinax had told me about being shadowed a few days earlier. What should I have done? Driven downtown, parked, gone into a department store, then ducked out another exit, caught a taxi, then a bus, like I was in some sort of spy movie? But I knew that even the broadcast of the question would probably tear the lid off things, even with my denial.

In the station's lead story that night, they reported that Gary was in fact at the task force headquarters cooperating with the police and leading them to skeletal remains, in exchange for no death penalty.

After more than a month of rampant speculation and a continual series of leaks, it seemed ridiculous to maintain the posture we'd all agreed on months earlier. I wished that Maleng hadn't been so insistent on keeping the secret. It only made us all look silly, I thought, like we still had something to hide.

As October arrived, Gary continued to direct the investigators to still more possible sites. By now, the interrogations of Gary had established that as many as a dozen victims who were never placed on the official Green River list could have been killed by him, including several victims up through the summer of 1998. And Gary *finally* admitted that he might have killed as early as the 1970s. He just couldn't remember any of the details. Even though I'd heard Gary confess to all sorts of heinous acts during my four months in the bunker, I couldn't escape being stunned as the victim toll shot into the sixties. I wondered if we would ever get to the end of this grueling, brain-shredding process, because it seemed like every time the detectives asked him about an unsolved case, Gary had something vague, if tantalizing, to offer.

Then, on Tuesday, October 7, the detectives dropped yet another bomb. Gary had for some months claimed that he'd taken a few bones from the place where he'd left Green River victim Shirley Sherrill's body—a spot off Auburn-Black Diamond Road in the rural southeastern part of King County—to Oregon. This happened at the same time when he'd taken April Buttram's skull and the skull of Green River victim Denise Bush to the Portland area, in an effort to throw the investigators of the time off his track in 1985, he said. He said he'd left the bones in two different locations in Oregon—Buttram's skull near the insurance office, where it could now not be found, and Denise Bush and Shirley Sherrill's bones at a rural location off Bull Mountain Road, some miles southwest of Portland. Both Denise Bush and

Shirley Sherrill's skulls had been found in 1985. That was one reason the investigators had rushed off to Oregon for a time in the spring of that year, exactly as Gary had hoped.

During our summer in the bunker, almost two decades later, we'd all gone out to the Auburn-Black Diamond Road site two or three times, looking for the rest of Shirley Sherrill. Todd and I both believed that Gary was telling the truth about leaving her body there, because Gary had maintained that he'd only taken a few of Shirley's remains to Oregon. But no matter how hard the Diggers dug and the Whackers whacked, there were no more remains of Shirley Sherrill, or anyone else, to be found off Auburn-Black Diamond Road.

Now we found out that Gary could have been lying about this, too.

"You understand what forensics is? That's what got you sittin' here today, OK?" Jensen began. Gary nodded.

"It's science," Jensen said.

"Science, yes," Gary agreed.

Jensen got Gary to agree that science was probably highly accurate.

"They say it's such and such," Jensen said, "then it probably is such and such."

"Um-hm."

Jensen now put a piece of paper down in front of Gary. It was a pathologist's chart, showing the bones that had been recovered at one of the body disposal sites.

"Guess who that is," Jensen challenged him.

"Um, Sherrill, it says on the top," Gary said.

"Yes, it is. All the bones that are colored in blue . . . were found in Oregon. Now you tell us that you picked up a skull and a few ribs."

"Yeah. Uh . . ."

"We've got, we have basically . . . what we have here, Gary, is prob'ly 75 to 80 percent of the body. OK?"

"Um-hm, right."

"The parts that are missing are parts that are typically missing, when a body gets, is decomposed in a place like Bull Mountain, and the animals drag some parts away," Jensen went on. "OK?"

Gary saw what Jensen was suggesting: there were far, far too many bones at the Shirley Sherrill site for Gary to have taken to Oregon—at least, too many if Shirley had been only a skeleton. Either Gary had driven a dead body several hundred miles in his car (on a trip that he said he'd taken with his nine-year-old son, Matthew, who had his bicycle in the trunk, so *that* was probably out) or possibly he'd killed Shirley Sherrill in Portland.[2]

Good grief! I thought. *It's the Yates problem all over again!*

"Right," Gary was saying. "Yeah, I thought I just took just the skull from . . . uh, and a few rib bones on the side, here. But evidently I took a lot more."

"You took . . ." Jensen began.

"Took uh, 90 percent of her, I think," Gary agreed.

"I believe you took 100 percent of her, Gary," Jensen said. "Now, this is where you get your chance to tell the truth, OK? You want a minute to think about it?"

"I don't need a minute to think about it, no. I only took, I only thought I took the, the skull and the bones here. I didn't remember takin' the rest. The rest of her is still over there at, uh, Black Diamond Road."

Jensen wasn't going to let Gary off the hook.

"The forensic anthropologists and the scientists that have looked at these bones . . . according to [them], it would probably have taken you the better part of an hour to an hour and a half to gather up all those bones—after they had been there for the amount of time that you say you let them lie there, before you went back."

"Um-hm."

Not only that, Jensen told Gary, the way Shirley Sherill's bones had been found when discovered in 1985 indicated that a whole body had decomposed at that site.

"It's because some animal worked the hell outta that," Jensen told him, apparently deciding to try to shock Gary into a more complete admission by being graphic in his description of the condition of Shirley Sherrill's remains. "They didn't sit there [off Auburn-Black Diamond Road] chewin' on that bone, okay. Dogs, coyotes, bears, wolverines, whatever . . . [It] takes a long time to chew the knob off of a femur. It's good eatin', but it takes a long time. And no self-respecting coyote is gonna . . . chew on that bone right there. He's gonna take it home to the kids, okay. He's gonna come back and he's gonna get the pelvis, there's a lot of good meat there too, okay?"

"Un-huh."

"Particularly when this body is decomposing. They're gonna find it right away when it starts to stink." The circumstances showed that the body had not decomposed where Gary had said he'd left it, Jensen said.

"Then I must of . . . I must of taken her down to . . . to Portland, but I don't remember takin' a whole body down to Portland. Don't remember takin' a whole body . . ."

"Where did this body decompose?"

"It . . . it probably decomposed in Portland, is the only thing I can say if . . . that's where most of the body was. But I thought for sure I took a body and took parts of a body out of the [Auburn-Black Diamond Road site]."

Jensen was exasperated with Gary's continued mushiness over facts he should have been able to remember.

"Are we ever gonna reach an understanding between you and me and you and your lawyers where you . . . you realize that you're caught in a fucking lie, and it's time to straighten it out? You can't . . . you shouldn't even be lying to *them*. They should know what the truth is so they can protect your ass. You're gonna have to reach a point where you trust somebody in this thing, okay? I don't care if you tell me, at least tell them, so somebody can protect you. So that you know what you can talk about and what you can't talk about, okay?"

"Un-huh."

"This body did not decompose [off Auburn-Black Diamond Road]. Where did it die?"

"It died in the back of my truck," Gary said. "It had to."

But Gary admitted that while he might have taken Shirley's intact body to Oregon, he just couldn't remember doing it. He still thought he'd left her off Auburn-Black Diamond Road.

After the session ended, Todd and I had another brief meeting with Gary.

"Day 117 and you're still not being truthful," Todd told him. "That's very disturbing."

"How many more surprises?" I asked Gary. "You *know* Jensen has held stuff back. Don't you see what he's doing? He's testing you. He already knows the answers, and he's just trying to see if you're gonna be honest with him. So you gotta tell the truth. All of it. The whole, ugly truth. The whole nine yards, like they say."

"I'm trying," Gary said. He turned his head and pondered. "I'm sure I only took a few bones. Maybe I did get most of them. I was in a hurry and not really paying attention."

"Yeah, fine," I said, sarcastically. "But what about other stuff Tom's got? Inserting stuff? Doing things with their clitorises? Liquids? Bleaches? Souvenirs? Trophies? Other jurisdictions? What other surprises are out there?" For some weeks, Jensen and the others had been asking Gary if he'd mutilated any of the corpses of the victims after killing them; I had the idea that they thought he might have used battery acid or even bleach or knives as part of the insertion fixation he could only talk about obliquely.

Gary shook his head but didn't say anything.

Todd made another pass.

"You are violating the plea agreement if you do not fully disclose everything," he said. "Do you understand? This is *not* a done deal yet."

"Yes," Gary said, quietly. "I know it's not a done deal."

"And we sure as hell don't want you to get 'Yates'd,' because you withheld the truth from me and Mark. Do you get me?"

"Yeah, I understand."

"Well, is there anything else you need to tell us now? Before we hear it from Jensen or Mullinax?" I could tell that if anything, Todd was even angrier than Jensen.

"No," Gary said. "There's nothing else." Gary's assurance was unavailing; by now we knew better than to believe him.

"I didn't do anything to them," he said. "I didn't use any bleach on them or nothing. I didn't keep any souvenirs or trophies. And I didn't kill anyone in Oregon. I didn't kill anywhere other than King County."

Unfortunately, Todd and I could no longer be convinced. We'd heard him say the same thing, with as much or more sincerity and certainty, when he told us he hadn't killed after 1985. Hell, I'd even heard him use that same tone of denial when he'd told me, back on November 30, 2001, that he hadn't killed anyone. And look where we were now.

44

As our beautiful summer rolled on into fall, and the days grew cooler and the leaves turned into their spectacular orange and red, the Kentwood Conquerors' girls' swim team moved through their season without a loss, a matter of great pride to me. In the mornings, I was on the pool deck, just as I had been two years before. Only this time it was the girls' team in the water, not Sean and the boys. And after the workout was over, I'd find myself going once more back to that chamber of recollected horrors, the bunker, where the grilling of Gary continued. In October, we made three more field trips, looking for places where Gary had said he'd killed his many victims.

Although we were trying to tie up as many loose ends as possible, it seemed that as Gary tried to answer the remaining questions, his answers were getting more and more ambiguous, less and less clear. Were they real memories? Was Gary just trying to please and satisfy his captors, as he often had in the past? Was he purposely trying to stretch the process out, so he could remain the center of attention? Or was he simply tired and confused, after all the months of questioning and confrontation?

Although Todd and I believed he had simply run out of information, some of the task force believed he was still intentionally withholding, keeping some secrets to himself.

I began drafting the official guilty plea, a document titled the Statement of Defendant on Plea of Guilty, while Jeff Baird prepared a summary of the state's evidence against Gary, which was to include the details gleaned from the five months of confession. This would be a critical part of Maleng's approach to the deal. He wanted to be able to tell the public that the case was truly over, solved, and the only sure way to do that was to be able to recite all the facts, almost exactly as they would be if they'd been presented through testimony at a trial. Maleng did not want there to be any doubt that the real, bona fide, one-and-only Green River Killer had been identified. So Baird had the job of writing up all the gory details. By the time he was finished, the public would have a document that would dispel any doubts, as well as turn a lot of stomachs. We were all aware that this guilty plea was going to be like no other in American legal history.

On October 9, we were back at the bunker for more interrogations. I think the cops and prosecutors could tell we were down and still reeling from the Sherrill revelation, and Gary's seemingly impossible denial. Maybe the detectives took pity on us, I don't know. But this was a much better day, as they kept everything positive and light. Even Gary picked up on this; he seemed in better spirits, and as a result he did a pretty good job remembering. For this session, though, we'd sat down with Gary and tried to get him to make a list of things he could remember so he could give the details to Jensen *before* Jensen could bring them up.

Mullinax and Jensen ticked their way down the list. Eventually, they came to the letter that Gary had claimed he'd written to the *Seattle Post-Intelligencer* newspaper in 1984, the one that reporter Mike Barber had turned over to the task force. Although Gary had long ago admitted writing a letter to someone—he couldn't remember to whom—the first time he was shown this letter, during the summer, he'd denied writing it. *Arghhh!* Now Jensen was showing it to him again.

This letter had forty typed lines, each of them numbered, with words that usually ran into one another, that is, without spaces. Some of the lines had highly relevant facts in them, and others did not. The heading and the first few items are as follows:

Whatyou eedtonoaboutthegreenriverman

dontthrowaway

1first onebokenordislocatarmwhy

2one iakinriverhadastoneinthevaginawhy

3whysomeinriversomeabovegroundsomeunderground

4instrancewhogotit

5whostogainbytheredeaths

And so on, down one entire lined page and at the top of a second. It was signed:

callmefred

Once the words were separated with spaces, it became clearer:

What you [n]eed to [kn]no[w] about the green river man

don't throw away

1 first one b[r]oken or dislocate[ed] arm why

2 one iak *[sic]* in river had a stone in the vagina why

3 why some in river some above ground some under ground

4 ins[u]rance who got it

5 whos to gain by there deaths

The letter had been postmarked on February 20, 1984, sent to the *Seattle Times* postal box but addressed to the *Post-Intelligencer*. "Very importent," the outside of the envelope read.

And here was a strange twist of fate: because the two newspapers had a joint operating agreement, sharing ad sales and production functions, many people believed the two papers were one and the same and housed jointly, as apparently Gary did. However, they were not in the same location, or even jointly owned, and their reporters remained competitive. Once the letter was received at the *Times,* it appears that someone at that paper decided to forward it to the *Post-Intelligencer* without opening it. At this point, in early 1984, the fact of the rocks in the vaginas of two of the victims was highly secret information. Although it was known to reporters at the *Times,* it had never been published. So the statement about the rocks would have demonstrated to reporters at the *Times,* at least, that the writer was very probably the real killer.[1]

There were, in fact, a number of assertions about the murders in the letter that conformed to facts that had been closely held by investigators at the time. For example, line number nineteen read, "momaplehadredwinelombruscsomefishanddumpedthere," which translated to "M.O. Maple [Valley] had red wine Lambrusco some fish and dumped there," which was a clear reference to Carol Christensen. Another read, "whytakesomeclothesandleaverest," obviously meaning, "why take some clothes and leave rest." At that point, the information about the wine, fish, and sausage found with Carol Christensen's body in Maple Valley was also a secret, as was the fact that though some victims had been found with clothing, the remainder had not. At the time the letter was received, Carol Christensen had not been considered a Green River victim, and certainly only the police and the killer knew about the wine bottle.

Despite these and several other valid assertions about the murders, there were also a large number of false statements, including assertions that the killer smoked, chewed gum, and was a long-haul truck driver. The FBI considered the letter a hoax and suggested that someone with access to the information held by the police had written it. This, to the detectives, seemed like a direct shot to their own integrity.

Now, almost twenty years later, Jensen wanted to get to the bottom of this letter issue. Had Gary really written it or not?

Jensen put the letter in front of Gary. Yes, Gary said, that was his letter.

"When did you write the letter?" Jensen asked.

"I don't remember, remember when I wrote it," Gary said. "'Cause I wrote *two* letters. The first letter I wrote was talkin' about a lotta things about young, young uh, always used 'ladies' in there. And then I redone the letter and that's what you got . . ."

"The one I showed you?"

"Um-hm."

"Sure you wrote that?"

"I'm 100 percent sure, yes."

"Why wasn't your DNA on the envelope?"

"'Cause I used water on the uh, seal."

"Why?"

"'Cause I didn't want uh, anybody to find out who did it."

"Find what? How would we find out who did it?"

"Oh, if I licked it, it'd be uh, uh, I just didn't use, I didn't, I used gloves and I uh . . . everything in there points to me. Everything in that letter points to me, and I, I wrote it, yes."

This seemed very wobbly. The absence of Gary's DNA from the seal seemed odd or so Jensen wanted Gary to believe. After all, in 1984, DNA hadn't been used as a forensic technique, so how could Gary have believed that it would unmask him? Why else use water to seal the envelope?

Gary insisted that he'd written the letter, including some of the details of the crimes in order to convince the police that the real killer had written it but also including other details to lead investigators to look at someone other than him.

"Thinkin' of little things to throw in there?" Jensen asked him.

"Little things to throw in there, to . . . I think I wrote some'n about the gum, gum wrappers. I don't chew gum, so . . . and everybody knows I don't chew gum, so that would throw ya off. Uh, cigarette butts, I don't smoke. I think I threw cigarette . . . and maybe I didn't write cigarette butts in there, but I did throw cigarette butts in there for throwin' ya off."

Jensen now went through the letter, all forty lines related by the writer; Gary told him what was true and what he'd made up to throw investigators off the track.

When Jensen reached the final point, the letter's signature, "callmefred," he pulled out another letter.

"I wanna read you somethin' here, Gary," Jensen said. "'Cause I . . . 'cause I want this on the . . . on the record. It's written by, uh, the eminent John Douglas, the FBI Academy."[2] Jensen began to read from Douglas's letter.

"'August 24, 1984,'" he read. "'Historically, we've had very few serial killers of this type who have communicated with the media or members of the investigation team. Serial killers in fact [who] did communicate . . . were very specific in providing details of their crimes, in order for them to establish instant credibility. This is part of their personal need, having feelings of inadequacies and lacking self worth . . . they must feel powerful . . .' Basically, uh, [Douglas is] talking about the letter and some other stuff. 'In summary, none of these communiqués were authored by the Green River Killer,'" Jensen finished, put Douglas's letter aside, and waited.

"Yeah, I . . . I wrote that letter, you guys know it," Gary said.

"Are you the Green River Killer?" Jensen now asked.

"Yeah," Gary said.

"All right," Jensen said. "Anything else?"

"I'm good," Mattsen said.

"OK, I got my dig in." Jensen had just put "on the record" what he thought of Douglas's 1984 advice, at least about the letter that Douglas had claimed the killer hadn't written.

Jensen's dig was both subtle and hilarious. Todd and I cracked up. Gary wasn't quite sure what was so funny. But it was a thing of beauty. A long, slow, winding setup by Jensen. An honest straight man in Gary. Todd and I watched and had no idea Tom was setting it up for a poke at John Douglas and the FBI. From my view, it appeared there was no love lost between the King County Sheriff's Department and the bureau. Just like in the movies, the feds thought they were hot shit and came in and tried to take over the show from the locals. Then the locals were left to clean up the mess left by the feds.

For his part, Douglas always contended that his profile, at least, had been accurate, if general, and suggested that it had never been a substitute for resolute, determined police work.

―〰―

It turned out that Gary wasn't lying about something else, too—he *had* stabbed a little boy when he was fourteen or fifteen years old.

After Gary told O'Toole about the stabbing, Detective Rafe Crenshaw of the task force got to work. In an incredible piece of detective work, Crenshaw located the boy, now in his thirties, living in southern California. The boy's story essentially confirmed what Gary had admitted to O'Toole, except he had a few more details. Specifically, the man [now] recalled that he'd asked his assailant why he had killed him. He said the teenaged Gary told him, after stabbing him, "You're gonna die," and that he'd laughed before adding, "I always wanted to feel what it would be like to kill somebody."

Confronted with this, Gary could not recall saying that but didn't dispute the man's account of the stabbing. Although the boy nearly did die, he recovered, obviously, and the police were never able to locate his assailant. For his part, Gary had been certain at the time, in 1963, that he was about to be arrested; he was sure the police would show the boy school yearbook pictures to determine his identity. One can only wonder how different things might have been if that had happened.

45

By late October 2003, the speculation and anticipation about the possible plea deal for Gary had reached a crescendo. It seemed as if every single day brought new television reports, or commentaries or newspaper articles, or another letter to the editor. The *King County Journal* and the Associated Press continued to take the high road: all of their articles contained attribution to named sources. The other news outlets often abandoned that most-desirable practice, however.

On Friday, October 17, a front-page headline in the *Times* informed us that if there was no death penalty for Gary, there might no longer be a death penalty for anyone in Washington State:

"Ridgway deal could change criteria for death penalty," it read.[1] Three other criminal defense lawyers, John Muenster, Mark Larranaga, and Tim Ford, all pointed out that sparing Gary from the ultimate sanction was likely to make it constitutionally, and morally, impossible to give anyone else the last needle. Muenster, representing a murder defendant in Snohomish County, just to the north of Seattle, argued just that point in a hearing for his own client.

"If they don't seek the death penalty in Ridgway's case, how can a prosecutor morally seek the death penalty against someone who's not a killer?" Muenster asked. Muenster's client had been accused of participating in the death of one woman but had not yet been convicted. Larranaga agreed.

"It's going to be very difficult for prosecutors and the Supreme Court to say that other cases that are less egregious [than the Ridgway case] deserve the death penalty," he said. And Ford, widely known as one of the nation's leading experts on the law of the death penalty, pointed out that the "proportionality" of the penalty—whether it was applied evenly among defendants—was a major constitutional problem, if one believed that the Constitution gave the same rights to everyone.

"I've been making this argument for thirty years," Ford said, "but this will be a very visible and a very dramatic example of a phenomenon that's happening all the time. So you've got to be wondering what Norm Maleng is going to do . . ."

Initially, I was distressed by the article and the timing of the sentiments expressed by my fellow defense lawyers. *Couldn't they have waited until* after *the plea before they brought that up?* I didn't want any more pressure on Maleng *not* to do the deal, and this certainly focused it on the prosecutor. The reporter who'd written the *Times* article, Ian Ith, aptly pointed out that one of the primary beneficiaries of our proposed deal, besides Gary, might be . . . Robert Yates, who'd made a deal like ours in Spokane. But he got the death penalty for another two murders in Pierce County anyway. The argument could be made by Yates that even though he'd killed "only" thirteen, Gary had killed nearly four times as many, so it was hardly fair for the State of Washington to give him the big drop for only the two Pierce County murders, while letting Gary live, when he was believed to have killed as many as four dozen.

And there it was, in the same article: "At the time, Maleng was an outspoken critic of Spokane County Prosecutor Steven Tucker for plea-bargaining away the death penalty."

Ouch! That certainly threw the issue back in Maleng's face.

Although I knew that Maleng had thought the whole position through long before, and that he was fully prepared to deal with the criticism, and that an article in a newspaper certainly wasn't going to change his mind, I just couldn't stop worrying about whatever could possibly go wrong—until the "ink was dry," as Satterberg had put it.

At noon on October 20, Patty Eakes, Jeff Baird, Brian McDonald, and Mark Larson came to Tony's office to meet with Tony, Todd, and me under the moose. There was an air of camaraderie among us, a sense of having survived a sort of horrific catastrophe and now were in the calm after the storm. Yet there was an unspoken anticipation for what still had to happen. We all knew we had a lot of work left to do before we could rest.

"We want to go ahead and do the guilty plea on November 5," Larson told us. "There will be no pre-plea announcement to the press. Norm and Sheriff Reichert will be notifying the families of the victims a few days before the plea."

"How many will he be pleading to?" I asked. They had not let us know yet exactly which cases would be included in the actual plea. I thought it would be between fifty and fifty-five murders. That would include either forty-five or forty-six out of the original forty-nine from the official Green River list. Gary still denied killing Amina Agisheff, Tammy Liles, and the unidentified skeleton found near Tammy Liles's body in Oregon. In addition, he'd never been able to give the detectives anything useful on the Rebecca Marrero case (she remained among the missing), so that one might be out, too. To the original Green River cases would be added Linda Rule, Patricia Barczak, Roberta Hayes, Marta Reeves, Patricia Yellowrobe, and the new set of as-yet-unidentified bones found in September at the Kent-Des Moines Road site, which hadn't been matched to any of the missing. That made the most likely total fifty-one. And I still wasn't sure what they would be doing with the Sherrill case.

Then there were also others that the investigators believed Gary had killed but that had varying degrees of corroboration. If they took a medium-angle view, they could loosely match his descriptions of murders to several other cases, as well as those of missing girls. If they took the most expansive approach, the one that took every admission as the gospel, Gary had admitted as many as seventy-one murders. Yet, as Tony now reminded all of us, even seventy-one murders was significantly less than the total of all the previously unsolved murders of young women in western Washington State when they were added up. That figure, adding the Red River to the Green River total, as well as others that had taken place somewhat farther afield, meant that there were at least 150 murders of young women over the past two decades—an awful blot on one of the most beautiful regions of the country.

"We're going to include forty-eight," Baird told us. They were taking the minimum, which was smart. If evidence against someone other than Gary ever developed for any of the crimes between forty-eight and seventy-one, the prosecution would not be precluded from charging that person.

"Here's a copy of our proposed Amended Information for you." He dropped it on the table and continued.

"You'll see we only charged forty-eight. . . . Boy, that sounded weird . . . *only* forty-eight? . . . only the cases where we had solid corroboration."

"We know he killed Keli McGinness, Patricia Osborne, and Kase Lee," Patty Eakes said. "But we don't have their bodies. Rebecca Marrcro, too. But we just don't have enough corroboration."

"And we also know he killed 'Water Tower Lady' and 'Limping Lady,'" Baird said, gently mocking the names we had all used to identify Gary's victims, "but we don't know when or where or anything else about them, other than that he was 'quite certain' he 'would have' choked them from behind. In his truck . . . or maybe in his house."

"We only want to include murders we could prove he committed," Brian McDonald added. "We decided we couldn't include one, if our only evidence was Gary's confession. For some reason . . ." McDonald paused and smiled, politely ". . . we just didn't feel that was enough." We all knew the reason, having listened to Gary stray all over the place on some of his murder confessions.

While we talked, I quickly glanced through the Amended Information. I was pleased to see that they had included the case of Shirley Sherrill. But this raised the question: How could the court legitimately take a guilty plea from Gary if he couldn't remember some of the most important details of his supposed crimes? How could he "knowingly waive" his right to a trial if he couldn't remember committing the crime on a specific date, and in a specific place, and against a specific person, as the law required?

"Under the circumstances," Baird said, "we may want to do a combination straight plea and *Alford* [no contest] plea. He can't necessarily recall specific details like exact dates and names, and that's understandable."

"That's a good idea," Tony said. "I was wondering how we'd deal with his memory deficiencies."

"Yeah," Baird said. "I can just see it now: 'Mr. Ridgway, what is your plea to the murder of Gisele Lovvorn on July 19, 1982?' . . . 'Um? Was I on days or nights then?'" We all shared a laugh, "quite certain" that Baird had pegged Gary's answer on the nose.

"No, no," Todd said, still laughing. "We'll have him prepared."

"We should do a dry run with him the day before," Baird suggested. "If that's agreeable with you guys."

"That's a good idea," Tony said. "Gary would appreciate that." We all knew that Gary was petrified at the idea of standing up to speak in public. He hated being seen as Wrongway Ridgway. Giving him a chance to practice his lines ahead of time couldn't hurt.

"One other thing," Larson told us. "Satterberg and Donahoe want to confer with you guys about the post-plea press conferences."

"Why?" I asked. "Do you expect some press coverage?" Always trying to inject a little levity. I guess it's been my way of dealing with stressful situations.

—⁓—

It poured that day, a rainy day record for Seattle—almost five inches of rain at once. For Seattle, the so-called Rain City, it was a monsoon. Typically, rain in Seattle is not something to make much of, mostly because it generally just drizzles, constantly but lightly, from late October to April. It rarely comes down in barrels, or even buckets. But not on October 20. That was a deluge.

After winding things up in Tony's office, I'd headed down to the pool to coach the Kentwood girls team. Then, while I was on the pool deck, my cell phone rang just before five. It was Eakes, so I took the call and turned the team over to Tricia, our assistant coach.

"Hi, Patty," I said. "What's up?"

"You're not gonna believe this one," Eakes told me.

"Try me," I said. "What could I possibly 'not believe' at this point?"

"The bunker is flooded," she said. "They're moving Gary."

"You're shitting me?" She said she wasn't. I couldn't believe it! But on the other hand, I knew she wouldn't be telling me something like this unless it was true. She's not as cruel and demented as Todd.

"No, no," Eakes laughed, "I'm serious. We're down here getting everything up off the floor. The carpet's soaked and the water's still rising. It's kind of like chaos right now. We just wanted to let you know tomorrow morning's bunker session will probably be canceled. I'll call you back to let you know where they're taking Gary. You can talk to him once they get him wherever they're going."

"Man. . . . This is incredible. . . . It's crazy," I said. "OK. Thanks for the information."

An hour later, Eakes called back. "Gary's been moved to the Blue Pacific Inn.[2] It's about a mile or so from the bunker," she said.

"The Blue Pacific Inn?" It just struck me as strange, ironic—funny, even. The Blue Pacific Inn had changed locations since back then, but in the early eighties, it stood near ground zero for the Green River Killer. Now Gary would be spending the night at the lodging establishment that had once been near the epicenter of his murderous efforts. Now he was going to be put up, at county expense, at the successor to the place that had once been near the center of his depredations.

After hanging up, I called Todd.

"Todd," I said, "the bunker has flooded. They're moving Gary to the Blue Pacific Inn."

"*Right,*" Todd said. "I suppose they're giving him a steak dinner and a massage, too?"

"Really," I said.

"You're just trying to get even with me for the 'bones' I found," Todd said, meaning his practical joke with the photographs two months before.

"I would never do that," I said. I thought maybe I should suggest that I'd see him in the bunker the next day; when he waded into the interrogation room, he'd find out that I had been "quite certain" when I told him that Gary had been moved to the Blue Pacific Inn. *Take that, Todd!* But eventually, I convinced him that this was no joke: Gary really *was* spending the night in a luxury hotel.

The next day, though, Dean Radford of the *King County Journal* called to inquire about the flooding at the bunker, which only precipitated the obvious question: "Where's Gary?"

"No comment," I said. The last thing I wanted was for Radford with a photographer in tow to troop down to the hotel to get a picture of Gary reposing in the lap of luxury—just as the jail commander had jocularly worried about so many months before, when Gary had first vanished from view.

As the bunker dried out over the next few days, Gary sat in his hotel room and watched movies with the task force detectives—the first time he'd seen a television, except for a tape monitor, for almost six months. I suppose he did get a nice dinner, but certainly no massage.

The day after that, October 22, we had a closed-door conference with Judge Jones. Besides the lawyers from the bunker, Captain Jim Graddon and Sergeant Ray Green from the task force attended to give the judge some advice on logistics and security. We met in the jury room in Judge Jones's court, and if this came off, it would be the only time such a room would ever be used to discuss the matter of *State* v. *Ridgway.*

Baird gave the judge a copy of the proposed Amended Information.

"We'd like to confirm the November 5 date for the plea, Your Honor."

Jones smiled slightly.

"OK. That's fine, counsel. How long should we plan on?"

Baird said he thought the whole thing would take several hours to get through.

Because of the enormous public interest in the case, we all knew that Judge Jones's courtroom would be far too small. Both sides agreed to hold the plea hearing in the venerable old courthouse's presiding courtroom, which had the seating capacity for a few hundred people, almost the same as a medium-sized church. Seats in this courtroom would be reserved for the victims' families, the task force, the prosecution, and our defense team, as well as the news media. Security would also be extremely tight: names would have to be put on an approved list, in order to gain admission. No one wanted the sort of insane violence that periodically erupts in courtrooms across the country for this denouement, and we all knew that Gary, because of his notoriety, might be a prime target for some fanatic.

Jones told us that the court intended to establish a Web site for the case, just to prevent the clerk's office from being overrun by people who wanted access to the documents that would be filed with the plea. That was something else that had changed since the time of the murders: twenty-one years before, a computer was something used by NASA. Now it had the capacity to give the entire public instant access to the records of a criminal case, simply with the click of something called a *mouse*—a device that did not then exist.

By now, the fact that a plea was in the works was probably the worst-kept secret in Seattle. Still, the authorities seemed determined to pull this off in a well-organized, even regimented fashion, as if there were no such things as leaks. It was very clear that the task force and the prosecutor's office had worked out the *choreography* of the deal down to the minute and had no intention of deviating from their plan. Well, I thought, it was their show—they were the ones who were going to have to do the really heavy lifting to justify things.

"The plan is for the Sheriff's Department and prosecutors to notify the victims' families over a three-day period before the plea," Graddon told us. "Sunday, Monday, and Tuesday, November 2, 3, and 4."

"Our office will issue a press statement, just saying there will be a 'significant hearing' on November 5, in the presiding court," Eakes said, "to be followed by a press conference with Norm and Sheriff Reichert. They'll know what's going on without being told." Eakes meant the news media people. If they didn't know what was going on by now, they hadn't been reading their own newspapers or watching their own broadcasts.

"I just want to commend counsel for getting to this point," Jones told us. "Good work."

46

Now that the date had been set for the formal guilty plea, our side thought we should make one last effort to excavate Gary's memory for any other murders. Although we were pretty sure that the state would not renege on the deal, we still wanted to be sure that there were no other crimes lurking in Gary's "wherehouse" that might allow the prosecutors to later bring new charges. In short, with the finish line just days away, it was our aim to get every conceivable criminal act covered by the terms of the bargain. Legally, once the plea was entered, there would be no bar to the state bringing new charges on information developed after Gary formally made his admissions, so we had to make sure the deal covered everything.

We brought back Dr. Judith Becker, the Arizona psychologist who specializes in sex predators. Dr. Becker had interviewed Gary earlier in the year, before the plea bargain had been negotiated, and we thought she'd been able to develop a good rapport with Gary. Our idea was that perhaps Becker could reach areas of Gary's "wherehouse" that he'd been holding back from the detectives or the state's psychologists.

By this point, Becker had seen the interviews Gary had given Wheeler and O'Toole, so she had a pretty good idea of how Gary's mind worked. She knew that Gary had a problem with years—for instance, he frequently confused 1998 with 1989. The numerals of the years seemed to jump around in Gary's brain, which frustrated the hell out of everyone. And even though, at first, this was seen as yet more evidence of Gary's lying and his desire to conceal, eventually people realized that without some exterior reference to some other event, this was just the way Gary's spotty memory worked—or rather did *not* work.

Still, we wanted Becker to see if she couldn't loosen any recollection of earlier murders—any, for example, that Gary might have committed in the early 1970s between his marriage to Claudia and his marriage to Marcia. O'Toole had been convinced that Gary had killed in this time frame, and Wheeler seemed at least halfway persuaded. But Gary, after confusing 1971 with 1981, eventually seemed to be fairly clear that the first person he'd ever attacked and maybe killed was in 1981. He remembered choking a woman, then leaving her near the high school he'd attended. But there seemed to be no record of this, and Gary wasn't sure if he'd really killed her or just choked her.

Like others, Becker wanted to find out why Gary believed that he'd slowed down his killing pace after 1985. Gary provided the usual reasons: meeting Judith, attending church, becoming more financially secure, having more to lose, having less time on his hands. But for Becker, he added a few new ones. One was Judith's car, which had velour seats. When he used the car to pick someone up, Gary told Becker, he didn't want to kill them in the car, because it would stain the fabric. And there was a second reason: by 1985, Gary had become worried that the FBI had assigned a space satellite to keep him under surveillance.

"I thought I had . . . the FBI came on the case, way back in '85 or '84 something like that. And I thought there was a satellite taking pictures of me . . . and that's why it stopped me from killing somebody outside, I think. I always thought maybe somebody was watching me and it might be I'm paranoid about that but . . ." From 1985 on, if he killed anyone, Gary indicated, he wouldn't do it outside of the rear of his truck, because of the fear that the spy satellite would detect it.

Becker asked how his relationship with Judith had slowed down his killing.

"I was more . . . after going with, you know, living with Judith and everything, it seemed to be getting more calm and more . . . somebody cared for me. But it comes . . . I've . . . I've never really talked about this before and . . . I don't know if it matters or makes any difference.

See, when I was younger . . . my first time I had sex, it was a nice woman and I'd have sex with her and fall asleep in her arms."

Gary began crying. He continued.

"What bothered me about this was, it's almost like the same thing as being with a prostitute. Having sex and having to get up because of hygiene. Maybe I needed to see a psychologist at the time. I figured even having sex with an ordinary women, you know, jumping up and having to wash off and then you lose that intimacy of falling asleep in a woman's arms."

"Um-hm," Becker nodded.

"Maybe that had something to do with the way I felt about women in '82 and '83. And after, you know, realizing with myself the intimacy of their, of holding 'em, falling asleep. The last thing you see is a woman in your arms, instead of like a prostitute, getting up and cleaning up."

"Mr. Ridgway, this is the most sadness that I've seen you show over the times that we've met . . . you know, talking about this," Becker said.

"Well, it does bother me about having sex with a woman, wife or whatever it is, and then getting up. Because you lose that intimacy, and that started on early in my life."

It was clear that Gary took this post-coital behavior as something of a personal repudiation. He didn't like it when his wives behaved this way, and he hated it with prostitutes. Yet Gary also admitted that there was rarely any chance of post-coital intimacy with his victims: instead, that was when he killed them.

Which raised another issue for Becker: at what point during sex did Gary have the urge to kill?

"So . . . so what do you think was more arousing to you, having sex with them after, postmortem, is what they call it? . . ."

"The majority of 'em I killed uh, right as I climaxed," Gary said. "Right after I climaxed." Gary admitted that murder during sexual climax seemed to intensify his experience. Until this point, with Jensen and the other detectives, Gary had denied that his murders were committed during orgasm, although Jensen had come to believe that Gary was not being honest about this in his denials.

Becker wanted to know how Gary could commit murder so often without it affecting the rest of his life, particularly his close relationship with his parents.

"Now how would it be for you, to visit your parents' home, knowing what you had been doing? You know, seeing uh, the dating and then . . . and then the killings. How . . . what would that be like, to be at your parents' house, knowing that that had been occurring?"

"What I might, might say it's uh, the two Garys. There's the uh, calm and uh, calm Gary around people and joking a little bit. And, and it's the Gary, uh, Serial Killer. When I pick up a woman to have sex, I was . . . and not kill her, it was the Gary just to have sex. And, but when I got to the stage of having sex with a woman and then killing 'em, that's when uh, it was more of the Green River Gary. Not . . . not separated . . . the same person, but I could uh, talk to women that I'd kill just the same as I talk to a woman that I didn't kill. But when I killed 'em, I was uh . . . uh . . . hide the body . . . um, do what I have to do to um, hide evidence. Um, and then try to go back bein' normal uh, the next day. You know, go home, maybe, after I'd dumped a body off and taken a shower, hop into bed, get up in the morning. Then, I didn't sleep very good anyway."

"Um-hm."

"And I never have . . . then high on caffeine all day. It was just a nor-mal Gary. I could joke and I could be just like any . . ."

Becker wanted to know whether Gary's parents had ever talked to him about sex, or masturbation.

No, Gary said.

"And, and had your mom or dad prepared you for that? Did they talk about changes that would occur in your body and that semen might come out of your penis? Did they?"

"No."

"They didn't talk [about sex at all]?"

"No, they didn't, they didn't talk to me about that at all. Uh, they, but basically was, it was drilled in my head never, never to, never to hit a woman."

"I'm wondering why your parents focused on that, and you might not know the answer. Why would that be the main thing that they would teach you as a child . . . is not to hit women?"

"I think, well, m-my dad prob . . . m-my mom like a lotta times wore the pants," Gary said.

Becker wanted to know how Gary felt after killing, particularly in light of this statement that he'd been raised to "never hit a woman."

"I, I cried a lot about 'em. I know takin' some of 'em out to 410, I'd c-cry all the way to the time I dumped 'em. And on, on Star Lake I'd cry when I'd pull 'em in to, to uh, cover 'em up or you know, hide 'em. And one I uh, pulled out a the tailgate and, and she fell on her head and I put her over the guardrail. I turned around and came back, parked the truck, and I cried all the way in to uh, where I, where I, where I put her and told her 'sorry, I, I dropped you on your head.' And, and she's dead, there's no feeling there, she's nothin' there but it's still . . . and that's uh, one that we couldn't find."

This, Todd and I recalled, was Federated Forest Lady, picked up in Tacoma in the mid- to late 1980s, someone Gary thought had been named *Darci*, or *Dorsey*, who had never been found—the day Gary had a flat tire on his truck, and the camper shell had blown off his truck while driving home from Highway 410.

His memory was bad but could be improved when people gave him cues, Gary said. Pictures, maps, some details usually triggered off some memory, or fragment, and thinking about it later led him to remember other details or what he thought "mighta been," "coulda been," or was "quite certain" were details. But Becker realized that in their eagerness to get details, they were treading a fine line between cueing and overcueing, as Gary was so prone to adopting others' ideas as the reality.

"In terms of when he [a detective] asked you to recall something, it was difficult to recall," Becker told Gary. "But if you're given certain cues about something, then, then that facilitates your recall?"

"That's exactly, 'cause I have the same words Sue [Peters] says. She says she almost had to, she comes in here sometimes and she says I almost have to uh, uh, give ya information or some'n like that." It was when he was given something to work with, Gary added, that his memory improved.

Becker turned to the old bugaboo, the missing jewelry. By this point, Gary had told the detectives that he'd left much of the jewelry at Kenworth. And here was something of a taunt by Gary, at least during the time of the murders.

"I threw it in the woman's bathroom and I was . . . I was more intrigued on uh, uh, that was another part a my fantasy, which ones a these gonna be turned in, which ones, w-women are gonna keep the stuff. I'd throw it in the bathroom above where I worked and I could go up and I could listen. I'd ask, 'is uh, so-and-so in the bathroom' and, as a woman comes out and says 'no, nobody at all in the bathroom,' then that's when my cue was to throw some'n in there."

"I see."

"And not to go in the bathroom. But to throw some'n in and, and come back down and, and listen to the reaction I got. There was, I kind of uh . . . but it's more like, which one a these women are gonna turn this stuff in? Which one of 'em's gonna be k-keepin' it? And then later on when I told this to the officers, it's just, which ones of these gonna come forward with jewelry they've had for twenty years? . . ."

"Hm," Becker said.

"And it was a way a getting back at some a the women at Kenworth, because uh, sometimes I had problems with women, uh, control."

I wrote on my note pad: "Understatement of the day."

Todd saw my note and wrote: "Total insight nugget."

"Um-hm," Becker said.

"Uh, I had troubles with women back in '82, when I started killing. . . . I was getting more controlled by women and I didn't like that."

"This was at work?"

"It was work," Gary agreed. "I'd be in there painting and one woman would sch-schedule things I had uh, and they'd get all the easy ones and we'd get the hard ones, so. And . . . so that was a, a way a getting back at 'em, in a way. And uh, I, I was playin', I was killin' the women and that was the thing, I was hiding that. I was hiding the jewelry at work and throwing them out for these women. And then uh, the other thing was the f-f-feeling of what the women did with the jewelry—if they turned it in."

It gave him pleasure to see his female coworkers at Kenworth wearing the victims' jewelry, Gary indicated, rather than turning it into the plant's lost-and-found, because it validated his low opinion of the honesty of women.

47

That night, still a week before anything was official, two television channels reported that Gary Ridgway would plead guilty to forty-eight counts of aggravated murder on November 5. By this point, the leaks didn't matter much to the defense. Maleng and Reichert had both planned to meet with the families individually a few days before the plea to tell them about it, but the television people scooped them. However it was leaked, it was not the right way for the families of the victims to learn about the plea arrangement.

The next day, television reporter Linda Byron contacted Tony, Todd, and me as we were leaving the bunker. As politely as possible, we each said one variation or another of the same old thing: "No comment." Later, Byron called me to confirm the previously unreported scoop that Marta Reeves and Patricia Yellowrobe were among the forty-eight charges to which Gary was pleading guilty.

"Sorry," I told her. "As they say, 'I can neither confirm nor deny.'"

"I knew you were going to say that," she said.

"Where did you get this stuff, anyway?" I asked.

"You know I can't reveal my sources," she replied.

"I knew you were going to say that."

—⁓—

The day after that, on October 30, Baird gave Todd and me a draft of his case summary—the whole sordid story of Gary's predations, including the necrophilia, totaling about 140 pages in length. Getting all the facts out to the public was the only way, we knew, that the public and the media would ever believe that the right guy had been arrested. We knew it would be devastating to Gary's family, but there was no way around it.

"You guys review this and see if there's any major objections," Baird told us. "It's pretty much all in there. I don't see changing much, but let me know if there's anything that's a real problem."

That same afternoon, we all had another meeting in Judge Jones's jury room. In addition to the lawyers and task force representatives, Captain Graddon and Sergeant Green, Judge Jones had also invited Frank Abe of the King County government cable TV channel and Paul Sherify of the King County Superior Court administration. Abe and Sherify would be responsible for media-related issues. The plan was to broadcast the plea and subsequent press conferences live on the county's cable channel, as well as the local channels and CNN—another way of making sure that all the facts could get out. Judge Jones had prepared a media packet outlining the procedures that would be followed, plus giving some background information.

Security was one of the major concerns. There was some chance that some deranged individual might try to take a shot at Gary or his lawyer, or even the prosecutors, and we were all well aware that courthouses had been the scene of emotional violence in the past. The first line of defense would be the regular metal detector at the courthouse doors, which had gone up a few years earlier. Bags and briefcases would be hand-searched. Another metal detector was to be set up at the courtroom door, just to make sure that someone passing the first barrier hadn't somehow previously secreted a weapon somewhere in the cavernous building. Besides this, the only people to be allowed inside the actual courtroom had to be on an approved list—victims' family and friends, law enforcement, and members of the news media.

"As a final precaution," Green said, "we'll be having Mr. Ridgway wear a vest." The bullet-proof kind, Green meant.

"Hey, Ray," I asked, "what if the shooter misses? Got any extra vests?"

"Sorry, Mark," Green said, his face completely straight. "We're only worried about Gary. Just duck."

Green was kidding. I think. On the way out of the meeting, he let me know they would give me one to wear if I wanted. I declined.

Over the next two days, I reviewed Baird's written summary of the facts. Despite its length, it was succinct, accurate, and despite the difficult subject matter, easy to follow. However, its substance was very hard to read, even after having listened to the awful details straight from Gary's mouth for the previous five months. I tried to imagine how it might seem to someone who'd never heard any of this stuff before. From that perspective, it was stomach-turning, given the monstrous things our client had done.

On Monday, November 3, Todd, Tony, and I met with Gary at the bunker to go over the formal plea documents. We spent a couple hours going over the guilty plea form and answering Gary's questions. He understood everything and was ready. As I knew, Gary's biggest concern was embarrassing himself in court. Having to stand where everyone would have their eyes on him as he performed his part of the proceeding reminded him of the thing he hated most about school—being publicly humiliated if he made any mistakes.

At noon that same day, Tony, Todd, Michele, and I met with Greg and Dorene at Tony's office. Gary's younger brother, Ed, and his wife, Tina, lived in a rather isolated, rural part of King County and preferred their quiet, anonymous existence. While they cared about Gary and his situation, they left the meetings with Gary's lawyers to Greg and Dorene.

The moose on Tony's wall gazed down on us impassively as we tried to prepare Gary's brother and sister-in-law for what was to come. For almost five months, they'd had no contact with Gary, and even no real idea of where he was, let alone what had been going on in the bunker. Judith Ridgway did not accompany them. We later discovered that the entire experience of seeing her husband arrested, then disappear from the jail, apparently to enter into plea negotiations (which implied that he had actually committed the crimes), had been too much for Gary's wife. Judith, it seemed, just wanted to put as much distance as she could between herself and the notoriety of having been married to the world's most prolific serial murderer. And who could blame her? After some sporadic contacts in the spring with Greg and

Dorene, Judith had moved in with relatives from her own family and ceased further contact with anyone from the defense. When I thought of Gary crying about what he'd done to Judith, I realized that this was by far his worst fear—that Judith would repudiate him. But when I looked at it from Judith's point of view, I couldn't help but have sympathy. It was an impossible situation for her.

"As I'm sure you already know from what's been reported," Tony told Greg and Dorene, "on Wednesday, Gary will be pleading guilty, and the state will be dropping the death penalty."

"How many?" Greg asked.

"Forty-eight," Tony said, as delicately as one could possibly say such a number. Greg and Dorene both winced.

"Well, we've been preparing for this news, but it's very difficult," Greg said, after a pause to contemplate the enormity of the situation. I couldn't begin to imagine *how* difficult it was for them. "We're going to get out of town so we won't have to deal with the press."

"That's a very good idea," said Todd. "Otherwise, they're gonna be camped out at your house."

"Yeah," Greg agreed. "We'd just as soon avoid that."

At this point, I handed Greg a copy of Baird's 140-page summary of the facts: the one that explained just exactly how and where and— as far as possible—why Gary had committed so many murders. Baird had approved this as long as Greg and Dorene agreed to keep it confidential until the actual plea. My reasoning was that Gary's family deserved a chance to prepare themselves, and Baird agreed.

"This is the document that summarizes the case against Gary, including all the stuff he admitted to during the interviews," I told them. "There's some pretty rough stuff in there." I was thinking not only about the necrophilia but also about the things that Gary had said about wanting to hurt his mother, the presence of Matthew in the truck when Gisele Lovvorn was murdered—some of this would be devastating for Greg and Dorene.

"You can have this copy to take home and read and react to it in private," I said. "Obviously, it's still all confidential. At least until Wednesday."

"Of course," Dorene replied.

As this difficult meeting ended, Greg and Dorene were extremely gracious and thankful, especially considering the circumstances.

Later that same afternoon, we had another defense team meeting at ACA, where members of the team had a chance to review the case summary. We briefed everyone on the process and what was going to happen from there out. There seemed to be a weird atmosphere, an ambivalence. No one knew exactly what the right emotion was: upset that our client was guilty, happy he wouldn't get the death penalty, sick that he could have killed all those girls. No one was entirely sure of how to feel. We were all happy the case was coming to an end, but none of us felt like celebrating.

———

The next day was Tuesday, November 4. Todd and I returned to the bunker for one last pre-plea meeting with Gary. We again went over the rights he was waiving, the sentence he was facing, and all the other legal details he had to officially be made aware of.

"So tell us, Gary, in your own words: What's all this mean?" Todd began.

"Well, basically I plead guilty. There won't be a trial. In exchange, they won't ask for the death penalty. I'll get life in prison." He nodded at Todd and me.

"I think you got it," I told him. "That's the bottom line."

Todd and I prepped him some more, just as if Gary were to have the starring role in the school play.

"Baird will say, 'Mr. Ridgway, you say you picked up so-and-so, intending to kill her, that you killed her, and then you left her body at such-and-such a place.' Then he'll ask you, 'Is that true?' And then what do you say?"

"I say, 'yes,'" Gary said.

"And then Baird will do this for each of the counts, right?"

"Right," Gary said.

"And you say, each time he does this—what do you say?"

"I say, 'Yes,'" Gary said.

After we'd made sure that Gary had it down, Baird, Eakes, and McDonald came into the interrogation room. Again we went through, slowly and deliberately, exactly what was going to happen and in what order things would occur. Baird went through three or four of the cases as examples of what all forty-eight would sound like, as we just had. Once he sensed that Gary had the idea, he stopped. All of us felt confident that Gary understood everything and was ready to go. Even Gary felt he could do his part without slipping up.

Todd and I met at The Annex afterward for a few beers. We plotted out some of our own responses to the inevitable questions *we* would face after the plea. We wanted to be ready for anything the news media might throw at us. After all, this was going to be the biggest guilty plea of all time. Besides that, we realized that some of the biggest questions would be about the future viability of the death penalty in Washington, and we wanted to be ready for those, as well.

That night, the hype on the news was even greater than I had foreseen. Expectation of the impending plea was all over the local channels as well as some of the cable news networks, so it was clear this was going to be a worldwide media event. Despite knowing that we had prepared everything as well as we possibly could, I still tossed and turned all night. What could go wrong? Nothing, it seemed. Everything had been scripted down to the last detail. Of that I was, well, "quite certain."

48

On the day of the plea, I arose at five A.M. The girls high school state swim championships were only a week away, and I had four girls and a couple of relay teams seeded in the meet and hoped our group would score high. Because I knew I'd be in Seattle that afternoon, we had a workout from six to seven that morning. So even though I couldn't sleep, I had to get up early anyway. When I thought of the early hour, I realized it wasn't only me who was making sacrifices for the defense of Gary Ridgway. So were my swimmers. So, indeed, were all the taxpayers of King County.[1]

In the shower, I thought of how nervous I would have been if I were about to go down to do the closing argument in the penalty phase of Gary's trial, if we had ever had one; instead, we were doing a guilty plea. *Piece of cake,* I told myself. *No big deal. I've done this literally hundreds of times before.* Just not to forty-eight counts of aggravated murder . . . and live on national TV.

I kissed Kelly to say good-bye. She was awake.

"I decided not to go," she said. "I think I'd rather just stay here and watch it on television. You're gonna be so busy."

"That's fine," I said. "I mean, it'd be fine if you wanted to come. Your name's on the pass list. . . . Fiona [Todd's wife] is coming. But it's going to be long—and pretty tough."

"Yeah," she said. "And I wouldn't want anyone to know I was connected to his lawyer." She pulled me close for a hug and whispered, "You know I'm just kidding. I'm really proud of you. This would never have happened without you. I love you."

"Thanks, hon. I love you too." And even though I'd played a role in the outcome, I didn't need to point out to her that she had a bias. But it was nice she thought that.

"I'll try to tape as much of it as possible," Kelly said as I headed out. "Good luck."

—⁓—

After the workout, I drove to Tony's office to meet with the rest of our team's lawyers. It was weird to hear the radio disc jockeys and newscasters, on every station, talking about the case that I was driving downtown to participate in. I put a Bob Marley CD in to help me try to relax. "*Don't worry about a thing. Every little thing's gonna be alright.*"

We all convened at Tony's by quarter to eight. One by one, each of us signed the original plea form, the one that Gary would also sign once the deal was formally done. There was an air of anticipation and excitement of being involved in something historic. Our conversation was mostly nervous chitchat.

We walked up the hill from Tony's office to the courthouse. There were all the big trucks usually associated with intense media coverage, dish antennas arcing toward the sky, cameras and reporters underfoot. We made our way through the throng, as the reporters peppered us for statements.

"No comment. Have to wait . . . We'll comment after the hearing." We made our way to Judge Jones's own courtroom, as a staging area before heading up to the presiding courtroom, the big one, which had been set aside for this hearing. Judge Jones wanted this one final meeting to make sure everything went off as planned. Everything seemed ready.

There was one change: Norm Maleng had changed the time of the state's news media briefing: instead of waiting until *after* our own briefing, which had been scheduled for fifteen minutes after the plea, now their press conference was to start fifteen minutes after ours—

essentially overlapping us and thereby forcing many members of the media to skip our statements to the news media. Todd cynically suggested that this was another move calculated by the government to drown out the defense point of view.

We took a back stairway up to the ninth floor, where the presiding courtroom was located. As we put our yellow legal pads and files at the counsel table, I glanced around: a courtroom packed with nearly three hundred people, television monitors for people in the back to watch, a jury box full of reporters, a couple different cameras, and cops and SWAT-team security everywhere. A special curtained-off area in the rear was set aside for still more media types.

Our side then adjourned to a small room just outside the courtroom, a place where the media couldn't get at us. This was where we were to meet the man of the hour when he was brought down from the holding cell atop the courthouse. A minute or so later, Gary arrived, manacled as usual hand and foot, clad in a clean red jail jumpsuit, plastic sandals on his feet, obviously bulked up by the concealed bullet-proof vest.

"Hello," Gary said, smiling. Outside of Todd, Tony, and me, Gary hadn't been seen by any other members of our team for five months. He appeared calm, relaxed, even happy. Todd, Tony, and I stood back as Eric, Fred, Dave, and Michele shook Gary's hand and exchanged their comments with him, reassuring him in their own way. He was clearly pleased to see everyone. He expressed his gratitude to everyone on the team. Pretty soon, Juanita, the judge's bailiff, came in and told us it was time. We all then filed into the courtroom.

—⁓—

We were all commanded to rise, and shortly after 9 A.M., Judge Jones took his seat on the bench.

"Good morning," he said. "Please be seated."

We sat.

Because everything had been worked out days in advance, the entire proceeding had an atmosphere of high formality, almost as if we were in a cathedral for some sort of religious service.

"Counsel for the state?" Jones invited. Baird stood up.

"Good morning, your honor. Your honor, this is . . . State of Washington versus Gary Leon Ridgway."

Baird introduced all of the lawyers, for the record.

"Your honor," Baird went on, "I have before me a motion and proposed order which would permit amending the information in this case to charge forty-eight counts of aggravated, first-degree murder."

Baird asked that the judge approve the amended information and said that we on the defense had reviewed it with Gary some time previously, which, of course, we had. He said we had agreed to waive formal reading of the new charges before entering a plea of guilty. Jones asked me if this was true.

"Yes, your honor," I said rising to my feet. "For the record, we have received a copy, do waive formal reading, and do intend to enter a plea of guilty to the charges as amended." I sat down again.

Baird gave the judge the amended information, and Jones approved it.

Baird next gave Jones a motion to withdraw the death penalty.

"Just as the [amended] information was filed with the understanding that Mr. Ridgway would plead guilty, so it was [also] filed with the understanding, by all parties, that the state would withdraw the notice of the special sentencing proceeding," Baird said, giving the formal, legal name for the death penalty hearing.

Tony rose to tell the court that we agreed with this, too, and sat down again.

Baird now asked the court to accept the filing of his 140-page summary of the evidence.

"This is a document that has been provided to the defense and court some days ago. . . . We'd like to make it part of the record . . . because it's our understanding that the court may review this document to see whether there's a factual basis for the plea."

Baird passed up his graphic summary.

Baird went on. "Your Honor, I have before me a Statement of Defendant on Plea of Guilty. Attached to that document . . . are two documents . . . the original plea agreement signed June 13 of this year, the other is the amended information filed this morning. With the court's permission, I would ask leave to inquire of Mr. Ridgway . . . I'd propose to ask him a few questions about that plea agreement."

Baird wanted to have it formally on the record that Gary had freely and without coercion or promises of any kind [other than the withdrawal of the death penalty notice] agreed to enter his guilty plea.

"I should state for the record that the plea agreement was made in June but not made public until today. I think the reasons for that are evident. Most importantly, perhaps to us, any disclosure of that would have seriously jeopardized the prosecution's ability to prosecute Mr. Ridgway. But I think the court should know that the plea agreement has been discussed by Sheriff Reichert, and the elected prosecutor, Mr. Maleng, with the victims' families and survivors. I can tell the court that these individuals are all in a state of grief, they're angry and upset. But I believe I can say with assurance that most of them, the majority of them, agree in principle with the plea agreement. There are a few I am told that do not."

The fact was that the new charges included forty-one cases that would never have been brought against Gary without his cooperation through the plea agreement, Baird said.

Baird now asked Gary if he was familiar with the plea agreement, and if he had signed it; Gary said he was and he had. Baird summarized the agreement and asked Gary if he agreed that that was what the deal was. Gary said yes. That was what he'd agree to: no death penalty for any crime he'd committed in King County, Washington, if he'd admit to them. In fact, Baird asked Gary had he agreed to tell "the complete truth" about all of his murderous activities in King County?

"Yes," Gary nodded.

He had also agreed to waive his right to a speedy sentencing on the forty-eight charges and that the sentencing could be delayed for as long as six months to give the authorities more time to interview him, Baird said. "Is that correct?"

"Correct," Gary said.

And Gary also understood, didn't he, that he would not be able to appeal any aspect of his plea, the finding of guilt, or his sentence?

"Yes," Gary said.

Baird asked Gary to initial the plea agreement at the place where he'd signed it five months before.

Baird asked Gary if he understood the plea agreement.

"Yes, I do," Gary said.

"Do you have any questions about it?"

"No, I do not," Gary said.

Baird asked Gary to look at the Statement of Defendant on Plea of Guilty, the sixteen-page recitation of just exactly what he was pleading guilty to. Did he understand this, and had he initialed it?

Gary agreed that he had.

Baird now put on the record the various rights that Gary was giving up by agreeing to plead guilty, including the right to a trial. Gary said he understood that he was giving up these rights and was doing so freely and voluntarily. All this was necessary so that Gary—or someone representing him—could not later claim that Gary didn't understand that he was giving up his rights under the Constitution in accepting the finding of guilt and the sentence.

"Yes, I know that," Gary said.

Baird asked if Gary understood that with the prosecutor's office withdrawing the death penalty request, he would serve a term of life in prison without the possibility of parole or any early release.

"Yes," Gary said.

And he also understood that any other murders in King County that he admitted to—before his formal sentencing would also not be subject to the death penalty. This was an additional inducement to Gary to continue his cooperation, because once sentencing was completed, any undisclosed King County murders *could* be the subject of the death penalty, under terms of the agreement.

"Yes," Gary said.

Baird told Gary that the prosecutor's office intended to recommend that all the life sentences be served consecutively—in other words, given Gary's life expectancy, a total term of nearly a thousand years in prison without any possibility of ever getting out. While serving that many consecutive life sentences was an obvious absurdity, it safeguarded the state in case one or more of the murder counts was later thrown out for some reason. As I've said, lawyers like to have everything nailed down completely tight.

Baird asked if anyone had threatened Gary with any harm—other than the prospect of the lawful death penalty—to induce him to enter the plea agreement; this was necessary to make sure that Gary had freely and voluntarily agreed to plead guilty.

"No," Gary said.

Baird asked if Gary understood that if there had been a trial, the state would have had to prove each and every element of each crime, including the *aggravation*—in other words, the common scheme or plan—to justify asking a jury to give him the death penalty. This was a way of putting on the record that the prosecutor's theory of the case—that serial murder *did* fulfill the aggravation definition, which had been the point of great dispute, was accepted as valid by Gary. Gary said he understood this.

Baird now noted that Gary had prepared a written statement of his guilt and asked the court for permission to read it into the record. We all stood up.

"It says," Baird began, "'I killed the forty-eight women listed in the state's second amended information. In most cases, when I murdered these women, I did not know their names. Most of the time I killed them the first time I met them, and I do not have a good memory for their faces. I killed so many women I have a hard time keeping them straight.'" Baird asked Gary, "Is that true?"

"Yes, it is."

Baird continued to read Gary's written statement. "'I am positive I killed each one of the women charged in the second amended information. I killed all of them in King County. I killed most of them in my house . . . and I killed a lot of them in my truck not far from where I picked them up. I killed some of them outside. I remember leaving each woman's body in the place where she was found.

"'I have discussed with my attorneys the common scheme or plan aggravating circumstance charged in all these murders. I agree that each of the murders I committed was part of a common scheme or plan. The plan was: I wanted to kill as many women I thought were prostitutes as I possibly could.' Is that true?"

"Yes."

"Your statement continues: 'I picked prostitutes as my victims because I hate most prostitutes, and I did not want to pay them for sex. I also picked prostitutes as victims because they were easy to pick up without being noticed. I knew they would not be reported missing right away, and might never be reported missing. I picked prostitutes because I thought I could kill as many of them as I wanted without getting caught.

"'Another part of my plan was where I put the bodies of these women. Most of the time I took the women's jewelry and their clothes to get rid of the evidence, and make them harder to identify. I placed most of the bodies in groups which I call clusters. I did this because I wanted to keep track of all the women I killed. I liked to drive by the clusters around the county and think about the women I placed there. I usually used a landmark to remember a cluster and the women I placed there. Sometimes I killed and dumped a woman intending to start a new cluster, and never returned because I thought I might get caught putting more women there.' Is that true?"

"Yes."

Baird now moved to the second part of Gary's statement: his admission as to each of the forty-eight victims.

"Your statement, pertaining to count one, reads as follows: 'In King County, Washington, sometime between July 8, 1982, and July 15, 1982, with premeditated intent to cause her death, I strangled Wendy Lee Coffield to death. I picked her up, planning to kill her. After killing her, I placed her body in the Green River.' Is that a true statement?"

"Yes."

"Is that your statement?"

"Yes."

And so it went, for forty-seven more victims, with Baird reading, almost intoning, "I picked her up, planning to kill her. After killing her, I placed her body . . ." over and over again, as he went down the list of victims, charge by charge and cluster by cluster, each time asking Gary if this was his statement and if it was true.

"Yes," Gary said. "Yes."

As the toll of the dead rolled on, the exchange of words almost took on a ritualistic quality, a call and answer as if in a prayer. And even though we were in a court of law, it was also as if some sort of ceremonial exorcism was being performed, admission by admission, truth by truth, as the darkness of twenty years was cast out by the light.

Twice during this litany, I thought Gary might break down. The first time came at the mention of Connie Naon. He started to choke up.

I leaned over to Gary and asked, "Are you all right?"

"Yes," he said, nearly inaudible.

He almost broke down a second time but again was able to maintain his composure. We had schooled him in not displaying emotion. We knew that if he, or we his lawyers, smiled or grimaced even once during the three-hour hearing, that's all that would be repeated over and over again on the nightly news. The last thing we wanted was for someone to think we were all having a grand time.

Once we reached the end of the admissions—it took over half an hour to do them one by one—Baird told Judge Jones that he believed that Gary's admissions were truthful and that they should be accepted by the court as part of the plea of guilty "in the interests of justice."

Judge Jones asked us if we agreed, and we said we did. The judge now summoned Gary to the bench, accompanied by Tony, Baird, and me.

Jones asked if Gary understood what he was pleading guilty to. Gary said he did. Once more, the judge asked if any untoward influence had been brought to bear to convince him to plead guilty, and Gary said there had been none.

After satisfying the judge that he understood his rights, that he was giving them up freely and voluntarily, and that he was satisfied with the advice he'd received from his lawyers, Gary was asked if he was agreeing to plead guilty because he believed that he was guilty of each of the murders.

"Yes," he said.

"Mr. Ridgway," the judge continued, "I'm going to ask at this time: How do you plead to the charge of aggravated murder in the first degree as charged in count one for the death of Wendy Lee Coffield?"

"Guilty."

Judge Jones went down the list, reading each name.

"Guilty," Gary said.

Guilty, guilty, guilty—forty-eight times.

49

Afterward, as Gary was being returned to the bunker, our side convened in an idle courtroom to answer questions from the news media.

I led off with a statement.

"We want to just start with the fact that today is a day to remember all the young women," I said, obviously referring to the victims. "Our thoughts and prayers are with their families and their loved ones, and we hope this resolution will bring some measure of peace and healing to the families. We want to commend Norm Maleng for his courageous and correct decision in this case. We believe that this resolution serves the interest of justice and serves the best interests of the people of King County and the State of Washington."

I expressed our thanks and appreciation to the deputy prosecutors and the detectives, as well as everyone else who'd been involved in the bunker siege of the past five months. Everyone, I said, had acted with professionalism throughout, despite all the stress that everyone had endured during the months of questioning.

"The King County citizens should be proud," I said. "They were well served by these professionals. They showed tremendous patience, endurance, and persistence. And I think it's high quality from top to bottom in that department.

"We'd like to ask you all to respect the privacy of Gary's family," I continued. "They obviously have to have some time to react to these events.

"This was a good result for Gary Ridgway. He will continue to co-operate to help locate other remains, as he has been for the past several months, and to help bring resolution to some of the other cases. It's a good result for the State of Washington and a good result for the criminal justice system. There's a lot more work to do, and there are some cases we won't be able to talk about, because they're pending investigations."

The first question was why—not why Gary had committed the murders but why he'd agreed to the plea.

"Mr. Ridgway wanted to live, did not want to face the death penalty," I said. "He also wanted to bring whatever help he could to closing the unsolved cases, which he did by providing information. That was certainly a big motivating factor for Gary, for providing information, and he should be commended for having the courage to come forward."

We were asked if the plea bargain signified a potential change in how the death penalty was applied in Washington State.

Tony fielded that one.

"The death penalty is an abomination that has no place in our society, and if we help get rid of it, that's another plus for us," he said.

We were asked if Gary had shown any remorse and if so, how?

"He's shown remorse in a variety of ways," I said. "Tears, and words."

"About the acts, or being caught?" a reporter asked.

"About the acts," I said.

"Does he have any sense at all of the evil that he committed and that many people think he's a psychopath?" another asked.

"Well, he certainly understands that he's not the most popular man in town," Tony said. "We've got to keep in mind that we're dealing with an individual with a modest education, and modest intelligence, if I can put it that way, and the depth of his feelings about what he has done is . . ." Tony gestured with his hands, as if to say it was impossible to say for sure. "You can write books about that for the next twenty or thirty years, and I'm sure there will be."

Someone else asked how anyone could believe anything that Gary said, if he was, as the prosecutor's summary contended, "a pathological liar."

"I don't know," Tony said. "I'm convinced and have been since June 13 that Gary has been doing his best to divulge whatever it is that's buried in the back of his mind. Whether we've been successful or not, I don't know. But we're going to keep on trying so we can get these things resolved. I don't think anybody will ever accurately know the precise number . . . what the number is.""

"Do you have any insight into what drove Mr. Ridgway to do what he did?"

"Rage," Tony said. "And you've got to get the psychiatrists and psychologists onboard. He was—and is—a very, very angry person. And the source of that—there are all kinds of theories. Some people go for the snap theory, some people say it's a development from his potty training. I just don't know, but he was consumed with rage."

"For the past several months, the focus has been on trying to get through the who, what, when, where," I added. "The 'why' question has been touched upon but not explored as deeply as it should be or needs to be."

Someone asked if we had considered an insanity defense for Gary.

"No," Tony said, shortly. "He's been diagnosed up one side and down the other, and he does not meet the Washington State definition of legally insane."

"Can you describe Mr. Ridgway's reaction when you told him that the plea arrangement had been accepted by the prosecutor?"

"He was relieved," I said. "A great relief. Part of the relief was that he was not going to have to face the death penalty, and I believe that part of the relief was the fact that this information was going to be released . . . what he was keeping inside of himself. I truly believe that. We noticed the change in his demeanor. He was refreshed, and looking forward to this day, and getting that out."

"He admitted to the murders, but is he sorry for them?" a reporter asked.

"Yes," I said.

Tony shrugged.

"He says he's sorry. I believe him. But I don't really know."

———

Afterward our team adjourned to the Merchants' Café. For some reason, there'd been a delay in the prosecution's own media briefing, so we were able to see it there.

At length, Maleng arrived and took his place at a podium. The prosecutor's media briefing was being held in the conference room of a downtown Seattle bank.

Maleng looked over the assembled crowd of reporters—probably close to one hundred of them—and then directly at the television cameras.

"Our Green River nightmare is over," he said. "We have seen the face of justice: it brings truth for our community and for the families of the victims. Now the healing can begin. This morning Gary Ridgway pled guilty to forty-eight counts of aggravated murder. In return for this plea, and the information necessary to solve and charge the crimes, we agreed not to seek the death penalty. This is a historic day for King County, one that will allow us to close this terrible chapter in our history. The Green River nightmare is over."

Maleng sketched in the events of the previous twenty years, ending with the discovery of the microscopic paint spheres.

"This new forensic evidence supported charging three more counts, for a total of seven," he said. "As exciting as this development was, we realized that we had exhausted our leads in the remaining cases. There were no more dramatic forensic-science breakthroughs left. It became clear that despite the scores of cases still under investigation, we would be left with only seven that could be charged."

He recounted our approach to his office in the spring, when we'd offered the deal.

"My immediate reaction was 'No!'" he said. "The question leaped out to me, just as it does to you: How could you set aside the death penalty in a case like this? Here we have a man presumed to be a prolific serial killer, a man who preyed on vulnerable young women. I thought, as many of you might, if any case screams out for consideration of the death penalty, it is this one. I realized, however, that this proposal had huge implications for families of victims, for the men and women of the task force, for the sheriff, and for the entire community. It deserved thoughtful consideration.

"I have long said that the mission of the King County Prosecuting Attorney's Office is not just to win cases, but to seek justice," Maleng continued. "One of the principles that we have followed in seeking justice is that we do not plea bargain with the death penalty. It is a principle I specifically mentioned with regard to this case at the time the case was filed. The reason for that policy is that it is not fair to defendants to use the death penalty as leverage for a plea to aggravated murder. The death penalty is too powerful a consequence to be used as a plea bargaining tool.

"But this case squarely presented another principle that is a foundation of our justice system—to seek and know the truth. I knew that there were many people waiting for the truth in this case. I spent three weeks considering the defense proposal. I listened to members of the Green River Task Force, and to Sheriff Dave Reichert. I listened to my own team of senior deputy prosecutors and staff. I knew that, in the end, this was my decision to make and mine to defend.

"I was searching for justice—what should be the legacy of this case? During this search I was reminded of the Biblical phrase from First Corinthians, chapter 13: 'For now we see in a mirror, dimly, but then face to face.' I finally saw a new face of justice. Before, I could only see the face of Gary Ridgway; but I began to see other faces—the mothers, fathers, sisters, brothers, and children of the victims. I saw that the justice we could achieve could bring home the remains of loved ones for proper burial. It could solve unsolvable cases the task force had spent twenty years investigating. It could begin the healing for our entire community. The justice we could achieve was to uncover the Truth."

Maleng explained, "We could have gone forward with seven counts, but that is all we could have ever hoped to solve. At the end of that trial, whatever the outcome, there would have been lingering doubts about the rest of these crimes. This agreement was the avenue to the truth. And in the end, the search for the truth is still why we have a criminal justice system."

Maleng said he realized that criminal defense lawyers from this point on would try to argue that if the death penalty couldn't be applied to someone guilty of murdering at least forty-eight women, it could never be applied to anyone who killed far fewer victims. But, Maleng said, that was a misreading of the requirements of the law, which required an individual consideration of the appropriate penalty in *every* case.

"The reasons supporting the resolution of this case are principled," he continued. "They are based in justice, not in cost or convenience. This resolution promotes justice. It will meet any so-called 'proportionality review' arguments made to our courts." This was his answer to John Meunster and other defense lawyers who said that the plea deal ruined any proportionality in applying the death penalty for people who committed fewer murders.

Maleng went on. "Gary Ridgway does not deserve our mercy. He does not deserve to live. The mercy provided by today's resolution is directed not at Ridgway, but toward the families who have suffered so much, and to the larger community. I have met with many of the families of the victims to share this news. Our meetings were very touching; their grief is still fresh, even twenty years later. They are people who have suffered life's most terrible hurt, the loss of a child. They are deserving of answers; they are deserving of truth; they are deserving of mercy. There are forty-eight families of forty-eight victims and none deserved their fates. We see photos of these young women, most taken during happier times in their short lives. They were young women, with troubles to be sure, but they each had their hopes and aspirations. They had moms and dads, sisters and brothers, and some had children. These victims were God's children, our children. They deserve our sympathy, our tears, and our mercy.

"When I see the face of justice in this case, it is those young women that I see. They deserve to have the truth of their fates known to the world. When I see the face of justice in this case, I will see each family impacted by these crimes. They deserve to know the truth about the fate of their loved ones. And the families who until recently have endured decades not knowing the whereabouts of their daughters— they deserved to be able to have a proper burial. They all deserve our deepest sympathy. Finally, the face of justice reflects our whole community. We have all suffered this terrible trauma known as the Green River murders. We deserve to know the truth and to move on. Justice and mercy: for the victims, the families, and the community. That is why we entered into this agreement."

From our table at the Merchants', we were all impressed by Maleng's statement. He had cut directly to the heart of the reason we have laws—not to exact personal revenge, not just to punish the guilty, but to defend the interests of the whole community. And in this case, Maleng had gotten it just right. Getting the truth was far more important for all of us than merely seeing Gary Ridgway die.

50

The post-plea media coverage was intense. We spent the following week doing a variety of media interviews—from CNN to the local *King County Journal,* as well as a number of others. Tony appeared on Geraldo Rivera's show on Fox, despite our misgivings. We were worried that the whole thing might be sensationalized in an unseemly way. But Geraldo was evenhanded and responsible in his presentation. When the plea deal was criticized by a pro-prosecution guest, Tony cut to the bottom line: "There are forty-eight families who now have received some solace," he growled.

Back at the bunker, although Gary had now entered his guilty plea, almost everyone thought that he still had some secrets to reveal, particularly in connection with murders he might have committed either before or after the Green River crimes. Some of the experts still had a hard time believing that Gary's love for Judith, or even Peaches the Poodle, could have caused him to slow down as much as he claimed he had in the late 1980s and 1990s. They thought that with more interviews, Gary might admit to having murdered more than the handful he'd acknowledged over the previous decade and a half. And as for his first murder victim, virtually no one accepted the proposition that he hadn't killed before Wendy Coffield. That meant that although he'd pled guilty to forty-eight murders, and the authorities had varying amounts of evidence on twenty-three others—seventy-one total, and maybe even more—the fact was, the final, awful total might never be known.

Still, to try to get a grip on this question, the police and prosecutors wanted to delay Gary's formal sentencing for up to six months to give them a chance to prod him some more. Most thought that Gary's cooperation had been sincere since at least the summer and that something might be gained by returning him to the bunker for still more interrogation sessions.

The prosecutors had already assured us that if Gary confessed to new murders that hadn't been included in the guilty plea, they wouldn't seek the death penalty for those. However, once the formal sentencing took place, they couldn't guarantee anything.

In other words, Gary had up until the day of sentencing to confess to every murder he'd ever committed, with no additional penalty. But if evidence came in after that day, of a murder he had concealed, Gary would be legally liable once more for the ultimate sanction. Both sides wanted to give Gary a powerful incentive to continue his cooperation. Gary was amenable to this. He seemed to understand what was at stake.

But first he wanted to see his brother Greg and sister-in-law Dorene for the first time since the previous spring, when they'd helped convince him to cooperate with the authorities in return for his life.

"I know Judith wouldn't want to see me," he told me, tears evident in his eyes, and I didn't know what to say about this, because I was sure he was right.

A few days later, I arranged for Greg and Dorene to meet with Gary at the Regional Justice Center. Gary would be taken from the bunker to the south county offices of the detectives for this one-time meeting. The detectives agreed that Gary had a right to see his brother and sister-in-law after his cooperation.

Gary, legs shackled but his hands free, was waiting in a conference room at the broad, bland, government-issue table on the day the meeting took place.

"If you want to meet privately, that's fine," one of the detectives said. "We'll just keep an eye on things from out of earshot." The officers were able to view Gary through a window in the door.

"Thank you," Greg said. He and Dorene sat down at the table. Michele Shaw and I chatted with them for a few minutes, trying to put everyone at ease. After a few minutes, we excused ourselves, leaving them to talk privately for about an hour. What was said between them, I do not know, but I had to believe it must have been an incredibly intense, emotional conversation. After all, Greg and Dorene were largely responsible for ending the entire case, more than twenty years after it had all begun. When I thought about it, without their intercession with Gary, we might have had to have an enormous trial, and then, even if Gary had been found guilty, no one would ever have known the whole, awful truth.

—◆◆◆—

Ann Rule, the author, had said publicly that she believed Gary Ridgway had stalked her, obviously prior to his arrest. Rule was by now working on her book on the case, which was eventually published in September 2004, as *Green River, Running Red*.

That's why, a few days after Gary met with Greg and Dorene, Mullinax showed Gary a photograph.

"Who's this?" he asked.

"Ann Rule, I think," Gary said.

"Why?"

"I've seen her picture on the back of her books. I heard she says I stalked her but I didn't."

"Ever go to her book signings?"

"No."

"You've mentioned her before. Do you read her books?"

"I read two of her books. Read 'em in jail."

"How about before jail?"

"No."

"Didn't you go to a bookstore when she was there?"

"No."

"What bookstores do you go to?"

"Half-Price Books. Goodwill." *He's not really a Barnes & Noble kind of guy,* I thought.

"Are the stories of you stalking her true?"

"No. That's false. . . . I just woulda walked up to her and introduced myself as the Green River Killer."

Jensen, Mullinax, and I cracked up. Gary continued, "She's not my type. No. I did *not* stalk Ann Rule."

Late in November, Dr. Wheeler returned for another go at Gary's memory, and eventually the conversation returned to the old reliable— the jewelry. Gary's previous admission that he'd left some of the victims' jewelry at the Kenworth plant had prompted the detectives to investigate this. Some jewelry, it now turned out, had been found by Kenworth employees as recently as 2001.

Which was a big problem. Because it seemed to suggest that despite his denials, Gary had actually been killing right up until his arrest at the end of November of that same year.

"Christ," Todd muttered. Gary just seemed to be incapable of telling the truth.

Wheeler now looped Gary's troubled "conscious," as he persisted in calling it, to this discovery of 2001 jewelry in an effort to get Gary to admit he'd murdered right up until the time he was arrested. In a way, it was ridiculous: all Gary had to do was admit that he'd killed someone, or even many someones, *before* the sentencing, and those murders could never get him the death penalty.

"So jewelry is found at the Renton plant in 2001," Wheeler said, referring to a second Kenworth plant, where Gary had worked in 2001.

"I didn't think I . . . I didn't think I hid any jewelry there."

Wheeler went to his Socratic parsing method:

"I guess . . . I guess you were wrong, though . . . when you hid jewelry, where did the jewelry come from?"

"I don't know."

"Jewelry is found hidden at the Renton plant in locations where you have said you hid jewelry. Let's first ask ourself . . ."

"I said the *Seattle* plant had jewelry," Gary said, meaning the Kenworth plant near Boeing field, just south of downtown Seattle, where Gary had worked in the 1980s, while most of the murders were going on. "I don't know if I told 'em that I had jewelry in the *Renton* plant. I mighta made a mistake, because in '82 I had all kinds of jewelry I took to the Seattle plant. I don't remember if I said Renton. I mighta made a mistake and said Renton plant, but . . ." Gary was caviling.

"Jewelry . . . let's . . . let's do this, OK? Jewelry is found in locations where you have previously said you hid jewelry. And it was found in 2001. Based on your insight and expertise, that you talked about earlier today, who would you suspect put the jewelry in those locations?"

"It has . . . has to be me," Gary admitted.

"OK, so we . . . we can agree that it's probably you."

"There's nobody else," Gary said.

"OK, all right."

"Nobody else."

"And if it was put there in 2001, what would you deduce from that as to . . . would you . . . first of all, if it was put there in 2001, would you be inclined to think it came from somebody that you killed?"

"It would be 100 percent chance that it's somebody I killed in 2001," Gary said. "Hundred percent, there's no other reason."

But try as he might, Gary could not think of anyone he'd murdered in 2001.

After the end of this long day, Todd and I had another discussion with Gary. Todd went on for a while.

"We can't help you without you being completely honest and making complete and full disclosure," Todd complained, all over again. "No one believes you wouldn't remember killing in 2001. What's going on?"

Gary now denied killing anyone in 2001 and continued to insist he was being as honest as he could be.

I was worn out and frustrated. Getting Gary to do what was necessary to save himself was incredibly fatiguing, especially when he didn't seem to understand that all this was being done for his benefit.

"We've tried to help you. It's on you now," I told him. "It's your ass." I realized I had finally begun to lose my patience with our client.

51

Despite the plan to continue to hold Gary at the bunker for up to the next six months, it soon became clear to all of us that trying to squeeze more from Gary was probably a fruitless exercise. Neither Todd nor I thought he was purposely withholding, only that there simply wasn't all that much more that could be rooted out of his mind, under the present circumstances. By now, Gary was thinking ahead to coping with life in prison, a major life change in its way, not much different than graduating from high school and going to college—except, of course, in Gary's case it would be forever.

"I don't know about you," Jeff Baird told me, after one interrogation session that had meandered aimlessly for several hours. "But I think I've had enough of this." I could see his point. But Todd and I wanted to be sure, so we asked for a little more time to try ourselves to pull anything else out of Gary's brain. We didn't want to let anything get by as long as the no-death window was still open. Baird agreed but insisted that we formally set the sentencing date, and we had to agree to this. The sentencing was scheduled for December 18. As noted, after that date, if the police and prosecutors found any new evidence to prove that Gary had committed a murder he hadn't confessed to, the state would be legally free to file new charges and this time ask for the death penalty. There was no doubt that they would get it from a jury, if this ever came to pass.

—⁓—

Thursday, November 27, 2003, was Thanksgiving, as well as my dad's birthday. The family gathered at Mom and Dad's house for the annual feast. I had earlier made arrangements with Sergeant Green and Captain Graddon to bring a slice of pumpkin pie to Gary, because the bunker was only about ten minutes from my folks' house. My mom made up a plate with everything—turkey, mashed potatoes and gravy, cranberry sauce, dressing, a roll, and pumpkin pie.

"Here," Mom said, handing me the plate. "Take this to Gary; I'm sure he's feeling pretty lonely and miserable right now. Even though he did what he did, he's still a human being. He did the right thing by pleading guilty. This is for him, for doing the right thing and bringing some healing to those poor families."

Kelly drove down to the bunker and waited in the van while I ran it inside.

"Here you are," I said, passing over the plate. "Happy Thanksgiving from the Prothero family."

"Oh, hey," Gary smiled. "Thank you. Happy Thanksgiving to you and your family. Thanks a lot. That's very nice."

"Well," I said, "my mom's a nice person and thought you could use a good home-cooked meal." To describe my mom as "nice" is an understatement. My mom's a saint. Not everyone could look beyond Gary's horrific past and treat him like a human being, deserving of a home-cooked Thanksgiving meal.

"Tell her thanks from me," Gary said.

"I'll do that," I said. "See you Monday."

Did I mention that Gary was a very polite serial killer?

—⁓—

With Gary's sentencing now set for December 18, Todd and I worked to get him ready for what we hoped would be his final public appearance. Michele had remained in contact with Greg and Dorene. They told her they did not want to attend the sentencing personally, a wise decision, we felt. Instead, they drafted a written statement and asked Michele to read it on their behalf at the proceeding.

As usual in criminal cases, those affected by the crimes had the opportunity to address the court in writing. In this case, there were well over a hundred letters, a pile several inches thick. Todd and I read these aloud to Gary on December 16 and 17, and of all the days we spent in the bunker, I think those were two of the hardest. The letters from those whose lives Gary had wrecked—or at least significantly damaged—were heartrending. I think that Gary, as he listened, for the very first time, got a glimpse of the enormous devastation he had caused for so many people.

On Thursday, December 18, we convened for the last time before Judge Jones, once again in the large presiding courtroom. As had happened with the formal plea a month and a half before, the room was packed. Almost all of the people whose lives had been forever altered by the horrible events—mothers, fathers, sisters, brothers, as well as the police officers who had devoted much of their own lives to seeing that this day would finally arrive.

This would be the first and only opportunity for those who had lost loved ones to formally participate in the legal process. Judge Jones had earlier asked that the victims' family members limit their comments to ten minutes. It might not seem fair—how can people express their feelings in only ten minutes? But it is just. Meting out justice isn't—or shouldn't be—a matter of revenge, but of addressing the needs of the whole community.

Still, these were the people that Gary had never thought of. The real people behind the seemingly faceless young women he had so heartlessly hunted down and killed. The mothers, fathers, sisters, and brothers he had ultimately robbed, people whom he had never imagined in his mind's eye, as he was choking the life out of his victims. We had tried to prepare Gary, as well as ourselves, for what we knew would be an intensely emotional event by reviewing the letters that had been written on behalf of the victims. That had been very difficult. But that was not nearly as painful as hearing this in person.

—⁓—

For the second time in less than two months, the large, high-ceilinged, presiding courtroom in the old courthouse was filled. Again we had the elaborate security precautions: the metal detectors, deputies waving magnetic wands, the invitation-only list, the bullet-proof vest for Gary. Once more, the room seemed like a church of sorts, row upon row of somber people, a couple hundred of them, mothers, fathers, brothers, sisters, and children, most more than twenty years older than the day that their loved ones had been taken from them so abruptly.

Gary sat between Tony and me, clad in a white, short-sleeved jail jumpsuit, with another red coverall beneath, whose longer sleeves extended from beneath the white. He'd showered and shaved, his hair was neatly combed, and his eyes were serious from behind his large glasses.

As each relative who chose to speak came forward to a podium, Gary turned to face them.

Many family members called Gary names: "animal," "demon," "monster," "devil," "parasite," "loser," "coward," "evil," "sick," "depraved," were repeated again and again. No one could fault any of them for their feelings. Though it was not pleasant to hear, this type of verbal onslaught was as expected as it was deserved.

More than ever before, as family member after family member excoriated Gary for what he had done, I felt the overwhelming impact, the widespread destruction, of his acts. So many tears, so much grief, so much anger over so many years. People who had lost their children; husbands who had lost their wives; children who had lost mothers they had never really known. I had suppressed all of this to make it through the case. I had focused on the evidence, not on the human impact. But on this day, the day of reckoning, it was no longer possible to avoid. The enormous human dimension of the case had been, until this day, something beyond my imagination. It was too huge and voluminous to comprehend.

"I was only five when my mother died and my dad told me I would never see her again," Carol Christensen's daughter, Sarah King, told Gary through her tears. "The one thing I want you to know is that there was a daughter at home, I was that daughter at home, waiting for my mommy to come home. I'm glad you didn't get death, because death is too good for you. You'll die someday, and you'll go to that place, and you'll get what you deserve."

For the next three hours, these and similar emotions filled the courtroom. Hatred, disgust, anger, pain, and sorrow seemed unrelenting, and as people spoke, their pain was palpable.

"If I could do what I want to do right now, you'd be gone right now," Jose Malvar Jr., Marie Malvar's brother, told Gary. "I'm angry. I will always be angry. I will never have my sister in my life. You broke my family apart. For twenty years, a lot of birthdays and a lot of Christmases were broken apart. I hope you rot in hell, you son of a bitch."

"I can only hope that someday, someone gets the opportunity to choke you unconscious forty-eight times, so you can live through the horror that you put our daughters, our sisters, our mothers through," Tim Meehan, Mary Meehan's brother, said. "May God have no mercy on your soul."

"Gisele was only seventeen years old," said Michelle Blair, Gisele Lovvorn's sister. "She was murdered by that animal sitting over there, who we have to call a man. He does not deserve to live, or breathe. But he doesn't deserve to die. Dying would be too easy for him." She remembered Gisele as a "wonderful, caring, loving young girl," who had gotten into minor trouble and run away from home. "It is impossible to put into words how much her murder has devastated and destroyed our family. . . . We miss her every day, and we'll never stop."

Yet, surprisingly, even through all the anger, some still had the capacity to see Gary as a human being.

"Even if you may say you're sorry, Mr. Ridgway, it won't bring back Opal," said Kathy Mills, the now white-haired mother of Opal Mills. "You have held us in bondage all these years, because we have hated you. We wanted to see you die. But it's all going to be over now. That is, provided we can forgive you. Gary Leon Ridgway, I forgive you. I forgive you. You can't hold me anymore. My life now is lived to one day be with little Opal."

As Kathy Mills spoke, I could see tears forming in Gary's eyes, and as she walked away, he dabbed at his eyes with a handkerchief.

"Mr. Ridgway, there are people here that hate you," said Robert Rule, father of Linda Rule. "I am not one of them. I forgive you for what you've done. You've made it difficult to live up to what I believe, and that is what God says to do, and that's to forgive, and He doesn't say to forgive just certain people. He says to forgive all. So, you are forgiven, sir."

The sister of Patricia Yellowrobe—Gary's last known victim—told Gary, "I don't hate you. This experience is going to make me stronger. It's going to make my family stronger."

Again Gary wiped his eyes.

I could feel myself also begin to choke up. For month after month after month, I had kept all of my own emotions in check, priding myself on my professionalism. But this forgiveness was so amazing that I began to feel my own tears coming. I took a deep breath then a drink of water to keep my emotions from busting out.

Over the past two years, I had witnessed the worst and the best of human beings: from the most depraved state of inhumanity to the most charitable and forgiving state of human emotion, all in one case. Gary had expected the hatred. He understood, we all understood, the bitter anger that so many felt toward him. But the capacity of some others to forgive him for his acts was beyond his capacity to understand, even if he could feel it and knew it was real.

Finally, after the victims' families had been heard from, it was our turn.

Rising, I told Judge Jones that we agreed with the state's recommendation of forty-eight consecutive life sentences, each without the possibility of parole.

"For the record, we acknowledge receiving copies of letters submitted to the court from victims' family members," I said. "For the past two days, we have reviewed every letter, many, many powerful letters, with Mr. Ridgway. It was very difficult; they had a profound effect on him, and on us, his lawyers. I have known him for two years and believe his remorse is sincere."

Michele Shaw now rose and read a statement that had been prepared by Greg and Dorene.

"The Ridgway family would like to express its deepest, heartfelt sympathies to all of the families and friends who have lost loved ones. We grieve the losses and are sorry that so many have suffered for so many years. We have prayed that truth and justice would prevail in this case. Be assured that we were shocked to hear that Gary could do the things he has admitted to doing. However, we love Gary, and believe that the Gary Ridgway America now knows is different from the person known by our family. Clearly, there were two Gary Ridgways. We have always viewed Gary as a kind and compassionate person, who was there when the family needed him.

"He was a responsible, hardworking husband to his wife, and was devoted to his parents until their deaths. He displayed loyalty while in the Navy and while working at his job. He never showed any tendencies to anger and never harbored ill will toward anyone. We saw a reliable, dependable, conscientious guy who negotiated calmly during difficult times, always putting the troubles of others before his own.

We had not seen anything that could be considered strange or abnormal. Had Gary shown anything that we thought was improper, we would have brought that to the attention of the authorities.

"We would like to thank the law enforcement officials, lawyers, investigators, and everyone who have labored for so many years. We thank them for never giving up on this case and for their commitment to justice. We were extremely grateful when Gary agreed to cooperate and accept responsibility for his actions. We pray that these proceedings will help everyone to heal who has been so profoundly affected by this tragedy."

It was then Gary's turn to make his own statement. He had written this out himself. He rose and began to read.

"I'm sorry for killing all those young ladies," he read. "I've tried hard to remember as much as I could, to help the detectives find and recover the ladies. I'm sorry for the scare I put into the community. I want to thank the police, prosecutors, my attorneys, and all others that had the patience to work with me and help me remember all the terrible things I did, and to be able to talk about them. I know how horrible my acts were. I have tried for a long time to get these things out of my mind. I have tried for a long time to keep from killing any more ladies. I'm sorry that I've put my wife, my son, my brother, and my family through this hell. I hope they can find a way to forgive me. I am very sorry for the ladies that were not found. May they rest in peace. They need a better place than what I gave them. I'm sorry for killing these young ladies. They had their whole life ahead of them. I'm sorry I caused so much pain for so many families."

Gary sat down.

Finally, it was Judge Jones's turn to address Gary.

"Mr. Ridgway," he began, "the time has now come for the final chapter of your reign of terror in this community. Today has been a long time coming for the brutal murders you committed. As an English poet, John Dryden, once wrote:

'Murder may pass unpunish'd for a time,
But tardy justice will o'ertake the crime.'"

Before pronouncing the sentence, Judge Jones told Gary to turn and face the courtroom. Killer and victims' survivors stared one another in the face.

"Mr. Ridgway," Jones said, "those are the families and friends of the people you killed. If you have a drop of emotion, you will be haunted by them for the balance of your life."

And to the families, Jones asked them to harbor no thoughts about revenge. It would be far better, he said, to think of others in trouble, as so many of the victims had been and to try to do something to help them.

"In this community, there are hundreds of women who don't have families who love them," he said. "Find them, help them. In this way, you can give [your loved one's] life true meaning and dignity."

The judge now addressed Gary, who turned back to face him.

"Today, Mr. Ridgway, is a day of justice for all of the young women you murdered. It is now time for our community to have peace from the Green River murders. . . . the remarkable thing about you, sir, is your remarkable, Teflon-coated emotions and complete absence of genuine compassion for the young women you murdered. . . . there is nothing in your life that was of significance, other than your own demented, calculating, lustful passion of being the emissary of death.

"As you spend the balance of your life in your cell in prison, much of which will probably be in solitary confinement, I truly hope that the last thoughts you have of the free world are the faces of the people in this courtroom. As you spend the balance of your life in that tiny cell, surrounded only by your thoughts, please know the women you killed were not throwaways or pieces of candy in a dish placed upon this planet for the sole purpose of satisfying your murderous desires. While you could not face them as you took their lives, if you have a drop of emotion anywhere in your existence, you will face those young women in your dreams and private thoughts of your grisly deeds. And sir, if you have that drop of emotion, you will be haunted for the balance of your life."

―――

After we left the courtroom, Gary was whisked away without any good-byes. He was returned to the custody of the King County Correctional Facility, to the eleventh floor, to await his transfer to the Washington State Penitentiary. This was the institution where the most violent offenders served their sentences. Located in Walla Walla, about three hundred miles southeast of Seattle, it's appropriately nicknamed "The Walls."

As we walked out of the courthouse, a woman approached me. I recognized her immediately. It was Mertie Winston, Tracie Winston's mom.

"You're Mr. Ridgway's attorney," she said. I couldn't help but wonder where this would be going. I stopped.

"Yes," I quietly replied, extending my hand. "I'm sorry for your loss."

She shook my hand and said, "You must have a very difficult job. I just wanted to tell you I think you've done a very good job. Thank you."

I was stunned and touched by her kind remarks. "Thank you," was all I could think to say.

"And not that I ever will," she continued, "but if I was ever in trouble and needed a lawyer, I'd want you by my side."

"I'm sure you won't," I said, "but thank you." To me, that was the best compliment I had ever received. Or ever will.

PART FIVE

The Truth

52

Three weeks later, on January 6, 2004, Gary Ridgway was transferred to The Walls. As an inmate at high risk of being murdered himself, Gary was assigned to the institution's intensive management unit, or "IMU." Although that meant that the other prisoners couldn't get to him, it also meant that for all practical purposes, he had to stay alone in his cell for all but one hour on Tuesday, Thursday, and Saturday. Most people would have a hard time with this, but I recalled what Ross Nooney of the task force had said about Gary: "Gary, hell, that's all he does for several hours a day . . . stare at blank walls. I've seen him just sit there for hours. He's amazing."

So what *was* going on in Gary's mind? What was the truth about the Green River murders? As the events of the two years from late 2001 to 2003 have begun to recede in my memory, I'm no longer sure what to think of my most notorious client. By the time he'd been sentenced to spending the rest of his life in prison, I was convinced that the weeping Gary *did* have remorse for his horrible crimes, that the real killer had been "the old Gary," and the "new Gary" truly understood the enormity of what he'd done.

But then I remembered that Gary's forte had always been his adaptability—his capacity to be whatever people expected of him. Despite his lack of education, despite his below-average intellect, Gary was, I think, the finest Method Actor alive. It wasn't conscious so much as it was instinctual. He could cry whenever he wanted to and shut it off just as abruptly. If you wanted remorse, he could do that. If you wanted him mad, sad, stupid, smart, embarrassed, boastful, sinful, or religious, he could do them all, and you'd be convinced. I'd seen all of these stages, and others, during the years since the night I'd first met him, and especially during our time in the bunker. He was, as Dr. O'Toole once observed, a chameleon, always blending in, always giving you what you expected, always ready to please. And that was, in fact, his deadliest trait.

Because, when I thought about it, I realized that what had begun as a method of social adaptation for the child Gary—compensation for his dyslexia and his family's arduous early poverty, as well as his allergies that always made him seem like he was crying, his emotional estrangement, indeed, all his other physical and behavioral problems—had eventually become the very core of his ability to kill over and over again.

He'd worked hard to blend in, to conceal his deficits, and had succeeded so well that none of his victims ever realized that the mousy little man with the snapshot of his child in his wallet was actually the deadliest sexual predator in the nation. He waited, literally until their backs were turned, and then struck, the trick who had the final, fatal trick that no one had ever suspected.

Over the years before he went to prison, many people had offered theories as to why the Green River Killer had killed so many. It was abundantly clear that Gary himself did not really know. Whenever he was asked the "why" question, he could only focus on the slights and angers he had received in his life—at school, at work, from his wives—but nothing he'd endured really served to explain the origin of the murderous rage that had animated him.

Mary Goody, for instance, came to see that Gary's killing had stemmed from a combination of his neurological problems and his frustration at being so often overlooked and discounted. She thought he hadn't started out to kill; instead, she thought that something had initially gone wrong during his sexual encounters and that his choking was a nearly automatic response when things went awry, a reaction to his disappointment at not having things evolve as he had idealized in his fantasies. Then, later, as Gary continued to kill, he began to take pride in his skill at murdering. "It was the only thing in his life that he'd ever done really, really well," she told me. "It was something that gave him power and helped him feel good about himself."

Dr. Judith Becker believed that Gary's killing stemmed from his frustration at never having true intimacy with anyone. Abandoned by his first two wives, he had sought solace with money, hating himself for being a sexual "loser," and yet ensuring, by his use of prostitutes, that he never could get the intimacy he craved—not for twenty dollars and ten minutes. It was not until he took up with his third wife, Judith, that some measure of this intimacy was finally attained, and even that was short of Gary's idealized desire, as his continued patronage of prostitutes, even after his marriage to Judith, showed. Still, when Gary said that he'd "slowed down" after meeting Judith, he was telling the truth, and in that sense, one can only wonder how many lives Judith unknowingly saved over the years.

Then there was O'Toole's "paraphilia" paradigm, one that seemed to put the onus squarely on Mary Rita Ridgway and Gary's early childhood. At first, I thought there must be something to this, especially in light of the prolonged bed-wetting that Gary told us about; and like others, I wondered whether there was some sort of seductive aspect in Gary's relationship with his mother that accounted for his later behavior as an adult. But eventually, I came to realize that this was insupportable—there was absolutely no evidence for it, despite the best efforts of Dr. O'Toole's "verification" process. I came to see Mary Rita as a woman who had done the best she could for her three sons, under what appeared to be very difficult circumstances. Certainly, the idea that Gary's murderous behavior stemmed from his childhood environment was not helped by the fact that two other sons in the same environment did *not* have Gary's problems. Which in turn seems to suggest that there may have been some sort of organic attribute of Gary's brain that prompted murderous behavior, something that science as yet does not understand.

Todd had still a different take on Gary. "Here was a guy in a low-end job, who was put down by people all the time, who developed this secret skill that gave all meaning to his life."

Referring to a surveillance video that the Green River Task Force had taken of Gary before his arrest, Todd pointed out that he was like a predatory animal in the forest. "When you watch it, you can see him look over his shoulder, almost as if he's scenting the air. He's completely in tune with his surroundings. He's checking everything, looking for potential threats, looking for potential game." Gary's hunting instincts were so ingrained, so masterful, had become such an important part of his personality, Todd believed, that he simply felt compelled to murder.

Tom Jensen, who had spent so many years studying the murders, and later, so many hours with Gary, put it very succinctly: "I think his brain is just wired different than the rest of us."

Later, Jensen expanded on this notion. "The short answer of why he did this is because he found he could and he found he liked it. To say that Gary is 'wired differently than the rest of us' may be oversimplistic, but I doubt that even the learned scholars who have studied the phenomenon could come up with an exact recipe for cooking up a serial killer. I believe that it is part genetics and part environment that creates the type of personality that could be a candidate to 'morph' into a serial murderer. Beyond that, I think that events in the life of the candidate are very critical to setting things in motion that eventually lead to that first kill and finding that they like it. Factors such as memory, fantasy, planning, stalking, and sex drive may help to dictate frequency, victim selection, and other paraphilic behaviors.

"In six months of interviews, we rarely saw the guy behind the Gary Ridgway mask. In his fifty plus years, he had become very adept at hiding and coping. His life was a lie and he found it very difficult to avoid doing the same in our interviews. He claimed that he picked up so many prostitutes over the years he could not recall where he found most of those that he killed. He said he killed so many prostitutes in the same manner and method that he recalled few specific details of individual cases. He acknowledged only those postmortem activities that he knew we were aware of. Then he blamed poor memory for things that he wanted to hold back. It's very difficult to prove that lack of memory is a lie."

Why? What has this all meant? What have the confessions of Gary Ridgway taught us? What have we learned about serial murderers? What can we learn from the mistakes we made and the lives that were needlessly lost? What have we learned about ourselves as a result of the Green River case? We need to ask these questions. The victims deserve no less.

Why? There is not and never can be a logical, satisfactory answer to why Gary murdered. There are clues that lead to theories and speculation, but no correct, definitive answer. Nothing where one would say, "Oh. Yes. I see. I understand now."

But we can and should research, ask questions, speculate, and theorize in the hope we hit on something, some bit of wisdom or truth that could shed some light on the darkness of serial murderers.

There is an obvious connection to prostitution, more than mere vulnerability and anonymity, given that Gary told us he would only kill prostitutes or girls who were selling sex for one sad reason or another. Yet he was addicted to sex with prostitutes. Sort of a love-hate situation taken to the extreme. I believed Gary when he told us he killed a "lady" if she was in a hurry or she only worried about money as opposed to a prostitute who would allow him to take his time. I believe this may have been a factor that was building up within him as he frequented prostitutes after his divorce from Marcia.

He got squeezed tighter and tighter financially, while he grew more and more frustrated and angry over the divorce. Marcia was hassling him over child support for Matthew. Two young streetwalkers stole his wallet. He boiled over and whatever violent tendencies had been planted earlier were allowed to come out. He choked a woman and it made him feel powerful for a moment. And it was free.

He progressed to his first kill and though it made him ashamed and guilt ridden, he found it exhilarating to have so much power and control. And, again, it was free. And, he quickly realized, it was easy. The ladies just got right into his car.

The second victim. The third. The fourth. And he was off. The sex was secondary, merely a necessary prelude to lull his victim into the killing position. He got off on the kill.

Where did this evil side of Gary come from in the first place? Certainly, he described some problems and weird things that happened as a kid; for example, having learning disabilities, wetting the bed into his teens, putting the cat in the cooler, having a mom who cleaned the floors with bleach, and, of course, stabbing the young boy. I initially favored the "Mommie Dearest" theory but thought that Gary was just not going to admit whatever bad things his mom may have done. Now, having reviewed everything, I do not subscribe to that theory. Although bleaching the floors is a bit much, I was not convinced that Mary Rita was a bad mom. I don't believe there was any real abuse, sexual or otherwise. In fact, I've come to believe that she tried to do everything she could for her boys. Perhaps she shouldn't have berated Gary for his learning disabilities and other shortcomings. That certainly could have been an early foundation for the anger Gary had toward women who had power or control over him. But it wouldn't turn a young man into a serial killer.

When Gary was asked why, he gave simple answers:

"I was so mad at Marcia."

"That way, I didn't have to pay."

Until he got right down to it:

"Because I liked to kill and could get away with it."

Which begs the question—why did he enjoy killing young prosti-tutes? Because he had the power and control. First, over the "ladies." He outsmarted the young girls that got in his car. As it snowballed and he didn't get caught, he felt superiority over the police. For someone who was berated by his mom for not being smart enough, some-one teased and held back in school, someone nicknamed "Wrongway" at work, outsmarting the sheriff and his detectives, even the FBI, had to be a great feeling. He *was* smart. And that gave him more power and control.

He was smart enough to keep this all to himself. For someone who was essentially ignored his entire life, someone always in the background—that is, unless he was being ridiculed—it had to be tempting to want to brag about his deeds. It's been the downfall of many other murderers. He did attempt the contact with the *P-I* but didn't pursue public communications after that. Keeping the secret to himself not only prolonged his freedom, but, as he realized, it also gave him more power and control over the police and their investigation.

Why did he do it? In twenty-five words or less:

Killing prostitutes gave him power and control over women and others in authority—power and control he wanted but lacked in his own existence.

—∿∿—

What can we learn to prevent this from happening again? I don't think this type of murder spree *will* happen again. Advances in forensics and computer technology will catch serial killers before they kill as many as Gary. Lessons learned from the Green River investigation have led to advances in investigation techniques in serial cases across the globe. Jon Mattsen, Randy Mullinax, and other Green River Task Force detectives have taught at many law enforcement training seminars, passing on things that they did, right and wrong, in their quest to put Gary away.

Earlier recognition of possible serial murder activity, better intra-agency and jurisdictional cooperation, crime scene investigation, and better evidence collection and preservation are among some of the lessons learned that will catch serial murderers much earlier in their hunt for victims.

Gary's case, along with other recently captured serial killers, such as the D.C. snipers and the BTK murderer in Wichita, blew away many of the preconceived notions of serial murder profilers. The behavioral scientists have to reevaluate and work to improve the analysis, including the data gathered in Gary's case. Unfortunately, in my opinion, the FBI was so determined to make Gary fit their mold that the opportunity to learn much more was missed. "We know what we know and it is what it is." With this type of close-mindedness, maybe this could happen again.[1]

——

For those who believe that most crimes are solved, that murder will out, the history of the Green River murders remains shocking. For apart from Gary's peculiar attributes, his skills at social camouflage, there were also a large number of wider causes that contributed to the gigantic death toll. Gary Ridgway was the killer and he was the one directly responsible for so many deaths, but the rest of us unwittingly helped him. We cared too little about his victims before they became victims; our Victorian-era attitudes about prostitution condemned Gary's victims to indifference even before Gary's hatred and lust took their lives. That some of our children could walk the streets selling their bodies in ever-present danger of possible assault and murder and that we allowed this, even taxed it in the form of fines, was a disgrace, especially because we preferred to pretend it did not exist. We were more interested in establishing our disapproval of their behavior than we were in making sure they were safe. We rousted them out of the motels and onto the streets, where they became the prey of people like Gary; it's worth remembering that Gary never killed anyone in a motel room, a far safer venue for prostitution, and if ever he had, he would have been caught long before.

"I firmly believe that the solution to the Green River cases was on the streets and could have come from the streets," Jensen said later. "We needed people who were invisible, who could watch the people watching the people on the streets. We needed to identify the Ridgways, who were sitting in the supermarket parking lot watching the hookers and the guys talking to the hookers and picking them up. The problem with this approach is that it does not produce any numbers or anything that can be quantified to justify its continued existence."

In addition, Jensen told me, the police bureaucracy was simply not organized to cope with the murders when they began and as they developed. Record keeping was rudimentary, evidence collection and analysis were far too fragmented, and psychological profiles of the perpetrator were far too unrefined. All of these things changed over time, he said, but by then it was too late.

"Law enforcement," Jensen said, "must get better at identifying and catching serial murderers, and the behavioral analysts must get better at predicting patterns and profiles. Better profiles will aid law enforcement in apprehending more killers that can then provide more data for profilers."

"Of course," he added, "you have a much better chance of analyzing a serial killer if you have not executed him."

Since Gary's transfer to the State Penitentiary in Walla Walla, I've made the long drive across the state nine times to visit him. Living in an eight-by-ten-foot cell, Gary is allowed out for exercise for one hour on three days each week. Those who think that life in prison is a breeze should try to imagine living in the same small space for 165 hours out of 168 hours a week, 8,580 hours a year, year after year after year, with very little human contact. No one could think this was pleasant.

Since his arrival in prison, Gary has done everything he can to maintain a low profile. He spent the first several weeks in the medical unit where he was checked out by the doctors and psychologists. In June 2004, he was moved to the IMU. He received some verbal abuse when he first arrived, but he said he just ignored it and didn't respond. It stopped within a couple weeks.

Gary has received numerous requests for interviews from a variety of people interested in his case: a forensic psychiatrist, a "wellness" therapist, a doctoral student in psychology, journalists and reporters, documentary filmmakers, and serial murder researchers. He has been willing to be interviewed but, following our advice, only in the presence of Todd or me. However, the prison has refused to allow visits for purposes beyond law enforcement, attorney visits, and family visits.

A few months after Gary's move to the IMU, I was contacted by the Missing Women's Task Force in Vancouver, B.C., Canada. They asked to interview Gary regarding his visits to Canada, although they were convinced that Gary was not involved in any homicides up there. They just wanted to cover all of their bases in anticipation of cross-examination by Robert Pickton's defense lawyers. Pickton, a B.C. pig farmer, was facing trial for the murders of twenty-seven women. In fact, the Canadian authorities also sought any insights Gary might have that could help their investigation and prosecution of Pickton. I contacted Gary, and he agreed to meet with them.

On October 6, 2004, I traveled to Walla Walla to be present for these interviews. The Canadian police officers politely and respectfully questioned Gary for a few hours. Gary discussed his various trips to Canada over the years and what he had done up there. He denied committing any crimes in Canada, and he denied having any knowledge of Pickton or his pig farm in Coquitlam, B.C. The only thing he could suggest, Gary told the Canadian authorities, was that they should appeal to Pickton to do what he could to help the families of his victims as a means of inducing the alleged Canadian killer to cooperate.

———

To my knowledge, as of this writing, Todd, Tony, and I (and the Canadian detectives) are the only ones to have visited Gary at Walla Walla. He has stayed in touch with Greg and Dorene on a weekly basis, through the mail and collect phone calls. He has told me he reads, writes letters, and exercises. He began to study the Bible with more intensity and spends a good portion of his time reading scriptures and completing Bible study assignments. Through his good behavior, he earned a small black-and-white TV, which he said he watches about two or three hours a day. He consistently receives letters from people from all over the country but is allowed to have no more than six in his cell at a time.

On occasion, when I feel the timing is right, I have asked him if he has remembered any additional information that could be helpful in trying to find those who are still missing. He has tried and tried to come up with something, but nothing of substance has yet materialized. And one other thing is clear: Gary still doesn't seem to have any real insight about the psychological forces that brought him to this point and what went wrong, so long ago.

For myself, things have also changed: in March 2004, both Greg Girard and I left Associated Counsel for the Accused, becoming partners in the private law firm of Hanis Greaney, in Kent. It had been a very long and arduous two years since the evening that Greg and I had first sat down with Gary, back before I really understood the enormity of what was to unfold. In some powerful way, the experience of defending Gary changed me utterly, and yet in other ways I remain the same.

Gary Ridgway killed at least forty-eight and possibly as many as seventy-one women, or maybe even more. We will probably never know the actual total. These murders took place over a period as long as twenty years. Five hundred years ago, we would have burned someone like Gary Ridgway at the stake. In our superstition in that age of religious unreason, we would have called him the Devil or at least considered him possessed. Even today, some would say that Gary is "pure evil." But this is only labeling, and when we use these words, we do nothing to explain how these things happen. And if there is anything of value to be gained from the nightmare, this is the least we should do. We owe it to those who died.

As for me, I make no apologies for helping to get Gary Ridgway life in prison rather than execution. Through this agreement, law enforcement was given a rare opportunity to get inside the mind of the nation's most prolific, and horribly successful, serial killer. Knowledge was indeed gained, knowledge that will help in future serial murder investigations.

And, hopefully, save some lives.

◦◦◦ Notes

Chapter Four

1. The defense lawyers soon discovered that this information reported in the newspapers was wrong—that DNA evidence had been found with Carol Christensen, Marcia Chapman, and Opal Mills, but not Cynthia Hinds. The difference was significant, in that Carol Christensen's body was found under circumstances that were radically different than the victims found in or near the Green River. At the time that he talked to the news media immediately after Gary's arrest on November 30, 2001, Sheriff Reichert certainly knew of this distinction. It appears that the reporters covering Reichert's initial press conference did not parse Reichert's words carefully and wound up adding two and two to come up with five. The defense discovered the error in the reporting the next day, and it was one reason they elected to be so cautious in their subsequent statements to the news media. This was Exhibit A insofar as the media's capacity for accuracy, they felt. (Carlton Smith [CS])

2. This is from a *Seattle Times* front-page story, published on December 1, 2001, by Ian Ith, Steve Miletich, and Duff Wilson.

3. See Note 2 above.

Chapter Five

1. Article by Ian Ith, Carlton Smith, and Thomas Guillen in the *Seattle Times*, December 3, 2001, p. A-1.

2. Article by Eric Sorensen in the *Seattle Times*, December 4, 2001, p. A-10.

3. The story, reported by Ian Ith, ran on the front page, above the fold, in the *Seattle Times*, December 4, 2001, p. A-1.

4. In this interview with reporter Ian Ith of the *Seattle Times*, published on December 4, 2001, Sheriff Reichert said he was confident that his detectives would "connect additional cases to Ridgway" but acknowledged that "it's

incumbent on us to be absolutely positive." Being less than absolutely positive, of course, opened the possibility that other people might have committed some of the murders. And in a bit of historical revisionism, in the
same interview, Reichert asserted that as the original lead investigator in the
case in 1982, "I was left alone, from the fall of 1982 to . . . late summer of
1983." This was actually not the case. From the fall of 1982 to the late summer of 1983, the same period of time that almost forty of the forty-nine
murders were committed, Reichert was assisted by four other detectives.

The primary reason why the initial staffing level for the investigation
was cut back from twenty-five investigators to five in the fall of 1982 was
Reichert's erroneous belief that he had identified the probable murderer
as cabdriver Melvyn Foster. During this period of time, several valuable
leads that would have led to the identification of Gary Ridgway were provided to Reichert and the other four detectives (including, possibly, the
license plate of Gary's vehicle in direct connection with the disappearance
of one victim at the end of October 1983), none of which were aggressively
followed up. These errors in the original investigation were one reason why
Gary Ridgway was able to kill so many women. Reichert had developed
"tunnel vision" focused on Melvyn Foster, as later police administrators
acknowledged. (CS)

5. Front-page headline in the *Seattle Post-Intelligencer,* December 4, 2001,
p. A-1, article by Mike Lewis, Vanessa Ho, and Tracy Johnson, December 4,
2001, p. A-1.

Chapter Six

1. According to King County Sheriff's Department spokesman John Urquhart, however, it was Reichert who first tried to restrain Maleng. At a meeting held in Maleng's office two days before Gary's arrest, Reichert asked the
Prosecutor to make no statements insisting on the death penalty for Gary
Ridgway. Reichert said that his detectives were far more interested in getting
the answers to enduring questions—such as the location of still undiscovered victims' remains—than they were in seeing Ridgway executed for the
crimes. He urged Maleng to make no unequivocal statement insisting on
the death penalty, in order to keep open the possibility of future negotiations. (CS)

2. Subsequently, when the defense team examined Dave Reichert's investigator
follow-up report, compiled between 1982 and 1987 when Reichert was only
a rank-and-file homicide investigator, not the elected Sheriff, they discov-

ered that the Green River investigators had debated the honesty of including only portions of the profile—just those parts that fit Gary Ridgway—
as a means of obtaining probable cause to search his property, when other
portions of the profile were significantly off. This issue had apparently become
so heated in 1987 that some investigators had asked for transfers from the
task force rather than participate in the 1987 search of Gary. (CS)

Chapter Eight

1. The Sheriff's Department, and Reichert, subsequently asserted that they
   had placed the river under surveillance but that the surveillance was blown—
   exposed—by the reports of a Seattle television station, KIRO. That was
   something of an evasion, however. The surveillance was not established
   until Sunday night, August 15, 1982, not three days earlier as implied by
   Reichert. Had the surveillance been put in place on August 12, 1982, it quite
   likely would have resulted in the capture of the killer at the very beginning
   of the murder series. This failure, of course, opened the way for the later
   victimization of nearly sixty-five women at the hands of the killer they had
   failed to watch out for, at a time when it might have done some good. A
   large part of this failure was the result of Reichert's initial insistence that
   Debbie Bonner's murder was not connected to the earlier murder of Wendy
   Coffield, an error that Green River Task Force commanders later acknowledged as one of the most critical failures in the entire investigation. (CS)
2. In fairness to Reichert, Melvyn Foster was given numerous polygraph examinations between 1982 and 1986 and showed deception on virtually all
   of them. Later, however, the quality of the King County polygraph expert's
   assessment of Foster's examinations was called into question; according to
   some members of the Green River Task Force, the examinations of Foster
   and numerous other potential suspects—including Gary Ridgway's "no
   deception" polygraph of 1984—were found by other experts to be flawed.
   So the use of the polygraph test as a screening tool for the early part of the
   Green River investigation was later judged to be essentially useless. (CS)
3. The word *cluster* was first employed by the *Seattle Times* in the mid-1980s
   in an effort to avoid the dehumanizing term "dump sites," then employed
   by police. Later the word was adopted by the police, the prosecutors, the
   defense team, and Gary Ridgway himself. (CS)
4. Using STR technology, the DNA recovered from Christensen produced a
   13-loci profile that was identical to Gary's 13-loci profile. According to the
   state's experts, based on population genetics and statistical calculations, that

profile would be found in 1 in 4.2 quadrillion (4,216,000,000,000,000) Caucasians, more than the total amount of people that have ever lived. The degraded DNA recovered from Marcia Chapman produced a 9-loci profile identical to Gary's at all 9 loci. The numbers were lower but still very damning: 1 in 10.6 million.

5. The computer, a then state-of-the art VAX minicomputer, was about the size of a large desk. It was financed by a grant from the State of Washington, and according to Green River Task Force members, it never did work very well. (CS)

6. The detective who had been contacted by Miley later told Mullinax that she had never provided a license plate number to him. But at the time of the tip, Reichert's crew of five detectives was very nearly overwhelmed with tips, and it was possible that the plate number was simply misplaced as the maelstrom of paper washed over the detectives' desks. (CS)

Chapter Nine

1. Reichert later wrote that the defense had no confidence in their case because we hired a mitigation specialist: "Gradually it became clear that Tony Savage and the other defense lawyers lacked real confidence," he observed in *Chasing the Devil* (2004), his book about the Green River case. "One sign was their hiring of a nationally known expert to delve deep into Ridgway's background for a 'mitigation report' that would be used to argue against the death penalty in the event of a conviction. Why would they begin this work so early in the pretrial period if they weren't worried about losing?"

The Sheriff's lack of knowledge on this point is surprising. Before making such a statement, he should have done a little research. He would have learned that the death penalty statute in Washington *requires* the defense to prepare a mitigation package to be presented to the prosecutor within thirty days of arraignment. He would also have learned that death penalty after death penalty, in Washington State and across the country, have been reversed by appellate courts, including the U.S. Supreme Court, because the defense did not fully prepare for the penalty phase. And one of the most common reasons for these reversals was the failure to retain a mitigation specialist at the very beginning of the case. Recent Supreme Court cases have held that it is ineffective assistance of counsel to fail to engage a mitigation specialist early in the case. A Washington case, *State* v. *Brett,* had just been reversed on those very grounds. The Washington Supreme Court had recently adopted a court rule *requiring* the defense to have a mitigation specialist on the team in death penalty cases, and recently published American Bar Association guidelines on defense of capital cases mandated retaining a mitigation specialist. It has nothing to do with "confidence" or lack of confidence in the defense case. A defense lawyer is required to "worry about losing." It's standard operating procedure in capital defense. (MP)

Chapter Ten

1. Mary Rita Steinman Ridgway died on August 15, 2001—the same day Gary's wife, Judith, had her fifty-seventh birthday. Coincidentally, August 15 was also the date of Gary's marriage to Claudia in 1969, as well as the date that the Green River murders first came to public attention with the discovery of the bodies of Marcia Chapman, Cynthia Hinds, and Opal Mills in 1982. (CS)

Chapter Twelve

1. The Loop goes right by Renton High School, where I graduated from in 1974. My friends and I "cruised The Loop" a few times in the mid-seventies. (MP)

Chapter Thirteen

1. Judith was dismissed as a defendant in this lawsuit three years later, in 2005. (CS)
2. This admission of childhood bed-wetting by Gary was to evolve as the next year unfolded. After initially saying that his enuresis stopped at the age of four or five, Gary later admitted—by stages—that this problem had lasted into his midteens. A Federal Bureau of Investigation–sponsored study of thirty-five multiple murderers, conducted in 1982, found that twenty-two reported bed-wetting as children, twenty as teenagers, and five as adults. See *Sexual Homicide: Patterns and Motives,* Ressler, Burgess, and Douglas, Lexington Books, 1988. (CS)
3. The White Shutters Inn, located at South 146th Street and Pacific Highway South, was near the epicenter of many of the Green River disappearances from 1982 to 1984. Many prostitutes used a bus shelter there to solicit passing motorists and often worked out of motel rooms across the street from the restaurant, which no longer exists. (CS)

Chapter Fifteen

1. Dr. Beaver administered some common preliminary tests: the Wechsler Adult Intelligence Scale III, the Wide Range Achievement Test 3, the Beck Depression Inventory II, the Rey 15-Item Memory Test, and the Validity Indicator Profile nonverbal subtest. (CS)

2. We considered a number of experts in the areas of forensic toxicology and neurotoxicology. Eventually, however, our efforts along this line were overtaken by other events—consequently, we never were able to say whether the chronic exposure to lead paint, solvents, thinners, and other toxins played any role in Gary's behavior or neurological deficits. (MP)

Chapter Sixteen

1. This $1.9 million, when added to the approximately $1 million that had already been committed by OPD, made the total authorization for defending Gary Ridgway for 2002 about $2.9 million. (CS)

2. *South County Journal*, June 13, 2002, p. A-8.

3. Satterberg's attempt to play the populist in this regard was a bit disingenuous. He certainly knew that the forty-five uncharged murder counts would be used by his office to prove the four charged counts and that a failure on the part of the defense to adequately investigate them would have resulted in a reversal of any conviction due to ineffective assistance of counsel. It was, however, the sort of statement that made Satterberg look as if he were defending the taxpayers, even if it was legally inane. (CS)

4. Colwell, interviewed years later by the police after his retirement, said as far as he could recall, Miley had never given him a license plate number. (CS)

Chapter Seventeen

1. As noted, much later, when the King County Sheriff's Department submitted three suspected perpetrators' DNA samples to the Washington State Patrol Crime Laboratory, Foster's was one of those offered for testing. Of the three, only Gary Ridgway was matched to the available samples from victims. Even after Gary Ridgway confessed to the crimes, Reichert refused to say that Foster had been cleared and declined to apologize to the one-time cabdriver. Experts later concluded that Foster's lie detector tests were significantly flawed in their interpretation by the county's polygraph expert—as was Gary Ridgway's. (CS)

Chapter Eighteen

1. *South County Journal,* Letters to the Editor, August 8, 2002, p. A-8.
2. The letter was dated July 22, 2002, received at our home on July 26. (MP)

Chapter Nineteen

1. *Seattle Post-Intelligencer,* August 7, 2001, Special Report by Lise Olson.

Chapter Twenty

1. Because of Webbe's obvious mental impairment, the state had already agreed not to seek the death penalty for him. He was sentenced to life in prison without parole in January 2003. So instead of being incarcerated in a secure mental facility where he might receive treatment for the illusory demons tormenting him, Roy Webbe will spend the rest of his life in a state penitentiary, where the demons are all too real. (MP)

Chapter Twenty-Three

1. Following Gary's arrest in 2001, there had been considerable speculation in Washington State political circles that Sheriff Reichert would run for the governorship of the state on the strength of the Green River case. In the end, however, he ran for Congress and was elected in 2004. (CS)
2. These names have been changed to protect any innocent persons.

Chapter Twenty-Eight

1. Rebecca Garde was the woman whom Gary had choked in the fall of 1982 but who had escaped by running to a neighborhood house. (CS)

Chapter Twenty-Nine

1. The audio-video feed was later transcribed by a contractor for the state and eventually represented 8,463 pages of typewritten material, virtually every-thing that was said between Gary Ridgway and his interrogators between

June 13 and December 16, 2003. The material excerpted for this book was taken directly from those transcripts, with only minor editing for clarity. The publicly anonymous transcribers did a fantastically good job of recording every utterance, right down to the omnipresent "uhs" so typical of such encounters. (CS)

Chapter Thirty

1. Much later, Jensen said that by this point, Sunday, June 15, 2003, he was wondering whether Gary had only committed some of the murders and was trying to claim responsibility for all of them, even those he hadn't committed, to secure his plea deal with the prosecutor. That's why he was so anxious to discover something from Gary that would tend to prove his claims. (CS)

Chapter Thirty-One

1. This admission shed light on two mysteries: first, how was it that a reasonably intact sperm sample had been recovered from Marcia Chapman's body, despite the fact that she had been killed almost two weeks before she was found; and two, why the heavy rocks had been piled atop both Chapman and Cynthia Hinds under the water. The cool water would have acted as something of a preservative of both remains, sufficient for a necrophiliac killer to return later to pull them out to have sex with them. That was the purpose of the heavy rocks and, possibly, the rocks placed inside the vaginas. (CS)
2. Carol Christensen was employed as a barmaid at the Red Barn Tavern on Pacific Highway South, a few blocks away from her apartment. On the day she was last seen, May 3, 1983, she had told a coworker she was going for a picnic with someone the following day. Her fully clothed body bore the marking of a thin ligature, possibly an electrical cord or clothesline. (CS)
3. This was the bottle of Lambrusco wine that had been found with Carol Christensen's body on May 8, 1983. (CS)

Chapter Thirty-Two

1. Gary had told the detectives that he'd taken Polaroid photos of two of the dead river victims and that he had stashed the pictures in a stairwell at the

Red Lion Hotel near the airport. Later, he said, he'd retrieved the photographs, tore them up, and threw the fragments into the Green River. After that, he said, he'd run over the Polaroid camera with his car in order to destroy it. One problem with the story, however, was that Gary had also told the detectives he'd never returned to the Green River after the bodies had been found: that was one reason the detectives didn't believe that he'd gone back to get rid of the images. A second reason was that the "book" on serial murderers predicted that they would invariably save such photographs in a secret cache rather than destroy them. (CS)

2. As noted previously, this letter was actually sent to the *Seattle Post-Intelligencer*. Reporter Mike Barber then turned it over to the Green River Task Force, which provided it to the FBI's Behavioral Sciences Unit. The FBI concluded that it had not come from the killer, however. (CS)

3. On the previous day, the detectives had suggested that they might return to the house that Gary had shared with Judith in Auburn at the time of his arrest to search for victims' jewelry. The house had already been sold to new owners. But this suggestion had clearly agitated Gary and may have been one of the reasons he became confrontational the following day. He apparently did not want the detectives to search the Auburn house. (CS)

4. Green River Task Force detectives had discovered the complete skeleton of a large dog intermingled with the skeleton of Sandra Gabbert at Star Lake in 1984. Some investigators wondered whether the killer had placed Sandra Gabbert's body at the same place where he'd previously placed a dead dog, but it now appeared that the proximity between Ms. Gabbert's remains and those of the dog was sheer coincidence. (CS)

5. Jensen later came to believe that the "bad Gary" was the real Gary and that the "good Gary" had tried to "sugarcoat" his admissions by claiming that he'd cared for some of the victims, such as Carol Christensen. "I believe that he had a certain 'persona' that he wanted to project to the world as The Green River serial killer," Jensen said later, when interviewed for this book. "That persona did not cross certain lines: (1) [He] only killed the 'un-innocents' (hookers). (2) Only engaged in mild postmortem mutilation (vaginal insertion of objects). Something we already knew. (3) Only strangled them so they did not suffer (no guns, no knives, no blood). The fact that he admitted postmortem sexual activity with the bodies seems to be contrary to this idea, but I believe that he may have thought that there was some scientific way to prove PM [postmortem] sex and felt he had to give it up. . . . Since I think that he thought we could detect PM sex, he had to have an explanation. I think that admitting that he 'kept' them for company portrayed him as the pathetic, lonely little wimp that he was, and he needed a stronger image for where he was going. If he was going to have PM sex, why

not have it under the best conditions (in the house)? What other reason was there to go to the trouble of taking them home?" (CS)

6. This site was near a large insurance company office visible near Interstate 5 south of Portland. Gary said he'd left the glove near the skull of someone he thought might have been April Buttram near the building's parking lot. That skull, however, was never recovered and so neither was the glove. (CS)

Chapter Thirty-Three

1. In the spring of 1982, Gary Ridgway had been having trouble making the payments on his house. As a result, he rented the house to a family and moved into the garage. The stress from this arrangement, and his worries about money, coupled with his ex-wife's demands for child support, were among the factors present when the series of killings began. The renters lived in the house until the following spring. (CS)

2. Robert Ainsworth's recollection was that he'd seen two men on the river-bank the afternoon of August 15, 1982, just before he discovered the bodies under the water. He was unable to identify Gary. Attempts to hypnotize him to enhance his recollection were unsuccessful. Even after Gary Ridgway confessed, it wasn't clear that Ridgway and Ainsworth were referring to the same encounter. The two men seen by Ainsworth could have been completely unconnected to the murders, although the similarity of accounts was striking. (CS)

3. Marcia Chapman was last seen on July 31, 1982, and Cynthia Hinds on August 11, 1982. So it appears that Marcia Chapman may have been placed in the river, weighted down by rocks, more than a week before Cynthia Hinds. Ridgway's admission that he had returned to have sex with one of the river victims' bodies after he had placed the remains under the water suggests that one reason he may have put rocks in the vaginas was to possibly preserve that portion of the anatomy from water damage prior to his anticipated return. (CS)

Chapter Thirty-Four

1. At one point in the first week, when Gary had been asked if he ever tortured or mutilated small animals, as some profilers have suggested was common in serial killers' childhoods, Gary admitted that as a teenager, he'd enclosed the family cat in an ice cooler, after an argument with his mother; the cat had suffocated. (CS)

Chapter Thirty-Five

1. Jensen later said that there was no evidence to support this story of Gary—
   except for the abiding belief that he had to have killed someone before
   Wendy Coffield. (CS)
2. Amina Agisheff, thirty-six, was found near Kerrington Road, near I-90 and
   Highway 18. She had last been seen on July 7, 1982, and had been considered
   the first victim of the Green River Killer. But Gary had previously denied
   killing her, although he now seemed to be backtracking a bit. Gary might
   have been confusing Kerrington Road with Kensington Road. (CS)

Chapter Thirty-Eight

1. This was "abhorrent" in the transcript, probably the result of a transcrip-
   tion error. (CS)
2. This "verification process" was the crux of the FBI's profiling methodology,
   which was based on statistical modeling. Dr. O'Toole's approach was to
   compare Gary's behavior and background against other known serial
   killers, which essentially involved getting him to confirm or deny certain
   things. This data would then be added to the pile and would help the bureau calculate probabilities as to the personalities of future offenders. (CS)
3. The FBI's behavioral profile of serial sexual offenders' remains based upon
   the study of such offenders completed by Ressler, Burgess, and Douglas and
   reported in *Sexual Homicide: Patterns and Motives*, Lexington Books, 1988.
   The paradigm includes such antisocial childhood acts as the torture and
   mutilation of small animals, arson, and, significantly, bed-wetting, among
   other behaviors. All of these behaviors were present in Gary's childhood,
   and perhaps just as important, all involved issues of control. (CS)
4. Although the word *paraphilia* and it's derivative, *paraphilic,* are now much
   in vogue among psychological profilers employed by law enforcement, they
   are a relatively recent invention, a joining of the Greek *para,* meaning beyond, with *philos,* Greek, for love. It has only recently come into more common use in connection with definitions of sexual deviancy. (CS)

Chapter Thirty-Nine

1. KIRO 7 Eyewitness News Investigative Reporter Chris Halsne, July 24, 2003.
2. This story ran in the *Seattle Times,* July 26, 2003, reported by Duff Wilson
   and Mike Carter, p. B-1.
3. Article by Kathleen Merrill and Dean Radford, in the *King County Journal,*
   August 1, 2003, p. A-1.

4. Reported by Steve Miletich in the *Seattle Times*, Sunday, August 3, 2003, p. A-1.
5. Of course, Mary Rita Ridgway's supposed "provocative" dressing hadn't been established by anything Gary Ridgway had said, but only through the description provided by Marcia in the search warrant affidavit, which Dr. O'Toole seems to have accepted as an established fact without further verification. (CS)

Chapter Forty-Two

1. Reichert eventually did write a book, *Chasing the Devil*, in which the devil, of course, was Gary Ridgway. (CS)

Chapter Forty-Three

1. Mario Mendoza, onetime infielder for the Pittsburgh Pirates. (MP)
2. At this point in early 1985, Gary was driving a Plymouth Satellite sedan; his pickup truck—the "PKV," as Patty Eakes referred to it, for "primary killing vehicle"—had been wrecked some months earlier. (CS)

Chapter Forty-Four

1. The *Times* would certainly have turned the letter over to the Green River Task Force, as the *P-I* did. A number of similar letters were received by the *Times* and provided to the task force, although none with this level of apparent detail about the killings. After receiving a copy of this letter from the *P-I*, the Green River investigators considered asking that its receipt and perhaps some of its contents be published, in the hope of stimulating further letters, but eventually rejected that tactic. Would the *Times* have published the contents of the letter, even if the investigators had asked that it be kept secret, given that the paper would have known that it had probably been written by the real killer? And would that have stimulated Gary to write additional letters, possibly leading to his earlier apprehension? These are both imponderable questions at this point, more than twenty years after the events. (CS)
2. John Douglas was one of the FBI's preeminent psychological profilers in the 1980s. He had consulted with the Green River Task Force throughout that

decade, providing advice about the likely characteristics of the killer. He later acknowledged that he'd erred in concluding that the "callmefred" letter was not from the killer. (CS)

Chapter Forty-Five

1. The front-page headline ran in the *Seattle Times,* October 17, 2003, p. A-1. Subsequent article by Ian Ith.
2. The actual name of the hotel is being kept confidential at the request of the sheriff's office. (MP)

Chapter Forty-Eight

1. At the State championships on November 15, one of my Kentwood swimmers, sophomore Courtney Eronemo, successfully completed a rare double, winning the 100 butterfly and 500 freestyle, both in All-American times. Kentwood finished second in the meet, and I was voted 4A Coach of the Year. It was a dream night. (MP)

Chapter Fifty-Two

1. Things may be improving. From August 29 to September 2, 2005, I attended a Serial Murder Symposium in San Antonio, sponsored by the FBI, bringing together a wide array of professionals involved in serial murder investigations, prosecutions, and research. Most agreed that profiling techniques must be reevaluated in light of cases such as Green River, BTK, and the D.C. snipers. (MP)

—◆— **About the Authors**

Mark Prothero, fifty, is a Seattle native. The younger of two sons of a renowned family of wooden boatbuilders, he was a champion collegiate swimmer at the University of Washington, twice selected to represent the United States in international competition, in Argentina in 1977 and in Amsterdam and Paris in 1978. He graduated in 1978 with a degree in history and then attended the University of San Diego School of Law, earning his J.D. in 1981.

In 1983, he was hired as a staff lawyer for Associated Counsel for the Accused (ACA), one of four nonprofit agencies who contract with King County, Washington, to provide legal defense for the indigent. Since 1983, he has defended many men and women in the courts of Washington State, including a number of high-profile murder cases, before undertaking the defense of Gary Ridgway. Among these other murder cases were the defense of James Cushing, the "Queen Anne Axe Murderer," a mentally ill man who terrorized a well-to-do Seattle neighborhood for six months in 1990; James Hutcheson, accused of murder-for-hire in a notorious love triangle case; Stephen Hollis, accused of rape, one of Washington State's earliest cases involving the use of DNA evidence; Kenny Ford, charged with a triple murder at a tavern in north Seattle; and Roy Webbe, a mentally disturbed native of the Virgin Islands accused of raping and murdering a young woman by nearly severing her spinal cord with one of her own steak knives.

During his time at ACA, Prothero also participated in many pro bono projects for accused criminals. He was a member of the Innocence Project Northwest, focused on freeing the wrongfully accused from prison. He is also a Judge Pro Tem in the Seattle suburbs of Kent, Tukwila, Des Moines, and SeaTac. He has been a frequent lecturer at continuing legal education seminars. Among the subjects he has presented on are forensic DNA, mental illness and mental defenses, and the death penalty. He is a member of the National Association of

Criminal Defense Attorneys (NACDL), the Washington Defender Association (WDA), and the Washington Association of Criminal Defense Lawyers (WACDL), having served on their Board of Governors since 2003 and having written three articles for their magazine, *Defense.*

Currently, Prothero is a partner in the law firm of Hanis Greaney, PLLC, in Kent, Washington, where he and Greg Girard formed the firm's criminal defense department.

In addition to practicing law, he also coaches swimming, which he has done since the summer of 1978. He currently coaches the Kentwood High School girls swim team and the Kent Swim and Tennis Club in the summers. He has also served as an announcer at several U.S. national swimming championships.

He and his wife, Kelly, whom he first met in high school, have two children, Sean, twenty-one, and Marley, sixteen.

Carlton Smith is an award-winning journalist, who has worked for the *Los Angeles Times, Willamette Week,* and the *Seattle Times.* In 1988, he was a finalist for the Pulitzer Prize in Investigative Reporting for his work, with Tomas Guillen, on the Green River murder case. In 1991, Smith and Guillen wrote *The Search for the Green River Killer* (Penguin-Onyx), a book about the frustrating early years of the investigation into the murders, at the time of publication still unsolved. The book became a *New York Times* best-seller and a finalist for the Helen Bernstein Award of the New York Public Library.

Since 1991, Smith has written nineteen other books dealing with murder and their associated investigative, psychological, and legal issues, including *Death of a Little Princess* (St. Martin's Press, 1996), about the Jon Benet Ramsey case in Boulder, Colorado; *Love, Daddy* (St. Martin's Press, 2003), about convicted family killer Christian Longo; and *Reckless* (St. Martin's Press, 2004), about the shooting of actress Lana Clarkson in the castle-like mansion of rock music producer Phil Spector. His most recent book, *The BTK Murders* (St. Martin's Press) is scheduled for publication in 2006.

In addition to these books, Smith has also written for a number of periodicals, including *Willamette Week, Seattle Weekly,* and *California Lawyer.*

He presently resides in South Pasadena, California.

～ Index